Contents

PART II | The Social, Environmental, and Health Contexts of Aging 121

5 Theories and Research in Explaining and Understanding Aging Phenomena 123

6 Social Structures, Social Inequality, and the Life Course 164

7 Health Status and Health-Care Transitions 193

8 The Lived Environment: Community and Housing Alternatives in Later Life 232

PART III | Aging, Social Institutions, and Public Policy 267

Preface

To be able to learn is to be young, and whoever keeps the joy of learning in him or her remains forever young.

— J.G. Bennett, 1897–1974

The objective of this book is to present a synthesis and interpretation of social science research concerning individual and population aging, with a focus on aging in Canada. The emphasis is on identifying, describing, and explaining patterns, processes, and current issues. This approach enables students and practitioners to acquire fundamental knowledge about older people and to develop a broad understanding of aging processes and issues that may be experienced across the life course. Reading the book involves more than accumulating information for a mid-term or final examination. As you read, personalize the information so that you are prepared to move through life, with reflection and understanding, to help family members as they age, to participate in an aging society as an employee or as a volunteer serving older adults, and to function as a concerned and well-informed global citizen who can lobby or vote concerning aging-related issues confronting your community, region, or province—or the world.

This is the sixth edition of this textbook. The 1983 edition was the first textbook on aging in Canada and was written at a time when few scholarly resources about aging in Canada were available. The second and third (1990 and 1998) editions reflected the growth of Canadian research about aging, and the fourth edition (2004) included even more "made-in-Canada" knowledge about aging. That is why, for the first time, the book was subtitled *Canadian Perspectives*. These first four editions were solo-authored by Barry McPherson who, along with Victor Marshall, taught the first courses on aging in Canadian universities.

I was invited to co-author the fifth edition (2008) with Barry and gladly accepted, in part because of my long history with both the author and the book. I met Barry McPherson in 1985, at which time I began a post-doctoral fellowship at the University of Waterloo under his direction. The first course that I taught in the area of sociology of aging (starting in 1985–6) was in fact Barry's course, a course that I have taught in different forms for almost 25 years. Over the years of my academic life course, I reviewed subsequent editions of the book so it was a natural process by which I eventually became a co-author on the fifth edition. We significantly revised the structure of that edition in response to suggestions from students and faculty who had read previous editions, including adding a new chapter on health and aging, expanded sections about the aging baby boom generation, Internet resources, a glossary, and updated literature on every topic.

With Barry in partial retirement mode and busy cycling the highways of North America and Europe, I assumed the role of lead author for the current edition. This edition has been further enhanced with expanded sections addressing poverty, gender, ethnicity, and their intersections; new research and program developments in areas such as longevity, innovative care models, and elder abuse; and an updated timeline of historical developments in the study of aging phenomena, with a focus on Canada (see the next section).

The field of social gerontology has grown exponentially, developing into a new interdisciplinary phase that makes research in, and the study of, all key areas challenging. We have maintained a Canadian focus without sacrificing developments in the field globally. In addition, where available as of 29 July 2013, all data in the text have been updated based on the 2011 Canadian census, labour force surveys, the Canadian Community Health and General Social Surveys, and international data from the Population Reference Bureaus and US Bureau of the Census. Each chapter opens with "Focal Points and Key Facts," a preview of some of the major issues, ideas, and facts discussed in the chapter. And to encourage debate and reflection and to develop critical thinking and observational skills, each chapter concludes with a section entitled "For Reflection, Debate, or Action." Hopefully, these two sections will enable you to become a more critical reader who questions commonly held assumptions, myths, and erroneous beliefs about aging and older people, both in your family and in your community. In each chapter, references are cited in the text or in a note. These serve a twofold purpose. First, they provide theoretical or research support for the ideas. Second, they are a resource to help you locate and use primary sources in the basic literature if you are required to write a term paper on a specific topic or if you wish to acquire additional information about a particular subject.

Before social policies and programs for older Canadians can be initiated, we must identify and verify that a problem or a situation exists. We must understand why and how the problem or issue evolved, clarify the role of complex and interacting elements, and then propose alternative solutions. Guesswork, hunches, or past practices are insufficient. Nor will programs and policies implemented in another community or country or for a particular ethnic, religious or cultural group work in every context. Rather, new information must be produced through research and then applied if efficient and effective policies and programs are to be developed and implemented. Moreover, research can refute prevailing myths or misconceptions about older persons, thereby changing or eliminating some of the negative stereotypes that we may hold about aging and about the later stages of life.

This book uses a variety of theoretical and methodological orientations to describe and explain aging processes. Although it might be desirable to write a book from a single theoretical perspective, our ability to do so is limited since the social science literature about aging and later life requires a number of perspectives, from a variety of disciplines, if we are to have a more complete understanding of aging phenomena. However, throughout this edition, the life-course perspective is employed as an overarching integrative framework since events, decisions, behaviours, constraints, and opportunities at earlier stages in life often have cumulative positive or negative effects at later stages, both for aging individuals (namely, you) and for aging birth cohorts (the baby boomers). Moreover, considerable content is based on knowledge generated by the interpretive perspective and by qualitative research, which reflects the extensive use of these approaches by the Canadian research community.

The material in this book is based on the premise that aging, as a social process, involves multi-level and complex interactions between individuals and various social structures and systems; within changing social, economic, political, policy, and physical environments; and across diverse cultural contexts, all of which vary at specific periods in history, as well as across one's life course. Thus, aging as a social process is considered from an interacting micro (individual) and macro (societal) perspective. This book has three general objectives:

1. To provide you with basic concepts, theories, and methodologies that can be used to understand social phenomena related to individual and population aging and to

develop critical thinking and observational and interpretive skills. Moreover, with this knowledge, you will be better prepared to identify, deconstruct, and help refute common misconceptions about aging and growing older. Where possible, the book presents alternative explanations for aging processes rather than a single description or interpretation of a process or problem.

2. To sensitize you to the fact that aging is not just a biological process but an equally complex social process. In fact, you may be left with the impression that there are more gaps in knowledge than answers. Herein lies a challenge to the curious, innovative reader who may wish to pursue a career in this field.

3. To make you aware of the dynamic interplay between your individual life course and the local, national, and global historical and cultural forces that shape your life experiences and opportunities. Aging, as a lifelong process, must be of interest and concern to people of all ages and in all communities, cultures, and countries.

In conclusion, there has been an enormous growth in knowledge about aging in Canada; however, the sociology of aging and social gerontology fields of study are still in the early developmental phases. Continued integration and synthesis of ideas from what previously were thought to be separate disciplines with distinct pillars of knowledge have resulted in innovative developments at the crossroads of disciplines. Critical thinking and reflection are essential skills to acquire, since gaps in knowledge, differing opinions and interpretations, and even controversy concerning issues, processes, programs, or policies for aging adults or an aging society are prevalent in contemporary Canadian society. Thus, we encourage you to become a critical reader and thinker, to ask questions about what you read, and to discuss with others the validity and applicability of research findings presented in any single study. One published article on a particular subject does not represent the absolute truth. Indeed, even many research studies on a topic may not provide a complete and valid explanation of a particular process, pattern, or problem. To illustrate, many studies describe only one slice of a particular social setting or community at one point in time. Other relevant social, individual, cultural, structural, or historical factors may not be considered in the analysis and interpretation of the results. Therefore, we encourage you to search for and debate the merits of alternative explanations and to be cautious in what you accept as fact—including what you read in this book.

Finally, the test of how well a book serves as a learning resource is whether students find the material useful, interesting, clearly written, and comprehensive. Please provide feedback about this book to your instructor and to the authors:

Andrew V. Wister, PhD, Simon Fraser University, Vancouver, BC (wister@sfu.ca)

Barry D. McPherson, PhD, Waterloo, ON (bmcpherson@wlu.ca)

July 2013

Acknowledgments

I assumed senior authorship of the sixth edition of *Aging as a Social Process: Canadian Perspectives*. Writing this edition required intensive work over a long period that could not have been completed without the support and assistance of family, friends, and colleagues. First and foremost, I would like to thank my wife, colleague, and life partner, Barbara Mitchell-Wister, for providing the inspiration, time, and feedback needed to tackle this project. Her expertise in the sociology of the family, theory, and policy helped to fine-tune sections of the new edition. My daughter, Kayzia Wister, provided the university student audience perspective. Over my career, I have also enjoyed the support of my parents Stephen and Iris Wister. I wish to acknowledge the continuing involvement of Barry McPherson, the originator of the text and my co-author, who provided conceptual and editorial input. Thanks are also due to the many professors, students, and practitioners across Canada who submitted constructive criticisms about the content and structure of previous editions. I received support from two graduate students from the Gerontology Department at Simon Fraser University: Laura Booi, a PhD student, and Maia Hillen, a master's student. Both assisted in searching Web-based resources to uncover new highlights, photographs, and bibliographic material. In addition, Ray Adams, Information Officer at the SFU Gerontology Research Centre, assisted with the updating of the Web-based resources shown in the Appendix. On the production side at Oxford University Press, we thank the many staff who contributed to the editing and production of this book. We are also deeply appreciative of the assistance provided by Colleen Ste. Marie, a freelance copyeditor, who significantly improved the manuscript with her creative, constructive, and rapid copyediting.

Developments in Social Gerontology since 1940 That Have Had a Major Impact on Canadian Research, Policy, and Practice

1948 Founding of the International Association of Gerontology in Liege, Belgium.

1940 Publication of the journal *Geriatrics*.

1962 The "Aging in the World" series included papers from the Fifth Congress of the International-Association of Gerontology held in 1960. These volumes, which illustrated the increasing global interest in aging, and the growing interdisciplinarity of the field, included the following: C. Tibbits and W. Donahue (eds.)/*Social and Psychological Aspects of Aging*; J. Kaplan and G. Aldridge (eds.)/*Social Welfare of the Aging*; N. Shock (ed.)/*Biological Aspects of Aging*; H. Blumenthal (ed.)/*Medical and Clinical Aspects of Aging*.

1959–60 These handbooks summarized the knowledge about a number of gerontology topics in the late 1950s: J. Birren (ed.)/*Handbook of Aging and the Individual: Psychological and Biological*; C. Tibbitts, (ed.)/*Handbook of Social Gerontology: Societal Aspects of Aging*; E. Burgess (ed.)/*Aging in Western Societies*.

1953 R. Havighurst and R. Albrecht/*Older People*.

1940 ——— 1950 ——— 1960

1945 Establishment of the Gerontological Society (later named GSA "of America") to hold annual meetings to promote the scientific study of aging from multi-disciplinary perspectives, and to stimulate communication among scientists, researchers, teachers, and professionals.

1945 The first issue of the *Journal of Gerontology*.

1948 O. Pollock/*Social Adjustment in Old Age*. This landmark report of the US Social Sciences Research Council shifted focus from problems of aging to the process of aging, and led to several theoretical developments in social gerontology.

1959 L.D. Cain, Jr. (ed.)/*The Sociology of Aging: A Trend Report and Bibliography: Special Issue in Current Sociology*.

1959 Ontario Longitudinal Study on Aging initiated under the leadership of L. Crawford. Followed 2000 men from 1959 to 1978, with follow-up in 1990.

1961 *The Gerontologist*: A second journal published by the Gerontological Society to focus on applied research, model programs, and policy initiatives for professionals working with·and for the aged.

1961 E. Cumming; W. Henry/*Growing Old: The Process of Disengagement*. The first attempt to develop a social gerontological theory to account for satisfaction in the later years.

1961 First USA White House Conference on Aging. These conferences are held every ten years in the United States to draw scientists and professional workers together to make recommendations for consideration by Congress.

1970 E. Palmore/*Normal Aging: Reports from the Duke Longitudinal Studies, 1955–69*. The first interdisciplinary longitudinal study.

1965 D. Schonfield/"Memory Changes with Age." Article published in *Nature* by a Canadian psychologist who mentored many first generation gerontologists in Canada.

1969 R. Havighurst et al./*Adjustment to Retirement: A Cross-National Study*.

1968 B. Neugarten (ed.)/ *Middle Age and Aging: A Reader in Social Psychology*. The first collection of readings on the social psychology of aging.

1974 National Institute on Aging (NIA) established in the United States to promote research on all facets of aging.

1974 D. Cowgill; L. Holmes/ *Aging and Modernization*. This book popularized modernization theory to explain the changing status of the elderly in primitive and developing societies.

1971 Founding of Canadian Association on Gerontology.

1971 Manitoba Longitudinal Study on Aging initiated. Elderly individuals living were interviewed first in 1971, and later in 1976 and 1983.

— 1965 ———————————— 1970 ———————————— 1975 —

1967 E. Youmans/*Older Rural Americans*. One of the few studies to consider aging in a rural context.

1968 M. Riley; A. Foner, (eds.)/*Aging and Society. Volume One: An Inventory of Research Findings*. This landmark volume presented and interpreted the empirical findings of social science research to this date.

1968 E. Shanas, et al./*Older People in Three Industrial Societies*. A cross-national comparative study of the social situation of older people in Denmark, Great Britain, and the United States

1969 M. Riley et al. (eds.)/*Aging and Society, Volume Two: Aging and the Professions*. A statement of the concerns and involvement of a number of professions in the care of older adults.

1970–2 First sociology of aging courses taught in Canada by B. Havens (University of Manitoba); B. McPherson (University Waterloo); and V. Marshall (McMaster University).

1972 M. Riley et al./ *Aging and Society, Volume Three: A Sociology of Age Stratification*. Presents a model of aging that stresses the interaction between history and the social structure as it affects various age cohorts.

1972 R. Atchley/*The Social Forces in Later Life: An Introduction to Social Gerontology*. The first textbook written exclusively for undergraduates in social gerontology courses.

1976–7 These handbooks represented the state of knowledge up to the mid-1970s: R. Binstock and E. Shanas (eds.)/*Handbook of Aging and the Social Sciences* (1976); J. Birren and K. Schaie (eds.)/*Handbook of the Psychology of Aging* (1977); C. Finch and L. Hayflick (eds.)/*Handbook of the Biology of Aging* (1977). Subsequent editions have been published every five to seven years.

1986 N. Chappell; L. Strain; A. Blandford /*Aging and Health Care: A Social Perspective.*

1986 Butterworths Perspectives on *Individual and Population Aging* published under the editorship of B. McPherson. The series, which ended in 1992, published a total of 15 monographs on major aging topics. The first monograph was by S. McDaniel/*Canada's Aging Population* (1986). Selected monographs are included in this timeline; and a summary of developments on most of the topics since the series ended appeared in *CJA* Vol. 30(3), 2011, edited by H. Northcott; M. Rosenberg.

1976 R. Butler/ *Why Survive? Being Old in America.* This book won a Pulitzer Prize, bringing aging to the attention of the media and the public of all ages.

1976 J. Schulz/ *The Economics of Aging.*

1979 Social Sciences and Humanities Research Council of Canada (SSHRC) Strategic Grants Committee on Population Aging was established to award research and to fund Aging Centers across Canada.

1979 *Research on Aging: A Quarterly Journal of Social Gerontology* first published.

1979 Program in aging established at the University of Toronto.

1975 ——————— **1980** ——————— **1985**

1975 R. Rapaport and R. Rapaport (eds.)/*Leisure and the Family Life Cycle.* The first examination of leisure within the family context across the life cycle.

1975 Association for Gerontology in Higher Education (AGHE) formed to facilitate leadership development for training programs that were being established in universities and colleges.

1980 The National Advisory Council on Aging (NACA) of Canada created to assist and advise the federal government on seniors' issues.

1980 Gerontology Research Council of Ontario established.

1980 V. Marshall/*Aging in Canada: Social Perspective.* This was the first reader presenting a collection of articles pertaining to aging and the aged in Canada. Second edition published in 1987 with considerably more Canadian content.

1980 P. Lawton/*Environment and Aging.* Development of person-environment fit theory.

Mid-1980s Undergraduate programs developed at McMaster University, the University of Waterloo, and St Thomas University.

1984 J. Myles/*Old Age in the Welfare State: The Political Economy of Public Pensions.* Early development of pension issues and challenges in Canada.

1983 B. McPherson/*Aging as a Social Process: An Introduction to Individual and Population Aging.* First Canadian text, now in the sixth edition (2013).

1982/83 Gerontology centres and programs funded by SSHRC established at Guelph, Manitoba, Simon Fraser, Toronto, and Moncton universities.

1982 *Canadian Journal on Aging* first published.

1995 S. Arber; J. Ginn/ *Connecting Gender and Aging: A Sociological Approach.*

1997 E. Moore; M. Rosenberg; D. McGuinness/*Growing Old in Canada: Demographic and Geographic Perspectives.*

1987 US Bureau of the Census/An Aging World. This is the first of nine publications on global aging, the most recent by K. Kinsella; W. He (2009).

1991 L. McDonald/ *Elder Abuse in Canada.* Butterworths Series.

1997 E. Gee; A. Martin-Matthews (Eds.)/*Canadian Public Policy/Canadian Journal on Aging Joint Issue—Bridging Policy and Research on Aging*, Volume XXIII (CPP)/Volume 16 (CJA).

1987 E. Gee; M. Kimball/ *Women and Aging.* Butterworths Series.

1991 A. Martin-Matthews/ *Widowhood in Later Life.* Butterworths Series.

1998 J. Giele; G. Elder/ *Methods of Life Course Research: Qualitative and Quantitative Approaches.* Connected life course theory and methods.

1987 W. Forbes; J. Jackson; A. Kraus/ *Institutionalization of the Elderly in Canada.* Butterworths Series.

1991 M. Minkler; C. Estes/ *Critical Perspectives on Aging: The Political and Moral Economy of Growing Old.* Development of a critical perspective in aging.

1999 R. Friedland; L. Summer/ *Demography Is Not Destiny.* This was the first book to address apocalyptic demography.

1987 N. Chappell; L. Driedger/*Aging and Ethnicity: Toward an Interface.* Butterworths Series.

1991 Canadian Study of Health and Aging initiated. A ten-year study with a focus on dementia and its care.

—1990——————————1995——————————2000—

1990s–present
Several graduate MA/MSc/ PhD programs in Gerontology were established in a number of Canadian universities.

1999–2003
B. Spencer; F. Denton/ Social and Economic Dimensions of an Aging Population (SEDAP) I & II (2005-11), a multi-disciplinary SSHRC-funded research program. Supported a network of researchers from across the country to develop a series of major papers on this topic.

1990 CARNET: The Canadian Aging Research Network established.

1988 L. Plouffe; F. Béland (Eds.)/*Canadian Journal on Aging Special Issue—Francophone Research in Gerontology in Canada*, Vol 7 (4). This was an important issue of CJA that attempted to make French-language gerontological research more widely known.

1996 B. Spencer; F. Denton/ Independence and Economic Security of the Older Population (IESOP) Program. Led to SEDAP in 1999.

1988 Research Centre on Aging, Sherbrooke, Quebec, established, funded by Fonds de recherché en santé du Québec (FRSQ).

1996 D. Foot/*Boom Bust and Echo: How to Profit from the Coming Demographic Shift.* First Canadian book to envisage population aging as the primary driver of social and economic change.

1988 J. Birren; V. Begtson/ *Emergent Theories of Aging.*

1996 Quebec Network for Research on Aging established, funded by FRSQ.

1988 M. Novak/*Aging and Society.*

2000 Canadian Institutes of Health Research (CIHR) created. The Institute of Aging (IA) was one of 13 institutes created by the CIHR to stimulate research on health issues related to aging.

2000 E. Gee; G. Gutman/*The Overselling of Population Aging: Apocalyptic Demography, Intergenerational Challenges, and Social Policy.* First Canadian book to critique population aging as apocalyptic.

2003 N. Chappell; E. Gee; L. McDonald; M. Stones/*Aging in Contemporary Canada.* Second edition 2008, without E. Gee who died in 2002.

2003 V. Marshall; W. Heinz; A. Verma/ *Restructuring Work and the Life Course.*

2003 W. Heinz; V. Marshall/*Social Dynamics of the Life Course: Transitions, Institutions and Interrelations.*

2002 J. McMullin; V. Marshall/ Workforce Aging in the New Economy (WANE). Project funded by SSHRC. One of the largest funded studies by SSHRC in aging.

2004 J. McMullin/ *Understanding Social Inequality: Intersections of Class, Age, Gender, Ethnicity, and Race in Canada.* Second edition published in 2010.

2006 B. Mitchell/ *Boomerang Age: Transitions to Adulthood in Families.* A life-course analysis of family transitions.

—2000————————————————————————2005——————

2001 17th World Congress of the International Association of Gerontology (IAG; now IAGG, Geriatrics added), Vancouver Canada. This was the first IAGG conference in Canada.

2001 A. Martin-Matthews; F. Béland (Eds.)/*Canadian Journal on Aging Special Issue— Northern Lights: Reflections on Canadian Gerontological Research*, Vol. 20.

2001 I. Connidis/*Family Ties and Aging.* Developed out of the original Butterworth's series (1989). A second edition published in 2010.

2001 G. Kenyon/*Narrative Gerontology: Theory, Research and Practice.* A first Canadian examination of narrative theory and analyses.

2001 Initial developmental meeting of the Canadian Longitudinal Study on Aging, CLSA, Alymer, Quebec.

2005 National Initiative for the Care of the Elderly (NICE). National network funded by the Networks of Centres of Excellence— New Initiative Program.

2005 A. Wister/*Baby Boomer Health Dynamics: How Are We Aging?* First Canadian book addressing health of the baby boomers.

2005 Public Health Agency of Canada/Report on Seniors Falls in Canada.

2007 National Seniors Council of Canada established, replacing NACA.

2008 N. Keating/*Rural Ageing: A Good Place to Grow Old?* Developed from an original Butterworth's book (1991) focusing on rural aging in Canada.

2008 A. Martin-Matthews; J. Phillips/ *Aging and Caring at the Intersection of Work and Home Life: Blurring the Boundaries.*

2010 Alzheimer Society of Canada/*Rising Tide: The Impact of Dementia on Canadian Society.*

2010 G. Gutman; C. Spencer/ *Aging, Ageism and Abuse: Moving from Awareness to Action.*

— 2010 — 2015 —

2009 V. Bengtson et al./ *Handbook of Theories of Aging.* Includes chapters on integrative theories in social gerontology. First edition published in 1999.

2009 Canadian Longitudinal Study on Aging launched. This will be the largest longitudinal study on aging in Canada with 50,000 participants aged 45 and over followed for 20 years.

2011 H. Northcott; M. Rosenberg (eds.)/ *Canadian Journal on Aging Special Issue—Individual and Population Aging: Commemorating the Butterworths Series and the Founding of the CJA.* Many of the original topics in the series are revisited.

Part I

An Introduction to Individual and Population Aging

Age is opportunity no less,
Than youth itself, though in another dress,
And as the evening twilight fades away,
The sky is filled with stars, invisible by day.

—Henry Wadsworth Longfellow, *Morituri Salutamus*

For centuries, humans have sought ways to prolong life and to be healthier in later life. The search for a magic elixir—through healthy lifestyles, drugs, surgery, the fountain of youth—has been primarily from a biological or medical perspective. Increasingly, however, researchers have discovered that social aspects of aging—such as historical, socio-cultural, and environmental factors, as well as biological factors and disease states—influence both individual and population aging in any society or community.

Given the rapid pace of population aging in Canada and the world, coupled with an increase in knowledge about the aging process, this is an exciting time to study these phenomena. The journey you are about to begin by reading *Aging as a Social Process: Canadian Perspectives*, 6th edition, like the life course itself, will be different for each person. The subject matter will present unique challenges, varying degrees of interest, and many opportunities for personal reflection. By acquiring knowledge, separating facts from myths, and applying this information, you can enrich your own life, as well as the lives of older adults in your personal family and social networks, and in society at large. Whether you are a student thinking about your future, a concerned citizen, a practitioner working with older adults, a person caring for an aging parent or other relative, a policy-maker, or a researcher, knowledge about individual and population aging is a lifelong pursuit and investment.

Part 1 of this book consists of four chapters that introduce facts, trends, and ways of thinking about aging and about growing older in a global society. Chapter 1 introduces the concept of aging as a social process, distinguishes between individual and population aging, defines four types of aging, and identifies some major issues and challenges, as well as images and myths about aging in Canada. In addition, the chapter introduces arguments as to why it is important to understand aging phenomena throughout the life course from a number of disciplinary and theoretical perspectives (see also Chapter 5). This chapter stresses that we do not age in a vacuum but, rather, in a highly interactive and ever-changing social world as we move through our individual life courses. It also stresses the need to treat older persons ethically and to protect their human and legal rights, especially as their physical and cognitive capacities decline.

Chapter 2 illustrates the diversity in the aging process and in the status of older people across time because of cultural differences and historical events. Aging, and being labelled as "old," "elderly," or a "senior," varies across time, both within and across countries. A major change in the status of older people is alleged to have occurred as societies moved from pre-industrial to industrial to postmodern states, especially after the onset of modernization. Within a multicultural society such as Canada, the process of aging varies within indigenous, language, ethnic, rural, and religious subcultures.

Chapter 3 briefly describes how the various physical and cognitive systems of the human organism change and adapt across the life course. The focus is on how physical and cognitive changes, which may or may not occur in all aging individuals at the same rate or to the same degree, influence the nature and frequency of social relations throughout the life course but more so in later life. Some of these natural and inevitable changes lead to a loss of independence, a lower quality of life, and a need for informal and formal support from others to complete such activities of daily living as dressing, eating, and bathing. For others, positive adaptations to these changes enable aging individuals to maximize well-being and fulfill their potential as human beings.

Chapter 4 presents an overview of demographic processes and indicators that describe the size, composition, and distribution of the population by age. Demographic facts from both developed and developing countries are introduced to place the Canadian situation in a global context. Demographic processes are dynamic, and this chapter discusses the implications of demographic changes over time, especially with respect to fertility, **mortality** (note that terms in bold throughout the text are defined in the Glossary), and immigration rates. The final section of the chapter examines the geographic distribution of populations by age across provincial and rural–urban boundaries and illustrates how immigration contributes to the diversity of Canada's older population. Population aging is a universal phenomenon that, at times, has been expressed as a fearful and negative event by some members of the media and government. They argue that "demography is destiny" and that population aging will lead to the bankruptcy of public pension systems and to the destruction of the health-care system through excessive use and costs. This chapter discusses whether this view is myth or fact.

1   Aging as a Social Process

A [person's] age is something impressive, it sums up his life: maturity reached slowly and against many obstacles, illnesses cured, griefs and despairs overcome, and unconscious risks taken; maturity formed through so many desires, hopes, regrets, forgotten things, loves. A [person's] age represents a fine cargo of experiences and memories.

— Antoine de Saint-Exupéry, *Wartime Writings*, 1939–1944
Translated from the French by Norah Purcell

Focal Points and Key Facts

- Why should we study social processes of aging?
- To what extent, and why, does population aging influence life chances, choices, and lifestyles throughout the life course?
- Why and how does age and aging matter in our everyday lives, and do the meanings of *age* and *aging* change across the life course?
- Are older people a burden to society, an untapped resource, or both?
- How do media images about being old influence the aging process?
- How do the culture and social structure of a society influence individual aging?
- Why and how are individual aging and population aging linked?
- Why and how should the human rights of older people be protected?
- In 2011, almost one in seven Canadians was 65 or older (4.95 million people), representing 14.8 per cent of the total population.
- There were 5825 Canadians 100 years of age or older (i.e., centenarians), according to the 2011 census.
- In 2011, baby boomers (born between 1946 and 1965), comprising 30 per cent of all Canadians, began to turn 65. As a result, the 60 to 64 age group is growing most rapidly, followed by centenarians.

Introduction: Challenges of an Aging World

The world is growing older as the number and proportion of older people in each country increases. In developed countries like Canada, this growth has occurred over the past 40 years as fertility rates decreased after the **baby boom** of 1946–65 while mortality rates have gradually declined. The boomers comprise 30 per cent of the total Canadian population—more than 10 million individuals in 2011 compressed into the narrow age range of 46 to 65. As additional cohorts of the baby boomers turn 65 and beyond, the proportion of persons 65 and over in the population will rise significantly. This growth is expected to level off after 2031 when baby boomers reach advanced age and their numbers begin to shrink.

In developing countries, much of the increase in population aging will occur over the next 30 to 40 years as fertility rates decline and sanitation and public health improve. That is, with fewer births, older people begin to comprise a larger proportion of the total population, and with improved sanitation and public health, people will live longer, also increasing the proportion of the population that is older. Population aging in these countries will occur at a faster pace than in developed countries because of more rapid drops in fertility and mortality rates. This global phenomenon, known as **population aging**, is illustrated by the following facts or projections (Kinsella and He 2009; Population Reference Bureau 2011; US Census Bureau 2012).

- In 2012, 8 per cent of the world's population was 65 years of age or older, estimated at 562 million individuals (US Census Bureau 2012).

- By 2040, one in seven persons could be 65 and older.
- In developed or modernized countries, 16.5 per cent of the population is 65 or over (US Census Bureau 2012). In some of these countries, the proportion is projected to reach one in four, one in three, or even one in two during the next 30 years (Kinsella and He 2009).
- In comparison, only 6.2 per cent of the population in the less developed nations is 65 and over (US Census Bureau 2012). However, this percentage will rise quickly over the next several decades.
- About 75 per cent of the world's older population lives in developing countries, given their large populations.

In 2011, 5825 Canadians were 100 years of age or older—an increase of 25.7 per cent since 2006—compared to almost 50,000 centenarians in Japan, the country with the highest life expectancy. We live not only in an aging world but in a society in which older citizens are healthier and more active. As individuals and as a society, we cannot ignore the challenges of population aging and the needs of older adults. Understanding and developing a society for all ages is essential—today and in the future when you and members of your family grow older. The effects of population aging permeate all spheres of social life: work, the family, **leisure**, transportation, politics, **public policy**, the economy, housing, and health care. Consequently, both challenges and opportunities exist for aging individuals, as well as for family members, politicians, employers and employees, health and social services personnel, and public policy–makers. Indeed, aging issues are linked to many of the well-known challenges facing societies, including **gender** inequality, intergenerational family relations, **retirement** and economic security, universal access to health care, and social assistance in later life, to name but a few.

We do not age in a vacuum. Rather, individually and collectively (as a family, **community**, or society), we live in a social world. In our lifelong journey, we interact with other individuals and **age cohorts** across time and within a unique culture, social system, and community. Just as individuals change as they grow older, so too do **social institutions**—such as the family, the health-care system, the labour force, the economy, and the educational system. In short, we do not age alone, nor do we have total freedom in selecting our lifestyle or **life course**. There is constant interplay among individuals and various social processes and social institutions across the life course (Heinz and Marshall 2003; Mitchell 2003, 2008; Pearlin, 2009; Dannefer and Settersten Jr. 2010). To illustrate, mandatory retirement at age 65, or its elimination, can restrict or increase work opportunities for the individual who attains 65 years of age, and provide economic advantages for society. Similarly, the state of our health at any stage in life is linked to personal decisions about diet and lifestyle; the cost, quality, and availability of foods; and the quality of care provided by the informal and formal support systems and by the health-care system. It was C. Wright Mills (1959), a well-known sociologist, who first stressed that we must understand and appreciate how and why the "private troubles," or personal responsibilities, of individuals interact with the "public issues," or public responsibilities, of a society—at the local, regional, national, and global level. This dialectical private–public debate and process pervades the study of individual and population aging, and it should be on the agenda whenever policies or programs for older adults are being debated. Highlight 1.1 summarizes why the study of aging processes and the social world of older adults is important—to you personally, to your family, and to your community and the larger society.

Highlight 1.1
Why Study Aging and Older Adults?

- to challenge, refute, and eliminate myths about aging and older people
- to "know thyself" and others by examining personal journeys across the life course
- to assist and support older family members as they move through the later stages of life
- to serve as an informed and effective volunteer in your community while assisting older adults
- to prepare for a job or career (as a practitioner, policy-maker, or researcher) in which the mandate is to address aging issues or to serve an older population
- to identify and understand significant changes in patterns of aging and in the age structure
- to understand intergenerational relations and the status of older adults in a multicultural society
- to critically evaluate policies and practices for an aging population and to identify where and why the needs of older adults are not being met
- to understand aging and older people from an interdisciplinary perspective—their potential, their competencies, their history, and the complex interactions of physical, social, and cognitive elements
- to enhance the quality and quantity of interaction with older people in your personal and professional life
- to help Canada become a healthy and active older society

Population Aging: Adding Years to Life

Throughout history, humans have been preoccupied with searching for a fountain of youth, for ways to look younger in later life, and for ways to prolong life (Gruman 2003). However, it was not until the twentieth century that enormous gains in longevity were achieved, as evidenced by an increase in the average and maximum lifespan of humans, in the average life expectancy at birth, and in the number of **centenarians**—those who reach 100 years of age and beyond. While each centenarian has a different life history, their longevity, in general, can be attributed to some combination of genetics, environmental factors, diet, and lifestyle choices.

Lifespan is the fixed, finite maximum limit of survival for a species (about 20 years for dogs, about 85 for elephants, and about 120 for humans). The longest-living human with a verified birth certificate was Madame Jeanne Calment, who was born in 1875 in Arles, France—before films, cars, or airplanes had been invented. She died at the age of 122 in 1997. Today, the oldest living woman and man are about 114 and 113 years of age, respectively, living in France and the US. The maximum lifespan for humans is unlikely to increase to any great extent in the immediate future because there are multiple and complex causes of mortality linked to genetics, lifestyle, and environmental factors that cannot be easily altered.

Life expectancy is the average number of years a person is projected to live at birth or at a specific age (such as 65). Average life expectancy has increased in the past 50 years and will continue to increase, although more in developing nations where life expectancy is still quite low because of high infant mortality rates, AIDS, and poor living conditions. In the early 1800s, average life expectancy in Canada was about 40 years; by the late 1800s, it had reached about 50 to 55; and by the late 1900s, it was 75 to 80. Life expectancy in China and Vietnam was about 40 years in the 1950s versus 70 years in Sweden; today, life expectancy has increased to 70 years in China and Vietnam but only to about 80 in Sweden (Population Reference Bureau 2011). These dramatic increases are part of an evolving "health transition" (Riley 2001; Land and Yang 2006) in which there are fewer deaths at birth and in infancy, and more individuals reaching advanced age. Not surprisingly, these gains in life expectancy have stimulated dreams of even longer lives but without all the physical changes that occur with age. To satisfy these wishes, entrepreneurs market anti-aging products that claim to slow, stop, or reverse the physical process of aging. However, there is little or no scientific evidence for such claims; indeed, some of the products or treatments (such as drugs or cosmetic surgery) have serious risks associated with their use (Olshansky et al. 2002; Mehlman et al. 2004).

Life expectancy varies by gender, culture, geographic region, ethnicity, race, education, personal habits (such as diet, exercise, smoking, and drinking), and birth cohort. Based on 2006 to 2008 data, the average life expectancy at birth for Canadian women was 83 years; and for men, 79 years (Statistics Canada 2011). But among Aboriginal people, life expectancy is lower—about 78 years for women and 73 for men. And because of the diversity of genetic, environmental, and lifestyle factors, some Canadians will die before reaching the average life expectancy for their group, and few will ever approach the theoretical maximum lifespan.

Increased life expectancy (i.e., lower mortality) is only part of the reason that the proportion of older people in a society increases. The most important factor is a significant decline in the **fertility rate**, which has the most direct and largest effect in shaping the age structure. For instance, the large baby boom generation was the result of increased fertility rates occurring after World War II. In 2012, Canada's birth rate was about 11 infants per 1000 population, down from a high of 26.9 per 1000 in 1946 when the baby boom started (Population Reference Bureau 2011)

Figure 1.1 shows the actual and projected growth in Canada's older population from 1921 to 2041. As the baby boomers age, the population of those 65 and older is projected to reach about seven million in 2021 and nine million in 2041 (almost one in four Canadians).

Population aging began in Canada after the end of the baby boom period (1946–65) when a "baby bust" period (from about 1966 to 1980) began. During this period, women had fewer than two children on average, and the first pregnancy was often delayed until a woman was in her mid- to late thirties (McDaniel 1986, 96). This "baby bust" period was followed by a small "baby boom echo" from about 1980 until the mid-1990s. However, the number of "echo" births was only about 30 per cent of the number in the original baby boom. Since the mid-1990s, fertility rates have fallen further to about 1.6 children per woman. This low fertility rate is below the "replacement rate" of at least two children per woman that is needed to replenish the population when normal fertility and mortality rates prevail. However, some of this population decrease is offset by immigrants arriving in Canada, which results in modest positive population growth.

Some politicians and media personnel claim that this rapid aging of the population will weaken the viability of the Canada Pension Plan, the Canadian economy, and the health-care system; that it will cause an enormous demand for long-term care and social support of older adults; and that it may lead to intergenerational inequities or conflict. Indeed, some consider population aging, and particularly the aging baby boomers, an impending crisis for our society.

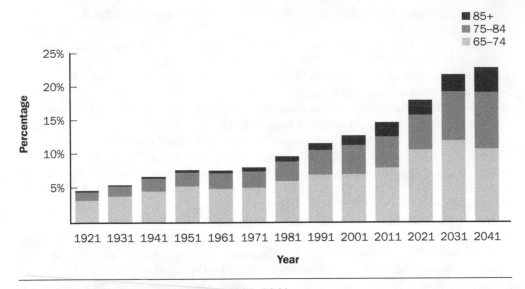

Figure 1.1 Canada's Aging Population, 1921–2041

Source: *Canada's Aging Population*. Public Health Agency of Canada, 2002. Reproduced with the permission of the Minister of Public Works and Government Services Canada, 2013.

At the turn of the millennium, Ken Dychtwald, an influential futurist in the US, contended that American baby boomers will face a pandemic of chronic disease and mass dementia, a caregiving crunch, conflict with other generations, and inadequate pensions, among other crises. He stated, "When I look into the future, I see a number of train wrecks about to happen—all of which are preventable, but only if we fully understand the relationship between our current decisions and their future outcomes and only if we initiate corrective action now" (Dychtwald 1997, 11). His views tend to be based on selected demographic and social "facts" and would seem to be exaggerations that instill fear in society. Highlight 1.2 features newspaper headlines and comments showing that these views continue to reappear whenever new statistics indicate an increase in population aging, a rise in public debt, or a perceived crisis in the social welfare or health-care systems.

Such fears can interfere with rational policy-making by focusing only on sheer numbers instead of taking into consideration other important social changes (Cheal 2003a). For instance, more careful and detailed analysis has demonstrated that with health promotion and health-care improvements, increased savings and private investments, higher levels of education, and creative and timely policy planning, an older population will not be a drain on societal resources. Indeed, healthier, better-educated, and more active older people are an untapped societal resource who can serve as volunteers, caregivers, or paid workers when the labour force shrinks (Gee 2000; Cheal 2003b; Fast et al. 2006; Gottlieb and Gillespie, 2008; Morrow-Howell, 2010).

This labelling of older people as a burden to society has been called "apocalyptic," "catastrophic," or "voodoo" demography, which results from a process of exaggerating or misinterpreting population statistics. Gee (2000, 5) describes apocalyptic demography as "an ideology . . . a set of beliefs that justifies (or rationalizes) action . . . wherein the beliefs converge on the idea that an aging population has negative implications for societal resources—which get funneled to the sick, the old, and the retired at the expense of the healthy, the young, and

Highlight 1.2
Journalistic Views of Population Aging

Raise Seniors' Taxes*

Ottawa should hit older people and their estates with new taxes to pay down the national debt, says a top tax lawyer. Seniors have benefited from a lifetime of economic growth boosted by government spending, and it is now time for them to pay the country back. . . . The $500-billion federal debt "belongs" to older Canadians, but younger generations are being asked to pay for it.

(*Toronto Star*, 11 November 1994)

Painful Decisions Must Be Made to Ensure Future of Social Programs*

If you think we are having a hard time affording our social programs today, just wait a few years. What is little understood is how the demographic clock is working against us and how fast it is ticking.

(Peter Hadekel, *The Gazette*, Montreal, 10 December 1994)

Pension Plan Pins Prospects on Market*

Faced with the daunting demographic challenges of an aging baby-boom . . . Canadians— younger ones in particular—are skeptical . . . will the CPP be around for their retirement. And they have every reason to worry.

(Shawn McCarthy and Rob Carrick, *The Globe and Mail*, 11 April 1998)

Rising prevalence of dementia will cripple Canadian families, the health-care system and economy

A report released by the Alzheimer Society today to mark Alzheimer Awareness Month reveals alarming new statistics about the projected economic and social costs of dementia in Canada.

(Alzheimer Society of Canada, *The Medical News*, News medical.net, 4 January 2010. Retrieved from www. news-medical.net/news/20100104/Rising-prevalence-of-dementia-will-cripple-Canadian-families-the-health-care-system-and-economy.aspx)

Canadians ill-prepared for the inevitable

The strain this lack of preparedness puts on family members at one end of the patient-care spectrum and medical professionals on the other could become intolerable in Canada.

(Editorial, *The Gazette*, Montreal, 23 July 2010)

It is argued that the very old (typically women) who enter hospitals, do so with multiple chronic conditions that can not be cured. This leads to wasted health care dollars on these "bed blockers."

(M. Wente Article, *The Globe and Mail*, Thursday, 11 November 2010)

*Source: Reprinted with permission from Gee and Gutman 2000, 6–7, with additions by authors.

the working." This way of thinking has been influenced by public policies designed for hypothetical average or typical people and by simplistic projections of the number of people who must be supported by public funds in the future. The media and policy-makers, faced with an increasing number of older people, ask such questions as the following:

- Will there be sufficient funds in the public pension system when future birth cohorts reach 65, or will the C/QPP (Canada/Quebec Pension Plan) become bankrupt while supporting the large baby boom generation that will retire from about 2011 to 2031?
- Will hospitals disproportionately serve frail older people and make it difficult for those in other age groups to receive hospital treatment?
- Will the number and proportion of individuals with Alzheimer's disease due to population aging create an economic and social crisis?
- Who will provide home care and social support to the large number of aging people, especially with a decline in fertility, more dual-career families, and an increase in older people experiencing singlehood and divorce?
- Will conflict emerge between younger and older generations over what are perceived to be intergenerational inequities favouring older people in the receipt of public services?
- Will an older society become economically stagnant with people aged 65 and over being out of the labour force?
- Will baby boomers place greater demands than earlier generations on the health-care system?

Some of these apocalyptic fears are magnified when there is a global or national economic recession and high government debt. These economic conditions, combined with projections of exponential increases in per capita costs for economic, health, and social support services, encourage governments to propose reducing economic or social support for older people. Governments also employ these arguments as they attempt to download more of these costs to lower levels of government or to individuals and families. To illustrate, in the past decade when governments were faced with an increasing public debt, they built fewer long-term-care facilities and reduced the operating budgets of existing facilities, thereby forcing more families to be involved, at greater personal and financial cost, in the long-term care of aging parents. Seldom were new, alternative, and more economical types of care proposed (see chapters 7 and 12). This issue of public support for older Canadians is a classic example of the debate proposed by Mills (1959) as to whether support in a welfare state should be a "public responsibility" of the state or a "personal responsibility" of the individual and the family.

Despite questions about the sustainability of Canada's universal pension and health-care systems, there is increasing evidence that the significant growth in population aging over the next 30 to 40 years will not bankrupt the pension system, will not be a major contributor to escalating health-care costs, and will not cause intergenerational conflict (Denton and Spencer 2000; Gee 2000; Evans et al. 2001; Hébert 2002, 2011; Myles 2002; Cheal 2003a, 2003b; Chappell and Hollander 2011; Wister 2011).

In the health-care domain, Hébert (2002, 2011) argues that the disproportionate use of health services by older adults in the future will not be a problem. He stresses that the demand for services will not be as high as projected, that there will be improved efficiencies in the health-care system, and that there will be greater use of home-care services to offset the need for costly hospital and residential care. Similarly, Evans et al. (2001, 188) concluded that "the actual evidence is absolutely clear. Whatever the trends in health-care expenditures, and whatever the 'sustainability' of particular financing arrangements (public or private), we have nothing to fear from the aging of the population, only from those who continue to promulgate the fiction of a doomsday scenario." However, the aging of the baby boomers will necessitate rethinking current health-care policies and programs, as well as creating new ones (Wister, 2011).

Consequently, despite periodic fear-mongering by politicians and the media, we should not fear population aging or view it as a crisis. Instead, we should look at population aging as a significant but manageable challenge. This will be especially true when baby boomers retire since the sheer size of this cohort will require reallocation of health and social resources. But members of this generation will spend their retirement years in better functional health with more education and economic resources; and they will be more physically and socially active than previous cohorts of older adults. Moreover, as they have done for most of their adult lives, they will continue to spend their wealth on leisure, travel, and health-care products. As Gee (2000) and others (Friedland and Summer 1999; Longino 2005) have concluded, "demography is not destiny." Changes in the age structure can be managed by policies, programs, and changes within social institutions. More will be said about these institutional changes and public policies in later chapters.

Individual Aging: Adding Life to Years

Scholars and policy-makers at one time focused mainly on the biomedical (Kaufman et al. 2004) and biological (Masoro and Austad 2006) aspects of aging that caused illness, frailty, dependence, and death in later life. Today, **individual aging** is viewed as the interaction of interrelated biological, clinical, psycho-social, and societal factors that affect aging over the life course and that may manifest themselves differently among tomorrow's older adults (Raina et al. 2009). We experience biological aging at different rates and with varying degrees of disease states. These changes often occur dynamically within social, cognitive, and environmental contexts that influence our **life chances** and **lifestyle**, including our degree of independence. For instance, depending on when we were born, whether we are female or male, and where we live out our lives, our health, lifestyle choices, and life chances as we age will be affected by unique social conditions and social change. Events such as economic depressions, natural catastrophes, wars, baby booms, technological revolutions, or social movements mould the life trajectories or pathways of individuals or age cohorts. The impact of these events on a given individual or age cohort usually depends on the chronological age or stage in life when the event is experienced.

To understand aging individuals and older age cohorts, a historical, dynamic, and developmental perspective is required. These criteria are met by the **life-course perspective**, which examines the interplay among individual life stories, our social system and institutions, and environments, and also looks at the effect of specific historical events at particular times in the life course of individuals or age cohorts. Through this approach, we understand how the problems, advantages, disadvantages, needs, and lifestyles of later life are shaped by earlier life transitions, decisions, opportunities, and experiences within specific historical or cultural contexts (Dannefer and Uhlenberg 1999; Hareven 2001; Heinz and Marshall 2003; Settersten 2005; Dannefer and Settersten 2010; Marshall and McMullin, 2010). Individuals are connected to one another because of the timing, direction, and context of their trajectories or pathways—what has been called "linked lives." The life course perspective provides a framework for understanding age-related transitions that begin with birth and entry into the school system and conclude with retirement, widowhood, and death in later life. This perspective reflects the heterogeneous, fluid, and interrelated nature of life transitions. It also recognizes that transitions can be reversible. For instance, an individual who retires from one employer may decide to re-enter the paid workforce after a period of time, or a person who is divorced or widowed may remarry, even in later life.

The life course construct also enables us to observe and analyze how different individual or societal events create variations in the aging process within and between cohorts and individuals. Some events (a war, an economic depression, a flu epidemic) will have an impact on some age cohorts but not on others or only on specific individuals within an age cohort. For example, the feminist movement that started in the 1970s has had a profound influence on the life course of women born just before and after the 1970s. But in general, the feminist movement has had little influence on most women who are now in the later stages of life (75 and older). Statistics Canada has created an interesting life course micro-simulation model of individual and family lives from birth to death (www.statcan.gc.ca/microsimulation/lifepaths/lifepaths-eng.htm). This model, entitled LifePaths, enables us to answer such questions as the following:

- What is the economic benefit, if any, of post-secondary education?
- Do people plan for their retirement?
- How long do we need to work and save to ensure economic security in retirement?

The model can also assist in developing effective policies by employing integrated life course data (Rowe 2003).

Figure 1.2 illustrates the cohort effects of being at a particular stage in life at a particular time in history. For example, during the late 1990s, a period of economic restructuring and high unemployment in Canada, members of cohort A, born in the early 1940s, were probably at the "empty-nest" stage and within 5 to 10 years of retirement. Many were likely coping well with the prevailing social and economic conditions, assuming they did not lose their job to downsizing by their employer. In contrast, some members of cohort B, born in the early 1970s, experienced unemployment or underemployment in early adulthood, and many delayed getting married and buying a house. Cohort C, born in the early 1990s, entered or are entering post-secondary institutions during the early 2010s at a time when there has been a significant downturn in the economy, and many will need to work part-time in order to cover increasing educational costs. Thus, past and current social conditions, as well as life histories, can have an impact on different age cohorts. Some of these factors have an influence on most members of an age cohort throughout their lives (for example, cohort B in the example above); others are affected at only certain periods of their lives. Or an event may have an effect only on some segments of a birth cohort (depending on social class, gender, race, or ethnicity).

At the societal level, your life course will be different from that of younger and older age cohorts and from others of about the same age in other countries and perhaps even in other parts of Canada. Such differences result from cultural, regional, economic, or political variations in opportunities, lifestyles, values, or beliefs. The events a person experiences throughout the life course will vary as well because of particular social or political events that affect some but not all individuals or age cohorts. The study of aging as a social process seeks to identify patterns in life course trajectories and link them to their causes and consequences.

Personal biographies interact with structural, cultural, and historical factors to influence how we age across the life course. Thus, we need to understand why there is diversity

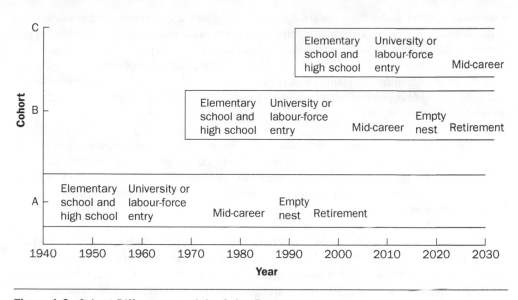

Figure 1.2 Cohort Differences and the Aging Process

in aging among individuals in the same birth cohort (all those born in the same year) and in different birth cohorts (those born at different points in history—you, your parents, your grandparents). Much of this diversity arises because of where an individual or a cohort is located in the social structure.

Social structure pertains to those elements of social life and society that constrain, promote, and shape human behaviour. Whether based on gender, age, class, or ethnicity, social structure creates or limits life course opportunities and leads to common ways of behaving and acting among segments of the population (Giddens 1984). The structural elements provide a set of guidelines or expectations concerning behaviour, and they may set limits on life chances and lifestyles. People's everyday actions reinforce and reproduce a set of expectations—the social forces and social structures that guide our daily lives. These elements, or rules of social order, can be changed—and are changed when people ignore them, replace them, or reproduce them in different forms across their life course. These structural factors interact and become cumulative as we age, often leading to extreme differences in the quality of life among older adults. For example, in later life there can be a cumulative advantage or disadvantage associated with income and poverty across the life course (O'Rand 1996). For instance, a single mother in middle-age can become a single individual living in poverty in her elder years.

While living within a social structure, we are not merely reactive puppets to social forces around us. Individuals in similar situations can act in different ways and make different decisions (Smith et al. 2000; Connidis 2010, 12–13). Within the life course perspective, this process is known as **agency**. Glen Elder, a pioneer in the study of the life course, argues that agency is a "principle," one of five defining principles of the life course (Elder and Johnson 2003, 57–71). These principles are described in Chapter 5. Elder defined *agency* as a process in which individuals construct their life course by making choices and taking actions. These intentional choices and actions are strongly influenced by the constraints and opportunities of social structures, by personal history and past experiences, and by significant others in our daily lives. Dannefer (1999, 73) argues that "human behavior is purposeful; it is not guided by instincts but by intentions." Similarly, Marshall (2000, 11) states that agency refers to the human capacity "to act intentionally, planfully and reflexively, and in a temporal or biographical mode throughout the life course." Marshall (2000, 9–10) also stresses the personal responsibility that we inherit to invoke agency:

> Agency has been seen as the production of a life. The agent is the producer; human development (the lived life, the narrative) is produced by agency . . . people not only react but act and, in acting, produce their biographical selves . . . agency refers to a culturally legitimated responsibility to act—on behalf of others, of organizations or ideas, or of one's own self.

Through agency we create unique identities, develop personal meanings, and decide which social groups are significant in our lives. Considerable variations in lifestyles, experiences, and quality of life evolve within different age cohorts in the older population. Consequently, Canada's population of older adults is a diverse group that, as we will see throughout the book, varies by chronological age, gender, culture, wealth and social status, health status, type and place of residence, and living arrangements. Treating older adults as a homogeneous group with common needs, interests, and experiences can lead to ineffective policies and programs. Some older adults are poor, and some are wealthy; some live alone, and some live with a partner; some live in urban areas and some in rural or remote communities; some are active, mobile, and independent, and some are sedentary, disabled, frail, and dependent; and most fall somewhere in between these extremes. Chapter 6 elaborates further on the relationship between the social structure and individual aging, and Chapter 8 explores the relationship between the individual and his or her lived environment (the search for person–environment "fit"), while Chapter 12 addresses policy issues for a diverse aging population.

Interacting Aging Processes

Although there are a number of separate aging processes, they do interact. For example, a decline in vision (a biological change) may lead to an inability to read or drive a car, thereby restricting a person's mobility, independence, and social interaction. Similarly, mandatory retirement (a social act) may have positive or negative psychological, economic, and/or social outcomes for individuals and for a society. Furthermore, there is variation within and among individuals in the onset and speed of aging among the various processes, which are introduced under separate headings below.

Chronological Aging

The passage of calendar time from one birthday to the next represents **chronological aging**. Our age in years determines our rights (often through legislation) and influences the way we live. Chronological age serves as an approximate indicator of physical growth and decline, social and emotional development, and expected patterns of social interaction. However, chronological age can be deceiving. A 50-year-old with facial features more like those of a 60-year-old may behave and dress more like a 30-year-old. Some may consider this person to be "old" for his or her age, while others may consider him or her to be "immature." Similarly, a person who appears "elderly" from his or her physical appearance may exhibit social, cognitive, or physical behaviour that is similar to that of a much younger adult.

The social meaning or value attached to a specific chronological age, as defined within a particular social context, is often more important than actual chronological age in determining social or cognitive behaviour (for example, people are told to "act their age"). However, such age-based norms are increasingly less influential if we live in an age-integrated rather than an age-segregated society. Consequently, actions or decisions pertaining to education, work, leisure, family, and health are less tied to chronological age than previously.

Chronological age defines "legal" age and thereby provides social order and control in a society, although it can sometimes cause conflict between generations when special benefits (discounts, free drugs) are provided to those at or beyond a specified age. However, legal definitions based on years since birth often constrain individual rights and freedoms. For example, mandatory retirement at age 65 implies that all citizens are no longer able to contribute to the labour force at that age! While some are not able to perform tasks as effectively or may not wish to continue working, others have the capacity, experience, and desire to continue as contributing members of the labour force.

Laws or regulations based on a specific chronological age—for example, the age we enter school or are eligible to drive a car, vote, purchase or consume alcohol, or retire—are established according to what was considered the best, or "normal," chronological age for the specific event at the time the law was passed. For example, legislation requiring individuals to retire at age 65 was originally passed at the beginning of the previous century when life expectancy was considerably lower. Age is used in law to assign advantages and benefits or to impose obligations or restrictions (Law Commission of Canada 2004; Kapp 2006). Sometimes legal age is based on the best available knowledge about capacity or potential at a specific age or on **chronological age norms**—how most individuals behave in a given situation or perform a particular task at a specific age. Or legal age may be influenced by functional age—how well an individual performs specific physical, cognitive, or social tasks (e.g., driving a car after 80 years of age). Or a law based on age may be established according to what is considered, at least by some, to be best for the society (e.g., mandatory retirement).

Functional age is often a more useful guideline than chronological age. It is based on the fact that aging is a multi-faceted, diverse process in which individuals at a specific chronological age are either "older" or "younger" than age peers in terms of some relevant skill or ability. For example, where retirement at a certain age is not required, the right to continue working might be based on a person's ability to work effectively and efficiently. But how we objectively measure physical and cognitive abilities is a difficult and so far unsolvable problem. Hence, functional age, as fair as it seems, has not received much support from employers, unions, or policy-makers. Some have argued that the traditional marker for "old age," 65 years, should be revised upward because of gains in both life expectancy and disability-free life expectancy (Denton and Spencer 2002). This has occurred in the United States, where the eligibility for full social security pension benefits is being increased gradually (through to 2027) from 65 to 67 years of age for those born after 1966. In Sweden, eligibility for pension benefits is indexed to gains in life expectancy. Others contend that flexibility is needed in accessing public pensions in order to reflect the diversity in working conditions experienced by older individuals, especially women (McDonald et al. 2000).

Biological Aging

Internal and external biological changes influence behaviour, longevity, and one's quality of life. **Biological aging** includes genetic and environmentally induced changes in the cellular, muscular, skeletal, reproductive, neural, cardiovascular, and sensory systems. The rate and occurrence of biological changes influence the number of years a person is likely to survive and the extent to which he or she is likely to experience illness or disability. These changes and their accompanying adaptations interact with the social and psychological processes of aging. For example, visible changes, such as greying of the hair and wrinkling of the skin, influence whether we are viewed by others to be young, middle-aged, or elderly. Similarly, our lifestyle, including the amount of stress or depression we experience, can slow down or accelerate the biological processes of aging. Although a detailed discussion of biological aging is beyond the scope of this book (Timiras 2002; Masoro and Austad 2006; Tollefsbol 2010), we should not ignore the effect of such changes when studying aging as a social process. In Chapter 3, we examine the influence of physical and cognitive changes on social behaviour and social interactions.

Psychological Aging

Changes in learning ability, memory, and creativity occur across the life course (Birren and Schaie 2006; Bialystok and Craik 2006; Craik and Bialystok 2006). **Psychological aging** involves the interaction of individual cognitive and behavioural changes with social and environmental factors, such as the loss of a spouse or a change in housing that affects our psychological state. A decline in memory or attention span can reduce or eliminate a lifelong interest in reading or learning. This in turn changes an individual's leisure habits and may lead to boredom, depression, and a deteriorating quality of life. Similarly, a stressful life event, such as divorce, the death of a spouse, or a serious health problem alters the emotional, behavioural, and cognitive processes of an individual at any chronological age. Adapting to stresses often depends not only on personal psychological capacities but also on the amount and type of social support and assistance received from the family and others in the community. Psychological aging is influenced as well by cultural differences, such as whether or not older people are valued. Chapter 3 describes some of the cognitive and personality changes associated with aging.

Social Aging

Biological aging and, to some extent, psychological aging are somewhat similar in all cultures. **Social aging**, however, varies within and across societies and across time, depending on the interactions between aging individuals and others in a particular family, society, or subculture at a specific period in history. Thus, an identical twin separated at birth from a sibling and raised in a different family and community would exhibit behaviour, values, and beliefs that were more similar to age peers in his or her own social world than to those of the sibling.

Patterns of social interaction across the life course are learned within a social structure, whether it be the nuclear family, the workplace, the local community, or Canada as a whole. The age structure of a society is stratified like a ladder. While earlier societies included only a few strata (childhood, adulthood, and old age), modern societies involve many **age strata**—infancy, early childhood, preadolescence, adolescence, young adulthood, middle age, early late life, and very late life. The behaviour and status of the members of each stratum are influenced, at least partially, by the rights and responsibilities assigned on the basis of age or age group and by attitudes toward specific age groups as defined by that society. In some societies, for example, older people are highly valued; in others, they are considered less attractive and are therefore less valued than younger people. In the latter society, being defined as "old" often means that one is marginalized and stigmatized.

Within each culture, social timetables define the approximate or ideal chronological age when we "should" or "must" enter or leave various social positions. Some of these transitions involve institutionalized rites of passage, such as a bar mitzvah, a twenty-first birthday party, a graduation from university, a wedding, or a retirement party. Within an age cohort, the meaning and significance attached to a rite of passage or to a particular age status also varies by social status. For example, marriage early in her twenties for a woman without much formal education may be considered more "on time" than it would be for a woman of the same age with a university degree because of class-based norms or values about the right age for women to marry. The meanings attached to membership in an age stratum or to specific events change as a society changes. For example, some people in your grandparents' generation may have believed that a woman who was not married by her mid-twenties was, or would become, an "old maid." Today, a single woman in her early or mid-thirties may be viewed as independent, "liberated," and modern. She may be praised for not rushing into an early marriage and for pursuing a career.

These variations in social values illustrate why chronological age is a poor indicator of the needs, capabilities, and interests of adults across the life course. Increasingly, the time when major life events take place is no longer dictated by chronological age. For example, women may give birth for the first time in their teens or in their early forties; parents may become grandparents as early as age 30 or as late as 70; and marriages take place at all chronological ages, including a first marriage or a remarriage for those in their sixties, seventies, and eighties.

Social aging is influenced as well by the composition of the age structure, which comprises many different birth or age cohorts. People born during the same period in history can exhibit considerable diversity because of variations in personal attributes, such as their gender or where they live. As the life course evolves for each cohort, social inequality on one or more of these dimensions accounts for different patterns of aging within the cohort. For example, two women born in the same year in the same community might follow different life trajectories depending on their education and their views about marriage, childbearing, and careers. Similarly, a child in a family where both parents earn an income will have different life experiences from those of a child born in the same year to a single mother who drops out of school to work and support her child.

No cohort ages alone. Aging involves interaction among cohorts and cohort succession. Each cohort is integrally linked to others through social interaction in family, work, or leisure settings. These inter-cohort relations have the potential to create both co-operation and conflict between generations. This is especially true if social differences in a society create age strata with higher or lower status and therefore greater or lesser power. In societies where older people are highly valued, intergenerational relations are generally positive, and each cohort moves from one age stratum to the next with little or no conflict. In contrast, in societies where youth is valued more highly than old age or where elderly people are marginalized, intergenerational rivalry and conflict are more likely. In such societies, elderly people often resent the loss of status and power they once held. It was this resentment and concern that launched the "grey power" movement in the 1970s (Pratt 1976) and an awareness of growing generational inequities in the 1980s and 1990s (Bengtson and Achenbaum 1993).

Dimensions of Social Aging

The Social World and Aging: History, Culture, and Structure

Aging and the status of older people in everyday life are linked to the period of history in which we live and to the culture and social structure of the society or communities where we are born and live out our lives. Our place in history and our culture influence the type and quality of life we experience, as Chapter 2 illustrates in more detail. For now, think of the differences in how we might age or spend later life if we lived at a time when we either did or did not experience or have access to drugs (for cancer, heart disease, or AIDS) and such medical devices as pacemakers and artificial hips; to mandatory retirement and a universal pension system; to nursing and retirement homes; to technological devices, such as computers, cellphones, home and personal alarm systems, and microwave ovens; and to subsidies for older adults for transportation, home care, or long-term care. As you consider aging issues, think about history and culture to understand fully the circumstances in which older adults in a particular society and as a member of a specific cohort spent their earlier and later years. **Culture**, the way of life passed from generation to generation, varies within societies and changes across time in a society. Our culture creates ideas, beliefs, norms, values, and attitudes that shape our thinking and behaviour about aging and about being old. Thus, to understand the lifestyles of individuals as they age and the views of a society about aging, one needs to consider the cultural elements prevailing at a particular period in history and the changes that occur in cultural values and meanings across generations.

Diversity in aging experiences and the considerable heterogeneity among those in older age cohorts occur because of both cultural and social differentiation in the social structure of a community or society. **Social stratification** is a process by which social attributes (age, gender, religion, social class, race, and ethnicity) are evaluated differentially according to their value in the eyes of the society. These attributes create a structure in which some people are considered superior to others. In North America, for example, individuals are generally evaluated more highly if they are young rather than elderly, male rather than female, and white rather than a member of a visible-minority group. These evaluations of social attributes influence our identity, life chances, and lifestyle throughout our lives and can foster social inequalities. To illustrate, we live in a "gendered" society. Gender distinctions are socially constructed so that women often have a lower position in everyday social and work life. Consequently, their situation and interpretation of growing old are different. There are many gender inequities in the aging process, as noted first by Susan Sontag, who spoke of the "double standard of aging" (Sontag 1972; Gee and Kimball 1987; Kimmel 2000; McDaniel 2004). Gender and aging are strongly connected across the life course, and as we will see in more detail in several later chapters, some consider aging to be primarily a "women's issue" (Arber and Ginn 1995, 2005; Moen 2001; Estes 2005).

In Canada, we live in a unique multicultural society. Approximately 19 per cent of Canadians are foreign-born (calculated using Statistics Canada CANSIM tables). A majority of these people belong to visible minorities who, in recent years, tend to originate from Asian, Caribbean, South American, eastern European, and African countries rather than from northern Europe. Today, there are at least 200 language groups in the country. As these individuals age, there will be increasing diversity within our older population (see Chapter 2).

Place of residence, while not generally considered a stratification system, is an important factor when discussing diversity in aging. There is considerable diversity in the lifestyles,

Highlight 1.3
Age-Friendly Rural and Remote Communities: A Guide

In September 2006, the Federal/Provincial/Territorial (F/P/T) Ministers Responsible for Seniors endorsed the Age-Friendly Rural/Remote Communities Initiative (AFRRCI). The Initiative has two main objectives:

1. To increase awareness of what seniors need to maintain active, healthy, and productive lives within rural or remote communities
2. To produce a practical guide that rural and remote communities across Canada can use to identify common barriers, and to foster dialogue and action that supports the development of age-friendly communities

In an age-friendly community, policies, services, settings, and structures support and enable people to age actively by

*   recognizing the wide range of capacities and resources among older people
*   anticipating and responding flexibly to aging-related needs and preferences
*   respecting the decisions and lifestyle choices of older adults
*   protecting those older adults who are most vulnerable
*   promoting the inclusion of older adults in, and contribution to, all areas of community life

Source: Federal/Provincial/Territorial Ministers Responsible for Seniors 2009.

backgrounds, and aging-related services and support systems of residents in rural versus urban communities (Keating 2008; Davenport et al. 2009). For instance, there has been an initiative in Canada and other countries to develop age-friendly communities, with a focus on improving social services and programs for older adults living in disadvantaged rural and remote communities (see Highlight 1.3).

The Social Construction of Old Age: Images and Labels

There are many myths and misconceptions about growing older and about being elderly. Before reading this section, you should assess your knowledge about aging by answering the questions[1] in Highlight 1.4.

Whereas chronological age is a precise measure of how many years someone has lived, it is seldom an accurate representation or definition of being "old" or of being at a specific stage in life. The reality of aging is clouded if chronological age is employed as the way to assign meanings to a specific age or stage in life—if, for example, 65+ means to be retired, dependent, and perhaps poor and frail. Such labelling creates and perpetuates **stereotypes**, which are exaggerations of particular attributes of a group of individuals, and fosters **age discrimination** and prejudices toward members of specific age groups; in short, it constitutes **ageism**. Such views may discourage older adults from participating in the labour force or in some social, leisure, or volunteer activities. Ageism can also influence how young adults are treated by others. To

Highlight 1.4
Some Facts about Aging: True or False?

Palmore (1977; 1980; 1981; 1988; 1990), Miller and Dodder (1980), Martin-Matthews et al. (1984), and Harris and Changas (1994) have developed versions of a true-or-false "Facts on Aging" quiz. The items in the test are based on documented research, and the following 10 questions represent the type of questions included in the various versions.

T   F   1. Older people tend to become more religious as they age.
T   F   2. Most old people are set in their ways and unable to change.
T   F   3. The majority of old people are seldom bored.
T   F   4. The health and socio-economic status of older people (compared with younger people) in the future will probably be about the same as it is now.
T   F   5. Older people have more acute (short-term) illnesses than people under 65.
T   F   6. The majority of old people are seldom irritated or angry.
T   F   7. Older workers have less absenteeism than younger workers.
T   F   8. The elderly have higher rates of criminal victimization than people under 65.
T   F   9. The majority of older people live alone.
T   F   10. Older people who reduce their activity tend to be happier than those who remain active.

Responses to the questions reflect one's knowledge of facts, and thus the quiz cannot be regarded as a direct measure of attitudes. In reality, any misconceptions—and they have been found in all age groups—often reflect the respondents' lack of personal experience with older adults, inaccurate conclusions based on personal observations of elderly people from a distance rather than through direct interaction with a friend or family member, or the unquestioned acceptance of myths and images presented by the mass media.

Source: Palmore 1977, 315–20; 1981, 431–7. Reprinted by permission of The Gerontological Society of America.

illustrate, students may be refused apartments because of stereotypes about the risk of renting to young adults, especially students!

"Old" age, being "elderly," or becoming a "senior" does not happen overnight when a person turns 65. Rather, the meaning of being "old," "elderly," or a "senior" is socially constructed and reinforced when cultural values and misconceptions define those who are 65 or over as "elderly," "old," or a "senior." These labels[2] are not based on an individual's abilities or health status. Rather, they are assigned to everyone on the basis of stereotypes about those who reach a particular chronological age. This process of labelling is institutionalized in a society when social policies require all citizens to meet some requirement based on age, such as mandatory retirement at age 65. These age-related public policies can influence older persons' sense of self and how others regard them, especially if the policy fosters labelling (Hendricks 2004). In addition, cultural elements produce verbal and visual images about aging or elderly people through the television, the Internet, literature,[3] art, films,[4] song lyrics, photographs, jokes, and birthday cards. Often these images express the view, with or without humour, that later life is equated with illness, losses, loneliness, asexuality, and poverty. To illustrate, Ellis and Morrison (2005) found that 67 per cent of the birthday cards sold in retail stores in a small Canadian metropolitan area depicted aging in a negative light although often humour was intended. Many images of older people presented on television, such as the cartoon show *The Simpsons*, are created to generate humour through references to asexuality, deafness, or forgetfulness, but in so doing they reinforce common (usually erroneous) stereotypes, albeit with a sense of irony that sometimes produces multiple meanings (Blakeborough 2008). Similarly, newspapers focus either on the horrors or tragedies of aging or the marvels of truly unique but atypical long-lived people who have accomplished feats unusual for their age or have celebrated birthdays beyond 90 years of age. In an analysis of 30 articles published in *The Globe and Mail* in 2004, Rozanova et al. (2006) found that both positive and negative stereotypes and images appeared. Common themes included the diversity of the older population, successful aging, and conflict between generations.

Media images seem to be changing over time. Miller et al. (2004) analyzed historical portrayals of older persons in US television commercials. They concluded that elderly persons tended to be shown in comical roles in the 1970s, with more negative portrayals in the mid-1970s and early 1980s, shifting to neutral ones in the later 1980s, and more positive ones since the early 1990s. More recently, Lee et al. (2007) found that older adults appeared in 15 per cent of advertisements on television, with older women being under-represented. The older persons played incidental roles in the advertisements and promoted a stereotyped set of products and services, although most characters displayed positive attributes and traits. Similarly, Robinson et al. (2007), in a study of 34 Disney animated films, argued that the media can serve as an important socializing function for children by supplying images that create or reinforce stereotypes. They found that while only 42 per cent of the older Disney characters were portrayed negatively (grumpy, mad, threatening, highly wrinkled), these portrayals might be influencing children to develop negative feelings about older people in general. The aging of the large baby boom generation will likely result in media portrayals of more healthy and wealthy older adults. However, closer examination of media portrayals of particular groups of elderly persons suggests variations in these patterns. For instance, Kessler et al. (2004) have identified common television themes of "powerful men" and "caring women," which contribute to the marginalization of women in society.

Negative or atypical images, when accepted as fact by the media, the public, and policy-makers, can shape public opinion about aging, influence which public programs are funded (should community recreational facilities be built for youth, older adults, or both?), and undermine the potential of adults as they move into the later years. In short, these socially constructed labels and images foster a self-fulfilling prophecy whereby some older adults believe they should think and behave like the stereotypes perpetuated by the media. This in turn can lead to a loss of self-esteem, isolation, and the labelling of oneself as "old." To illustrate, currently older adults are often heard stating, "I'm having a senior moment!" The phrase could refer to anything from a brief memory lapse about a name, place, or date, to a moment of confusion, to severe cognitive impairment (Bonnesen and Burgess 2004). This is an ageist expression that older persons have adopted as an excuse when they forget something in the presence of others. The popularity of the term suggests that some negative stereotypes of older adults remain socially acceptable.

Another example of a socially constructed label applied to some older adults late in the life course is the term *frailty*. But in fact, most older people do not experience frailty—a severe biomedical condition. Indeed, the conditions implied by this label may never appear or may only apply to those who, through a natural progression of aging, lose strength, endurance, weight, and perhaps some degree of cognitive functioning, especially in the last few months or years of life (see Chapter 3). The cultural construction of old age as a biological phenomenon is also propagated by anti-aging technologies and science, which often view aging as a negative medical problem (Vincent 2008). Yet science can also counter ageist discourse as we will see.

We must be careful in the creation, selection, and use of labels about older people and later life. The language we use can affect the behaviour of older persons or influence the behaviour of others, who may avoid or ignore older persons or apply the stereotypes as they interact with older persons. Moreover, such labels or images mask the considerable heterogeneity among older people. In short, there is no "typical" older person who can be depicted or defined by one image. Similarly, it is difficult to discuss or promote the idea of "successful" aging or to develop a model for "successful" aging that could be used for developing policies for the entire older population. In a recent critique of the construct of "successful aging," Bowling (2007) argued that there is little theoretical justification for the **concepts** or definitions included in this construct and that the definitions vary widely because they reflect the academic disciplines of the proponents—for example, the biomedical models of successful aging emphasize physical and mental functions, while the socio-psychological models emphasize social interaction/functioning, life satisfaction, and the availability and use of psychological resources. If an ideal and workable model of successful aging is to be developed, it must be multi-dimensional; it must involve a continuum of success; and it must be reflexive and include the views of older people on what constitutes successful aging, especially variations in values across gender, across socio-economic status, across cultures, and across the social structure.

Images of Aging and Their Influence on Individuals and Society

Stereotypes

Many stereotypical images are based on the changing appearance of the aging body (e.g., wrinkles, changing body shapes, baldness for men, greying hair) or on reported or observed changes in the social, physical, or cognitive behaviour of some older persons. In some cultures, wrinkles are a sign of high status and wisdom; in others, they are a sign of decay and a symbol of being less attractive, less valued, and less useful. Similarly, paintings in some earlier eras indicate that short, plump women were admired whereas today, photographs and paintings idealize women who are tall and very thin. This latter example illustrates how images are socially constructed and how they can change over time (de Beauvoir[5] 1970; Featherstone and Hepworth 2005).

Misleading stereotypes of older adults can also be found in elementary school texts, children's literature, and adult fiction in which older people are seldom, if ever, portrayed in illustrations. Older people are usually peripheral to the plot, have limited abilities, and play passive rather than active roles. Furthermore, they are usually under-represented in relation to their proportion in the real world. And older women are even more under-represented even though they comprise a higher proportion of the older population than men. Not surprisingly, elderly members of **minority groups** are seldom included in books, except in literature written by or specifically about members of particular ethnic or racial groups. Thus, there is a constant need for education to eliminate false images and to eradicate stereotypes.

We must not assume that a misleading and stereotypical view of aging and older adults is acquired solely through literature or by watching television. There is no proof of a direct causal relationship between the reading of books in which older people are ignored, under-represented, or misrepresented and the adoption of negative attitudes toward older people. Furthermore, since school textbooks are interpreted by teachers, elementary school students could be more sensitive to the realities of aging issues, depending on the supplementary material presented by a particular teacher. Nevertheless, given the pervasiveness of negative **attitudes** about aging in our culture, these attitudes are often reflected in affective, cognitive, and behav-ioural responses of individuals and groups of all ages (Hess 2006; Davis and Friedrich, 2010) and affect some older individuals in a negative way.

Stereotypes can, with time and research, be refuted. For example, in recent years, older people have been portrayed in a wider variety of occupations and social roles that more closely coincide with reality. Today, they are depicted as active, independent, influential citizens and family members and as having skills and experiences of value to society. The presentation of a more positive view of aging and older people is due, partly, to the mass media's recognition of the changing demographic profile of society in general and of television viewers in particular. The change is also due to entrepreneurs' recognition that a large, wealthy "senior market" is emerging. By some estimates, people over 50 control more than 80 per cent of the savings in Canada, making them the most economically advantaged age group. Negative stereotypes of older adults are being challenged and eliminated as well by increasingly politically active and age-conscious older people. This pressure can lead to a deconstruction and reconstruc-tion of the images and discourse about aging and later life. Negative and inaccurate social images and words are being replaced by more accurate, modern pictures and descriptions of active, vibrant, and independent older adults. By challenging the current discourse, such images help to refute the apocalyptic view of population aging and its hypothesized dreaded outcomes for a society.

Many realistic images of aging and of the meaning of being older are developed through interviews with and reflections by older adults. Much of the credit for the emergence of more accurate images belongs to anthropologists and sociologists, who employ a qualitative approach to understanding social behaviour, and to humanists, who employ biographical narratives to identify the meaning of later life (Kenyon et al. 2001; Randall and Kenyon 2004). These scholars present the voices of women and of people from diverse ethnic groups, social classes, or regional environments. Older adults, by telling their life stories and by sharing their thoughts and feel-ings, enable us to understand later life as it is experienced by those living that life. Highlight 1.5 describes aging in the words of older people.

Age Identity: Not Just a Number

Age identity is the result of a subjective experience that represents the psychological and social meaning of aging rather than chronological age. This concept, sometimes referred to as "subjective age," illustrates how aging is socially constructed. Social and age-related identities are renegotiated in different social contexts or as an individual's health or visual appearance changes (Lin et al. 2004). In this sense, the aging self is a managed identity (Biggs 2005). People of the same chronological age (e.g., 65) may report a wide range of age identities. Some may feel younger and report feeling like 55; others may feel older and identify with 75-year-olds, although this "age as older" identification seldom happens except on days or during periods when health and energy are low. Increasingly, the clothes we wear are central to expressing how older bodies are experienced, presented, and understood in our culture. Clothing can be used

Highlight 1.5
Voices of Older Adults

People Living in the Community

I think it's quite normal to be anxious about aging. For all of us it means entering unknown territory, with its attendant fears. The reality for me is that growing older has meant a time of much greater freedom. My children are grown and increasingly independent. I am free to develop my own person, in a way that I never had the courage to do when I was younger. I am discovering strengths and recognizing weaknesses. I don't need to apologize and explain as much as I used to. I wish I'd known 10 years ago that getting older would be this interesting, because I have spent too much time in the past worrying about it.

(Rodriguez 1992, 26. Reprinted by permission.)

My life has been more happy than sad, much more good than bad. Still, for the past several years, I learned about the troubles of aging as my strong and vigorous husband gradually became weaker and more ill. When he was young, I thought he was like a great oak tree and that nothing could ever bring him down. Yet he is gone, and I, never particularly strong or robust, remain well and active and learning to manage on my own. . . . I drive my car, baby-sit grandchildren, and make plans to travel and visit around the country. I spend a great deal of time just being thankful for many things younger people take for granted. I am thankful to still have so many people to love and share my life—children, sisters and their families, many other relatives and good friends, and the many nice people around this city.

(Adapted from *Are You Listening? Essays by Ontario Senior Citizens on What It Means to Be a Senior.* 1989. Toronto: Office for Seniors' Issues, Ministry of Citizenship. Reprinted by permission.)

Residents of Long-Term-Care Facilities

When my wife had her stroke, she spent almost a year in a hospital. I lived alone and was terribly depressed. When we both got accepted here I was really glad to be with her again. I have to admit that living like this with her is sometimes depressing for me. We only have one room and the children can't come very often. But I've adapted. At least I'm not lonely for her anymore.

They take care of me here but they don't do it the same as I would myself. I can't take care of myself because I'm all "crippled up." Sometimes I think this place is run more for the convenience of the staff than for the residents. I resent having to go to bed so early just to suit them. . . . I only have $90 a month to get by on. That is not very much. It is very hard for me to take a bus to go anywhere.

(*The* NACA *Position on Canada's Oldest Seniors: Maintaining the Quality of Their Lives.* 1992. p. 54–5. Ottawa: National Advisory Council on Aging. Reproduced with the consent of the National Advisory Council on Aging (NACA) and the Minister of Public Works and Government Services Canada, 2004.)

to express an age identity and to resist or define the dominant meanings of being older (Twigg 2007). Age identity is shaped by social experiences—how individuals view the self and how individuals think that others view and react to them. Kaufman and Elder (2002), in a study of grandparenting and age identity, found that those who become grandparents in their thirties and forties felt older than those who acquire this role "on time" (i.e., later in life). Older people who enjoyed being grandparents felt younger, believed that people become "old" at older ages, and hoped to live longer than those who reported that they did not enjoy being grandparents.

In reality, many older people do not think of themselves as old and often report feeling and acting younger than their chronological age. In an examination of five dimensions of age identity in later life, Kaufman and Elder (2002) found that as people age, their subjective and desired ages become further removed from their actual chronological age. That is, personal age identity changes as we age, but these personal perceptions and definitions lag behind our real age. The identification of the self as younger than our actual chronological age is more likely among those who are in good health and physically active and among those who are employed. Individuals from lower socio-economic strata often experience an earlier onset of health limitations and a faster rate of decline in functional ability. Consequently, they tend to hold "older" identities (Barrett 2003). For some older people, negative societal attitudes about aging are a threat to self-esteem. For others, however, old-age stereotypes are functional in that the individuals may, in comparison with the stereotypes, see that they are better off than most elderly people.

Older people often define themselves as being different from others of the same age by presenting themselves as active and healthy. For example, a 91-year-old woman in Finland, in response to questions about how she interprets old age and how she views herself, talked about "dancing," "racing around," and "walking up stairs and around the yard." She concluded the interview by stating, "I haven't taken to a walking stick yet. And there are others here who go around with a stick and a walker" (Jolanki et al. 2000, 366). This respondent defines herself as being more active and more independent than those who are younger or of the same age in her retirement home. Similarly, Hurd (1999), in a study of older women who attended a senior centre in central Canada, found that older women distance themselves from those they consider old and that they actively work at presenting an alternative image of what it means to age. The demonstration of "active aging" is a form of identity management that is often related to higher levels of life satisfaction and subjective well-being (Westerof and Barrett 2005).

Ageism: A Form of Discrimination

In 1968, the public housing authority in Chevy Chase, Maryland, applied to convert a building in a white, middle-class suburb into housing for older citizens. The public hearings degenerated into a riot as residents of the area fought to keep "all those old people" out of their community. As a result of this incident, Butler (1969) coined the term "ageism." He considered ageism to be similar to racism and sexism in that inherent biological factors are used to define **personality** or character traits. Butler defined ageism as a process of systematic stereotyping of and discrimination against people because they are old. Ageism can be expressed, fostered, and perpetuated by the media, by public policies, in the workplace, and in casual daily interactions with older people. Indeed, even those who work with or study older people may employ unintentional, insensitive ageist language (Palmore 2000; 2001). A large body of literature has examined the attitudes and behaviours of various age groups toward aging and older people, as well as the effects of those attitudes on the older persons.[6]

Attitudes toward aging are influenced by a number of factors, including the age, ethnicity, education level, gender, and socio-economic status of the respondents. Those with more education consistently show more positive attitudes toward aging, perhaps because they have more knowledge about aging. Similarly, those who have frequent and meaningful interaction with older people, especially in a family, have more positive attitudes, primarily because the frequent contact provides factual, personal knowledge that refutes the myths and stereotypes about aging encountered elsewhere in society.

Ageism is a socially constructed way of thinking about and behaving toward older people. It is based on negative attitudes and stereotypes about aging and older people and involves an assumption that the passing of time represents decay and is therefore grounds for discrimination or marginalization. Ageism is the one source of disadvantage, oppression, or discrimination that we all might face from others in later life. And we may even oppress ourselves later in life if we adopt ageist attitudes and beliefs. When negative attitudes and stereotypes become pervasive and institutionalized, they can be used to justify prejudicial and discriminatory legislation or regulations, such as mandatory retirement at a specific chronological age. Or, on the basis of age, people may be excluded from social interaction or denied equal access to services in the public and private sectors. Where ageism exists, older people are devalued, and their human rights are compromised. In short, there is both *individual* ageism, the acceptance of negative feelings and beliefs that influence our thinking and behaviour, and *institutionalized* (or structural) ageism, as expressed in legislation, advertisements, the mass media, and anti-aging products, all of which can lead to social and economic inequalities across society (Bytheway 2005b).

With the onset of population aging and increasing awareness of the changing age structure, age has been used to "explain" the limitations, rights, abilities, and characteristics of people of a certain chronological age. Age is also used to "explain" withdrawal from the labour force or the onset of illness, disability, or dependency. As with most forms of discrimination, it is difficult to obtain reliable research evidence to explain the extent of ageism or why it exists (Cohen 2001; Nelson 2002; Palmore et al. 2005). It may be that the occurrence and degree of ageism is closely linked to demographic and economic factors in a society. For example, when a significant proportion of the aging baby boom cohort reaches retirement age between 2011 and 2031, the skills of older people may be needed to meet the demand for labour. In that case, structural ageism could ebb or disappear because of the need for more flexible work and retirement schemes (Longino 2005). In another 15 to 25 years, older people will be a near-majority group in the social structure, and ageism may be much less common, especially if older people are perceived as necessary and useful contributors to the labour force and the economy.

Regardless of what social changes the future may bring, "age" should not be employed as a convenient benchmark for behaviour or rights or as an explanation for processes or outcomes in later life. Cooper (1984, 4) states,

> Most would agree that ageism is not the total experience of age. . . . But only if we learn to recognize ageism—name it, resist it, refine our understanding of it, stop participating in it—only then can we separate growing old from the fog of ageism which diminishes us. Then, and only then, are true acceptance and celebration of age possible.

Similarly, Bodily (1991, 260) argues that the study of "age effects" should be abandoned and that "age differences" are not synonymous with "differences due to age":

Gerontologists do not study the effects of age; rather, they study processes, the effects of which tend to surface among older populations, not because these people are older, but because the processes themselves take time or depend on other processes which take time. This distinction is crucial because it preempts the possibility of casting "age" as a cause, thereby making room not only for variations "between" different age groups, but variation "among" the same age group. People age differently both because they are subject to different events and processes and because the same events and processes affect them differently.

As members of a society become better informed about aging, chronological age as the defining marker of being old will be eroded. Increased research, a longer life expectancy, and visible, more active, and independent older people are revising the definition of later life. However, some members of the media, as well as some politicians, are still enamoured of the use of chronological age as a marker for labels or rights and still rely on stereotypes and ageist images when forming their opinions or policies. Chronological age should not be a criterion when framing legislation that affects older adults. In Belgium, strict anti-discrimination legislation requires that all legislation be reviewed for its use of 50 or more years as an age criterion (Breda and Schoenmaekers 2006).

The Field of Gerontology Grows Up

Gerontology, traditionally a multidisciplinary field of study, is the study of aging processes and aging individuals, as well as of the practices and policies that are designed to assist older adults. Gerontology includes research conducted in the biological and health sciences, the behavioural and social sciences, and the humanities, as well as analyses of policies and practices developed at the global, federal, provincial, regional, or local level. Increasingly, the field is becoming even more interdisciplinary in terms of the questions asked and the perspectives and methods employed to answer the research questions about aging phenomena (Alkema and Alley 2006). The latest information in the field can be found in the proceedings of conferences; in articles in newspapers, magazines, and research journals; in government documents; and on the Internet.[7] **Geriatrics**, not to be confused with gerontology, is a sub-specialty of medicine that focuses on the physical and mental diseases of later life and on the clinical treatment and care of elderly patients by specialized physicians.

Social gerontology, a subset of gerontology, studies the social processes, issues, practices, and policies associated with aging and older people. It was not until the 1960s that scholars in Canada began to study aging processes and individuals in later life. This early research was concerned with two aspects of aging: first, with developing, evaluating, or critiquing welfare programs or social policies for older people; and, second, with describing and explaining aging processes and older adults' status and behaviour. The researchers in the second category were affiliated with a traditional discipline, such as sociology, psychology, political science, geography, history, demography, or economics. Since the 1980s, aging phenomena and issues have also been studied by practitioners and scholars in professions such as social work, nursing, dentistry, education, architecture, pharmacy, law, criminology, urban and regional planning, recreation and leisure, and kinesiology and physical education. More recently, scholars in disciplines such as philosophy, literature, fine arts, communication and film studies, women's studies, men's studies, and cultural studies have been offering critiques of the way that old age and older people are depicted in the arts, the media, and scholarly publications.

Gerontology has become a discipline in its own right, as reflected in the significant growth in the quantity and quality of educational programs about gerontology in Canada and every other developed country, as well as in the discipline's recent expansion to developing countries. Ferraro (2006) published an editorial in *The Gerontologist* entitled "Gerontology's Future: An Integrative Model for Disciplinary Advancement." He argued that the field of gerontology has developed into a discipline, based on four elements critical to its evolution: theory, research methodology, formalized organizations supporting the field of study, and a common vernacular. He distinguished between a multidisciplinary (pillar model) and an interdisciplinary (integrative model) approach to research and educational training. He speculated that "with greater emphasis on interdisciplinary work in educational programs, a paradigm shift may commence with academic and research institutions moving away from aging scholarship based on a single perspective toward valuing the unique contributions that gerontology offers as an integrative discipline" (Ferraro 2006, 580).

Gerontology can be further divided into two general components: the academic community, which produces research, theory, and critiques about the aging process and the situation of older people; and the professions, which apply research knowledge and theory to the development and implementation of policies, programs, and services to enhance the quality of life for older adults. The Canadian Association on Gerontology (www.cagacg.ca), which welcomes student members, includes researchers, graduate students, government policy-makers, and practitioners in the public or private sector who are employed in a variety of positions that serve older adults. This diverse group of members meets annually to share information that will advance knowledge and improve the lives of older Canadians.

The timeline displayed just before Part I of this textbook provides key advancements in the field of social gerontology in Canada in education, research, and policy. While it is impossible to include all major events and publications, the timeline does identify significant milestones. During the early periods (prior to 1945), there was primarily isolated work related to aging, with little organization through formal organizations. Between 1945 and 1960, the first-generation scholars began to form "networked" organizations, conferences, and the first journals on aging in an attempt to develop a distinct area of research and training. A second generation of researchers was trained in the 1961 to 1975 era, some of whom received their education in gerontology programs and centres. This period experienced growth in key knowledge development in a number of sub-fields or clusters. Between 1975 and 2000, social gerontology became a recognized discipline, with a critical mass of researchers and practitioners. Since the millennium, we have witnessed an enormous growth in the field of social gerontology and the integration of knowledge across disciplinary boundaries.

In Canada, courses on the sociology of aging and social gerontology have been taught since the early 1970s. The first Canadian reader and textbook with a focus on social aging were published in the early 1980s by, respectively, Marshall (1980) and McPherson (1983). In 1971, the Canadian Association on Gerontology was founded, and in 1982 the association launched the *Canadian Journal on Aging*, a quarterly research journal (Martin-Matthews and Béland 2001). As well, a number of major research initiatives have contributed to our knowledge base in Canada. The Canadian Health and Aging Study focused on the epidemiology of dementia wherein 10,000 elderly Canadians were studied over a 10-year period from 1991 to 2001. In June 2000, the CIHR Institute on Aging was established as one of 13 institutes of health research in Canada. CIHR supports the development of the Canadian Longitudinal Study on Aging, which will collect population health and social data from the cellular to the societal level on 50,000 Canadians from 2010 to about 2030. Earlier, provincial longitudinal studies on aging were initiated in Ontario in 1959 under the leadership of Lawrence Crawford; and in Manitoba, in 1971, under the leadership of Betty Havens. Other notable developments that have increased our knowledge and awareness of aging in Canada include the formation of centres on aging at universities or colleges; the development of diploma, undergraduate, or graduate programs in many universities and colleges since the 1980s; the creation of provincial gerontology associations; the funding of the Canadian Aging Research Network (CARNET) from 1990 to 1995; the National Initiative for the Care of the Elderly (NICE) since 2005; the creation of the National Advisory Council on Aging (NACA) (replaced by the National Seniors Council in the mid-2000s); the Division of Aging and Seniors, Public Health Agency of Canada, Ministry of Health, and various other departments or ministries concerned with aging issues at federal, provincial, regional, or local levels of government; and many research networks, grants, and contracts funded by provincial and federal agencies since the 1980s (Martin-Matthews and Béland 2001, 25–81, 205–11).

The study of aging processes and older adults is thriving in Canada (see Sheets and Gallagher 2013). Many government agencies produce regular reports about aging issues and older adults (Statistics Canada, Public Health Agency of Canada, Employment and Social Development Canada, the Minister of State (Seniors), the National Seniors Council, Veterans Affairs). Globally, more than 200 journals publish gerontological research, and most of them have the words *aging*, *gerontology*, or *elderly* in their titles (see www.sfu.ca/iag/links/journals.htm). With the aging of the population expected to reach new heights over the next 30 years, jobs or careers in aging-related fields should present good opportunities for employment.[8]

Three Conceptual Dimensions to Understand the Study of Aging

Many methods can be used to study aging phenomena (see Chapter 5). Before these methods can be studied, we must understand a number of conceptual dimensions upon which we can develop our questions and focus our analyses. Each of these dichotomies represents a dimension with two extremes: personal troubles and public issues; agency and social structure; and the micro (individual) and macro (structural) elements of daily life. They refer to different aspects of social life that are interrelated and interdependent. However, we separate them, conceptually, so that we can understand more completely an extremely complex social world.

Personal Troubles and Public Issues

To understand our social world, we need to consider relationships and links between individuals and their society. In his influential book, entitled *The Sociological Imagination*, C. Wright Mills argued that this dialectic needs to focus on how social order and change are created out of the disparate needs and motivations of the many diverse individuals who make up a society, group, or organization. Often, this view of the relationship between personal troubles (of individuals) and public issues (responsibilities of society) exaggerates the degree to which individuals are influenced by structural forces that control and guide their lives, depending on where they are located in the social structure. This view is therefore limited because it ignores the presence of agency—how individuals interact with social structures.

Agency and Social Structure

Agency involves individual or group action, based on the ability and willingness to make decisions that affect social relationships. We develop individual or group identities as we interact with others and form social relations across the life course as a result of individual action within the constraints and opportunities of our social world. We have the potential, as individuals or groups, to construct and change our social world, at least within the boundaries of the social structures and social contexts in which we live. Or, as Giddens (1984) noted, agency refers to the ability of human beings to make a difference in the world. The individual or group can act as an agent of change, with varying degrees of freedom, to shape social structures, institutions, and cultural artifacts.

Social structures provide the social context or conditions under which people act and form social relationships. Most components of this structure—gender, race, ethnicity, and class—are present from birth and endure across the life course. To summarize, "the agency-structure issue focuses on the way in which human beings create social life at the same time as they are influenced and shaped by existing social arrangements" (Layder 1994, 5).

Micro and Macro Analyses

The third vector influencing our conceptualization of social life across the life course is the micro-macro distinction. This dialectic analyzes the interaction of those elements that focus on personal, face-to-face social interactions in the daily life of individuals or small groups (a micro-analysis) and those that focus on the larger, impersonal structural components of a society—organizations, institutions, and culture, and their sub-elements of power, class, and resources (a macro-analysis).

Critical Issues and Challenges for an Aging Society

As you begin your journey toward increased understanding of and sensitivity to aging processes and older adults, a number of issues and challenges should be at the forefront of your critical thinking skills and your personal actions. They will be addressed in more detail throughout the book. At this point, you should note the following:

- Aging is not an illness or a disease state—avoid the medicalization of aging view and the view that aging can be decelerated, reversed, or "cured" through anti-aging medicines and modalities (Fisher and Morley 2002; Binstock 2003; Mehlman et al. 2004; Hudson 2004; Bayer 2005).
- Aging is primarily a women's issue—women live longer, often alone, and face more challenges in later life, such as poverty and discrimination, especially if they are divorced or widowed or have never married.
- We live in and are connected to an aging world. Much of the growth in population aging in the twenty-first century will occur in developing countries.
- Aging, as a social process, occurs in a changing social world with diverse structural opportunities and barriers—there is inequality in the aging process and in later life because of lifelong variations in life opportunities and choices.
- Individual and population aging are inevitably linked and constitute an evolving dialectic

wherein aging issues and experiences manifest themselves in larger societal spheres, such as retirement, pensions, health care, and social support policies and programs.

- As birth cohorts grow older, there is increasing diversity among members of the cohort—in health status, lifestyles, income, attitudes, mobility, and independence, to name only a few dimensions. This diversity or heterogeneity must be considered in the development of policies, programs, and services at all levels of government.
- As the large and diverse baby boom generation continues to move into later life, the relationships among individual and population aging will become more complex and require the development of unique policies and practices, such as home care and long-term care, before this generation moves into their seventies and eighties.
- Social institutions, policies, and practices for an aging society must evolve to avoid perpetuating inequities or inadequate services. For example, the emphasis in public policy debates may shift from a concern about decreased availability of pension funds to a concern about labour shortages and the need to keep older workers in the labour force through delayed or partial retirement.
- Population aging will not weaken or destroy a society, as proponents of "apocalyptic demography" would have us believe. But population aging will present us with challenging policy and political issues to resolve.

To meet the needs of an ever-changing, increasingly diverse older population, a balance of collective versus individual responsibility must evolve, especially with respect to economic security, health care, and social support and personal care. This will require a change in view from believing that population aging is a threat to one in which it is viewed as an opportunity—to make social and economic gains for society and to enhance the quality of life for longer-living older Canadians. Population aging is a life-course, society-wide issue as much as it is an older person's issue. As the United Nations has argued with respect to global population aging, we need to build "a society for all ages." This will require a transformation of national and international thinking (Hicks 2003). Two essential steps in this direction involve ensuring the ethical treatment of older people, especially those who are vulnerable, and ensuring that human rights in later life are protected.

Ethics in an Era of Population Aging

Ethics represents an objective and reflective way of thinking about how one should act in a specific situation by taking into account the best interests of everyone involved in the situation—the individual, family members, professional workers, society. Thus, ethical caregiving ensures that care for an older person is based on a concern for the self and for others (Voyer 1998). For both individuals and the state, ethics involves the following:

- "should" questions (e.g., Should life-sustaining technology be used for those with a terminal illness?)
- ethical issues (how to prevent elder abuse by caregivers) and ethical dilemmas (e.g., Does a physician prevent or delay death or initiate death through physician-assisted suicide?)
- decisions about what is right, good, or appropriate for an individual or for society (e.g., Who should make decisions about ceasing treatment, extending life, or employing costly surgery, and when should those decisions be made?)

Ethics, as an area of study, does not provide a set of rules for decision-making or behaving, or a set of easy answers or solutions. Rather, a set of culturally induced principles and values (fairness, privacy, autonomy, freedom, honesty) are employed when debating and resolving moral, religious, or social issues. Ethics involves an *ideological* dimension (Should individualism or collectivism guide public policy and in what proportion?), a *practice* dimension (Should an 85-year-old receive a heart transplant, a hip replacement, or kidney dialysis?), and a *professionalism* dimension (adherence to the Hippocratic oath taken by physicians; the development of standards of care for home-care workers; a bill of rights for those living in a long-term-care facility).

The onset of population aging, along with biomedical technological developments that foster new ways of thinking and acting, raises legal, moral, philosophical, and ethical questions about aging and older adults.[9] Some questions and issues operate at the level of the individual; others, at the level of society. Discussions and debates concerning ethics should recognize that there will be individual differences of opinion. Debates might address some or all of the following topics, which would make for interesting discussions in class or with parents, grandparents, siblings, or friends:

- Should "age" or "need" be a criterion for entitlement to economic security or expensive elective surgery?
- Should economic and health resources be rationed, and priority given to young people?
- Should we privatize the health-care system, and, if so, to what degree and how?
- Should people pay a portion of their health-care costs if they smoke or engage in other unhealthy behaviours?
- Should families be responsible for the care of their dependent elders?
- Should older people have the right to die a "good death" with dignity and at a time of their choosing? If so, should they make the decision in advance or at the time, as autonomous individuals, or should a third party be involved? Who should make a decision if an older person is not competent to decide?
- Should an older person's driver's license be suspended or revoked, and, if so, when and according to what criteria?
- Should an older person who cannot carry out the basic and necessary activities of daily living be removed from his or her home? How much home care should be provided in the home before an elderly person is moved into a long-term-care facility?
- Who should make decisions about living wills, the use of protective restraints and drugs in nursing homes, and euthanasia?
- Should genetic testing be employed to identify who is most at risk for certain illnesses, and should this information be used to treat individuals differentially within the health-care system?
- Should medical technology be used to extend a person's life if the quality of life deteriorates significantly or below an acceptable level because of a terminal illness or severe dementia?
- How should autonomy, privacy, and the rights of institutionalized and cognitively impaired older people be protected? Who should have access to information about dependent elderly persons?

In all debates and decision-making around ethical issues, we must ask whose best interest is being served by any decision or action—that of the older person, a caregiver, an organization, or society. And we must decide what is best at this time, in this situation, and for a specific dependent person. As much as possible, the older person, a family member, or both should be a partner in decisions about personal matters and public debates about ethical issues pertaining to later life, such as whether euthanasia should be legalized. Many decisions about home or health care in later life involve competing or conflicting values, beliefs, or opinions. Often, laypeople and professionals disagree on issues with an ethics dimension. They may disagree about what treatment or outcomes would best serve a dependent older person, the family, or society. Yet many decisions are made, or influential advice given, about an elderly person by medical or social services personnel or by family or friends on behalf of the older adult, who is not consulted, even if he or she is able to make personal decisions.

Ethical issues and dilemmas emerge and evolve over time; therefore, they need to be debated frequently and resolved because of the possible implications of an unethical decision or situation for an individual or for society. Throughout the book, you will find discussions of specific ethical issues, such as conducting research with older adults (Chapter 5); driving in later life and living in a long-term-care facility (Chapter 8); ensuring economic security for an aging population (Chapter 10); elder care and elder abuse (Chapter 12); and end-of-life decisions, such as assisted suicide, euthanasia, and the use of technology to sustain life (Chapter 12).

Protecting Human Rights in Later Life

Respect, autonomy, and dignity must be assured as rights for older adults, especially if they are likely to experience discrimination,[10] ageism, neglect, abuse, poverty, homelessness, or malnutrition. Increasingly, some "seniors" issues are being addressed as an integral component of a rights-based society that seeks to improve the standard of living and the quality of life for all older adults (Morgan and David 2002). Human rights should be permanent, consistent, and universal across the life course—not devalued or lost as one ages and becomes more vulnerable or at risk.

To protect human rights in later life, a Declaration of the Rights of Older Persons (Highlight 1.6) was presented to the Second United Nations World Assembly on Ageing in April 2002 (Butler 2002). This declaration, which pertains to societies as well as to individuals, concludes with a call for action to improve the quality of life of older adults throughout the world.

What Do Older Canadian Adults View as Important Issues?

In April 2009, the Special Senate Committee on Aging published its final report, entitled *Canada's Aging Population: Seizing the Opportunity*. Under the Hon. Sharon Carstairs, Privy Council, Chair, and the Hon. Wilbert Joseph Keon, Deputy Chair, the committee travelled across Canada speaking to seniors and experts, and reviewing programs and services, with three major aims: (1) to identify priority areas for political leadership and multi-jurisdictional coordination; (2) to provide support for research, education, and the dissemination of knowledge and best practices; and (3) to provide direct services to certain population groups for which it has direct responsibility. From coast to coast, the committee discovered that many of the personal stories of older adults themselves provided the foundations of their report. Highlight 1.7 illustrates some of the major ideas that the committee learned concerning both positive messages and gaps in services and programs. These issues are critically examined in more detail throughout the book.

Highlight 1.6
United Nations Declaration of the Rights of Older Persons

Preamble

At the first United Nations World Assembly on Ageing in 1982, some consideration was given to human rights issues, and in 2000, Mary Robinson, United Nations Commissioner on Human Rights, emphasized the importance of protecting the human rights of older people. At the second United Nations World Assembly on Ageing in April 2002, the International Longevity Center–USA, in collaboration with its sister centers in Japan, France, the United Kingdom, and the Dominican Republic, proposed that the following Declaration of the Rights of Older Persons become the basis of action as well as discussion at the Assembly and beyond.

Declaration of the Rights of Older Persons

Whereas the recognition of the inherent dignity and of the equal and inalienable rights of all members of the human family is the foundation of freedom, justice, and peace in the world,

Whereas human progress has increased longevity and enabled the human family to encompass several generations within one lifetime, and whereas the older generations have historically served as the creators, elders, guides, and mentors of the generations that followed,

Whereas the older members of society are subject to exploitation that takes the form of physical, sexual, emotional, and financial abuse, occurring in their homes as well as in institutions such as nursing homes, and are often treated in cruel and inaccurate ways in language, images, and actions,

Whereas the older members of society are not provided the same rich opportunities for social, cultural, and productive roles and are subject to selective discrimination in the delivery of services otherwise available to other members of the society,

Whereas the older members of society are subject to selective discrimination in the attainment of credit and insurance available to other members of the society and are subject to selective job discrimination in hiring, promotion, and discharge,

Whereas older women live longer than men and experience more poverty, abuse, chronic diseases, institutionalization, and isolation,

Whereas disregard for the basic human rights of any group results in prejudice, marginalization, and abuse, recourse must be sought from all appropriate venues, including the civil, government, and corporate worlds, as well as by advocacy of individuals, families, and older persons,

Whereas older people were once young and the young will one day be old and exist in the context of the unity and continuity of life,

Whereas the United Nations Universal Declaration of Human Rights and other United Nations documents attesting to the inalienable rights of all humankind do not identify and specify older persons as a protected group,

Therefore new laws must be created, and laws that are already in effect must be enforced to combat all forms of discrimination against older people,

Further, the cultural and economic roles of older persons must be expanded to utilize the experience and wisdom that come with age,

Further, to expand the cultural and economic roles of older persons, an official declaration of the rights of older persons must be established, in conjunction with the adoption by nongovernment organizations of a manifesto which advocates that the world's nations commit themselves to protecting the human rights and freedoms of older persons at home, in the workplace, and in institutions and offers affirmatively the rights to work, a decent retirement, protective services when vulnerable, and end-of-life care with dignity.

Source: Reprinted with permission from Butler 2002.

Highlight 1.7
Special Senate Committee on Aging Final Report: Canada's Aging Population: Seizing the Opportunity

What the Committee Learned

- Seniors need to be recognized as active, engaged citizens in our society.
- Older adults should have the right to age in the place of their choice.
- All Canadians need to place as much importance on adding life to years, as on adding years to life.
- The aging population should be viewed as an opportunity for Canada.
- Seniors are often unjustly stripped of their rights.
- Inappropriate care decisions are made because we do not provide the right service at the right time.
- The unequal rate of population aging across the country creates challenges for the provinces to provide a necessary range of services.
- Some seniors live in isolation or in inappropriate homes because of inadequate transportation and housing.
- Current income security measures for our poorest seniors are not meeting their basic needs.
- The current supports for caregivers are insufficient, and some Canadians, especially middle-aged women, are forced to choose between keeping their jobs and caring for the ones they love.
- The voluntary sector is suffering as volunteers themselves are aging.
- Canada faces challenges in health and social human resources as doctors, nurses, and social workers are themselves aging.
- Technology, if known and used, provides new opportunities to deliver care.
- The Canadian government is both a leader and a laggard in providing care to seniors under its jurisdictional responsibility.

Selected Report Recommendations

1. Promote active aging and healthy aging and combat ageism.
2. Provide federal/national leadership and coordination through initiatives such as a National Integrated Care Strategy, a National Caregiver Strategy, a National Pharmacare Program, and federal transfer payments to provinces with the highest proportion of the aging population.
3. Ensure the financial security of Canadians by addressing the needs of older workers, developing/proposing pension and income security reform.
4. Facilitate the desire of Canadians to age in their place of choice with adequate housing, transportation, and integrated health and social care services.
5. Implement changes for those population groups for which it has a specific direct service responsibility, and in relation to Canada's official language commitments (e.g., Aboriginals).

Source: Adapted from the Special Senate Committee on Aging (2009). *Final Report: Canada's Aging Population: Seizing the Opportunity*. Ottawa: The Senate. Retrieved from www.parl.gc.ca/Content/SEN/Committee/402/agei/rep/AgingFinalReport-e.pdf

Summary

The older population, which is growing rapidly in Canada and throughout the world and will continue to do so for the next several decades, consists of a heterogeneous group of individuals with a variety of personal characteristics, social attributes, and life experiences. An appreciation of this diversity is essential as you study aging processes, work directly with older adults, or design and implement policies or programs for middle-aged and older adults. Indeed, there has never been a more exciting set of challenges facing society or students of gerontology. The study of aging processes is complex and requires the identification and understanding of salient trends and patterns and how to connect these to the larger society in which we live.

The aging process is influenced by the social, economic, and age structures of a society; by a variety of social processes; by social, political, and economic change within a given culture or subculture; and by major historical events. These factors influence both individual and population aging, and they interact with biological and psychological factors to shape social opportunities and social behaviour throughout the life course. This may appear complex and all-inclusive at this stage; however, as we move further into the book you will gain a deeper understanding of these important processes. Furthermore, as you study aging processes and elderly persons, question the validity of images of aging that you confront (are they myths and stereotypes?), and search for cross-cultural or subcultural variations in the aging process, particularly with respect to the treatment and status of older adults in different segments of Canadian society (from homeless older persons, to elderly Aboriginal people living in remote northern communities, to recent, impoverished immigrants or refugees, to upper-class, wealthy Canadians living in affluent neighbourhoods in metropolitan areas).

Above all, remember that we are not puppets acting and behaving according to formal roles and rigid social structures as we proceed through the life course. We do not all age in a similar way, but we are not totally autonomous, either. We act with agency and play out our individual life course as part of a dynamic age cohort. Our life course evolves within social structures that foster equity or inequity across the life course. As well, our life chances and lifestyles are influenced by the cultural, historical, and structural factors that pervade our particular social world. This social world involves living in different neighbourhoods and communities and being a social actor in a variety of ever-changing social institutions (i.e., family, peer group, education, religion, work, government, etc.). We do not age in a vacuum but, rather, in a highly interactive and changing social world where our life course is intertwined with other individuals, groups, and social institutions, both within Canada and globally.

As you reflect critically on the various topics and issues introduced in this text and in other sources, you will find that a number of common themes pervade serious discussions and examinations of aging as a social process. These themes include the following:

- Aging occurs across the life course—it is not just an event in later life.
- Diversity or heterogeneity, on a number of social, cultural, cognitive, and physical dimensions, is common among older populations.
- Aging processes are complex, but they can be understood by careful research and study.
- Aging is a gendered experience that tends to favour men, except with respect to longevity and selected other domains.
- Individual aging and population aging are linked processes.

- Agency interacts with social structures to influence the nature and quality of the aging experience.
- Demography is not destiny—population aging will not destroy society.
- Aging, especially in the public-policy domain, is either a private trouble (for the individual and family) or a public issue (for society or an institution)—or both.
- Individuals employ human agency to change social institutions (such as through voting).
- Older people seek dignity and respect and strive to remain independent and to function as autonomous beings.
- Aging involves continuity and change across the life course.
- Aging is a holistic process involving biological, cultural, environmental, economic, social, and psychological processes that interact to influence life chances and lifestyles across the life course.

For Reflection, Debate, or Action

1. Interview members of your extended family to identify historical and cultural factors that may have influenced the process of aging for earlier generations. Identify some problem or issue they have experienced while aging, and try to determine why the problem arose and how or whether it was resolved.
2. Identify some factors in your life course to date that may or may not have an impact on your journey across the life course.
3. Identify the living generations in your family, and define and contrast the characteristics and life situation of the oldest woman (the matriarch) and man (the patriarch).
4. Ask your oldest living relative(s) to tell stories about their parents and grandparents and about the everyday life and challenges of earlier generations in your family.
5. Meet with an older person who is not a member of your extended family and has lived in a different neighbourhood or community from that of your parents and grandparents. Ask the person to tell you a story about his or her life in general, or ask them to reconstruct a few significant events that may have changed their life course or have given special meaning to aging or to being elderly at the present time. Contrast this person's life with that of someone about the same age in your family.
6. Select one or two television shows and watch them over a three- or four-week period. Observe, record, and interpret whether and how older characters are portrayed.
7. Administer the Facts on Aging Quiz (Highlight 1.4) to four or five friends and four or five family members. Note any differences in the responses, in general or to specific questions, by chronological age. For any erroneous responses, inform the person why their response is incorrect.
8. Think about how the lessons learned and recommendations made by the Special Senate Committee Report on Aging can be best addressed or implemented.

Notes

1. The correct responses are: 1–F; 2–F; 3–T; 4–F; 5–F; 6–T; 7–T; 8–F; 9–F; 10–F.

2. When we study aging and later life, there is no commonly agreed-upon terminology to refer to older adults—"seniors," "elders," "third agers," "golden-agers," "the old," "the oldest old," "the old," "the frail elderly," etc. And preferred terms vary in usage across time and in different domains. For example, government personnel use "seniors" in much of their written and oral communications; scholars use "older persons" or "older adults" to generically describe people in later life. The perfect term, and a commonly accepted term, has yet to be derived.

3. Some excellent fiction and non-fiction books about aging include S. de Beauvoir, *The Coming of Age*, 1970; M. Laurence, *The Stone Angel*, 1964; W. Booth, *The Art of Growing Older*, 1992; R. Yahnke and R. Eastman, *Literature and Gerontology: A Research Guide*, 1995; M. Albom, *Tuesdays with Morrie*, 1997; Joan Barfoot, *Exit Lines,* 2010.

4. The Audiovisual Reviews section of *The Gerontologist* includes reviews of both educational and feature-length films with aging themes (see *The Gerontologist* 39 (4): 504–10 for a review of many feature-length films produced before 1999).

5. Simone de Beauvoir (1970), in an early study and critique of aging, presented a history of thought about aging from early Egypt to the modern era and examined aging as a subjective experience.

6. See Bytheway 2005a, 2005b; Hagestad and Uhlenberg 2005; Nelson 2005; Palmore et al. 2005; the fall 2005 issue of *Generations*, which focused on the theme "Ageism in a New Millennium"; Davis and Friedrich 2010.

7. The endnotes to each chapter and the appendix (Study Resources) list many websites, as well as a number of books, periodicals, and government reports.

8. For job or career ideas, scan www.cagacg.ca, www.aghe.org, and www.geron.org, and contact representatives of provincial gerontology associations, as well as faculty working in colleges and universities. Some universities now require that students complete some type of community experience on a volunteer basis. If this is a requirement, or a recommended activity at your university, seek out opportunities to work with older adults in the community or in an institutionalized setting, such as a retirement home or a long-term-care facility. Local social-service agencies, retirement and nursing homes, and hospitals may provide volunteer opportunities to work with older adults.

9. For a discussion of ethical questions and dilemmas, see NACA 1993a; Cole and Holstein 1996; Moody 1996; Morgan 1996; Smith 1996; Johnson 1999; Clements 2002; Ross et al. 2002; Cantor 2006; and current and past issues of the *Journal of Ethics, Law and Aging,* the *Journal of Medical Ethics,* or *Ethics and Values in Health Care. The Soul of Bioethics* covers such topics as palliative care, dementia, ethics in caregiving, and ensuring autonomy for dependent adults.

10. In June 2002, the Ontario Human Rights Commission released a Policy on Discrimination against Older Persons Because of Age. The policy emphasizes issues pertaining to the older worker, housing for the elderly, and special needs in health care and transit services (www.ohrc.on.ca).

2 Historical and Cultural Perspectives on Aging

We may have different religions, different languages, different colored skin, but we all belong to one human race.

— Kofi Annan, past UN Secretary-General

Focal Points and Key Facts

- In what way is our life course influenced by the period of history in which we live?
- How does culture shape the meaning of being older in a society, and how does culture influence the challenges, experiences, and outcomes of the aging process?
- In what ways have modernization and other technological advances changed the status of elderly people in different cultures and at different times?
- What can the study of other cultures, past and present, teach us about growing older in our society?
- Does being a member of a subculture influence how older members are viewed and supported in later life?
- According to 2006 census estimates, 1,172,790 Canadians reported Aboriginal identity—including North American Indian (First Nations), Métis, or Inuit—of which 56,460 (4.8 per cent) are aged 65 and over.
- To what extent and why are aging Aboriginal people disadvantaged in Canadian society?
- In 2011, about 19 per cent of Canadians were foreign-born (approximately 6.5 million people); most of them are members of a visible-minority group.
- Canada admitted about 1.1 million immigrants between January 2001 and May 2006; 4.1 per cent of these immigrants were 55 to 64 years of age, and 3.4 per cent were 65 years of age or older.

Introduction: Diversity in Aging across Time and Place

Individual and population aging are universal phenomena, but the processes vary at different periods of history and in different cultures. There are differences within and across cultures in how "old age" is defined. The definition is based on the following: average life expectancy (which can range from about 40 to 80 years); the extent to which older people are valued, supported, and cared for in later life; the cultural stereotypes of aging and of being elderly; and the roles that older people assume in a society and the extent to which these are valued. Sensitivity to cultural differences and similarities is essential for the development of effective policies and service programs, for meeting the unique needs of older people with different cultural roots, for refuting myths about aging, and for understanding the future of aging. This chapter examines diversity in aging experiences and in the status of older persons in selected cultures throughout history, as well as in a few Canadian subcultures.

The meaning of age and aging, and the social position of older people in their communities, is studied in many cultural and ethnic groups.[1] Although biological aging is a universal experience, different patterns of social aging are found in different cultures throughout the world, in different historical periods, and in different parts of a multicultural society like Canada. Our culture, and the period of history we pass through, influences how we age and the extent to which we are valued and supported in our later years. To illustrate, in the eighteenth century terms such as *gaffer*, derived from *godfather*, and *fogy*, meaning "a veteran," were positive labels for older people. However, by the nineteenth century both had become derisive terms reflecting a reversal in society wherein deference for the oldest members was replaced by contempt and perhaps neglect. In the twentieth century, Fry (1996) noted that the following terms were used to express the low status of older persons in North American societies: *hag, old geezer, old maid, codger, fuddy-duddy,* and *fossil.* Today, *senior, third ager, elder,* and *retiree* generally have positive meanings when used to refer to older persons, but stereotypes and questions about the status of older persons remain.

To understand the cultural basis of aging in a global context, four common research approaches have been used: (1) a historical comparison of early and later societies (from pre-literate to postmodern); (2) a comparison of two or more somewhat similar societies at the same point in time (e.g., England, Canada, and Sweden today); (3) a comparison of Eastern with Western societies (e.g., Japanese and Canadian); and (4) a comparison of developed with developing regions or countries (e.g., Canada and Africa). An example of one of these approaches can be found in Bengtson et al.'s (2000) comparison of the responsibility of families and the state for supporting and caring for elderly persons in Eastern and Western societies. Following are some of the findings of the *differences* between Eastern and Western societies:

- **Filial piety** (respect and a feeling of responsibility for one's parents) is embedded in Eastern cultures; such a general guiding principle is not found in the West.
- Rapid population aging occurred in modernized Western societies in the twentieth century; it will occur in developing Eastern societies in the twenty-first century. (It has already happened in Japan.)
- In Eastern cultures, the eldest son and his wife are usually responsible for caring for his parents (often in a multigenerational household); in Western cultures, a daughter or a daughter-in-law is more likely to be responsible.
- In Western cultures, state-supported economic assistance, housing, and health care for older adults are common; these programs are just beginning to appear in Eastern cultures.

Some of the *similarities* in Eastern and Western societies' treatment of elderly persons include the following:

- The family is the primary support system for the daily lives of older adults.
- With population aging, an increasing number of older adults are economically dependent on the state and/or their families for survival in later life.
- Fertility rates are declining, and smaller families, including some with no children, are more typical than in the past. (China, for example, has a one-child policy.)
- Debates about the relative responsibility of the state and the family for providing support to older adults are common in both cultures.

Aging in Canada's Multicultural Society

Canada's open-door immigration policy has created a multicultural society in which the mosaic of later life has become increasingly heterogeneous. If we are to embrace diversity and design effective programs and policies for all older Canadians, the past, present, and future cultural fabric of our aging population must be understood. Our population mix is different today from what it was in the middle of the twentieth century. From the 1940s to the 1960s, most immigrants were white, they came from Europe, and they lived in both rural and urban communities. Many had little education, and they usually, at least among the first generation, found employment as labourers.

Over the past 40 years, as members of many different cultural and linguistic groups arrived, our immigrant population became larger and more diverse. Currently, there are more than 200 language groups in the country (Statistics Canada 2012), and about 19 per cent of the Canadian population is foreign-born. The largest proportion of immigrants is comprised of visible minorities because more immigrants are now coming from Asian, Caribbean, South American, eastern European, and African countries, rather than from northern Europe (Statistics Canada 2012).

There is now much greater variability in level of education and economic status on arrival (from Hong Kong millionaires to political refugees from impoverished, developing nations), and most (about 69 per cent) settle in the three largest urban centres—Montreal, Toronto, and Vancouver. As well, there are significant variations in the rate at which members of different groups are assimilated into mainstream society. Moreover, a general label, such as Asian, and one general policy that "fits all" is no longer adequate when describing or serving a specific group because of the considerable diversity within the group. Furthermore, unlike earlier times, some immigrants arrive late in life (under the family reunification program) and are supported by children who immigrated to Canada in early or mid-adulthood.

About 8 per cent of family reunification immigrants are over 65 years of age. Older members of ethnic groups can be divided into two types with distinct needs: (1) those who arrived years ago and have grown old in Canada and (2) those who arrived here in later life. Many immigrants who arrive in their elder years are sponsored by a relative who is a permanent resident in Canada, through Citizenship and Immigration Canada's (CIC) Family Class reunification policy. Under this policy, the older relative must undergo medical, criminal, and background checks to meet eligibility criteria. This policy also requires that the sponsoring relative promise financial and social support for the immigrating relative for a period ranging between three and ten years (CIC, 2010), depending on their relationship. The sponsored older immigrant does not have access to certain social programs (i.e., Old Age Security, Home Support, etc.) until he or she has lived in Canada for this predetermined period of time. Although most older reunification immigrants make contributions to their families and Canadian society, this policy has the unintended consequence of increasing dependency, especially if the older adult is limited in his or her functional or cognitive ability (Koehn et al. 2010), or is unable to read or speak English or French.

Immigrants' language, cultural, and religious differences create unique challenges for service delivery, and for workers and policy-makers who provide health care, community and home care, institutional care, and economic assistance. Some older members of ethnic minorities do not speak English or French, are not knowledgeable about social or health-care services, and have specific cultural beliefs about health care, death and dying customs, and the responsibility of the family versus the state in supporting older people. Moreover, many of these immigrants adhere to their traditional diet, which can create dietary and adaptation problems in hospitals or long-term-care facilities. These factors are especially challenging when trying to reduce or eliminate gender inequality. Many immigrant women experience **marginalization** because of these factors, which may be compounded by illiteracy, poverty, and lack of transportation (Mjelde-Mossey and Walz 2006; Shemirani and O'Connor 2006; Stewart et al. 2006; Connidis 2010; Mitchell 2012).

The Multiple Meanings of *Culture*

Culture provides a symbolic order and a set of shared meanings to social life and includes values, beliefs, attitudes, norms, customs, and knowledge. These elements are represented in our language, art, technology, mass media, literature, music, appearance, ceremonies, and games. The most highly valued elements of a culture become institutionalized and are transmitted from one generation to the next. These elements may or may not be adopted by immigrants through a process of assimilation and **acculturation**, or they may be adopted at different rates among different ethnic groups depending on whether or not they live in a concentrated ethnic neighbourhood or community.

Values, beliefs, and norms are of particular importance in understanding a society's social organization. **Values** are the internalized criteria by which members select and judge goals and behaviour in society. Values are trans-situational (that is, they are held and used in many situations) and are found in most institutions in a society. They include principles such as democracy, equality, freedom, achievement, competition, and respect for older people. **Beliefs** represent an individual's conception of the world. They are a statement about what is thought to be true as opposed to what is real or desirable. Beliefs are unique to a given culture or subculture and are learned through socialization processes via parents, teachers, peers, and the mass media. **Norms** define acceptable or expected behaviour in specific social situations. Many norms concerning how we dress and act, how we spend our leisure time, or how we select living arrangements are related to our stage in life or our social position. Our values, beliefs, and norms generate images and stereotypes about people and can lead to discrimination toward members of a specific group, including older adults.

Some cultural elements are similar from one society to another, although they may be expressed differently. For example, all societies have some form of political, social, and economic organization, as well as a set of values, a common language, and a way of socializing their members. In most societies, there is a high degree of agreement about what people value and how they behave. This is reflected in the phenomenon known as **ethnocentrism**, in which members regard their mainstream culture as superior to all others. Ethnocentric beliefs influence how we behave toward people from other cultures, including members of subcultures in our own society, who themselves hold and express a unique set of values, beliefs, norms, and customs. Ethnocentrism can foster insensitivity to those who are different and can influence practices such as the kind of food served in long-term-care settings that primarily house those from mainstream society.

Historical and Comparative Approaches to Understanding Aging Processes

The study of aging from a comparative perspective began with the publication in 1945 of Simmons's classic descriptive study of elderly people in a variety of primitive societies (Simmons 1945). The studies that followed found that chronological or perceived age is an important factor in the stratification of many societies and that the status of older people varies *between* societies and *within* a society at different historical periods.

More recent scholars (especially since the late 1970s) have sought to explain cultural variations in the aging process. First, historians, anthropologists, and sociologists identified patterns of thought and behaviour by older people that are repeated in many cultures, as well as those that are found only in a specific culture, subculture, or historical period. Historical studies of aging, for example, have verified that the status of older adults has not always been as low as it is today in some societies or as high as it was once assumed to be in some Eastern societies. A second development was the study of aging from a cultural anthropological perspective, employing mainly observational ethnographic studies. The anthropology of aging investigates how culture shapes the social and economic status of older people in a society, the social roles of adults at different stages in life, the rituals associated with aging and dying, and whether age discrimination is a factor in a society's social organization. Anthropologists have identified more than 3000 societies in the world, with considerable variations found in both the process of aging and the status of older people (Fry 1985, 1996, 2010; Schaie and Elder 2005; Gilleard 2007, 2009). These societies are categorized according to their level of industrialization and modernization into one of three types: (1) primitive hunting-and-gathering societies; (2) pre-industrial societies; and (3) post-industrial and postmodern societies. Today, many international organizations (e.g., the United Nations, the World Health Organization) use a relatively crude dichotomous category: developed and developing nations. Most studies describe variations within a specific society over time, and only a few have directly compared aging processes in two or more cultures.[2]

As the social structures of modern societies have become more complex, scholars have studied the diversity within a society and the structural factors that influence the experiences and opportunities of aging adults, especially across gender lines, social class, and ethnicity. Topics studied within unique cultural backgrounds include gender roles; attitudes toward aging; spiritual rituals; diet, housing, and income; and variations in access to family and friendship support networks and to formal health and social support services in a community or institution. These studies have shown that unique policies and services are often needed to enhance the quality of life of an older person in a specific cultural group and to reduce later-life inequities between members of the dominant group and minority groups.

A third development is the "unpacking" of meanings of old age as they are reflected in historical accounts, which mainly stem from North American and Western European sources. Achenbaum (2010, 21) identifies a number of archetypes of age that have predominated historical accounts of old age, including the following: (1) physical features of old age; (2) differences between old and younger members of a society; and (3) the relevance of gender in constructing old-age imagery. Thus, historical and cultural variations in aging necessitate an understanding of the continuity and change in societal meanings attached to age in a global and historical context.

According to Achenbaum (2010), older persons have been typified in negative imagery in historical accounts in terms of physical deterioration and weakness, such as missing teeth, wrinkled faces, and small stature. This has been balanced by positive images of wisdom and mystical or spiritual traits. The archetype of older women has been particularly negative in historical accounts in part because they were deemed to have fewer resources, a loss in beauty, and a loss in overall status in old age (since men dominated religious positions). The exception was in portrayals of older women as healers. Historical depictions of older women have also been primarily written by male historians and have therefore since been deconstructed using a critical feminist lens (see Chapter 5).

The Modernization Hypothesis and the Changing Status of Older People

Before the Industrial Revolution (before about 1750), only two types of societies existed: primitive hunting-and-gathering tribes and agrarian-peasant communities. In primitive hunting-and-gathering societies, the oldest members were considered a valuable source of knowledge about rituals and survival skills. Knowledge was a source of power, and when knowledge was no longer needed (when mechanization arrived with the Industrial Revolution) or when knowledge was acquired and held by the young, elderly people lost power and status. Before such developments, social differentiation was based largely on age, and elders held influential positions in the social, political, and religious spheres of life. The oldest members of the community contributed by performing economic and household chores; by teaching games, songs, traditions, and survival skills to the young; and, for men, by serving as "elders" or "chiefs" (Simmons 1945, 1952). As an illustration of the current importance of older people in developing countries, the past United Nations secretary-general Kofi Annan, at the opening of the World Assembly on Ageing in April 2002, stated that "in Africa, when an old man dies, a library disappears . . . without the knowledge and wisdom of the old, the young would never know where they come from, or where they belong."

In agrarian-peasant societies, the oldest citizens controlled the land and were the heads of extended families, which often included at least three generations. In these farming societies, the oldest people had the most knowledge about and experience with survival skills, animal care, growing crops, rituals, and laws. When no longer able to contribute as labourers, they "retired" and transferred control of the family resources, usually to the oldest son, whose family would care for the elder.

With the onset of the Industrial Revolution, the need for labour in towns and cities led to a rapid increase in migration from rural to urban areas, especially among young adults. New social structures, institutions, and processes evolved, and these had a profound impact on the lives of all age groups, including older adults, as shown in Highlight 2.1.

The process by which a society moved from the pre-industrial to the industrial world was known as **modernization**. Cowgill and Holmes (1972) were among the first to argue that modernization and the accompanying social, political, and economic changes led to a decline in the status of older people. Older adults lost power and status because they no longer played essential roles and were no longer the major source of knowledge. Also, because adult children no longer lived in the family home, some believed they were no longer obliged to support their aging parents. To test their hypothesis that the status of older people declined with modernization, Cowgill and Holmes (1972) examined the status of older people in 15 different cultures and subcultures. They concluded that modernization does account for the declining status of older persons, except in societies where they continued to perform valued functions.

For many years this somewhat simplistic "before and after modernization" explanation for the changing status of elderly people was accepted. However, in the 1980s, modernization theory was challenged and re-examined by historians and anthropologists.[3] First, they expressed serious doubts about the assumption that the status of all older people declined dramatically after the modernization of Western societies. Quadagno (1982), presenting evidence from nineteenth-century England, concluded that the onset and degree of industrialization, or modernization, differed considerably by region and industry. She found that in some industries and in some regions, the position of older people improved with increased mechanization. To illustrate, Quadagno (1982) noted that the invention of the sewing machine increased the output of older seamstresses who worked at home. Because economic conditions did not favour the construction of new factories, the contributions and status of these older women actually increased in the post-industrial era.

Similarly, Hendricks (1982) noted that modernization occurs first in core areas of a country or in core countries. Beyond this regional or international core is a peripheral region that fails

Highlight 2.1
Ways That the Industrial Revolution Changed the Lives and Status of Older People

1. A shift from home to factory production meant that the family was no longer the centre of economic production (as it had been on farms). This meant a separation of work and home and a dramatic increase in the number of people, including older people, who became dependent on non-family employers for economic security.

2. Increased migration to cities, especially by young people, resulted in greater social differentiation across age groups, the development of multiple social groups (family, work, and neighbourhood), exposure to new values and norms, and the establishment of public schools.

3. A breakup of the extended family and the emergence of the nuclear family, often saw young families living in a different community from older parents.

4. The rise of large organizations (that is, factories and unions) and the creation of new occupations required skills that young people could acquire through apprenticeship or formal schooling. Many of the skills possessed by older people became obsolete, and mandatory retirement was introduced. A minimum level of formal education became a prerequisite for employment in certain occupations, leisure-time increased due to standard work hours, and personal wealth increased for many.

5. A rapid growth in new knowledge meant that the knowledge and power held by older adults through experience was no longer relevant or valued.

6. An improvement in the quality of medical care, with a reduction in the rates of infant and childhood mortality, created an increase in life expectancy, and a larger population.

Source: Adapted from Burgess 1960; Cowgill 1974a.

to modernize at the same rate and perhaps not at all. A current example is the rapid modernization of urban Beijing and Shanghai compared to the rural regions in China. As an alternative explanation for the all-or-none view of modernization, Hendricks (1982) proposed an "internal colonialism" or "dualistic development" model. According to this model, control over resources resides in a nation's metropolitan regions. Older people living closer to a metropolitan area are the first to lose status, especially if they are members of an already devalued group. Those in peripheral (rural) regions may not lose status, although they may lack social assistance in later life if their children migrate to large urban centres or immigrate to other countries.

A second criticism of modernization theory noted that the social status of older people in pre-industrial societies was not always as high as assumed. For example, Stearns (1982) argued that in pre-industrial France, elderly persons were never highly valued. A pessimistic image of old age prevailed and was held by all age groups in France at that time. This view resulted from the cultural belief that old age is an unpleasant time and that older people are a nuisance, with certain exceptions (such as the clergy). Because these beliefs persisted both before and after modernization in France, modernization cannot be held responsible for a change in the status of older people in that country.

Another perspective is that the status of older persons in modern societies is no lower and may indeed be higher than it was before industrialization. In some post-industrial societies, such as Japan and Korea, older people are supported by their children, their economic status has improved because of income security plans, programs of social support have enhanced rather than diminished their position, and mandatory retirement has relieved them of the burden of work and rewarded them with freedom and leisure time. Laslett (1985) contends that any loss of status by elderly people occurred as much as a century or more *after* the beginning of industrialization. Such changes coincided with the demographic transition to lower fertility and mortality rates that characterize postmodern societies.

Ng et al. (2002), in a study of Hong Kong, concluded that as societies modernize, changes in family structures and in traditional values weaken the informal social support network previously supplied by the family. The breakdown of the traditional multi-generational household (where an older parent often lived with an adult child) is due to smaller families, smaller dwelling sizes, increased employment by daughters and daughters-in-law, and the immigration of children to other countries, such as Canada. The reality in modern Hong Kong, and in the urban areas of other Asian societies (Sung 2001), is that older people now lead more independent lives without the immediate, available support of family members. These patterns are further complicated by the differential effects of social forces linked to modernization. For instance, Cheung and Kwan (2009) found that while filial piety declined in more modernized cities in China, filial piety was actually less prominent among individuals with higher education, suggesting that educational policy can sustain filial piety in the face of modernization. Highlight 2.2 examines the ideals and complex expression of elder respect in the modern East Asian societies of China, Japan, and Korea.

In summary, there is conflicting evidence concerning the status of older people in pre-industrial societies. In some earlier societies, elderly people were held in high esteem, while in others they were abandoned. Similar patterns can be found in contemporary societies; however, an important difference is that life expectancy has increased from below 40 years in pre-industrial societies to about 80 in current developed ones, resulting in very different social contexts in which older people find themselves, as we will see.

The next two sections present brief descriptions of aging in selected pre-industrial and industrial societies. The descriptions are based on accounts from each society at a given point in history. Thus, we see only a snapshot of a specific period in a society's development, or a historical account based on records and artifacts.

Aging in Pre-industrial Societies

Preliterate Societies

In preliterate societies (those in which there was no formal education system), knowledge, beliefs, and survival skills were located in the memories of those with the greatest experience: the elders. The economic system, whether the people were hunters and gatherers or farmers, was based on production and consumption within domestic kinship groups, and the dependence of children on their parents was linked to a degree of obligation toward the oldest people in the family or tribal unit.

The status of elderly people was highest in societies that had a surplus of food and where

Highlight 2.2
Filial Piety: Elder Respect in Three Modern East Asian Societies

Throughout history, respect for elderly people has been a common value in many societies, especially where Confucian teachings prevail, such as China, Japan, and Korea. Filial piety requires children to acknowledge and appreciate the care and assistance they received from parents as children. In return, there is an obligation for children to respect their parents, and all elderly people, and to provide support for their parents in later life. But as Sung (2001) notes, "respect" is an abstract concept. Hence, there is confusion as to how respect should be demonstrated, in general, and specifically in Asian societies. Sung (2001, 17–21) identified 14 types of respect for elders:

- care respect: providing care and services for elders
- victual respect: serving food and drinks of elders' choice
- gift respect: bestowing gifts on elders
- linguistic respect: using respectful language in speaking to and addressing elders
- presentational respect: holding courteous appearances
- spatial respect: furnishing elders with honourable seats or places
- celebrative respect: celebrating birthdays in honour of elders
- public respect: respecting all elders of society
- acquiescent respect: being obedient to elders
- salutatory respect: greeting elders
- preferential respect: giving preferential treatment to elders
- funeral respect: holding funeral rites for deceased parents
- consulting respect: consulting elders on personal and family matters, customs, and rituals
- ancestor respect: worshipping ancestors

Using these categories, Sung (2001) analyzed how younger Asians in three societies express respect. While there is general adherence to the belief in elder respect at the level of society (toward elders in general), the amount of respect shown to elders in a specific family depends on personal beliefs, experiences, resources, and education. Whether elders are actively or passively respected and which forms people use to express respect also vary by culture and age cohort. As Mehta (1997) and Sung (2001) found, there is a shift in the meaning of respect from obedience and subservience to courtesy and kindness, from listening to parents and obeying them to listening but not always obeying or behaving as expected, from bending forward (bowing) to greet elders to shaking hands with them, and from treating all elders equally with respect to treating those with more resources and greater achievements with higher respect. As acculturation occurs in Canada across generations of Asian immigrants, mandatory expressions of respect are likely to be modified, weakened, or abandoned.

Source: Adapted from Sung 2001, 17–21.

the oldest members controlled property; had knowledge of survival skills, rituals, and customs; or held religious roles. In societies where food was scarce, where property was nonexistent, or where leadership was based on ability rather than on longevity or family ties, older people

Highlight 2.3
The Status of Older People in Preliterate Societies

In nomadic societies, elderly people were devalued if they became a burden and had no specialized knowledge or skills, if cultural values dictated that they were no longer worthy of life (because of declining physical strength), or if children sought revenge on parents. Thus, abandoning ill and frail elderly people was relatively common. Holmberg (1969, 224–5) reported that the Sirino tribe in Bolivia abandoned elderly people when they became ill or unable to walk. The Yakuts of Siberia forced elderly people to become beggars and slaves. The Chukchee of Siberia killed frail elderly people in a public ceremony before the tribe (de Beauvoir 1972).

In other preliterate societies, elderly people served as "information banks" for the society and were held in high esteem if they passed on useful skills and information to younger people. In another important study, Maxwell and Silverman (1970) identified six major functions that elderly people performed in these societies: (1) hosts of feasts, games, or visiting groups; (2) consultants about survival skills or rituals; (3) decision-makers for the group; (4) entertainers; (5) arbitrators of disputes; and (6) teachers of the young. The authors found a strong relationship between the amount of useful information held by older adults and the respect accorded to them by other members of society. Today, we observe these functions among North American Aboriginal groups.

Elderly people in preliterate societies might contribute to their tribes, even in old age, in the following ways: older chiefs conducted political meetings; elders had major roles in spiritual or religious rituals; and elders educated and entertained children in the evenings (Simmons 1960; de Beauvoir 1972).

were sometimes abandoned or put to death. In both types of preliterate societies, older men commanded greater respect than older women. Highlight 2.3 illustrates the status of elderly people in a variety of preliterate societies.

Literate Pre-industrial Societies

The status of older people in literate pre-industrial societies varied according to living conditions, religious beliefs, cultural values, and the degree to which they were nomadic. For example, elderly people appeared to have high status in early Hebrew, Roman, and North American societies. The higher status of older people due to religion was particularly pronounced during the Dark Ages (the fifth to tenth centuries), at which time power within the Christian Church was dominated by senior clergy. However, this privilege did not extend to women, who were excluded from these positions of power (Gilleard, 2009). Highlight 2.4 describes the status of elderly people in several literate pre-industrial societies.

Diversity of Aging during Modernization

The onset of industrialization and modernization occurred very differently across societies and cultures. Below are some snapshots of modernization and its impact on the diversity of aging in different societies.

Highlight 2.4
The Status of Older People in Literate Pre-industrial Societies

The Ancient Hebrews: A Patriarchal Order

The ancient Hebrews were one of the earliest societies for which there are written records and well-preserved artifacts. This society was one of the first to view long life as a blessing rather than a burden. In the years between 1300 BC and AD 100, the Hebrews were a nomadic desert tribe comprising large extended families. The family included a patriarch and his wives, concubines, children, slaves, servants, and any others who attached themselves to the domestic group for protection. In this relatively stable yet nomadic culture, aging, at least for men, represented increasing wisdom and power.

Ancient Greece and Rome: Survival of the Fittest

According to ancient Greek literature, the Greeks feared old age. Greek gods were depicted as eternally youthful, and much of the literature commented on the declining physical and mental strength of older people, at least those fortunate enough to reach age 30 to 40 or above—considered old at that time. Evidence from burial remains indicates that average life expectancy may have been only 20 to 30 years. In ancient Greece, power was more likely to be associated with wealth than with age.

Elderly Romans, unless they were wealthy, lost power and influence as they grew older. Death, even by suicide, was considered preferable to suffering the indignities of physical, mental, and social deterioration. In the later years of the Roman Empire, the threat from the barbarians placed a premium on youth and strength, and survival of the fittest prevailed as a necessity.

Ancient Byzantine Society: Respect Thy Elder

The Byzantine empire followed the fall of the Roman empire (410 AD) and continued until the fifteenth century. In contrast to the ancient Greek and Roman empires, the Byzantines held all aged persons in high esteem (Gilleard 2007). Influenced by the Christian Church and a conservative moral order, Byzantine society created a number of state and individual charities and services aimed at helping older people—what Gilleard has called a "prototype

The Anishinabe of Georgian Bay: Elders' Shifting Status

The Anishinabe, a term meaning "original people," inhabited the islands and mainland of Georgian Bay in Ontario (Vanderburgh 1987). The elders played a traditional role by transmitting knowledge and culture to the children of the tribe. Specifically, they taught mythic and local history, the language, healing methods and beliefs, and tribal rituals.

With the arrival of Christian missionaries and the creation of schools on the reserves, missionaries and teachers began to control the knowledge and culture that was transmitted to the younger generations of Anishinabe. Skills needed for survival in the "modern" world were taught: English, mathematics, and science. By the 1960s, the role of elder had disappeared, and the older members of the tribe lost prestige and a sense of being useful and needed. In the 1970s, however, the Native elderly regained some importance when the federal government created Native Cultural/Educational Centres across Canada. Vanderburgh (1987) describes how, in 1974, the Native elders welfare state." Old age, therefore, became a less marginalized status and was integrated into medicine, art, and culture.

Feudal/Medieval England (1400–1750): Rise of the Poor House

The Roman Church, after the decline of the Roman Empire, became the ruling authority throughout feudal England and western Europe. Although the status of older people should have improved with the rise of Christianity, this was not the case. The church was more interested in recruiting new members than in performing social work. However, by the sixteenth and early seventeenth centuries, when life expectancy remained about 30 years, values such as charity, hospitality, and care for others became basic tenets of parish life, regardless of denomination. The state became formally involved in supporting older people with the passage of the Elizabethan Poor Laws in 1603. Henceforth, elderly persons without families to care for them were looked after by a parish, with some limited financial assistance from the state.

Colonial America (1620–1770): The Protestant Ethic

The rigours of colonial life placed a premium on strong, healthy adults. Consequently, the colonies were initially a young, male-dominated society, with a median age of about 20 years. Less than 2 per cent of the residents were over age 65. Being highly religious, the Puritans adhered strictly to biblical teachings. Elders were honoured by having them occupy leadership positions. However, this status was not based solely on religious beliefs; it was also related to wealth. Even in this religious society, the poor were sometimes driven from town so that they would no longer be an economic burden. As in many societies, older women did not receive the same respect as older men and were often denied access to influential positions.

According to Fischer (1977), the declining status of elderly people in North America began not with industrialization, urbanization, and higher levels of literacy but with a change in cultural values after the American Revolution, which led to an emphasis on equality based on performance and income and to a westward migration away from the influence of parents.

of the Anishinabe were recruited by the staff of a centre on Manitoulin Island to record and transmit elements of their traditional culture. The oldest-surviving members became "volunteer elders" in the traditional sense: passing on their knowledge to young children concerning rituals, crafts, language, and related anecdotal narratives about the early life and history of the Anishinabe.

Japan: Modernization and Care of the Elderly

Understanding the status of elderly people in Asian cultures requires an understanding of Asian philosophical and religious principles. While the cultures vary in many respects, they have some common elements. First, many Asians believe that age represents an accumulation of wisdom. In addition, the Confucian concept of filial piety, or respect for parents, is linked to the principle of ancestor worship, maintaining a link with the past and ensuring respect and status for parents, who will be the next ancestors to be worshipped.

Modernization began in Japan in the Meiji era (1868–1912) and intensified during Japan's reconstruction after World War II. Today, Japan has a rapidly decreasing birth rate (a total fertility rate of 1.3 children per couple) and the highest life expectancy in the world. Hence, it is also the most rapidly aging society in the world. In 2011, life expectancy in Japan was 80 years for men and 86 years for women, and people 65 years of age and over made up about 23 per cent of the population (Population Reference Bureau 2011). But it is projected that by 2020, about 28 per cent of the population will be over 65.

A number of other changes are redefining traditional cultural ideology (Takagi and Silverstein 2006). First, young adults are moving to large cities, far from their rural roots, where traditional norms and values prevail. Second, traditions such as respect for older people and caring for one's parents are weakening (Ogawa and Retherford 1993; Ikels et al. 2004). Third, because of a shortage of special housing for older people, retirement communities are being built, and older affluent persons are seeking a more independent lifestyle (Hashimoto and Ikels 2005). Finally, the role of Japanese women is changing as more young women earn university degrees and work full-time. Consequently, they have less time to care for an aging parent or parent-in-law and less interest in doing so. Grassroots organizations are being created as well to improve the status of women, including older women. While the leadership and control of most senior citizen clubs in Japan still rests with men, these traditional rights are being challenged by women.

At the institutional level, the status of older people in Japan is supported by Respect for the Elders Day, an official national holiday on 15 September; by the special celebration for a person's 60th birthday (i.e., *Kanrecki*); and by the practice of giving up one's seat to an older person on public transit. In 1963, the Japanese government passed the National Law for the Welfare of the Elders, which requires that elderly people be given respect, the opportunity to work, and the right to participate in social activities. Since then, many other laws or national policies have been initiated to institutionalize the care of and respect for older people in Japan.

Research suggests that the status of older adults in Japan may be affected in the longer term due to a shift in responsibility of care from families to the state. Japan has recently undergone reform to its long-term health-care system and tertiary-care system to meet the needs of an aging population (Tsutsui and Muramatsu 2007). Consequently, the burden of care for elderly parents is increasingly being shifted from adult children, for whom it is a personal trouble, to the state or place of former employment, where it becomes a public responsibility.

Israel: Aging in a Kibbutz—Communal Benefits and Challenges to Aging

The first kibbutz in Israel was established in 1909 by Jewish immigrants. A kibbutz contains 50 to 1000 people living in a self-sustaining economic and household community. For the most part, kibbutzim are agricultural co-operatives (although some have established industries) characterized by common ownership of property and equality in production and consumption.

All members of the kibbutz must work to produce sufficient food and goods for themselves. The oldest men and women in the kibbutz are called *vatikim*. In addition to receiving the same benefits as regular members, the *vatikim* usually have better housing. They also benefit from close family bonds, since two or three generations usually live within the kibbutz.

Although elderly people are opposed to retirement because it represents a life without purpose or meaning, they nevertheless engage in a process of gradual retirement that involves lighter tasks and reduced hours of work. As a result, some kibbutzim have established industries in which older people are assigned easy but tedious tasks, thereby enabling them to continue contributing to the community in some functional capacity.

The Israeli kibbutz represents a model in which many of the basic problems of aging—economic security, family and community relations, health care, and retirement—have been addressed and partially solved because of a religious and social commitment to equality and care, regardless of age. However, there are increasing reports of intergenerational conflict between younger members, who want farming to become more mechanized, and the *vatikim*, who adhere to a tradition that manual labour is needed to produce goods. This conflict is rooted in the changes that have been made to many kibbutzim: outsourcing of services, a greater emphasis on profits, the use of hired workers, less input into decision-making by all members on an equal basis, and differential rewards according to one's contribution or social position (Leviatan 1999).

Aging in Subcultures

The Concept of Subcultures

Members of a **subculture** adopt a set of values, norms, customs, behaviours, and attitudes that differ from those of mainstream society. In a multicultural society such as Canada, a subculture may be created when a subgroup uses a different language and separates itself physically or socially from mainstream society in homogeneous communities, such as Chinatown. However, subcultures may be formed among those who live in a commune, a trailer park, or a retirement village if they adopt a common identity (as, for example, retirees) and hold unique values, norms, and experiences that differentiate them from others in significant ways.

Convergent subcultures are subcultures that are eventually assimilated into the larger culture. An example would be the descendants of Italian immigrants who arrived in Canada after World War II and were assimilated over two or three generations. Other subcultures, such as the Old Order Mennonites or Hutterites, are *persistent subcultures* because they maintain a totally separate and unique identity, lifestyle, and place of residence, often in rural areas. In the following sections, issues of aging and the status of elderly people are examined for indigenous, racial, ethnic, and religious subcultures.

Indigenous Subcultures: The Aboriginal People of Canada

Cultures and Lifestyles

Aboriginal people are those whose ancestors were the original inhabitants of a region or country. Statistics Canada defines Aboriginal people as "those who report themselves as identifying with at least one Aboriginal group (North American Indian, Métis or Inuit), and/or those who report as being a Treaty Indian or a Registered Indian as defined by the Indian Act, and/or those who were members of an Indian Band or First Nation" (Statistics Canada 2001). Overall, there are more than 55 sovereign Aboriginal peoples in Canada.

According to the 2006 census, 1,172,790 Canadians reported Aboriginal identity (North American Indian, Métis, and Inuit), an increase of approximately 20 per cent since 2001 (compared to an increase of only 4.9 per cent for the non-Aboriginal population) (Statistics Canada 2008a). Most live in Ontario and British Columbia, in terms of absolute numbers, but Manitoba, Saskatchewan, and the three territories have the largest percentage of Aboriginal people. In total, Aboriginal people comprise only 3.8 per cent of the population, and only 4.9 per cent of this population is 65 and over, compared to 13.7 per cent of the non-Aboriginal population (Statistics Canada 2008b). But while the population is growing, fewer people are able to carry on a conversation in a Native language. In 2006, about 30 per cent of the Aboriginal population was under 15 years of age, largely because of a higher fertility rate than that for other Canadian women. First Nations people (North American Indians) comprise about 61 per cent of the total Aboriginal population; the Métis, about 34 per cent; and the Inuit, about 5 per cent excluding multiple origins (Statistics Canada 2008a). Collectively, "Aboriginal people" appears to be the preferred label, although government reports and the popular press use "Native" and more specific terms such as First Nations, Indian, Treaty or Status Indians, Registered Indians, Métis, or Inuit.[4] While about 50 per cent live in cities (Newhouse and Peters 2003; Statistics Canada 2003a, 2003b), it is those who live in defined communities in rural areas, in isolated northern settlements, or on reserves who constitute a subculture.

The Canadian Constitution recognizes three groups of Aboriginal people: Indians, Inuit, and Métis. These groups are three separate cultures with unique heritages, languages, cultural practices, spiritual beliefs, and degree of assimilation into mainstream society. For example, in the Northwest Territories, there are nine recognized "official" languages (NACA 2005). Thus, just as we should not label all people from Asia, India, and the Far East as "Asians," not all members of all sovereign groups should be labelled as "Aboriginal."

In comparison to mainstream Canadian society, relatively little is known about the diverse subcultures in the Aboriginal population or about elderly people in the small, often isolated communities.[5] There is considerable diversity in beliefs, values, and customs, both among the various tribes, bands, and nations and among generations in each community. These differences are due to geographical isolation, economic conditions, out-migration of younger people, and the degree of government support or intervention in a community.

Nevertheless, some structural and cultural conditions are common to many communities and have an effect on elderly Aboriginal people (Indian and Northern Affairs Canada 1995). Traditional Aboriginal cultures share the following elements:

- a large kin network, with strong family ties and orientation
- a close-knit community, sometimes suspicious and resentful of mainstream society
- a respect for elders, who are a source of tradition and wisdom
- a preference for informal support from relatives over formal care from public services
- a wide variety of spiritual beliefs, which guide everyday life
- a preference to remain in the community in later life rather than to live in an institution in another community
- an adherence to traditional healing practices and beliefs

Demographically, Aboriginal communities are characterized by the following:

- high fertility rates, with infant mortality rates twice as high as the Canadian average
- families headed by a single parent (about 20 per cent), of whom the vast majority are women
- an earlier age at death because of an average life expectancy that is approximately six years less than the national average, although the gap is narrowing (Health Canada 2002)
- more disabilities in adult life than within the general population

- a projected tripling in the number of Aboriginal "seniors" by 2016 (Health Canada 2002)
- less formal education than other Canadians

From a structural perspective, Aboriginal people face inequalities and a difficult lifestyle, characterized in general by the following:

- high levels of unemployment or irregular employment
- low average incomes, economic deprivation, and a dependence on government subsidies, with many living below the poverty line
- substandard housing and few housing options, especially in later life
- few retirement residences, nursing homes, or geriatric care facilities in remote communities
- poor health, including a high incidence of chronic diseases related to lifelong malnutrition, alcoholism, and misuse of drugs, and to inadequate health-care services and facilities, including a lack of hospitals and health-care workers in the community
- higher incidence of being victims of crime, especially violent crime, and of spousal or child abuse
- lack of formal community-based social and welfare services, such as home care, and under-use of formal services even when they exist, owing to a preference for support from relatives

Despite increased interventions through federal health and financial assistance programs (Health Canada 2002, 33), Aboriginal people still suffer higher unemployment, much worse living conditions, lower levels of physical and mental health, and greater poverty than any other group in Canada. While improvements have been recorded in terms of standard of living, health, and well-being among Registered Indians of older ages over the last few decades, there remain significant gaps when they are compared to other elderly Canadians, particularly with respect to income and male life expectancy (Cooke et al. 2008). Whereas most ethnic groups are assimilated into the dominant culture over time, at least to some degree, most Aboriginal groups, especially those living on reserves or in northern outposts, remain both culturally and physically isolated from mainstream society. Since Aboriginal people have a shorter life expectancy than other Canadians, it has been argued that the eligible age for federal assistance should be lowered from 65 to 55 years of age. In this way, fairness and need would be addressed, and a larger number of Aboriginal people would be eligible for social assistance earlier in life, at the time when it is needed.

Although significant improvements in education are occurring, many Aboriginals have not completed high school or even elementary school. Many women are widowed early in life or have been single parents for many years. Because the extended family is a central institution, many elders live with their "family," which also includes dependent children and grandchildren. In this situation, the extended family often lives on a very small income. This living arrangement does provide access to an informal support network in later life. Others, however, live alone, often in substandard housing conditions. "Elders" are still respected to some degree because of their experience, their past contributions to the community, and their knowledge of traditions. Native elders are important for cultural transmission, and consequently, more elders are becoming proactive and forming groups to provide leadership in their communities. Highlight 2.5, based on an autobiography by Chief Simon Baker of the Squamish Nation in BC, illustrates why and how some First Nation elders have held more than 20 gatherings over the years.

Highlight 2.5
The Formation of First Nation Elder Groups

First Nation elders of British Columbia formed a provincial elders group that meets periodically around the province. In 1989, Chief Simon Baker of the Squamish Nation was named King of the Elders. He called the group Síiyuxwa—the old elders. He states in his book,

> something I believe in is the importance of the elders. People always keep saying, "why don't you go to the elders? Why don't you talk to the elders" . . . Well they are not going to talk if they feel that nobody's interested. So we formed our first elders group. . . . We had our program set so that the young people could take part. We followed the theme, Elders Teach—Youth Reach. I told them [w]e have gone in the wrong direction. We were spiritual people. We paid great homage to our Creator and we must get back to that way of thinking. Spirituality, culture and language must be emphasized for our young people to know who they are. Education is the tool necessary for self-determination.

Source: Baker and Kirkness 1994, 175–6.

Health Inequality among Aboriginals

The health of Aboriginal people who live in cities and towns (the off-reserve Aboriginal population) is significantly poorer than that of the non-Aboriginal population with respect to self-perceived health, chronic conditions, long-term restrictions on activity, depression, and reported unmet health needs (Statistics Canada 2002, 73–88, 2003a, 2003b; Wilson et al. 2010). In general, Aboriginal people living on reserves and in remote northern settlements also have high levels of poverty, morbidity, and mortality, although these are slowly improving. Life expectancy is lower than that of the non-Aboriginal population because of high rates of infant mortality; alcohol and substance abuse; family and community violence; high suicide rates; and a high incidence of chronic diseases, HIV infection, obesity, and disability (Goins and Spencer 2005; Goins et al. 2007; NACDD 2010; Wilson et al. 2011). Many communities lack adequate health-care facilities, and it is difficult to recruit and keep health-care workers in remote regions. However, Wilson et al. (2010) found that health disparities between Aboriginal and non-Aboriginals tend to converge at the highest ages.

Elderly Aboriginal people experience barriers to health-care facilities (Health and Welfare Canada 1992; Wister and Moore 1998; Jervis et al. 2002; Finkelstein, Forbes, and Richmond 2012). Wilson et al. (2011) contends that older Aboriginals face a number of barriers to access to health services, including loss of traditional approaches, geographic isolation, and legal divisions with Aboriginal communities. They often also require high levels of care (Buchignani and Armstrong-Esther 1999; NACDD 2010), thereby placing a burden on the middle generation, which, because of high fertility rates, still has many child-care responsibilities. Among Aboriginal elders, the prevalence of self-reported chronic conditions such as heart disease, hypertension, diabetes, and arthritis is often double or triple the rate reported by other Canadians in the same age group (Health Canada 2002). These conditions are compounded by the fact that many are not eligible for extended health plans that cover vision and dental care, prescription drugs, and new health technologies. Most reserves and many communities do not have nursing homes. Thus, elderly people who need continuing care must enter a nursing home away from their community. There, they seldom receive the kind of food they prefer, and their family and friends are unable to visit frequently. There is also a need to address knowledge gaps in the provision of health care as well as the accessing of care, especially for specialized diseases such as dementia (Finkelstein, Forbes, and Richmond 2012).

Racial and Ethnic Subcultures

In multicultural societies, some ethnic or racial groups are labelled as minority groups. Because of prejudices and stereotypes, members of these groups often experience discrimination and marginalization. The relative status of a minority group in a society at any particular time determines whether a particular group is viewed as a "minority" group and is subject to some degree of discrimination and inequality. Moreover, individuals in the same ethnic or racial group are ranked differently depending on their gender, education, or occupation. This may place the individual or group in a situation of what has been termed **multiple jeopardy**—the presence of several attributes (i.e., ethnicity, gender, and class) that raise the likelihood of marginalization and differential treatment. Being an older, poor, ethnic woman negatively affects quality of life.

There are variations between and within ethnic groups in terms of the length of time a group has lived in the host country, the amount and type of discrimination directed toward members of a group, and the extent to which a group is assimilated into the host society. The location of a group in the ethnic and racial stratification system can change the process of aging and that group's social status. These differences arise because subsequent generations are likely to be assimilated into mainstream Canadian society. Later generations are better educated, have higher incomes, and may discard the traditional values, language, and customs of their parents and grandparents. If structural and cultural assimilation does not occur, cultural background remains an important ascribed factor that persists across the life course. Some ethnic groups live primarily in an ethnic neighbourhood throughout their lives. While this housing location provides security and support in the early years in a new society, it can also lead to isolation in the later years as children move away from the ethnic neighbourhood or as the neighbourhood changes.

Most health and social welfare policies and services are designed for members of the majority group. In fact, some racial or ethnic groups underutilize the social services available in a community because they do not know what services are available or because their language, customs, or beliefs make it difficult for them to access or use the services, especially in long-term-care institutions. Highlight 2.6 illustrates how cultural values and family dynamics influenced the understanding of disease and access to health care among one Japanese family.

Racial subcultures are characterized by physical features (colour of skin or shape of eyes) that distinguish them from the dominant culture. However, it is not the physical characteristics that set members of racial subgroups apart socially, politically, or economically. Rather, it is the social meanings that the dominant group assigns to these features, combined with the extent to which members of the subgroup adhere to their unique values, identities, and attitudes.

Ethnic subcultures are groups that share cultural characteristics, such as language, beliefs, religion, or national origin. Some ethnic groups that immigrated to Canada during specific historical periods have been assimilated into mainstream society and no longer constitute

Highlight 2.6
The Influence of Language and Cultural Barriers in Health Care

Mr T is a 73-year-old retired Nisei (second generation) Japanese-Canadian fisherman, who was referred by his family physician for clinical evaluation at an outpatient clinic for Alzheimer's disease (AD). Some of Mr T's family believed that he was suffering from AD because of confusion and memory loss. Others believed that he was having problems dealing with retirement because everyone in the household was busy and working except him, leading to depression and suicidal thoughts. Others felt he was having difficulty dealing with the loss of his parents, his sibling, and was experiencing post-traumatic syndrome resulting from his internment during the Second World War. They were reluctant to label his problems as a mental disease. Mr T's son accompanied him to the clinic for a number of tests and evaluations, and the clinic's neurologist diagnosed Mr T with having symptoms consistent with AD based on standard criteria, although Mr T could not complete the standard neurological testing because of both his poor English and his son's inability to translate test items into Japanese. The psychiatrist did not diagnose Mr T with depression but felt that he should be monitored. The interesting aspect of the case is not Mr T's symptomology but rather the distinct variations in family members' explanations of the causes of the problem. Interviews with the family members revealed two prominent cultural values—*oya koh* (filial obligation) and *haji* (shame). *Oya koh* was present among some family members in that if the clinical evaluation confirmed that Mr T was depressed, they would not be blamed as being insensitive and neglectful. *Haji* was present in the family's acceptance of AD as a cause of Mr T's mood and behaviour in public, since the disease would absolve the family from feeling shame. This case study also shows how language barriers in health care may influence patient outcomes.

Source: Smith and Kobayashi 2002.

a major subculture. Some examples are the descendants of Irish immigrants who settled in Montreal and Ukrainian immigrants in the Prairie provinces. Some large language and cultural groups, on the other hand, such as the French Canadians in Quebec or the Chinese in a "Chinatown," have formed a distinct, visible, and persistent dominant culture, often with their own social, economic, and religious organizations.

Ethnic groups provide members with a framework of common history, values, identity, and social networks. For example, although Chinese and Japanese Canadians form two distinct subcultural groups, they have relatively similar cultural backgrounds. The first generation, born in China or Japan, adhere to traditional values: the importance of the family for social support and the necessity of obedience to and respect for the eldest members of the family and community. Many of these first-generation Canadians have experienced difficulties as older adults in a foreign culture. Highlight 2.7 describes some of the unique features of aging in Chinese and Japanese subcultures. These groups are selected as examples because considerable research about them has been published in Canada. However, in a multicultural society like Canada, there is an urgent need for new studies on the many ethnic and religious groups that are "invisible in aging research" (Salari 2002). For example, in Arab, Middle Eastern, and Muslim immigrant groups (the fastest-growing visible-minority group in Canada), there are

Highlight 2.7
Aging in Chinese and Japanese Subcultures within Canada

Chinese Canadians

The Chinese emigrated to Canada in three main waves (Chui et al. 2005). The first to come, the Cantonese, were young, illiterate, unskilled labourers who began to arrive in the 1850s to build the railways and work in western gold mines. Most intended to make a fortune and return to China in their old age. However, many settled here permanently. Experiencing discrimination and hostility in mainstream society, many withdrew into the relative security of urban Chinatowns or lived in small towns, where they operated laundries or restaurants. The first Chinatown, consisting of tents and mud huts, was built on Cormorant Street in Victoria, BC, in 1858 (Lai 1988).

The second wave of Chinese immigrants, the Mandarins, arrived after 1948 when the communists occupied mainland China. Most of these immigrants were older, and because of their age, few learned English. As a result, they often lacked knowledge about services available to them in mainstream society and lived most of their lives in the Chinatowns of larger cities. The third wave, many of them affluent, well-educated entrepreneurs from Hong Kong, have been arriving since the 1980s, settling mainly in Vancouver, Toronto, and Montreal.

The situation of elderly Chinese people is often related to whether they spent their childhood in China or in Canada. Those socialized in China are more likely to adhere to traditional Chinese values, which are often quite different from those of their children, who were raised in Canada. They are ineligible for many forms of government financial and social assistance and, if single in later life, have limited incomes, often living with others in a single room in Chinatown. Others live in public housing, where security may be low and their neighbours may not speak Mandarin or Cantonese. They often lack information about social and medical services and may be unable to pay for medical care. Their later life becomes more difficult if they are moved to a nursing home, where they are often unable to communicate with staff or fellow residents and where they are not served traditional foods. Now long-term-care facilities, special housing, and services are being established by and for members of the Chinese community. Increasingly, Friendship Clubs and Benevolent Aid Societies in Chinatowns provide leisure activities, social services, and housing for elderly Chinese.

Recent elderly Chinese immigrants are more likely than non-Asians to live with their children or other Chinese families. Chappell and Kusch (2007), in a study of more than 2200 Chinese seniors in seven Canadian cities, found that 9 per cent live alone and 13 per cent live with a spouse only, while 73 per cent live either with their spouse and a child or, if widowed, with a child. Those between 55 and 59 years of age are nearly twice as likely to live with a child than non-Asians in the same age group, and by age 80 to 85 they are almost four times more likely to live with a child, especially if their income or wealth is near the poverty line. These living arrangements are most common in the case of elderly persons who are ineligible for pension benefits, cannot speak English or French, and are recent arrivals in a repatriation of the family.

Japanese Canadians

Japanese immigrants first arrived in North America in the nineteenth century. The first wave (the *Issei*) were primarily unskilled labourers, many of whom migrated because their older brothers had inherited the family land and wealth in Japan. Unlike early Chinese immigrants, the *Issei* required their children to learn English and attain an education

Continued

so that they could obtain better jobs. Despite being interned as possible traitors and forced to sell their property during World War II, Japanese Canadians have attained a higher socio-economic status than many other immigrant groups. Today, only about 15 per cent of elderly Japanese Canadians are foreign-born, compared to over 90 per cent of elderly Chinese Canadians (Kobayashi 2000).

Most elderly Japanese people are widows who enjoy good health and live as independently as possible, since housing is not generally a problem. Elderly Japanese of the *Issei* generation knew little English; the third (*Sansei*) and fourth (*Yonsei*) generations know little if any Japanese. This language gap creates communication problems for some elderly Japanese, but it does reveal that the Japanese are more acculturated and less tied to their cultural roots than the Chinese.

Despite the social mobility and cultural assimilation of second- and third-generation Japanese, the quality of relationships with elderly parents has not significantly declined. Research indicates that, regardless of different historical life course experiences and acculturation processes among second- and third-generation Japanese living in Canada, both generations continue to embrace filial obligations as important elements of family life (Kobayashi and Funk 2010). Elderly parents receive assistance from their children and seem to adjust to a state of dependency and reduced authority without losing self-esteem. This occurs because both generations adhere to the tradition of group goal-orientation rather than to an individualistic ethic. Kobayashi (2000), who interviewed 100 second-generation (*Nisei*) and 100 third-generation (*Sansei*) Japanese Canadians, found that more than 60 per cent have a high commitment to filial duty as a cultural value, even though only about 50 per cent report high identity as a Japanese Canadian. She found that this commitment influences the amount and quality of emotional support provided to parents but has little or no influence on the financial or service support they provide.

many unique aging issues pertaining to family support, housing and health-care needs, use of services, and discrimination that require specific programs and policies. Some of these issues are related to religious beliefs about medicine or diet; others, to economic status that makes medications or private home care unaffordable.

Currently, about 30 per cent of all Canadians over 65 years of age were born outside of Canada. But most of them immigrated as children or young adults and have lived in Canada for most of their lives. Others have arrived in recent years to be cared for by adult children who have lived in Canada for many years. Recent elderly immigrants are often widowed and are more likely to be women than men. Many leave their birthplace and encounter a foreign culture, a different value system, and, frequently, a family lifestyle that is foreign to their way of thinking. In 2011, 12.6 per cent of older adults spoke a non-official language at home. If they are unable or unwilling to learn the language, and if the youngest generation cannot speak the language of their grandparents, communication with those inside and outside the home becomes difficult, if not impossible. In such a situation, they often become housebound and totally dependent on their offspring for survival and mobility in the community. Many cannot understand their children's busy "Western" way of life and feel isolated and abandoned in their child's home. Older men, especially, miss the traditional power and status they enjoyed in their homeland, and older women, who are often lonely and depressed, feel that they live in an alien environment. Highlight 2.8 describes an elderly widow's unhappiness in later life after coming to Canada to live with one of her children.

Highlight 2.8
A Mother's Plea for Independence

My Dear Family:
How happy I felt coming to Canada to live with you! I thought all my dreams would come true: Enjoying the company of my children, watching my grandchildren grow up, learning English, having a job, making new friends. . . . Look at me now. . . .

Oh! If you knew how many times I have tried to write this letter, my dear daughter, my beloved grandchildren. But I preferred to hide my feelings in order not to make you suffer, too. Did you ever think of the consequences when you sponsored me to come to this country? Why didn't you tell me how things really were? Then I could have thought twice before deciding to make this enormous change in my life. Now it's too late. I don't have my house, my friends, my independence. I don't have money I can spend freely, and I think I'm also losing my family!

Please do not think I don't value your efforts. I know you have to work hard and don't have much time for housekeeping or taking care of your children. But I did not know you wanted such help from me. It's my pleasure to baby-sit my grandchildren from time to time, but I didn't think this would be a daily obligation. When I told you that I wanted to learn English so I could go out by myself and feel more secure, your answer was, "Mama, you are very old, you cannot learn English. Besides that, I need you here." For years, I didn't venture to ask again. I thought the least I could do was help you, since I was already a burden on the family. But, to tell you the truth, I cannot stand it any more! I couldn't even go to church on Sundays, if your husband was tired or not in a mood to drive me there, because you were afraid that I would get lost if I went by bus.

You came to this country very young. You have already adapted to the culture and customs here. For me, as a senior, the process is very difficult. I cannot even communicate with my grandchildren because they haven't learned to respect the old ones. When I ask the eldest to go with me to a store, he refuses, because he doesn't want anyone to know that we speak Spanish. He's ashamed to go out with his grandma. I feel so lonely and frustrated. . . . When I lived in my homeland I used to go everywhere, saying hello to everybody, solving problems, helping people, receiving friends in my home. Now, when your friends come over, I prefer to go to the basement and cry silently in my room, because your friends aren't mine and I do not feel welcome to join you. You don't seem to care about talking in English, although you know I don't understand. And I don't have the confidence to invite over some people I have met at church. This is not my house. I just have a dark little room in the basement. . . .

However, things are going to change now. A friend opened my eyes. She asked me, "Why don't you go to school? Why don't you have coffee with us when we invite you? Why do you seem so sad?"

I know you were very surprised when I told you about my registration in a seniors' English class. I know you were mad at me because I wouldn't have lunch ready for the family, or be home to baby-sit until you returned from work. But dear one, I need to have a life, too. I can help you. As your mother, I am willing to do that. But you know, I need my own activities and friends, too. I know that I'm capable of learning English, although you laugh at me and try to convince me not to go back to classes because "I'm wasting my time." Now I ride the bus, I have joined a seniors' club, and I don't need anyone to take me to church. Certainly I am old, but I have rediscovered the valuable person inside me. I hope you'll understand.

I want to lead my own life, a life worth living, as long as I am alive. Let me live,
Your loving mother.

Source: Herrera 1994. Reprinted by permission of the author.

Being a member of, and having a strong sense of identity with, a racial or ethnic group can be a liability in later life, depending on one's personal situation. For those with strong ethnic or racial identities and ties to the heritage group, there may be a conflict between adhering to traditional as opposed to mainstream practices with respect to the use of health-care services or the use of family as opposed to formal support mechanisms. As some ethnic elders are discovering, the formal support system in Canada can be insensitive to cultural needs. Koehn (2009) discovered that among ethnic minority seniors, language problems, immigration status, and limited knowledge of the health-care system and of specific service providers were major barriers to accessing health care. In addition, many long-term-care institutions fail to serve the linguistic, dietary, or health-care needs of their ethnic residents. For example, Yeo (1993) found that bilingual nursing home residents with advanced dementia often stop speaking English and revert to speaking their first language with staff and visitors. With more than 200 different language groups in Canada, culturally relevant services for an aging multicultural society must be developed. In particular, members of various ethnic groups should be hired as employees and volunteers in social and health-care settings for older people.

Religious Subcultures

In Canada and the United States, the Amish, Mennonites (Bond et al. 1987; Quadagno and Janzen 1987; Longhofer 1994), and Hutterites are examples of religious subcultures that live in rural areas, while Mormons, Jews, and Muslims tend to live in cities. In other societies, individuals and groups are formally or informally stratified by religion, and sometimes they are separated geographically (Sikh and Hindu in India, Catholic and Protestant in Ireland). These religious communities have a profound impact on the process of aging and on the rights, privileges, and status of older people. Highlight 2.9 illustrates the impact of a religious subculture on the status and lives of elderly Druze men and of Mennonites living in rural regions of Canada and the United States.

Summary

Understanding the historical and cultural differences experienced by older adults across the life course is essential if we are to meet their needs in later life. The meaning of aging, the situation of being older, and the processes of aging vary at different periods in history, as well as in different places, even in the same society. Although there are some universal commonalities in the aging process, cultural and subcultural differences are vital to our understanding of aging. Sensitivity to cultural differences is essential for ensuring that all members of an increasingly diverse mosaic of older Canadians will receive equal and relevant services and be treated without discrimination or ageism. In Canada, there are many ways to age and experience later life beyond that of mainstream society. The unique cultural beliefs, identities, values, traditions, and life-course experiences of Aboriginal people and immigrant groups present a challenge. Our goal, while creating a civil society, is to understand and respect diverse cultures and traditions and to incorporate them into our public policies and personal practices. In this way, all Canadians will experience a meaningful and satisfying later life.

Highlight 2.9
Aging in Religious Subcultures

The Druze in Syria and Israel

The Druze, a minority religious sect (Gutmann 1976), live in the highland villages of Syria and Israel. They follow a traditional way of life with an agricultural economy. To coexist with the dominant Muslim world from which they are geographically separated, they raise their sons to be policemen and soldiers for the government of Syria or Israel. Religion is central to their identity and way of life, particularly for men. The basic tenets of the religion are kept secret from the outside world, from all Druze women, and from young Druze males, who are labelled *hajil*, or "the unknowing ones."

When a Druze man enters late middle age, he is invited to become an *agil* and receives a copy of the sect's secret religious text. If the invitation is accepted, he gives up alcohol and tobacco and devotes a great deal of time to prayer, and his life becomes almost completely ruled by religious duties. Admittance to the religious sect gives men increasing power as they age, because they are thought to serve as a passive interface between their god Allah and the community. As Gutmann (1976, 107) notes, the older Druze "switches his allegiance from the norms that govern the productive and secular life to those that govern the traditional and moral life." Religion enables men to continue being active in the community but on a different level and for a different purpose than when they were younger.

Old Order Mennonites in Rural Canada and the United States*

Many Mennonites who immigrated to North America from Europe settled in rural areas of Canada and the United States. Isolated from mainstream society, the "Old Order" Mennonites maintain traditional ways of life: clothing is simple but somewhat formal, electricity and farm mechanization is not used, and transportation is by horse and buggy.

Following the traditional teachings and practices of Mennonite law, Old Order Mennonites adhere to the codified practices of inheritance and caring for elderly parents that were established in Europe. Parents are respected by their children to the extent that one child will remain single and live in the family home to care for aging parents. Parent-child relations are strong, and most children live close to their parents. Families are large, and religious teachings require that children inherit the farm property or an equivalent cash gift. Basic to this process of inheritance is a desire to preserve family stability, to support all members throughout their lives, and to provide security and care for parents in later life. If children are not present, others in the church provide assistance and care, either informally or through church-sponsored nursing homes.

* Adapted from Bond et al. 1987 and Quadagno and Janzen 1987.

For Reflection, Debate, or Action

1. If you are a member of an ethnic, racial, or religious group, or if you know someone who is, identify any unique cultural values, beliefs, norms, practices, or experiences that might influence the status and quality of life of elderly members.
2. Discuss with an elderly person outside your extended family whether there are any historical events or social changes during their lives that have had a major effect on how they have grown older or on how they are adapting to later life.
3. Interview a social or health-care worker to determine how cultural differences among their elderly clients or patients pose unique challenges in the delivery of services or programs.
4. Examine census data for your home community or province to identify the location and size of major cultural groups, and indicate the percentage of each cultural group in each of the following age groups: 45–64, 65–79, 80+.
5. Examine new policies or programs as they are announced by local, provincial, and federal agencies or organizations. Identify the extent to which they are likely either to serve or to neglect Aboriginal people and immigrant groups.
6. Identify some of the needs of aging people in Canada's racial, ethnic, and religious subcultures for housing, transportation, health care, and home care. Propose new or revised government policies that would meet these needs, especially policies that might improve quality of life and reduce language barriers.

Notes

1. Sources about the cultural and historical aspects of aging include the following: Fry 1996, 1999, 2010; Keith 1985, 1990; Achenbaum 1996, 2010; Sokolovsky 1997; Elliott 1999; Ikels and Beall 2001; Andersson 2002; Katz 2005; NACA 2005; Schaie and Elder 2005; Angel and Angel 2006; Haber 2006; Yoon and Hendricks 2006; Gilleard 2007, 2009. Articles about aging processes and older people in a variety of countries are also published in the *Journal of Cross-Cultural Gerontology*.
2. Some exceptions are Simmons 1945; Shanas et al. 1968; Havighurst et al. 1969; Cowgill and Holmes 1972; Fry 1980; Keith 1982; Shin and Lee 1989; Keith et al. 1994; Sokolovsky 1997; Bengtson et al. 2000; and Schaie and Elder 2005.
3. For discussions of modernization, see Cowgill 1974b, 1986; Fischer 1977; Amoss and Harrell 1981; Quadagno 1982; Stearns 1982; Foner 1984; Fry 1985, 1988, 1996; Albert and Cattell 1994; Ng et al. 2002; and Haber 2006.
4. Statistics Canada has published a list of definitions of Aboriginal groups in Canada (www.statcan.gc.ca/concepts/definitions/aboriginal-autochtone-eng.htm).
5. Sources of reports about Aboriginal people include the First Nations and Inuit Health Branch of Health Canada (www.hc-sc.gc.ca/fniah-spnia/index-eng.php); Newhouse and Peters 2003; White et al. 2003; NACA 2005; Turcotte and Schellenberg 2007, 221–69; and publications by Statistics Canada (1998, 2001, 2003a, 2003b, 2008a, 2008b).

3 Individual Aging: Physical and Psychological Change across the Life Course

Wrinkles should merely indicate where smiles have been.

— Mark Twain, *Following the Equator*

Focal Points and Key Facts

- Is physiological aging a disease, or a complex set of processes?

- In what way do physical and cognitive changes across the life course have positive and negative influences on the social behaviour, social interaction, and social networks of aging individuals?

- Do the motor, sensory, and cognitive systems decline to the same degree and at the same rate?

- Are older adults sexually active, and, if so, to what extent?

- Can adults delay, or compensate for, natural physiological and cognitive losses with age by engaging in physical activity in middle and later life?

- Does personality remain stable or change throughout a person's life?

- More than 40 per cent of Canadians 65 and over report having at least one disability that influences, to some extent, their ability to perform activities required in daily life.

- Only about 8 per cent of Canadians aged 65 to 74 experience any kind of diagnosed dementia, but this percentage increases to about 32 per cent for those aged 85 and over.

- It is estimated that the number of new cases (incidence) of dementia in Canada will rise from 103,700 per year in 2008 to 257,800 in 2038.

- Will rates of dementia become so high that Canada will not be able to sustain its health-care system?

Introduction

Why do some people "age well" while others "age poorly"? To understand fully how people interact with others and function within their environment in later life, we need to understand the changes that occur *within* most individuals across the life course. Aging involves a process of change, from birth to death, in our interacting sensory, physiological, and psychological systems. These changes take place at different rates and to varying degrees but, in later life, tend to influence a person's health, functional capacity, interaction with others, daily lifestyles, and quality of life (Aldwin et al. 2006).

Aging is not a disease, but some diseases, such as Alzheimer's disease, Parkinson's disease, and strokes, are more prevalent in later life. And the cumulative effect of having certain diseases, such as arthritis or diabetes, earlier in life can become serious in later life. Adopting safe, healthy habits concerning diet, drugs, alcohol, smoking, sex, and physical activity can slow the processes of aging, increase longevity, contribute to independence, and help a person adapt to age-related changes over the life course, such as loss of muscle strength, reduced endurance, and weakened immune function. In contrast, both genetic factors (McClearn and Vogler 2001) and environmental factors (e.g., low socio-economic status, inadequate housing) can speed up normal changes in aging or health for those who are predisposed to disease states and malnutrition. Thus, aging processes should be considered to be the result of a combination of individual choices and external constraints. Issues related to individual and population health in later life are discussed in Chapter 7. In the present chapter, we focus on continuity and change in the physiological, sensory, perceptual, cognitive, and personality systems across the life course (Birren and Schaie 2006). These changes can lead to cumulative advantages or disadvantages in later life, which are reflected in health status, extent of independence, and degree and type of mobility.

It is beyond the scope of this chapter to present biological or genetic-level explanations as to why changes occur in the human organism.[1] However, because these changes influence behaviour and cognition in aging adults and how we interact with a changing social and physical environment, the emphasis is on describing normal aging processes in order to separate myth from fact. The most prevailing myth is that aging involves degenerative changes in our physical and psychological systems that lead, inevitably, to frailty and ultimately to total dependence on others. While that may be true for some people (usually not until the last few months or years before death), disabilities and frailties are observed at any age because of genetics, injuries, diseases, environmental factors, and living habits.

A **disability** is a "reported" difficulty in performing the activities of daily life (ADLs), such as dressing, getting out of bed, grooming oneself, or using the toilet, or in performing instrumental activities of daily life (IADLs), such as shopping, banking, cleaning and maintaining a home, and driving a car. Or a disability is a physical or mental condition, or a health problem, that reduces the kind or amount of activity that can be completed (Statistics Canada 2007). A reported disability can range from a backache to an inability to walk even with an assistive device such as a cane or a walker. Older people report more disabilities than younger people; and older women, more than older men, report one disability or more. The 2006 Participation and Activity Limitation Survey found that 40.5 per cent (about 1.5 million) of Canadians 65 and over reported having at least one disability (Statistics Canada 2007). The number of disabilities and their severity increase with age, and by age 75 and over, 53.5 per cent of older Canadians report having a disability. Among people over 65, the disabilities reported most often were mobility problems (80 per cent of those with a disability), pain, agility (difficulty getting dressed), and confusion (about 4 per cent of all problems). Although these disabilities restrict functioning in later life, whether they increase dependence or lower someone's perceived quality of life depends on such factors as tolerance of pain, personality and self-esteem, formal and informal social support, type of environment, and whether the individual lives alone.

Frailty, often associated with aging, is neither well defined nor well understood (Ferrucci et al. 2006; Kuh et al. 2007; Karunananthan et al. 2009; Weiss et al. 2010). It is *not* an inevitable consequence of aging but rather a disease state that is susceptible to intervention and reversal in some cases (Bortz 2002; Morley et al. 2002; Bischoff et al. 2006). Frailty is characterized by impairments across physiological systems that often entail imbalances in systems, such as weaker lung capacity and loss of leg strength (Weiss et al. 2010). Frailty often includes the following: muscle weakness, especially in the legs; fatigue and diminished energy reserves; decreased physical and social activity; unintentional loss of weight; poor posture; and a slow or unsteady gait. Clinicians often label someone as frail if they have three or more of these characteristics. Frailty is strongly related to increased risk of falling and fractures, social isolation, dependence, utilization of home care or other community services, hospitalization and institutionalization, cognitive decline, and nearness to death. The causes of frailty include genetic traits related to the metabolic, cardiovascular, and immunologic systems; the onset of disease or injuries that limit physical activity; poor nutrition; sedentary living whereby lack of regular physical activity in later life leads to loss of muscle strength and endurance in the legs; and the onset of normal aging processes, such as dementia and sarcopenia (loss of muscle).

Having briefly discussed two possible outcomes of individual aging—disabilities and frailty—the remainder of this chapter presents an overview of aging processes that influence social and intellectual behaviour and performance in later life. Important in this discussion is the realization that disability and the disablement processes are socially constructed, and that disability is not a normative part of human existence. Rather, it is a societal label that is experienced differently across the life course (Kelley-Moore 2010).

As we age, we all experience some decline in health and gradual losses of physical, motor, and cognitive efficiency and ability. However, most people, at least until very late in life, do not experience functional losses that seriously change or affect their social or cognitive behaviour.[2] Indeed, most people do *not* spend their later years in a state of dependence. Rather, the varying degrees of physical, perceptual, or cognitive losses require some type of adaptation. This process of adaptation is influenced by a variety of past and present social and environmental factors, such as previous lifestyle, personality structure and coping style, support from informal and formal support systems, degree of social engagement, socio-economic status, race, gender, and living arrangements (who lives in the home). Adaptation to changes in the physical and psychological systems are influenced as well by historical events, such as recessions and health program and policy changes, and by unique life events, such as a change in marital status, retirement, or health transitions (such as becoming disabled or developing a serious chronic illness). Increasingly, adaptation is influenced by the availability of assistive devices and by the willingness of an older person to use devices such as canes, scooters, wheelchairs, computers, grab bars, or smart home monitoring systems (see Chapter 8).

Aging, Physical Structure, and the Physiological Systems

The structure and function of the human organism attains full maturity and its greatest strength and energy in early adulthood. From early adulthood on, there is a gradual and progressive decline in the structure and function of the body's various systems and a resulting decrease in activity level. The rate of decline is influenced by genetic and external factors, such as lifestyle, nutrition, and the quality of health care and the environment. In general, with each aging cohort we have observed a lengthening of life expectancy and a reduction in the onset of disability such that health and energy levels are maintained longer, at least until there is a sudden decline before death. Some of these system changes, such as those related to the elasticity and texture of the skin, are external and highly visible. Others are internal and are not noticed until they begin to influence the activities of daily living, social interactions with others, or work performance. Moreover, there are differences within each individual in the rate of decline for each organ or system. For example, a person who is 65 years old may have the strength, energy, and external physical appearance of a 50-year-old but may have hearing or vision problems more commonly experienced by an 80-year-old.

This interaction of physiological and psychological aging has a unique impact on an individual's behaviour, attitudes, and ability. This impact is reflected in the dynamic interplay between an individual's personality and personal coping style; in others' attitudes, perceptions, and interaction; and in an individual's subsequent "presentation of self" and type and frequency of social participation. For instance, some individuals adapt to a chronic condition (arthritis) better than others. The effect of these changes is related to the severity of change, the degree to which changes occur at the same time or rate, and the extent to which an individual considers changes to be threatening or limiting. The reactions of significant others (i.e., increased social support, lack of interest, or decreased interaction) also influence an older person's perceptions and behaviour.

As you read this chapter, remember that typical patterns are presented and that there are considerable differences *within* and *between* individuals. These differences are due to genetic, lifestyle (health practices, physical activity, diet, etc.), social support, and environmental factors, including socio-economic status, gender, diet, race, ethnicity, occupation, geographic location, body type, and age cohort.

Changes in the Structure and Composition of the Organism

External Changes

As we age, visible changes occur in the skin, the hair, and in the shape and height of the body. In later life, the skin becomes wrinkled as it loses thickness, elasticity, and subcutaneous fat. Similarly, hair becomes thinner and loses its original colour. Because of negative social meanings frequently attached to the presence of wrinkles and grey hair, some people actively fight a "cosmetic battle" so as to appear younger than their chronological age. Not surprisingly, a profitable cosmetics industry has evolved to meet this social need. As well, entrepreneurs actively market anti-aging gimmicks, programs, and products (foods, drugs, creams). Researchers have begun to question the anti-aging enterprise because it tends to view aging as a biological problem requiring a biological solution, without consideration of social and cultural issues (Vincent et al. 2008; Binstock and Fishman 2010).

For many adults, body weight increases up to about 50 to 60 years of age, although there is often a decline thereafter because of a change in body metabolism. This increase in weight is due to an accumulation of fat and a reduction in muscle tissue, which appears most frequently in the abdominal area of men, and in the limbs and abdominal area of women. These changes are more pronounced with poor diet and lack of physical activity. As a result, body shape may change from a lean and youthful appearance to a more rotund or mature appearance. Obesity in later life has both physical and psychological effects (Himes 2004; Reynolds et al. 2005). While research on the effect of obesity on the life expectancy of older adults has uncovered contradictory results (Auyeung et al. 2010; Berrington de Gonzalez et al. 2010; Orpana et al. 2010), obese adults are more likely to spend more of their later life with one or more disabilities, which lowers their independence and quality of life (Reynolds et al. 2005). Fluctuations in body weight are associated with disability and mortality among older adults, likely because this is an indicator of underlying health problems (Arnold et al. 2010). Being underweight is also linked to mortality.

Today, aging adults are faced with a cultural ideal of a youthful body and an active life. To cope with the changes in their appearance and with the inner changes that they feel (less efficiency, decreased energy, and aches and pains), older adults adopt various cognitive or behavioural strategies. A healthy adaptation to changes in body composition or shape is to exercise regularly and eat properly. However, many people are unwilling or unable to invest the time and energy to do so or do not know how or where to initiate an exercise program.

Another visible sign of aging is a shortening of stature that begins in late middle age. This is caused by changes in the structure and composition of the spine: vertebrae collapse or intervertebral discs compress. These changes are seen in an increased "bowing" of the spine, the loss of a few inches in height, rounded or stooped shoulders, and back pain. Again, more women than men experience these structural changes.

External visible changes with age influence how a person perceives himself or herself and how others perceive and interact with that person. A visible change in body shape may cause others to consider a person older than his or her actual age. For those who are secure and live in a supportive social environment, physical changes are seldom traumatic. However, for those whose identity and social interaction are closely related to their physical appearance, attempts to alter the presentation of the physical self may become a time-consuming battle.

Internal Changes

Internal physical changes have more effect on the performance of physical tasks than on social perceptions, attitudes, or behaviour. These changes include the following:

- a decrease in muscle mass (sarcopenia), strength, and elasticity
- a decrease in water content and an increase in fat cells in relation to muscle cells
- a decrease in bone mass and minerals so that bones become more brittle, which increases the likelihood of fractures, especially among menopausal women
- a deterioration in the range, flexibility, and composition of the articulating surfaces and joints, which enhances the likelihood of fractures or arthritis, particularly after 80 years of age

Many of these changes lead to decreased mobility, changing leisure activities, and an inability to perform household tasks in the later years. Also, they can increase the incidence of accidents or falls, particularly where there are steep stairs, insufficient lighting, slippery floors, or a bathroom without grab bars.

Changes in Physiological Systems

Over time, most physiological systems become less efficient and less capable of functioning at maximum capacity. Decreased functional performance is usually noticed during strenuous work or leisure activities. However, regular physical activity can delay or reduce the effects of physiological age-related changes. If physiological systems function efficiently, especially under physical or mental stress, day-to-day functioning and self-image can be enhanced.

The Central Nervous System

This system begins to slow down with age, as evidenced by a longer response or reaction time, the earlier onset of fatigue, hand tremors, and a general slowing of the autonomic nervous system (Williamson et al. 2010). Neurocognitive disorders may also appear in later life (Kempler 2005). Changes in the autonomic nervous system may lead to changes in metabolism, in the structure and function of a number of organs, and in nervous receptors, processors, and reactors. Some of these changes are seen in the slower execution of a task although, contrary to myth, the quality of performance seldom decreases. Changes in the autonomic nervous system influence emotions and behavioural reactions and are related to the onset of senile dementia.

The Muscular System

Age-related changes in the muscular system result in a decrease in strength and endurance, although the rate and degree of loss depend on the frequency and intensity of physical activity. Sarcopenia (a major loss of muscle mass and loss of muscle function), which is an age-related process, is a major cause of disability and morbidity among older people. Furthermore, a decrement in the muscular-skeletal system increases the likelihood of falls: there may be reduced leg lift when walking, which increases the chance of tripping, or there may be greater difficulty in regaining balance after stumbling. In addition, the time required for a muscle to relax or contract, and the time required before it can be re-stimulated, increases in later life. This occurs partly because of changes in the contractile tissue in the muscle and partly because of neurological changes. A decline in muscular endurance also reduces the efficiency of other body functions, such as the respiratory system. The efficiency of the muscular system can be enhanced in the later years by regular physical activity (Ferrucci and Simonsick 2006; Rejeski et al. 2010).

The Cardiovascular System

Among the many physiological changes that occur with age, the most visible (and the most significant for behaviour) are those in the cardiovascular system: there is a decrease in maximum attainable heart rate, a decrease in maximum cardiac output and stroke volume, and an increase in blood pressure. These factors combine to lower the system's efficiency and to hasten the onset of fatigue during physical activity (Freiheit et al. 2010). These outcomes, in turn, limit the duration and type of work and leisure activities that older people can pursue. But these cardiovascular changes are not inevitable. It is possible, with a regular and sufficiently intense exercise program, to lower the resting heart rate, to increase the maximum heart rate during work or exercise, and to increase cardiac output.

It is more difficult, however, to retard the onset of arteriosclerosis and atherosclerosis. Arteriosclerosis, a loss of elasticity in the arterial walls, restricts the flow of blood to the muscles and organs, thereby lowering endurance during work or play. Atherosclerosis, characterized by a hardening and narrowing of the arterial walls, results from the accumulation of fatty deposits that partially or completely block the flow of blood. These cardiovascular diseases, which are especially prevalent among men, are difficult to prevent or treat because their pathology is still not fully understood. However, low-cholesterol diets and regular physical activity throughout one's life are related to a lower incidence of these diseases.

The Respiratory System

The efficiency of the respiratory system decreases with age for a number of reasons, including decreases in elasticity of the lungs, in vital capacity (the amount of air that can be forcibly exhaled after a full inspiration), in diffusion and absorption capacities, and in maximum voluntary ventilation and oxygen intake. These changes reduce the efficiency of intake and inhibit the transportation of oxygen to organs and muscles.

The coordination and efficiency of both the respiratory and the cardiovascular systems are highly interrelated in determining a person's physical fitness capacity (Weiss et al. 2010). Unless people engage in regular endurance exercise throughout the adult years, by 60 to 75 years of age there may be as much as a 50 per cent decrease in physical work capacity from the maximum value attained in early adulthood. In the absence of training, a less fit person has few reserves for emergencies, and during stressful situations, fatigue begins earlier and the recovery period is longer. Obviously, these physiological deficiencies limit the type, intensity, and frequency of some forms of social activity, such as sports, playing with grandchildren, walking or hiking, gardening, sexual relations, and shovelling snow.

The Benefits of Physical Activity

Physical activity has a number of benefits for the aging person (see Highlight 3.1). Many studies have found a positive relationship between the amount of participation in physical activity at

Highlight 3.1
Physiological Benefits of Regular Physical Activity

- slowing of cellular degeneration
- increased blood flow through the capillaries
- increased muscle mass, endurance, and strength
- decreased body fat and a lower body weight
- increased flexibility and coordination
- increased cardiovascular endurance
- decreased systemic blood pressure
- increased and more efficient blood flow from the extremities to the heart
- increased maximal oxygen intake and physical work capacity
- lowered resting and exercising heart rate
- more rapid heart rate recovery after strenuous exercise
- more rapid oxygen-debt repayment after strenuous exercise
- increased use of anaerobic energy reserves
- increased neural regulatory control, including faster reaction time
- increased bone density

work or play and the level of physical and mental health (Shields and Martel 2006; Baker et al. 2009; Phoenix and Grant 2009; Rejeski et al. 2010; Williamson et al. 2010). Yet physical inactivity is common across the life course, especially in the later years (Prohaska et al. 2006), which has serious health consequences for the individual and for society. Recent studies have found that more physically fit older people score higher on tests of cognitive functioning (Williamson et al. 2010), thereby suggesting a relationship between physical activity and mental performance (a version of the "sound body, sound mind" theme). Similarly, there is an inverse relationship between the amount of physical activity at work or play and mortality rates.

Patterns of Physical Activity through the Life Cycle

The pattern of declining involvement in physical activity begins relatively early in life and appears to be virtually universal, although it varies somewhat from nation to nation, from community to community, and from cohort to cohort. Many children withdraw from involvement in physical activity because of unpleasant experiences in sport programs; because there is no alternative to or an overemphasis on elite sport, which discourages those who are less skilled; or because facilities or programs are not available. For those who remain involved past childhood, physical activity has a lower priority as adolescents search for personal identity, assimilate into the youth culture, and reject some societal values, including physical activity or sport as part of a healthy life. Coupled with an increase in food consumption, including more processed and "fast food," many individuals are living unhealthy lifestyles that increase their risk of chronic diseases. Consequently, childhood and adulthood obesity is becoming a global epidemic health problem, including in Canada. In some countries, 20 to 30 per cent of adults are considered obese; and the World Health Organization (WHO) reported in 2005 that an estimated 2.6 million people die, annually, as a result of being overweight or obese (WHO, 2005).

Although most people are aware of the health benefits of physical activity, a majority of Canadians do not meet the minimum guidelines recommended for achieving real health benefits. Research shows that while about four of five Canadians view physical activity as health-enhancing, two out of three report actual levels below those recommended to maintain or improve health (Spence et al. 2001; CLFRI, 2009). The *Canadian Physical Activity Guide to Healthy Active Living* and its sister document for older adults provide recommended activity guidelines. However, it is estimated that only 20 per cent of all Canadians are aware of these guidelines, and many experts feel that the barriers to physical activity make them unattainable (Spence et al. 2001). Current recommended levels of physical activity are being reviewed and possibly will be lowered in order to make them more attainable.

Based on the 2007–2008 Canadian Community Health Survey, about 50 per cent of men aged 65 and over and 38 per cent of women that age were at least moderately active (CFLRI, 2009). While a majority of mid-life and older Canadians are currently considered below that level (i.e., inactive), there is evidence that rates of regular participation in physical activity have increased over the past several decades (see Chapter 7), especially in communities where health-promotion messages advocate regular physical activity. Regardless of these positive trends, there is room for improvement in the physical activity levels of older Canadians.

Explanations for Varying Degrees of Involvement by Older Age Cohorts

Differences in the type and frequency of participation in physical activity are due both to declining physical capacity and to a number of sociological and psychological factors. Less involvement in physical activity across the age spectrum is a more pronounced pattern among the less educated, those with lower incomes, rural dwellers, those in manual occupations, and women (Wister 2005).

Negative attitudes toward physical activity, sometimes because of unpleasant experiences early in life, are also a factor in low participation rates. These attitudes can be reinforced by myths, such as the following: the need for exercise decreases with age; middle-aged and elderly people do not have or have lost the skill to perform most physical activities; physical activity is dangerous to one's health; or older people should "take it easy" as they age. Even among adults who do exercise, many think they are getting enough when in fact their exercise level is often insufficient to improve or maintain adequate health levels. From a societal perspective, the myth that an older adult cannot benefit from regular exercise often discourages the establishment of physical activity programs for older people. The public sector offers fewer facilities and programs to older adults than to younger groups; however, the aging boomers are demanding more programs geared toward a growing and heterogeneous older population.

Age grading, or ageism, is further entrenched in a society when physically active role models are not available. However, the increase in the number of physically active adults of all ages in recent years has weakened the restrictive age norms concerning involvement in physical activity in the middle and later years for both men and women. Moreover, there is increasing scientific evidence that physical fitness can be improved at all ages and, more important, that it enhances physical and mental health as well as competence in later life (Baker et al. 2009; Phoenix and Grant 2009; Rejeski et al. 2010; Williamson et al. 2010). Thus, physical activity is becoming more socially acceptable and desirable for adults of all ages, especially among baby boomers. Highlight 3.2 illustrates the range of possible involvement in sport and physical activity by older people, while Highlight 3.3 demonstrates how people can adopt new physical activity patterns during their senior years.

Highlight 3.2
Physically Active Older Adults at Play and Competition

Given the increased interest in physical activity and sport among the general population, the mass media periodically report the accomplishments or unusual athletic feats of aging adults. These individuals, although still exceptions to the norm, show what can be accomplished in later life and set an example for other people their age:

- A 61-year-old potato farmer in Australia won the 875-kilometre Sydney-to-Melbourne marathon.
- A 66-year-old, who holds 28 age-group track records, runs 32 kilometres every other day.
- A 71-year-old cycled 1479 kilometres in 10 consecutive days, including riding over the 3687-metre Independence Pass to Aspen, CO.
- A 72-year-old sophomore on a college tennis team hits 130 practice serves daily and competes in slalom and giant slalom skiing events in the winter.
- A 70-year-old ran from Vancouver to Halifax in 134 days, 16 days faster than he did when he ran the same course at age 62.
- Sixteen men (62 to 77 years of age) and six women (49 to 70 years of age) bicycled 7700 kilometres from Victoria, BC, to St. John's, NL, in 100 days, averaging approximately 90 kilometres per seven-hour day.
- Never physically active before age 65, a 75-year-old woman jogs 14 kilometres four or five nights a week. Three mornings a week, she conducts an aerobics class for women aged 25 to 45.
- A 77-year-old nun is the oldest woman to finish the famous Ironman Triathlon, which includes a 3.9-kilometre swim, a 180-kilometre bike ride, and a 42.2-kilometre run.
- Golfer Tom Watson almost won the British Open at age 59, 30 years past what was thought to have been his prime.

Aging and the Motor and Sensory Systems

In a previous section, it was noted that changes in the central nervous system occur with increasing chronological age. The most noticeable of these changes is a general slowing of motor, cognitive, and sensory processes. A number of explanations for this phenomenon have been proposed, including loss of neurons, which are not replaced; deterioration of telomeres in our DNA, which influence cellular division and aging; a decrease in the size and weight of the brain; diseases such as manic-depressive psychosis, coronary heart disease, stroke, or depression; hormonal changes; or loss of motivation or concentration.

Motor Performance

Motor performance in a multitude of daily tasks on the job, at home, while driving, or at leisure involves perceiving and evaluating information received from the sensory organs, storing and processing this information, and responding through the voluntary muscles. The most significant changes in motor performance with age are a loss of speed in making decisions and a concomitant increase in reaction time. These changes are most evident when a complex

Highlight 3.3
Eleanor's Story: It's Never Too Late

In Eleanor Mills' opinion, "it's absolutely never too late" to start exercising. When she was 68 years old, Eleanor was almost bedridden and "barely able to teeter across a room." When she was 81 years old, however, she was leading 5 km walks in cities across the country.

Eleanor had advanced osteoporosis, a disease in which the bones become so thin and brittle that they break easily. In time, several of her vertebrae collapsed, and three years later she suffered further fractures. "With the pain and agony and the lack of activity—because I could hardly do anything at all—I went down to 46% bone density. I really began to feel like a china cup walking around, because it really is about half the strength you should have."

Eleanor knew that one of the best ways to improve her condition was to be active. She started challenging herself to walk a little bit each day. "I was in terribly bad shape," she says. "I only kept going because I knew that if you keep still, you lose more bone than ever. It goes much faster." Through exercise, good nutrition and medical treatment, Eleanor eventually increased her bone density by 20%.

A turning point came when Eleanor first tried a walker. "I simply flew along, and I said to myself, 'Gee, I could walk to Vancouver with this?'" It was Eleanor's idea to form what was called the "Boney Express," a series of walks to raise money for, and awareness of, osteoporosis.

Eleanor admits that when she first used the walker, she felt a little strange and wondered what people would think. "There are many people who have resisted getting a walker because it sort of labelled them as unable. And I did feel a little odd pushing around what seemed like an empty chair, because my walker has a seat. But that is so much offset by the value of the walker, that I very soon got over it. I think we should welcome all the aids we can find, and we must be proud that we can do so much more when we use them."

One of Eleanor's goals is to try walking for the whole day. As she puts it, "I just want to see how far I can go."

Source: Keeping Yourself Healthy and Active. www.phac-aspc.gc.ca/seniors-aines/publications/public/injury-blessure/safelive-securite/chap5-eng.php. Public Health Agency of Canada, 2012. Reproduced with the permission of the Minister of Public Works and Government Services Canada, 2013.

decision is required and when the individual must respond rapidly. The loss is compounded if the situation is stressful, such as driving under dangerous conditions or writing a test with implications for present or future employment. This observable slowing down decreases the capacity for physical work, increases the chances of mistakes and accidents when fast reaction time is required, and has a direct effect on social behaviour, which can lead to stereotypes of older people—such as the slow, overly cautious driver. In fact, with advancing age there may be a slowing of speed to ensure accuracy. This **cautiousness**, a generalized tendency to respond slowly or not at all because of the possible consequences of a mistake, occurs in many situations when a decision must be made, such as while driving in heavy traffic.

Reaction time, the period from perception of a stimulus to reaction, is a complex phenomenon and is not well understood. A slower reaction time has been explained as a physical problem resulting from a number of physiological processes. These include a decline in signal strength as neurons and nerve cells die; an increase in reflex time for skeletal muscles; a loss of efficiency in central processing mechanisms so that more time is needed to monitor incoming signals; and a general deterioration in the sensorimotor mechanisms. A loss of reaction time can be offset by practice and a strong desire to succeed at the task and by spending more time monitoring the input stimuli before a response is made. With unlimited time to perform a task, older people perform about as well as they did when they were younger. In fact, with unlimited time to monitor stimuli, an older person is often more accurate than a younger person.

If a job demands speed in decision-making and performance, an older worker may be disadvantaged; more so than if the job merely requires physical strength. Although speed and accuracy at work decline slightly with age, experience can compensate for the onset of slowness. However, many of those who cannot continue to perform because speed and accuracy have decreased end up leaving their jobs, either voluntarily or involuntarily. In the social domain, a slowing of reaction time and decision-making, especially if accompanied by some of the sensory changes noted in the next section, reduces the frequency, quality, and type of interaction with others and with the environment. That is, individuals' perception of the social world changes, and others may see them as slow, old, or incompetent. Less social interaction can lead to further sensory deprivation, culminating in emotional and behavioural problems, such as loneliness, isolation, depression, and decreased activity.

Changes in motor control can influence mobility in later life. With normal losses in balance and a change in gait or posture, which becomes less stable and upright, older people are more susceptible to falls. These losses in postural control, and the onset of increased sway while standing, are compounded among older adults with Parkinson's or Alzheimer's diseases (Newell et al. 2006). Balance is controlled in the cerebellum, which loses about 25 per cent of its cells with aging. Falls are a major cause of hospitalization and institutionalization, dependency, and premature death in later life. With advancing age, people walk more slowly and take shorter and more frequent strides (this gait is often referred to as shuffling). These changes in gait also increase the likelihood of falls and can be influenced by an individual's balance confidence (Ketcham and Stelmach 2001; Liu-Ambrose et al. 2009). Once an older person has had a fall, he or she may begin to fear falling again and may avoid physical and social activities. However, a physical activity program that maintains or increases muscle strength, flexibility, balance, and posture can help to prevent falls.

Sensory Processes

Communication with others, either face to face or indirectly, is essential throughout our lives. To interact with the physical environment and with other people, we must have the capacity to send, receive, and process information. This ability depends largely on sensory receptors that permit information to be transmitted to and received by the brain. As we age, greater stimulation is needed in order to send information to the brain. The quality and quantity of information processing is reduced when age-related changes occur in the major sensory receptors and processors. If the receptors become less efficient, a person's interest in communicating and in their capacity to understand information is reduced. Changes in these systems are seldom abrupt and may not even be noticed at first. If the **impairment** is not severe, people may compensate for the loss through a variety of means: using another sense to a greater extent (e.g., reading to compensate for loss of hearing), intensifying the stimulus (e.g., using a hearing aid), or correcting the deficiency (e.g., with glasses). Or they may depend on experience to predict or identify the stimulus (such as recognizing a stop sign by its shape). If two senses decline simultaneously, as vision and hearing often do later in life, people may have difficulty with their job, with walking, or with social interaction. Moreover, sensory impairment can contribute to depression, loss of self-esteem, or social isolation, as well as to significant increases in both personal and societal health-care costs (Margrain and Boulton 2005).

Vision

After middle age, structural, sensorineural, and functional changes in the visual system have an effect on social behaviour (Kline and Scialfa 1996; Fozard and Gordon-Salant 2001; Schieber 2006). These changes include the following:

- a thickening of the lens and a decrease in the diameter of the pupil, both of which limit the amount of light reaching the retina
- less flexibility in the lens (**presbyopia**), which decreases the ability to focus on objects at varying distances
- a decrease in threshold adaptation to darkness, glare, and rapidly changing light levels
- a yellowing of the lens that filters out green, blue, and violet at the shorter wavelength end of the spectrum, resulting in loss of colour vision

In addition to these alterations in the visual system, people experience loss or impairment of vision if they suffer from glaucoma (less than 5 per cent of the population) or from some degree of cataract development (as much as 60 per cent of the older population).

As a result of these changes, a person may need a brighter light for reading and working and may have difficulty in adjusting to changes in illumination when walking or driving at dusk or when moving from well-lit to dark areas. Indeed, vision problems may account for as much as 25 per cent of falls among older people. Some people may also be unable to perceive blue, green, and violet tones in the spectrum. While none of these changes are totally disabling, they detract from the pleasures of daily living and can lead to depression (Tolman et al. 2005). For example, if declining eyesight prevents people from driving at night or at all, their mobility is limited and they become increasingly dependent on others or socially isolated. To offset vision losses, living and transportation environments need to be redesigned (brighter lights, less glare, and larger lettering on signs and in books) to make the environment safer, more functional, and more enjoyable for older people.

Hearing

Unlike visual problems, which can be recognized and then corrected more readily, hearing impairment is less noticeable to the individual and to others. The older person, unaware that his or her hearing is declining, may have communication problems. A major type of hearing loss is the progressive inability to hear higher-frequency sounds in music and speech (**presbycusis**). This impairment, caused by the loss of fine hair cells in the inner ear, appears after about the age of 50 and is more common among men, especially those who have been exposed to industrial noise. As much as 40 per cent of older people have some degree of impaired hearing. This rate may rise through exposure to loud music at concerts, and through technological devices such as earphones, which are more frequent among upcoming cohorts of older adults.

A hearing impairment affects performance on the job and the ability to function safely and efficiently in one's environment (for example, an inability to hear doorbells, telephones, or car horns). Presbycusis creates stress in social situations, inhibits communication (especially if there is background noise), decreases the quality of social interaction (missing the punchline of a joke, for example), and can cause fear and embarrassment or lead to depression. A spouse may have to change communication patterns and the frequency or type of interaction with a partner (usually a male) who has a hearing impairment. A common example of such a change is when a family cannot continue to watch television together because the husband has the volume so high that other family members cannot tolerate it (Wallhagen et al. 2004). Some older people with hearing difficulties begin to avoid social events, and what began as a natural hearing loss leads to social isolation. Hearing aids provide partial compensation for losses, but other adaptive means are also necessary, such as facing a speaker, lip reading, and interpreting hand gestures and facial expressions.

Taste, Smell, Touch, and Pain

By about the age of 60, individuals experience a higher taste threshold for all five taste sensations: salt, sweet, bitter, sour, and the recently discovered umami (monosodium glutamate). In addition, they produce less saliva and lose some of their taste buds. These changes are compounded by smoking, wearing dentures, and regular use of certain prescription drugs. Further, the ability to detect or identify odours declines with age.

Sensory problems tend to be minimal until individuals reach more advanced ages, such as 75 or 80, but increase substantially after that age (Schumm et al. 2009). If the sense of taste and smell decline at the same time, a person may derive less enjoyment from food and may restrict eating, with a consequent decline in nutrition. A person who is living alone may be less inclined to prepare food, especially if it no longer provides pleasure. These changes in eating habits can result in health problems, such as dehydration, diabetes, or extreme weight loss. Moreover, a severe loss of taste and smell deprives people of an early warning system that alerts them to spoiled foods or dangerous odours, such as natural gas and smoke. And some older people not only have a poor sense of smell and taste but also weaker cognitive skills to enable them to identify odours.

With advancing age, some individuals experience a loss of sensitivity in touch and to vibration in some but not all parts of the body. However, the prevalence of pain increases with age, and the main sources of chronic pain in later life are arthritis, rheumatism, angina, and vascular disease. Chronic pain has a serious effect on physical and emotional well-being, and when it becomes severe, it affects many aspects of people's daily lives. It is unclear whether pain thresholds remain constant or decrease with age. Part of this uncertainty stems from the difficulty of separating the physiological variable of the pain threshold from the social and psychological elements of pain.

Sexuality

Sexuality involves expressing feelings of passion, intimacy, and affection for another person through various forms of sexual activity, as well as the subjective meaning and quality of the experience for both partners. This topic is an ideal example of the need for interdisciplinary research about aging, since it requires a biological, medical, sociological, and psychological perspective for a full understanding.[3] Sexuality could have been discussed in Chapter 7 as a form of healthy aging, or in Chapter 9 in the discussion of intimate family relationships (although sexuality is expressed as well outside family or marital bonds), or in Chapter 11 as a form of leisure and social participation. Here, sexuality is discussed as part of a number of interrelated aging processes that occur across the life course, including in later life, although the frequency, meaning, and form of sexual expression may change.[4]

Sexuality can be a significant component of the intimate relationships that are needed in later life and is associated with good self-esteem (Langer 2009). Contrary to a once-popular belief, lack of interest in sex on the part of older adults is not the norm. The common image of sexual decline, lack of interest, and dysfunction is being replaced by the view that active sexuality is an essential part of one's identity in later life and of successful aging (Katz and Marshall 2003). The marketing of lifelong sex is especially directed toward men during the current "Viagra age" (Vares et al. 2007). Ironically, and somewhat comically, such marketing can trigger a vicious cycle, as noted in the following quotation from a letter to the *New England Journal of Medicine*. Written to draw attention to an increase in vaginal irritation among the middle-aged partners of men using erection-enhancing drugs, the writer stated,

> The man's pill makes the woman need a lubricant. The woman's lubricant makes the man need a penile sensory enhancer. The man's sensory enhancer makes the woman need a desire additive. The woman's desire additive makes a man need an energy stimulant. The man's energy stimulant makes him need anti-anxiety medication. And so on. (Tiefer 2001, 90)

Sexual desire and the ability and need to engage in sex are, of course, highly dependent on physiological and cognitive functioning. Hormonal changes in women and the general neuro-muscular slowing with age among men are normal outcomes of the aging process. It may take longer to become aroused, there may be less stamina, and it may take longer to reach satisfaction. Thus, while sexual desire and behaviour decrease as men and women age, the decline is not as fast, nor does it reach as low a level, as early research and popular belief would have us believe (Carpenter et al. 2006; DeLameter and Moorman 2007). Both heterosexual and homosexual intimacy are possible well into the later years, although sexual intercourse is not always possible or necessary to express feelings. Physical changes, chronic illness (diabetes, heart disease, arthritis), and some prescription drugs may reduce or eliminate sexual desire and behaviour among older adults. Rather than physiological deficiencies, however, the more likely explanations for reduced sexual activity in later life are psychological or social problems (fear of sexual inadequacy); the psychological side effects of drugs; negative attitudes on the part of adult children, physicians, friends, or staff in retirement or nursing homes; and lack of opportunity (not having a partner or privacy).

Sexuality also varies across cultures, time periods, and age cohorts. Some religious sub-cultures believe that sex is only for reproduction; some cultures encourage and promote sex at a very early age; others discourage sex at later ages. Sexuality is influenced by ageism and sexism in a society, especially if advertising images feature only attractive young men and women. Whether someone is interested or engaged in sexual behaviour in later life is greatly influenced by attitudes toward and knowledge about sex, by past practices and experiences, and by whether one has an interested partner (Clarke 2006; DeLamater and Moorman 2007). That is why we observe cultural or cohort differences in expressed attitudes and behaviour about intimacy and sexuality with each new generation of older adults.[5] Many people now entering later life were part of the sexual revolution and the women's liberation movement of the 1960s and 1970s. They have always had more freedom to express sexual desires, and some have been involved in serial relationships, both inside and outside marriage. Among the baby boomers, who have been transitioning into their elder years since 2011, many have experienced serial common-law or marital relationships, some have never married, and there are more gay and lesbian partnerships (Mitchell 2012). Thus, the definition and parameters of sexuality for aging boomers will be different from those observed among earlier cohorts of older adults.

It is still difficult to determine accurately how many older adults engage in heterosexual or homosexual behaviour, with what meaning, and how frequently. Research into aging and sexual behaviour is growing rapidly. A number of studies show that the meaning of sexuality shifts from an emphasis on the importance of sexual intercourse and passion to a greater appreciation for companionship, cuddling, affection, and intimacy (DeLamater and Moorman 2007; Langer 2009). This research also shows that a greater number of older people report that they are sexually active or willing to be active. This increase reflects a cohort effect (people are healthier and have more positive attitudes toward sex) and also greater honesty in responding to questions about sexuality. The most sexually active older people are those in good physical health, with high self-esteem and an interested partner, who have continued a high level of sexual activity throughout adulthood, and who live in their own home. A growing dilemma faced by nursing home personnel is how to accommodate the sexual needs of older residents, married or unmarried. The lack of privacy and the segregation of men and women, including married couples, is a major obstacle to sexual expression, and in some retirement or nursing homes, policies, practices, and lack of training in this area prevent or discourage sexual intimacy (Bauer et al. 2009).

Aging and Cognitive Processes

Just as aging individuals must adapt to physical and social changes, so too must they respond to changes in the cognitive systems—that is, memory, intelligence, wisdom, learning, and creativity (Craik and Salthouse 2008; Birren and Schaie 2006; Charness 2007; Wolinsky et al. 2009; Abrams et al. 2010; Jeste et al. 2010). These changes occur at different rates and to different degrees within individuals (aging effects) and among different cohorts or generations (cohort effects). As in the physical domain, there is a generalized slowing of the cognitive processes in later life, but there is considerable intra-individual variability and some age-related slowing is specific to particular kinds of tasks (Craik and Salthouse 2008; Hultsch et al. 2008; McGue and Johnson 2008). Understanding the complex interplay of neurobiological changes (e.g., shrinkage of neurons and cellular reproduction slowing) and psychosocial adaptation (e.g., behavioural alterations when driving) continues to challenge researchers attempting to understand cognitive functioning and aging (McGue and Johnson 2008). Recent developments in genetic research and neuroimaging are allowing researchers to connect brain physiology and behavioural research about cognitive aging. While a detailed coverage of the growing field of cognitive aging falls outside of the aims of this textbook, several major cognitive changes associated with aging, and some of the underlying implications for social processes of aging, are discussed/introduced.

Declines in cognitive functioning may result from normal aging processes, the onset of dementia disease states, or nutritional deficiencies, especially among frail elderly persons (Gillette-Guyonnet et al. 2007; Smetanin et al. 2009). These states represent a general and major decline in cognitive functioning that is reflected in memory impairment, losses in the ability to use judgment or language, or an inability to engage in abstract thinking. Depictions of an inevitable and sharp decline in cognitive functioning as people age has led many to believe that older people are incapable of learning or thinking, are forgetful, and may be unable to be creative or solve problems. Not only has this led to the fuelling of negative stereotypes of older adults, but research has shown that these images can result in a self-fulfilling prophesy—that is, some older adults fail to use their available resources to offset cognitive declines, such as memory loss, because they accept cognitive loss as inevitable (McDaniel et al. 2008).Yet a large body of research shows that declines in cognitive processes are less rapid and less severe than declines in the motor, physiological, and sensory systems (Craik and Salthouse 2008). Furthermore, there is more variability within any given age group than between younger and older people in general (McGue and Johnson 2008).

One of the most serious threats to cognitive health is dementia, of which about 70 per cent is of the Alzheimer's type (Albert 2008). Based on the Canadian Study of Health and Aging, one of the major dementia studies in the world, only about 8 per cent of Canadians between 65 and 74 years of age experience any form of diagnosed dementia at a mild, moderate, or severe level. However, this percentage increases to about 32 per cent for those aged 85 and older (Hogan et al. 1999). Moreover, changes in cognitive processes are influenced by illness or disease, low motivation to perform emotion, substance abuse, and level of education (Carstensen et al. 2006).

Intelligence

Intelligence is a multi-dimensional construct consisting of abilities such as verbal comprehension, reasoning, abstract thinking, perceptual speed, numerical facility, problem solving, knowledge, and word fluency (Schaie 2005; Ackerman 2008). However, psychologists disagree on the number, meaning, and measurement of these abilities. Moreover, it is important to distinguish between **competence** and intelligence: intelligence refers to underlying abilities that can be applied to many situations, while competence refers to adaptive behaviour unique to a specific situation or class of situations.

Adults demonstrate two types of intelligence. **Fluid intelligence**, influenced by neurological capacity, represents incidental learning that is not based on culture. Fluid intelligence is the ability to adjust one's thinking to the demands of a specific situation and to organize information to solve problems. It is measured by performance tests that are scored according to accuracy and speed. **Crystallized intelligence**, a product of education, experience, and acculturation, is based on learning and experience. Consequently, there are individual differences that vary by level of education, socio-economic status, and gender. Crystallized intelligence is measured by verbal comprehension tests that stress vocabulary and the continual addition or restructuring of information and knowledge within the cognitive system.

The acquisition of knowledge over the lifespan in different domains is often used to assess intelligence levels. An investment in developing fluid intelligence over one's lifespan leads to greater levels of crystallized intelligence (Ackerman 2008). Both cross-sectional and longitudinal studies confirm that fluid intelligence peaks during adolescence and is therefore susceptible to age-related declines, although it is not usually observable until people are in their mid- to late sixties. In contrast, crystallized intelligence increases with age, at least to the mid-seventies, and is therefore relatively resistant to aging effects (Sternberg and Grigorenko 2005). Studies indicate that more recent generations have experienced gains in both fluid and crystallized intelligence, but there are greater gains in fluid intelligence. Overall, there is little significant decline in intelligence until after age 60, at the earliest. In addition, examination of gender differences shows that women have higher levels of health-related domain knowledge and men have higher levels of academically related domain knowledge, which are likely the result of personality, self-concept, and interests rather than inherent sex differences (Ackerman 2008). These knowledge differences may benefit women, given the importance of health knowledge in

Highlight 3.4
Factors Influencing Intelligence-Test Performance in Later Life

In the absence of illness and disease states, the differences observed in intellectual performance can be accounted for by a variety of past and current social and environmental factors. Factors that may either increase (+) or decrease (−) test performance include the following:

1. Experience, motivation, and training concerning material in the tests (+)
2. Higher levels of education completed and fewer years since leaving school (+)
3. The absence of stress and fatigue in test situations (+)
4. The use of appropriate and meaningful test items (+)
5. The use of feedback, instruction, and practice in taking tests (+)
6. The presence of stereotypes that define older people as incompetent, thereby lowering expectations and the level of test motivation (−)
7. Living in an environment that is conducive to intellectual stimulation (+)
8. A decreased emphasis on speed of performance (+)
9. The onset of personal crises, including major changes in job, marital, financial, or health status (−)

These environmental explanations for performance on intelligence tests have led to remedial programs and attempts to change some elements of the environment in order to modify both crystallized and fluid intelligence (Schaie 1996, 2005; Willis et al. 2006; Sternberg and Lubart 2001; Sternberg and Grigorenko 2005; Ackerman 2008).

the aging process. Highlight 3.4 identifies factors that influence the intelligence-test performance of older people.

Older people demonstrate a range of intellectual abilities. Whereas some individuals experience little or no decline throughout adulthood, others experience severe intellectual loss. Moreover, although some elderly people perform more slowly on intellectual tasks or have difficulty with novel tasks or situations, such as computer games or automated banking, aging processes do not significantly diminish the ability to solve problems (Ackerman 2008). In fact, older people can use their accumulated knowledge and experience to offset any loss of speed in intellectual tasks.

Differences in intelligence among older people are more closely related to heredity, socialization, education, life experiences, and cohort differences than to chronological age. The greater intelligence demonstrated by younger cohorts is due to more and better education, more experience in test situations, better health care during infancy and childhood, and a greater likelihood of having learned the skills demanded by intelligence tests. Given a stimulating and supportive environment, gains rather than losses in intelligence are the more typical pattern.

Learning and Memory

Learning involves the acquisition of information or behaviour, while memory involves the storage and retention of the learned behaviour. Learning and memory illustrate the classic "chicken-and-egg" dilemma. For material to be acquired and stored in memory, it must be learned. Similarly, to demonstrate that material has been learned, the person must recall it from his or her memory before the material can be used. This underlines the importance of distinguishing between learning and performance. When a person cannot perform what was learned earlier, it is difficult to determine whether the material was not learned, whether it was learned but not remembered, or whether it was learned and stored in memory but cannot be retrieved for performance. Performance, rather than learning or retrieving per se, is influenced by age-biased or unsuitable learning tasks in tests, anxiety in a test situation, temporary physiological or psychological states (fatigue, lack of motivation, or depression), and the need to perform or demonstrate learning in a short period of time.

Learning

The belief that "you can't teach an old dog new tricks" is still widely held. However, research evidence suggests that while there are individual differences within and between age cohorts in learning ability, older adults can learn new skills, ideas, and concepts if adequate personal and situational conditions are present (see Chapter 10). Older adults have the capacity to learn, but it often takes them longer to search for, code, recall, and respond. When individuals set their own rates of speed, learning is more likely to occur.[6] Using memory strategies, prioritizing multiple tasks, and practicing retrieval strategies can offset age-related declines (McDaniel et al. 2008). Learning potential may be restricted because of a decreased ability to distinguish relevant from irrelevant information. This problem is more acute for women, and studies have indicated that they are more likely than men to attend to irrelevant stimuli in a learning situation. It is important to eliminate distractions in the environment for older learners and to enhance the learning environment with supportive instructions and guidance.

Non-cognitive factors also influence the ability to learn at all ages. First, people must be willing and have the confidence to use their physical and mental capacities. The level of motivation is most likely to be high for meaningful and relevant tasks. Second, learners not only must have a sufficient level of intelligence to acquire information but also must have experience in learning situations. Learning capacity involves acquiring and using the habits and skills of learning. Thus, older adults who remain involved in learning, education, or retraining across the life course are more likely to maintain mental fitness (Cusack and Thompson 2003). Another important factor in learning in later life is health. Generally, healthier individuals learn with greater ease.

Memory

Memory is involved in almost all stages of information processing (McDaniel et al. 2008). A simple three-stage model of how memory works was developed by Murdock (1967). During the first stage, information is received and temporarily placed in "sensory stores." For example, auditory information (the sound of a siren) is stored in the "echoic memory," while visual information (the face of someone you have just met) is stored in "iconic memory." In the second stage, this information, if it is considered important and is not interrupted by competing stimuli, is transferred by the "attention" process to "short-term memory." From here, by additional rehearsal of the stimuli, the information is transferred at the third stage to more permanent "long-term memory." Information can be lost in the first stage (sensory storage) by decay or replacement; at the second stage (short-term memory), by forgetting if the information is not repeatedly rehearsed; and in the third stage (long-term memory), through a failure of the retrieval system to find what has been stored. For example, there is often a decline with age in both recall and recognition tasks, thereby suggesting that both acquisition and storage processes may change with age.

Research suggests that there are different forms of memory and multiple systems of memory (Hoyer and Verhaeghen 2006; McDaniel at al. 2008). For example, "episodic" long-term memory represents the acquisition and retrieval of information acquired in a particular place at a particular time for a given individual (a trip, a meaningful event, or a first love). "Semantic memory" represents common knowledge, vocabulary, or concepts that are shared by most people, such as the colour of stop signs or the meaning of "Caution" signs or the fact that a round object rolls. Other types include short-term or episodic memory, working memory, and prospective memory (Braver and West 2008). Performance in short-term memory is most strongly predicted by life habits and personality, whereas performance in semantic and episodic memory is best predicted by autonomy and life habits (Hansson and Hagberg 2005).

A progressive decline in memory performance is not inevitable, and age-related deficits vary by type of memory. Older people are more likely to have the ability to remember distant events (episodic memory) than recent happenings. This type of memory is related to reminiscence, in which significant personal events from the past are frequently recalled and therefore rehearsed for later recall. There is considerable variability among the older population in the degree of impairment to episodic memory. Episodic memory is better among women, those in good health, those with more education, and those who are more engaged in social, cognitive, and physical activities. However, as in learning experiments, older people need more time to retrieve information from both their short- and long-term memory, especially if there are many competing stimuli in the environment or if stored material must be manipulated or reorganized before the question can be answered.

Why "memory loss" or slower and less efficient recall occurs is not clearly understood. However, it appears that many factors contribute to a decline in memory performance, including lower intelligence, not using stored information, not using various retrieval processes and strategies, changes in executive control and task-related function, interference in the recall process while learning new information, interference from the large amount of information already stored, and, the acceptance of stereotypes (a belief that older people are forgetful). To illustrate this latter point, Hawley et al. (2006) found that older adults endorsed stereotypical views of normal memory aging more often than younger groups, which may contribute to poorer memory performance.

Slower and less efficient memory processes are not totally due to biological changes. Therefore, it is possible to diagnose a problem and improve the efficiency of the memory process in later years through practice and intervention that involve support mechanisms (Hoyer and Verhaegen 2006; Newson and Kemps 2006; Braver and West 2008; McDaniel at al. 2008). Memory can be enhanced by the following:

- learning and adopting strategies to facilitate memorization, such as direct training and instruction
- practising
- providing more time for acquiring, rehearsing, and retrieving information
- using meaningful material to be learned and remembered in experimental situations
- relying more on recognition than on recall
- reducing interference during the learning process
- informing older adults that "forgetting" and "memory loss" are not inevitable and that they do have the capacity to remember, although it might take longer to do so

- improving cardiovascular fitness levels and good eating habits
- seeking and/or experiencing cognitive enrichment experiences/situations in everyday life
- making memory retrieval interesting and challenging to stimulate the brain

What people believe and feel about their memory may be as important as their actual memory. That is, a person who thinks that his or her memory is deteriorating may experience anxiety and a loss of control and may make less effort in memory-demanding situations; all of that may, in turn, contribute to declines in memory performance in later life.

Cognitive Style: Thinking and Solving Problems

"Cognitive style" refers to the characteristic way that individuals conceptually organize their environment, manipulate the knowledge they possess, and make decisions or solve problems. Two contrasting cognitive styles have been labelled **field-dependent** and **field-independent**. "Field-dependent" individuals are more aware of their social environment, more people-oriented, and generally more conventional in their behaviour. In contrast, "field-independent" people are more analytical, more internally directed, and less constrained in their behaviour by tradition and convention. Cognitive style is revealed, as well, when a decision involves some risk, such as driving.

An individual may be reflective (i.e., have a longer response time and fewer errors) or impulsive (i.e., have a fast response time with less accuracy). Older people are generally more cautious and cognitively rigid and are sometimes reluctant to make difficult decisions, especially when a situation is ambiguous, when speed is required, or when they are afraid of failing. Thus, in some situations, older people react with caution by substituting accuracy for speed; in others, they may be rigid in their thinking and resort to prior learning or experience, even if it is no longer suitable. Cautiousness may also indicate an unwillingness to take risks.

Complex thinking is limited by a general slowing of behaviour because of changes in the central nervous system, a loss of speed in all stages of information processing, and a change in health, particularly with the onset of dementia, coronary heart disease, or cerebrovascular disease. The slowing may also be due to "divided-attention" deficits (difficulty in trying to listen to two conversations) or "selective-attention" deficits (difficulty in ignoring irrelevant information, such as a conversation on the radio while talking to another person).

People may compensate for loss of speed in information processing by relying on past experience and knowledge, by employing memory aids, or by eliminating irrelevant stimuli. These compensating mechanisms are particularly important in problem-solving or decision-making tasks. Thus, with increasing age, adults become not only less accurate in problem-solving but also slower, although a task considered as high priority usually leads to an appropriate or better decision (Marsiske and Margrett 2006). Thus, changes in cognition do not necessarily produce difficulties in daily life (Newson and Kemps 2006).

The ability to solve problems declines with age because of a slowing down of behaviour and because of an unwillingness or inability to use newer, more efficient strategies that might lead to a solution or decision (Willis et al. 2006). However, declines are related, as well, to education and to the type of task. The decline in ability is lower among better-educated older people and for tasks similar to those used in a person's occupation. A cohort effect may therefore be present because of changes in educational and occupational experience that improve cognitive skills, such as computer use or the use of other technologies.

Creativity and Wisdom

Creativity and wisdom are related to, but different from, intelligence, and they reflect a person's cognitive style. Often, these two cognitive elements are thought to function at opposite ends of the life course—creativity is expressed when one is younger; wisdom, when one is older. Both concepts are difficult to define and measure (Sternberg and Lubart 2001; Brugman 2006; Cohen 2006; Jeste et al. 2010). **Creativity** involves the ability "to produce work that is novel, high in quality, and task-appropriate" (Sternberg and Lubart 2001, 510). It involves knowledge, personality, cognitive thinking, motivation, and a consideration of environmental influences. Creativity can lead to a solution to an old problem; the identification of a new problem; the creation of a unique cultural product that is valued by others (a work of art, music, or literature or a scientific invention); or the development of a new concept, product, theory, or practice.

Creative "potential" often peaks at about age 40, with a decline appearing after about age 50. However, there are individual differences by occupation. For example, the peak of creativity in mathematics and chemistry occurs when people in these professions are in their thirties and forties, while in literature and history, where experience and a larger investment of reflective time in a single project are necessary, the peak occurs in people's fifties or sixties. The pattern of creativity throughout a person's life is influenced by such factors as socialization, health, motivation, energy, personal lifestyle, competing interests, expectations of significant others, and other aspects of the social environment. For example, older people may have a capacity for creativity but lack a social environment that provides the stimulation or the opportunity to pursue ideas to completion. Nevertheless, with maturity and advancing age, many people become more reflective, integrative, and interpretive in their thinking and behaviour, thereby enhancing their creative potential.

With significant accomplishments by people in their sixties, seventies, or eighties, it is clear that with the right environment, older people are capable of highly creative work well into their later years. These individuals have been referred to as "Ulysseans" (McLeish 1976), and a number of societies have arisen using this title (google "Ulyssean Societies"). They view later life as a challenge, and the production of further creative works, as an adventure.

Wisdom is an ancient concept that has been defined in many ways, often with similar dimensions. Based on the Berlin Wisdom Paradigm (Baltes and Staudinger 2000)—that is, one of a number of studies that have begun to develop multi-level conceptualizations and measures of wisdom in gerontology—wisdom is defined as expert knowledge in the basic pragmatics of life that facilitate exceptional insight, judgment, and expert advice about complex life situations. The word *paradigm* connotes an overarching model that connects the various dimensions and definitions of wisdom. The acquisition of wisdom is not guaranteed, and not all older persons are viewed as possessing wisdom. Studies have suggested that wisdom involves some balance of advanced cognitive ability (such as being able to think on multiple levels with advanced decision-making skills) and creativity (Jeste et al. 2010). Wisdom may also be related to personality and to being "open" to new experiences. It is assumed that wisdom increases to a maximum in the older years because of experience, education, and creative energy, and many seeds of wisdom are planted in adolescence and early adulthood. Baltes and Staudinger (2000) contend that wisdom is associated with "successful aging." However, later in life, if the cognitive functions of memory and reasoning begin to decline, wisdom may be expressed or demonstrated less often.

Personality Processes and Aging

To explain changes in behaviour with age, social scientists have investigated the relative influence of personality factors, and the complex ways in which they interact with the social and biological systems in the aging process. Personality involves individual differences in diverse human characteristics, such as traits, emotions, moods, coping strategies, cognitive styles, goals, and motives, that are unique to an individual. Different elements of these characteristics may be expressed as an individual interacts with others in a variety of social settings.

Most personality research focuses on the early developmental years of childhood and adolescence. It tries to describe and explain characteristic ways in which individuals think (their cognitive style) and behave (their lifestyle). Two questions dominate personality research: (1) Is behaviour determined internally by personality traits or externally by the social situation? (2) Is personality, once established, stable, or does it change as people grow older? To understand the influence of personality on behaviour throughout later life, we need to address these questions.

Social Behaviour: A Function of Personality Traits or the Social Situation?

Is behaviour determined by **personality traits** or by the social environment? According to the "trait" approach, individuals, through a combination of heredity (genes and gene expression), early socialization, and interaction with significant others, develop personal traits and characteristics, a cognitive style, and a temperament. These behavioural dispositions are thought to be relatively stable over time, and they enable individuals to respond consistently and predictably to their social and physical environments.[7]

In contrast, the "situational," "behavioural," or "state" perspective argues that behaviour is determined by the social situation and that individuals learn to behave in a way that is appropriate to a given situation. According to this perspective, a "personality" per se does not exist. Or if it does, it has little stability, since an individual's behaviour is determined by external social norms and sanctions unique to specific situations, such as the workplace, the home, or a leisure situation.

As with many bipolar views of the world, neither position has received overwhelming support in the research literature. Rather, an interactionist perspective has evolved as a more realistic view in which behaviour results from continuous two-way interaction between a person with unique cognitive and emotional traits and a particular social situation. Thus, an individual's personality influences his or her behaviour and adaptation to specific situations while the situation itself influences which traits from the available repertoire are expressed and in what way.

Personality: Stability or Change across the Life Course?

This question is still being debated, although longitudinal studies suggest that after early adulthood, people demonstrate reasonable consistency in attitudes, values, temperament, and traits. Many individuals make a conscious effort to maintain consistency in the behavioural and cognitive presentation of the self. When behaviour and personality are assessed and averaged over a large sample of situations, stability is the normal pattern in the absence of serious health problems. However, researchers agree that there is a significant amount of intra-individual variation over time, wherein some people remain stable while others change to some degree

(Hultch et al. 2008). For example, it has been found that some people "rate" themselves as extroverted at one testing point and as introverted at other times (Mroczek et al. 2006).

However, evidence from surveys and individual case studies indicates that two patterns of personality change may be noted at or beyond middle age in some people. First, most members of a cohort exhibit changes over time in some traits, but a person's relative position in the group does not change. The most dependable person at age 20 is the most dependable person at age 50, even though the average score for the cohort may increase. A second pattern finds that all members of a cohort change on some trait but that some people change much more than others. The person who was most aggressive at age 25 (perhaps he or she was a high-achieving professional person), for example, may be among the more passive at age 50 (the person may have retired and achieved all of his or her objectives). Personality changes can be initiated at any stage in life by agency, when people actively seek to bring about behavioural changes in themselves; by the interaction of genetic factors with social or physical environmental factors; or by transitions or traumatic life events, such as work overload, health losses or gains, the death of a spouse, or divorce or remarriage in later life (Staudinger 2005; Mroczek et al. 2006).

How are these changes explained? A developmental perspective argues that people change and adapt as their individual lives evolve. A relatively new concept in personality research proposed by the famous developmental psychologist Erik Erikson (1985) is **generativity**, a process that begins in mid-life and in which individuals become less concerned with self-identity, the self, and a focus on themselves and more concerned with leaving a legacy to the next generation by helping others, such as younger co-workers, children, grandchildren, or other kin. This is achieved by becoming a leader, mentor, or volunteer in the broader community without the expectation of reciprocity (Ryff et al. 2001; Narushima 2005; Hagestad 2006; Valliant 2007).

Self-concept is a subset of personality that is the outcome of our motivations, attitudes, and behaviour relevant to our self-definition (how we define and present ourselves to others) and our personal meaning of life. The "self" has three basic components (Giarrusso et al. 2001, 296): (1) cognitive (who we think we are); (2) affective (feelings about who we are); and (3) conative (our action on the basis of self-perceptions). There is both stability and change in the self-concept as we age. We use our physical, cognitive, and social resources to maintain or change our self-concept as social or cultural situations change. George (1996) argued that there is a reciprocal relationship between life-course experiences and the content of the self as we age. Life-course events shape the self, and the content of the self influences life-course experiences. Moreover, the self is influenced not only by current social circumstances but also by culture and our place in the social structure earlier in life.

Research about the self attempts to understand how adults cope with stressful situations that emerge in later life—retirement, widowhood, death of friends, failing health, dependency, and institutionalization.[8] Ruth and Coleman (1996, 309) defined *coping* as the "constantly changing cognitive and behavioural efforts to manage specific external or internal demands that are appraised as taxing or exceeding the resources of the person." Through self-evaluation processes, we cope and adapt by making social comparisons and noting discrepancies in how we react, behave, or think compared to others in similar situations. This process involves social cognition; that is, we focus on the content and structure of social knowledge (our understanding of social reality) and on the cognitive processes involved in accessing such knowledge (Hofer and Alwin 2008).

Demonstrated changes in personality over the life course reflect underlying latent needs and characteristics that could not be or were not expressed earlier in life. As social situations change with age, people are less inclined to present the self in a traditional outmoded or inappropriate way. For example, as a person who was striving and ambitious in early adulthood moves into middle or later life, he or she may devote less time to work, become more relaxed in interpersonal situations, and demonstrate a different presentation of the self in all social situations.

Finally, emotions are at the "heart" of social relations, and they influence how and why we care about outcomes. Joy, fear, anger, guilt, love, and other emotions are expressed to varying degrees across the life course, depending on the social context. Age does not affect emotional intensity per se, but it may increase the chance that certain events may occur that affect them in negative or positive ways, such as changes in health, retirement, loss of a spouse, or changes in economic security.

So, does personality change as people age, or is it stable? The answer to the question is "yes" and "yes." The evidence increasingly supports the "co-occurrence of persistent traits and unfolding development linked to changing life tasks" (Ryff et al. 2001, 492; Mroczek et al. 2006; Craik and Salthouse 2008; Hofer and Alwin 2008). While most people do not experience major personality changes with age, some change their patterns of social interaction as situations or demands evolve. Similarly, others, aware of shifting norms, change their behaviour or cognitive pattern to "fit" with contemporary lifestyles or social expectations. Some personality changes may be related to physiological, medical, or cognitive changes; others reflect latent character traits, fewer opportunities, or a changing social environment.

Many cross-sectional studies have measured single or multiple personality traits[9] to determine whether differences exist by age or whether age is a more significant factor in personality differences than other social variables, such as gender, socio-economic status, race, ethnic background, or birth order. Some common personality traits[10] are aggressiveness, anxiety, authoritarianism, cautiousness, conformity, conservatism, creativity, decision-making style, egocentrism, ego strength, emotionality, introversion, extroversion, happiness, irritability, need for achievement, passivity, perceived locus of control, reminiscence, rigidity, risk-taking, self-concept or self-image, self-esteem, and sociability. Generally, it is agreed that there are five major factors or traits in personality development, the so-called "big five": neuroticism, extroversion, openness, agreeableness, and conscientiousness (Chapman et al. 2006; Mroczek et al. 2006). Most recent studies report that stability over the life course is high for the "big five" traits. If there is change in later life, the pattern tends to be a decline in neuroticism, extroversion, and openness and an increase in agreeableness and conscientiousness (Mroczek et al. 2006; Terracciano et al. 2006; Craik and Salthouse 2008).

For most traits, the evidence in favour of either age differences or age changes is equivocal. Some studies find differences between age groups or changes with age while others are unable to demonstrate any differences or changes. Despite the inconsistency of the findings, the current cohort of older people are generally more conservative, cautious, egocentric, introverted, and passive and less emotional than younger age groups. It is unclear whether these differences are due to lifelong characteristics related to cohort effects, learned changes with age, or forced changes with age because of decreasing opportunities, stereotypes, or changing interaction patterns with younger cohorts. It is highly unlikely that the baby boomers will exhibit the same traits as earlier generations, given their different life trajectories, such as involvement in social and political revolutions.

Other personality traits are more dependent on social learning and social interaction and are more likely to change with age. For example, self-esteem (how people think and feel about themselves and how they think others view them) is a learned characteristic and a product of lifelong social interaction and social experiences. Most older people report a positive sense of self-esteem. However, the degree of self-esteem is related to health, socio-economic status, life events, and social relationships. Thus, it is not surprising that a loss in self-esteem may accompany the loss of a job, being discriminated against as an older worker, a decline in health, a divorce, the onset of a disability, or declining independence. Moreover, withdrawal from or less frequent interaction with significant others also reduces self-esteem. McMullin and Cairney (2004) argue that self-esteem is lower among those with less power, and therefore they have fewer life chances because of a structurally or cumulatively disadvantaged position in society. Consequently, an age-based power structure in society acts as a detriment to self-esteem in later life. They found lower levels of self-esteem among both men and women in older age groups, but in all age groups, women in general reported lower levels of self-esteem than men.

Age differences and age changes in personality traits are neither universal nor inevitable. Some people are stable, others change; and those who change on one personality dimension may not change on another (Mroczek and Spiro 2003; Mroczek and Little 2005; Mroczek et al. 2006; Craik and Salthouse 2008). Some personality change in old age can be attributed to changes in health (Small et al. 2003) and others to the social environment. In turn, personality traits can influence our responses to questions about perceived health and well-being (Chapman et al. 2006), as well as behavioural reactions to health losses and pain. And in later life, a change in personality accompanies the onset of Alzheimer's disease.

Personality Types among Older Adults

The early years of social gerontology were characterized by attempts to identify **personality types** that would explain life satisfaction or "successful" aging.[11] This body of descriptive research generated many labels for older people who appeared to think and behave in similar ways—stable, rocking-chair, passive-dependent, integrated or unintegrated, disengaged, active-competent, and husband-centred (for women). The labels were thought to describe lifestyles that had been built over the life course and that persisted in later life and explained "adjustment" to the demands of aging. Most of these "types" were derived from a single research study, usually with men, and using samples of fewer than 100 older people. Unfortunately, these labels were sometimes adopted and propagated by the media, by practitioners, and by older people themselves, thereby contributing to ageism in society and to self-fulfilling prophecies about behaviour in later life. This perspective on personality is not well accepted today, however, since "labelling" is considered ageist and inaccurate and is not useful in accounting for diverse personalities in later life. Moreover, if successful aging could be defined or explained, it would involve many other factors, not just personality.

Summary

Aging is not a disease. As people go through life, they experience inevitable but gradual changes in physical structure (height, posture, and shape) and in their motor, sensory, cognitive, and personality systems. There are enormous variations, both within and between individuals, in the rate and degree of loss or gain in these domains because of personal factors (heredity, health, education, gender, and lifestyle) and environmental factors (work, housing, and neighbourhood) that require coping strategies and adaptation. These factors require longitudinal studies in order for researchers to fully understand them. These complex changes that take place as people age influence personal behaviour and lifestyles as well as the way in which others react to the aging person. A positive attitude may help to overcome some age-related cognitive changes. Personality is both relatively stable and subject to change across the life course in different social situations and as health changes or major role transitions occur. In short, the rate, degree, and nature of individual aging influences social interactions and lifestyles throughout life.

For Reflection, Debate, or Action

1. Go to www.growyouthful.com/gettestinfo.php?testtype=quizb and complete the Biological Age Test. How could this test be improved?
2. Using information in this chapter, develop an argument to support or refute the claim that the human lifespan can be extended beyond its current limit of about 120 years.
3. Can any of the cognitive processes be altered in early or later life to slow the amount of cognitive loss or impairment? If so, which processes, and how might interventions slow down such losses or impairments?
4. If you think of two or three older people in your family, to what extent does personality, lifestyle, and health distinguish those who are adapting well to growing older from those who are having some difficulty?
5. Develop a plan to enable more older adults to share their wisdom for the betterment of society.
6. Looking ahead to age 80, to what extent do you expect that you, as an individual, will have changed and in what ways (both physiologically and psychologically)?

Notes

1. For detailed discussions of psychological and biological changes, see *Handbook of the Psychology of Aging* (Birren and Schaie 2006); Kirkwood 2005; *Handbook of the Biology of Aging* (Masoro and Austad 2001, 2006); *Handbook of Cognition and Aging* (Craik and Salthouse 2008); *Handbook of Cognitive Aging: Interdisciplinary Perspectives* (Hofer and Alwin 2008); and current and past issues of the *Journal of Gerontology: Biological Sciences*, the *Journal of Gerontology: Medical Sciences*, the *Journal of Gerontology: Psychological Sciences; The Gerontologist*, the *Canadian Journal*, the *Canadian Journal on Aging* and *Psychology and Aging*.
2. This does not imply that gross changes in behaviour do not occur because of organic deterioration or the reaction to physically or mentally stressful events. Rather, it suggests that, contrary to the prevailing myth, most older people do not encounter such problems. Indeed, only about 5 per cent of older adults in Canada are living in institutions, and when they are, it is most often in the last few years or months before death.
3. Biologists, psychologists, sociologists, social workers, and medical personnel have studied such topics as sexuality and aging; sexual identity in the later years; the physiology of sex and age; sex and institutionalized elderly people; love in later life; homosexuality and aging; and male and female sexual needs, interests, activities, and problems in later life.

4. For discussions about sexuality in later life, see Katz and Marshall 2003; Carpenter et al. 2006; Clarke 2006; DeLamater and Moorman 2007; Bauer et al. 2009; Langer 2009; and Mitchell 2012.

5. Some of the highlights in Chapter 9 present examples of love and intimacy in later life.

6. For example, university-level correspondence courses in which lectures are provided on audiotape, videotape, or on Web-based tools with printed learning aids may be a more effective learning situation not only for older people but for all adults who have been away from formal schooling for many years. This method allows people to learn at their own pace, without having to take notes in a classroom from a professor who speaks rapidly, and they can replay the lessons as many times as necessary.

7. Although most studies have focused on measures of one or more personality traits (for example, introversion, sociability, aggressiveness, egocentrism, achievement-orientation, dependency), a few have used multi-dimensional scales to arrive at personality types (e.g., Type A versus Type B; or integrated, passive-dependent, work-centred, person-oriented, and rocking-chair). A variety of instruments have been used to measure personality traits or types, such as personality inventories like the Cattell 16PF; projective techniques like the Thematic Apperception Test or the Rorschach inkblot test; laboratory behavioural tests; and content analyses of life histories, diaries, memoirs, or autobiographies.

8. For a discussion of the self in later life, see Ruth and Coleman 1996; Ryff and Marshall 1999; Giarrusso et al. 2001; and Mroczek et al. 2006.

9. The instruments used most often are the Guilford-Zimmerman Temperament Survey, Cattell's 16 Personality Factor (16PF) Inventory, Eysenck's Personality Inventory, and the Minnesota Multiphasic Personality Inventory.

10. Sometimes traits are measured as isolated characteristics; at other times they are measured in such a way that clusters are formed. For example, on the 16PF instrument, sociability, impulsiveness, and dominance combine to represent the personality factor of extroversion. Many question whether we can assume that personality traits are independent of one another or whether the traits are interrelated to create a personality structure.

11. For a discussion of the influence of personality on successful aging, see Havighurst 1969; Mroczek and Little 2005; Mroczek et al. 2006; Hofer and Alwin 2008; and Cavanaugh and Blanchard-Fields 2011.

4 Population Aging: A Demographic and Geographic Perspective

Population aging is a complex issue that concerns not only the well-being of today's older Canadians but also broader areas and sectors affecting the total population, such as health, labour markets, and public finances.

(cited in *Government of Canada 2002*)

Focal Points and Key Facts

- Why do populations age, at what rate do they age, and how do we measure population aging?
- Why is population aging a global concern, especially in developing countries?
- How and why can demographic statistics be misused and misinterpreted?
- Have dependency ratios been used to create an aging crisis?
- Where do the elderly live in Canada—rural or urban areas, central city or suburbs, eastern or western provinces, metropolitan areas or small towns and cities?
- How can demographic statistics and indices be used to develop or revise policies, programs, and practices?
  - Globally:
    - It is projected that the population aged 65 and over will increase from about 562 million worldwide (8 per cent of total population) in 2012, to 1.3 billion by 2040 (14.7 per cent), with about three-quarters living in developing regions.
    - At some point around 2018, people aged 65 and older will outnumber children under five years of age.
    - The "oldest" countries (highest percentage of the population 65 and over) in 2012 were Japan (23.9), Germany (20.7), Italy (20.5), Sweden (20.2), and Greece (19.8).
    - The "youngest" countries (lowest percentage of the population 65 and over) in 2012 were Qatar (0.8), United Arab Emirates (0.9), Nauru (1.7), Uganda (2.1), and Kuwait (2.1).
  - In Canada:
    - The 2011 census found that there were 4.95 million people over 65 years of age, representing one in every seven persons, or 14.8 per cent of the total population.
    - More than one million people (1.33 million) are over 80 years of age; and 5825 Canadians were centenarians, one of the fastest-growing age groups in the country.
    - Based on 2007–9 data, the life expectancy in Canada is 78.8 for males and 83.3 for females.
    - According to the 2011 census, Nova Scotia has the oldest population of the provinces (16 per cent) and Alberta has the youngest (11.1 per cent) although the three territories comprise the youngest regions because of high fertility rates and a lower life expectancy (Nunavut: 3.3 per cent; Northwest Territories: 5.8 per cent; and Yukon: 9.1 per cent).

Introduction

Population aging statistics illustrate past, present, and future trends. In recent years, demographic facts have been used to raise concerns about the possibility of rapidly increasing costs of pension plans and health care, intergenerational conflict over scarce resources, a rapidly shrinking labour force, a changing family structure, and outmoded public policies that could advantage or disadvantage one age cohort more than another. These statistics highlight the need to plan, individually and as a society, for a future in which more people live longer lives free of disability. However, these same statistics can be misinterpreted, or they can be used to introduce irrational fears about the future—fears that have been attributed to "apocalyptic" or "voodoo" demography (Gee and Gutman 2000).

To understand the social processes associated with aging, we must understand, as well, the present and possible future age structure of our country and of other parts of the aging world. We live in an interdependent global society where global aging is, and will be increasingly, tied to the global economy, to geopolitics, and to global humanitarian issues. Worldwide, the population of persons aged 65 and over is growing by almost one million a month (Kinsella and Phillips 2005; Kinsella and He 2009; Bloom et al. 2010). Nationally, regionally, and locally, changes in age structures and in the geographical location where older people live (because of immigration or migration) require that public policies and service programs for an aging population be designed or redesigned. These policy domains may include health care and community services, housing, pensions and income support, education, home care, long-term care, public transportation, retirement, immigration, and leisure services. For example, members of a community might have to decide whether their priority, in a time of limited resources, should be to build a new elementary school, a senior citizen centre, or a long-term-care facility. And the building that they choose must meet the needs of that community for the next 30 to 50 years. Demographic trends and projections provide objective facts to help politicians and private-sector investors reach the best decision for the future (see CIHR 2010). To address economic and social problems arising from population aging, federal and provincial governments debate questions such as the following:

- Should the retirement age be raised or eliminated?
- Should some health-care needs be privatized and paid by individuals who use these private services?
- Should public pension benefits be reduced?
- Should pension contributions be increased?
- Should the number of immigrants be increased?
- Should incentives be created to encourage couples to have more children?

These questions illustrate how, on a societal level, population aging is posing significant challenges for the labour force, the economy, the health-care system, and the family, all of which must adapt to an age structure that is becoming older. History has shown that the school and university systems adapted when the baby boom entered school and that, later, the labour force absorbed this large birth cohort. Now, society must adapt as the baby boomers leave the labour force and enter the later years of life.

Demographic patterns can also be used by entrepreneurs to decide what type of new products to develop and where to sell new products in the health-care, travel, leisure, housing, or clothing sectors (Foot and Stoffman 1998). Personal preferences, life experiences, and societal change influence individuals' choices and predict patterns of consumer demand. For example, in later life, baby boomers will likely consume more products than prior generations because they have always been avid consumers.

Demographers conduct cohort analyses to understand the unique social and historical events affecting the life course of specific age cohorts (such as the baby boomers, who were born between 1946 and 1965), the effect of such a unique cohort on the age structure over time, and its interaction with earlier or later birth cohorts (Wister 2005). To preview your future life course, take the year you were born and add 25 (assuming you are in your early twenties). In that year, you will probably be a full-time member of the labour force. Add 40 to your year of birth: at this point you will probably be a parent and a homeowner. Add 60 or 65 to your birth year, and this will give you the period during which you will likely retire. You now have an approximate profile of the years when you and your birth cohort will experience some major life transitions.

The Study of Demography

This chapter presents a brief, non-technical introduction to the field of **demography**, including the size, composition, and distribution of the population in Canada and throughout the world, as well as emerging issues that will need to be addressed by individuals and government policy-makers. Demographers study why and how populations change over time and become smaller, larger, or older, due to the interrelationships among fertility, mortality, and migration patterns. For example, with declining fertility rates and very little immigration, later in this century Japan and many countries in Europe will experience a slow but significant decrease in population size as the baby boomers die. By comparison, in developing countries the rate of fertility and mortality decline has been faster such that their rate of population aging will increase more rapidly.

To analyze these issues, demographers develop profiles of a nation, region, or community; explain past, current, and future trends; and, based on varying assumptions, make projections—but not predictions—about the future size, composition, and location of the population. Often, these projections include economic, social, and policy issues to be addressed or the possible consequences, positive or negative, of demographic changes for a society or community (Foot and Stoffman 1998; Rosenberg 2000; Connidis 2003; Kalache et al. 2005; Kinsella and Phillips 2005; Population Reference Bureau 2006, 2011; United Nations 2007a; Kinsella and He 2009; Bloom et al. 2010; Martin 2011).

Demographers use tables and figures to illustrate demographic trends and patterns, for Canada and the world, about the past and also about the future. While you need not memorize all of the numbers, you should understand the major trends and their implications, along with why changes in patterns might be occurring. The Statistics Canada website (www.statcan.ca) and the government publications section of most libraries[1] contain a wealth of demographic information. You should be interested not just in those who are over 65 at present but also in comparison with other age groups. Characteristics of age cohorts who will be 65 and older in the next 20 to 30 years (e.g., persons aged 45–64) are relevant for future patterns. Keep in mind that statistics should be interpreted with knowledge of the values, beliefs, situations, lifestyles, and past experiences of different cohorts (see age-period-cohort analyses in Chapter 5, "Methodological Issues in Aging Research").

To illustrate, Easterlin (1996) stressed that lifestyle and value differences between the baby boomers and their parents are quite significant: boomers spend more of their income; fewer of them marry; more of them experience divorces and remarriages; they have fewer children; more of them are childless couples and people who have never married; more of them are dual-career families; and some will inherit vast amounts of money or property from their frugal parents or grandparents. Consequently, as the baby boomers enter later life, their financial, family, and leisure circumstances will be quite different from those of their parents and grandparents: some will have only limited savings, whereas others will have large inheritances; they will have fewer children or in some cases none at all to look after them; and a larger percentage will live alone because they are divorced, were never married, or do not live in a common-law relationship. They are also very consumer- and leisure-oriented.

Demographic statistics become dated quickly, in part because there is often a two- or three-year delay from the time data are collected through a census[2] or survey until the information is published or available for analysis. And statistical summaries can be confusing if they use different sources and/or years of data, or use different groupings or indices.[3] Consequently, we must ensure that we have the latest information and that we interpret and use such information correctly.

Global Demographic and Epidemiological Transitions

In many developed countries prior to the twentieth century, fertility rates were high, and large families were common, although many children died in infancy or succumbed to epidemics, acute infectious diseases, or food shortages in early childhood. Even those who survived beyond early or middle childhood often died in early or middle adulthood. That is why average life expectancy at birth was only about 30 years in 1800 and barely reached 50 years until after 1900. By the late 1850s and thereafter, mortality and morbidity rates declined, and populations started to grow larger and older. Then, as land became scarce in the United Kingdom and Europe, many young adults immigrated to North America, thereby increasing the population of both Canada and the United States.

In the late 1800s and beyond, changes in the population size and age structure of many developed nations occurred because of four interrelated demographic elements, all of which contributed to a **demographic transition**—that is, a shift from high fertility and high mortality in a society to low fertility and low mortality, which usually takes about 100 years. Typically, mortality rates drop faster than fertility rates, which results in significant population growth. Less developed countries have been experiencing this transition at a faster pace than did more developed countries, largely because of the global distribution of food, medicine, and technology. The first phase of the demographic transition was a **population explosion** in which the world's population increased from about one billion in 1800 to about six billion at the beginning of the twenty-first century. It is projected that if fertility rates remain constant in most developed countries and decline in developing countries, the world population will total about nine billion by 2040. Of this total, 25 per cent will live in the more developed countries and 75 per cent in the developing countries (Kinsella and He 2009). A second phase of the demographic transition was **population implosion**. That is, the population of most countries became concentrated in a relatively small area, primarily when young adults migrated to cities in search of work and an urban lifestyle. **Population displosion**, the third phase, began when the population of a specific geographic area became increasingly heterogeneous owing to in or out migration and immigration. Finally, as a country modernized, a **technoplosion** (the rapid spread of new technological developments) created major changes and improvements in public health (such as disease control, public sanitation, and health promotion), individual health and longevity, work and leisure lifestyles, and quality of life.

In the later stages of a demographic transition, there are often improvements in the health of a nation—a health transition. As a population ages, the leading causes of death usually change from infectious, parasitic, and acute illnesses to chronic and degenerative diseases. This phenomenon, known as an **epidemiological transition**, begins once there are improvements in food distribution, nutrition, water quality, personal hygiene, public sanitation, education, and economic development. As a result, life expectancy at birth rises, and the leading causes of death become the chronic and degenerative diseases of later life. In Canada during the twentieth century, the leading causes of death changed from pneumonia, tuberculosis, and infectious diseases in early life to cardiovascular diseases, respiratory diseases, and cancer in middle and later life.

These demographic and epidemiological changes, especially the increase in life expectancy, happen at different rates in different societies and primarily result from personal decisions (agency) and changes in public health policy (Riley 2001). A new stage of the epidemiological transition occurs when social and geographic factors affect the health of specific groups and where new emerging infectious diseases (HIV/AIDS, SARS) and social pathological diseases (cirrhosis, obesity, suicide) combine with chronic illnesses to affect population health, especially among older adults (Kinsella and He 2009). In developing countries, survival rates in the early years are increasing dramatically with improvements in nutrition, sanitation, and access to food and medicine. But, at the same time, their health-care systems are facing a "double whammy"— they must prevent and treat non-communicable diseases and eradicate infectious diseases such as AIDS/HIV, SARS, and tuberculosis while at the same time introducing community care and long-term-care services for the increasing number of citizens who survive into later life.

Demographic Variations among Generations and Age Cohorts

Demographic analyses enable us to understand some of the variations in the lifestyles and life chances of different generations and birth cohorts. Although several definitions exist as to what constitutes a generation, there tends to be agreement on three principal characteristics: (1) A **generation** is comprised of a set of individual birth cohorts (e.g., boomers born from 1946 to 1965); (2) it includes individuals who share particular life experiences at a particular stage in their life course; and (3) it typically exhibits characteristics or "watersheds" that distinguish it from other generations, characteristics that are related to the size and composition of the cohorts comprising the generation and the attributes of the individuals it contains (Morgan 1998; Pruchno 2012). While a generation is made up of birth cohorts, these terms are not necessarily synonymous, as Wister (2005, 4) argues:

> The age at which individuals of a particular birth cohort (age effects), who share social experiences at the same point in life as their age peers (cohort effects), are exposed to particular historical events (period effects) will define a generation. For example, in North America, the large birth cohorts of the baby boom transitioned from teenage years into young adulthood during the turbulent 1960s and 1970s, which distinguish them from earlier generations in significant ways. During their teenaged and young adult years, baby boomers reacted against the values held by their parent's generation (formed in the 1940s and 1950s), choosing to embrace a spirit of individualism and freedom of behaviour that included experimentation with drugs, sex, and new forms of music and art. They also reacted against the Vietnam War, racism, and other mainstream socio-political forces and normative structures in society.

Often, demographic analyses involve a comparison of the size and composition of one generation or birth cohort with those of earlier and later ones. For example, Foot and Stoffman (1998, 19–31) devote special attention to the "boom," "bust," and "echo" generations:

- The "baby boom," born between 1947 and 1966 (others use 1946–65), had about 9.9 million members in 1998 (about 32 per cent of the Canadian population).
- The "baby bust," born between 1967 and 1979, comprised about 5.6 million people in 1998. Members are currently in their late twenties to mid-forties.
- The "baby boom echo" (children of the baby boomers), born between 1980 and 1995, included about 6.5 million people in 1998. Members include teenagers to those in their early thirties.

At the height of the baby boom, Canadian women were averaging about four children each, concentrated in a shorter period than for previous generations. The net result was the highest fertility rate in the industrialized world at that time. The baby bust was characterized by significantly lower fertility rates because of changing roles of women in conjunction with increased educational and employment opportunities and changing attitudes and values about large families. The baby boom echo resulted in a small population bulge as a result of baby boomers having children, albeit at half the rate of their parents.

There is considerable diversity within the large baby boom generation (see Pruchno 2012). For instance, about 17 per cent are foreign-born. Thus, when decisions or projections are being made about economic investment, social services, or public policies, one policy may not fit all. For example, those born in the late 1940s, the "front-end" boomers, have always had an economic and social advantage (Owram 1996). Currently, the first members of this subgroup are in their early sixties and are contemplating retirement, although many are extending their work lives for economic and social reasons (Carrière, and Galarneau 2011). The "back-end" boomers, the approximately 3.2 million people born between 1961 and 1966, are now in their late forties and early fifties; they have been labelled "Generation X" (Foot and Stoffman 1998, 26–8). When members of Generation X were ready to enter the labour force in the late 1970s and early 1980s, Canada was in a major economic recession, and they experienced high rates of underemployment and unemployment. Out of economic necessity, many of these adult "back-end" boomers (boomerang children) returned to live with their parents at some point (Mitchell 2006), and they may seek to retire later in life to make up for lost income.

As in the case of the baby boomers, there is diversity within the older population. Thus, research analyses and projections should divide older persons into a number of generations or cohorts (Pruchno 2012). To illustrate, age groups for analysis might include 10-year age groups or generations (often estimated to be about 20–25 years apart). Each group has had different life experiences and opportunities, and public policy needs to reflect their different stages in later life with respect to interests, needs, capacities, and potential. At the same time, we must examine relationships among generations and age cohorts within the age structure. For example, in periods of high unemployment, as observed in the 2009–13 period, if a large proportion of the population between 18 and 25 is unemployed and if a large proportion over 50 is also unemployed because of downsizing or forced early retirements, conflict between these two cohorts could emerge as they compete for a scarce resource—namely, a job. An increase in the number and proportion of older adults in the future can result in a number of possible social issues, such as a need for more pension funds or the encouragement of older adults to continue working; a need for older adult education and retraining centres; and the need to provide more health, social, transportation, and recreational services.

Demography Is Not Destiny:
The Misuse of Demographic Statistics

The possible implications of demographic aging for public policy and for the lifestyles and life chances of different age cohorts has led to some misuse or misinterpretation of demographic facts about aging and older people. Sometimes facts are manipulated by the press, which uses alarmist headlines to increase newspaper sales; by politicians, to justify increasing taxes, reducing pension or health-care spending, or transferring more elder care responsibilities from the state to the family; or by the health-care system, to justify requests for larger budgets and more facilities. The use of demographic statistics for these purposes has been called "alarmist" (Friedland and Summer 1999) or "apocalyptic" or "voodoo" demography (Peterson 1999; Gee and Gutman 2000; Longino 2005).

Alarmist or apocalyptic interpretations argue that older people, as the fastest-growing segment of the population, are becoming a burden to society (Dychtwald 1997; Lascelles 2004; Chappell and Hollander 2011). However, others argue that a negative and unrealistic view of aging is being created by these catastrophic fear-based projections. If the elderly are blamed for the current social and economic problems facing society, older people may be marginalized to an even greater extent than at present. Such projections, and the resulting media headlines, fuel the argument that generations are being treated unequally or that there is "generational inequity." Some of these crisis-oriented and alarmist projections can be seen in the following headlines that were published in the North American press throughout the 1990s and into the early years of the twenty-first century:

- "Retiring Boomers Set To Detonate a Demographic Time Bomb"
- "Poll Suggests Boomers Are the Real 'ME Generation'"
- "Population Aging Creates Intergenerational Inequities"
- "Age Limits Needed for Expensive Health Treatments"
- "Baby-Boom Pensioners Will Bankrupt the Pension System"
- "Elderly Create Housing Crisis"
- "Elderly Caregiving Costs (Time and Money) Escalate"
- "Aging Immigrants and Refugees Deprive Older Canadians of Social Services"

Cheal (2000, 2003) identified some fears about population aging that came about during the 1990s as a result of demographic changes:

- The public pension system will have to support an increasing number of recipients. Therefore, if the system is to remain viable, an unfair burden will be placed on people of working age to contribute to Canada's "pay-as-you-go" pension system (those currently employed must make sufficient contributions so that benefits can be paid to those currently retired).
- Older people will create a large, unsustainable demand for costly medical services.
- The increase in the number of elderly people who will need public assistance cannot be met by current budgets.
- The economic output of Canada will be greatly reduced because so many older workers are leaving the labour force.
- The social and economic burden of responsibility for the care and support of older adults will fall on fewer people.

Most of these alarmist scenarios have been triggered by fears about the impact of the baby boomers moving into later life over the next 30 years. But demographic changes per se must be separated from other historical or period effects that increase a nation's debt or deficit and decrease individuals' net worth. To separate reality from rhetoric and myth, a more balanced, comprehensive analysis is necessary, not only of demographic facts but also of how individuals behave and make decisions and of how political, economic, and social welfare and health institutions react to changing population dynamics (Friedland and Summer 1999; Gee and Gutman 2000; Hayward and Zhang 2001; Cheal 2000, 2003; Graham 2004; Rozanova et al. 2006; Chappell and Hollander 2011). There is no question that population aging creates economic pressures for a society because of increased pension payments, increased expenditures for social and health services, and loss of tax revenue when large numbers of people retire or when revenue is forgone as a result of subsidies for older people (e.g., tax deductions or "senior" rates for public transportation). (In Chapter 7, we revisit fears about increased life expectancy and increased numbers of elderly people causing a "drain" on the health-care system. Fortunately, many of these fears are unfounded.)

Highlight 4.1
Demography Is Not Destiny

Drawing on the discussions and conclusions of a 13-person Expert Working Group, Friedland and Summer (1999) identified five messages and five policy principles that policy-makers should include when considering the future needs of a rapidly aging population.

Messages

- Population projections are fraught with uncertainty, especially those for the distant future. Projections vary widely in their accuracy, depending on the assumptions employed.
- Projections are not statements of absolute facts. They are based on assumptions, which are conditional statements about what will happen if and only if certain other things happen. As more information becomes available, the accuracy of those assumptions will become clearer, and the uncertainty of the projections decreases; therefore demographic facts must be monitored constantly.
- In the past few decades in many countries, the older population has grown dramatically in absolute size and as a proportion of the population without dire consequences.
- It is easier to make statements about the future that are based only on demographic facts than on all the interactions among people, communities, and institutions. Factors such as economic growth, changes in people's values, expectations, and behaviour, and changes in public policies can also alter the future situation for older and younger citizens.
- Today is different from the past. The elderly of today and those in the future are and will be, in general, healthier, wealthier, and better educated than previous generations. However, this does not mean that all older persons are coping well or having their needs met. Hence, future policies must strive to eradicate inequities in service, support, and assistance for older adults.

Continued

Policy Principles

- Policies that promote economic growth, redistribute incomes, influence individual behaviour, or alter the demographic age-sex structure will change our future.
- An aging and longer-living population may lead to higher public and private expenses.
- Sufficient economic growth should mean that projected government spending will be no larger as a percentage of national income than it is today.
- There are financial risks associated with health care, long-term care, and pension income regardless of financing decisions.
- Prudent public policy for an aging population requires action today but should be flexible enough to be adjusted as circumstances change.

Source: Adapted and reprinted with permission from Friedland and Summer 1999, 1, 55.

As you read demographic projections and the media's coverage of these projections, question and verify the assumptions that these projections are based on and the interpretations that are drawn from the demographic facts. While the facts may be accurate, are there hidden political, economic, or policy agendas in the publicized interpretations? Many countries in Europe, which comprise a much older population than Canada's, have adapted successfully to population aging and are providing high-quality support to their older citizens. Highlight 4.1 summarizes the main messages and policy principles from a report entitled *Demography Is Not Destiny* (Friedland and Summer 1999). Although based on an analysis of US data, the messages apply to any modernized country, including Canada.

The Demography of Aging

Introduction: An Aging and Changing World

The United Nations (2002b) reported at the Second World Assembly on Ageing that population aging (1) is *unprecedented* in the history of humanity, and the number of older people in the world will exceed the number of young people for the first time by 2050; (2) is *pervasive*, globally, and will have an impact on every citizen regardless of age; (3) is *profound* and will have an impact on all aspects of human life—economic, social, political, health, housing, and migration; and (4) is *enduring* and likely irreversible.

How each nation and community adapts to changes in the age structure requires careful planning and rational decisions by national and local political leaders, as well as by international agencies, such as the United Nations, the World Health Organization, the World Bank, and other financial institutions that invest in different regions of the world. To understand the evolving socio-cultural, economic, health, and population conditions of the twenty-first century, a demographic foundation is needed.

One concern has been that population aging will deplete economic growth because of labour-force shortages and reductions in productivity. Highlight 4.2 provides four economic reasons why global aging will *not* create an economic crisis.

In the twentieth century, from a global perspective, most interest in population aging was focused on the "developed" or "more developed" countries or regions; in this century most attention will be focused on the "developing" or "less developed" countries and regions (Martin 2011).[4]

Highlight 4.2
Global Aging and Economic Performance: Four Reasons to Be Optimistic

1. Declining fertility has led to, and will continue to lead to, greater female labour force participation. This will counterbalance age-related labour force declines associated with population aging.

2. Fewer children generally mean healthier, smarter, and better educated children as parents divide their resources among fewer offspring. Insofar as health, cognition, and education translate into higher adult productivity, lower fertility rates thus induce a further boost to economic growth.

3. Demographic projections indicate further gains in longevity, including gains in healthy life expectancy (living longer free of disability). Increased longevity is expected to provide a boost to savings rates as people accumulate more capital in expectation of longer future periods of retirement. Savings translate into investment, which fuels accumulation of physical and human capital and technological progress, which drives economic growth.

4. It appears natural for people to respond to longer lifespans by planning on longer work lives. Tight labour markets in the future will provide a strong impetus for countries to increase legal retirement age and change pension policies to entice longer work lives, which will increase the absolute size of the workforce. Developed and developing countries will have to adopt different approaches to addressing age-related labour market issues due to different resources and institutional supports across these countries.

Source: Adapted from Bloom et al. 2010.

These two categories are used for comparative purposes, but they are crude measures that may not accurately reflect differences at a given time because of different rates of economic and social development (e.g., Hong Kong versus mainland China; rural China versus the Shanghai region).

Employing census[5] data and vital statistics registrations,[6] demographers examine rates of fertility, mortality, migration, and immigration to describe the size, shape, and geographic distribution of past, present, and future age structures. They also collect and analyze statistics dealing with the distribution of the population by geographic region, age, sex, income, language, labour-force participation, occupation, race, and ethnic background. But demographers also search for possible explanatory factors for significant patterns, such as social, political, economic, or historical events, as well as the consequences of these changing rates. To arrive at plausible and realistic population projections,[7] demographers use a variety of demographic, social, economic, political, and environmental factors as "assumptions." They usually incorporate a range of assumptions to arrive at low, medium, or high projections of fertility, mortality, and immigration rates; population size; the **sex ratio**; and other demographic indices. For example, the current fertility rate in Canada (the average total number of children born to each woman during her childbearing years—from age 15 to her early forties) is about 1.6 and is projected to fall to 1.3 by 2021. However, low, medium, and high projections about population size might be based, respectively, on fertility rates of 1.2 (low), 1.4 (medium), or 1.6 (high). Each scenario would result in a different population size in the year 2021.

Aging in Developing Countries: The Compression of Aging

Globally, in 2012, 8 per cent of the world's population was 65 or over, but in the more developed regions the figure was 16.5 per cent compared to only 6.2 per cent in the less developed regions (US Census Bureau 2012). However, it is projected that by 2040, the proportion of persons aged 65 and over, globally, will increase to 14.7 per cent, whereas in the developing regions that figure will more than double to 12.9 per cent and rise at a slower rate to 25 per cent for more-developed countries. In China, which has about 20 per cent of the world's total population, 9.1 per cent of the current total population is 65 and older, and, hence, it is the country with the largest absolute number of older people. Moreover, in China the percentage of older people is projected to rise to 24.1 per cent by 2040 (US Census Bureau 2012), largely because of the "one child per couple" policy and that country's increasing life expectancy.

The rate of population aging is therefore higher in developing nations—and compressed into a shorter period. The changes in age structure in developing countries began in the early 1950s as fertility rates began to decline from an average of about 6.2 births per woman, and are projected to decline, depending on the country, to between 3.3 and 1.9 births per woman by 2025 (Kalache et al. 2005). At the same time, life expectancy in these countries is projected to increase, on average, from 40 to 76 years (Hayward and Zhang 2001) but with extreme variations by country. As a proportion of all older people in the world, it is estimated that by 2040, 75 per cent will live in the less developed countries, compared to about 63.5 per cent in 2012 (US Census Bureau 2012).

To put this compression of aging in perspective, Table 4.1 illustrates, for a number of countries, the length of time it has taken or will take for the population 65 years of age and older to double from 7 per cent to 14 per cent. Compared to the speed of aging in France and Sweden, developing countries will experience population aging over a very short period (20 to 41 years). Thus, the less developed regions of Africa, Latin America and the Caribbean, Asia (excluding Japan and Hong Kong), Melanesia, Micronesia, and Polynesia are aging more rapidly than the more developed regions of the world. This rapid demographic change does not give these countries much time to create policies and an infrastructure to meet the health and social needs of older citizens.

As noted earlier, percentages can mask reality, and therefore we must know the absolute numbers, real and projected, for a country or region (Kalache et al. 2005; Kinsella and He 2009). To illustrate, although the percentage of older people in sub-Saharan Africa will not change much between 2012 and 2040 (from 3.1 per cent to 4.4 per cent), the numbers for this age group are projected to increase from about 28 million to 73 million (US Census Bureau 2012).

The speed of population aging in a developing country such as China, where the number of older people 65+ is likely to increase from an estimated 122 million in 2012 to about 327 million in 2040, could be described as a population tidal wave. Many developing countries like China are young, and a major priority is providing education and jobs for young people. In a few decades, however, these nations will be faced with an aging society. Yet China may be ill-prepared to cope with these changes for a number of reasons:

- China's economic development is uneven, especially across regions.
- The country has no formal pension system.

Table 4.1   Speed of Population Aging

Country	Years for Population 65+ to Double from 7% to 14%
Developed countries	
France (1865–1980)	115
Sweden (1890–1975)	85
United States (1944–2013)	69
Canada (1944–2009)	65
United Kingdom (1930–75)	45
Japan (1970–96)	26
Developing countries	
Azerbaijan (2004–37)	33
China (2000–26)	26
Sri Lanka (2002–26)	24
Thailand (2002–24)	22
Brazil (2011–32)	21
Colombia (2017–36)	19
Singapore (2000–19)	19

Source: Adapted from Kinsella and He 2009, Figure 2-6.

- It has no comprehensive health-care system.
- The population is less educated, in general, than in the developed countries.
- Young adults are emigrating from China to developed countries (Canada, Australia) or migrating to urban regions (Beijing, Shanghai, and the new economic regions) and are not available to care for their aging parents.
- Jobs previously held by older people, often until near the end of their lives, will be eliminated, and as a result there will be economic hardship for older people without pensions.

These changes will have even more pronounced effects in rural regions, where fewer older people have pensions or social services, where there is limited access to health care, and where poor nutrition prevails. In terms of maintaining a workforce, some of the aging effect could be counterbalanced by an increase in rates of female labour-force participation in some developing countries where these rates have historically been low (Bloom et al. 2010). Highlight 4.3 depicts a bleak scenario for the oldest citizens of another impoverished developing region, sub-Saharan Africa.

An Expanding Older Population

A Global Perspective[8]

It is projected that the world's older population, currently at about 562 million (8 per cent of the total population), will reach 1.3 billion by 2040 (14.7 per cent), with about three-quarters

Highlight 4.3
Aging in Sub-Saharan Africa

In stark contrast to the rapidity of aging in other parts of the less developed world, most of sub-Saharan Africa remains in an intermediate stage of demographic transition. Fertility and mortality rates are quite high by global standards, and the regional age structure is changing only gradually. Women in sub-Saharan Africa still bear 5.5 children on average, compared with only 2.8 in North Africa and 2.4 in Asia. Although infant and maternal mortality rates are comparatively high, the large number of babies born each year ensures that the base of the population pyramid will remain quite broad. At the same time, life expectancy at birth for the region is approximately 50 years, 13 years below the average for all less developed countries. The scourge of HIV/AIDS has pushed the average life expectancy below 40 years in some sub-Saharan nations. "Old age" in Zimbabwe or Mali has a very different chronological interpretation from what it does in Switzerland or Japan.

The proportion of older people in Africa is expected to increase only modestly in the coming decades, although the absolute number of older people will rise steeply. While aging as a socio-political issue is not a high priority, there are unique features of many African societies that bear directly on older people. One is the impact of HIV/AIDS, which thrusts older adults back into the role of primary child-care providers (while also dealing with poverty). Another is the rapidly growing number of widows and the role that polygamy may play in their well-being or lack thereof. Also, sub-Saharan Africa is rapidly urbanizing, and the implications of migration patterns for the well-being of older Africans in rural areas are not well understood.

Source: "Aging in Sub-Saharan Africa", from Kinsella and Phillips, "Global Ageing: The Challenge of Success", *Population Bulletin*, Population Reference Bureau.

living in developing regions. Table 4.2 illustrates the current and projected growth for two segments of the older population in different regions of the world.

Those 80 and over constitute the fastest-growing segment of the world population. Indeed, globally, the 80+ population will increase 175 per cent between 2012 and 2040, whereas the 65+ population will grow 133 per cent over the same period (US Census Bureau 2012). In 2012, those who were 80 and over (termed the "oldest old") made up about 20 per cent of the world's older population (65+), meaning that about one in five older people were 80 and over. There is a higher percentage of oldest old as a proportion of all older people (27.5 per cent) in developed countries than in developing countries (16.3 per cent) (US Census Bureau 2012). At the beginning of the twenty-first century, about 53 per cent of those 80+ live in just six countries: China, the United States, India, Japan, Germany, and the Russian Federation (Poon et al. 2005). In China, the number of baby boomers born in the 1950s and 1960s will mean that the number of those aged 80 and older will grow from about 21.5 million in 2012 to 70 million by 2040 (US Census Bureau 2012). Moreover, a large percentage of these oldest Chinese citizens will be women, many of whom will be widowed, illiterate, and poor and have physical or cognitive disabilities. At present, 70 to 90 per cent of older women live with a family member. But this family support will not likely be as available, if at all, in the future.

The onset of lower fertility rates and decreased immigration rates increases the proportion of older people in the total population, whereas an increase in fertility and immigration

Table 4.2 Percentage Distribution of the Older Population by Region, 2012 and 2040

	2012		2040	
	65+	80+	65+	80+
Region				
World	8.0	1.6	14.7	3.6
More developed regions	16.5	4.5	25.0	8.6
Less developed regions	6.2	1.0	12.9	2.7
Northern Africa	5.2	0.8	11.7	2.6
Sub-Saharan Africa	3.1	0	4.4	0.7
Asia (excluding Near East)	7.5	1.3	16.4	3.6
Near East	4.7	0.8	10.4	2.1
Eastern Europe	15.0	3.6	25.9	8.5
Western Europe	18.5	5.3	27.0	8.9
Latin American/Caribbean	7.1	1.4	15.4	3.8
North America	13.8	3.8	20.9	7.2
Oceania	11.6	3.0	18.2	5.7

Source: US Census Bureau 2012.

Table 4.3 Percentage of the Population 65 Years and Older, by Country, 2012

Eight Highest		Eight Lowest	
Japan	23.9	Qatar	0.8
Germany	20.7	United Arab Emirates	0.9
Italy	20.5	Nauru	1.7
Sweden	20.2	Uganda	2.1
Greece	19.8	Kuwait	2.1
Bulgaria	18.6	South Sudan	2.2
Austria	18.5	Zambia	2.4
Belgium	18.4	Rwanda	2.4

Source: US Census Bureau 2012.

rates decreases their proportion in the total population. Currently, there are about 25 countries where at least 15 per cent of the population is 65 years or over, and about 25 countries where less than 3 per cent of the population is 65 or over (see Table 4.3). Canada will reach the 15 per cent level in 2012 or 2013.

A Canadian Perspective

The growth of Canada's older population started to accelerate in 2011 when the front edge of the baby boomers turned 65 years of age. Currently, the baby boom generation (born 1946 to 1965) comprises 29 per cent of the population in Canada, about 9.6 million people (Statistics

Canada 2012b). And, according to 2011 census data, 4.9 million (or 14.8 per cent of) Canadians were 65 years of age or older, which represents one out of every seven Canadians and a 14.1 per cent increase since 2006 (Statistics Canada 2012a). In contrast, the number of children under the age of 14 increased by only 0.5 per cent. A new trend was that the number of children aged 4 and under increased 11 per cent between 2006 and 2011 due to the children of the baby boomers moving into their family-building years (Statistics Canada 2012a). The 2011 census also found that 1.35 million Canadians were over 80 years of age, an increase of about 25 per cent from 2006. Moreover, there were 5825 centenarians, an increase of 25.7 per cent since 2006, making them one of the fastest-growing age groups in Canada. Not surprisingly, four of every five persons over 100 years of age were women.

The Significance of Demographic Indices

The proportion or size of the population aged 65 and over, or the proportion or size of other age groups, paints only a partial picture of demographic change. In this section, a number of the common indices used by demographers are introduced. These indices show past trends, the current situation, and projections of the future, or they can be used to compare different countries or parts of countries (regions, provinces, communities).

Median Age

Median age is the chronological age at which the population divides into equal numbers of younger and older people. When the median age rises, a population is aging. Today, the median age for the world is about 28.4 years and is expected to rise to over 30 by 2050. The median age in most developing nations is below 25, with that of the youngest country, Niger, at 15 (US Census Bureau 2012). In contrast, Japan has a median age of about 45 today, but that is projected to rise to around 55 by 2050 (Kinsella and Phillips 2005). The median age in Canada was 41 in 2012 (US Census Bureau 2012).

Life Expectancy

As mentioned in Chapter 1, life expectancy is the average number of years of life remaining for an individual at a given age. It is determined by applying current age-sex specific death rates to a hypothetical cohort of individuals to construct "life tables," which are typically calculated for men and women separately because of their different mortality rates. Remember that life expectancies are "averages" based on chronological age—some do not live as long as the average; others live longer. The index also underestimates actual life expectancy when mortality rates are improving.

The two most frequently cited statistics are life expectancy at birth and life expectancy at age 60 or 65. Most of the improvement in life expectancy has occurred over the past few decades, primarily because of declines in infant mortality (especially in developing nations), reduced mortality at all ages, and reduced morbidity in the later years. However, there is growing debate over whether the prolongation of life is accompanied by an increasing number of co-morbidities, disabilities, and frailty and whether people remain healthier for longer periods of life (Jeune and Christensen 2005; Parker and Thorslund 2007; Kinsella and He 2009; Martin et al. 2009). While we leave this debate until Chapter 7, we note here that most research shows that on subjective reports, older people report reasonably high levels of well-being, quality of life, and perceived health, despite age-related losses and/or constraints. It may be that older adults show a resiliency and an ability to adapt to personal and environmental changes in their lives, especially given limited time horizons.

In early Roman times, the average life expectancy at birth, globally, was about 20 years. By 1800, it was about 30 years, increasing to 45 to 50 by the 1900s. In 2011, life expectancy was 70 years, and it is projected to rise to 76 by 2050 (Riley 2001). Life expectancies for all countries can be found in the World Population Data Sheets (Population Reference Bureau 2011 [www.prb.org]). Life expectancy is 10 years higher in developed versus developing countries (78 vs. 68). Among the developed countries, current life expectancy at birth varies for males and females, respectively, as illustrated by Japan (80 and 86), Australia (79 and 84), and Hungary (70 and 78). In developing countries, gender differences are less pronounced, and life expectancy, in general, is lower, as illustrated by India (63 and 65), Zambia (49 and 49), Brazil (70 and 77), and South Africa (53 and 54). Where the HIV/AIDS epidemic is prevalent, as in Botswana, Namibia, and Zimbabwe, life expectancy at birth may be reduced by more than 25 years (Kinsella and Phillips 2005; Kinsella and He 2009).

Variations in life expectancy throughout the world at any time are influenced by the same factors affecting the demographic and epidemiological transitions. In North America, life expectancy at birth is higher for women, for urban residents, and for those with more education and a higher income. Life expectancy also varies within a country by region or municipality. These differences are due to variations in wealth, education, standards of living, climate, or the migration patterns of particular age groups. To illustrate, using 2007–09 data, the Canadian average life expectancy at birth for women was 83.3 years; and for men, 78.8 years (Statistics Canada 2011). The gap between men and women is narrowing, perhaps because women are involved in similar work and leisure lifestyles and fewer men smoke than in previous decades.

In Canada, average life expectancy varies by province, community, and even within different sectors of a metropolitan area. Life expectancy is an indirect indicator of a population's health, and people living in the largest cities and urban centres are among the healthiest in Canada. However, the poorer the neighbourhood, the shorter the life expectancy of its residents at birth, although the gap between rich and poor neighbourhoods is narrowing. Life expectancy varies from 83.9 for women and 79.5 for men in British Columbia to 78.2 for women and 72.5 for men in the Northwest Territories (including Yukon, Northwest Territories, and Nunavut) (Statistics Canada 2011). Life expectancy can vary by as much as four years above or below the national average, often because of differences in income, education, living conditions, exercise, and nutrition among different social groups.

Given the gains in life expectancy in the twentieth century, can we expect the same in this century? Olshansky et al. (2001) conclude that any significant gain will occur only if there are large reductions in mortality among older people and that significant gains in the future cannot be achieved by lifestyle modifications. In contrast, Oeppen and Vaupel (2002) assert that given past gains, it is reasonable to assume that life expectancy will continue to increase by about 2.5 years per decade, as in the past. If this projection were to hold, average life expectancy would reach about 100 years around the year 2060.

An improvement in life expectancy does not necessarily mean, however, that the health or quality of life of the population has improved (Hogan and Lise 2003; Jeune and Christensen 2005; Parker and Thorslund 2007; Kinsella and He 2009; Martin et al. 2009). Rather, ill or disabled people may experience a prolonged illness and a delayed death. Thus, life expectancy should be measured, as well, by qualitative indices that measure disability-free, healthy, or **active life expectancy** to assess *quality* of life more than *quantity* of life.

Active life expectancy, sometimes also called healthy or disability-free life expectancy (see Chapter 7) measures the average number of years a person can expect to live without chronic disability (Robine et al. 2003). The measures reveal how longevity and morbidity interact to influence differences in the quality of life. The most commonly used measures assess the ability to perform activities of daily living (ADLs), such as eating, using the toilet, and walking, and such instrumental activities of daily living (IADLs) as shopping, cooking, and using private or public transportation. Globally, healthy life expectancy varies from less than 28 years in Sierra Leone to a high of 75 years in Japan.

In Canada, compared to an average life expectancy of about 80 years, the disability-free life expectancy is about 69 years. This means that, on average, Canadians can expect to live 11 years with some mental or physical disability before they die (Statistics Canada 2002b). Those with higher education and those who live in urban areas have a higher disability-free life expectancy, as do people who live in certain geographical regions. For example, in 2001, the disability-free life expectancy index ranged from a high of 72.8 years in Richmond, BC (where life expectancy is 81.2), to a low of 61 years in the Nunavik region of Quebec (where life expectancy is 65.4).

A 2006 Participation and Activity Limitation Survey (Statistics Canada 2010a) found that at least one disability was reported by 43.4 per cent (about 1.5 million) of the population who were 65 and over, by 33 per cent of those aged 65 to 74, and by 56 per cent of those who were 75 and over. The most common disabilities were problems with mobility, agility, pain, hearing, and sight. Approximately one-third of all those with disabilities reported having "severe" or "very severe" limitations. The majority of these older adults were women, reflecting women's longer life expectancy.

Birth and Death Rates

A population grows or declines (without immigration as a factor) as changes occur in the number of births and deaths in a society. For much of human history, there were more births than deaths in any one year, but this ratio is changing. When fertility rates were high, especially above the natural replacement ratio of 2.1,[9] populations grew. But the worldwide average number of children per woman has decreased from about 5 in the 1950s to about 2.5 today (Population Reference Bureau 2011). At the same time, there are still wide variations in birth rates, ranging from 7.0 in Niger to 1.2 in Singapore and 1.1 in Hong Kong (Population Reference Bureau 2011). In Canada, the fertility rate (the average number of births per woman, assuming that current age-specific birth rates remain constant throughout her child-bearing years) is about 1.6, with a high of almost 3 in Nunavut. Projections for 2025 suggest that the number of deaths (338,000) will exceed the number of births (336,000) for the first time, thereby leading to a zero or negative **natural growth rate** (births minus deaths). But since immigrants number more than 200,000 per year and emigration is relatively low, population growth will continue in Canada. However, incentives to have more children could appear on some public policy agendas, as they have in Quebec and Newfoundland.

Crude birth and **crude death** rates record the number of births and deaths per 1000 people during a one-year period. They provide rough indicators of births and deaths, although they are influenced by changes in the age structure. Generally, in developed and developing societies, both rates have fallen since the early 1900s, apart from the increase in birth rates during the baby boom years, leading to population aging. In Canada, crude birth and death rates for 2011 were 11 and 7 per 1000 people, respectively (Population Reference Bureau 2011). Highlight 4.4 describes Statistics Canada's graphic representation of Canada's "population pyramid" as it evolved over the past 50 years.

Highlight 4.4

A Dynamic Representation of Population Pyramids for Canada

Population pyramids illustrate changes in the size of the population, by cohort and gender, over a period of time. The shape of age pyramids changed from that of a wide-based triangle to a more rectangular shape over the past half century. To fully appreciate these changes to the age structure, use the link below to locate the Statistics Canada animation of the age pyramid of the population of Canada from 1956 to 2006 (dates are updated periodically). Click on "flash" to run the animation and watch the baby boomers move through the age structure across this 50-year period, followed by the baby bust (drop in fertility) and the echo effect (fertility of baby boomers). Also observe the larger female side of the pyramid at the older ages. Use the arrows to control the speed of the animation. You should also run the age pyramid for your province (www12.statcan.gc.ca /census-recensement/2006/as-sa/97-551/vignettes/cda06pymd.swf).

The Sex Ratio

The sex ratio is the number of males per 100 females in a population. A ratio of 1 indicates an equal number, and a ratio of less than 1 indicates that there are fewer males than females in a particular age group. Although males outnumber females at birth (about 105 male births per 100 female births), females outlive males as chronological age increases. This changing sex ratio results from a higher incidence of mortality among men, primarily because of fatal accidents before middle adulthood, degenerative diseases in the middle and later years, and events such as wars or natural disasters. This is particularly significant for gerontology because it is an indicator of the shifting gender composition in later life, which affects virtually all dimensions of aging.

In North America, men outnumbered women in the early 1900s because of higher immigration rates for men. However, the trend since World War II has been a steady *decrease* in the ratio of men to women at all ages but particularly after age 65 (see Figure 4.1). This trend can be explained by a number of related factors. First, a shift in immigration patterns occurred in that more women than men immigrated to North America in the 1930s and 1940s. Many of those women are now elderly widows. Second, despite significant medical advances in this century, men's longevity has not increased significantly in relation to that of women's, since men have a higher incidence of cardiovascular disease than women. Third, men of all ages are more likely than women to die accidentally (for example, in workplace or traffic accidents).

Globally, the sex ratio for those 65 and older is 79 men per 100 women, and for those 85 and older, the ratio is 45 men per 100 women (O'Brien 2012). But there are great variations in the sex ratio among populations of older people—from 46 men per 100 women in Russia (because of deaths in World War II) to 117 men per 100 women in Bangladesh and 245 men per 100 women in Qatar (Kinsella and Phillips 2005). The sex ratio over the next 30 years is projected to increase in developed countries as the gender gap in life expectancy narrows and to decrease in developing countries as the gender gap in life expectancy widens.

The sex ratio for Canadian older adults aged 65 and over in 2011 was 80 males per 100 females, which continues the decline in the ratio of 104 men per 100 women in 1941 to 94 in

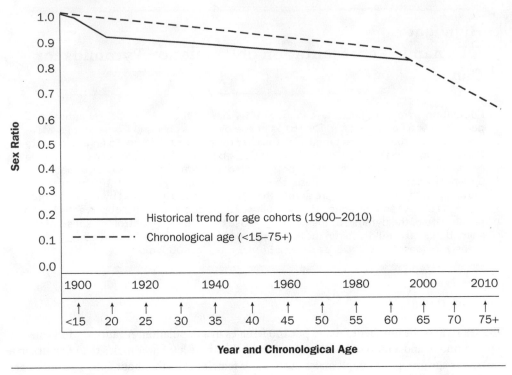

Figure 4.1 The Decreasing Sex Ratio by Year and by Chronological Age in North America

Source: Adapted from reports by Statistics Canada and the United States Bureau of the Census.

1961, 75 in 2001, and 77 in 2006. At age 80 and above, there are only 59 men per 100 women. The significantly larger number of older women has implications for social policies, which will be discussed in subsequent chapters.

The Dependency Ratio

The aging of the Canadian population has many important social and economic implications, one of which is the extent to which society must support individuals who are not in the workforce and therefore not contributing to the public purse. **Dependency ratios** (sometimes called demographic dependency ratios) have been developed to approximate this type of dependency and the ability of a society to support itself financially. Figure 4.2 portrays past and projected dependency ratios (youth, senior, and total) between 1971 and 2056. The *total dependency ratio*, which is most commonly used, is constructed by dividing the number of people under 19 and those 65 and older (the young and old dependents) by the number of people who are "eligible" to be in the labour force, i.e., all those from age 19 to 64. The total dependency ratio peaked around 1971. Between 1971 and 2011, it fell from 89 to 59 dependents per 100 workers. The relative stability of the total dependency ratio throughout the 1980s and 1990s was attributable to a decreasing youth dependency ratio that was offset by an increasing old-age (or senior) dependency ratio (explained below). In the future, Canada's total dependency ratio

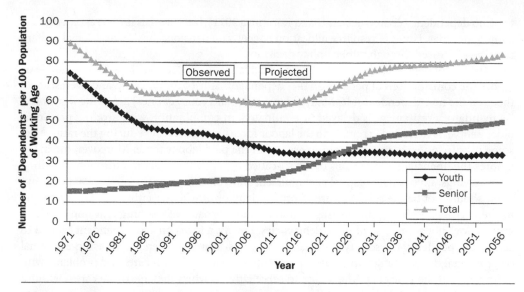

Figure 4.2 Observed and Projected Youth, Senior, and Total Demographic Dependency Ratios, 1971 to 2056

Source: Statistics Canada 2010b. Dependency Ratio. Retrieved 14 September 2012 (www.statcan.gc.ca/pub/82-229-x/2009001/demo/dep-eng.htm).

is projected to rise to 84 dependents for every 100 people of working age by 2056, mainly due to population aging (Statistics Canada 2010b).

The **old-age** (senior) **dependency ratio** is the number of people aged 65 and over divided by the number of people aged 19 to 64. It is usually expressed as the number of dependents for every 100 people in the population of working age. Canada's old-age dependency ratio rose from 15 in 1971 to 22 in 2011. By 2056, it is projected that there will be 50 seniors for every 100 people of working age 20 to 64. Projections of dependency ratios can vary due to the fertility, mortality, and migration assumptions used (see McDaniel and Rozanova 2011).

In contrast, the *young-age* or *youth dependency ratio* has been declining. In 1971, it was 74 youth for every 100 working-age people. This dropped to 36 youth in 2011 and is projected to drop further to 34 youth for every 100 working-age people by 2056. The decreasing youth dependency ratio and the increasing senior demographic dependency ratio show that more people are moving out of the working age range than into it (Statistics Canada 2010b). However, when moving in opposite directions, the effect of the youth and old-age dependency ratios partly cancel each other out, in terms of total dependency on society.

Dependency ratios (as well as the percentage of those aged 65 and over, and other statistics) can be calculated for Canada by province/region/health region using the Statistics Canada CANSIM data generator (www5.statcan.gc.ca/cansim/pick-choisir?lang=eng&p2=33&id=1095326).

Many who have used dependency ratios have been criticized for supporting an apocalyptic demography argument that an aging and dependent population will break the health, pension, and social-service systems. However, while the old-age dependency ratio has increased, the total dependency ratio has not done so in any significant way because there has been a decline in the number of Canadians under 20 over the past several decades. At present, there appears to be no dependency crisis (McDaniel and Rozanova 2011), but if a crisis is to be avoided in the coming decades, issues of resource allocation concerning pensions, health, and social welfare must be addressed through public policy decisions.

The use of dependency ratios has been criticized, as well, because they underestimate or ignore the contributions of persons on the "dependent" side of the equation and overestimate those on the non-dependent side. Many older people (and younger ones) are in the workforce. As mandatory retirement is delayed or eliminated, in combination with eroding pensions, older people have tended to remain in the labour force longer, thereby reducing the ratio. Also, some people in the 20 to 64 age group are not in the paid labour force. Moreover, the index ignores the financial contributions of the so-called dependent population through spending, taxes, savings, investments, capital accumulated, and voluntary unpaid labour. Paid employment should not be the sole measure of productivity or of whether citizens are contributing to their society. Refining the measures to fine-tune estimates of working and non-working groups does not address all of these deficiencies. Finally, a focus on age-dependent criteria to estimate dependency in a society masks underlying or systemic problems, such as large national or provincial debts, changes in transfer payments supporting health care, and problems with financing and the efficiency (the ability to serve citizens when they need the care—without long wait times—and the quality of that care) of the health-care system.

Geographic Distribution of the Aging Population

Geographic data are collected to provide profiles of the composition and distribution of the population in specific communities or regions. They are also used to analyze changes and to project future scenarios that may require new policies or programs. Most geographic information is presented at the national level. However, any change in population composition or size is felt most directly at the provincial, regional, or local level, where health-care, social, housing, transportation, and leisure services are actually delivered. In this section, we examine the geographic location and immigration patterns of the older population, globally and by region within Canada. We introduce information on the migration decisions and patterns of older Canadians in Chapter 8 when we discuss later life changes in housing.

A Global View

Global statistics record the number and proportion of older people by whether they reside in a "more" or "less" developed region or in a "least developed" country. The level of economic development is a key factor in categorizing the size, location, and health of the older population (see Table 4.2).

Internationally, migration is at an all-time high, whether it involves labour migration, family reunification, refugee asylum, or illegal immigration. An estimated two to four million people a year leave their homeland for another country. Whereas the largest immigration flows used to be from Europe to North America, they are now from Latin America and Asia to North America and from eastern Europe, the former Soviet Union, and north Africa to northern and western Europe. Most of these immigrants settle in large urban centres.

Urbanization is a global phenomenon, with about 50 per cent of the global population living in an urban area. It is projected that by 2030, more than 80 per cent of the population of North America, Europe, Australia, and Latin America and more than 50 per cent of Asia and Africa will be living in urban areas (Kinsella and He 2009). While rural areas may have a higher proportion of older people, urban areas have higher absolute numbers of older people—meaning that most older people live in urban areas. One might expect that large cities would be younger because of youthful migration, but globally there is no clear trend toward disproportionate reverse aging of the largest cities in the world (Kinsella and He 2009).

A Canadian View[10]

In 2011, there were 4.9 million Canadians aged 65 and over, more than twice the number in 1981. The growth of older people in Canada will accelerate in future years as the baby boomers move into the upper levels of the age structure. By 2036, the number of seniors will double again, reaching between 9.9 and 10.9 million, depending on the growth scenario used (Statistics Canada 2010c). But there will be significant differences among the provinces and territories over this period—in Alberta, the senior population is projected to increase by 200 per cent (doubling), whereas New Brunswick's senior population could increase by 118 per cent. The greatest proportional increases in seniors should occur in the northern regions due to high fertility rates in the past (similar to compression of aging in developing countries). For instance, population aging should occur at a faster rate in the Northwest Territories, increasing by 355 per cent between 2012 and 2036. Of course, most older people will still live in the four largest provinces: Ontario, Quebec, British Columbia, and Alberta. Table 4.4 reports the provincial and territorial variations in the geographic distribution (proportion) of those aged 65

Table 4.4   Geographic Distribution (Proportion) of Canadians 65+, 2011 and 2036, by Province/Territory

Province/Territory	2011 (%)	Projected for 2036* (%)	% Change/ Increase
Newfoundland and Labrador	15.8	30.6	194
Nova Scotia	16.5	28.5	173
Prince Edward Island	15.8	27.3	173
New Brunswick	16.2	19.1	118
Quebec	15.7	25.1	160
Ontario	14.2	23.4	165
Manitoba	13.9	22.0	158
Saskatchewan	14.6	24.5	168
Alberta	10.8	21.6	200
British Columbia	15.3	22.3	146
Nunavut	3.2	10.2	319
Northwest Territories	5.6	19.9	355
Yukon	8.8	16.5	188

*Based on Medium Growth Scenario 3 (using 1988–2006 growth), see source for full definition.

Source: Statistics Canada, CANSIM Table Generator (www5.statcan.gc.ca/cansim/pick-choisir?lang=eng&p2=33&id=1095326); Statistics Canada 2010c Retrieved 14 September 2012 (www.statcan.gc.ca/pub/91-520-x/91-520-x2010001-eng.pdf).

and older in Canada in 2011 and as projected for 2036, and the percentage increase over that 24-year period.

In 2011, 81 per cent of the Canadian population lived in an urban area while about 79 per cent of those 65 and over lived in urban areas. But among Canadians who live in rural areas, a large percentage are people 65 years of age and over who "age in place." Thus, aging of rural areas and small towns is the result of youthful migration to obtain employment in urban areas, while older people stay or others return to the home town from urban areas if they have left. In Canada, older communities tend to be those that are retirement destinations, those where young people have left, or due to historical trends of migration. Some notable examples of "older" communities as of the 2011 census are Kelowna, BC, with 19.2 per cent of its population aged 65 and over; and Elliot Lake, Ontario, with 35 per cent, and Parksville, BC, with about 38.6 per cent of their population aged 65 and over. Parksville also has the highest proportion of people aged 80 and over (11 per cent). At the other extreme, Barrie, Ontario, and Thompson, Manitoba, are examples of "younger" communities, with 18.8 and 24.7 per cent of the population, respectively, aged 14 and under.

Among the three largest metropolitan areas, the median age of the population is approximately 40 in Montreal and in Vancouver, and about 39 in Toronto. Because neighbourhoods develop at different times, variation in the average age of the residents is common. If the proportion of elderly residents increases in a neighbourhood or community, resources need to be shifted to meet the needs of retirees. For example, community recreation departments may increase spending on facilities and programs for middle-aged and older adults.

From one census to the next, the size and composition of the population changes in regions, provinces, and municipalities. These changes are monitored, and explanations are sought for any large growth or decline in the relative proportion of older and young adults. Are the changes due to increased or decreased economic opportunities in the labour force for young adults, who may, for example, leave Nova Scotia and move to Alberta? Are they due to lifestyle choices of the young, who may move from small towns to large cities? Or is it a case of migration by retirees, who may move either temporarily or permanently to a more temperate climate or less expensive region or return to a community where they lived earlier in life?

Immigration in Later Life

Although less important than fertility and mortality rates in determining the size and composition of the age structure, immigration has contributed to the multicultural diversity of both the total and the older population. Immigration has also contributed to population growth in Canada, but the effect on total population aging is modest because most immigrants arrive before they are 30 years old and then age along with the rest of the population. About 25 per cent of Canadians aged 65 and older were born outside Canada; most of them immigrated as young adults. At first, they increased the proportion of people under 65, but as they have grown older, they have contributed to the growth in size of the oldest age cohorts. Between 2001 and 2006, about 3.4 per cent of all adult immigrants were 65 years of age or older. Many older immigrants come to Canada to join their children, and most come from developing countries.

Until the 1970s, most immigrants came from European countries. In the past decade, however, immigrants were more likely to come from Asia, especially India and China, and an increasing proportion of new immigrants are identified as "allophones" by Statistics Canada—that is, their "mother tongue," or native language, is neither English nor French. In the 2011 census, Canadians reported more than 200 languages under the category "mother tongue," and about 7.2 million (21.8 per cent or more than one out of five) were identified as allophones, an increase of 14 per cent since 2006. After English and French, the most commonly spoken languages in Canada in 2011 were, in order, Chinese, Punjabi, Spanish, German, Italian, and Arabic.

According to the 2011 census, approximately 70 per cent of immigrants during the previous five years settled in Toronto, Montreal, and Vancouver, and they are increasingly living in "ethnic" neighbourhoods, which Statistics Canada defines as those where more than 30 per cent of the population is from one ethnic group. The number of ethnic neighbourhoods in the three cities increased from 6 in 1981 to 254 in 2001, with 157 being Chinese (most do not live in the traditional inner-city Chinatowns); 84, South Asian; and 13, black. To what extent this housing pattern contributes to isolation, less integration, and service delivery issues in later life remains to be seen. This linguistic concentration and diversity presents a challenge to those serving the needs of Canada's future older population.

Approximately 5 per cent of Canadians aged 65 and over in 2011 spoke neither English nor French. Many older immigrants use only their first language and adhere more closely to their ethnic culture than do younger generations in the family. Older immigrants are also likely to be economically disadvantaged in later life. This is especially true of refugees, some of whom arrive after age 50 with little or no formal education.

Summary

The number and proportion of people aged 65 and over in every developed country grew significantly in the twentieth century. This aging trend is primarily the result of lower fertility rates. However, longer life expectancy as a result of better health care and higher standards of living, as well as changing immigration trends, also contributed to the growth in many countries. During the next 20 to 30 years, this pattern of increasing longevity and a proportional growth in the number of people over age 65 (age compression) will occur quite rapidly in developing countries as their fertility rates fall and the standard of living rises.

Although older people remain a numerical minority, they make up an increasingly large proportion of the population in all countries. In this century, the older population will include an increasing number who are 80 and older, including some who will reach 90 and 100 years of age. Women live longer than men, and the ratio of women to men increases over the life course. Most older people live in urban centres where they have lived for most of their adult years. However, in small towns, villages, and farm communities, older people make up a higher than average proportion of the population.

To understand aging phenomena, and to plan policies and programs for the future, policy-makers need demographic and geographic facts. Successful planning requires accurate interpretations of the assumptions used to make demographic projections and a constant updating of the information at the local and regional level. It is also important to use demographic statistics within the broader societal context to avoid misinterpretation. Policies for an aging population must be constantly revised in light of new demographic data if Canada is to meet the needs of our aging population.

For Reflection, Debate, or Action

1. Search for current demographic and geographic facts and indices about your home community or the community where one of your grandparents lives (provincial or census data). Develop a brief demographic profile, and suggest what public policies and programs for older residents might be needed in that community in the next 10 to 15 years.

2. Visit www.Livingto100.com, and complete the "Living to 100 Life Expectancy Calculator." Then complete the Northwestern Mutual Life Insurance Company "Longevity Game" (www.northwesternmutual.com/learning-center/the-longevity-game.aspx). What do the results of these exercises tell you about life-course planning?

3. Assume that you have a position in the United Nations or World Health Organization, where you have responsibility for developing global public policies. Think about population aging around the world and identify what you think are three top priority areas and actions.

4. Think about the future needs of your grandparents and parents, and identify three products or services that could generate a profitable financial investment for you or a business or industry.

5. Statistical reports, tables, or figures, especially demographic projections, are sometimes interpreted in more than one way, or they may be misinterpreted. Examine one or more of the tables or figures in this book, and suggest how the data could be interpreted in at least two different ways. Discuss the implications for policies, programs, or beliefs and attitudes if one or the other of those interpretations is widely accepted.

Notes

1. Statistical sources, available in the periodical or government publication sections of most libraries, include the following: publications from the United Nations Department of Economic and Social Affairs, Population Division (www.un.org/esa/population/unpop.htm), such as the *Annual Demographic Yearbook*; Statistics Canada (www.statcan.gc.ca), including the *Canada Yearbook, Annual Report on the Demographic Situation in Canada, Social Trends*, and the *Daily Bulletin* (available on the Internet); the World Bank (www.worldbank.org); the Population Reference Bureau (www.prb.org), which produces a useful *World Population Data Sheet* on a periodic basis; the US Census Bureau International Data Base (www.census.gov/population/international/data/idb/informationGateway.php); and city or provincial social and government agencies. Other sources include journals such as *American Demographics* (www.demographics.com), *Demography*, the free on-line *Demographic Research* (www.demographic-research.org), *Canadian Public Policy*, and numerous gerontology journals and demography sourcebooks that publish recent research on individual and population aging (Health Canada 2002; United Nations 2002a, 2002b; Kinsella and Phillips 2005; Wister et al. 2006; Turcotte and Schellenberg 2007; Kinsella and He 2009; Martin 2011; Statistics Canada 2010a, 2010b, 2010c, 2011, 2012a, 2012b, 2012c).

2. The most recent Canadian census was conducted in May 2011; the data were released starting in 2012 and will continue throughout 2015 (see www.statcan.gc.ca/start-debut-eng.html).

3. Some sources use 60+ to define the older population; others use 65+.

4. The United Nations employs a classification system that includes "more developed regions" (all nations in North America and Europe, including some nations that were part of the former Soviet Union, and Japan, Australia, and New Zealand) or "less developed regions" (all the remaining nations of the world), and "least developed countries" (most of which are in Africa). Other agencies use the terms "developed" and "developing" countries or regions, but the countries in each category are usually the same as in the UN classification.

5. Most countries conduct a census every 10 years and attempt to count every citizen. In Canada, a complete census is conducted in years ending in 1. In addition, there is often a partial census halfway between the complete censuses (in 2006, for example).

6. Vital statistics are collected when a birth, death, or marriage is registered or when a person immigrates, obtains a driver's licence, buys a house, files an income tax return, or pays property tax. Population estimates vary in accuracy, especially in the developing countries, because of incomplete or inaccurate vital statistics registration and severe undercounting in censuses.

7. Population projections are made by taking the existing population and then making assumptions about future fertility, mortality, and immigration rates. These assumptions make it possible to project the size and proportion of the population at some point in the future. Globally, projections are made regularly by the United Nations, the United States Census Bureau, the World Bank, and the International Institute for Applied Systems Analysis. The assumptions used and the number of outcome scenarios vary greatly among these four agencies.

8. It should be noted that most of the statistics used in this section are from the US Census Bureau's International Data Base Program. Projections are estimates based on data derived from the source countries and may have variability in accuracy.

9. The "replacement level" fertility rate in developed societies is 2.1. This represents the rate necessary to maintain the current population size if there is no immigration or emigration (McKie 1993).

10. There are some excellent sources of geographic and regional demographic statistics in Canada. These include Northcott 1992; Elliott et al. 1996; Centre on Aging 1996; Moore and Rosenberg 1997; Northcott and Milliken 1998; Moore et al. 2000; Wister et al. 2006; and Northcott and Petruik 2011.

Part II

The Social, Environmental, and Health Contexts of Aging

The greatest wealth is health.

—Virgil

Part 2 examines the social, environmental, and health contexts in which individuals age. Chapter 5 introduces the main perspectives and theories that describe, explain, and interpret aging phenomena from a social science perspective. Two levels of analysis are required for a full understanding of aging processes: the micro (or personal) level, which pertains to individual aging, and the macro (or societal) level, which pertains to the aging of a cohort or population. These are not separate processes—throughout life and history, there is constant interaction between individual and population aging and among individuals, their culture, and the social structures in which they age. To help you interpret research findings, and perhaps conduct research, Chapter 5 introduces the goals and methods of scholarly inquiry and specific methodological issues that arise in the study of older persons and aging processes. Two unique challenges in the field of aging are (1) the timing and sequencing of processes, events, and behaviours, and (2) the need to address the temporal aspects of aging phenomena. As well, researchers must use ethical procedures and practices to protect older participants in research studies. Some of these issues are introduced in Chapter 5.

Our social world involves a number of interacting social structures that influence individuals' life chances, lifestyle, health, and actions throughout their life. Society is stratified by social class, gender, race, and ethnicity, and age interacts with these dimensions of social differentiation to create opportunities and barriers across the life course. Chapter 6 discusses the influence of social structures on the process of aging. This discussion examines such outcomes as social inequality and differentiation due to age and aging; age-segregated and age-integrated structures; and, ageism, age grading, and age norms across time. The chapter also presents social processes and issues, such as cohort flow, structural lag, the changing status of older persons, intergenerational equity and transfers, and whether a generation gap is myth or reality.

Chapter 7 recognizes that individuals pursue and experience health and illness in different ways, and that the health-care system is linked to these individual troubles and patterns. This chapter discusses individual and population health in later life, including health transitions and determinants, health behaviours, and health-care systems. Special attention is paid to the social structural determinants of health, the health trajectories of the baby boomer, health issues, patterns of health and illness among older adults, self-perceptions of health, health promotion in later life, mental health, and the costs of health care for older adults.

The lived environment influences the quality of our lives throughout the life course, but even more so in later life. As we grow older, an ideal person–environment fit requires adaptation if we are to "age in place" in the family home rather than move to a retirement or nursing home. Some older people suffer falls, lose their means of transportation, and develop a fear of crime, all of which limit their mobility and the way they live. Chapter 8 examines relationships between aging individuals and elements of their lived environment. Issues addressed include urban versus rural living; age-integrated versus age-segregated housing and neighbourhoods; transportation options; fear of crime; the risk, avoidance, and outcome of falls; technology and independence; and homeless older people. The chapter also discusses a range of housing options in later life (from independent living to assisted living to dependent living) and the mobility and migration of older people.

5 Theories and Research in Explaining and Understanding Aging Phenomena

The sociological imagination enables its possessor to understand the larger historical scene in terms of its meaning for the inner life and the external career of a variety of individuals.

— C. Wright Mills, from *The Sociological Imagination*

Focal Points and Key Facts

- What is a theory? Why are theories constructed, and how are they used to explain and interpret aging phenomena?

- Which theories best explain and interpret individual and population aging and the link between individual aging and the social structure; and how do we synthesize theories?

- Why and how do we conduct research?

- Are unique research methods required for studying older adults?

- How can an older person's rights be protected through ethical research practices?

- Why does an understanding of aging phenomena increasingly require a multi- and a trans-disciplinary approach (in theory and methods) to questions and issues about growing and being older?

Introduction

As you read and assimilate information from research journals, scholarly books, government reports, and the mass media, you will find descriptions of many facts, patterns, and observations about individual and population aging. But description represents only the first level of understanding. We also need to know *why* a fact or observation exists (why women are the primary caregivers for the elderly); why a process, problem, or event occurs repeatedly (why ethnic elders may experience discrimination in the health and social-welfare system); and why there are variations in the facts, patterns, and observations (across individuals, communities, regions, or countries). If we can better understand, explain, and interpret the meaning of a phenomenon, then we are more likely to improve the everyday life of older people by developing effective policies and programs that equitably meet the needs of *all* older persons.

To enlarge the knowledge base and enhance our understanding about individual and population aging, theoretical perspectives and well-established research methods are employed. Theoretical perspectives provide a set of concepts by which scholars share frameworks, ideas, and meanings with which to study a phenomenon. In a similar way, common research methods enable us to answer a specific question, interpret social reality, or solve a specific problem within our social world.

The Goals of Scholarly Research

The ultimate goal of scholarly inquiry is to offer plausible, explicit, and complete interpretations of, and explanations for, observations or empirical findings in our social world. Scholars theorize and engage in research for the following reasons:

- to satisfy a need to know about some question, pattern, problem, or observation. (Why and how, for example, does a social pattern or problem occur? Why do people, individually or collectively, behave in a specific way?)

- to refute myths or verify assumptions—for example, that the elderly are a burden to society.
- to identify inequities in the social world—such as the poverty of elderly widows or the lack of adequate health care and housing for older people—and suggest how they might be reduced or eliminated.
- to produce reliable and valid information for the development, implementation, and evaluation of policies and programs.

The most crucial goal of research is to explain observed relationships or patterns and to interpret the meaning of a **social phenomenon** observed in everyday life. Examples of social phenomena discussed in this book include why some are socially advantaged while others are at a disadvantage (e.g., ethnic, gender, and social class differences in aging); cross-cultural variations in the status of older people; the consequences of population aging for both society and individuals; fear of crime among older adults; elder abuse; the desire to age in place; and adaptation to retirement and widowhood in later life.

Human behaviour is multi-faceted; therefore, different scholars study a given phenomenon or problem by using different theories, assumptions, and methods. These different and often competing approaches sometimes confuse students or laypeople. However, they are necessary for advancing knowledge about a phenomenon that you or others observe. The presence and emergence of alternative theoretical perspectives and explanations for the same issue or question stimulate researchers to better understand complex aging phenomena. Unfortunately, unlike researchers in the natural and physical sciences, social scientists seldom reach one ultimate explanation for some facet of the social world that could be expressed as a "law."

Laypeople and journalists also pursue the goals of description and explanation as they study or observe aspects of aging behaviour in everyday life. However, the major difference between a scholarly and a non-scholarly approach to understanding is that scholars use well-defined concepts and theoretical perspectives to guide their thinking, coupled with rigorous and standardized scientific methods to help them reach their conclusions.

Although there is no universally accepted definition of **theory**, it is a set of interrelated ideas that presents a logical, systematic, explicit, and reasonably complete understanding of a process, situation, or observed fact. A social theory represents "a process of developing ideas that allow us to understand and explain empirical observations" (Bengtson et al. 2009, 4), and provides "a broad view of the fundamental processes underlying social structure and social life" (George 1995, 51). Theory is used as both a research tool and an outcome of scholarly inquiry. As a research tool, a theory

- provides a common set of assumptions, definitions, and meanings for key concepts and **variables**, and **hypotheses**
- summarizes, connects, and synthesizes many existing facts, empirical findings, or observations to help build a coherent, systematic, and cumulative body of knowledge
- provides a critical awareness and a focus on large, highly relevant research questions or issues facing society (such as age and gender inequality)
- guides and stimulates thinking by introducing new research questions and identifying gaps or flaws in the existing state of knowledge
- stimulates the search for more complete or alternative explanations

As a product of scholarly activity, a theory

- provides a model of how the complex social or physical world operates and thereby opens key issues for discussion
- advances knowledge by helping to answer the "why" and "how" questions
- interprets and explains findings, observations, and meanings
- stimulates the development and accumulation of knowledge and the translation of that knowledge into the institutional fabric of society
- facilitates social interventions through the development, implementation, and evaluation of policies and programs

Foundational Perspectives

It is useful to begin with a discussion of the fundamental schools of thought upon which many aging-related theories have been based. Foundational perspectives, sometimes labelled as schools of thought, such as the **normative perspective** (or functionalism), **symbolic interactionism**, and the **conflict perspective**, provide a general orientation to developing research questions in social research. They explain research findings and help to interpret observations or meanings about aging phenomena. Dawe (1970) identified two contrasting foundational perspectives that have guided general sociological research since its inception: the normative perspective and the interpretive perspective. The normative perspective assumes that norms (established rules) and **status** levels exist in society to provide social control or social order. This order is deemed necessary for the survival of a society. According to this perspective, individuals learn social rules by internalizing shared norms (how to behave at a social event) and values (respect older people) through a process of **socialization**. Most individuals in a society adhere to these rules (that is, conformity prevails). When rules are broken (deviation from the norms), varying types of sanctions are imposed by the formal agents of social control (parents, teachers, or the police). This perspective is often associated with the positivist approach to understanding, which assumes that the social world is similar to the physical world of chemistry, biology, or physics in that there is a cause and effect process to explain outcomes.

In contrast, the **interpretive perspective** (which includes symbolic interactionism) views individuals as social actors who, through a process of negotiation, define, construct, and interpret their place or situation in society. In this way, individuals, through agency, create and change the social order. Institutions and structures are changed when agency is used and when people engage in interaction. Here, the focus is on interpreting and understanding the meaning of everyday life as expressed and interpreted by actors in the situation. The emphasis is on definitions of a situation (the meanings) and how they emerge and are managed through social interaction (Berger and Luckmann 1966). According to this perspective, sometimes termed the social constructionist, interactionist, or social phenomenological perspective, the world is composed of "meanings," not "things" (Longino and Powell 2009). The facts themselves are not essential for understanding social life. Rather, what matters is how the facts are interpreted and constructed into common meanings and knowledge, and how these create our social reality or multiple realities. Different interpretations of the same fact or situation can occur (multiple realities) because of social differentiation (men and women view caregiving responsibilities differently) and different cultural experiences, beliefs, and values. And interpretations shift over time (from the elderly being highly respected to being viewed as a burden on society).

A third foundational perspective is the conflict perspective, which is rooted in the work of Karl Marx and George Simmel (Turner 1982). Whereas the normative perspective sees the social world as normative and static, the conflict perspective views society as dynamic and changing. According to this perspective, conflict is inevitable, since society is comprised of competing groups. If one group has more authority, power, and money, others believe that they are deprived, exploited, or manipulated and therefore strive to obtain some or all of the resources from those in control. Conflict theorists believe that changes must be made so that all groups have an equal share of the resources. Viewed from a conflict perspective, social interaction involves negotiation and compromise to resolve conflict, and only in extreme cases does conflict lead to a civil war or a revolution.

Adherents of the conflict perspective search for power groups or organizations and attempt to explain how they maintain power, control, and advantage over other social groups. For example, some have argued that modern industrialized societies are dominated by white, middle-aged, wealthy males. This has led to conflict either between young people, who have yet to gain power, and middle-aged people, who have the most power, or, more recently, between older people, who have lost their power and authority, and middle-aged and younger people. That is, conflict among age groups evolves because of perceived inequities in power and inadequate access to valued resources. Another example of conflict is that between women and men for power, status, positions, and money that contribute to accumulated advantages or disadvantages over the life course for women. It was this power struggle over gender inequity that fuelled the feminist movement and feminist theories. The conflict perspective has spawned, as well, the political economy approach, which seeks to explain inequity created by the social structures and policies of a society, as will be seen later in this chapter.

More recently, the conflict approach has led to another variant—the **critical perspective**. This perspective argues that there are inherent inequities in the social structure that have important consequences for the life chances and lifestyles of some members of a society. Advocates of this perspective critically study and interpret (by gender, class, race, age, and ethnicity) the experiences, meanings, and actions of the disadvantaged and less powerful members of a society (see the section on "Critical Gerontology" later in this chapter).

Developing Knowledge: The Use of Perspectives and Theories

This section introduces a number of perspectives and theories for understanding aging phenomena from both the individual and societal perspective. Although terms such as *theory*, *model*, *perspective*, and *framework* are often used interchangeably, in this book a theory or model refers to a formal, specific explanation for some facet of the social world. A perspective or framework is a more general or global view, which often encompasses one or more theories or models that, in general, take a similar approach to the study of social phenomena.

Just as different research methods are needed to answer questions, different theoretical perspectives are necessary for increasing our knowledge. Each perspective or theory is based on different assumptions and employs different concepts. Currently, scholars are attempting to integrate or synthesize theories across disciplinary boundaries (sociology, biology, psychology) and within a discipline across epistemological approaches (the normative/positivist, interpretive, or critical perspectives) in order to more fully understand complex aging phenomena. An integrative theory of social gerontology is "one that draws on the elements that have emerged over the years and places them in a context that is acceptable to a wide range of investigators" (Bass 2009, 360).

Throughout most of the history of gerontology, theories were developed at either the micro-level (individual) or the macro-level (societal/structural), although some have served a "bridging" or "linking" function between the two levels (Marshall 1996; Bengtson et al. 1997, 1999, 2009).[1] In reality, if aging processes and the situation of older people are to be understood, both types of analysis are required. That is, we need to link the lives of individuals (agency) with social structures across the life course (Marshall 1999, 2009). To date, much of the research has focused on aging individuals and on how they adjust to or cope with their micro-worlds. Hagestad and Dannefer (2001) argue that we need to move away from this "microfication" in aging research and pay more attention to the wider social context—namely, the processes influencing stability and change in the culture and social structure of communities, nations, and the global village in different historical periods. This approach reinforces Mills's (1959) well-known plea to connect the "personal troubles" of individuals with the "public issues" inherent in the structures and institutions of society. The everyday aging experiences of individuals, which are the subject of the micro-level of analysis, are connected with the macro-level historical, cultural, demographic, political, economic, and social situation in which aging occurs. In this way, individual biographies and social history are interconnected (Marshall and Mueller 2003; Bass 2009).

Theoretical Perspectives[2]

The following sections summarize the major theoretical perspectives that can be applied to aging, the principal micro-macro bridging theory in gerontology (the life-course perspective), and some theories specifically constructed to study aging phenomena. These are presented in a way that lets you identify their foundational perspectives, assumptions, and similarities and differences. You will gain a better understanding of these theories as we apply them in subsequent chapters.

The Structural Functionalist Perspective

Developed by North American sociologists in the 1950s and 1960s, structural functionalism is rooted in the normative perspective and focuses on the relationships between social structures and social institutions, as well as on the resulting influence on the individual. For example, advocates of this perspective might ask what purpose the family, as a social institution, serves in society and what influence the family and its structure has on aging. This perspective argues that there is a commonly accepted social order (or structure) in a society; that it is essential to maintain the existing forms and functions of social institutions, such as the family, the political system, or the economic system, so that society can function efficiently (much like humans need different organs and internal systems to live); and that each element of the structure can be viewed analytically as having manifest (intended) or latent (unintended) functions.

The essential concepts of functionalism are norms, **roles**, and socialization, which regulate behaviour so that society runs smoothly, rather than agency, which implies a more proactive role of individuals in shaping it. This perspective assumes that all components of the social structure are necessary, are interrelated, and exist to maintain consensus and conformity within the social system. Social norms determine the roles available to different age groups. For example, mandatory retirement, which removes older individuals from a major social role, is viewed as "functional" because it enables younger people to enter the labour force. Since the older worker is required to accept and adapt to this role loss, society creates and legitimizes the non-work role of the "retiree," and many societies provide an economic reward in the form of a pension (see "Disengagement Theory" later in this chapter).

For structural functionalists, aging is a process in which an individual adjusts to inevitable new roles, such as a retiree or widow. This perspective argues that an individual's failure to adapt to role changes (from worker to retiree) represents an inability to fit into the existing social structure, not that the structure is ineffective or unsuitable for that individual or period in history. However, some role changes may be dysfunctional. For example, mandatory retirement could be viewed as a dysfunctional process in that it eliminates from the labour force those who have the most experience and knowledge.

Structural functionalism employs *quantitative* research methods and adheres to the principles of scientific discovery used by the physical sciences. Increasingly, this perspective is criticized as being overly reductionist, static, and supportive of the status quo. Consequently, scholars have proposed alternative perspectives.

The Social Constructionist Perspective

Social constructionists apply an interpretive lens to understand social life by examining the meaning of cognitive, symbolic, or behavioural acts. They are more concerned with challenging common assumptions and asking new questions than in perpetuating the social order (the normative approach). Understanding is reached when an individual defines the social situation in terms of what it means to him or her (Thomas 1931). Through verbal or symbolic interaction with others (type of dress, hand gestures or body language, verbal language, and facial expressions), a specific situation is defined in personal terms. Individuals also observe and interact with others in order to arrive at a definition of the "self" (Cooley 1902). Through this process, meanings emerge as we interpret and evaluate how others view us. Goffman (1959) refers to this process as "the presentation of self." Individuals are viewed as actors who decide how they will present themselves to others when in different roles in terms of dress, body language, content of verbal interaction, and general and specific behaviour. For example, as university students, you may present your "self" differently to others during a job interview, at home with your parents, or at a party with people your own age.

The interpretive perspective, a form of micro-level analysis, is derived from symbolic interactionism, phenomenology, and ethnomethodology (Longino and Powell 2009). This perspective studies individual processes of aging in a natural setting (home, workplace, senior centre), especially the interpretive meanings of age and of everyday aging experiences, and the agency individuals use to shape their social worlds. The social definition and meaning of the setting and of aging are derived through observations and personal narratives of older people. This perspective does not normally consider the larger social system in which the specific individual is found. Rather, it is interested in how individuals in a specific setting interpret and assign meaning to specific events, behaviours, or situations and in how these meanings influence the person's life. A study that used this perspective was Chaudhury's (2003) analysis of life stories to understand how reminiscence of "home" (called place-therapy) influences the creation of "self" and quality of life for persons living with dementia in long-term-care facilities. Highlight 5.1 provides insights based on Chaudhury's interpretive analysis.

The Social Exchange Perspective

At both the individual and the societal level, social interaction is viewed as a process in which we seek to maximize the rewards we receive and to reduce the costs, whether they are material

> ## Highlight 5.1
> ## Excerpts from "Quality of Life and the Meaning of Home"
>
> ---
>
> Respondents in the study journeyed back into time to retrieve memories of places, events and people. . . .
>
> The childhood home that is *recollected* is not in its entirety, but signifies its fragmented and highlighted portions that the person remembers. . . .
>
> Memories of the home bring up descriptions of physical features and social contexts that are not photographic images of the historical home, but are a personal reconstruction of the place. At a temporal level, recollections are about the *past* that occurs in the *present*. Likewise, the *self* carrying out the recollection is not the identical *self* of the past. The elderly resident who recollected her childhood home is no longer the child who had the original experience of the home. The passage of time aside, it is the accumulated life experiences that have influenced the child-self into becoming her late-adult-self.
>
> Source: Chaudhury 2003, 99–100.

(money, goods, or services) or non-material (friendship or social support). Social interaction involves reciprocity (give and take) whereby each actor in a relationship brings resources (often unequally) and strives to balance his or her costs and rewards. Since reciprocity may occur over a long period, researchers have described the rebalancing of relationships, such as between family members, as global reciprocity (Mitchell 2012). For instance, if a parent helps out an adult child with child care (i.e., babysitting grandchildren when age 65), the adult child may reciprocate years later when their parent requires caregiving support in advanced old age (when the parent is 85). While the quantity element is important, we increasingly focus on the quality of exchange relations.

A basic assumption of the social exchange perspective is that individuals search for social situations in which valued outcomes are possible and in which their social, emotional, and psychological needs can be met. Since this goal may involve acquiescence and compliance by an individual or a group a fair exchange may not be readily apparent, or possible, in every social relationship. Thus, social scientists seek knowledge about past experiences and current personal needs, values, and options before they determine the amount of equality or inequality in a specific social exchange relationship. This is especially the case when one attempts to explain the type and amount of exchange among individuals of different ages, particularly since roles, decision-making, and resources can shift with advancing age. For example, emotional, physical, and financial support in later life is often reversed between aging parents and adult children. Unbalanced exchanges may also lead to problems, such as abuse (see Chapter 12).

In reality, most social relationships are not reduced to participants seeking a "balanced" budget. Rather, most relationships include some imbalance in which one side cannot or will not reciprocate equally, at least at that point in time. In most exchange relationships, participants strive to maximize their power while maintaining a fair outcome. Not surprisingly, some status characteristics—for example, being white, male, highly educated, wealthy, or young—strengthen one's position in the negotiation process. If a person is black, female, illiterate, poor, or elderly, he or she is often at a disadvantage in social interactions. Having two or more of these lower-valued status characteristics leads to even greater disadvantages in social exchange relationships (see Chapter 6).

One outcome of exchange relationships is that older people may become increasingly dependent on others, and their social power may diminish. For example, at the macro-level, if the occupational skills of older workers become outmoded or obsolete, they are forced to accept early retirement in return for a modest pension benefit, social assistance, and leisure time. Similarly, when individuals are considered no longer able to care for themselves, they are forced into residential institutions and cared for as a repayment for past contributions. In reality, however, most older people have resources to exchange, including love, experience, wisdom, time, skills, money, and real estate, and they do continue to participate in an exchange process. In chapters 6, 9, and 12, we will learn, respectively, how exchange influences intergenerational relationships, parent–child relationships across the life course, and the caring for parents in later life by adult children.

The Postmodern Perspective

Originating in philosophy but now used widely in the social sciences and humanities, post-modern thought challenges the notion that positivist science provides an objective, reliable, and universal way of understanding human behaviour. Rather, science and knowledge are inexorably linked to social control and power (Powell and Wahidin 2006; Bengtson et al. 2009). Post-modernists employ two basic intellectual approaches to understanding: social construction and deconstruction (Hazan 1994). Both of these processes are interpretive, phenomenological, analytical, interactive, critical, and change-oriented. As discussed above, the social constructionist (interpretive) approach argues that truth and reality are dynamic and cannot be observed objectively. Rather, reality is socially constructed and evolves as we actively interact with others or record our thoughts and meanings (Longino and Powell 2009). As Hare-Mustin and Marecek (1994, 52) note, "our understanding of reality is a representation, not an exact replica. . . . Representations of reality are shared meanings that derive from shared language, history and culture." For example, Ray (1996) argued that the conclusions of some scholars and practitioners about the experience of later life may reflect their own perceptions or interpretations rather than those of older people themselves.

The deconstructionist (or post-structuralist) approach contends that language is a social concept that must be deconstructed in order to understand and explain the "real" meaning of thoughts and behaviour. In this approach, literature, laws, policies, and value systems are "unpacked." An understanding of the "real" meaning of social life is acquired by emphasizing what is included and not included, and by highlighting inconsistencies and consistencies in what has been written and said by others. To illustrate, Ray (1996, 677) suggests that a postmodern feminist who deconstructs the term "caregiving" might find that the activity involves intimacy and connection (care) and that the care is offered freely (is given rather than demanded or paid) to meet the needs of another person. She could find as well, contrary to public opinion, that the term excludes the notion of care as hard work performed for remuneration (by a home nurse) or the idea that care begins because of a sense of duty or responsibility (by a daughter). Similarly, postmodernists critique the language and discourse of the research and policy literature that biases our knowledge about the thoughts, needs, feelings, and situation of older women, and they are therefore connected to feminism and critical gerontology.

The Feminist Perspective[3] and Masculinity Theory

Feminist gerontology emerged in the 1990s because of the failure of aging theories to adequately address issues of gender and inequality (Calasanti 2009). This perspective argues that gender is an organizing principle for studying social life across the life course, and it can create inequities that advantage men and disadvantage women, especially in the later years. Across the life course, unequal roles, opportunities, access to resources, and social status accrue to individuals according to gender. Through the gendered stratification of such institutions as work, the family, the polity, the economy, the media, and religion, as well as in everyday interaction, women are viewed as oppressed and disadvantaged compared to men (Moen and Chermack 2005; McMullin 2010). In **gender relations**, men hold power that is derived from participation in the public sphere of social life; women lack power and often are restricted (this was especially so in the past) to the private world of the home.

Feminist scholars emphasize that the male view of the world should not be the norm and that the situation of women can be understood only through an examination of women's social experiences, by women or by men, using a feminist perspective. They argue that understanding, and therefore equality, can be attained only through analysis, theory development, and political and social action. Hence, the goals of feminist research are to understand social reality through the eyes and experiences of women, to eliminate gender-based oppression and inequality, and to improve the lives of women. The process involves a consciousness-raising experience for the researcher and the participants (Neysmith 1995). Feminist scholars and practitioners seek explanations for how gender hierarchies are created and sustained and why women are subordinated. They also develop strategies and actions to confront and eliminate the inequalities created by a gendered social world and seek to construct new images and possibilities for women by changing attitudes and eliminating stereotypes.

Although feminists have emphasized the diversity among women based on race and ethnicity, class, health, and sexual orientation, the study of aging women received relatively little attention until the past two decades (Thompson 1994; Arber and Ginn 1995; Kimmel 2000; Cruikshank 2003; Calasanti 2004a, 2004b, 2009; Bengtson et al. 2009). As McMullin (1995, 31) observes, gender has been an "add-on" to other theories in mainstream sociology and in gerontology. Consequently, she argues for the development of a theory that explains the link between gender and age-based systems of inequality. Feminist scholars interested in aging have criticized general gerontological theories as being conservative and incomplete, since they are based on the experience and interpretations of white middle-class males, who for the most part have been the developers of theory and research in the field. Similarly, scholars and practitioners are criticized for failing to study gender relations or the experiences of women in the context of aging.[4]

Studies of older women that employ a feminist approach often focus on their everyday experiences or on the economic and power relations between women and men. To illustrate, Blieszner (1993), employing a critical feminist perspective, examined the economic and social consequences of widowhood. At the individual level, she studied both widows and widowers from different classes, racial or ethnic backgrounds, and age cohorts to understand the "meaning" of widowhood. As well, at the societal level, she examined how capitalism and patriarchy, which encourage class exploitation and the gendered division of labour, influence the experience of widowhood.

Feminists argue that the factors influencing the onset of poverty in later life differ between women and men (McDaniel 1989, 2004; Moen and Chermack 2005; Calasanti 2009). First, because of their irregular work histories, elderly women have few if any pension benefits.

Second, some older women are not eligible for survivor's benefits when their spouse dies. Third, women live longer than men and are more likely to exhaust their savings. Fourth, when older women become ill, they seldom have a partner to care for them. Poverty, as seen from this perspective, is less an aging problem and more an issue for women who live a long life. Feminists conclude that older women are devalued and powerless in a male-dominated society that oppresses all women and that this situation is even worse for women who live a long life. For example, Estes (2004) argued that the welfare state and the capital and gender systems render women vulnerable and dependent throughout their life course. In reality, the impoverishment of older women is socially constructed and imposed. Hence, feminist perspectives encourage us to view the experiences of aging through the eyes of women.

Men and women experience the life course and later life differently. Nevertheless, feminist theory increasingly includes the study of women and men in their linked experiences across the life course. This perspective is also embedded within the political economy and critical perspectives, which critique gendered access to key material, health, and caring resources that can alter the experience of aging for women and men. To illustrate, Moen and Chermack (2005) propose a dynamic model of the intersection between gender, health, and life course in which the gendered nature of occupational and family-care paths produce disparities in health-related resources, relationships, and feelings of mastery and control. Feminists argue that women occupy an inferior status in later life because they live in a capitalist and patriarchal society in which they have been disadvantaged throughout their lives. MacQuarrie and Keddy (1992) note that power relations between the genders influence the current situation of older women for a variety of reasons, including the following:

- Most older women have accepted, without question, the patriarchal structure and men's domination of their social and work lives.
- Gendered processes in organizations throughout the life course determine what types of jobs are available to women (often part-time and clerical) and, therefore, the size of the pension they receive because of the type of job, as well as because of an irregular work history due to pregnancy, child-rearing, or caring for elderly parents.
- A conflict exists between production (work) and reproduction (family) because of the gendered division of labour and gender ideology.

Feminists argue that social reform is needed to change the social and economic structure, as well as gender relations, so that there will be social, economic, and political equality between the genders (Lynott and Lynott 1996). Gender inequities across the life course are socially constructed, institutionalized, and perpetuated by dynamic social, economic, and political forces rather than by individual choices (Cruikshank 2003). Both genders experience ageism and patriarchy, but they experience it differently because of different life experiences, meanings, and expectations in relation to work, family, and leisure. Gender-based public policies also favour males in terms of eligibility and benefits. To illustrate, feminists stress that the burden of caring for elderly parents or parents-in-law falls on women, not because they have natural (biological) nurturing needs but because of a gendered socialization process. This process, reinforced through public policies, creates an expectation that women will perform this type of labour, perhaps because they have been socialized to perform or are willing to engage in unpaid domestic work (Stoller 1993; Ray 1996). Feminist gerontologists question the fairness of caregiving, which is primarily a woman's responsibility.

Recently, gender theorists have drawn from feminist gerontology to develop and apply masculinity theory to older men. Masculinity theory attempts to explicate the unique dimensions of men's identities and lives as they age (Calasanti 2004a; Calasanti and Bowen 2006; Van den Hoonaard 2010). This theory has been used to understand older men's experience of health and illness (see Chapter 7), of caregiving roles, of social relationships, and of widowhood. Some research has suggested that older men maintain traditional gendered identities even when crossing gendered boundaries in roles such as caregiving (Calasanti and Bowen 2006). Others suggest that there is a blurring of gendered identities and roles in older age and, moreover, have been able to identify separate and unique experiences of the social processes of aging for men. For instance, Van den Hoonaard (2010) found that older men experiencing widowhood do not conform to stereotypical images of being helpless and desolate but, rather, redefine their masculinity through a process of developing new roles and identities. Masculinity theory, like feminism, gives voice to older men in an effort to show the significant diversity and complexity in their aging experiences.

The Life-Course Perspective:[5] *A Dynamic Bridging Approach*

As noted above, some perspectives bridge individual and structural approaches to social phenomena. The life-course perspective is one of these approaches, and it has played a major role in advancing the discipline of gerontology (Alkema and Alley 2006; Dannefer et al. 2009). It is therefore important to understand life-course theory and its interconnections with the other theories presented in this chapter. Our journey through life is like a road map: it involves many possible routes and many alternative destinations or outcomes. The pathways we follow as we age are a product of our place in history, of our place in the social structures of our world, of agency and the decisions we make, and of the consequences of earlier decisions we made. There is both continuity and change in adult lives over time, and our experiences in later life are shaped to some degree by those we encountered earlier in life. Hence, there is considerable variability among older adults in shared experiences across the life course and in later life (Settersten 2006). Experiences and decisions we make early in life that may impact our situation in later life can be related to education, work history, leisure, family circumstances (married, divorced, widowed, never married), and health status (stress, illness, disabilities). O'Rand (2006) notes that the opportunities we are presented with, the constraints we face, and the decisions we make across the life course are influenced by two factors: life-course capital and life-course risks. Capital involves stocks of resources (education, wealth, genetics, health, social relations, identity, competence) that may be accumulated or dissipated over the life course. This capital can be exchanged or converted, if available, to meet needs and wants or to follow a particular pathway. Risks emanate from structural sources (class, race, ethnic, age, or gender stratification) that can create structural opportunities (advantages) or adverse conditions (disadvantages) that influence the accumulation, protection, or depletion of life-course capital. In this sense, advantages and disadvantages accumulate throughout our lives and affect our aging experiences.

The life-course perspective provides an analytical framework for understanding the interplay between individual lives and changing social structures, between personal troubles and public issues, and between personal biography and societal history (Holstein and Gubrium 2000; Elder and Johnson 2003; Heinz and Marshall 2003; Marshall and Mueller 2003; Settersten 2003, 2005, 2006; Dannefer et al. 2009; Marshall 2009). The approach requires a consideration of the interaction among historical events and social changes occurring at the structural (or macro) level, the individual (or micro) level, and the public policy (or meso) level. These capture the opportunities we have and the constraints we face in decision-making as we move through our life paths. As George (1996) noted, "we are architects of our own lives," but our choices are linked inevitably to social structure and culture.

It was once assumed that the life course involved timely, orderly, and sequential transitions along a relatively clearly defined and common or "normative" trajectory or path. These transitions, significant life events, and branching or turning points usually happened at a certain age or time in life and were often accompanied by rites of passage, such as a graduation, a new job, a wedding, or the birth of a child. Or the transitions occurred with the onset of critical events or experiences, such as retirement, divorce, a major illness, or widowhood. Today, pathways through the life course (sometimes termed paths) are deemed to be more variable, and less linear and "normative" than early formulations of this theory (Dannefer et al. 2009). And the time at which major transitions (marriage, child-bearing, divorce, widowhood, retirement) occur can vary widely. A given route depends on which events occur at the branching points and on their timing and context. Thus, our life course is composed of multiple, interdependent trajectories relating to education, work, family, and leisure (Mitchell 2003). What happens along one trajectory, such as education, often has an effect on other trajectories, such as work, marriage, and leisure. The branching points, when connected, represent an inverted tree, and many trees of different shapes and sizes are possible for individuals, groups, or cohorts. The life-course trajectory changes direction or shape when a new event leads to a branching point. The decision to move in a new direction may be voluntary or involuntary and may be influenced by external historical, geographical, social, or political circumstances.

Compared to the past, fewer transition points today are related to one's age per se. The trajectories are less orderly along the life course and may even reverse or boomerang, such as when young or middle-aged adults return home after an initial departure from the nest (Mitchell 2006), when people move in and out of retirement, or when individuals move out of a long-term-care setting back into a community dwelling setting. Transitions are also more diverse: older people date and remarry or live common-law after being divorced or widowed; men father children at age 60; people become unemployed at 40 or retire at 45; adults graduate from university after age 65; women are widowed or become grandmothers at 40. These asynchronous transitions, which may create strains in relationships or personal stress, can be the result of earlier decisions or situational contexts that have a cumulative effect, such as inequality.

The influence of early life events on our life path and on later life is not well understood because of its complexity and a limited number of longitudinal studies. However, using an extensive longitudinal analysis of the meaning of the Depression for those who were children during this difficult economic period, Elder and Johnson (2003, 57–71) derived five principles that can guide our study of aging and later life:

1. Human development and aging are lifelong processes; many early experiences, meanings, events, and transitions are linked to later life opportunities and experiences.
2. Agency prevails: individuals construct their own life course through the choices they make and the actions they take within the opportunities and constraints of history and their personal circumstances, such as their advantages or disadvantages because of their location in the social structure (stratification by age, gender, race, ethnicity, and social class).
3. The life course of individuals is embedded in, and shaped by, the historical times and places they experience over their lifetime. Individuals and birth cohorts at the micro

level are affected by large-scale macro-historical events, including wars, economic depressions, or natural disasters.

4. The antecedents and consequences of life transitions, events, and behaviour patterns vary according to when they happen in a person's life. Different but adjacent birth cohorts can be affected differently by the same historical event.

5. Lives are lived interdependently, and social-historical influences are expressed through these shared relationships—lives are not lived in isolation. Our actions are determined by, and in turn influence, the actions of those to whom we are closely linked. Losing a job in middle age can create stress in a marriage or make it difficult for children to attend university.

One approach to studying aging from a life-course perspective is to reconstruct the lives of individuals or cohorts. In this approach, people are interviewed about their life histories, and lifelines are drawn to identify crucial events and turning points at each chronological age and stage of life, thereby providing a biography, or road map, for an individual. Respondents are asked what important events happened at a specific time or age, and why, and what the event meant to them at that time and later in life (Schroots 1996, 123; Giele and Elder 1999). For example, a personal experience, such as getting married at the time of a major historical event (war), may alter an individual's expected life course. To better understand this approach, interview a grandparent or an elderly neighbour to find out how a few significant decisions or social or historical events at one stage in life influenced his or her life history and life opportunities. What were the "roads taken, or not taken" and why?

Theories to Explain Aging Phenomena

Since the 1960s, a number of theories have been specifically developed to explain aging phenomena. Most of the early theories (activity, disengagement, and continuity theories) focused on *individual* (micro) adaptation in later life, whereas more recent theories (age stratification, political economy, and critical gerontology) focus on the *structural* (macro) aspects of aging—age and social structures, the state, and social inequality.[6]

Activity (Substitution) Theory

This was the first theory that sought to explain "successful" or ideal aging in the later years of life. Rooted in the symbolic interactionist perspective, the theory argued that individual adaptation in later life involved continuing an active life. Continued social interaction would maintain the self-concept and, hence, a sense of well-being or life satisfaction (Havighurst and Albrecht 1953). Later, Burgess (1960) suggested that old age should not be viewed as a "roleless role" but that individuals should replace lost roles or social activities with new ones. Maintaining an active life involved replacing lost roles by either re-engaging in roles played earlier in life or learning new ones. Engaging in activities provides opportunities for role-related interaction, and one's identity is confirmed by receiving positive feedback from others (Reitzes et al. 1995). The basic hypotheses stemming from this theory are that (1) high activity and maintenance of roles is positively related to a favourable self-concept and (2) a favourable self-concept is positively related to life satisfaction—that is, experiencing adjustment, successful aging, well-being, and high morale.

For a number of years, this theory was accepted without question and in fact was the basis for many of the social programs and services provided to older people—on the assumption that if they were kept busy with a range of activities and social roles, they would age "successfully." Some studies have supported activity theory while others have failed to support it.

Because the evidence to support activity theory has not been overwhelming, a number of scholars have expressed criticisms and reservations about the theory. Opponents of activity theory argue that activity levels can decrease without a loss of morale, that some people have never been socially active in their lives yet exhibit satisfaction, and that not everyone has the economic or interpersonal resources to replace lost roles. The notion of "successful aging" can produce stigma for those not meeting the inherent expectations of this concept, for instance, an older person who is either unable to maintain active roles, or one who chooses to relinquish roles and embrace a more private life. Moreover, there has been little consideration of the quality or meaning of the activity. To keep busy at mundane, repetitive, socially sanctioned tasks may not result in a high sense of morale or life satisfaction. It has been noted as well that activity theory illustrates the chicken-and-egg dilemma: are older people satisfied because they are active, or are people who are satisfied more likely to be involved in social roles and activities? Most evidence suggests that aging involves selective replacement of, and selective disengagement from, some roles and activities as well as the acquisition of new roles.

Disengagement Theory

Disengagement theory (Cumming et al. 1960; Cumming and Henry 1961) was developed as an alternative explanation for the "successful" aging view proposed by activity theorists. This theory represented a shift from an emphasis on the individual to an emphasis on the interaction between the individual and society. Disengagement theory was based on the assumption that change and adaptation in the later years of life are necessary, both for the individual and for society. The inevitability of death, the probable decrease in physical and/or mental ability as one ages, and the high value placed on youth led to the belief that both the individual and society benefit from disengagement.

This theory, rooted in structural functionalism, argued that only through a process of disengagement by older people can young people enter the labour force. Thus, for the mutual benefit of individuals and society, aging should involve a voluntary process by which older people disengage from society and society disengages from the individual. In reality, however, many forms of disengagement, including mandatory retirement, widowhood, and illness, are not voluntary.

Theoretically, the process of disengagement results in less interaction between an individual and others in society and is assumed to be a universal process. Disengagement is believed to be satisfying to individuals because they are released from pressures to behave as expected (on the job) and have more freedom to deviate from societal norms without criticism. Through disengagement, it is argued, individuals experience a high level of satisfaction and well-being in the later years of life.

To support or refute this explanation of successful aging, many research studies were conducted in the 1960s and 1970s, resulting in some revisions and clarifications of the theory by the original authors (Cumming 1963; Henry 1964). The major criticisms of the theory were that the process was not universal, voluntary, or satisfying and that not everyone disengages from their previously established role set. Clearly, a comparison of pre-industrial societies, where there was no retirement and older people had a high status, with modern industrialized societies suggests that the process is not universal across time.

A number of studies found that withdrawal is not a typical pattern. Moreover, there are different types of disengagement, and people in different social situations disengage to varying degrees. For example, a person may be physically engaged in a job but psychologically disengaged if work no longer has interest, meaning, or value for him or her. Similarly, a person may be disengaged organizationally from religion if he or she no longer attends religious services but may be engaged non-organizationally if he or she prays in private or participates in religious services via radio or television. Some older people are forced to disengage when their health or financial means decline or when friends die or move away. Additionally, some individuals are socially or psychologically "disengaged" throughout their lives while others are fully engaged in work, volunteer activities, and social interaction until they die.

In summary, there is little research evidence to support the idea that decreased role involvement and social interaction are universal and inevitable processes. Nor is there evidence that this decreased interaction is related to higher levels of life satisfaction or morale. Nevertheless, the simple "concept" of disengagement, more than the full "theory" of disengagement, may be useful in explaining individual behaviour. For example, older people in poor health have less opportunity to be engaged in social roles and may consciously narrow their social world by withdrawing from social roles (Johnson and Baier 1992). In all likelihood, the way in which individuals adapt in the later years may be related to maintaining role flexibility in a manner that meets their needs, desires, and expectations. That is, some roles and activities are continued, some are discontinued, some are intensified, some are reduced, and some are initiated for the first time.

Continuity Theory

This theory argues that as people age, they strive to maintain continuity in their lifestyle. Indeed, there are pressures within society to stabilize lifestyles, role relationships, and activities throughout our life. Drawing from symbolic interactionism, this theory argues that people adapt more easily to aging if they maintain a lifestyle similar to that developed in the early and middle years (Atchley 1971, 1989). Thus, it may be unreasonable to expect that a person who has always preferred solitary activities will adjust to retirement by becoming more socially active, joining voluntary associations, or taking a trip with a tour group. Similarly, a person who has led an active life will not likely disengage unless there is a strong reason for doing so, such as failing health.

In reality, aging involves both continuity and change. Continuity does not, however, imply an absence of change. Rather, maintaining continuity involves adapting to both internal changes (i.e., in attitudes, values, beliefs, temperament, and identity) and external changes (i.e., in role relationships, activities, and the environment) and coping with discontinuity because of illness, disability, role loss, or loss of skills.

Age Stratification: The Aging and Society Paradigm[7]

This model of aging has evolved over a 30-year period from a static to a dynamic view of aging, with new concepts being added as further knowledge about aging processes emerges.[8] The approach finds its origins in the structural functionalist perspective and was specifically developed to link people's lives with social structures[9] (Riley 1971, 1985, 1994; Riley et al. 1972, 1999). More specifically, Riley et al. (1999, 327) argued that

> the paradigm is a conceptual framework, or approach, for designing and interpreting studies of age and illuminating the place of age in both lives (as people age) and the surrounding social structures. . . . Changes in people's lives influence and are influenced by

changes in social structures and institutions. These reciprocal relationships are linked to the meanings of age, which vary over time.

The early focus of this theory was on studying age cohorts to identify similarities and differences among them across time, but it later developed into a broader theory addressing both structural and individual aspects of aging. It has become a component of life-course theory given its emphasis on the dynamic nature of cohort aging.

According to this theory of aging, society is segregated by age, and the common example given by Riley and her colleagues was that there are three main age strata, each with a specific purpose: childhood and adolescence for education; young and middle adulthood for work; and the later years for retirement and leisure (see Figure 6.1, p. 178). Through a process of role allocation or age grading, individuals gain access to social roles on the basis of chronological, legal, or social age. Age is a criterion for entry into and exit from many social roles. However, such an age-related status system can lead to inequality and exclusion. In this model, structures and institutions provide opportunities and barriers at particular ages in people's lives and tend to force people to interact primarily with those in the same age stratum. In the early stages of developing the theory, agency was ignored, and it was assumed that individuals passively accept and adhere to social norms based on age. Hence, conflict between the age strata was not envisioned.

In the second phase of development, Riley and others recognized that cohort differences arise when cohorts born at different times experience a different life course as societal changes occur in values, in economic and educational opportunities, and in the use of technology. That is, the lives of those who are older today (your grandparents) are not the same as the lives of those who were older 30 years ago (your great-grandparents) or those who will be older in 20 years (your parents) or in 40 years (your own cohort). The process of **cohort flow** and succession (Riley 1973) was introduced to account for the aging of cohorts in a dynamic world characterized by social, economic, political, and structural changes. These changes may or may not have an influence on specific age cohorts.

These interdependent changes in people's lives, and in structures and institutions pertaining to age norms for social behaviour and the allocation of social roles, changed our thinking from a society that is age-segregated to one that is age-integrated. Highlight 5.2 illustrates one example of a change in age-based norms concerning both the pursuit of formal education and interaction among diverse age cohorts.

A third stage of development of the age stratification theory moved beyond a consideration of age stratification alone to a consideration of other structural elements in a society. One of the early criticisms of age stratification theory was that it not only ignored the possibility of conflict between age strata but failed to account for the interaction of age with other social categories—race, ethnicity, gender, and social class—that could also produce conflict within or across age cohorts. Age conflicts can arise when members of subsequent birth cohorts have different opportunities (e.g., more formal education), different attitudes (e.g., concerning equality in society), and different beliefs (e.g., whether women should pursue careers). These beliefs arise when unique social and historical experiences suggest that resources, rewards, and social roles should be allocated in different ways. If an age stratum consciousness develops, a cohort interprets events through its own unique experiences, thereby generating a cohort-centric view of the world. **Cohort-centrism** makes it difficult to understand or accept the views of other cohorts, and the possibility of resolving differences becomes more difficult. Thus, age cohort conflict may emerge over differing values, beliefs, experiences, or interests.

Highlight 5.2
It Is Never Too Late

The first day of classes our professor challenged us to get to know someone we didn't already know. As I stood up to look around, a gentle hand touched my shoulder. I turned around to find a little old lady with a smile that lit up her entire being. She said, "Hi handsome. My name is Rose. I'm 87 years old. Can I give you a hug?" I laughed and enthusiastically responded, "Of course you may! Why are you in college at such a young, innocent age?" She jokingly replied, "I'm here to meet a rich husband, get married, have a couple of children, and then retire and travel." "No, seriously," I asked. "I always dreamed of having a college education, and now I'm getting one!" she told me.

After class we walked to the student union building and shared a chocolate milkshake. We became instant friends. Every day for the next three months we left class together and talked non-stop. I was always mesmerized listening to this "time machine" as she shared her wisdom and experience with me. Over the course of the year, Rose became a campus icon and easily made friends wherever she went. She was living it up.

At the end of the semester we invited Rose to speak at our football banquet, and I'll never forget what she taught us. As she began to deliver her prepared speech, she dropped her three by five cards on the floor. Frustrated and a little embarrassed, she leaned into the microphone and simply said, "I'm sorry I'm so jittery. I gave up beer for Lent and this whiskey is killing me! I'll never get my speech back in order so let me just tell you what I know." As we laughed, she cleared her throat and began: "We do not stop playing because we are old; we grow old because we stop playing. There are only four secrets to staying young, being happy, and achieving success. You have to laugh and find humour every day. You have to have a dream. When you lose your dreams, you die. We have so many people walking around who are dead and don't even know it! There is a huge difference between growing older and growing up. If you are 19 years old and lie in bed for one full year and don't do one productive thing, you will turn 20 years old. If I am 87 years old and stay in bed for a year and never do anything, I will turn 88. Anybody can grow older. That doesn't take any talent or ability. The idea is to grow up by always finding the opportunity in change. Have no regrets. The elderly usually don't have regrets for what we did, but rather for things we did not do. The only people who fear death are those with regrets." She concluded her speech by singing "The Rose." She challenged each of us to study the lyrics and live them out in our daily lives.

At the term's end, Rose finished the college degree she had begun all those years ago. One week after graduation Rose died peacefully in her sleep. Over 2,000 college students attended her funeral in tribute to the wonderful woman who taught by example that it's never too late to be all you can possibly be.

Source: www.geocities.com/koalagrey_au/never.html.

To illustrate, the counterculture movement of the 1960s involved primarily middle- or upper-middle-class university students in their late teens or early twenties who comprised the largest birth cohorts in history. This generation rebelled against the middle-aged and older cohorts of society, which they believed held too much economic and political power. Comprised mainly of the baby boom generation, these individuals are becoming the elderly of tomorrow. The current counterculture, represented by punks and indies (bohemians) and originally comprised of lower-class youths, has been spreading to other classes. This counterculture has expressed discontent—through music, literature, film, and art—concerning the way the United States government has conducted the "war on terror."

Age strata interact with other elements of social stratification to initiate change across society. As a result of new social movements, such as the women's movement, gender roles have changed to some extent in the attempt to eliminate inequalities based on gender. This continuous process of cohort norm change involves "behaviours and attitudes that develop within a cohort in response to social change, and they become crystallized as new norms or ideologies—new meanings—that then pervade and influence all age strata and social structures" (Riley et al. 1999, 339).

Another development in the third stage of this theory was the recognition that age-based changes in individual lives and in social structures do not occur simultaneously or in sync. This asynchrony creates "imbalances between what people of given ages need and expect in their lives and what the social structures have to offer. These imbalances exert strains on both the people and the social institutions involved, creating pressures for further change" (Riley et al. 1999, 336). Most of this imbalance is at the social structural level and is known as **structural lag** (Riley et al. 1994). For example, women seeking career advancement may find that economic institutions block their opportunities or that society cannot create enough opportunities to meet individual needs. Or with rapid population aging, community services and institutional facilities lag behind the needs of the increasing number of older people who are no longer able to live independently in their homes. Imbalances created by structural lag, once recognized, become a stimulus for change to restore the balance between individual lives and social structures.

The Political Economy of Aging

This critical perspective emerged in the 1980s as older people were beginning to be viewed as a burden on society, especially in financial terms. The view of political economists is that the market economy and public policies are interlocking systems that influence inequality (Kail et al. 2009).

To understand the economic status of older people in a modern welfare state, researchers study the social institutions, structures, and processes that influence the meaning and experiences of aging that contribute to inequality in later life.[10] According to this view, politics and economics, not demography (demography is not destiny), determine how old age is constructed and valued in a society. This theory argues that the onset of dependency and a diminished socio-economic status and self-esteem in the later years are an outcome not of biological deterioration but of public policies, economic trends, and changing social structures. Public policies concerning retirement income (pensions), health care, and social services are an outcome of power relations and social struggles within political institutions that result in the unequal distribution of resources.

According to Estes (1991, 31), a political economy approach to aging is based on the following premises:

- The social structure shapes how older individuals are viewed and how they view themselves, thereby affecting their sense of worth and power. The experience of aging is shaped by the social structure and the social policies that constrain opportunities, choices, and lifestyles in later life.
- Labels such as "the elderly" or "seniors" shape not only the experience of old age but also society's decisions concerning public policy.

- Social policy and the politics of aging mirror both the inequalities in a social structure and the outcomes of power struggles that emerge because of structural factors, such as gender, class, and racial stratification. Thus, social policy is an outcome of the perceived advantages and disadvantages experienced variously by those representing capital and labour, by whites and non-whites, and by men and women.
- Social policy embodies the dominant ideologies and beliefs that enforce, support, and extend the cumulative advantages or disadvantages in the larger economic, political, and social order.

This approach links the structural and personal aspects of aging, and it has been used to study such aging issues as the following:

- the retrenchment (decline) of the welfare state, including the amount of public expenditure required for retired people on health care, pensions, housing, and home care
- the social, political, economic, and legal rights of older people
- how population aging changes the distribution of public funds, sometimes creating a heavy public debt for later generations
- whether retirement should be mandatory or voluntary
- age-restrictive policies that marginalize older workers in the labour force or exclude them from the labour force

Another assumption of the political economy perspective is that older people, as an age group, are impoverished and lack power. Yet this view conflicts with the experiences and feelings reported by many older people. Like other perspectives, this macro-level approach to the study of aging must be integrated with micro-level approaches to account for the variety of individual and cohort aging experiences in modern industrialized societies. In effect, the political economy perspective illustrates how private troubles become public issues and how public issues create private troubles. To understand whether public policy reduces, removes, or increases social inequalities in later life, we must consider the intended and unintended consequences of policies for persons with different characteristics. Some social welfare policies and programs have the potential to reinforce gender, age, and racial stratification, thereby reproducing inequality across the life course. Moreover, inequality can accumulate over one's life course and across generations (Kail et al. 2009). Thus, this perspective on aging phenomena can be combined or synthesized with a life-course perspective for individuals and cohorts who live their lives within a specific but changing political, social, and economic context.

Critical Gerontology

This theory emerged when scholars[11] began to question the assumptions of much of the social gerontology research of the 1970s and 1980s, especially the ideas based on essentialism—a position that seeks a universal, single, or multiple cause for some social phenomenon (Laws 1995). Baars et al. (2006) defined critical gerontology as "a collection of questions, problems and analyses that have been excluded by established (mainstream) gerontologists." Some examples of questions that critical gerontologists have addressed include the role of the state in the management of later life, the purpose and meaning of old age and growing old, the meaning and outcome of the lack of power in later life among disadvantaged members of society, and the gender and regional inequities in access to health care, technology, and wealth. Minkler and Estes (1999) and Minkler and Holstein (2008) add that critical gerontology consists of two paths—the political economy of aging and a more humanistic path based on the deconstruction of meanings in communication (note the roots in phenomenology and the postmodern perspective outlined earlier).

Critical theorists critique the prevailing ideology and social order. They challenge the status quo, including prevailing myths and assumptions about pervasive and unacceptable social conditions and the hidden interests and goals of power groups. This approach involves praxis—active involvement in understanding and changing the social construction or meaning of everyday life. To critical theorists, the search for causes of a social phenomenon (based only on a positivist approach) ignores the complexity of our daily lives, which are lived in unique historical, social, cultural, and geographical circumstances (Katz 2003). Recently, attention to the role of globalization in public policy for old age and in the social construction of aging has added a further critical dimension to the study of later life in modern societies (Phillipson 2003, 2009). In particular, globalization has produced new forms of anxiety and uncertainty (called the "risk society") because of greater awareness and direct experience with cultural and social diversity linked to global aging (Phillipson 2009, 629).

Much of the early thinking and research in gerontology emphasized the views of white, urban-dwelling, middle- and upper-class older people, primarily men. Critical gerontology, like many of the more recent perspectives, seeks to be inclusive and to emphasize the experiences of older people who are under-represented or disadvantaged within a number of social institutions, including the labour force, leisure, housing, health care, and social services, or who live in developing rather than developed countries. This critical approach has generated knowledge of what it means to grow old within specific class, gender, racial, and ethnic boundaries, as well as how to empower older people to improve their lives. For example, Calasanti (1996, 2003) stresses that the "voices" of retirees—whose power in social relations is reduced because of the outward signs of aging or social characteristics, such as gender, race, ethnicity, or class—must be acknowledged in our research and policy agendas. She argues that a more inclusive approach to the study of aging phenomena enables us to understand that aging experiences are fluid, contextual, dialectical, and changeable through agency and political action.

Research Methods: The Search for Answers

The Link between Theory and Research

To advance our understanding of aging phenomena, the previous sections introduced a number of concepts, theories, and perspectives. But theories alone cannot guarantee that we will understand social reality. Rather, research is needed so that we can discover, describe, and interpret facts, behaviour, patterns, and relationships that we observe in our social world. Research is needed to both develop new theories and test present ones.

Philosophers of science have often debated which comes first: theory or research. While there is no agreement on this question, there is agreement that both theory *and* research are essential components of scholarly inquiry and that they are linked in a creative dialectical process. The nature and importance of this link was summarized by the social theorist Derek Layder (1994, vi):

My guiding assumption is that theory is never completely isolated from problems of empirical research, any more than empirical research is free from theoretical assumptions. The really interesting questions concern the nature of the relations between theory and empirical research and not whether either domain has some divinely given priority.

Research refutes or supports hypotheses, theories, and perspectives; initiates the revision of existing theories or perspectives; or leads to the construction of new ones. In practice, most scholars employ a composite approach: observations, surveys, interviews, and textual analyses begin after some preliminary theoretical work, and theory construction and revision do not proceed too far without testing its propositions through some type of research.

Some critics argue that much research in the social sciences and in social gerontology is "theoretically sterile," "atheoretical," and mainly descriptive (George 1995; McMullin 2000; Biggs et al. 2003). As Featherstone and Wernick (1995, 1) warned, we must avoid an approach to generating knowledge that is "data rich and theory poor." Therefore, as you read articles, books, or reports about aging phenomena, you should question the content and completeness of the theories and theoretical perspectives, look for underlying theories or explanatory models that are sometimes assumed or omitted, critique the research methods upon which conclusions are based, and search for alternative explanations and interpretations rather than mere description about the problem or issue. Above all, strive in your own thinking and actions to incorporate a theoretical approach and to expect or demand plausible and complete explanations and interpretations for the phenomena you observe.

The Research Process

Research "matters" because it is an essential part of the development and advancement of knowledge-based societies. Research is termed "basic science" when there is a need to know more about the topic without any immediate practical applications. Or it can be more "applied" or practical when it is undertaken to evaluate service programs or to develop, evaluate, or change current policy, or when it attempts to translate knowledge derived from research to the public. In order to advance knowledge, researchers use an integrated research agenda, involving many theoretical perspectives, disciplines, and research methods.

Figure 5.1 illustrates an intellectual framework developed by the Canadian Institutes of Health Research to guide health research on topics related to four primary research sectors. To illustrate, when the intellectual framework is applied to aging research, the horizontal axis represents a continuum of research from the cellular and molecular level (namely, biology and genetics) to the community or population level (that is, history, demography, epidemiology, sociology, and economics). The vertical axis represents a range of different types of research from basic (that is, research in chemistry or biology) to applied, such as program evaluation, clinical procedures and practices, and public policy analysis.

The Selection of Research Methods

Selecting which research method or methods to use in a study is guided by the research question to be answered. A decision to ask a specific question or to study a particular setting is influenced by observations of everyday life, reviews of the literature, or critical analyses of a program and policy. Once a question is asked or a gap in knowledge is identified, the creative insight of a scholar frames the question based on a theoretical perspective and selects a method

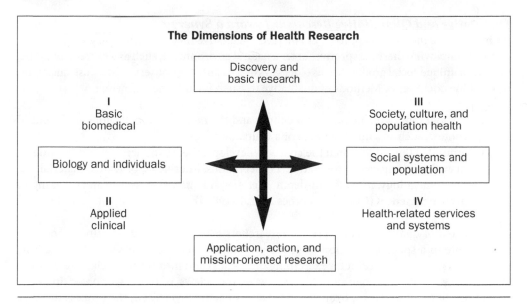

Figure 5.1 A Model to Guide Research

Source: Halliwell and Lomas (1999). Reprinted with permission.

or methods to arrive at answers or explanations. For example, a sociologist might be interested in understanding whether and to what extent childless older adults substitute child–parent support with other forms of social support and whether this affects how they cope with aging processes. The sociologist is likely to draw on accumulated knowledge in the literature about models and theories of social support, caregiving, and well-being and may compare different types of childlessness (voluntary and involuntary) across various marital status groups and family types. This may include, for example, comparisons of patterns of support, gender differences, socio-economic status, and well-being among these groups or in-depth interviews with childless older persons (as well as with those with children).

Many different research methods can be employed to study aging processes and older people. Often, they are classified as *qualitative* (based on observations, open-ended interviews, or analyses of textual material to interpret the meanings of what people say, do, or think) or *quantitative* (based on surveys or analyses of existing data to reach conclusions statistically). In the early years of research on aging topics, quantitative methods dominated. More recently, qualitative methods or a combination of both approaches (multi-methods) are common (Singer and Ryff 2001; Krause 2002; Etches et al. 2006). Singer and Ryff (2001) argue that the multi-method blending of "numbers" from quantitative research and "narratives" from qualitative research enables us to more fully understand life histories, aging processes, and older people. A mixed-methods approach draws upon various types of information to obtain a complete picture (Etches et al. 2006). A specific method may be more suitable at one stage or level of research—for example, qualitative methods for understanding at the individual level and quantitative methods for understanding at the societal level—or there may be an advantage to employ both in a multi-method approach.

Qualitative and Quantitative Research: Toward a Synergy

As interpretive theoretical approaches emerged, qualitative methods of inquiry were needed. Scholars employing these perspectives enter a natural environment, such as a retirement home, or study a unique social group, such as older gays or lesbians. They observe, listen, ask questions, or examine documents. Methods of qualitative research include the following:

- ethnography, which describes a culture and the meaning of behaviour in a cultural context, such as a nursing home or a Chinatown
- grounded theory, in which the goal is to develop a theory inductively and "ground" it in evidence collected through direct observations, interviews, or textual material
- phenomenology, in which in-depth interviews identify the essence and meaning of lived experiences (Cobb and Forbes 2002, M198–9)

The goal of qualitative, interpretive researchers is to understand, as fully as possible, how people in a specific situation or group view and experience their social world. This approach is particularly useful for examining the context and meaning of social interactions. It is achieved through an analysis of letters, diaries, interviews, or reports, or observing what is said or done in the setting from the individual's perspective. Then, the process involves searching for and interpreting commonalities and variations in the experiences and meanings of aging, of being old in a particular environment, or of having certain characteristics, including class, race, ethnicity, sexual orientation, or state of health. For instance, health diaries have been used to explore health and well-being as experienced by frail elders (Milligan et al. 2005).

The quantitative researcher, who is often separated from his or her "respondents" (they may never meet face-to-face, unless this type of interview is conducted personally), employs statistical analyses; the qualitative researcher, on the other hand, observes and/or interacts directly with the "informants" and analyzes and interprets their words, symbols, experiences, beliefs, and actions in the context of their social setting. Thus, whereas research reports based on quantitative studies contain statistics, graphs, tables, and figures, reports by qualitative researchers contain many observations and/or quotations that reflect the experiences and voices of older adults. Finally, there are also differences in how the two types of research are evaluated and assessed as contributions to knowledge. For quantitative research, the criteria for evaluation are internal and external validity, reliability, generalizability, and objectivity. For qualitative research, the evaluation criteria are credibility, transferability, dependability, and confirmability (Cobb and Forbes 2002; Windsor et al. 2004). But for both types, the main criterion is whether we understand the phenomenon more completely and accurately as a result of the research.

Types of Research Methods

Secondary Analysis of Data Sets

In a secondary analysis, the researcher, to answer emerging research questions, re-analyzes data sets (surveys or a census) that were collected at an earlier time and often for some other purpose. The goal may be to answer new research questions, to analyze data that were not used when the original study was completed, or to study changes by comparing earlier data with current data. A serious weakness of secondary data analyses is that the data set may lack essential **independent** (or control) **variables** that could provide a more complete and valid explanation for any age differences or age changes that are discovered.

Secondary Analysis of Textual Materials

In this method, the researcher analyzes textual material, such as diaries, letters, photographs, films, biographies, or newspaper articles, for qualitative themes to understand a social phenomenon. Highlight 5.3 illustrates how we can understand the influence of stereotypes about aging by analyzing articles in a newspaper.

Historical and Literary Methods

These methods are used to describe and analyze an individual, a setting, or an issue to understand a process or an event of everyday life in an earlier period or in another society or to develop case studies or biographies of aging individuals across their life course. This method involves detailed interviews with older respondents about their life course; an examination and interpretation of relevant personal documents, such as photos, letters, and diaries; and interviews with relatives and other significant others in their lives. Similarly, literary and discourse scholars in cultural studies and in aging studies[12] analyze books, poems, plays, and letters to discover meanings about aging and being old, about attitudes toward older people, and about social relationships in later life—for example, between older parents and their adult children.

Highlight 5.3
A Content Analysis of Media Stereotypes of Seniors in *The Globe and Mail* in 2004

Rozanova et al. (2006) analyzed how seniors are portrayed in *The Globe and Mail* through a content analysis of 30 articles published in 2004. An analysis of these articles revealed that there were six different contexts within which seniors were portrayed, including family, work/retirement, community networks, scientific studies of population aging, social and health-care policy, and social attitudes toward aging. The authors found that ageism is portrayed in both positive and negative stereotypes. Seniors of different genders, ages, health statuses, abilities, and needs were reflected in both positive and negative ways. Older adults were also characterized through intergenerational comparisons with younger age groups and through intra-generational comparisons. There was some evidence that intergenerational conflict exists, especially with respect to competition for scarce resources linked to the health-care or pension systems. Older adults were also described as a burden to younger persons and society in many of the articles, supporting an apocalyptic perspective of population aging. Intra-generational ageism was evident from portrayals in which some seniors (healthy, wealthy, and active ones) were depicted as aging successfully, whereas others (frail, poor, and the oldest seniors) were not. This contrast produces the notion that the latter group are to blame for not aging successfully, fostering stigmatization among those not meeting the expectations of "aging well." This blaming may divert attention from the need for society to be supportive of persons as they age, regardless of the degree to which they require societal resources or assistance from informal social networks.

Source: Adapted from Rozanova et al. 2006.

Narrative Gerontology

As both a method and a way of thinking about aging processes, narrative gerontology assumes that we are biographical beings with stories to tell and that in the process we become the stories.[13] The stories told by individuals function as a lens through which continuities and discontinuities, transition points, crises, and the meaning of those events in our lives are revealed (Kenyon and Randall 1999; Randall and Kenyon 2004; Phoenix et al. 2010). Advocates of this method often justify such an approach to understanding phenomena with the phrase "we are biographical as well as biological entities." Narrative gerontology considers agency to be important in our lives but stresses that "when we are told a tale, we do not necessarily have to believe it" (Biggs 2001, 315). That is, narrative gerontologists must tease out the truth in the stories they are told (Phoenix et al. 2010). One weakness of this method is that it may not work with people who are very reserved, not very articulate, not highly educated, or not very fluent in English, or who have lost some of their memory. Highlight 5.4 illustrates how the biographical method interprets the broader context of a person's life by understanding the meaning of physical activity in an older woman's life.

Survey Research

This method, which uses random or purposive samples, employs face-to-face or telephone interviews or questionnaires that are mailed, accessed through the Internet, or delivered to a respondent. Survey research is conducted for the following reasons:

Highlight 5.4
A Narrative Approach to Understanding Physical Activity Involvement in Later Life

To understand the meaning of physical activity as a leisure or social activity in later life, Grant (1999) used a life history approach, based on the interpretive perspective, to get "inside" the concept of active aging, as expressed by those living this type of lifestyle. Through interviews, he reconstructed the experience with sport and physical activity of older adults across the life course, and the role of physical activity in their lives generally. He then set these biographical narratives within the broader social context of an older person's social world (see the opening paragraph below). Based on interviews with Beryl, a 78-year-old widow, we learn that her experiences with active aging in later life were not due to any single set of determinants. As you read the thoughts expressed by Beryl, Grant suggests that you try to "identify some experiences that have been influential in shaping how she makes meaning about the role of physical activity in her world."

> Monday morning was washing day. The clothes were boiled, put in a tub of rinsing water, then put through the wringer. Then they were hung on the line. . . . Then the ironing would start, and that took time. So that was Monday gone. Tuesday was similar but another routine, and so the week went. Of course it was also my job to organize the kids and be responsible for all the meals. I had many years of that lifestyle. It was all I knew, and compared to others I thought I had a great life. But when I look back . . . well it's hard to imagine how I coped.
>
> For years Roy and I used to play bowls at the same club, and I loved it. However, a few years after he died, I had my left hip done [replaced] and couldn't play like I used to. I got so frustrated that I eventually stopped playing. . . . As

- to describe or discover social or personal facts, such as the number of widows over 70 who live below the poverty line or the percentage of men over 50 who have specific types of disabilities
- to discover whether a relationship exists between variables, such as between chronological age and voting behaviour in a local election
- to determine attitudes, beliefs, or behaviour before and after specific events (for example, a questionnaire or interview with people shortly after they retire might be repeated one year or five years later to discover whether attitudes or behaviour have changed)

A major advantage of survey research is that information is collected from samples that are representative of much larger populations by using statistical techniques. It can also provide information in a relatively objective, repeatable manner. However, this method can be very expensive and time-consuming. A survey involving a mailed questionnaire is less expensive than personal interviews, but researchers are unable to probe and obtain a more detailed interpretation of what is meant by a particular answer to a question.

There are also a number of disadvantages or limitations when surveys are used with older respondents. Older people are more likely to agree than disagree with some statements, use extreme response categories (high or low), or give the same answer to all the questions in a set of questions that have similar response categories. Reasons for responding in set ways may include fatigue in the case of long questionnaires or interviews, declining physical or mental health, lack

---

you can imagine, I was a bit low for a few years, quite lonely . . . didn't really do anything at all. Had to get some help from the hospital but I'm fine now.

It was during one of those lonely moments that I decided life needed to change. I used to just sit around, it wasn't me. . . . I needed a thrill in my life, take a risk; I wanted to do something different. So I arranged to go sky diving, you know, strapped to the instructor. My friends thought I had lost my marbles, but the doctor gave me a clearance, probably wanted to get rid of me. . . . What an amazing experience, such a beautiful feeling, just floating along like a bird.

After sky diving, I got a new lease on life and realized I could do things if I was determined. I joined a dancing group, although I hadn't danced since my daughter's wedding back in the mid-60s. I also signed up for a plant propagation course and played around with that for a while, but it was too complex. Recently I went to a daytime class on interior designing because I wanted to paint the bathroom. But you know what surprised me the most? On my walk one damp morning, I popped into the local gym. I'm still not sure why, maybe it was to get dry or the weird music aroused my curiosity. I had sometimes seen others about my age going in there and wondered what they did. After a tour of the place and a chat, I signed up.

On my next visit they took my blood pressure, and they gave me a few pamphlets to read about blood pressure, osteoporosis, and some stretching exercises to do at home . . . but I never do them. When I'm there, I just love playing around on the rowing machine. They [instructors] know me now and just leave me to myself. It's funny though because even after a couple of years my friends still don't understand why I bother going and I don't understand why they don't want to go.

I was 75 when I started doing most of those things. I think I found a new freedom. You know, sometimes I can hardly believe myself. Up until a few years ago I would have shied away from all this. But now I feel like a flower that's about to bloom. Roy would be so proud of me.

Source: Adapted from Grant 1999 and Grant and O'Brien-Cousins 2001.

of experience with multiple-choice questions, or a desire to be viewed as co-operative. Older respondents are also less likely to answer questions about income or savings, death, personal health problems, or sexual matters, all of which they view as private and confidential matters.

Participant Observation

In this method, scholars observe or interact with individuals as they carry out everyday living in one or more natural social settings over a period of time. This method is most commonly employed to understand the meanings and context of aging in a special setting, such as everyday life in a retirement home or in a senior citizens centre. The qualitative interview with older informants requires careful consideration of participants' abilities and the style of questions to be used (Rubinstein 2002). In some studies, the researcher's role is not disclosed to the people being studied until after the project is completed. This unobtrusive approach may prevent the subjects from behaving unnaturally or misrepresenting information. In other studies, a researcher's identity is disclosed, and he or she participates, often as a regular member of the staff (by leading an exercise class or serving as a volunteer) or as a passive but visible observer (Maxwell 2005). Participant observation enables a researcher to

- obtain information about specific cultural, subcultural, or social environments
- understand the nature, quality, and meaning of social interactions, not just their frequency
- study phenomena if informants or respondents are unwilling or unable to report directly or accurately
- adapt and change the design or emphasis of the study as the research progresses

The main limitations of this method are as follows: (1) often, participant observation does not use standardized instruments, such as a questionnaire or interview schedule, and, consequently, other scholars find it difficult to repeat the study; (2) it is very time-consuming; (3) the sample is small and may not be representative of the situation in another, similar setting (Luborsky and Rubinstein 1995); and (4) the participant observer must be highly skilled in observation, conversation, listening, analysis, and interpretation. Moreover, these studies are seldom replicated in similar settings to verify that the interpretations of thoughts and behaviours are typical and representative of the phenomenon in question.

Evaluation and Intervention Research

This method is a form of applied research that evaluates or provides feedback about the efficacy or effectiveness of a specific program, policy, or service. Use of this type of research is increasing because policy-makers are under pressure to be more accountable and to use public funds fairly, efficiently, and effectively (Windsor et al. 2004). With the aging of the population, it is essential to know which policies and programs work, for whom they work, and where they work best (Pillemar et al. 2003, 5). Either qualitative or quantitative methods, or a combination, can be used, sometimes referred to as process and outcome evaluations (Windsor et al. 2004). This type of research is used to make informed decisions about whether or not specific programs or policies should be changed, continued, or eliminated when budget cuts are required. However, sometimes such evaluations are funded by an agency that has an interest in either terminating or continuing a policy or program. Thus, we must be alert to possible hidden agendas when program or policy evaluations are commissioned.

Evaluation research is conducted for the following purposes:

- to assess needs before a policy or program is started
- to determine whether any progress has been made toward a specific goal, such as greater independence or well-being among older residents or participants
- to measure whether and how a program's objectives have been attained, whether a policy is effective, or whether an intervention has been successful
- to measure cost-effectiveness at any stage of a program or policy after it has begun
- to identify gaps or inequities in existing policies or programs, and to improve the efficacy of the program
- to ascertain whether and to what extent a program can be generalized to wider populations

Evaluation research can alert us to social change and to the diverse or changing needs of different age cohorts. For example, an intervention program designed to address the transportation needs of urban residents over 60 years of age living in the central core of the city in 2012 may be totally inadequate for the needs of the same age group who live in the suburbs of the same city.

Action Research
Action research is undertaken to change and improve the situation of people living in particular circumstances, such as elderly people who are homeless, poor, or living in inadequate housing. This type of research often leads to changes in programs or policies (McWilliam 1997) that can improve the lives of older people. There are three key principles of action research (Reason and Bradbury 2001; Weisman 2003):

- The research process is done *with* people rather than on or for people—that is, participants are partners in the research process.
- The search to understand specific, detailed contextual factors (through case studies) is as important as understanding general patterns.
- The research should produce knowledge that helps people who are in the situation to understand and solve some social problem or issue they have encountered.

Action research begins with identifying some problem, as viewed by those in the setting, then discussing, with the people involved, alternative courses of action that might solve or eradicate the problem. Once a best course of action is agreed upon, action is initiated, and an evaluation phase at the end reviews the action's effectiveness and consequences. This cycle is repeated as often as necessary until the problem is considered solved. Throughout the process, collaborative knowledge is built by incorporating input from the clients, from practitioners in the field, from consultants, and from researchers. This process has been used to solve micro environmental problems in specific settings, such as nursing homes. Highlight 5.5 describes a case study in which action research was employed to design a state-of-the-art long-term-care facility.

Cross-National Research
A comparison of cultures, social structures, policies, statistical data, or individual characteristics in various countries is a useful way to discover and understand differences and similarities

Highlight 5.5
Action Research in Gerontology: A Case Study

Redesigning Brewster Village

Drawing on the principles of action research (Weisman 2003), a team of individuals representing four organizations (a county health centre, an architect's firm, a construction company, and a research institute) guided the development of a new facility over a five-year period. Project goals were developed through site visits to other facilities and focus groups with stakeholders. These goals departed from the traditional design of long-term care for older persons (private rooms and a decentralized dining area). Meetings with stakeholders over a seven-month period resulted in the development of the following principles to be used in creating a non-institutional environment: promote sensory and social stimulation; create clusters of 13 to 14 residents; provide spaces for social interaction; facilitate spatial and social orientation; and create secure outdoor spaces. During this process, staff and other participants were taught how to read architectural drawings and how to envision how the space would be used. Once the facility was completed, a post-occupancy evaluation of residents, staff, and families was conducted to assess whether the goals were attained. Quantitative measures showed positive change along 11 dimensions for the residents, including activity, mood, and anxiety levels. Staff experienced positive changes in working conditions and in emotional climate. Families enjoyed a more home-like atmosphere for visiting and noticed an increased quality of life for the residents. Action research is iterative, and therefore environmental and operational monitoring continues so that, if necessary, changes can be made.

Source: Adapted from Scheidt and Windley 2006, 116–20.

among older people throughout the world. Cross-national research provides information on where we stand in comparison to other societies, and it enables us to acquire new ideas from countries where some aging issues we will encounter in the future have already been addressed. To provide valid, reliable, and useful comparative knowledge, this type of research, using any of the methods described above, must employ common concepts, definitions, measurements, and language in the collection of data or in the observations made in each country. In aging research, cross-national comparative research has studied similarities and differences in cultural characteristics; work and retirement patterns; private savings and wealth; family, work, and leisure structures; intergenerational transfers of wealth; health and disability statistics; and general well-being in later life (National Research Council 2001).

Methodological Issues in Aging Research

Interpreting Data and Observations

The production and translation of new knowledge involves not only asking "relevant" and "interesting" questions but also answering the research questions with the appropriate methods. The interpretation or explanation of observations must be valid and not extend beyond the information collected. Most aging research examines differences among age groups on one or more characteristics: changes in meaning, behaviour, status, or lifestyle within age groups or individuals as they pass through various stages of life. Social scientists—and you as readers of their work—must conclude whether the research findings are due to individual aging effects, cohort differences, or period effects (the influence of unique historical or societal events).

Aging varies within and among individuals, cohorts, and cultures. To understand why, universal processes of aging must be separated from culture-specific processes. For example, there are different conceptual and methodological issues to consider when research is conducted in a rural environment (see Chapter 8) rather than in a large urban community: What is the definition of a rural area? Are the respondents in the rural setting lifelong residents or recent migrants to the area? Moreover, the heterogeneity within an ethnic or racial group by gender, income, or education must be recognized. Similarly, it is a major conceptual error to classify all older people who came to Canada from mainland China, Hong Kong, Vietnam, Southeast Asia, or Korea as "Asian." In the same vein, not all older Aboriginal people have common backgrounds, values, or experiences. Such labels mistakenly imply that those with the same label have had the same kind of cultural and lifelong experiences.

Issues in Quantitative Research Designs

Cross-Sectional Designs: Identifying Age Differences

A cross-sectional design involves recording observations or responses of individuals at different ages at one point in time and reporting the results for each age group. For example, the results of a descriptive study of the relationship between age and attendance at movies in 2004 might be reported as in Table 5.1.[14] While a quick reading of this table might lead to the conclusion that movie attendance declines with age, the method of collecting data means that we cannot conclude that the differences between age groups are due to growing old—that is, to an aging effect. Rather, we can only conclude that at one point in history (in 2004), there were age differences in the frequency of movie attendance. The table shows that younger age cohorts are more likely to attend movies three or more times a year. Depending on the questions asked, it is often possible to identify variations *within* age groups that are significantly different from those *between* age groups. For example, Table 5.1 shows that males of all ages attend movies more often than females. Thus, the low frequency of attendance by those over the age of 55 could be partially explained by the fact that there are more women than men in the older age groups.

A cross-sectional design identifies differences between age groups but does not enable us to explain the reason for the differences. Nor can it provide explanations about the process of aging experienced by a given cohort. For example, those over 65 may never have attended movies to any great extent at any time in their lives. This pattern may have evolved either because going to the movies was not popular in their early years or because they could not afford to go to movies when they were young. In either situation, this cohort, unlike later generations, may never have acquired the habit of going to movies. Consequently, in later life, they do not spend any of their fixed income on movies.

A cross-sectional design alerts us to patterns of behaviour that vary by age group. The differences among age groups could also indicate generational or cultural differences (immigrants may be less inclined to attend movies), changes with age, or the influence of specific historical events (a depression or an energy crisis) on a particular age group at some point in their lives. Therefore, alternative research designs are needed to determine whether attendance at movies declines with age and is therefore an aging effect (see list of Canadian surveys in Sheets and Gallagher 2013).

Table 5.1   A Cross-Sectional Design: Age and Movie Attendance, 2004

Age	Percentage of Those Who Attended Movies Three Times or More per Year in 2004		
	Males and Females	Males	Females
14–19	58	65	52
20–24	54	62	50
25–34	45	52	39
35–44	33	41	25
45–54	20	31	14
55–64	15	20	10
65–74	11	19	9
75 and over	8	12	6

Note: The data reported here are hypothetical.

Longitudinal Designs: Identifying Changes with Age

Longitudinal designs involve collecting and analyzing data over time, including samples of different people (a trend design) or the same people at different points in time (a panel design). A panel longitudinal design provides more accurate and complete explanations of the aging process because the same individuals or groups are studied over time, and the information can be used to identify and explain patterns and relationships associated with age and aging. Specifically, to explain whether social, cognitive, or physical differences among individuals or cohorts at a particular age have always been present or whether these change with age, we need longitudinal data. Hence, a multi-disciplinary longitudinal study of health and aging in the country—the Canadian Longitudinal Study on Aging (CLSA)—has begun. Funded by CIHR and the Canadian Foundation for Innovation (CFI) the CLSA has begun to collect data on 50,000 Canadians aged 45 to 84, covering many aspects of aging at the biological, physiological, psychological, and social level, in order to support interdisciplinary research on aging (Raina et al. 2009).

Until CLSA, only a limited number of panel longitudinal studies had been conducted because they are expensive and time-consuming.[15] Moreover, subjects in such studies may move away, refuse to continue participating in the research project, or die.[16] Longitudinal research allows direct observation of changes in individuals and groups as they age, either in prospective studies (in which the subjects are studied at regular intervals over a period of years) or, although less desirable, in retrospective studies (in which individuals reply to similar questions pertaining to earlier stages in their lives). This method is used as well to examine the rate at which events occur or to illustrate that changes occur across time (Mendes de Leon 2007). This latter technique, known as event history analysis (Campbell and O'Rand 1988), enables us to study how much time passes before a consequent event occurs: the length of time between a serious illness or onset of a disability and retirement, between having a restricted licence and a motor vehicle crash, between moving into a nursing home and death, or between a divorce or widowhood and remarriage. Using a longitudinal design, researchers can study variations by gender, social class, education, place of residence, or ethnicity for aging-related events.

Table 5.2 presents hypothetical data for a longitudinal study of two birth cohorts. These data, collected from 1925 to 2005, indicate the frequency of movie attendance across the life

Table 5.2   Longitudinal Design: Age and Movie Attendance by Birth Cohort

Year	Age	1910 Birth Cohort Attending 3 Times or More per Year (%)	Year	Age	1940 Birth Cohort Attending 3 Times or More per Year (%)
1925	(15)	10	1955	(15)	58
1935	(25)	15	1965	(25)	62
1945	(35)	42	1975	(35)	60
1955	(45)	40	1985	(45)	57
1965	(55)	30	1995	(55)	52
1975	(65)	22	2005	(65)	40

Note: The data reported here are hypothetical.

course for two birth cohorts, one born in 1910 and one in 1940. Note that few in the 1910 cohort attended movies before 1945. Yet after World War II, a larger percentage of this age cohort attended movies. This effect on a particular age cohort at a particular point in the life course is known as a *period* effect. It represents a change in behaviour resulting from environmental, historical, or social events rather than from reaching a specific chronological age (35 in this case). But unless a research project has a large sample, studied over a long time frame, period effects at a particular stage may be missed or confounded with age effects.

Table 5.2 also illustrates how to avoid cohort-centrism—interpretations in which generalizations about the aging process and the status or behaviour of older people are derived on the basis of studying only one age cohort. Since each birth cohort experiences a different life course, longitudinal studies should include at least two age cohorts to control for possible cohort differences in life experiences—that is, allow for the identification of potential period effects. Unless more than one age cohort is included, possible between-cohort differences may be missed, and conclusions based on the study of one age cohort can be misleading or inaccurate. For example, Table 5.2 shows that the 1940 birth cohort attended movies more frequently at all ages than the 1910 cohort. Furthermore, the 1940 cohort demonstrates a relatively stable pattern of movie attendance across the life course, with only a slight decline in attendance occurring in the later years. Are they an atypical or a typical cohort with respect to patterns of movie attendance?

As in cross-sectional designs, any intra-cohort variations by gender, social class, marital status, ethnicity, educational attainment, or other relevant variables should be observed and noted. However, these controls are often neglected in longitudinal studies since more emphasis is placed on changes or differences at subsequent time periods. That is, variation within a cohort may increase or decrease because of either maturation or specific period effects. For example, movie attendance at age 35 may be significantly lower than at age 25 for those in each cohort who become parents and therefore have less time (because of work and child-rearing demands) for leisure outside the home (this is a maturation or life-course effect). Or attendance may decrease at a certain point in history for all adults, regardless of chronological age—perhaps because the movie industry has to compete with different type of media (a period effect), such as the growing use of DVDs, digital TV, the Internet, or satellite dishes. As well, large TV screens with surround sound may reduce actual movie attendance more for specific age cohorts than for other cohorts. Yet their frequency of actual movie "viewing" rather than attendance at theatres may increase with the use of new technology.

Cohort Analysis: Isolating Age Changes and Age Differences

Cohort analysis was developed in response to the limitations of cross-sectional and panel longitudinal designs for studying aging processes across time (Schaie 1965, 1988; Wolinsky 1993). This design uses similar information from different individuals who were born at different times and who are studied at different times. That is, a number of sequential cross-sectional trend data sets with the same information are used (e.g., census survey data for 1981, 1986, 1991, 1996, 2001, 2006, and 2011). In order to identify age changes, cohort differences, and period effects, one must examine repeated patterns in the data related to each of these effects (Wolinsky 1993). While there are more sophisticated methods of attempting to estimate age/period/cohort effects by using panel data, the tabular method shown below is useful when only cross-sectional trend data are available. For example, national surveys (health surveys, opinion polls, and the census) often ask the same questions at regular intervals. However, at each interval, different people represent the specific birth cohort. This eliminates the need for a panel longitudinal study in which the same individuals must be followed for many years. To illustrate this design, imagine we are in the year 2015 and have constructed a table based on one item (movie attendance) that has been included in a national survey every 10 years since 1945. Table 5.3 illustrates hypothetical patterns of movie attendance across the life course for three birth cohorts that might represent three generations within a family: grandparents, parents, and grandchildren.

In this type of analysis,[17] it is possible to do the following:

- Observe cross-sectional age differences (read down column 5 for the year 1985).
- Study age changes within a cohort over time (read across row a, b, or c).
- Compare patterns of movie attendance by cohorts of the same chronological age (at 35 years) at different points in history (compare cells 3a, 5b, and 7c).
- Note whether patterns of attendance over time vary among different cohorts (compare rows a, b, and c).

For example, the hypothetical data in Table 5.3 suggest that, except for the 1930 cohort, which began to attend movies relatively late in life (compare cells 1a and 2a versus cell 3a), there seems to be increasing frequency of movie attendance by the younger birth cohorts, both initially (compare cells 1a, 3b, and 5c) and later in life (compare cells 4a, 6b, and 8c). Moreover, despite increasing attendance by the younger cohorts, attendance is lower among all cohorts after age 35 (see cells 3a to 7a, cells 5b to 8b, and cells 7c to 8c). For the two most recent cohorts, this trend begins sooner in that the peak for attendance is reached at about age 25 and age 15, respectively (compare cells 4b and 5b and cells 5c and 6c).

A cohort analysis compares the influence of period effects on each cohort. For example, to determine whether high ticket prices during a period of high unemployment might have been a factor in decreased movie attendance around 1995, an investigator might note that there was a sharp decrease in attendance by the 1930 cohort. But this might be expected because of retirement and individuals having less discretionary income, and the decrease might be found in all cohorts when they reach 65. However, an examination of cells 5b, 6b, and 7b and cells 5c, 6c, and 7c suggests that for both the 1950 and the 1970 birth cohorts as well, attendance fell in 1995 before rising slightly and then continuing the overall pattern of declining by age. Therefore, we might be able to argue that there were unique period and historical events around 1995 that partly explain why all three cohorts attended movies less often. It should also be noted that while we can never completely separate age/period/cohort effects by using this method,

Table 5.3   Cohort Analysis: Age and Movie Attendance by Birth Cohort

Birth Cohort	% Attending Movies Three Times or More per Year (Age in Years)							
	1945 (1)	1955 (2)	1965 (3)	1975 (4)	1985 (5)	1995 (6)	2005 (7)	2015 (8)
a) 1930 (Grandparents)	10 (15)	12 (25)	33 (35)	30 (45)	21 (55)	11 (65)	4 (75)	–
b) 1950 (Parents)	–	–	58 (15)	62 (25)	60 (35)	41 (45)	52 (55)	40 (65)
c) 1970 (Children)	–	–	–	–	72 (15)	60 (25)	69 (35)	61 (45)

Note: The data reported here are hypothetical.

since they often occur simultaneously (known as interaction effects), it is possible to identify significant patterns in these effects. This helps us to understand whether an association with age is due to aging effects, period effects, cohort effects, or some combination.

Issues in Qualitative Research Designs

Emergent Research Designs

Rather than the more formulaic research designs used in quantitative research, qualitative research employs an "emergent" research design (Marshall and Rossman 1999). This type of design is more flexible and can be modified as new ideas and understandings surface during the research study. The process of qualitative research moves from broad questions at the start to more specific questions as the study evolves.[18]

Unlike quantitative designs, where data are analyzed after being collected, in qualitative research, interpretation and analysis are continual and subject to reinterpretation as new evidence is uncovered. Rather than the large random samples that are necessary in quantitative research, qualitative research employs smaller, nonrandom samples in which key informants, identified by others in a setting, are added at any time. Thus, the sample size is seldom predetermined as it is in quantitative research, where formal statistical methods dictate the minimum sample size required for the findings to be accurate and generalizable to the larger population.

Researcher as Participant

Unlike the quantitative researcher, who strives for objectivity and distance from the research participants, the qualitative researcher can be part of the study. In this style of research, he or she must be a sensitive, adaptable, patient, and astute observer and listener and must be as tenacious as possible in probing for more information. Yet at the same time, the researcher must avoid having his or her personal prejudices or preconceptions interfere with gathering and interpreting observations or information (Cobb and Forbes 2002). In quantitative research, the researcher could be fooled by responses to poorly worded or misinterpreted questions. In qualitative research, the researcher uses interviews with respondents, observations of the respondents in the setting, and a review of any available or relevant personal data to help verify information or to revise an earlier interpretation of the phenomenon being studied (Maxwell 2005).

The Setting

Because the setting or context is so essential to the interpretation of evidence, it must be fully and accurately described and analyzed, including both the physical and social structure. Within the setting, activities and interactions are observed, and any events, including those that might negatively influence the study's success, are noted. In short, this method is a complex, dynamic process that requires a complete understanding of the assumptions, language, and procedures of qualitative research. The approach does not merely involve adding a few open-ended questions to a survey or "hanging out" and watching older people in some social setting.[19]

Sampling Issues: The Selection of Respondents and Participants

When studying older people, researchers must consider the heterogeneity of the elderly population before reaching any conclusions. If a representative sample is needed in quantitative studies where the intent is to apply the findings back to the general population, lists of those in the population who are 65 and older, typically with age and sex details, are needed to create a random sample. However, such data may not always be available. Hence, researchers sometimes depend on nonrandom samples comprised of readily available and visible older people, such as volunteers or people who attend senior citizen centres. Those who are less visible, less active, or less healthy or who live in nursing homes are, consequently, less likely to be included. Moreover, people of any age who volunteer are often better educated, healthier, more mobile and social, and perhaps more liberal in their values, beliefs, and lifestyles. These sampling matters can introduce significant bias and non-representativeness into a research study and thereby limit the generalizability of the findings.

In qualitative studies, while the intent is to understand the actors and the social interaction in a particular setting, sometimes settings are selected for reasons of convenience; for example, the researcher may know a resident of a particular retirement home or may have met the director at a professional meeting. The selection of one setting rather than another may not be an issue for some aging topics, but it may be for some types of research questions. For example, the findings of a study involving older Aboriginal people in a northern settlement will not be applicable to older Aboriginal people in general because many now live in large cities. Or to study older gays and lesbians in a small university community because that is where the researcher is located may not yield findings that are representative of the lives of most gays and lesbians who live in large metropolitan centres or of those who live in conservative, rural communities. Similarly, a study of the residents of a single retirement home may ignore the unique circumstances of retirement home residents elsewhere who are members of a particular ethnic, religious, or racial group, or who live in a rural setting.

Regardless of whether a study is qualitative or quantitative, potentially relevant characteristics of all older people and real situations in their everyday lives are often under-represented or neglected in aging research. For example, studies often do not include frail and institutionalized older people, members of less well-known immigrant groups (East Indian, Vietnamese, or Brazilian), members of minority religious groups (Muslims and Hindus [Salari 2002]), those in the lower socio-economic stratum (including homeless older persons), those living in a household with family members, gay and lesbian older people, divorced or never-married older men and women, those whose first language is neither English nor French, widows or widowers living alone in their home, and those living on farms or in small towns in remote areas of the country. Therefore, studies sometimes target individuals with these characteristics. To illustrate, in a study of the caregiving and care-receiving patterns of older women, researchers must consider differences in ethno-cultural characteristics, family network, and socio-economic status because these factors do influence caregiving and care-receiving. Contrary to common assumptions, not all women over 65 are retired, married or widowed, and grandmothers.

Issues in Collecting Information from Older Adults

Special skills, techniques, and instruments are needed for research involving older people. First, researchers must establish trust and a good rapport with older respondents, who may view research personnel suspiciously as strangers, especially if researchers telephone or arrive at the older person's home without warning or permission.

Surveys conducted by mail may not be completed for a variety of reasons: the respondent has literacy problems, the print is too small, the sentences are too complicated or contain jargon, the respondent is unable to choose a single answer to a multiple-choice question, or he or she refuses or forgets to return the survey. Even if the survey is completed, the answers may not be accurate because older respondents may give what they think are socially acceptable responses. In addition, they may be more likely to respond with "no opinion" or "don't know," and they may be unwilling to answer very personal questions about death, finances, health, sexual relations, or family relationships.

Interviews are a much more effective way to gather information from older people because a face-to-face situation builds rapport and enables an interviewer to clarify the questions and to probe for additional information. But even with interviews there can be difficulties. First, once rapport is established, the respondent must be kept focused on the topic. He or she may want to share all kinds of information or to turn the interview into a social visit. Or when interviews are conducted in the respondent's home, a spouse or other people in the household may interject their opinions or answers or influence the interviewee's responses. Second, the gender of the interviewer matters. For some topics, older people may feel more comfortable responding to interviewers of the same sex, or they may mention or emphasize different issues or give quite different answers, depending on whether the interviewer is of the same or opposite sex (Stephenson et al. 1999). Similarly, an interviewer of the same age, race, or ethnic background can increase the depth and quality of information collected.

Regardless of whether a questionnaire or an interview is used, language is an essential component of the research process. Ageist language and labels should be avoided. Similarly, questions that begin "When you were younger . . ." do not elicit as detailed and useful responses as more specific questions that begin, for example, "When you were 25 to 30 years of age . . ." The language used when studying older people from a specific subcultural or cultural group must be appropriate for the respondents. Interviews and questionnaires should be conducted in the respondent's first language as those who are not entirely fluent in English may not fully comprehend the questions in an oral interview or a questionnaire. Members of the specific group should be involved in the design and pre-test of a questionnaire or interview guide, as interviewers, and in the interpretation of the information collected.

The very old (85 and over), including those who are frail regardless of their age, are difficult to find and are often excluded from research studies. Yet they constitute an important and growing segment of the older population (Wister and Wanless 2007). These segments of the older population are important when we need to study such issues as loss of independence, elder abuse, adequacy of social support and caregiving, and the quality of life in residential institutions. An interpreter, caregiver, or family member can be used (as a proxy) when deafness, lack of comprehension, or confusion on the part of the older interviewee might otherwise interfere with the collection or quality of the information (Russell 1999b). One approach to studying this subpopulation is to use the **Minimum Data Set** for comparing health outcomes among frail older people. This procedure involves implementing a standardized assessment for all patients in chronic-care hospitals or nursing homes (Hirdes and Carpenter 1997; Hirdes et al. 1999). Finally, the frail, institutionalized elderly person is often viewed by long-term-care administrators and staff as powerless and incapable of being studied. Moreover, administrators, who fear what residents might say about the quality of care, may refuse a researcher's request to interview or observe residents in their institution. In short, special effort must be made to include frail and institutionalized older persons in research studies.

Ethics in Research: Procedures to Protect Older Participants

Regardless of the setting or the competence of potential research participants, participation in research must be voluntary and fully informed. Older adults who participate in research projects must understand what is expected of them, and why, and must give their consent freely and without coercion to be interviewed or observed or to have their personal records examined (Ries 2010). The process of acquiring informed consent must allow participants time to consider whether they wish to be involved or not. If the potential participant has dementia, the concept of informed consent may not be understood, in which case a family member or a **guardian** with the legal power to make such a decision must give consent (Ries 2010).

All research involving older respondents must ensure privacy and guarantee protection from harm. The research process must protect participants from any physical or mental harm, such as worry, anxiety, or physical or mental anguish. Locher et al. (2006) have addressed some of the ethical issues involving research conducted with homebound older adults. Often, these persons are socially isolated and may not be monitored closely by others. Therefore, they could be vulnerable to unsafe or threatening situations during a research project. The authors identified two major ethical issues that might arise when conducting research with homebound older persons. First, older people may experience "therapeutic misconceptions" wherein they mistakenly believe they are to receive some form of treatment or cure for some illness or disability that is of concern to them. And second, the researcher may experience role conflict as to whether to continue the research with a given person if the researcher becomes aware of a situation in the home that is immediately or potentially harmful to the participant, such as personal neglect or abuse or exploitation by a caregiver (see Chapter 12). Those who live in a retirement or nursing home or who are cared for by others in their own home must be protected from any possible retaliation by caregivers who may be criticized by an older person during an interview. Protection from harm also involves refraining from asking questions, especially questions about death, if they appear to disturb the respondent, as well as ending an interview or observation immediately if the older person becomes severely disturbed or appears uncomfortable.

A particularly difficult ethical issue involves how to respond if the observer or interviewer suspects, or is told by the older person, that physical, psychological, or financial abuse or neglect is occurring. Who should be informed, how, and when: these are difficult decisions, especially if concrete evidence is lacking or if there is no legislation clearly defining what must be reported, to whom, and what the consequences are for the "whistleblower" or for non-reporting. These are issues that researchers and their staff must understand and resolve before entering the field to conduct interviews or observations involving older people.

Summary

This chapter introduced theories and perspectives to help you explain, interpret, and understand data and observations about aging processes and the situation of older people in a variety of settings. At present, no single theoretical perspective or methodological approach dominates. Rather, as in many fields of study, a variety of methods and theories are needed to stimulate creative thinking, to increase our knowledge, and to provide alternative explanations for or interpretations of a process or situation. Some theories and methods are used primarily to study micro-level (individual) aging questions; others are used for macro-level questions (issues at the level of society or the population). Increasingly, the micro and macro levels are interdependent, and theories and methods must address and answer questions at both levels. And we must take a longer and broader view of aging phenomena at both the individual and societal level, across historical periods, in different cultural settings, and across the life course of a specific individual or age cohort.

You may never become a theorist or a career researcher. However, an understanding of current theoretical perspectives and research methods is essential for your development as a creative and critical thinker, as an informed citizen, as a student, and later in a career that may or may not relate to aging issues. Use theoretical perspectives and theories and their concepts to critique what you read and observe in the mass media, government reports, and research articles. They can also guide your thinking about the development and evaluation of policies and programs concerning the older population. Similarly, an understanding of research methods and their inherent strengths and weaknesses will enable you to assess more accurately the quality, reliability, and credibility of the information you read about in research articles and the print media, or that is reported in the electronic media, including the Internet. Finally, do not always accept what you read as the truth or as the only explanation for an outcome or event. Interpret and critique the ideas and conclusions of others, look for mounting of evidence from multiple studies, and search for new or more complete explanations or interpretations. And above all, in any interactions with older adults, especially those who are frail and dependent, adhere to ethical practices and principles in both research and practice.

For Reflection, Debate, or Action

1. Select a fact, a pattern, or an observation about aging or older people that is of interest to you, and, employing concepts from three theories about later life and aging, attempt to explain or interpret why the phenomenon occurs regularly.
2. Select a public policy, and use one of the theoretical perspectives on aging to explain why the policy is, or may not be, successful in meeting the intended objectives.
3. Select an article from a recent issue of the *Canadian Journal on Aging*, and critique the research design and methods used. Are they appropriate for the research questions being asked? Do they facilitate or inhibit a more complete understanding of the topic? What other design or method might have been used to address the same topic and why?

4. Select two diverse theoretical perspectives, and, with a classmate, debate why and how the perspectives can or cannot contribute to better policy-making for Canada's aging population.

5. Select a newspaper or magazine article about a topic in aging, and state whether and how the article reflects a particular theoretical perspective. If the article is atheoretical, suggest a theoretical perspective that might have been used to provide a more in-depth, consistent, and accurate interpretation or explanation of the issue being discussed.

6. Select a program aimed at supporting older people and think about how you would evaluate its goals and whether it reaches the right people.

7. Among the many theories and theoretical perspectives, which ones, and why, would be most useful in addressing the perennial question as to whether support in later life is a public issue or a private trouble?

Notes

1. For a detailed and historical discussion of theoretical issues in social gerontology, see George 1995; Bengtson et al. 1997, 1999, 2005, 2009; Calasanti 1996; Lynott and Lynott 1996; Marshall 1996, 1999; Schroots 1995; Bengtson and Schaie 1999; Minkler and Estes 1999; Garner 1999; McMullin 2000; Hagestad and Dannefer 2001; Biggs et al. 2003; Estes et al. 2003; Marshall and Mueller 2003; Powell 2005; Powell and Wahidin 2006; Hitlin and Elder 2007; Marshall and Clarke 2007; Biggs 2008; and Achenbaum 2009.

2. Additional perspectives and theories are introduced throughout the text to explain specific phenomena, such as modernization (Chapter 2), environmental press (Chapter 8), intergenerational family dynamics (Chapter 9), and caregiving (Chapter 12).

3. The feminist perspective includes many theoretical approaches: micro, macro, normative, interpretive, and critical (Gee and Kimball 1987; Calasanti 1993, 2009; Hamilton 1993; Osmond and Thorne 1993; Lopata 1995; Marshall 1996; Ray 1996; Bengtson et al. 1997, 2009; Garner 1999; McDaniel 2004; Bengtson et al. 2005, 2009; Moen and Chermack 2005; McMullin 2010) and many research methods (Reinharz 1992; Neysmith 1995; Calasanti 1996; Moen and Chermack 2005; Mitchell 2012). Articles representing the different approaches can be found in the *Journal of Women and Aging*, the *Journal of Aging Studies*, and *Canadian Woman Studies*.

4. For feminist critiques, see Gee and Kimball 1987; McDaniel 1989, 2004; MacRae 1990; Calasanti 1992, 1993, 2004a, 2009; MacQuarrie and Keddy 1992; Calasanti and Zajicek 1993; Arber and Ginn 1995; McMullin 1995, 2010; Ray 1996; Garner 1999; Bengtson et al. 2005; and Moen and Chermack 2005.

5. "Life course," "lifespan," and "life cycle" are sometimes used interchangeably in the literature (Hagestad 1990). However, from a sociological and gerontological perspective, life course is the preferred term, whereas psychologists employ "lifespan" to refer to universal "stages" of development from infancy to old age.

6. See Bengtson et al. (1997) for a historical analysis of the development of three generations of theories in social gerontology, and Achenbaum (2009) for a metahistorical perspective on theories of aging.

7. Originally called "age stratification theory" when first proposed in 1972 (Riley et al. 1972), more recently it has been relabelled the "aging and society paradigm" in recognition of its evolving, broader view of aging (Riley et al. 1999).

8. The work of Riley et al. (1999) provides an illustration of how theoretical developments occur over a period of time.

9. In the work of Riley and her colleagues, social structures refer to "societal institutions, such as the family, the economy, and educational, political and religious organizations; their component roles; their rules and resources; their built-in culture and values; and the social environments" (Riley et al. 1999, 341, n. 5).

10. Adherents of the political economy of aging perspective include Myles 1989; Minkler and Estes 1991; Estes 1991; Estes et al. 1996; Quadagno and Reid 1999; Walker 1999; Phillipson 2005; Minkler and Holstein 2008; Kail et al. 2009.

11. For examples of the critical perspective, see Moody 1988, 1993; Minkler and Estes 1991, 1999; Cole et al. 1993, 2000; Calasanti 1996; Minkler 1996; Phillipson 1998, 2003; Ray 1998; Estes 1999; Estes et al. 2003; Biggs et al. 2003; Holstein and Minkler 2003; Katz 2003; Minkler and Holstein 2008; and Baars et al. 2006.

12. Examples of this type of research are found in the *Journal of Aging Studies*.

13. Narrative gerontology is represented by the work of Cole et al. 1993, 2000; Birren et al. 1996; Kenyon and Randall 1999; Biggs 2001; Katz 2003; Randall and Kenyon 2004; and Phoenix et al. 2009.

14. Please note that the data reported in Tables 5.1, 5.2, and 5.3 are fictitious. These hypothetical results are presented to illustrate research designs and possible interpretations of the data.

15. For more information about the CLSA, see the Special Issue of the *Canadian Journal on Aging*, 28, 2009. Two other major Canadian longitudinal studies that have been completed over the past several decades include the Ontario Longitudinal Study and the Manitoba Longitudinal Study.

16. Because respondents may be lost over the course of the study, researchers can always ask and examine whether the final sample is similar to the original sample. For example, in a longitudinal study of movie attendance, those who no longer wish to be in the study may be those who no longer attend movies because of such factors as low income, declining vision, or loss of mobility.

17. Ideally, this type of analysis is completed for both males and females and with controls for relevant factors, such as race, income, education, or religion. However, to simplify the explanation of cohort analysis, only patterns for the total population in Table 5.3 are reported.

18. Excellent sources for learning how to design and interpret qualitative studies include Gubrium and Holstein 1997; Crabtree and Miller 1999; Marshall and Rossman 1999; Russell 1999a; Denzin and Lincoln 2000; Munhall and Boyd 2000; Cobb and Forbes 2002; Rubenstein 2002; Rowles and Schoenberg 2002; Maxwell 2005; Milligan et al. 2005; and Etches et al. 2006.

19. An excellent example of qualitative research is Sarah Matthew's in-depth study of how siblings (sisters and brothers) support their aging parents (Matthews 2002). Case A in Highlight 7.4 (page 216) illustrates how insights about a situation (concerns about and care for a parent with Alzheimer's disease) can be acquired through the use of qualitative research.

6

Social Structures, Social Inequality, and the Life Course

One generation plants trees, and the next takes it easy under their shade.

— Chinese proverb

Focal Points and Key Facts

- How does age define and structure our lives and influence social relations and opportunities across the life course?
- In what way do social structures and agency interact to influence social relationships and to shape life-course trajectories?
- Why and how are life chances and social relations across the life course, and in later life, influenced by social inequalities based on social class, gender, race, age, or ethnicity?
- Why do some members of society experience a cumulative disadvantage in later life, in particular, older women?
- How much of our daily social life is age-segregated as opposed to age-integrated and why?
- Are there gender gaps and generation gaps in the family and/or in society?
- The baby boomers comprise approximately 10 million Canadians or one-third of the population. Will their retirement and needs in later life foster generational equity, generational inequity, or intergenerational independence?

Introduction

Our identities are created and modified through interactions with social structures, which guide and limit the nature and type of social relationships. As people engage in social relationships, they acquire or are assigned unequal amounts of power and status because of the rights or duties attached to their social positions, such as doctor versus patient or parent versus child. A social structure is created when a pattern of interrelated statuses and roles coalesce to constitute a relatively stable set of socially constructed relations.

Personal histories are constructed within evolving and intersecting social structures based on social class, race, ethnicity, gender, and age. These dimensions organize social life in hierarchical structures, and they shape social identity and social opportunities. They influence how, and to what extent, we gain access to power and other valued resources in a society or organization. Or, as McMullin (2010) succinctly argues, class, age, gender, ethnicity, and race are interlocking sets of power relations that structure social life and therefore contribute to and perpetuate social inequality across the life course. They may also foster conflict among social groups.

This chapter is concerned with the interaction of **age structures** and other key structures affecting the lives of people as they move through their life courses. Age structures are socially structured relations among individuals and age **cohorts**, and they create structural-level processes, such as cohort flow, intergenerational transfers of wealth and support within families and in society at large (e.g., child–parent caregiving within families or tax support of education or health that benefits a particular generation in society), age grading, and structural lag. Age is the structural dimension of interest in this chapter. For example, "old age," per se, is socially constructed and defined in different ways at different historical times and in different religions and cultures. Consequently, across history and within some cultures, we have observed a shift from emphasizing filial piety to apocalyptic demography to intergenerational conflict as the status of older persons is constructed, deconstructed, and reconstructed (Johnson 2005). Age interacts with class, race, gender, and ethnicity to create and intensify power relations and life chances across the life course and across age cohorts.

Before we examine social structures and their effect on an individual, three caveats must be noted. First, while the focus here is on the structures or power relations based on age, class, race, gender, and ethnicity, we must not ignore agency. Structures do not fully determine or control an individual's life course or outcome. The structural elements establish boundaries within which agency is invoked by individuals or groups. Social movements (the feminist, black power, or grey power movements), changing roles and norms, and changing status systems over time present different opportunities and barriers to individuals or cohorts as they invoke agency across the life course. Agency can change life trajectories and facilitate social mobility, whereby new occupational or income statuses emerge (or are created). Agency is invoked when we acquire and develop social, human, and cultural capital by pursuing higher education and by joining social networks. Although advantage and disadvantage can be passed on through direct transfer of economic capital across generations in families, agency enables individuals to change society or to improve their social status by acquiring their own social, human, and cultural capital.

A second caveat is that, at present, no single theory or perspective can guide our thinking about social structures and aging. The age stratification perspective focuses on inequality but minimizes the interaction of age with other systems of inequality. Similarly, the political economy and feminist perspectives focus on power relations in society but devote less attention to age per se and to the interaction of age with other dimensions of power. And while exchange theory may help us to understand intergenerational transfers in the family, it is not very effective in accounting for transfers at the societal level. The life-course perspective can bridge some of these elements, but it is difficult to test multi-dimensional theories. As McMullin (2000, 526) noted, one set of these power relations, whether based on age, class, gender, ethnicity, or race, does not have more weight than the others, at least theoretically. Until a new macro theory emerges that synthesizes the full set of power relations, we, as students of aging phenomena, must conceptually consider all five dimensions (McMullin 2010).

A third caveat is that individuals experience social structures and processes related to aging in multiple and diverse ways depending on their social characteristics and the situational contexts. Social structures do not determine behaviour but, rather, form a context in which individuals experience the aging process.

Social Structures and Aging

Variation in Life Chances and Lifestyles

To survive and attain its goals by ensuring social order and stability, each social system—whether a married couple, a business organization, a university, or a society—requires a division of labour and responsibility among its members. Positions are ranked, formally or informally, according to whether they have more or less status, power, or prestige than other positions and whether there is variation in the rewards. Associated with each position are rights and obligations, together with social norms that represent common agreement on how individuals should behave.

Social inequality connected to one's position in the social system influences our life chances and lifestyles and facilitates or inhibits social interaction within and between the various strata of the social structure (O'Rand 1996, 2001, 2006). This structural differentiation fosters either the integration or isolation of individuals or groups in a variety of social systems. For example, a 65-year-old man whose occupation is defined as labourer may have a moderately high status in the age structure of society because of his chronological age; a very high status in the family structure because he is the patriarch and primary wage earner; but a low status, responsibility, or power at his place of employment or in the community at large because of his low level of education and type of job. However, social statuses also vary according to attributes, such as being female. Compared to the illustration of the 65-year-old man above, a woman with the same characteristics could experience lower statuses than the man in all areas because of patriarchal social structures.

Social Stratification: Unequal Access to Opportunities and Rewards

In pre-industrial societies, a simple three-tiered social structure based on age and gender often prevailed: a group of elderly men who ruled as a gerontocracy, all other adults, and children and adolescents who had not been declared "adults" by some rite of passage. Today, the social structures of modern societies represent a complex mosaic of intersecting dimensions on a variety of social attributes and across a number of social institutions: family, education, work, leisure, the state, and religion.

Individuals in a society, an organization, or a group may be ranked higher or lower than others. When this ranking occurs, a system of unequal access to opportunities and rewards is created and is usually perpetuated across time because they become part of the social fabric of society. Social positions, with variations in status and power, are assigned on the basis of either *ascribed* attributes (race, gender, ethnicity) or *achieved* attributes (class, age, and education), all of which represent social constructs. These stratification systems mean that some people have higher (or lower) status and more (or fewer) opportunities to acquire valued rewards, and they experience different lifestyles, challenges, and opportunities as they move through life. This leads to competition for, and sometimes conflict over, scarce resources among occupants of the various social strata (O'Rand 1996, 2001). These status differences are reinforced, if not created, by government policies that allocate resources and define the eligibility for rewards on the basis of the status and needs of certain lower-status groups—minority racial groups, poverty groups, children, elderly people, or women. But changes can and do take place in status rankings and in the composition of a social structure as a result of population aging, changes in the number and type of immigrants, and changes in opportunities for disadvantaged groups.

Inequality involves an uneven distribution of wealth and poverty; unequal opportunities for education, health care, and leisure; differential access to power and rewards; and differential use of agency. For example, studies have shown that in modern societies, there is a strong relationship between socio-economic status in childhood and functional and health status in later life (Zarit and Pearlin 2005; Guralnik et al. 2006). Also, in our complex social world, stratification systems interact and intersect to create and perpetuate structured social inequality (McMullin 2010), for instance, being an older female who is a member of a marginalized ethnic group. Thus, we must understand how the age stratification system and chronological age interact with other stratification dimensions across the life course. These dimensions produce, maintain, and transfer elements of social inequality from one generation to the next, and they interact to influence opportunities, challenges, and lifestyles in later life. For example, economic security and health in later life are related to lifelong constraints imposed by gender, race, ethnicity, and class (especially the level of education) and to one's marital and employment history across the life course. The following subsections discuss relationships between age and stratification systems, and discuss the possible cumulative effect, for individuals and society, of these status systems in later life.

Social Class and Age

Most societies are structured into a number of interlocking social classes, or strata, that are socially constructed. The number of strata range from two (aristocrats and peasants) or three (professionals, white-collar workers, and blue-collar workers) to a more complex structure with many divisions, such as observed in Canada (upper class, upper middle class, middle class, lower middle class, upper lower class, and lower class). In modern societies, the social class structure is strongly influenced by the level of formal education; the prestige allocated to each occupation; and the wealth of an individual, a family, or a social group. Education, as an investment, leads to skills, employability, a healthier and longer life, and higher standards of economic and social well-being. It can also facilitate upward mobility. Educational status influences attitudes, values, behaviours, friendships, job opportunities, health, and income throughout life. Different age cohorts and specific members of each cohort have had differential access to education throughout history. In general, until the late twentieth century, few people, especially women, completed a university education. Today, however, a majority of the baby boom generation, especially women, have completed an undergraduate degree, and an increasing number have earned graduate degrees.

In each class stratum, common values, beliefs, types of behaviour, and lifestyles emerge, many of which are passed from generation to generation by the family of origin. This outcome is explained by *cumulative inequality theory* (Ferraro et al. 2009). That is, unequal or disadvantaged status and the accumulation of risk early in life can contribute to unequal situations and hardships later in life (O'Rand 2001, 2006; O'Rand and Hamil-Luker 2005; Ferraro et al. 2009). To illustrate, O'Rand (2006) noted that early and sustained poverty can predict higher rates of disability in later life as well as earlier mortality. Other research has shown a link between early childhood living conditions, such as exposure to conflicts in the home and low parental socio-economic status, and poor cognition in later life (Fors et al. 2009). In short, O'Rand (2006, 156) concluded that "early advantages increase access to beneficial opportunity structures throughout the life course, while early disadvantages may increase the likelihood of persistent disadvantages." Highlight 6.1 illustrates the influence of social class on the lives of two elderly widows: one from a lower-class background; the other, with the advantage of an upper middle-class background throughout her life.

Gender and Age

Sex refers to the genetic and biological difference between males and females. **Gender**, however, is a socially constructed concept that defines what it means to be male or female in a given society and what types of behaviour and roles are expected of females and males at different stages in their lives.[1] Pyke (1996, 530) defined gender as

> an emergent property of situated interaction rather than a role or attribute. Deeply held and typically nonconscious beliefs about men's and women's essential natures shape how gender is accomplished in everyday interactions. Because those beliefs are molded by existing macrostructural power relations, the culturally appropriate

Highlight 6.1
Social Class Matters: Diversity in Widowhood

The transition to widowhood, itself a traumatic experience, can lead to unforeseen changes in the way one lives because of variations in social class. Alma and Betty are 70 years of age, live in the same city, and have both been widowed for five years. Here the similarities end, partly because of class differences and their related life experiences and opportunities.

Alma is among the invisible poor in society, because when her husband died, his pension benefits were lost. A housewife most of her life, Alma lacks her own pension, has few savings left, and is totally dependent for her survival on the government old age security (OAS) and guaranteed income supplement (GIS). Since she was unable to find work, she has recently moved from her rented house into a sparsely furnished rooming house. In her small room, she cooks, eats, and sleeps, sharing a bathroom with other lodgers. Faced with declining strength and mobility, she finds the climb to the third floor more difficult, as is shopping for food and other necessities. She lives in a deteriorating neighbourhood with a high crime rate, and so she never ventures out at night. She has become a "prisoner in her own room" because her children and friends live too far away to provide help and transportation. For Alma, the "golden years" have not materialized. The next transition will probably be a move to publicly funded housing, where, in fact, her quality of life may improve.

Betty, in contrast, having raised her family, entered university at age 50 and upon graduation began a career as a journalist. Now, at 70, she is constantly seeking new challenges and adventures. She has written a successful novel and contributes a weekly column to a number of newspapers. Betty lives in a downtown condominium, consults her stockbroker weekly, plays tennis three times a week, has a wide circle of female friends, and dates regularly. Volunteer work at a local elementary school one day a week keeps her in touch with the younger generation. She has considered "wintering" in the south, but she prefers to take three or four trips a year to more exotic destinations in Europe or the Far East. For Betty, widowhood does not represent a loss of economic or social resources. In reality, the transition to being single has provided freedom and an incentive to reap the benefits of later life.

Source: "Ideal Types of Age Structures," from Riley and Riley Jr, "Structural Lag: Past and Future," in Riley et. al., eds, *Age and Structural Lag*. Reprinted with permission of John Wiley & Sons, Inc.

ways of producing gender favor men's interests over those of women. In this manner, gendered power relations are reproduced.

Gender shapes social life through agency and gender stratification; it is a central organizing principle of our social world, like class and race. Women's experiences and situations are socially constructed in a male-dominated world where social norms and institutionalized structures are shaped by the division of power between men and women. That is, the lived experiences and perceived or real problems encountered by women are more structurally conditioned than they are a product of individual behaviour and choices (Estes 2005; Calasanti 2009). Throughout the life course, and in all societies, males and females play different roles, receive different rewards, and experience different realities. For women, these gendered realities often include the following:

- less access to education, income, property, power, and pensions
- more responsibility for unpaid family caregiving and less involvement in the paid labour force
- more poverty, in general, and often in later life
- more victimization through violence, abuse, or neglect
- a more difficult later life—widowhood, poverty, living alone, being institutionalized or homeless—owing to cumulative disadvantages, many of which originate earlier in life as a result of divorce or exclusion from the labour force

Definitions of gender vary by culture and across time and age. They also vary by race, class, ethnicity, sexual orientation, education, and region of the country. Our gendered selves (males and females) interact within gendered institutions of education, work, family, leisure, politics, the military, the mass media, and religion to create a gendered world as well as social and economic inequalities.

When age and gender intersect to create gendered social processes and outcomes across the life course, including in the later years, women in general are more disadvantaged, and gender inequalities are most cumulative and visible among older women (Ven et al. 2011). Recognition of these problems has been magnified by the fact that there are many more older women than older men, especially of advanced ages. Because of gendered pathways through life and the situation of women in later life, aging has been described as "a woman's issue." Calasanti (1999, 45) argues that "gender relations are socially-constructed power relations between men and women which become institutionalized in various social arenas." These power relations emerge in the family, education, work, leisure, and politics. They spill over into society at large, becoming embedded as well in the larger context of differences by race, class, ethnicity, and age at different stages in life, including the later years. According to Ven et al. (2011), a "gendered lens" is needed in order to fully understand the unique experiences of aging women and men, both separately and in relation to one another.

The gender differences we observe or that individuals experience are the outcome of gender identities interacting in gendered institutions to create gender inequality. As gender inequality is reduced, gender differences between women and men will shrink, although they are unlikely ever to fully disappear, at least not in the immediate future. Men and women are not from different planets, as one popular book—*Men Are from Mars, Women Are from Venus* (Gray 1992)—would have us believe! We are more alike than different, and in some social groups and in some institutions, the gender gap is narrowing (Kimmel 2000).

However, despite social change and progress, there remain "enduring inequalities by gender across the life course, producing for women an accumulated disadvantage, and a lifetime of cumulative advantage for men" (Moen 2001, 184). Gender matters because men and women, as gendered individuals, are differentially located in gendered social structures that foster different roles, relationships, and the accompanying opportunities and barriers. Gender reflects power differences in which inequities are created so that some men have power over women, some women have power over other women and men, and some men have power over other men (McMullin 2010). Consequently, Kimmel (2000) concludes that not all masculinities and femininities are created equal. To illustrate, because of lifelong gender differences and experiences, women may

- be valued less in society
- be victims of discrimination and sexist attitudes and practices

- be victims of violence
- be underemployed or unemployed
- work exclusively on unpaid labour in the home, which deprives them of pension benefits
- have major responsibility for family caregiving
- have truncated or random work careers

In later life, gender differences are further magnified because women followed different life trajectories at work, at leisure, and in the family; and they experienced different lifestyles from those of men. These differences reflect the "feminization of later life." Clearly, more, but not all, older women are vulnerable in later life because of lifelong gender differences.

The financial and health implications of having less education, moving in and out of the labour force, and having major responsibility for the home, for child care, and for parent care are magnified in later life. Inequalities are more likely to occur if an older woman survives her spouse, receives a reduced pension when she is widowed, and depletes her savings if she lives into her eighth or ninth decade. The economic situation of older women is compounded by gender-based pension policies in the past, which were based on the assumption that all women were married and dependent on their husbands. Ven et al. (2011) contend that women are therefore disadvantaged in accessing adequate pensions due to the following:

- life events, such as marriage and child care, which affect labour-force participation rates
- working part-time or withdrawing from the work force, thereby reducing pension benefits
- engaging in unpaid activities, such as caring for sick or older parents
- receiving lower earnings and fewer advancements in the work force than men
- living longer than men so that pensions must be spread over more years of life
- experiencing widowhood, which significantly reduces income level and thereby increases the need for pensions (see Chapter 10)

However, because men's life expectancy is growing, because more older women are independent and wealthy, and because new co-habitation arrangements are possible and likely for divorced or widowed women in later life, Arber and Ginn (2005) suggest that there may be fewer "feminization of later life" issues in the future. Similarly, Moen and Spencer (2006) suggest that there is a trend to greater convergence in lifestyles and opportunities in later life as the pathways for men and women across the life course become more similar with changes in age and gender-related institutions and norms.

As with most aspects of aging, descriptions of ideal, generalized patterns of aging by one social category—gender—are insufficient. Women are not a homogeneous group but, rather, vary by age, education, wealth, marital status, ethnicity, race, and social class, just as men vary on the same attributes. Gender relations do foster gender differences, but gender relations in terms of roles, power, and prestige are changing, at least in domains like the family and leisure, and in some sectors of the labour force. In later life, if older people in general are valued less and assigned a low ranking by society, their life situation becomes even more difficult if they also hold another lower-status attribute, such as being a woman with little education, a gay woman, an Aboriginal woman, or an immigrant widow. Consequently, we must understand the intersection of these various stratification systems when developing research, policies, or social programs that pertain to older women.

At one time, scholars and practitioners in gerontology labelled this multi-dimensional impact as double jeopardy (age and gender), triple jeopardy (age, gender, and race), or multiple jeopardy (age, gender, race, and class). Serious difficulties in later life were attributed to the interaction of racism, sexism, and ageism; and with negative effects that are more than the sum of their parts. You may still encounter the "jeopardy" label when you read the literature. However, a more useful way of understanding later life is to realize that stratification systems interact to create structural inequalities for some individuals as they move through the life course, including during the later years.

Today, research and policy analysis focus on the extent to which the outcomes of the stratification systems are cumulative and additive throughout the life course (O'Rand 1996; Ferraro 2001; Arber and Ginn 2005; Moen and Spencer 2006). Inequality in power, prestige, and privileges exists throughout the life course within and between all cohorts. The effects of these risk factors accumulate through a person's life to increase the heterogeneity of older cohorts and thereby increase the inequality experienced by some older people. Inequalities in later life are not random. Economic or health disadvantages later in life are partially attributable to the cumulative effect of early structural disadvantages (poverty, less education, and child-care responsibilities), institutionalized discrimination, and agency (personal decisions or actions taken or not taken at key transition points).

As with many topics in gerontology, aging must be understood within the context of complex processes that occur at the individual and structural level and include both aging effects and cohort effects. An individual elderly woman with lower-class roots in a racial or ethnic group may be among the most impoverished people in later life with respect to income, housing, and health. But she is also likely to be among the least educated, and she has probably had a lower income and poorer than average health all her life. Being female, poorly educated, and a member of a minority ethnic or racial group has created lifelong disadvantages, and the later years may not significantly increase her already disadvantaged situation. Some of these heightened disadvantages in later life can be offset by policies that provide income or services based on need. Such policies, if delivered fairly and effectively, have the potential to reduce inequities at all stages of life, but especially in later life (O'Rand 1996). Highlight 6.2 provides a blog from the Canadian Association of Retired Persons' (CARP) advocacy page on its website that encapsulates a woman's life-course trajectory into poverty.

Race, Ethnicity, and Age

Canada's "open door" immigration policy has contributed to considerable variation in the number of language and cultural groups in most age cohorts. Some immigrants never experience full **assimilation** into Canadian society; others, often those in the second generation, become structurally assimilated while still retaining many of their cultural traditions and values. For many first-generation members of racial or ethnic groups in Canada and for some individuals in subsequent generations, poverty or lower-class status is synonymous with race and ethnicity, thereby fostering and perpetuating social inequality across the life course. Because of prevailing prejudices and stereotypes in mainstream society, members of these groups may experience discrimination in access to services and opportunities. With less education, lower incomes, and

Highlight 6.2
Women Aging into Poverty

This is a guest blog from the Older Women's Network

November 26, 2010—Poverty has many facets and many features, but low income is always the defining factor.

By any definition, women 65-plus (and especially those unattached) represent a substantial number of those living on low income. Single or widowed women are significantly more likely to be poor than seniors living in families.

Women's average CPP (Canadian Pension Plan) income is less than half that of a man. And, 14% of women receive no CPP. Almost two-thirds of women 65-plus get OAS (Old Age Security) or GIS (Guaranteed Income Supplement) which is meant to help seniors with lower income or zero income.

Why are older women so much more likely to have low income? The problem begins way before retirement. Women are more likely to go into "women's work"— caring for and teaching children, nursing the sick, cleaning, preparing food, serving others. At any time 40% of all working women are doing some combination of part-time, casual (temporary), contract, and self employed work. Result: Women earn 71% of a man's wage. When you look at just part time and seasonal work, women make just over half of what men make (54¢ to his $1.00).

During her working career she is far more likely to take unpaid leave, to take care of the children, parents, and/or a spouse. There goes some of her earnings toward CPP or work pensions. She is more likely because of family pressures to be unable to take the high level jobs that require large amounts of travel, long hours, and being available 24/7.

The federal government likes to talk about the "Three Pillars of Retirement"—CPP/QPP, OAS/GIS and RRSPs and employment pension plans to support a retirement house. Instead, for many, especially women, the pillars are somewhat rickety. In the ideal situation, CPP/QPP is supposed to replace 25% of average life-work earnings, OAS/GIS provides a maximum of just over $14,000 a year, and work pensions and RRSPs are supposed to provide the rest.

Here is a description of your "average" woman 65-plus (remember to get the average you include those who retire with an excellent pension). She may have had to take a leave to look after her children and/or grandchildren, she may have nursed a sick husband and/or her elderly parents or in-laws. She was more likely working in a lower paying job and more likely to have worked part-time or intermittently. If there was a family business, she is more likely than her husband to have not received a salary. She may have lost workplace pensionable earnings (or even pension contributions) by her more intermittent work pattern. So the only "pillar" she can count on is OAS/GIS—a little over $1000 a month.

Her only hope is a basic structural change to the pension system. There is a lot that can be done to help older women, but a few things stand out. OAS and GIS should at least bring seniors up to the poverty line and CPP should not penalize the casual or intermittent worker as much.

Source: CARP (2010). Advocacy, www.carp.ca/advocacy/adv-article-display.cfm?documentID=5269

a lower quality of housing throughout their lives, and less state support, they are more likely to experience poor health and poverty in their later years (Williams and Wilson 2001; Kaida and Boyd 2011). For many women in later life, these differences are further magnified because they followed different life trajectories at work, at leisure, and in the family and experienced different lifestyles from those of men. Their situation is compounded further at all ages, including later life, if they head a household as a single parent, if they are the sole wage earner, and if they are a member of a minority group. Moreover, men and women in Canada who cannot read or speak English or French face additional difficulties in later life—when seeking income security, social services or health care, for example, or when living in an institution where staff cannot speak their primary or sole language.

Nevertheless, not all members of a racial or ethnic group are disadvantaged. Their status depends on educational attainment and opportunities for social mobility, especially for those in the second and third generations. But those born into a family with low income, little education, and little power experience a lifelong negative impact on their employment opportunities and income, health, quality and location of housing, and access to health care and other services (Koehn 2009). These lifelong disadvantages accumulate to create additional hardships in the later years as health and income decline further.

The location of a specific group in the ethnic and racial stratification system changes over time and leads to variations among generations in the process of aging and in the status of older people. Moreover, the status of one group improves when other even more disadvantaged groups arrive in Canada, when the amount or type of institutionalized discrimination directed toward a group decreases, or when the group becomes assimilated into mainstream society.

Finally, members of minority ethnic and racial groups may be disadvantaged in terms of receiving public benefits and social services since most social programs are developed with the needs of mainstream society in mind. For instance, Kaida and Boyd (2011) found that poverty among older Canadian immigrants has remained, whereas poverty rates have fallen among older adults born in Canada. The higher poverty among elderly immigrants is attributed to inadequate state income support; however, it may be reduced by financial assistance from kin. This form of systemic inequality is subtle and often unintended. But if policies and formal services are insensitive to varying cultural or language needs, people outside mainstream society may be unaware of or not know how to obtain a service or benefit. Facilities such as nursing homes may not meet their needs with respect to diet, health-care practices and beliefs, or language. Yeo (1993) found, for example, that bilingual nursing home residents in advanced stages of dementia often revert to speaking their first language with staff and visitors and thus cannot make their needs known.

Age Structures and the Life Course

Introduction: Concepts and Social Processes

Age structures are fundamental to the process of aging at a societal level and at the family level. To understand the influence of age structures across the life course in a society or a social institution, such as the extended family, three major concepts are employed: "cohort," "generation," and "generational unit" (Marshall 1983).

Concepts

A cohort is composed of everyone who was born in a specified year (2008) or in a specific period of years (2005–10). We are often interested in the size and socio-demographic characteristics of an age cohort and whether these elements influence the life chances and lifestyles of cohort members at different stages of their lives.

A generation is more than a group of people (an age cohort) born during the same period (Mannheim 1952). It represents a unique grouping of adjacent birth cohorts, many of whom have experienced a significant socio-historical event (a depression or war) in a similar manner or whose members tend to think and behave in a similar way because they interact frequently or adopt similar values (e.g., the baby boomers—see chapters 4 and 7). Some generations create significant conflict and change in a society or institution (the hippies or counterculture generation of the 1960s). That is, members of a generation often develop a historical or social consciousness or bond that gives unique meaning to their lives and sets them apart from other birth cohorts. The social construction of a generation does not occur among all adjacent age cohorts that emerge, however. There have been four significant generations[2] in North America in the twentieth century:

1. Adults who had just entered or were about to enter the labour force during the Depression of the 1930s (the "Depression" generation).
2. People who were children of this Depression generation and who were influenced throughout their lives by the fact that they were children during this calamitous economic period in history. Many became parents of the baby boomers (Elder 1999).
3. The large baby boom generation born in the years following World War II (Foot and Stoffman 1998; Wister 2005).
4. Children of the baby boomers, who were born after 1970 (Adams 1997) and variously labelled in the 1990s as "Generation X," "twenty-somethings" (Coupland 1992; Thau and Heflin 1997), "Generation Next" (Kotash 2000, 2004), or "Nexus Generation" (Barnard et al. 1998), primarily because of their unique values and lifestyles.

When scholars, the media, and laypeople use the term *generation*, they may be discussing three quite different groups (Alwin 2002, 43):

• all people born in the same year (e.g., 1996) or period (e.g., 1991–2001)
• a unique position in a family's line of descent (the second or third generation to attend a specific university or enter a specific occupation or be employed by a specific company)
• a group of people self-consciously defined, by themselves and by others, as part of a historically based social movement, such as the "hippie" generation of the 1960s, or a major demographic event, such as the birth of the baby boomers or Generation X

It is important to note that in the media, and sometimes in scholarly research, *generation* and *cohort* may be used interchangeably, although this is neither correct nor appropriate.

To this point, we have implied that a generation defines a group at the societal level of analysis. However, as a concept, *generation* applies as well to different age groups in an extended family system (Price et al. 2000; Silverstein 2005; Connidis 2010; Mitchell 2012). The structure of a family lineage system influences the interaction patterns within and between generations. Most kinship systems include two generations (parents and young children or adolescents) or three generations (grandparents, parents, and children). But with increasing longevity in modern societies, a four-generation family (great-grandparents, grandparents, parents, and children) is also possible, at least for a brief time. However, with childless marriages or never-married children among the second generation, a new type of two-generation family is emerging, consisting of parents and adult children. In time, this latter group will become a one-generation family consisting of older adults with no children, ultimately leading to the extinction of a particular kinship system.

At the societal level, each generation may include subgroups with different world views or with a unique group consciousness, such as university students compared to people of the same age working in blue-collar occupations. These unique subgroups are known as **generational units** (Mannheim 1952). In some generations, there may be no generational units, or a number may form depending on the social, political, or economic circumstances of a particular historical period. For example, in North America among the youth generation of the 1960s (variously labelled the "hippie," "beat," or "counterculture" generation), it was college students rather than working-class youth who were the more radical generational unit in seeking social change. In contrast, in England, working-class youth ("punkers") were the more radical and rebellious generational unit in the youth culture of that period. In short, generational units coalesce and form around existing social characteristics, such as class, race, or ethnicity, and they are related to political or social values, beliefs, and perspectives (liberalism, conservatism, or socialism), which in turn are often class-based.

Social Processes

Three interrelated social processes are influenced by age structures and require examination: cohort analysis, generational analysis, and lineage effects. Cohort analysis refers to the use of quantitative or qualitative methods to study the characteristics of, or meanings associated with, a specific birth cohort, whether for a single year or for a five- to ten-year period, as it moves across the life course. Cohort analysis is used, as well, to study social change and stability over time. The relative size of a cohort compared to others born earlier or later shapes the experiences of its members. To illustrate, individuals born in 1961 (members of one of the largest birth cohorts) compared to persons born in 1945 experienced crowded classrooms and much more competition for a finite number of jobs when they entered the labour force.

Generational analysis involves comparing specific cohorts or groups of adjacent cohorts that comprise a generation (the baby boom and the baby bust generations) on the basis of sociohistorical experiences. This approach, at the macro-level of society, seeks to understand how cohorts maintain continuity in the existing social order or how and why they initiate change in the social order. These outcomes are known as *generational or cohort effects*. This type of generational analysis examines the influence of emerging age cohorts on the stability of social structures and considers interaction patterns within and between members of age strata. Generational analysis examines the impact on society of social consensus, conflict, change, or inequality among generations. It also examines the extent to which age stratification interacts with other dimensions of **social differentiation** and how this interaction affects individuals or society.

Generational analysis has also been used to study similarities, differences, or conflicts among generations in an extended family. Here the outcomes are known as **lineage effects**. For some family members, particularly adolescents and young adults, the influence of the family as opposed to that of the peer group, which may adhere to different values and practices, creates strain and perhaps leads to social conflict and change for society if a generational consciousness emerges. Thus, generational "conflicts" or generation "gaps" may reflect either a cohort gap across society or a lineage gap in an extended family, and become even more complicated when we compare different ethno-cultural or socio-economic groups. For example, parents' and grandparents' views about premarital sex generally conflict with those of teenagers and young adults. Are these differences due to aging effects, to different cohort values, or to a more deep-rooted difference based on changing cultural or religious values in specific extended families?

Age Grading and Age Norms

Age grading is the process by which chronological age influences elements of social life, such as social positions, roles, norms, and structured social relationships. This process results from a system of age stratification (see Chapter 5) that is present not only in the society at large but also in social groups, organizations, and institutions (O'Rand 1996, 2001, 2006). Age grades provide a cultural definition of the expected rights, behaviour, and responsibilities of an individual at a particular stage or age in the life course. These age-based cultural definitions become the basis for self-identification and for allocating positions in a society or institution.

Two types of age norms are internalized and adopted to varying degrees across the life course. *Ascriptive age norms* are based on rules and constraints determined for a specific chronological age, such as retiring at 65, voting at 18, or driving at 16. *Consensual age norms* provide an approximate age range in which specific roles or types of behaviour are appropriate or should be given up. They define the approximate age for transitional events, such as leaving home, entering the labour force, getting married, having children, or retiring. Age norms also influence lifestyle factors, including what kind of dress, language, or type of social or leisure activities are considered suitable for different ages.

Age norms provide some degree of social control and stability by constraining our behaviour in social situations ("Act your age!"). Where clearly defined norms for older people are present, and accepted, they often refer to behaviour that should be avoided at a particular age, such as dating or wearing certain styles of clothing. Obviously, age norms change over time; can be disregarded by some individuals; and vary within a cohort by class, race, gender, ethnicity, and place of residence.

Age Structures: Segregated or Integrated?

Age structures include people who are of different chronological ages and who are at different stages in the life course. The age strata are interconnected, and there are varying degrees of interaction between the strata.[3] An individual's location in the age structure influences his or her behaviour, attitudes, and values in a number of domains. Similarly, age creates behavioural expectations in structured relations with others, both within and outside the age stratum to which an individual belongs by virtue of year of birth. Some age-related expectations become institutionalized and lead to self-fulfilling prophecies and stereotypes that magnify the differences between age strata. For example, at one time it was believed that older people should "relax, retire, and cease being productive." However, today, a greater number of older people have the potential and desire to be creative and to remain productive, including as volunteers.

This need would not be fulfilled if they accepted a socially constructed age norm that expected them to "take it easy" or "disengage" after they retire.

A long-standing debate in the aging literature has been the question of whether a society and its institutions should be *age-segregated*, as university residences and nursing homes are, or *age-integrated* like families and workplaces.[4] This debate was stimulated by age stratification theory, which conceptualized society as age-segregated, and by the related question of whether an age-segregated structure stimulated or prevented age or generational conflict. Riley and Riley (1994) conceptualized two "ideal" types of social structures across the life course; one was more typical in the past (age-segregated) and one reflects the present and future structure (age-integrated). Figure 6.1 illustrates that in an age-segregated structure, different periods or stages in life were associated, in general, with specific activities or responsibilities: youth, with education; middle age, with work; and old age, with leisure. In contrast, the contemporary view is that age structures are integrated and should permit, as well as encourage, opportunities for education, work, and leisure at all ages (see chapters 10 and 11).

Over time, age-graded roles and expectations have become blurred as people of different ages interact more frequently and develop more common interests. Public policies also change the meaning and significance of age for structured relations and thereby either reduce or enhance barriers for age-based interaction (Walker 2000). Age integration has been fostered through formal intergenerational programs in which people of different ages interact frequently and thereby come to understand and respect people of other ages (Kovacs and Lee 2010; MacKenzie et al. 2011). Examples[5] include the following:

- adopt-a-grandparent programs in which young children are paired with older non-relatives in their community
- retired people serving as teaching assistants in elementary schools or as volunteers in youth after-school programs

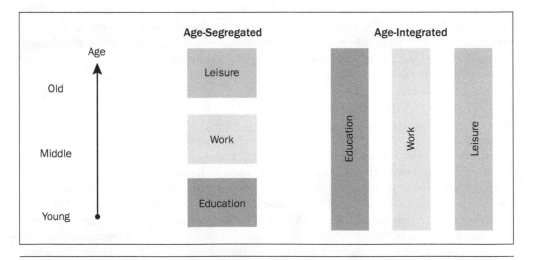

Figure 6.1 Ideal Types of Age Structures

Source: M.W. Riley and J.W. Riley, Jr (1994). Copyright © 1994. "Structural Lag: Past and Future", in Riley et. al., eds, *Age and Structural Lag*. This material is used by permission of John Wiley & Sons, Inc.

- university social work students working with a consortia of community service organizations targeting older adults to assist with mutual learning
- older people attending university classes (see Highlight 5.1, page 130)

As Hamil-Luker and Uhlenberg (2002) note, later-life educational pursuits promote age integration and increase the likelihood that older people will make a productive contribution to society, either as employees or as volunteers. However, they caution that there are still many age-related role expectations that create barriers or lead older people to believe they should not enter formal education programs. As we will learn in Chapter 11, Silver Colleges in Japan, Universities of the Third Age, and Road Scholar programs provide educational opportunities for older people, but they also reinforce an age-segregated society. In contrast, at the institutional level, many universities encourage older adults to attend age-integrated classes, where they share life experiences with young adults. Are there any older people in your classes? If so, introduce yourself, and spend some time learning from these lifelong or later-life learners.

Age Structures and Social Change

Structural Lag

Over time, there have been changes in the number of age strata, in the shape of the age structure, and in the relative prestige of positions, both in the same and in different age strata. For example, in pre-modern societies, the oldest men generally held the most prestige and power. In modern societies, with more age strata, power has shifted to middle-aged individuals. That is, social meanings based on age vary from one culture and historical period to another. To illustrate, in earlier centuries, those over 40 years of age were considered old, whereas in the twentieth century people were not defined as old until about 65 years of age. At present, the definition of old age is moving toward 70 or 80 years as life expectancy increases and the health of older people improves for most of the population. However, among Aboriginal people, because of a shorter life expectancy, "old age" may include those in their fifties.

Many policies and programs lag behind changing definitions and the changing needs of older adults. For example, because of healthier lifestyles, new programs and facilities for a healthy, active, and more heterogeneous older population are required. But they may not be available because of outdated ideas, policies, or programs. The outcome of individual or cohort needs changing faster than social values, ideas, and norms or faster than changes in institutional structures is known as structural lag, a term derived from age stratification theory (Riley et al. 1994; O'Rand 1996; Cutler and Hendricks 2001). To illustrate, in developed countries, "there is a disjuncture between opportunity structures and the capabilities of older persons, and between roles open to them and their potential contributions" (Cutler and Hendricks 2001, 465). And in developing countries, public pensions, continuing care, and health-care facilities lag far behind the needs of a rapidly increasing number of older people.

Social structures and values often lag behind changes in family values, such as the filial obligation to care for one's elderly parents, especially in Asian countries where education levels are rising quickly (Cheung and Kwan 2009). In Taiwan, Hsu et al. (2002) found that this practice was declining as children emigrated or established their own household after marriage rather than living with a parent. Adult children are much less likely to live with their aging parents than previously, and, hence, they are more likely to contribute financial support, paid household services, and emotional support. Hsu et al. (2002) quote an old Chinese proverb that expresses the new reality and a need for new policies: "nearby neighbours are better than faraway relatives." They argue that volunteer support networks and community-care systems should be established to eliminate the structural lag in caregiving. But in Taiwan, the needs of elderly people are not being met by the family or by government policies and programs, creating structural lag.

Examples of structural lag in which policies and programs for older people have not kept up with emerging needs include the following:

- few opportunities for formal education throughout life
- lack of flexible pension and retirement systems for work histories that involve many jobs, with many employers, rather than one career in the same organization
- absence of flexible work schedules and pension rights for women to recognize the time they spend on child-rearing and caregiving
- few employment options permitting both early retirement and working beyond 65 years of age
- little social support for dual-career couples who care for or help their aging parents
- absence of age-neutral policies to recognize a shift from an age-segregated society to an age-integrated society in which age structures and age norms become less important

Cohort Flow

Cohort flow is the process by which birth cohorts succeed one another over time. As cohorts pass through life, they become smaller and comprise a larger percentage of women. Each cohort experiences the life course in different ways (Uhlenberg and Miner 1996). While each cohort includes individuals with different social characteristics and experiences, all members of a cohort experience some similar events, thereby making them different from members of other cohorts—especially older or younger cohorts far removed from the trajectory of the cohort being studied.

Cohort and Generational Effects

Social structures are relatively static at specific periods in history, but over time they are changed by social conflict or by the adoption of new ideas, values, and beliefs. As a result of social change, cohorts and generations age in different ways and have the potential to introduce further social change. As noted in earlier sections, a society and the social institutions in that society are characterized by social differentiation and social stratification. At the societal level, whether there is change, and if so how much, is influenced by whether successive cohorts accept, redefine, or reject the values and status quo that preceding cohorts have institutionalized. Newer cohorts initiate change when elements of the social stratification systems are no longer considered acceptable or just. For example, when older people perceive ageism, discrimination, segregation, or isolation, they seek to change the status quo by educating others, through political processes (see Highlight 6.3), or by rebelling and no longer conforming to social expectations.

Sometimes social change involves generational conflict. This conflict may be unavoidable because members of two or more competing generations are at different stages of life, because they live during unique historical periods when competing values or conditions prevail, or because one generation experiences social inequalities that they seek to reduce or eradicate.

Highlight 6.3
Two Examples of Social Change by Older Adults

Grey Power

Political participation across the life course generally involves a low-level beginning in late adolescence, an increase through late middle-age, followed by a decrease in the post-retirement years. In recent decades, however, older adults have expanded their political consciousness and activism. Inspired by the charismatic leadership of Maggie Kuhn in the United States, who founded the Gray Panthers in 1970 (www.graypanthers.org), people over 65 in many countries began to lobby and speak out on their own behalf. Most of this activism, labelled "grey power," is focused on inadequate government policies and programs concerning such issues as taxes, old-age security systems, housing, and access to home care, drug plans, or health care.

Older political activists participate in public dialogue on radio and television, in mail and Internet messages to politicians at all levels, and in protest marches and sit-ins to bring their concerns to the attention of politicians, private-sector businesses, the media, and younger age groups. They have also formed advocacy groups to promote the needs, interests, and rights of older people (e.g., Canadian Pensioners Concerned, Canadian Association of Retired Persons' [CARP]). Governments, to seek advice, have created local, provincial, and national advisory groups (e.g., the National Seniors Council [NSC], the Senate of Canada Committee on Aging). These groups incorporate older adults in the decision-making process and/or invite them to comment on existing and possible future government policies. Older citizens do have ideas, needs, and dreams, and they must be consulted about policies, programs, or events that affect them personally, now and in the future. Visible and vocal advocacy groups sensitize governments to the important issues that affect the quality of life of middle-aged and older Canadians and help to empower "senior" voters.

Grandmothers to Grandmothers Campaign

The Stephen Lewis Foundation launched the Grandmothers to Grandmothers Campaign in March 2006, in response to the emerging crisis faced by African grandmothers as they struggled to care for millions of children orphaned by AIDS. What began with only a few groups of committed Canadian grandmothers has since evolved into a dynamic and responsive movement, made up of grandmothers and "grandothers" working to mobilize support in Canada for Africa's grandmothers.

The Campaign currently boasts more than 240 grandmother groups across the country. Many of the groups have organized into regional and national networks in order to support each other's development, fundraising and advocacy networks.

Funds from the Grandmothers Campaign are used to support African grandmothers with food, health care, school fees and school uniforms for their grandchildren, income-generating programmes, counselling, social support, essential shelter, and other necessities. Throughout Africa, grassroots organizations run by and for grandmothers are sharing insights, deepening their expertise, collaborating with other local organizations, and building their capacity to turn the tide of AIDS at community level.

Members of the Grandmothers Campaign share three goals. They work to:

Continued

- Raise funds to meet the needs of African grandmothers and the children in their care;
- Listen to African grandmothers, respect their expertise and amplify their voices, in order to promote authentic and substantive responses to the pandemic in Africa;
- Build solidarity among African and Canadian grandmothers in order to motivate and sustain the vital work of turning the tide of AIDS in Africa.

Canadian grandmother groups are tremendously active in their communities. They put on concerts, organize card tournaments, sell jewellery, and march on Parliament Hill. They visit countless schools and community organizations. They bake, cook, sew, knit, paint, write, organize cycle tours, walks, and even ride motorcycles—all to raise funds and awareness for grandmothers in sub-Saharan Africa through the Stephen Lewis Foundation.

Source: "About the Grandmothers to Grandmothers Campaign." The Stephen Lewis Foundation, www.stephen-lewisfoundation.org/get-involved/grandmothers-campaign/about-the-campaign

Generational conflict may also arise because of cohort-centrism, in which members of a cohort interpret all social or historical events from their own point of view (Morgan and Kunkel 2011). Cohort-centrism may develop an age-group consciousness and solidarity, thereby leading to possible discontinuities or conflict between age groups. Ultimately, this may lead to social or political change. Highlight 6.3 illustrates the increasing political involvement and empowerment of older age cohorts, which has resulted in social and political change.

Generations, like gender, class, race, or religion, become a common explanatory factor to account for differences among groups in a society or to explain why a society changed. Too often, changes or differences are attributed to generational succession—that is, the characteristics common to one or more older age cohorts are replaced by those of younger age cohorts. Alwin (2002), however, notes that changes in attitudes, beliefs, and behaviour result from both historical events (such as the tragic destruction and death toll in New York on September 11, 2011) and from agency, by which people change as they grow older and respond to specific social movements or historical events. Clearly, the civil rights movement in the United States and the worldwide women's movement were unique and distinctive experiences for those who were young adults at that time. These events influenced the development of unique world views among many, and these views remain an influential force as these cohorts age. But these world views also changed the lives of older cohorts, not just the lives of those in much younger cohorts.

Most studies of generational succession and social change are based on cross-sectional rather than longitudinal studies. Hence, most conclusions about the influence of generations are based on a snapshot at one time. Moreover, the specific issue or question addressed in a survey at one point in time can influence interpretations. Alwin (2002, 42) concluded that whether generational succession explains social change depends more on the issue or question that is being used to represent change.

Generation Gaps: Myth or Reality?

Is there a "generation gap" in the extended family? Or at the societal level? Or among the young, middle-aged, and older segments of the population? In the family and extended kinship system, there are likely more similarities in values, ideals, and behaviour than there are at the societal level. These similarities, despite age and gender differences, provide some continuity and stability across generations in the extended family. Structured social relations in the extended family also involve negotiation and the provision of opportunities for agency and change, especially by younger members. When intergenerational strain arises, it could lead to generation "gaps" or "inequities." To understand why this might happen, it is necessary to examine social, economic, political, and historical events, or changes in values and beliefs, that create social dissension among generations at the lineage or cohort levels. Each new generation experiences existing social institutions with a new perspective—this is the phenomenon of "fresh contact" (Mannheim 1952)—and they may or may not attempt to change social, political, or economic conditions to meet evolving needs and interests.

Lineage Gaps

Discussions between members of two or three generations in a family concerning differences in opportunities, values, rights, and behaviour can lead to action and change, or they may remain at the level of interesting or at times frustrating debates. Where a gap is *perceived* ("I don't understand my kids"; "My parents are out of date"), the size and seriousness of the gap are evaluated differently by each generation. The older generation tends to minimize the gap, arguing that it is merely due to less maturity and experience on the part of the younger generation. They also believe that any differences in music, clothes, body piercing, hairstyles, sexual activity, racial or gender equality, or political ideologies are temporary and will eventually disappear. In contrast, members of younger generations exaggerate perceived differences in values, norms, beliefs, or behaviours. They claim that members of the older generation do not understand and that middle-aged and older people interfere with their need and right to establish distinct social identities.

Conflict often occurs in immigrant families when the cultural values and experiences of different generations begin to clash. Second- or third-generation youth, socialized by parents or grandparents who were born and raised in another country, face the dilemma of having to choose between the traditional values held by older members of their family and the customs of their peers, mainstream society, and the media. In such a situation, intergenerational strain and conflict does arise in the family. However, these generational differences tend to narrow and disappear as subsequent generations become assimilated and adopt the cultural norms of mainstream Canadian society.

A perceived generation gap may be reported more frequently if different generations live together. That is, frequent daily interaction can create intergenerational disagreements, which may be seen as a generation gap. Of course, such a housing relationship can also create greater understanding and appreciation of generational differences. That is, such disagreements may be due to living arrangements and to differences in behaviour because of one's stage in the life course rather than to a real generation gap.

There appear to be three possible explanations for apparent lineage gaps in an extended family. First, differences in values and attitudes arise because generations are at different stages of development or maturation. In this situation, members of the older generation expect (or hope) that young people will grow out of their adolescent values and attitudes as they move into early adulthood. A second explanation is that differences arise because of a generational or cohort effect. Members of a particular generation, socialized at a different time in history, acquire habits, attitudes, and beliefs that are relevant to that era. A third possible explanation for generational differences is based on historical or period effects. That is, social, economic, or political events, such as a war, a major new public policy, technological advances (such as computers, cellphones, smart phones), or the election or defeat of a corrupt government, change the behaviour and beliefs of a specific generation. In this situation, even though the event has an influence on other generations, one generation may be more affected. For example, many of those who were young adults during the Depression of the 1930s have tended to be thrifty and cautious in personal financial management throughout their lives. They saved much of what they earned, and they cannot understand the consumer spending habits of their children or grandchildren.

One reason why there appear to be relatively few generational differences within the nuclear family is that conflicts tend to be resolved through daily negotiation and compromise between parents and their children. At the family level, individuals usually coexist peacefully with respect to value or behavioural differences. Tensions are more likely to develop over visible interpersonal and lifestyle matters, such as etiquette, dress, study habits, or music preferences, rather than over political or religious issues. Differences in political and religious beliefs and affiliations generate healthy debates and are often viewed as a normal and desirable part of maturing. Often, these differences between parents and children persist only during adolescence or young adulthood, although they can last a lifetime.

Societal Gaps

Any attempt to determine whether a generation gap exists at the societal level, rather than within families, must consider social class, ethnicity, educational attainment, religion, gender, and place of residence. These factors, rather than age or cohort differences, could account for major observed generational differences in society since people who have similar life experiences are more likely to share the same world view, regardless of age.

Another limitation in understanding whether generational differences exist at the societal level is the diversity in attitudes, values, beliefs, norms, and lifestyle behaviours throughout modern societies. We cannot conclude that a generation gap exists on the basis of studying only one or two of these factors, such as a specific political, religious, or sexual belief, or only one or two groups in a society. There may be a generational difference on one value dimension but not on others. Similarly, there may be differences among elements of a specific domain (politics). For example, there may be a disagreement among generations about which political party to support but agreement about the performance, positive or negative, of a current political leader or a particular government policy.

The debate continues over whether real and persistent generation gaps exist, whether there are societal or only lineage gaps, and to what extent a gap, if it exists, leads to generational conflict, social disharmony, or social change. Most of the evidence from studies that have examined both societal and lineage differences among three-generation families suggests that no significant gap exists at either the societal or lineage level (Bengtson et al. 1990, 1996). The generation gap is more imaginary than real, and there is more consensus than conflict among and between generations. If a study finds that a generation gap does exist, the gap usually centres on a specific value, belief, or behaviour. Moreover, respondents are more likely to detect a generation gap in society than within their families, often replying, "Yes, there is a generation gap, but not in my family" (Bengtson and Cutler 1976, 145).

The generation gap debate has also addressed major social change in society—in particular, the influence of technology. Highlight 6.4 presents support for this development.

Highlight 6.4
Is the Technology Generation Gap Widening?

The generation gap of technology adoption between younger and older North Americans is widening, spurred on by Gen Y's rapid integration of mobile and social technology. Based on a mail survey of nearly 43,000 consumers, in both the U.S. and Canada, the Forrester's North American Consumer Technographics Benchmark reported results for Gen Y (ages 18 to 30), Gen X (ages 31 to 44), younger boomers (ages 45 to 54), older boomers (ages 55 to 65), and seniors (age 66 and older). Gen Y and Gen X outpaced baby boomers and seniors on almost all measures of technology adoption, especially mobile technology. Among Gen Y and Gen X, 23 percent of consumers own a smart phone, while 17 percent of all ages own one of these devices, up from 11 percent one year ago. Gen Y is particularly mobile savvy: 85 percent of these consumers regularly send or receive SMS/text messages, compared with 57 percent of consumers over the age of 18; 27 percent of Gen Yers access social networks on their mobile devices, compared with 14 percent of all consumers; and 37 percent of Gen Yers access the mobile Internet, compared with 23 percent of all consumers.

"The digital attitudes and behaviors that Gen Y and Gen X are cultivating will follow them as they age and will only be multiplied in the generations that follow them," said Forrester Research consumer analyst Jacqueline Anderson. "Gen Y in particular is living and breathing a digital social life. In almost every online or mobile behavior, Gen Y leads the adoption curve. About two-thirds update or maintain a profile on a social networking site, which for them is a way to facilitate all social aspects of their lives. . . . On the other hand, Gen X is the master of maximizing the functional benefits of technology. In many activities, Gen Xers closely rival Gen Yers in adoption. For example, both spend about 17 hours online a week. But Gen Xers have mastered the art of using digital tools in a more functional manner, especially if it supports their family's needs," Anderson said.

Source: Adapted from Talent Management, "Is the technology generation gap widening?" Harvard Business School, Cambridge, Mass Sept. 26, 2010. Retrieved 6 July 2013 from http://clomedia.com/views/articles/is_the_technology_generation_gap_widening/

Based on data such as that given in Highlight 6.4, the question remains as to whether and to what extent generation gaps are widened due to the adoption of new technologies, perhaps because persons are influenced differently depending on their age of exposure and pace of adoption to these societal changes. While some degree of generational separation may occur because of the influence of technology on social relationships among age-peers, it may also bring generations together if the technologies facilitate communication and are adopted by individuals across generations. A good example of this is anecdotal reports of grandchildren and grandparents communicating through social media and other new technologies besides email.

Role Transitions

Our journey through the life course involves learning and playing a sequence of social roles, many of which interact in the family and work structures. This process of acquiring and discarding roles is often influenced by either chronological or social age norms. Some major role transitions include moving from being a student to being an employee, from being single to being married, from having children at home to having an empty nest, from being married to being divorced or widowed, and from working to being retired. At some of these transition points, rites of passage such as a wedding or a retirement party celebrate the transition. Throughout the life course, in each society or subculture, there are relatively well-accepted beliefs concerning the right age and order for such events as completing an education, leaving the parental home, entering an occupation, marrying, or retiring.

The ideal timing and sequence of events and role transitions across the life course is socially constructed (Gee 1990; Settersten and Hagestad 1996a, 1996b; Ferraro 2001; Hareven 2001; Moen 2001; Marshall and Mueller 2003; Longino and Powell 2009). Informal and formal age norms evolve to create an approximate timetable for events in key areas of social life across the life course (Foner 1996; Dannefer et al. 2009). Today, there is more room for agency and social change, with age norms viewed as flexible guidelines for the timing and order of how life trajectories might evolve. Age norms are less likely than in the past to be taken as rigid and compulsory. There are also fewer and less severe consequences if one ignores an age norm (by remaining single until age 40 or 50), skips an expected life event (a married woman who has no children), or experiences a life event in a different sequence (having children before or without being married or completing a university education in mid or late life) (Mitchell 2012).

Intergenerational Transfers

We all function in a complex web of intergenerational relationships, first in the family and later at work and in society at large (McDaniel 2002; Larkin et al. 2005; Connidis 2010; Mitchell 2012). Social order and the stability and continuation of a society, an institution, or an organization are dependent on intergenerational transfers, which are "the essence of societal reproduction, continuity, interaction and exchange" (McDaniel 1997, 2). Transfer of money, property, formal services, or "in-kind" donations (child or parent care, housework) is a long-standing tradition in family units. In developing countries, the transfer of services represents a form of mutual aid between generations, while in developed Asian countries, where filial piety is still valued, transfers often involve household labour and child care by an elderly parent in exchange for housing, money, and food (Silverstein 2006). Intergenerational transfers represent, as well, an inherent principle in a welfare state, where public transfers pay for education, health care, home care, and income assistance.

Some transfers are directed to the oldest generation; others, to the youngest. Some are compulsory, others voluntary; some apply to everyone in an age cohort, others only to those who can demonstrate need; and some are taxed while others are tax-free. McDaniel (1997, 14–15) proposed four criteria for evaluating and understanding intergenerational transfers:

1. The direction of the transfer: old to young, young to old, middle-aged to old or young. Most are downward, but some are upward.
2. The sector: public or private or both in some proportion (public pensions and an inheritance from their parents to support older people in their later years).
3. The content of the transfer: money, services, in-kind gifts, time.
4. The nature of the transfer: direct or indirect, voluntary or coerced, from the individual or family rather than from the public or the workplace, planned or unplanned, large or small.

Table 6.1	A Typology of Intergenerational Transfers		
	Receiving Generations		
	Children	Parents	Grandparents
Giving Generations			
Children			
Private	———	Social joys/continuity Community links	Social joys, continuity
Public	———	Public debt[a] Support, transfer potential	Support, transfer potential
Parents			
Private	Child support Attention, care Socialization	Security Attention, care	Attention, care Support
Public	Education Health care Transfers, i.e., social assistance, public health, etc.	Transfers, i.e., employee insurance, regional equities, social assistance, etc.	Pensions, health care Public debt[a]
Grandparents			
Private	Attention, care Bequests, gifts Values, heritage	Attention Bequests, gifts, support Values, heritage	Attention, care Pooling resources
Public	Public infrastructure Societal wealth	Public infrastructure Societal wealth	Transfers from well-off to less well-off

[a]Cremer et al. treat public debt as a transfer from children to parents, or from parents to grandparents, since they see the latter benefiting from taxes and the former paying taxes without benefiting as much from public expenditure.

Source: Adapted from Cremer et al. (1994: 218) and McDaniel (1997).

Table 6.1 illustrates the types of transfers along two dimensions: (1) upward or downward across three generations; and (2) transfers from the public (government or employer) or private (family) sectors.

Intergenerational transfers are related to the concept of "linked lives": the idea that different cohorts at the societal level and different individuals in the family are linked together over time. Over time, a social compact, if not a legal contract, emerges by which "we repay the generosity of the preceding generations by giving to our successors" (McDaniel 1997, 6).[6]

Public Transfers

Public transfers occur from the state to individuals or families. Because of the inherent inequality and diversity in intergenerational relationships (Tindale et al. 2002), changes in values and beliefs led to arguments that society's resources must be redistributed to those who are disadvantaged. Public transfers include the education system for children, adolescents, and young adults from kindergarten to the level of either an undergraduate education or specific job skills training; public pensions and, for retired people in the lower-income group, a guaranteed income supplement; and subsidies to retirees for health care, home care, institutionalized housing, and transportation. Most public transfers are funded by those currently paying taxes, including those in the labour force as well as many older adults not in the labour force.

Maintaining public transfer systems is expensive, especially in periods of population aging when the public debt or unemployment rates are high. Transfer payments lead to debates about "generational inequity" and "generational conflict" or to "apocalyptic," "catastrophic," or "voodoo-demography" warnings that the public pension and health-care systems are on the verge of bankruptcy. Individuals who pay much of the cost of supporting older people begin to question the society's guiding principles and policies. They forget, however, that someday they too will be eligible to receive such transfers and will perhaps have a greater need for them than the current cohort does. Often, these arguments are made by the more advantaged members of the society, who forget or ignore the inequalities in society as a result of race, ethnicity, age, or gender. It is these inequities, especially those based on gender and class, that are not captured fully in the intent of many public policies. Members of younger generations argue that their generation is being penalized by having to bear the cost during difficult economic times. But as McDaniel (2000) and others stress, population aging is not the cause of inequities. Rather, it reveals underlying weaknesses in the funding and coverage of safety-net policies in a welfare state undergoing retrenchment.

Concomitantly, at various periods in history, a state may question whether it can still afford its various transfer systems. This raises the question: what is the right balance of public (a public issue) versus private (a private trouble) responsibilities and transfers? In recent years, the boundary between public and private transfers has become blurred as adjustments to financial support are made. When this debate emerges, the state looks for ways to offload costs or services to the family, for example, through home care for the elderly rather than hospitalization or institutionalized housing.

Private Transfers

In many traditional, pre-industrial societies, private transfers in the family took place when land was passed to the eldest son and when the eldest son (or daughter) took care of aging parents in return for housing or some other component of wealth. When the state reduces its transfer of resources to the family or older individuals, there is a need for more private transfers within family units. Today, intergenerational family transfers involve caregiving and care receiving, as well as financial transfers and housing. Caregiving transfers primarily involve time and work, rather than money, and are usually one-way, from parents to young children or from adult children to aging parents (Martin-Matthews 2000; Connidis 2010; Mitchell 2012).

Transfers begin in childhood when parents or grandparents give the children gifts, money, or opportunities, such as music lessons, trips, or participation in competitive sports. The practice continues with encouragement and financial support to attend university, financial assistance for the purchase of a car or home, and the inheritance of accumulated wealth when the grandparents and parents die.

In a study of why and how older people make financial transfers in the family, Ploeg et al. (2003) found that the oldest generation provides funds to grandchildren primarily for education (in the form of cash or RESPs), discretionary spending, or trips; and to adult children for the purchase of a home or car, a wedding, living expenses, trips, or cash for spending or investing. Many transfers are made either at a time of need (a divorce, an illness, or unemployment) or in relation to a major life-course transition (marriage, purchase of a first home, birth of a child, or entry to post-secondary education). Transfers are more likely to be made by an older married couple than by a widow and when there are enduring, stable, and high-quality relationships in the extended family.

In the family unit, transfers have the potential to maintain relative economic advantage from one generation to the next or to facilitate higher standards of living than those experienced by earlier generations. But there is also the potential for conflict if some or all members of a younger generation do not receive transfers, or equal transfers, and if they harbour feelings of resentment (Connidis 2010). This situation occurred in earlier times when the eldest son or the first-born child inherited the land while his or her siblings were left to fend for themselves. The inability of parents to leave enough wealth to all their children, or their failure to do so, was one reason for the creation of almshouses, homes for the elderly, and a public pension system and for immigration by children to other countries.

Generational Equity at the Societal Level

Most discussions of **generational equity** are linked to economic fears generated by apocalyptic demography (see chapters 1 and 4). Issues in this debate were raised in a *Globe and Mail* article entitled "A Generation Bequeaths a Terrible Mess to the Next" (Simpson 1997, A14). The article stated that people under 65 pay significantly more into the Canada Pension Plan than did the oldest generation, which now receives what is perceived to be a generous pension from the plan. The article also pointed to inequity in that those in the middle-aged and oldest cohorts created large government deficits and debt, which would have to be reduced or eliminated by subsequent generations. Similarly, other sources allege that the elderly receive a disproportionate share of public resources for income maintenance, health care, and social services—at the expense of younger members of society (Kohli 2005, 2006). But as McDaniel (2000) noted, population aging is only a triggering event for this discussion, not its essence. The generational equity debate—about how to achieve equity, whether equity can be achieved, and whether there should be equity among generations—is really about fairness in the distribution of scarce public resources across a society and about how to finance transfers, such as income assistance, health care, and subsidies, to needy individuals (Williamson et al. 1999). This debate is also about ensuring justice among age groups and generations (Kohli 2006; Holstein 2010).

Over time, an informal or formal intergenerational "social contract" emerges, which assumes that generations with relatively common expectations and obligations work together to ensure solidarity, support, and an orderly generational succession across the life course. In this way, regardless of stage in life, generations are treated equally in terms of their economic, social, and political needs, especially in later life when some members have greater needs. The ideal world is a "win-win" situation in which both children and older adults receive the support they need. Later, in Chapter 12, we will see this issue re-emerge when we discuss whether public policies and programs should be based on automatic entitlement or evidence of need.

With the onset of population aging, increasing concern has been expressed about the loss of generational equity—for a number of reasons:

- the rising cost of health and elder care, which will have to be borne by younger generations
- a decline in the economic status of many young people owing to high unemployment and underemployment

- the unequal distribution of wealth, which favours a small segment of the middle and oldest generations
- public policies that give more to members of one generation than to others—such as tax deductions for retirees and lower fares for older people on public transit
- a shift in government policy in which responsibility for social welfare and health care has changed from being a "public issue" to a "private trouble"

In recent years, each of these issues has been magnified by escalating government deficits and debts. Some argue that these debts can be eliminated as follows:

- if those now in the labour force pay higher taxes than previous workers (the retirees)
- if higher tax rates are imposed on those over 65 for their accumulated wealth and for entitlement to pensions and income supplements they "earned" earlier in life
- if governments reduce services or make them more efficient
- if a combination of these approaches is applied

These policy changes could trigger charges of unfairness on the part of those most affected by them. Specifically, there has been a growing feeling among younger generations that the benefits older people receive from publicly funded programs are disproportionate to their current or past contributions or to their real need. Their opinions include the following:

- Eligibility for social benefits should be based on need, not on attaining a certain age.
- Tax-sharing responsibilities are shifting too fast from older to younger groups.
- Other groups in society, such as single mothers and the homeless, have a greater need for public benefits or services than do older people.
- Too many older Canadians are wealthy, greedy, and uncaring.

Generational equity continues to be debated in Canada as part of a discussion of changes in intergenerational relations and public policy that are needed to address population aging, both of which are complex issues. Foot and Venne (2005) predict that generational equity will become an even more prominent subject of debate in Canada as our population ages. Apocalyptic demography is often invoked in these debates to justify shifting responsibility for transfers from the public to the private domain (Gee 2000). At the same time, there is insufficient recognition of past intergenerational contributions by older people at the family and societal level. There is also a need to recognize contributions among older generations in the form of volunteerism and other helping activities directed at younger generations, a process known as generativity (see Chapter 3) (Valliant 2007).

Insufficient effort goes into ensuring that society's resources are more equitably distributed, taking into account the differences in class, gender, age, race, and ethnicity in the total population. Consequently, scholars and public policy–makers continue to monitor intergenerational relations, and the possible effect of public policies on these relations, to identify structural inequities and the generation they affect, and to change policies to ensure that the needs of all generations are met equitably. Kohli (2006) introduced the concept of "intergenerational interdependence," in opposition to the idea of generational equity, as the ideal goal through which burden-sharing and solidarity among the generations may be realized. Perhaps the concept of interdependence will dominate public-policy debates in future decades, thereby reducing or eliminating the ideas of conflict and equity.

Summary

This chapter, using cohort and generational analyses drawn from the age stratification and life-course theories, examined the influence of the social structure and a number of social processes on aging and the status of older people. Lifelong social or economic differentiation is important in understanding the situation and status of older people, especially women and members of disadvantaged groups.

Chronological age, which influences an individual's location and status in society and in specific social institutions, is one criterion for entering and leaving social positions. Laws based on chronological age impose responsibilities, prescribe eligibility for benefits or programs, and influence our life chances and lifestyles (Kotash 2004). In an age stratification system, age-based norms provide cultural definitions of the expected rights, appropriate behaviours, and responsibilities of individuals at particular times in their lives. To some extent, these norms regulate individual thought and behaviour and social interactions. And they help to define when life events should occur and in what order. But there are few age-related norms to guide the behaviour of older people. The few norms that do exist usually specify what behaviour should be avoided after a particular chronological age.

When they do exist, cohort, generational, and lineage gaps often lead to social change. It is likely that as the baby boomer generation ages, members' experiences with social change will be reflected in their level of social activism and social participation. Older baby boomer women, in particular, may be active in effecting change in society due to their exposure to the cultural changes of the 1960s/70s and their higher levels of education and material resources compared to previous generations of older women.

A generation gap, especially in extended families, appears to be more imaginary than real. There is little empirical evidence to support the existence of a generation gap at either the societal (cohort) or family (lineage) level of analysis. When a cohort or generation gap is noted, however, it tends to be at the societal level and to involve specific values, beliefs, or behaviours. When lineage differences are observed, they are often related to lifestyle and developmental issues among the youngest generation, many of which disappear with the transition to early adulthood. Increasingly, scholars and public-policy personnel are concerned with the emergence of issues surrounding the creation and perpetuation of generational equity or intergenerational interdependence.

For Reflection, Debate, or Action

1. Find two or three situations in your social world where age interacts with class, gender, ethnicity, or race to disadvantage some members of society. How would you eliminate these disadvantages to render aging a more equitable process?

2. Identify possible sources of structural lag in your social world, and suggest how the lag might be reduced or eliminated.

3. Debate whether, why, and in what way there is a generation gap in your family and/ or in society in general.

4. Identify ascribed and achieved attributes that create unequal access to opportunities in your world. In what instances might an older person have more opportunities than the younger person, and when might an older person have fewer opportunities?

5. Think about the generations in your extended family, and describe any differences in behaviour, attitudes, or beliefs that you could attribute to aging or cohort effects.

6. Interview someone from another generation in your family, and ask their opinion about the younger generation's beliefs, values, and lifestyle and about their taste in movies, music, and dress. Do their responses differ from your views, and if so, how? Why do you think there are differences, if any?

7. Debate whether it is reasonable and fair to use age as a criterion in legislation, laws, public policies, or public programs.

Notes

1. For a discussion of gender, see Matthews 1979; Gee and Kimball 1987; Hendricks 1993; Thompson 1994; Nichols and Leonard 1994; McMullin 1995, 2000, 2004, 2010; Moen 1996, 2001; Arber and Ginn 1995, 2005; Calasanti 1999; Hatch 2000; Kimmel 2000; Worell et al. 2000; Calasanti and Slevin 2001; Sinnott and Shifren 2001; Arber et al. 2004; Estes 2005; Moen and Spencer 2006; van den Hoonaard 2007; Connidis 2010; Ven et al. 2011.

2. A specific label may apply to only one generation throughout history, although the label may not apply in all societies to those who belong to that generation. That is, particular social or historical conditions may not occur in all societies at the same time, or ever, and the historical conditions (e.g., the Depression, the sexual revolution, the feminist revolution) that spawned the generation may never occur again.

3. For a discussion of age strata, see Foner 2000; Riley and Riley 2000; Uhlenberg 2000; and Walker 2000.

4. Interaction among people of different ages can be measured or classified according to frequency, duration (how long it lasts), equality (whether it is one-way or two-way), quality, intimacy (the nature of the topic discussed), complexity, and outcome (co-operation, conflict, or consensus).

5. For specific examples of intergenerational programs, see *Journal of Intergenerational Relationships*.

6. This discussion is based on the political economy perspective and exchange theory as described in Chapter 5.

7

Health Status and Health-Care Transitions

The seeds of healthy aging are sown early.

— Kofi Annan

Focal Points and Key Facts

- What is health and what constitutes good health?
- What models of health and health care are used or could be used in Canada?
- Are older persons becoming healthier over time? Are the baby boomers healthier than prior generations?
- Are health and health behaviours influenced by perceptual, cultural, lifestyle, and social structural factors?
- Does an inability to cope with change and stress in later life, including a decline in physical health, lead to mental-health problems?
- Will older people destroy the health-care system because of their increasing numbers and overuse?
- Approximately 43 per cent of persons 65 and over have a disability.
- In 2011, about 57 per cent of older adults had two or more chronic conditions; in 2011, the most common illnesses among older adults living in the community included arthritis (44.4 per cent), hypertension (49.5 per cent), heart disease (19 per cent), diabetes (17.1 per cent), chronic obstructive pulmonary disease (COPD) (7.5 per cent), and asthma (7.3 per cent).
- In Canada, about 8 per cent of persons aged 65 and over and about one in three aged 85 and over have mild, moderate, or severe dementia.
- Between 10 and 20 per cent of older adults are diagnosed with mild to severe depression.
- About 40 per cent of hospital days are used by the 5 per cent of patients who are hospitalized for more than 30 days. Of these patients, two-thirds are 75 years of age and over.
- Canada spends only 15 per cent of its public funds for long-term care on home care, whereas the Netherlands, France, and Denmark spend 32 per cent, 43 per cent, and 73 per cent, respectively.

Introduction: What Is Health?

Health is a multi-dimensional concept involving interrelationships among a number of dynamic human processes, social structures, and social policies, including the following:

- individual genetic, biological, physical, psychological, and social dimensions
- the social and physical environment
- lifestyles (health behaviours)
- the health-care system (medical care by physicians and in hospitals)
- public policies and private insurance plans concerning coverage, payment, and access

The World Health Organization (WHO) broadly defines good **health** as the absence of symptoms of illness or signs of disease; the presence of well-being and a sense of being healthy (or not ill or sick); and the capacity to perform activities of daily living (ADLs) and to function with some degree of independence. There are many excellent discussions of the meaning and measurement of health and its various components.[1] Illness is both a subjective experience and a personal and professional assessment of symptoms. Subjective feelings and experiences are important when reporting self-perceptions of health in social surveys ("Do you rate your health as excellent, good, fair, or poor?") and when reacting to and coping with an apparent change in one's health ("Has your health changed over the last year and in what way?"). Professional assessments and diagnostic tests of symptoms usually result in a diagnosis of disease that can be termed *acute* or *chronic*.[2] Faced with symptoms, we have many possible courses of action. Do we treat them ourselves (via self-care) with rest, home remedies, or over-the-counter drugs? Do we seek advice from family and friends? Do we visit a health-care specialist, such as a physician, pharmacist, therapist, psychologist, psychiatrist, or geriatrician (physician specialist in aging)? Do we visit a health-care clinic or a hospital's emergency department? Do we seek out complementary or alternative therapies, such as chiropractic, acupuncture, or massage? Or do we decide to change our health behaviour through exercise, diet, or decreased smoking or drinking?

Health and illness are processes that have causes and consequences across the life course. Stability and change in health is not just a biological or medical process. Rather, health is a significant social process that involves the interaction of agency (decisions made or not made about health and lifestyle matters), personal history (heredity, personality, and lifestyles), social conditions (our place in the social structure, environmental factors, where we live, and our social networks and social relations), and the social construction of health (George 2003; Segall and Fries 2011). The concept of **health transitions** captures this dynamic interplay between individual and structural factors that shape our health as we age, sharing many of the same tenets of life-course theory (see Chapter 5). Our health perceptions also shape these transitions in that many older adults see their own health in a more positive light than others do.

The incidence of acute and chronic illness varies as individuals move through life, and how older adults react to illness, frailty, and impending death varies greatly. Some older people experience chronic health problems in their sixties, others not until well into their eighties. For most older adults, however, the longer they live, the greater their risk of experiencing chronic diseases and physical or cognitive impairments. In later life, there is variation in the **incidence** (rate of new cases), **prevalence** (current rate), and progression of diseases and disability states, such as arthritis, rheumatism, hypertension, strokes, cancers, cardiovascular disease, diabetes, osteoporosis, Parkinson's disease, and Alzheimer's disease. At some point, these conditions, especially if there is **comorbidity** (more than one condition at the same time), may lead to decreased functional capacity and loss of independence; decreased well-being; isolation; stigmatization as frail, sick, dependent, or disabled; and the need to move from one's home to a long-term-care facility.

Models of Health and Health Care

There are several interrelated models of health and health care in Canada. Like the theoretical models of aging discussed earlier, these models are not completely distinct from one another. Rather, they are ideal types. Furthermore, there are variants of each of these models. The *medical* model dominated our thinking, especially when life expectancy was shorter and disability rates among older adults were higher. This approach focuses on the incidence, causes, and treatment of disease, and the emphasis is on treating or curing health problems with surgery, drugs, bed rest, rehabilitation, or, for elderly patients, moving them to a facility offering 24-hour nursing care. This model perpetuates the idea that health status is caused by physiological and biological systems. It has been criticized for "over-medicalizing" people—making them too dependent on formal health care when they should be taking greater control of their own health and illness and using community services and clinical health care services. Illich (1977), for example, discusses several types of **medical iatrogenesis**—illness that is induced by the medical system (unnecessary surgery such as a hysterectomy, the negative impact of over-prescribing drugs, blood transfusions that may carry serious infections, and other health problems caused by health professionals or a stay in a hospital). Another outcome of this medical model has been the perpetuation of negative images of aging—that later life is a time of decay, inactivity, frailty, dependence, and incompetence.

The *social* model of health care builds on the medical model. It views health as having a social (one's socio-economic status or social support network), psychological (stress), physiological, biological, and genetic basis. This model stresses the role of agency in health decisions, self-care, and any changes in health behaviours and beliefs. Thus, it places more emphasis on prevention and less on drugs, surgery, and hospital stays. The model also includes a continuum of care in which health care and social services are provided in homes, in the community, and in residential facilities so that the "right services, in the right place, at the right time" can be delivered to older people as their health and support needs change (Stephenson and Sawyer 2002, 3). The idea is to ensure that a safety net is in place to prevent older people from "falling through the cracks" as they might in a fragmented system of service delivery. Proponents of the social model maintain that the medical model is only one part of the system and that an integrated model of health-care delivery is more efficient, especially for frail elders, since it connects appropriate health and community services with individual needs through a comprehensive case management system by a multi-disciplinary health team (Béland et al. 2006; Hébert et al. 2010). However, the social model has been criticized, mainly by members of the medical profession, as being an unnecessary and largely ineffective "add-on" to the medical model. There are studies that indicate the opposite (see "Integrated Models of Care Delivery" later in this chapter). Unfortunately, we do not have adequate research evidence to evaluate many aspects of the model.

An offshoot of the social model is the *health promotion* model (HPM), which promotes healthy behaviours by targeting individuals or groups in a community or across a society (Epp 1986). Developed within Health Canada, the HPM is aimed at achieving health for all Canadians by (1) addressing health challenges (reducing inequalities, increasing prevention, and enhancing people's ability to cope); (2) supporting the mechanisms of health promotion (improving health knowledge, self-care, mutual aid, and healthy environments); and (3) implementing community strategies (fostering public participation, strengthening community health services, and coordinating healthy public policy). This model seeks to empower people and communities and to foster equal access to health-care resources. The HPM also recognizes the impact of the physical environment (pollution, occupational hazards), which tends to be outside the control of the individual.

An extension of the HPM is the *population health model* (PHM), which was developed in the 1990s in response to a growing interest in identifying determinants of health (see below). The HPM and PHM have been combined into the *population health promotion model* (PHPM). Hamilton and Bhatti (1996) developed this three-dimensional model based on health policy and health practice, which includes (1) the determinants of health (income and social status, social support networks, education, working conditions, physical environment, biology and genetics, personal health practices, child development, and health services); (2) health promotion strategies (strengthening community action, building healthy public policy, creating supportive environments, developing personal skills, and reorienting health services); and (3) the different service levels that are needed (society, sector/system, community, family, and individual). The model identifies key domains and mechanisms of change and places them within a health policy/institutional framework. It can be used to identify priority areas for promoting and facilitating healthy aging.

As a result of a number of major government reports (Lalonde 1974; Epp 1986; Hamilton and Bhatti 1996; Romanow Commission 2002) and the research of many health scholars in Canada and abroad, there has been a gradual shift to an integrated population health and health promotion model that conceives healthy aging as the culmination of life choices and life chances that occur against the backdrop of a changing society. Health transitions at the individual level, as well as population health, require consideration of micro (individual), meso (policy), and macro (structural) forces, sometimes referred to as the "determinants of health." To further explore the complex interrelationships between health and aging, we address two fundamental questions about the mid-life and older populations in the following two sections.

Is the Older Population Healthier over Time?

The research community generally believes that the health of older people, on average, is improving in most industrialized societies because of advances in nutrition, in environmental and housing conditions, in health promotion, and in health care (Segall and Fries 2011). In particular, life expectancy has been steadily rising, making the likelihood of individuals reaching their 90th and 100th birthday more common (Wister and Wanless 2007; Perls 2012). The average life expectancy of Canadians now exceeds 80 years when males and females are considered together, although women still outlive men by about four years. There is disagreement, however, over whether or not extension of life has occurred mainly because of **morbidity compression**[3]—the tendency for the onset of disease in later life to be compressed into a shorter period at the end of life (Fries 1983). If this compression is taking place, then people are living longer with an extended period of good health, and future cohorts of elderly persons might use fewer health-care resources.

While compression of morbidity has been supported by a number of researchers (Fries 1983, 2003; Hubert et al. 2002; Crimmins 2004; Mor 2005; Manton et al. 2006; Wolf et al. 2007; Manton 2008; Keefe et al. 2012), other studies have shown a worsening of health over time among older adults (Roos et al. 1993; Parker et al. 2005). This health paradox is probably due to the fact that health status is complex and is measured in a variety of ways, with different research designs and different sets of underlying causal factors, and that it is examined in different populations (some studies ignore those living in institutions) and in different health systems (Wister 2005; Parker and Thorslund 2007). How do we resolve this health conundrum to ensure that effective policies and practices are developed *and* implemented to benefit future cohorts of aging Canadians?

It is well known that as age increases, the likelihood of disability and activity restriction also increase among older adults. Hogan et al. (1999) found that 75 per cent of those 85+ had a functional disability, which increased to 89 per cent among those surviving five years to 90 and over. Statistics Canada (2007) reported that 43.4 per cent of persons 65+ in 2006 experienced restrictions in their daily activities, up from 40.5 per cent in 2001 (Statistics Canada 2002a). The rate for persons 75+ was 56.3 per cent. To further examine whether disability rates are increasing over time among older adults, the **disability-free life expectancy** (also known as healthy life expectancy) measure is frequently used to estimate the average number of years of life remaining (at a given age) without disability. Most research finds an increase in disability-free life expectancy in a number of countries, including Canada, the United States, and France (Robine et al. 1998; Crimmins and Saito 2001; Manuel and Schultz 2001; Wilkins et al. 2001; Manton 2008). This trend implies that as people live longer, they are also free of disability for longer periods before death, suggesting that there is a **compression of disability** rather than a more general compression of morbidity, or at least of all morbidities.

Recent research has also discovered a delayed onset of severe disability but that the rates of recovery from severe disability are decreasing (Wolf et al. 2007). That is, people are experiencing severe disability much later in life, but once they experience it, the chance of recovery has declined, as might be expected. Parker and Thorslund (2007) confirm that while disability measures (usually measured as an inability to carry out day-to-day tasks) show improvement, there is a concurrent pattern of increasing chronic conditions and functional impairments (defined as health components that require health-care resources). For society, a compression of disability may be accompanied by an expansion of other health problems that place greater demands on limited health-care resources (Mor 2005; Keefe et al. 2012). Clearly, the relationship between disease and disability has become more complex over time. A reduction in reported disability over time may, in part, be the consequence of better support systems (see Chapter 12) and environmental designs (see Chapter 8) that enhance independence, or of a more effective and/or efficient medical system.

Acute conditions, many of which are treatable with drugs, therapy, or surgery, occur less frequently than chronic conditions among older adults. But when acute conditions do emerge among older adults, they often require a longer period of recovery than they do for younger people, and when these conditions combine with a chronic illness or frailty, they deplete the older person's physical or mental capacity to adapt or function.

Most people experience one or more chronic illnesses at some time in their lives, and Statistics Canada (2012) estimates that approximately 57 per cent of older adults have two or more chronic conditions.[4] As shown in Figure 7.1, which is based on the 2011 Canadian Community Health Survey, the most common chronic illnesses among older adults living in the community include arthritis (44.4 per cent), hypertension (49.5 per cent), heart disease (19 per cent), diabetes (17.1 per cent), chronic obstructive pulmonary disease (COPD) (7.5 per cent), and asthma (7.3 per cent). The major causes of death in Canada are coronary heart disease, cancer, strokes, and respiratory system diseases. There is a perception that a new emphasis on public health has lowered the prevalence of disease among older persons (65+) over the past several decades. However, a rise in certain chronic diseases (diabetes, high blood pressure, and dementia) has been shown by using national data (Statistics Canada 1999a, 2012) (see Figure 7.1). Thus, while there appears to be a compression of disability, the incidence or prevalence of many disease states is not declining as the population ages. As elaborated in the next section, this may be due to actual changes in health conditions over time or to changes in the efficiency of diagnosing diseases through an improved health-care system, or a combination.

Is the Mid-Life Population Healthier over Time?

Are persons in mid-life today more or less healthy than those in previous generations? The answer to this question may shed light on health patterns for future cohorts of older persons. Among Canadians aged 45 to 64, there were significant decreases between recent decades in the prevalence of arthritis/rheumatism, hypertension, heart disease, and bronchitis/emphysema

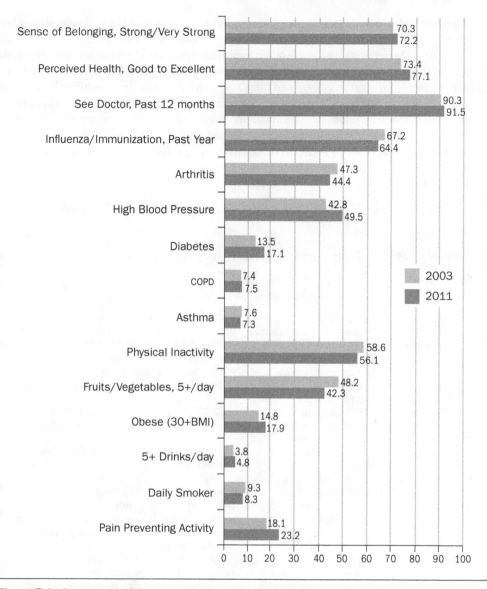

Figure 7.1 Percentage of Persons 65+ Reporting Selected Health Indicators, Canada, CCHS 2003 and 2011

Source: Adapted from Statistics Canada, 2012 (CANSIM Tables 105-0501).

(Statistics Canada 1999b; Wister 2005). But there were significant increases in the prevalence of diabetes, asthma, and migraine headaches. Thus, trends among various diseases appear to differ depending on the type of illness under investigation and the age group studied. Another unanswered question is whether the decreased incidence of specific diseases among mid-life persons will be sustained into old age, or whether the onset of some of these conditions will merely be delayed.

Significant changes in the health-care system have occurred over the past several decades. On the one hand, pharmacological treatments may have improved the control of some chronic conditions (e.g., hypertension). On the other, improved screening and more accurate diagnosis of illnesses (such as breast and prostate cancer) may contribute to the increased prevalence of certain diseases (Martin et al. 2009). And there has been substantial growth in the health-care industry, suggesting that fewer illnesses are going undetected and untreated. Also, because of more effective health promotion, individuals are more aware of disease symptoms than ever before, prompting visits to health-care professionals. Highlight 7.1 addresses how the baby boomers are aging, which may hold part of the answer to questions about the immediate future of our health-care system.

Highlight 7.1
Are the Baby Boomers Healthier Than Previous Generations?

The front edge of this generation turned 65 in 2011, beginning a rapid rise in population aging. Will the baby boomers be healthier than previous generations? Wister (2005, 2009) demonstrates that the baby boomers' rates of smoking and unhealthy exercise (defined as exercise that is below the minimum recommended level) is about 40 per cent lower than the rates for persons who were their age about 26 years earlier or a generation apart (comparing 1978/79 and 2005 data). As well, their rate of heavy drinking is lower by half. However, obesity rates among boomers have doubled in just over two decades—increasing to 15.5 per cent in 2005 from 8.2 per cent in 1985. Further analyses indicate that obesity rates have increased steadily to 22 per cent in 2011 for the baby boomers (Statistics Canada 2012).

In addition, baby boomers report a significantly higher rate of chronic illnesses overall in 2005 compared to persons of the same age in 1978/79, a higher rate of hypertension, and more than twice the rate of diabetes, as well as an approximately 60 per cent increase in consulting a doctor three or more times a year. Research also shows that these individuals use prescription drugs significantly more than the previous generation at their age. These findings suggest that baby boomers are experiencing more complex health patterns and are more medicalized than the previous generation.

One major conclusion is that regardless of whether baby boomers will have more or less illness or disability as they age, the health and illness landscape is changing. For instance, diseases and conditions that are associated with diabetes are going to rise as baby boomers age, whereas those associated with smoking will decline. Also, cognitive dementia, for which there are few treatments, appears to be increasing in prevalence. This suggests the need for a health-care system that is flexible and can be both proactive and reactive with respect to acute and chronic illness as well as in the prevention of illness. Furthermore, expectations of the health-care system developed by boomers over their life course may be as important as actual health status in determining future utilization patterns. These expectations stem from baby boomers' tendency to have greater health knowledge than prior generations, more experience with bureaucracies, and a stronger sense of entitlement, partly due to paying higher taxes over their life course.

Source: Adapted from Wister 2005 and 2009.

Increasing Longevity and Centenarians

Researchers frequently study centenarians (persons who reach 100) to help unlock the mystery of youthfulness and longevity. The rapid rise in their numbers (5825 in 2011, a 25 per cent increase since 2006) is redefining aging (Perls 2012). Coles (2004) contends that the maximum human lifespan, the highest potential age we can attain under ideal conditions, is approximately 125 years. The oldest person on record was 122 years of age at the time of her death (see Chapter 1). Longevity is attributed to genetic predisposition and biomarkers (Perls et al. 2002; Evert et al. 2003; Gruenewald et al. 2006), healthy lifestyles, social involvement and connectedness, and exposure to particular environments (Stessman et al. 2005; Wister and Wanless 2007; Butler 2008). The increase in survival into and beyond 100 years is due to a reduction in mortality among octo-genarians (those in their eighties) and nonagenarians (people in their nineties) (Vaupel and Jeune 1995). Some researchers argue that centenarians possess no particular "secret." Rather, they may be extreme cases in their cohort who aged later, developed chronic diseases later in life, and/or have milder forms of these diseases (Jeune 2000). However, in all likelihood, there are combinations of genetic, lifestyle, and environmental factors that enhance an individual's ability to reach advanced ages. According to Evert et al. (2003), evidence suggests that there may be multiple routes and phenotypes to longevity, such as *survivors* (those who experience an age-related illness before age 80 but make it to 100+); *delayers* (those who do not experience an illness until after age 80 and make it to 100+); and *escapers* (those who reach 100 without experiencing an age-related disease). There are also pockets of extreme longevity found around the world. Highlight 7.2 describes three communities in which large proportions of the population are centenarians.

Highlight 7.2
Secrets to Longevity

Three different communities in very different parts of the world have high numbers of centenarians. One of these hotspots for longevity (called "blue zones") is in Sardinia, Italy, especially in the mountain communities, where some of their longevity secrets include walking and working outdoors at high altitudes, drinking red wine in moderation, sharing work burdens within families, and eating a Mediterranean diet (see "Nutrition, Weight, and Obesity" later in this chapter), including foods high in omega-3 fatty acids. More male than female centenarians are found in that region, which may occur because the older men engage in more physical activities than the older women.

Some of the oldest people in the world have been found in Okinawa, Japan. Their lifestyle includes maintaining lifelong friendships, eating small food portions comprised mainly of rice, fish, and vegetables, and finding purpose in life.

The third location is Loma Linda, California, home to many Seventh-Day Adventists. These people have a diet high in nuts and beans, they observe the Sabbath, and they exhibit strong spirituality and community connectedness.

The three communities have many commonalities that may be linked to longevity. None of the communities have high rates of smoking; they all highly value and are socially engaged with their family, friends, and community; they are physically active every day; and they eat plenty of fruits and vegetables. Although good genes play a role in long and healthy lives, much of the secret to longevity lies in adopting and maintaining healthy lifestyles.

Sources: Adapted from *National Geographic*, November 2005; Poulin 2001.

Dimensions of Health and Illness

Health status influences both the quality and the quantity of life. How an individual reacts and adapts to declining health, including a major disability or a terminal illness, may have more influence on the quality of life than the illness per se. For this reason, we must understand all the factors associated with **morbidity** and with the reaction to an illness in later life: the *personal* factors (adaptation to stress and pain and coping strategies); the *social* factors (the availability of a support system); the *structural* factors (gender, age, class, and ethnicity); and the *cultural* factors (ethnic/religious health beliefs and medical practices).

Living with Illness and Disability

The influence of a disease or an illness on an older person varies greatly, depending on the illness's severity and duration, the individual's coping mechanisms, and the availability and use of social support, health care, and adaptive devices. Most acute illnesses involve only temporary restrictions or changes in lifestyle. However, chronic conditions, which range from minor aches and pains to a long-term physical or mental disability, often restrict social interaction, mobility, the ability to care for oneself, and the fulfillment of family responsibilities. This is particularly problematic when individuals face more than one chronic condition, known as comorbidity or multiple morbidity.

Furthermore, more serious chronic condition(s) act as a barrier to engaging in healthy lifestyles. Older adults experiencing the onset of chronic illness do not adopt new changes to health behaviours, such as increased physical activity, reduced drinking, or improved diet, although smoking cessation is more frequent as is maintaining health behaviours among those who have engaged in them over their life course (Newsom et al. 2012). Highlight 7.3 illustrates some of the health challenges facing older adults.

Activity limitation or "an impairment" represents the loss of physical capacity (e.g., hearing, vision, use of the legs) or of mental capacity and typically requires the use of health-care resources (Moore and Rosenberg 1997; Parker and Thorslund 2007). If sufficiently severe, an impairment becomes a disability that prevents the person, partially or totally, from performing activity related to work, leisure, or personal care. Multiple impairments, or comorbidities (often connected to an index disease—i.e., one that is the primary interest of the health researcher, such as diabetes), result in increasing vulnerability and perhaps in the person being labelled as "frail" (Hogan et al. 2003). Trajectories in ADL disability (difficulty in performing the activities of daily life) have been shown to be variable over time. However, a sudden increase in disability is often predictive that some type of institutionalization will follow in a few months (Li 2005). Unfortunately, disability is increasingly viewed as a form of dependence and frailty and is linked to old age and, consequently, to the perpetuation of negative stereotypes about aging. This suggests the need for a reconceptualization of disability (Stone 2003) and an examination of "living well" and positive adaptive strategies (Zarit et al. 2004). In later life, pain from arthritis, osteoporosis, diabetes, angina, cancer, or muscular and joint trauma restricts social, physical, or mental activities. Pain, and drugs taken to reduce pain, can disturb sleep, suppress appetite, and cause depression, drowsiness, and unclear thinking. Above all, pain influences mobility, social interaction, subjective health, well-being, and quality of life (Zarit et al. 2004).

Highlight 7.3
Health Challenges in Later Life

Vignette 1

A 64-year-old woman had a major stroke eight months ago, causing paralysis of her right side. She is unable to get out of bed and into her wheelchair or onto the toilet without physical assistance. Her 71-year-old husband, who has some minor health problems, finds it difficult to help her and is only just managing. Also, he is having trouble coping emotionally with seeing his wife in such a weak condition. Their only source of income is the government old age pension, so they are unable to afford private help.

Vignette 2

An 81-year-old widow, managing well on her own despite arthritis in her hips that limited her mobility, fell and broke her left hip, which required an operation. She was sent to a convalescent hospital where she received physiotherapy. Despite recovering quite well, she has not been able to regain her previous level of function. The staff at the hospital is considering discharging her, but they are uncertain whether she will be able to cope unassisted in her own apartment. She is unable to afford a private nursing home, and the waiting time for a publicly funded facility is at least six months. She cannot stay in the hospital that long, so other arrangements must be made.

Vignette 3

A 76-year-old man with Alzheimer's disease lives with his wife in an apartment where a community nurse visits him every week. He has no understanding of his illness and gets upset, and at times aggressive, when anyone tries to get him to do something against his will. He tends to get more agitated at night and has trouble sleeping. He has reached the stage where he requires supervision for most activities and cannot safely be left alone for any length of time.

His wife, who is 72 years old, is in reasonable physical health but is becoming exhausted because of the demands of having to take care of her husband. She is unable to get a good night's sleep and cannot rest during the day because she is afraid her husband will wander and get into trouble.

Source: Wolfson et al. 1993. Reprinted by permission of The Gerontological Society of America.

Self-Perceptions of Health and Health Beliefs

The prevalence of serious, chronic health conditions increases with age, and between 70 and 90 per cent of adults 65 years of age and over report having at least one chronic illness, activity limitation, or mobility limitation. In addition, although disability related to mobility affects about 2 per cent of persons aged 15 to 24, about half of those aged 75+ are so affected (Statistics Canada 2007). Yet numerous surveys (in this case the 2011 Canadian Community Health Survey) have found that the majority (about 77.1 per cent) of older people say that they are "well" or that their health is "good," "very good," or "excellent," and this does not differ by gender (Statistics Canada 2012). These patterns occur even among persons reaching extreme old age. For instance, Wister and Wanless (2007) found that approximately three-quarters of male and two-thirds of female nonagenarians reported good to excellent perceived health. However, people tend to overestimate their subjective health status, perhaps because people use as a comparison point persons their own age. That is, older people compare themselves and their situation with age peers or with common images of the expected health of someone their age, rather than with their own health 10, 15, or 20 years before. These favourable subjective assessments of personal health generally come more frequently from older people with higher levels of social involvement and education, positive attitudes about life, and positive personality characteristics, from those who are married, and from those who receive social support from family and friends.

There is some evidence that subjective measures are predictive of impending death. Menec et al. (1999) reported that those who rate their health as "bad/poor" or "fair" were more than twice as likely to die within three to three-and-a-half years following the survey than those who perceived their health as "excellent." There is no clear explanation for this relationship, but it may be that personal feelings are more sensitive to an individual's actual health than some objective measures (Ferraro 2006a). By the same token, people with a low level of perception may not notice that something is wrong and fail to take action either by seeking treatment or deciding to live a healthier lifestyle.

Older individuals hold a number of health beliefs about what makes them healthy or sick and whether seeking professional help will improve their condition when they are ill. The *health belief* model (Rosenstock 1974) identifies a number of interacting components of health beliefs (perceived seriousness of and susceptibility to illness; motivational cues to action that influence the propensity to alter health behaviours or seek treatment). This model demonstrates that health beliefs are the result of our social experiences over the life course and explains how they affect health and help-seeking behaviour (Segall and Fries 2011). **Self-efficacy**—the perceived confidence that one can accomplish a behavioural change or adopt a new behaviour—is a necessary precursor to making a shift in behaviour (Chou and Wister 2005). This suggests that the promotion of health among older adults needs to address a variety of belief systems embedded within society.

The Social Determinants of Health: What Makes Us Healthy in Old Age?

Health in later life is determined not only by biological or genetic factors but also by the following:

- socio-economic status
- lifestyle choices and behaviour
- socio-demographic factors, such as age, sex, marital status, nativity, and ethnicity
- physical environment, including pollution, housing and neighbourhood conditions, and safety
- social environment, including the amount and type of informal and formal social support
- work environment, such as exposure to stress, unemployment, pollution, or safety hazards

These factors operate across the life course and can have cumulative effects on an individual's health in later life. The **social determinants of health** include socio-economic status; living and working conditions; and social support from family, friends, and the community (Frank and

Mustard 1991; Canadian Public Health Association 1997; Health Canada 2002; Chappell and Funk 2011; Prus 2011). These determinants interact with healthy lifestyle behaviours, as well as with genetic and physiological determinants of health, and are cumulative over the life course.

The concept of **social capital** has been added as a major determinant of health (Wanless et al. 2010; Health Canada 2006a). Lomas (1998) defines social capital as the physical and social structure of a community that facilitates mutual support, caring, self-esteem, sense of belonging, and enriched social relationships. To illustrate, the Jerusalem Longitudinal Study found that financial security, volunteer activity, regular exercise, positive perceived health, and activities of daily living (ADL) modify the genetic influence on both survival and daily functioning (Stessman et al. 2005).

Structural *inequalities* create different life chances, experiences, and lifestyles across the life course because of differential access to social resources and can cause health *inequities* throughout life (Armstrong and Armstrong 2003). For instance, lower health status is associated with having less education and income, having smaller social networks, being female, living in rural or remote locations, and being a member of an ethnic group. The following subsections examine several key social determinants of health in old age connected to the social structure.

Social Class, Health, and Aging

One of the strongest social determinants of health is a person's economic position in society. Socio-economic conditions in life affect a number of risk and protective factors that influence people's health and their help-seeking patterns (Herd et al. 2011). Older individuals in the upper-middle and upper socio-economic status (SES) levels, as compared to the bottom levels, of Canadian society, are more likely to report and enjoy good to excellent health for a longer period of time and to live longer lives (Cairney 2000; Buckley et al. 2004; Prus 2007). Social class also affects access to a range of health-care services, partly because our health-care system is not fully publicly funded (about 30 per cent of services are privatized), but also because knowledge, attitudes, and access to health services are linked to SES. Our economic position in society affects the likelihood of being disabled, influences our exposure to health risks because of where we live, and determines, to some degree, the health behaviours and lifestyles we adopt (Berkman and Kawachi 2000).

From a global perspective, "we know that the longest life expectancies are found not in the wealthiest countries (USA) but in those countries (Japan) with the smallest spread of incomes and the smallest proportion of the population in relative poverty" (Martin-Matthews 2002, 21). Higher education, and the continuation of education over the life course, helps people to better understand health risks, educational material, and health-care instructions by physicians (Wister et al. 2010). Moreover, good literacy skills enable older people to assimilate health information from the media, from books, and from the Internet.

Researchers have found support for the hypothesis of cumulative disadvantage, especially as a result of poverty, which influences health in later life if it is present across the life course (Shaw et al. 1999; Dannefer 2003; Prus 2004). Using Canadian data, Prus (2007) found that the SES-based gap in health disparity appeared to increase over the life course (also see Chapter 6). Also, O'Rand and Hamil-Luker (2005) found that economic hardship in childhood can be cumulative and can increase the chance of heart disease later in life. From a life-course perspective, while policy interventions need to intervene in early and mid-life in order to break the cycle, there is also a need to focus on the health of older adults, especially given that many health problems and utilization rates increase in later life (Herd et al. 2011).

Gender, Health, and Aging

Gender differences exist in both subjective (perceived) and objective (diagnosed) health status. As Gee and Kimball (1987, 31) note, "Women get sick but men die." Women are more likely to report a greater number of physical and mental-health problems than men do. Therefore, although women live longer, they live alone and experience more years with some disability, with nonfatal chronic diseases, with more co-morbid or multiple health conditions, and with more stress and anxiety, especially after they are widowed (Maxwell and Oakley 1998; Clarke 2000; Laditka and Laditka 2002; Chappell et al. 2008; McMullin 2010; Segall and Fries 2011). Moreover, women are more frequent users of health-care services, drugs, and residential-care facilities. As well, they experience more days of restricted activity, spend more days confined to bed, and make more visits to physicians.

Older women engage in more self-care than older men by paying attention to nutrition and treating symptoms arising from common ailments, such as a cold or flu. They also use complementary and alternative therapies (chiropractic, massage therapy, acupuncture, herbal remedies) more often than men (Votova and Wister 2007). Older women are more likely than men to have chronic conditions (osteoporosis, arthritis, cataracts, high blood pressure) and physical limitations (deafness, difficulty in walking) and twice as likely to require help with one or more daily activities (housework, personal care). In addition, women have more skin allergies, migraine headaches, hip fractures, and adverse reactions to drugs, sleep disorders, memory loss, pain, anxiety, and depression (Maxwell and Oakley 1998).

These higher rates of morbidity and health-care utilization among older women may well reflect a process of cumulative disadvantages. Such disadvantages may be both socio-economic and social, for example, responsibility for multiple roles across the life course (see feminist theory, Chapter 5). Women may also have a greater proclivity than men to discuss health problems due to socialization differences (Chappell et al. 2008).

Concern for older men's health has also been on the rise, given their unique aging circumstances. For instance, a special issue of the journal *Generations,* published in the spring of 2008, focused exclusively on a variety of issues, including socialization and health-care use, sexual health, sleep, driving cessation, prostate cancer, and post-traumatic stress disorder.

Ethnicity, Health, and Aging

The proportion of immigrants who are 65 or older has increased to 19 per cent, largely because of the aging of those who came to Canada shortly after World War II. Life expectancy and general health are higher for immigrants than for persons born in Canada, and non-European immigrants have higher life expectancies than European immigrants (D'Arcy 1998; Perez 2002; Gee et al. 2004; Newbold and Filice 2006). This difference between immigrants and those born in Canada is known as the **healthy-immigrant effect**. The effect is strongest among recent immigrants because healthier people are more likely to emigrate and because health requirements in the Immigration Act screen out people with serious medical conditions (Gee et al. 2004; Newbold and Filice 2006).

The longer immigrants live in Canada, however, the more their self-reported health resembles that of the rest of the population (Clarke 2000, 131–2). For example, Newbold and Filice (2006) found few differences in health status between foreign-born and native-born persons aged 55 and over in Canada. Gee et al. (2004) tested the healthy-immigrant effect for both middle-aged (45–64) and older people (65 and over). They found that middle-aged immigrants who had arrived within the previous 10 years had better functional and self-rated health than their Canadian-born counterparts and that this gradient declined the longer they were in Canada. However, older (65 and over) recent immigrants, especially women, had poorer health than longer-term immigrants and Canadian-born age peers.

Ethnicity is related to class, and more recent immigrants have incomes that are often below average. Thus, we might expect to find poorer health over time in immigrant ethnic groups because of cumulative disadvantages stemming from poor living and working conditions, change of diet, discrimination, or ineligibility for some health services. As well, studies have indicated that immigrants make less use of health services, especially mental and preventive health services, often feeling marginalized in an unfamiliar society. For example, Chinese immigrants, like Aboriginal people,[5] often adhere to their traditional medical practices and beliefs (Chappell and Lai 1998). Identification with Chinese health beliefs has been shown to be associated with better physical health, lower number of illnesses, and fewer limitations with daily activities, and may suggest the need to make the health-care system more compatible with their unique needs (Lai et al. 2007).

Immigrants may make less frequent use of health services because they face language barriers or do not know about services available in the community or how to access them (Koehn 2009, 2012, 2013). Because some immigrants do not understand English or French, they may encounter diagnostic or treatment problems, especially in a stressful hospital setting or in conversations involving medical terminology or instructions in a physician's office (Sudha and Mutran 2001). In a multicultural society like Canada, in which there are more than 113 ethnic groups and more than 200 language groups, health policies must address the need for different health services to serve older recent immigrants, especially if family reunification is to be encouraged.

Rural and Remote Living

Although rural areas are often defined by geographical location or density of the population, they are more aptly defined in terms of interrelationships among people, culture, environment, and health-care access (Keating et al. 2011; Ory et al. 2011). Most surveys indicate that residents of rural and remote communities have poorer health than people who live in urban centres and that the farther a community is from a large urban centre, the poorer the health of the residents. When communities with different socio-demographic profiles are compared, rural and remote living accounts for 25 to 55 per cent of any variation in residents' health status (Statistics Canada 2002b). For example, the 2000–01 Canadian Community Health Survey found that rural regions had average life expectancies lower than the Canadian average; higher disability and accident rates; and rates of smoking, obesity, and heavy alcohol consumption above the Canadian average. This suggests that unhealthy lifelong habits are more prevalent in rural areas. As well, a lower SES adversely influences health states in rural communities, and health information and promotion are less likely available in smaller rural or remote communities.

Recent research indicates that additional elements of rural life may influence health among older adults. In a comparative study of rural and urban Canadian older women, Wanless et al. (2010) found that older women (65+) residing in rural areas had more chronic conditions, hypertension, diabetes, and heart disease than those in urban areas. Moreover, the health of rural elderly women appears to be influenced by factors different from those influencing the health of urban older women. These factors include diet, lifelong health habits, and perhaps a rural culture that fosters different health beliefs and practices.

Since many rural and remote communities have a shrinking population base, it is difficult to develop a sufficient and efficient health-care system for them. While more than 20 per cent of older Canadians live in rural areas, many public policies overlook this sector in the alloca-tion of health-care resources (Keating 2008; Keating et al. 2011). The situation has worsened in recent years with fragmentation of services, the closing of small rural hospitals, restructuring and regionalization of health services, and the continuing difficulty that rural communities encounter in attracting and retaining physicians and other health-care and social-service work-ers. It is therefore not surprising that Allan and Cloutier-Fisher (2006) found that older adults in rural and remote BC areas had a lower rate of using physician services than those living in urban areas. Fewer health and social services in rural areas also likely contributes to longer hospital stays among rural seniors (Allan and Cloutier-Fisher 2006). For instance, there are fewer rehabilitation facilities and home-care programs supporting early discharge from hos-pitals in rural areas compared to urban ones (Mitchell et al. 2006).

In rural and remote areas where young people have moved away from the community, where distances to urban centres are great, and where fewer services are available, older people experience inequities in access to health services (Keating 2008). Acute-care services may be located in another town, and the region may lack physical therapy services, rehabilitative or palliative care, mental-health services, and home and community care. Moreover, rural com-munities seldom offer many, if any, alternative housing options for older people who can no longer live in their home. An older person who cannot drive is even more disadvantaged. Thus, rural residents throughout adulthood, and especially late in life, are disadvantaged in terms of both health status and access to health and social services necessary for maintaining an independent life.

Healthy Lifestyles and Health Promotion across the Life Course

Healthy lifestyles entail clusters of health behaviours that influence the health risk of individ-uals as the result of life chances and choices and the social context in which they occur (Wister 2005). For example, health behaviours such as poor nutrition, obesity, low levels of physical activity, smoking, and heavy drinking significantly inflate the probability that an individual will suffer from disease or premature death (Hubert et al. 2002; Prus 2011). Approximately two-thirds of older adults report no efforts in the prior year to change or improve their health behaviours, and the same proportion feel that no change is necessary (Newsom et al. 2004). Merely adopting one preventive health behaviour or practice does not necessarily mean that a person will adopt any others. But it is never too late to initiate health promotion programs and to initiate practices to prevent or reduce disease (Morley and Flaherty 2002; Wister 2003). Health promotion programs should target older adults, including the frail and chronically ill as well as those who are aging in a positive way (Keating 2005). Targeting a program to indi-viduals who are ready to change a specific behaviour (smoking, eating habits, physical activ-ity, drinking patterns, stress management), as well as to specific health barriers, is important in the design of health promotion programs (Wister and Romeder 2002). Health promotion also involves disease and injury prevention—flu shots, self-care, self-screening for acute and chronic diseases (prostate and breast cancer, depression, diabetes), and preventing accidents by ensuring one's home is safe.

Healthy aging in Canada is a major policy and practice priority (Healthy Aging and Wellness Working Group 2006), and communicating health information is essential in the promotion of healthy aging. Health promotion through the Internet, called **E-health**, reaches large segments of the older population. According to Health Canada (2006b), E-health is "an overarching term used to describe the application of information and communications technologies in the health sector." To increase the level of **health literacy** (ability to seek and understand health information) among older people, the Public Health Agency of Canada operates a "seniors" section on its website (www.phac-aspc.gc.ca). Even though growing numbers of older adults (more than half) use the Internet to seek health information, many people do not or cannot access this resource. As well, many people are concerned about privacy and security and worry that their confidential health information may be revealed on the Internet (Cain et al. 2000). Strategies to address these concerns and to overcome technological, educational, cultural, language, and other barriers must be developed.

Self-Care

Older people are encouraged to engage in **self-care**, sometimes called self-management, in order to improve or maintain their health, to prevent illness or disease, and to respond to illness and frailty (Gottlieb 2000; Morrongiello and Gottlieb 2000; Gallant et al. 2007). This practice includes seeking health information, reading about self-care ideas, examining oneself for symptoms of disease, adopting healthier habits, and treating oneself for minor ailments (colds, flu, fevers, sprains, headaches, or rashes) with rest, over-the-counter medications, or a visit to a physician. Self-care also includes attending programs on such topics as fall prevention, medication management, dental health, weight loss, and physical activity, and joining self-help groups for mutual aid, social support, or coping skills (these groups can help people with a chronic illness or with alcohol or gambling problems and also provide support for caregivers to Alzheimer's or Parkinson's patients). By engaging in self-care, older individuals demonstrate independence, become empowered, lower the cost of community and health care, and improve their quality of life. While only about 2 to 4 per cent of seniors join self-help groups, 80 to 95 per cent do engage in self-care before seeking medical advice (Morrongiello and Gottlieb 2000). Older women (more than men) and people who perceive their health as more important are more likely to engage in self-care (McDonald-Miszczak and Wister 2005). The coping strategies we learn throughout our lives for dealing with pain and minor acute illnesses carry over when chronic health problems or disabilities emerge in later life. In addition to medical professionals, family and friends can also influence self-care but sometimes this can have outcomes that are either positive (e.g., help with medication management, dietary activities, physical activity, sharing health information, and health-care appointments) or negative (e.g., cooking meals that do not follow dietary guidelines, discouraging physical activity, giving unwanted advice, and not understanding the reality of living with a chronic illness) (Gallant et al. 2007).

Nutrition, Weight, and Obesity

Although many lifelong dietary choices and eating lifestyles persist in later life, changes in appetite and in food preferences do occur in the later years. Major dietary changes may be caused by poorly fitting dentures or other oral health problems, a diminished sense of taste or smell, depression and cognitive impairment, alcohol or drug dependency, difficulties in preparing and cooking food, the increasing cost of some foods, problems in chewing or digesting certain types of food, or the use of multiple medications that depress appetite or change the taste or smell of some foods. In addition, retirement, widowhood, inability to shop, or a low income can lead to poor eating habits, perhaps resulting in malnutrition. Older adults are also more susceptible to fad diets or miracle foods advertised as nutritious and essential for health. Many older adults unknowingly generate a dysfunctional cycle of poor eating habits, which lead to malnutrition and loss of weight, strength, and energy, and then a further loss of appetite. In contrast, the active lifestyles of many older adults have encouraged some nutritionists to argue that the "recommended" daily caloric intake is too low for these individuals. Some studies have also shown a protective effect of being slightly overweight among older adults (Public Health Agency of Canada 2010).

Changes in eating habits can result in lower energy reserves and increased susceptibility to illness. Consequently, community service agencies and families should monitor the older person's nutritional status, especially if he or she lives alone. For instance, Green et al. (2008) found that current levels of public pensions are not high enough to sustain a nutritional diet among older adults living in single households. Interventions to change and improve nutritional habits include prescribed and over-the-counter nutritional supplements, as well as education on selecting and preparing foods. One of the most successful programs in ensuring adequate nutrition is Meals on Wheels, a service that provides at least one hot meal per day to an older person at home.

While weight loss can be a problem for the very old, obesity is a problem for many older adults (Jenkins 2004; Wister 2005). Although the estimates vary, conservative rates among community-living elderly persons show that about 18 per cent are obese (with a body mass index [BMI] equal to or greater than 30), and another about 39 per cent are overweight (BMI from 25 to 29.9) (Statistics Canada 2012). Obesity tends to result from lifelong overeating and physical inactivity (Himes 2004). Jenkins (2004) has shown that among older adults an increase in body weight of more than 5 per cent raises the likelihood of lower-body functional impairment (joint pain or dysfunction, which affects walking, climbing, and stability functions). Being overweight is also associated with a number of chronic illnesses, including diabetes, heart disease, and arthritis (Urster 2008; Public Health Agency of Canada 2010).

The rise in obesity is partly due to an increase in the average size of food portions and in the consumption of foods high in saturated and trans fats (Binkley et al. 2000). People who consume a Mediterranean-style diet (more vegetables, fruits, legumes, olives and olive oil, nuts, whole grains, fish, poultry, and red wine, and smaller amounts of red meat) generally enjoy better health (Hu et al. 2000; Hu 2003; Urster 2008). Hu (2003) found that persons following such diets may extend their longevity by 25 per cent over that of persons following a Western diet (greater amounts of red meat, processed meat, refined grains, and sweets).

Physical Activity and Health

Since the early 1990s, health promotion programs have stressed the importance of an active life to reduce the risk of numerous diseases, increase disability-free years, increase the quality of life, and enhance longevity (Prohaska et al. 2006; Gilmour 2007; Colley 2011). In fact, the economic impact of inactivity has been estimated to be $5.3 billion or about 2.6 per cent of total health-care spending per year in Canada (Gilmour 2007). Regular physical activity involving, at a minimum, brisk walking for about 30 minutes most days is considered sufficient to generate positive health outcomes. Physical activity provides a number of benefits for aging adults:[6]

- increased life satisfaction, confidence, and sense of self-worth
- reduced morbidity and mortality
- reduced risk of cognitive impairment
- improved physical health and functional ability, especially in flexibility, balance, strength, and endurance
- less stress and depression
- a higher self-reported quality of life

An increasing number of middle-aged and older adults are physically active. The proportion of Canadians aged 65 and over engaging in leisure-time physical activity[7] at an active or moderate level increased from approximately 38 per cent to 43.9 per cent between 1994 and 2011 (Statistics Canada 2001, 2012; Public Health Agency of Canada 2010). Although this reflects improvement, it also means that more than half (about 56.1 per cent) of all adults 65 and over (and about half of those aged 35 to 64) are in the inactive category and therefore not enjoying or reaping the benefits of physical activity. This is even more pronounced when using the new Canadian physical activity guidelines, which recommend 10,000 steps per day of activity (Colley et al. 2011). Some of the common perceived barriers to exercise include physical ailments, fear of falling, lack of motivation or time constraints, and a lack of understanding as to what can be achieved and how to engage in physical activity in later life (Lees et al. 2005; Prohaska et al. 2006).

Inactivity is more pronounced among women, the less educated, those with lower incomes, those who live in rural areas and small towns, and those employed in manual occupations. There is also an east-west provincial difference in physical activity levels, with those living in the western provinces being more active. Again, structural inequalities and regional cultures affect leisure norms, opportunities, and the desire to participate in regular physical activity.

In recent years, however, greater numbers of older adults are demanding activity opportunities. These visible, active older adults are helping to remove restrictive age norms that discourage older men and women's involvement in physical activity. Moreover, scientific evidence has demonstrated that moderate to high levels of physical activity are possible at all ages and that regular activity enhances physical and mental health. "Master," "veteran," or "senior" sport competitions, including marathon runs, are held for older adults by age group. Reasons for older adults' increasingly active lifestyle include the following:

- greater knowledge about the benefits of lifelong physical activity
- changing portrayals of older people in the media and changing societal values and norms regarding exercise and activity, especially for women
- effective health promotion programs with physical activity as a key component
- cohort changes in physical activity levels
- a desire to continue existing active lifestyles into the later years
- an increased understanding about which activities to initiate or continue, and of how to correctly perform activities, and with what intensity

Smoking Cessation

Although smoking declines significantly with age, about 9 per cent of adults over the age of 65 smoke, with 47 per cent being former smokers. More older men than women report daily smoking, and rates of smoking are higher among Aboriginal elders (Public Health Agency of Canada 2010). Smokers tend to have lower incomes and education levels, and Quebec has a higher rate of smoking than other provinces. In Canada, the economic costs of tobacco use for the health-care system range between $3 billion and $3.5 billion as a result of the many deleterious effects of smoking on health (Cataldo 2003; Makomaski Illing and Kaiserman 2004). Smoking is a major risk factor for cardiovascular disease, respiratory disease, and lung cancer, although quitting smoking at virtually any age may significantly reduce the health risk (American Council on Science and Health 1999). Studies have shown that older adults are highly responsive to smoking cessation programs and should not be overlooked in anti-smoking campaigns.

Oral Health

Often ignored and certainly under-researched, oral health is an essential component of health maintenance in later life (Gift et al. 1997; MacEntee et al. 2011). Oral infections, gum disease, and poorly fitting dentures cause pain and discomfort, interfere with chewing and swallowing, and lead to loss of appetite and inadequate nutrition. Uncomfortable dentures (about 50 per cent of older people wear dentures) influence an older person's self-esteem and well-being, since ill-fitting dentures alter a person's facial appearance and create difficulties in speaking and eating. This discomfort in turn can make a person avoid eating in public or refrain from interaction with others because of slurred speech. Reduced social interaction in turn detracts from the quality of life.

For some older people, dental treatment is too expensive, especially if they do not have a dental plan. For others, poor oral health stems from lack of knowledge (oral health should be covered in health promotion programs), inadequate lifelong dental care, or cognitive impairment (forgetting to brush or floss). Effort has been given to enhancing oral health care for frail elders, but there is little agreement on how the care should be regulated or financed within the LTC sector (MacEntee et al. 2011).

Mental Health

Most older adults report that they are in good or excellent mental health; however, about 20 per cent of community living older adults are estimated to have a mental-health issue, with estimates reaching 80 to 90 per cent in institutions[8] (Public Health Agency of Canada 2010). The most common age-related mental health illnesses or disorders among the older population are depression, dementia, anxiety, delirium, and delusional disorders. Women tend to have higher rates of mental illness than men, especially for depression and the dementias.

In later life, some loss in the ability to remember and to make decisions is normal. These changes are challenging and require coping strategies and social support from others (Chappell and Funk 2011). If significant or rapid declines in cognitive, behavioural, or emotional functioning occur, they are often the result of disease processes or stressors in daily living. Stressors can be triggered by the loss of physical health, the death of a partner, moving out of the family home, financial difficulties, social isolation and loneliness, or the loss of social support. The ability to cope with stress decreases as our strength, energy, and cognitive functioning decline and when more than one of these events happens at the same time.

An inability to cope with change and stress in later life can lead to mental-health problems, which impede one's ability to interact with others and their surrounding environments. In Canada, the most commonly cited definitions of mental health and mental illness (or disorders) are as follows:

> **Mental health** is the capacity of each of us to feel, think and act in ways that enhance our ability to enjoy life and deal with the challenges we face. It is a positive sense of emotional and spiritual well-being that respects the importance of culture, equity, social justice, interconnections and personal dignity. **Mental illnesses** are characterized by alterations in thinking, mood or behaviour—or any combinations

thereof—associated with some significant distress and impaired functioning. Mental illnesses take many forms, including mental disorders, schizophrenia, anxiety disorders, personality disorders, eating disorders and addictions such as substance dependence and gambling. (Standing Senate Committee on Social Affairs, Science and Technology 2004)

Until recently, little attention was paid to the promotion of mental health or to the prevention and early detection of mental illness among older persons (Knight et al. 2006). Yet there is much that the older person and his or her caregivers can do to foster good mental health in later life:

- engaging in social, physical, and intellectual activities to maintain competence
- being connected to others in social networks or self-help groups/networks for social interaction and social support (Social isolation is a risk factor for mental-health problems.)
- maintaining independence and control over one's life through empowerment and personal decision-making
- attending educational programs to learn coping and adapting strategies for normal aging losses and changes
- ensuring that older people live in a safe, secure, and familiar environment
- providing financial assistance to low-income older people to relieve some uncertainty and stress in daily living
- screening periodically for declines in cognitive function
- providing support at times of stress and loss—retirement, death of a partner, an acute illness or injury, or moving from the family home
- encouraging older people with symptoms of mental illness to use mental-health services (Many will not refer themselves because of the stigma associated with mental illness and the fact that many family physicians do not notice mental illness symptoms during brief medical visits.)

Mental health contributes to the quality of life of older people and their caregivers. A failure to prevent, detect early enough, or treat mental-health illness or problems often leads to premature institutionalization. Therefore, strategies to promote mental health among older adults are needed, including early detection, regular access to primary health care, and the provision of home-care services.[9]

Depression

Fiske and Jones (2005) define two types of depression. The first is major depression, which is characterized by a depressed mood or loss of interest or pleasure. This is typically accompanied by appetite loss, physical agitation, difficulty in concentrating or making decisions, and feelings of worthlessness or guilt. The second type is dysthymia, which includes depressive symptoms that may be less severe than major depression but that usually last for at least two years. Taken together, these two types of depression affect 2 to 5 per cent of older persons; however, prevalence rates are considerably higher in long-term-care residences (estimated at 14 per cent to 42 per cent), and are higher among older women than men (Fiske and Jones 2005; Public Health Agency of Canada 2010).

Depression may be triggered by multiple concurrent personal losses, lack of social support, living alone, drug interactions, chronic pain, disability, physical illnesses (heart disease, Parkinson's disease, strokes, cancer), dementia, fear of falling, the strain of caring for a frail spouse, or the diagnosis of a terminal illness (Public Health Agency of Canada 2010). Outcomes include withdrawal from social interaction, decline in physical and/or cognitive functioning, increased dependence, and risk of suicide (if severe and prolonged, especially among men). Late-life depression results from the interplay among biological, psychological, and social influences that change over the life course. If social support and professional care are available and used, depression can be treated and thus controlled or eliminated (Blazer 2003).

Delirium

This common but usually temporary cognitive disorder involves fluctuation in consciousness, an inability to focus, hallucinations, periods of disorientation, and bizarre behaviour at random moments. Delirium is related to insomnia, the onset and progression of chronic diseases, the onset of either sensory deprivation or sensory overload, bereavement, relocation to a new residence, or drug interactions. It is more common among hospitalized seniors or residents of LTC, but often goes undiagnosed (Canadian Coalition for Seniors' Mental Health 2009).

Dementia

Dementia, an organic brain disorder of later life, impairs memory, thinking, and behaviour. It has been defined as "an acquired global impairment of cognitive function, sufficient to impinge on everyday activities, occurring in clear consciousness (the person is awake and alert)" (Woods 2005, 252). Memory impairment is the main outcome, and it usually results in behavioural changes, depression, anxiety, and delusion. In Canada, dementia affects about 8 per cent of persons aged 65 and over and about one in three people aged 85 and over (Hogan et al. 1999). Some projections indicate that the number of older people in Canada with any type of dementia was 480,600 (1.5 per cent of the Canadian population) in 2008 and might reach 1,125,200 (2.8 per cent) by 2038. The economic costs of care were estimated to rise from approximately $15 billion in 2008 to $153 billion in 2038 (Alzheimer Society of Canada 2010). The prevalence is greater among women and increases with age. As well, persons with dementia are more likely to live in rural areas (Forbes et al. 2006). While dementia appears to be on the increase (Menec et al. 2005; Alzheimer Society of Canada 2010), it is possible that it may not be increasing in prevalence, per se, but rather that more people are living beyond 80 and being diagnosed. It is also controversial whether dementia will "overwhelm the health-care system" as stated by the Alzheimer Society of Canada. While the number of dementia cases will increase as baby boomers age, there are potential advancements in health-care systems and treatments for older adults that may offset some of the expected increase in cases. In addition, improvements in some health behaviours (lower smoking, increased physical activity, etc.) and reductions of potential environmental risk factors (trace metals, toxins, pollutants, etc.) may also lower dementia rates over time. Indeed, in a recent controversial UK study, researchers determined that the prevalence of dementia among persons aged 65 and over declined by 24 per cent between the 1990s and 2011 (Matthews et al. 2013), an opposite trend from that found in most other studies. Clearly, more research is needed to understand these emerging developments.

As it progresses, dementia is characterized by the following severe losses in more than one aspect of cognitive, emotional, or social abilities:

- cognitive abilities: impairment of short-term memory and in comprehension, language use, and reasoning
- emotional abilities: inability to express emotions, onset of aggressiveness and shouting
- social abilities: inability to start a conversation, difficulty in planning and making decisions, aggressiveness, inappropriate or repetitive behaviour, and wandering

These losses interfere with daily functioning and reduce independence and quality of life (Burke et al. 1997; Tierney and Charles 2002). Differentiating between depression and dementia is difficult as both involve memory impairment as a symptom (Holstein 1997). Yet an accurate diagnosis is essential to prevent incorrect labelling and to ensure that appropriate treatment is provided, including drugs and therapeutic programs. There are a number of tools that have been developed for assessing cognitive functioning and dementia, but there is controversy as to their accuracy. The most common type of dementia is Alzheimer's disease (AD), a degenerative disease of the brain that begins with the loss of short-term memory and progressively destroys most cognitive functioning.[10] Age-related memory impairment and cognitive impairment are often precursors to AD. But loss of memory capacity alone does not constitute a diagnosis of AD. The rate of progression is unpredictable, and various levels and types of care are required, depending on the symptoms. We must not label all those with memory problems as AD patients unless the other symptoms emerge and progress. There are no simple tests to confirm a diagnosis of AD. Rather, the disease can only be accurately diagnosed by a brain autopsy after death, although expensive magnetic resonance imaging (MRI) of the brain over a period of time can reveal changes in the brain's structure.

As AD progresses, it may involve personality changes, disorientation (both temporal and spatial), wandering, added confusion at sundown, agitation, hostility, and the loss of self and a core identity (see Highlight 7.4). The disease interferes with the functioning of the mind, devastates family members—especially a spouse if he or she is the primary caregiver—and creates increasing and significant demands on the health- and social-care systems.[11]

Whereas we celebrate increasing longevity and improvements in the treatment of cancer and heart disease, relatively little progress is being made in the prevention, early detection, or treatment of AD (Alzheimer Society of Canada 2010). Thus, more people are living longer with the symptoms. Ultimately, 24-hour care may be required, and AD may be the major factor in a decision to move an older person into a residential care facility. Such relocation is necessary for the person's care and safety, as well as for the relief of family caregivers who can no longer cope with such problems as agitation, verbal or physical aggressiveness, wandering, repetitive behaviour, and incontinence. Some studies report that more than 50 per cent of the residents of long-term-care facilities have AD.

Interventions for dementia involve prevention (such as physical activity and a healthy diet), coordinated home care, drugs to calm the person and to slow the process, and recreational therapy programs at home or in the community. Interventions for caregivers involve the acquisition of knowledge about the disease, skill building, support groups, respite care, and the training of health professionals and provision their services to caregivers (Grossberg and Desai 2003; Alzheimer Society of Canada 2010). Highlight 7.5 describes the recommendations for a national dementia strategy.

Highlight 7.4
The Ravages of Alzheimer's Disease

The Case of Tom[*]

At age 65, Mr Tom X retired from a successful career as a journalist. Tom hoped to write a book of reminiscences of his journalistic exploits. For the next six years, he enjoyed his retirement and sprinkled his leisure time with an assortment of freelance writing assignments as well as working on his book. However, his wife began to notice slight changes in his personality—her husband, whose "bread and butter" had been a keen memory and tremendous initiative, seemed to be having difficulty in remembering where he put things, with whom he had spoken, and what time it was. He began to make mistakes when paying their bills and making change in stores. He couldn't find the right words for objects. He took longer to do routine things. Gradually he grew worse.

Tom had frequently said, "I don't want to live a long life if my mind goes." Cognizant of some of the changes that were taking place, he became at times anxious and at times depressed. He recognized that the considerable body of knowledge he had accumulated and his imagination, in which he took pride, were crumbling away, but he did his best to fabricate an outer facade to conceal from others the advancing decay beneath.

As his condition worsened, he became less and less aware of what was happening. He became hostile, even assaultive, when his wife tried to feed or dress him. He would wander outside if she did not keep a watchful eye on him. His wife and companion of 40 years, herself suffering from crippling arthritis, was unable to care for him at home any longer, so, with a mixture of shame and regret, admitted him to a nursing home, putting her own financial security at risk. There, he deteriorated rapidly. Incontinent and often reverting to speaking the Norwegian language of his childhood, he eventually could not even recognize himself in the mirror. In the near-final phase he became a "screamer" and was hopelessly confused. The end stage was coma. The death certificate read, "Cause of death, aspiration pneumonia." But what first killed his mind and then his body was senile dementia of the Alzheimer's type.

[*]Reproduced with permission from Butler, R. 2003. "Senility: The epidemic of the twenty-first century of longevity". Unpublished essay in the Imagining Longevity Series. New York: International Longevity Center. www.ilcusa.org.

Barriers to Mental-Health Care

Older adults with mental-health problems or disorders are vulnerable people. They present a difficult challenge to society and to their family, especially if they cannot leave the home for treatment. And an increasing number of older women experience mental-health problems and disorders (Malatesta 2007). Early screening and diagnosis is essential, but this seldom happens. There are a number of barriers to mental-health care (Conn 2002; Canadian Coalition for Seniors' Mental Health 2009; Préville et al. 2009), including the following:

- failure of partners or other family members to refer a person to a mental-health clinic
- a lack of understanding of mental illnesses and treatments
- inadequate funding for mental-health care versus physical care
- a shortage of trained personnel for geriatric mental-health services
- a shortage of mental-health clinics in a community, especially ones that encourage attendance by older people and that are staffed by psycho-geriatricians

Highlight 7.5
Recommendations for a National Dementia Strategy

1. Accelerated investment in all areas of dementia research;
2. Clear recognition of the important role played by informal caregivers by providing information and education, supporting their roles as care partners and providing financial support;
3. Increased recognition of the importance of prevention and early intervention for these diseases, for both health care professionals as well as the general public;
4. Greater integration of care and increased use of accepted frameworks or "best practices" in chronic disease prevention and management, community support and community care coordination;
5. Strengthening Canada's dementia workforce by:
    a. increasing the number of specialists including geriatricians, neurologists, psychiatrists and advanced practice nurses with specialized knowledge of dementia;
    b. improving the diagnostic and treatment capabilities of all frontline professionals;
    c. making the best use of general and specialized resources through inter-professional collaboration;
    d. supporting patient self-management and caregiver participation in care coordination;
    e. leveraging the capabilities of the voluntary sector.

Source: © 2010. "Rising Tide: The Impact of Dementia on Canadian Society." Alzheimer Society of Canada. All rights reserved. www.alzheimer.ca

- a lack of coordination between the primary-care system (physicians and acute-care hospitals) and mental-health and aging service personnel in the community
- a lack of support groups or peer counselling programs for mental illnesses, such as depression, distress, and AD
- inadequate treatment for mental-health problems in long-term-care facilities
- a lack of outreach programs in the community for screening, diagnosis, and intervention
- mis-prescribing or overprescribing psychotropic drugs and inadequate monitoring for drug interactions
- a lack of mental health promotion
- a lack of education about mental health for home-care workers and family caregivers
- a lack of trained personnel to cope with diverse cultural and ethnic beliefs and practices concerning health care in general and mental-health care in particular

Suicide in Later Life

In most countries, suicide rates increase with age. Males 85 and older are most at risk, with an average of 29 suicides (per year) per 100,000 in Canada compared to about 20 for all persons aged 65 and over (Public Health Agency of Canada 2010). Because of reporting errors, these rates are likely under-representations. Men who attempt suicide are more likely to be successful while women are more likely to be unsuccessful and to be hospitalized. Suicide is one outcome of severe depression that is not diagnosed soon enough or treated successfully.

Suicide is not the leading cause of death among older people, but rates are rising as longevity increases. Prevention includes monitoring those who live alone and have recently suffered multiple losses, providing social support, making sure that someone is in regular contact by phone or in person, and encouraging a person who appears depressed to seek professional help. Among the risk factors for suicide are a history of suicide or dysfunction in the family, distressing life events such as the death of a partner or financial problems, a feeling of uselessness, an inability to satisfy basic needs to belong or feel safe, alcoholism or drug addiction, living alone and feeling isolated, the availability of a firearm or drugs in the home, and the presence of a life-threatening or debilitating disease (Legris and Préville 2003; Beeston 2006).

Canada's Health-Care System and Population Aging

Overview of the Medicare System

The federal government implemented a universal medicare system in 1972 based on the Medical Care Act (1968). The Canada Health Act of 1984 established that the federal and provincial governments would share the costs 50/50. Medicare is responsible for health protection, disease prevention, health promotion, and for health-service delivery to specific groups (veterans, inmates of federal prisons, Aboriginal people living on reserves, and military personnel) (Health Canada 1999). The management and delivery of health services to all other Canadians is the responsibility of each province and territory.

To be eligible for federal funding, provincial and territorial health insurance plans must adhere to five criteria (known as "the principles") in the Health Act. These principles state that health services must be as follows:

- *publicly administered*: This is on a non-profit basis.
- *comprehensive*: All "medically necessary" services provided by hospitals and physicians must be insured, including drugs, supplies, and diagnostic procedures within a hospital; some out-patient services are covered; and chronic care services are covered if accommodation costs are shared by the resident (however, there is considerable provincial and territorial variation in access, cost sharing, and quality of long-term-care facilities).
- *universal*: All eligible residents are insured equally.
- *accessible*: No additional fees can be charged for insured services, and there must be no discrimination on the basis of age, income, health status, gender, or ethnicity.
- *portable*: Residents are fully insured when they travel within Canada and to some extent when they travel abroad and are fully insured when they move to another province.

However, a number of problems with our health-care system have been revealed in recent years. For example, lack of funding and excessive wait times for service or surgery have received considerable attention as generic problems (CIHI 2005). For older adults, the fragmentation of services in the health-care system is another growing concern. It means separating acute care from health promotion and failing to integrate services in an ideal continuum of care: from acute hospital and physician care to community social and health care to long-term care (CIHI 2011a). Fragmentation is most evident when those who suffer cognitive decline and chronic illnesses in later life need support and care (see "Integrated Models of Care Delivery" later in this chapter). In the current system, cognitive impairment and mental illnesses tend to receive less attention than physical diseases, especially in the early stages. Fragmentation is evident, as well, when health-care workers in one part of the system do not communicate with other workers in related areas. For example, a hospital discharge planner may not notify the community home-care workers that an older patient is being sent home to recuperate.

Older People in the Health-Care System

How well does the health-care system serve older Canadians? Although persons over 65 constituted 14.8 per cent of the population in 2011, they accounted for more than 50 per cent of the patient days in acute-care hospitals, and about 45 per cent of health expenditures. In general, more older men than older women are admitted to hospitals because of a greater incidence of heart disease and stroke. The average stay for those aged 65 and over is 17 days, compared to 10 days for those 64 and under. By age 65, a person is 33 per cent more likely to spend time in a hospital than a person 45 to 64 years of age. And for persons aged 75 and over, the difference rises to over 70 per cent. Overall, however, most studies find that older people do not misuse or make unreasonable use of the health-care system (Chappell and Hollander 2011a).

In spite of their growing numbers, there has been a decrease in the length of acute-care hospital stays among older people in recent years. This may be due to faster recoveries as a result of greater use of drug and other nonsurgical kinds of treatment, increased self-care, more day surgeries, and an increase in the availability of home care or private care during convalescence. And because older people may have to wait longer for help with using the toilet, getting in and out of bed, and eating during their acute-care stays, they may be motivated to return home earlier (Pringle 1998; Saunders et al. 2001). Moreover, acute-care patients of all ages are being discharged from hospitals much earlier than in the past to create beds for waiting patients. Unfortunately for older patients, an early discharge, especially to the family home without adequate assistance, can increase the risk of falls, malnutrition, and self-medication problems that may lead to a cycle of readmission and eventually longer average stays. This issue illustrates the need for a coordinated and integrated system that provides suitable treatment at the right time; home support when needed; and suitable placement in a rehabilitation hospital, in the home, or in a long-term-care facility. Currently, Canada spends only 15 per cent of its public funds for long-term care on home care, whereas the Netherlands, France, and Denmark spend 32 per cent, 43 per cent, and 73 per cent, respectively.

Population Aging and the Cost of Health Care

Health care is financed primarily through federal, provincial, and corporate taxes and by individual contributions to insurance plans that provide supplementary health benefits. However, in some provinces, sales taxes, health-care premiums, and lottery sales supplement the revenue generated by taxation. The federal government's contribution to the provinces is transferred as a combination of funds and tax credits. Figure 7.2 illustrates this complex funding structure.[12]

Between 2004 and 2010, the total expenditure for health care in Canada rose from an estimated $130 billion to $200 billion, amounting to an increase in expenditures as a percentage of gross domestic product from 10 to 11.6 per cent (CIHI 2005, 2011b). About 70 per cent was derived from government revenues, and about 30 per cent was privately funded from

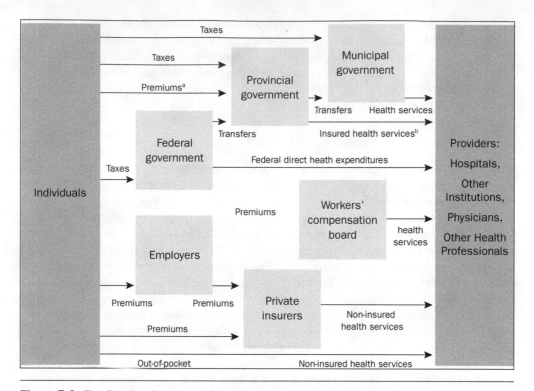

Figure 7.2 The Funding Structure of the Health System in Canada

[a] Two provinces, British Columbia and Alberta, levy health premiums.
[b] Medically necessary hospital and physician services.

Source: Canada's Health Care System. Health Canada, 1999. Reproduced with the permission of the Minister of Public Works and Government Services Canada, 2013.

individuals outside of medicare. Of the total cost for health care, the provincial government contributes about two-thirds (CIHI 2010). In 2010, approximately 29 per cent of the total expenditure was allocated to hospitals, 16 per cent to drug prescriptions, 14 per cent to physician payments, 7 per cent to dental services, 5 per cent to home care, and about 29 per cent to other institutions and services, such as vaccine centres (CIHI 2005). Between 1975 and 2010, inflation-adjusted rates of health-care spending have approximately doubled (CIHI 2010).

Given the rapidly rising costs and recent cutbacks in spending and services by hospitals, Canadians are seeking reform and improved services. They wonder whether the health-care system is sustainable. But these fears may be exaggerated. For example, Armstrong and Armstrong (2003, 157) concluded that "Canadian public spending on health care is not significantly out of line with that of other countries, not out of control, and not disproportionately concentrated in acute-care facilities . . . what is growing disproportionately is drug expenditures." Those who claim that health-care costs can be contained and that the system will remain sustainable argue that we have time to change the system before the baby boomers reach and exceed 75 (at which point health utilization rates will escalate). Some claim that the boomers will be healthier than previous generations in the early years of later life.

While baby boomers may live longer, those who live into their eighties, nineties, and even to age 100 and above will likely require more health services. Using the LifePaths microsimulation model, Légaré and Décarie (2007) estimate that between 2001 and 2031 the elderly population in poor health will increase by a factor of about 2.5. Baby-boom seniors may also expect and use more formal care in the health system, perhaps because of their higher levels of education, health literacy, and expectations of the system (Black et al. 1995; Wister 2011). Increases in the absolute and relative number of older adults in the future will undoubtedly place increasing pressures on the system, and these pressures may be exacerbated due to the more rapid rate (or speed) of population aging (Wister 2011). Moreover, the baby boom generation is not homogeneous; there are subgroups (single mothers, refugees) that have experienced cumulated disadvantages in health over their life course, with significant health-care consequences.

Population Aging and Health-Care Utilization

In an article entitled "Apocalypse No: Population Aging and the Future of Health-Care Systems," Evans et al. (2001) provide data from BC that undermine the popular belief that population aging is the cause of skyrocketing health-care costs, or what has been termed "apocalyptic demography" (see Chapter 1). They note that illnesses increase with age; people are living longer and need more health care; and the Canadian population will have more older persons, both as a proportion of the population and in absolute numbers. The authors conclude that population aging accounted for about 10 per cent of the increase in health-care expenditures between 1975 and 1992. In addition, the Canadian Institute for Health Information (CIHI) (2011a) reports that population aging has added less than 1 per cent to public-sector health spending each year over the past decade. In comparison, hospitals, physicians, and prescription drugs account for about 59 per cent of health-care expenditures in Canada. According to the CIHI (2010), on the supply side, the primary reasons for health-expenditure increases in Canada include hospital costs and the use of new technologies, pharmaceuticals, home and community services, and salaries and benefits for health workers.

Regarding hospitals, Evans et al. (2001) demonstrated that it costs more each year to provide health care to a person entering a hospital, and health technologies and treatment procedures have become more sophisticated and expensive. There is a higher intensity of health service to the elderly, especially the 75+ age group, but population aging, per se, is a trivial factor in these patterns. Indeed, CIHI (2011a) states that it is the increase in the number of chronic conditions rather than the increase in the number of seniors that is at the root of increased demand for health-care services. Also, there are areas for improvement in the system. For instance, in Manitoba, 42 per cent of the patient days in hospital among persons aged 75 and over were spent waiting either for transfer to another level of care (a nursing home) or for medical tests or treatments, and almost half of all stays were accounted for by only 5 per cent of patients (De Coster et al. 2005).

Another area of concern is the increased use and cost of pharmaceuticals (Sheets and Gallagher 2012). Total expenditures on drugs have almost doubled between 1975 and 2010 (CIHI 2010); however, costs appear to be levelling off in recent years, mainly due to generic drug policies that enforce the prescribing of less expensive drugs. At present, Canada does not have a national pharmacare program, but the Canadian public is in favour of implementing such a program (Sheets and Gallagher 2012). At present, coverage for prescription drugs in Canada involves a mix of private and public coverage, and there is considerable variation among the drug plans of the provinces. These differences include who is covered, what drugs are covered, whether there is co-payment, how large the deductible is, and whether there is a maximum amount of coverage per year. There is very little interprovincial portability in drug plans, and people often have to wait three months for coverage after moving to another province.

As drug costs escalate and pharmacare coverage decreases because of rising costs and greater prescribing practices, some older people reduce or quit their medications because they can no longer afford the cost. Depending on where they live, seniors may have to pay significant amounts for their medications because of the enormous provincial differences (up to a 21-fold variation) in out-of-pocket costs for those aged 65 and older (Grootendorst et al. 2003). These are some of the driving forces behind the attempt to introduce a national pharmacare plan. The Romanow Commission (2002, 189–210) recommended creating a "catastrophic drug transfer" plan to protect people who have excessively high drug costs because of the critical nature of their illness. This insurance plan would reduce disparities in the level of reimbursement across Canada. Unfortunately for the Canadian population of older adults, this recommendation had not been implemented as of 2013, although some provinces such as BC have implemented catastrophic drug plans for all residents. The commission also recommended creating a national drug agency to evaluate and approve new prescription drugs, evaluate existing drugs, negotiate and contain drug prices, and provide comprehensive and accurate information about prescription drugs and drug usage to the public and to health-care providers. This is particularly important in the face of many new and expensive drugs being placed on the market for Alzheimer's disease, Parkinson's disease, cardiovascular diseases, cancer, sexual dysfunction, and so on. The Health Canada Drug Product Database (DPD) provides information on 15,000 drugs and drug companies, including product specific information on drugs approved for use in Canada (www.hc-sc.gc.ca/dhp-mps/prodpharma/databasdon/index-eng.php). However, the DPD is fundamentally descriptive in nature and does not meet the function of a national drug agency.

We have witnessed rapid increases in drug costs and in the intensity of health services for the elderly. This has occurred during a period of improvement in some health indicators associated with older adults, in particular life expectancy and disability-free life expectancy. We also know that education and health literacy influence how people use the system and that the level of education of older people is increasing. These facts suggest that new policies and practices are needed to reduce drug, diagnostic, and caring costs. Finally, greater efficiency in assessing older people and in electronic centralized record-keeping would ensure that all of an individual's needs are known and addressed by all health-care personnel.

The Anti-aging Movement

Throughout history, a variety of anti-aging methods have been proposed to achieve **prolongevity**—a significant extension of average life expectancy or the maximum lifespan (Gruman 2003). Today, a commercial and clinical anti-aging movement offers a variety of products, treatments, and surgical procedures aimed at slowing or reversing physiological and psychological aging processes (Binstock et al. 2006). These include efforts to reduce wrinkling of the skin, replace hair for men, increase muscle mass or strength, enhance memory, reduce obesity, lower the risk of major chronic illnesses (cardiovascular disease, cancer, arthritis, osteoporosis), and enhance sexual function. The anti-aging movement is estimated at somewhere between a $43 and $64 billion industry in the US, offering a growing number of treatments and products, such as cosmetic surgery (e.g., facelifts, Botox, liposuction); exercise and other physiological therapies and aids; and various medications, vitamin therapies, and mineral supplements. A variety of educational programming and resources dealing with anti-aging are provided on the WorldHealth.net website, as well as at the Annual World Congress on Anti-Aging Medicine and Regenerative Biomedical Technologies (www.a4m.com/). In addition, many of these treatments and products are available in the offices and clinics of medical professionals, in drug and vitamin supplement stores, and via television and the Internet. These products and services may appeal to baby boomers since they represent a consumer culture. Yet because of some recent deaths during or following anti-aging surgery, it is clear that this way of fighting aging is not without serious risks.

Butler (2003) contends that the anti-aging movement promotes ageism, is class-based, and requires careful monitoring by government agencies to protect consumers from scams and the side effects of unproven drugs and therapeutic modalities. In his most recent book, *The Longevity Revolution,* Butler (2008) contends that there are many unanswered moral and ethical questions. Is prolongevity desirable, and what are the unintended consequences of this growing movement? What are the implications of increasing the lifespan by 20 or 30 years for families, work, leisure, marriage, politics, medicine, death and dying, and quality of life?

Drug Use, Misuse, and Abuse

Most studies find that the number and frequency of medications increase with age and that many older adults take more than one drug per day (a practice known as polypharmacy). To illustrate, in BC on average, each person under the age of 65 fills approximately 10 prescriptions (involving one or more medications) per year compared to about 16 for persons aged 65 and over (British Columbia Ministry of Health Services 2004). In later life, drugs are prescribed for chronic conditions such as arthritis, heart disease, memory loss, Alzheimer's disease, insomnia, depression, anxiety, and Parkinson's disease. Drugs can alleviate symptoms, including pain, hand tremors, or agitation, but most do not cure the underlying condition. In general, women take more drugs than men, partly because they consult doctors more often and because they live longer. In contrast, members of some cultural groups (e.g., Chinese Canadians, who prefer traditional Chinese medicine) use fewer drugs than their age peers because of their cultural beliefs and practices about illness and healing (Tjam and Hirdes 2002).

Increased self- or prescribed medication use among older adults has raised a number of issues pertaining to the cost of drugs, the need for more rigorous research to ensure that new drugs are safe and effective for older adults, and the need for education about medication management (Tamblyn 2000; Tamblyn and Perreault 2000; Maddigan et al. 2003; Ballantyne et al. 2005). Unsuitable medications can alter the way older people think, move, or express their feelings. Some drugs, especially if taken in conjunction with other drugs, with caffeine, or with alcohol, can cause drowsiness, falls, accidents, nausea, convulsions, or even death (see Chapter 8, the section "Falls and Injuries: Risk Factors and Prevention"). These interactive conditions are more likely to occur if a person overmedicates by taking more than one drug, if prescribed drugs are shared, or if over-the-counter drugs are taken without medical supervision. Overmedication also results when an older person gets a prescription from more than one physician or has his or her prescriptions filled at more than one pharmacy (CIHI 2010). Overmedication results as well from drug plans that cover most costs and therefore indirectly foster increased use of drugs.

In addition to the overuse of medication, noncompliance with a prescribed drug regimen (forgetting when or how to take the pills) creates similar outcomes. Tamblyn (2000) reports that the rates of adherence to prescribed medication among elderly adults varies from 16 to 73 per cent. This noncompliance may be due to forgetfulness or confusion, the complexity of the instructions, changes in the underlying condition, difficulty opening the bottles, or an inability to read instructions (Tamblyn 2000; McDonald-Miszczak et al. 2005). Older people are also more likely to hoard or share drugs or to use drugs beyond the expiry date. Underuse occurs as well when older adults stop taking a prescribed drug because of side effects or cost and do not inform their physician.

With increasing age, there are changes in the rate of drug absorption by the body. As a result, older people are more sensitive than younger people to some drugs and may experience more side effects. This requires either reducing the dosage or not prescribing the drug for older adults. Prescribing errors, along with polypharmacy, account for 19 to 36 per cent of drug-related hospital admissions (Tamblyn 2000). A list of drugs called the Beers list identifies those drugs that are deemed inappropriate for seniors because they are ineffective, pose an unnecessarily high risk when alternatives are available, or should not be used by persons with a particular medical condition (Fick et al. 2003). A study in Alberta, Saskatchewan, Manitoba, and New Brunswick (using the Beers list) found that the rate of inappropriate prescription drug use among seniors declined from 33 to 25 percent between 2004 and 2006 (CIHI 2007). In all four provinces, the rate of chronic use (drug claims made on a regular basis) of inappropriate drugs among seniors was highest among women and those aged 85 and over (CIHI 2007).

To ensure safe and effective use of necessary prescription drugs, older adults and their families need more education about their use and compliance; physicians and pharmacists need to communicate with each other about drugs prescribed for and purchased by a specific patient; and the possibility of over-prescribing should be considered if a person makes repeated visits to a physician or pharmacist.

Barriers to Health Care

Health care at one time referred to treatment by a doctor in an office or by other health-care workers in an acute-care hospital. Today, there are three interacting levels of service: self-care (described earlier), community and home care (described in Chapter 12), and formal medical care. Since the mid-1990s, however, regardless of the size of their community, Canadians have been complaining about waiting lists: for services and waiting times for elective surgery, for appointments with specialists, for diagnostic tests, and for a bed on a ward rather than a stretcher in an emergency department (Chen et al. 2002).

There is also considerable variation in the amount, regularity, and continuity of health care for older adults. Some older people (acute-care patients) have a high amount of use for a short time; some (outpatients) have a low amount of use but for a long period of time; and still others (chronic-care patients) have a high amount of use for a long period of time. The rate of health care use by older people is influenced by a variety of factors:

- predisposing, or structural, factors (age, gender, beliefs, attitudes, ethnicity)
- enabling factors (presence or absence of a spouse or family, rural or urban place of residence, availability of health-care personnel or facilities)
- need factors (subjective perceptions and objective diagnoses)

Barriers to access include lack of transportation, not living close to needed services, language and cognitive deficits, and cultural differences (Chipperfield 1993; Ferraro 2006b; CIHI 2010). To illustrate, members of some ethnic groups do not seek medical care because of differing cultural beliefs about health care, lack of knowledge about the availability of services, or language barriers when they do seek assistance. In addition, health-care personnel may not understand the unique cultural norms, beliefs, and values that ethnic groups bring to a health-care centre. Similarly, elderly people living in remote or rural communities may not seek medical care if they have to travel a long distance to a hospital in another community. While telemedicine and related communication technologies to provide health care from a distance are growing, hands-on medicine is still needed.

Health-Care Reform and Renewal: Toward a Better Future

Health-care reform has been discussed across Canada and around the globe. In Canada, since 2001, inquiries, commissions, and public consultations at both the provincial level of government (the Fyke Commission in Saskatchewan, the Clair Commission in Quebec, the BC Conversation on Health) and the federal level (Kirby 2002; Romanow Commission 2002; and the 2014 federal/provincial/territorial Health Accord: www.canadians.org/2014accord) have critiqued and analyzed the health-care system and recommended improvements. These reports deal with the future health-care needs of all Canadians, but if their recommendations are adopted, they will have a major impact on future cohorts of older Canadians. Similarly, the reform of health policies has been debated around the globe (Quadagno et al. 2005), and some of these reviews have led to significant changes. For example, in the UK, physicians are paid a salary in combination with incentive payments for meeting health targets (e.g., the proportion of patients with fewer cardiovascular risk factors, such as high blood pressure and high cholesterol) in lieu of a payment schedule as in Canada (although 27 per cent of clinical payments to Canadian physicians are made through alternative payment methods, such as salaried physicians in universities) (CIHI 2010).

The impetus for reform stems from a range of issues and problems:

- accountability and the spiralling cost of primary health care and the need to decentralize services and responsibilities away from hospitals
- an emphasis on enhancing the quality of life at the end of life, including empowerment, choice, and dignity for the patient who is dying (see Chapter 12)
- reduced accessibility to primary-care services owing to waiting times for emergency care, for transfer from an emergency ward to an acute-care bed (sometimes as long as three or four days), for surgery, and for personal assistance with eating, toileting, bathing, and pain management in a hospital
- too much emphasis on primary health care (the use of doctors, medications, and hospital care) and too little on disease prevention, health promotion, and home and community care
- the shortage and high turnover of health-care personnel, including family doctors and specialists such as geriatricians, and a shortage of modern diagnostic tools and treatment facilities in many communities
- the need to fairly, effectively, and efficiently serve all members of the diverse Canadian society, especially Aboriginal people, ethnic minorities, immigrants, residents of rural and remote regions, and those with lower levels of income and education
- whether health care is a public or a private responsibility and in what proportion—the merits, if any, of privatizing health-care[13] services and of imposing user fees to be determined

- "scope of practice"—that is, who should perform which tasks: general practitioners or specialists, doctors or nurse practitioners, nurses or nurses' aides, other allied health professionals, or home-care workers
- federal–provincial–regional disputes over transfer payments, cost-sharing, and the devolving of jurisdictional responsibilities (At the end of 2011, the federal government announced that it will continue the 6 per cent per year increase in transfer payments to the provinces, but will tie subsequent transfers to economic growth in each province.)
- whether the Canada Health Act should be expanded beyond the "medically necessary" criterion to include post-acute and chronic illness care, home care, palliative care, pharmacare, rehabilitation services, counselling for mental illness, and more benefits for those in long-term-care facilities
- the inflationary cost of drug research and the need to protect against catastrophic (poverty-inducing) prescription drug expenses for individuals (some individuals have drug expenses in excess of $5000 a month), for example, by implementing generic drug programs to reduce costs

Thus, an evolutionary process is required that will "build on values" (Romanow Commission 2002) and result in a new, efficient, and effective system that meets the needs of all Canadians equitably and promptly. With enhanced health promotion and the adoption of healthy lifestyles, older adults would require fewer health-care services in later life (assuming that expectations of the health-care system do not increase dramatically among future cohorts of older adults[14]). This can be facilitated by more self-screening and self-care, which is based on increased knowledge, much of which can be obtained on the Internet.[15]

For older people who are having difficulty living in their home, a single access point (one-stop access or a community-care access centre) enables case workers to make a full and coordinated assessment of their medical, cognitive, and physical needs; and of home safety and environment issues (see next section). The Romanow Commission (2002, 50–2) recommended that Canadians adopt a health covenant that would

- state the objectives of a health-care system for the public, patients, and health-care providers
- inform, educate, and support better decision-making within the health-care system
- serve as a common foundation for collaboration among governments, the public health care providers and managers

Over the next 10 to 20 years, there will be many debates about health reform. As concerned citizens, you must become involved in these debates. Your future quality of life is at stake, as well as that of your parents and other members of your current or future extended family.

Integrated Models of Care Delivery

In the 1980s and early 1990s, there was a movement across Canada to provide integrated care delivery systems for older adults that included case management for home care (i.e., short-term care at home typically after a hospital stay); home support (i.e., short- or long-term assistance with daily tasks at home for anyone meeting functional status assessments); community services to enhance independence and quality of life; residential care; and some aspects of acute care in hospitals (Hollander et al. 2007, 36).

Concerns about the rising costs of health care and the potential effects that an aging population may have on these patterns has led to a critical examination of models of health care for older adults. Recently, a number of integrated models of health-care delivery for older adults with functional impairments have been proposed (Gross et al. 2004; Tourigny et al. 2004; Béland et al. 2006; Hollander 2007; Hollander and Prince 2008; MacAdam 2008; Hollander et al. 2009; Hébert et al. 2010; CIHI 2011a; Chappell and Hollander 2011a; Hébert 2011). These models would create a more seamless delivery system for elderly persons that would combine health, housing, and social services. Integrated models of care aim to improve coordination between acute care (hospitals and clinics), continuing care (home care and support services), and long-term care (residential and nursing homes)—that is, the coordinated assessment and management of older patients/clients despite a fragmented health-care system (Chappell and Hollander 2011b).

An integrated model of care delivery has been shown in studies to actually lower costs since some patients/clients will be redirected from higher cost hospital and institutional care toward less expensive services delivered in the community, such as home care (Béland et al. 2006; Hollander 2007; Hollander et al. 2009; Hébert et al. 2010). While there are many integrated models or systems of care delivery in Canada and around the world, and different definitions, most include such features as the following: (1) a single entry point/location; (2) a case management approach; (3) geriatric assessment by multi-disciplinary teams; (4) coordination of hospital and nursing home care; (5) single assessment instruments for care options; and (6) simplified payment and financial coordination (Hollander 2007).

Chappell and Hollander (2011b, 87) recently defined an integrated model of care for older adults as follows:

> Our view is that an integrated system [of care] needs to be broad and combine a wide range of health and supportive services, including case management, home care and home support services, supportive housing and residential care, and geriatric assessment units in hospitals. It should also have a single administrative authority and a single funding envelope that allows leaders in that system to increase value for money by making proactive trade-offs to substitute lower-cost care for higher-cost care, while maintaining the same, or better, quality of care.

Figure 7.3 provides a best practices framework for organizing an integrated model of continuing/community care services.[16] There are three major components of the model: philosophical and policy values, best practices, and linkages with other parts of the healthcare system. There are several key features of this model (Hollander and Prince 2008; Chappell and Hollander 2011b):

1. It requires a single administrative authority and funding envelop to facilitate tradeoffs between different levels and "packages" of care to maximize cost efficiency and quality of care.
2. It is based on a case management model that uses multidisciplinary teams of health professionals.
3. It requires a complex Health Information System in order to organize movement through the system.
4. It would provide potential linkages between continuing care and hospitals by funding geriatric assessment, quick response teams, and elder-friendly services.

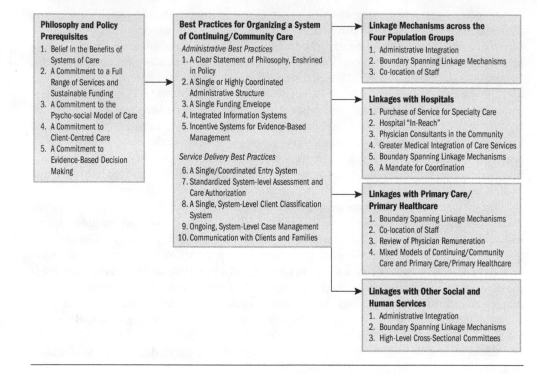

Philosophy and Policy Prerequisites
1. Belief in the Benefits of Systems of Care
2. A Commitment to a Full Range of Services and Sustainable Funding
3. A Commitment to the Psycho-social Model of Care
4. A Commitment to Client-Centred Care
5. A Commitment to Evidence-Based Decision Making

Best Practices for Organizing a System of Continuing/Community Care
Administrative Best Practices
1. A Clear Statement of Philosophy, Enshrined in Policy
2. A Single or Highly Coordinated Administrative Structure
3. A Single Funding Envelope
4. Integrated Information Systems
5. Incentive Systems for Evidence-Based Management

Service Delivery Best Practices
6. A Single/Coordinated Entry System
7. Standardized System-level Assessment and Care Authorization
8. A Single, System-Level Client Classification System
9. Ongoing, System-Level Case Management
10. Communication with Clients and Families

Linkage Mechanisms across the Four Population Groups
1. Administrative Integration
2. Boundary Spanning Linkage Mechanisms
3. Co-location of Staff

Linkages with Hospitals
1. Purchase of Service for Specialty Care
2. Hospital "In-Reach"
3. Physician Consultants in the Community
4. Greater Medical Integration of Care Services
5. Boundary Spanning Linkage Mechanisms
6. A Mandate for Coordination

Linkages with Primary Care/ Primary Healthcare
1. Boundary Spanning Linkage Mechanisms
2. Co-location of Staff
3. Review of Physician Remuneration
4. Mixed Models of Continuing/Community Care and Primary Care/Primary Healthcare

Linkages with Other Social and Human Services
1. Administrative Integration
2. Boundary Spanning Linkage Mechanisms
3. High-Level Cross-Sectional Committees

Figure 7.3 A Best Practices Framework for Organizing Systems of Continuing/Community Care Services

Source: Hollander and Prince 2008.

5. It would provide linkages between continuing care and primary care systems, for example, in the area of chronic disease management.
6. It would provide tertiary prevention and care for older people with lower level care needs, such as housekeeping in their home or falls prevention, to prolong independent living in the community and delay higher cost hospital and institutional care.

Long-term-care insurance models have developed in a number of European countries (e.g., Denmark, France, the Netherlands), in an effort to provide funding structures that support an integrated model of continuing care with a long-term-care component (Hébert 2011). While there are different funding models, Hébert (2011) suggests an "autonomy support benefit" (ASB), which would allow individuals to make care choices ("cash-for-care") based on a pre-assessed level of need. The amount for each individual would be based on functional disability tools/measures in existence. Long-term-care insurance would be publicly funded, which could originate from mandatory premiums, taxes, and possibly co-payments.

One reason why the integrated model of care delivery has not been more widely implemented is that health care and community care are funded from different provincial envelopes. In most cases, the ministries (health, social and community services, housing) do not communicate with each other to develop an integrated policy, nor are they willing to share resources or co-fund an integrated system that involves more than one ministry or level of government (municipal, regional, provincial). Future developments in health policy for the elderly in Canada will require a restructuring of funding mechanisms and jurisdictional responsibilities to allow for long-term funding of new models of care. A second reason for a failure to implement an integrated model is that there are philosophical and policy debates pertaining to a commitment to expand the health-care system to cover a broader range of health issues, including those that address functional disability, chronic disease management, mental health, and prevention. We revisit these issues when we discuss the continuum of care and home care in Chapter 12.

Summary

Physical and mental health issues are major concerns as people move into the later years. Health in early and middle life influences health and functional independence in later life. Clearly, health is determined by complex interactions among biology, heredity, health behaviours, and our place in the social structure. Chronic illnesses and mental-health disorders are major factors influencing the quality of life in later life. Mental-health disorders are the hidden enemy in the health of many older adults. They are often undiagnosed or misdiagnosed, especially depression, and older people are not always referred to mental-health professionals and often do not seek such help. The dementias, especially Alzheimer's disease, are neither well understood nor well treated; their prevalence is growing, and they are devastating for individuals, families, and caregivers.

Our health-care system is not broken, but it is under severe stress—not because of population aging per se but because of financial cutbacks and rapid inflation in the cost of providing high-quality health care and producing and prescribing drugs. The sheer number of older adults with health needs will increase significantly as baby boomers reach advanced old age, which will create added pressures on the health-care system. Recent provincial and federal health inquiries and commissions have recommended reforms to the Canada Health Act to cover more than "medical" treatments. Some needed additions are a national home-care program; a national pharmacare program; coverage of palliative-care costs for a dying person; increased mental-health services; healthy aging programs; and more facilities and services for rural and remote areas. If Canadians of all ages are to have equitable and timely access to health-care services, regardless of age, economic status, or place of residence, changes must be made in the health-care system. The recent development of integrated models of care for older adults presents both opportunities and challenges as we move into a new era of health-care reform.

For Reflection, Debate, or Action

1. Examine your health habits, and consider how they might be improved to enhance your quality of life across the life course.
2. What policies and programs might reduce inequalities in health across the life course? What model of health and health care do you support and why?
3. Consult some of the websites listed in note 15, and critically review some of the health information that is presented.
4. Debate whether health care and home care for older people should or should not be rationed. If you believe they should be rationed, who should make the decision about an individual, and what criteria should be employed to make a fair and objective decision?

5. Support an argument, with research evidence, that the arrival of baby boom seniors will or will not reduce health-care costs.

6. What is an integrated continuing care system, and why do you think it could be an important development in Canada?

Notes

1. For a discussion of health concepts, definitions, and the health-care system, see Clarke 2000; Alexander 2002; Statistics Canada 2002b; Armstrong and Armstrong 2003; Johnson 2005; Binstock and George 2006; and Segall and Fries 2011; issues of the *Journal of Aging and Health*, the *Canadian Journal on Aging*, *The Gerontologist*, the *Journal of Aging Studies, Research on Aging*, and the *Journals of Gerontology*; and major government reports, such as Lalonde 1974, Epp 1986, and the Romanow Commission 2002.

2. *Acute* conditions are of a limited duration; they include flu, colds, and minor or major surgery. Chronic conditions persist over time, even though they may begin with an acute condition such as a heart attack or hip fracture. They are treated to reduce symptoms, pain, or trauma but are less likely to be cured. Examples are heart disease, cancer, diabetes, asthma, and arthritis.

3. The compression of morbidity thesis argues that most of the chronic and severe health problems that older adults experience are compressed into the last few months or years of their lives. This compression is thought to occur later in life because of improvements in health promotion, health prevention, and health care.

4. Sources of information concerning health statistics and health status include Health Reports published quarterly by Statistics Canada (also see CANSIM table 105-0501, health indicator profile); CIHI 2002, 2003, 2004, 2005, 2007, 2010, 2011a, 2011b; the CIHI website (www.cihi.ca); and the Public Health Agency of Canada (www.publichealth .gc.ca).

5. The health of Aboriginal people is discussed in Chapter 2 under "Indigenous Subcultures: The Aboriginal People of Canada." See also *Improving the Health of Canadians* (CIHI 2004).

6. See the *Journal of Aging and Physical Activity* (http://journals.humankinetics.com/ japa) for many articles on the social, physiological, and psychological benefits of engaging in regular physical activity throughout the middle and later years; Wister 2003; Public Health Agency of Canada's Physical Activity Tips for Older Canadians (www.phac-aspc.gc.ca/hp-ps/hl-mvs/pa-ap/08paap-eng.php); and *First Step to Active Health* (www.firststeptoactivehealth.com).

7. Leisure-time physical activity level is calculated by using a measure of energy expenditure (EE), which is calculated by multiplying the number of times a respondent engages in an activity (walking, exercise, gardening, swimming, dancing, etc.) over a 12-month period, times the average duration in hours of each activity, times the metabolic energy cost associated with each activity (kilocalories expended per kilogram of body weight per hour of activity), converted into daily levels. Active individuals have an EE that is equal to or greater than 1.5, and inactive persons are below that level.

8. Professionals in psychiatry and clinical psychology rely heavily on the guidelines laid out in the *Diagnostic and Statistical Manual of Mental Disorders* in order to classify mental disorders. While it is a useful tool, many problems have been identified, including its validity and reliability as a diagnostic tool, cultural biases, and superficial symptoms. In addition, the guidelines may support an over-medicalized population due to the rapid escalation in new diagnostic categories.

9. The Canadian Mental Health Association (www.cmha.ca) published two useful guides in 2002: "Supporting Seniors' Mental Health through Home Care: A Guide" and "Supporting Seniors' Mental Health: A Guide for Home Care Staff." Another source of information is the Canadian Coalition for Seniors' Mental Health (www.ccsmh.ca).

10. The other major but less prevalent type is vascular dementia, which is caused by arteriosclerosis, a hardening of the cerebral arteries. Vascular dementia deprives the brain cells of nutrients and oxygen and leads to the atrophy and destruction of brain tissue.

11. A poignant and courageous personal account of the onset and progression of Alzheimer's disease is chronicled in a book by DeBaggio (2003).

12. Feder et al. (2001) describe the different funding system for health care in the United States.

13. Privatization of health care, as it is available in the United States, is a contentious issue in Canada (Romanow Commission 2002, 6–9). It raises the possibility of a two-tier system in which the wealthy receive better care and sooner; it could mean inaccessibility and inequality and a greater burden on families who cannot afford private services; and it could lead to costly competition to generate a profit. On the other hand, privatization could reduce waiting times, reduce public expenditures, provide higher-quality diagnostic and treatment procedures, and offer more free choice as to where to obtain treatment. Reflecting this diversity of opinion, the Kirby (2002) report recommended that private care be permitted, whereas the Romanow Commission (2002) did not make a recommendation and discouraged any developments in this direction.

14. Wister (2005) discusses the possible scenario wherein baby boomers may have higher expectations of the health-care system because of their life-course experiences and health knowledge, which may override improvements in some health status indicators.

15. The following are useful websites pertaining to health knowledge, policy, and statistics: Canadian Institute for Health Information (www.cihi.ca); Public Health Agency of Canada (www.phac-aspc.gc.ca/index-eng.php); Canadian Mental Health Association (www.cmha.ca); Canadian Health Care Association (www.canadian-healthcare.org); Statistics Canada (www.statcan.ca); Canadian Women's Health Network (www.cwhn .ca); Canadian Institutes of Health Research (www.cihr-irsc.gc.ca/e/193.html); CIHR Institute on Aging (www.cihr-irsc.gc.ca/e/8671.html); Canadian Foundation for Healthcare Improvement (www.chsrf.ca); Canadian Coalition for Seniors' Mental Health (www.ccsmh.ca); WebMD (www.webmd.com).

16. For a full description of Figure 7.3, see Hollander and Prince 2008, and Chappell and Hollander 2011b.

8

The Lived Environment: Community and Housing Alternatives in Later Life

Home is where the heart is.

Focal Points and Key Facts

- With whom, and where, do older people live?
- What environmental challenges must older people conquer to remain independent and mobile in their community?
- Why is "aging in place" the preferred housing choice in later life?
- To what extent, and why, do older people move or migrate—to a different kind of housing or to new neighbourhoods or communities?
- What are the potential benefits of age-friendly communities for older adults?
- In 2011, about 24.6 per cent of the population aged 65 and over (about 1.2 million people) lived alone (a rate of 31.5 per cent for women and 16 per cent for men) while 7.1 per cent of persons aged 65 and over (352,205) lived in care facilities—nursing homes, chronic care, long-term-care hospitals, and residences for senior citizens.
- Also, in 2011, about 19 per cent of older Canadians lived in rural areas, with some rural villages and towns having 20 to 25 per cent of their residents aged 65 and over.
- In some studies, as many as 50 per cent of seniors express fear that they may be victimized, or they report changing their travel patterns, especially at night, to avoid being victimized.

Introduction

Well-being and quality of life are influenced by the community and neighbourhood in which we live, the type of living arrangement (with whom we live, if anyone), the quality and type of housing, and the availability of transportation and community services. These elements in our physical and social environment become even more important in later life as changes in physical and cognitive capacities require us to make more complex adaptations in order to remain as independent, mobile, and safe as possible (Golant 2011a).

The study of the behavioural, social, and psychological implications of encounters between older adults and their **environment** is known as environmental gerontology (Golant 2011a). This field of study develops interventions to create a better fit between older individuals and their environments, thereby maximizing independence and improving their quality of life, as well as their physical and subjective health, including longevity (Wister 2005). To illustrate, Scheidt and Windley (2006, 105) describe four scenarios in which the local environment can create stress and change the lifestyles of older persons:

1. A 75-year-old woman cancels a shopping trip after considering the problems posed by heavy traffic, poor sidewalks, and a user-*un*friendly bus system.
2. An elderly married couple experience stress and unhappiness when forced to move from their lifelong home to an assisted living facility several miles away from their community.
3. Healthy rural elders, with strong attachments to their homes and small rural town, struggle to "age in place" as community supports dwindle and the town's physical and service infrastructure deteriorates.

4. An elderly widowed woman who speaks and understands only her native language (Mandarin) is forced to leave the family home and move into a retirement residence where most or all staff do not communicate in her language.

Whether older people "age in place" or move, they must adapt not only to a changing or different physical milieu but also to a changing or new social network. To meet the needs of a heterogeneous older population, a variety of housing and living arrangements, as well as supportive programs and services, should be available in every community.

One goal of public policy should be to create "age-friendly" communities where citizens can maintain active lifestyles and live independently for as long as possible.[1] The World Health Organization's Global Age-Friendly City Project (www.who.int/mediacentre/news/releases/2007/pr53/en/index.html) encourages cities to achieve this goal (see www.phac-aspc.gc.ca/seniors-aines/afc-caa-eng.php). According to the World Health Organization (WHO), an "age-friendly" community has policies, services, and structures related to the physical and social environment that support and enable older people to "age actively"—that is, to live in security, to enjoy good health, and to continue to participate fully in society. This approach draws from ecological models, emphasizing the social connectivity of older persons through linkages among the policy, community, service, and family environments (Menec et al. 2011). For instance, public and commercial settings and services, including parks and recreation centres, are made accessible to people with varying levels of ability. As well, age-friendly service providers, community leaders, and business people are present who

- recognize the diversity among older persons
- promote their inclusion and contribution in all areas of community life
- respect their decisions and lifestyle choices
- anticipate and respond flexibly to aging-related needs and preferences

If healthy, active-living communities are created, health-care costs are reduced, and fewer older people are housed, for fewer years, in long-term-care institutions. However, thus far, age-friendly community initiatives have not been adequately evaluated, in particular as to whether they reach the most vulnerable older adults in a community (Golant 2011a; Menec et al. 2011). Developments in Canada have been supported by collaborations between researchers and the Canadian Association on Gerontology (see Age-Friendly Communities Canada Research & Stakeholder Inventory and Research Reports: http://cagacg.ca/age-friendly-communities/).

The Multiple Meanings of *Community*

Community has a number of meanings that we must understand in order to have successful policies and programs for older people. On the simplest level, a community is a geographical space defined by political or natural geographical boundaries. A community may range in size from a few adjacent streets in a neighbourhood to a small city to a large metropolitan area. Some even refer to the world as a global community or a global village. A community can vary, as well, in location—rural, remote (as in Canada's northern areas), urban, or suburban—with each location posing different challenges for aging individuals and for those responsible for public policies and social services.

This sense of "community" arises through meaningful and persistent social relationships in which members engage in mutual trust and co-operation, known as social capital, and have shared interests, goals, values, and traditions. Thus, one can live physically in a community but not feel part of it if there is little or no meaningful social interaction with other people. One may also feel connected to, or a part of, several communities (e.g., a neighbourhood, an ethno-cultural group, an age-based retirement community). An overlooked aspect of the residential experience are the ethno-cultural and immigrant dimensions of communities, given that these individuals often face limited access to community and housing services and have unique needs within unique contexts (Chaudhury and Mahmood 2008; Mahmood et al. 2008).

Across the life course, community matters to individuals because it represents an anchor point and is a source of cumulative advantages (e.g., a safe, upper-middle-class neighbourhood) or disadvantages (e.g., an unsafe, deteriorating lower-class area). These differences in the size, type, and quality of communities in which aging occurs have implications for older adults' social and economic health and well-being (Robert 2002; Golant 2011a; Golant 2011b). Although most older people prefer to age in place for as long as possible, the quality of the community can influence whether they move to a different place or remain in the same place.

Communities may be *age-integrated* (i.e., people of varying ages who work and live together), or they may be *age-segregated* (i.e., people of similar ages, as in a retirement home or a rural village where most of the residents are older people). In general, most older people favour age-integrated communities.

Aging in Rural or Remote Communities

Rural communities vary in size, location, availability of public services, occupations of residents, age of the labour force, types of housing, economic base, ideology, and culture (Statistics Canada 2004; Keating 2008; Keating et al. 2011). Statistics Canada defines "rural and small towns" as those populations that live in towns or municipalities outside of the commuting zone of centres with populations of 10,000 or more (du Plessis et al. 2001). According to Keating et al. (2011, 327), there are 3000 rural communities in Canada with an average population size of 1736; 52 per cent of these have fewer than 1000 residents.

Different challenges and opportunities face those who age in such diverse rural settings as an isolated Newfoundland fishing port, a farm in northern Saskatchewan, or a rural village in southern Ontario. In Canada, some rural communities, such as those in the northern territories, are also "remote," that is, far from cities (more than 350 kilometres is typically used). This diversity means that one policy for rural Canada will not meet the needs of all rural or remote older residents. Moreover, some have lived in the area all their lives whereas others may be recent migrants to a rural retirement area.

This diversity in location, in socio-economic status, and in the composition of residents makes it difficult to agree on a definition of *rural*. Keating (2008) argued that any definition of rural life needs to consider several elements. First, occupations in rural communities have expanded and become more diverse, and we need to distinguish between "farm" and "non-farm" occupations. In the Canadian census, "farm," as an occupational category, is defined as "all persons living in rural areas who are members of the households of farm operators living on their farms for any length of time during the twelve-month period prior to the census" (Statistics Canada 2003a). Second, population density and distance from a metropolitan centre must be considered. And in rural areas, population densities and living conditions are quite diverse. Statistics Canada (2003c) considers rural areas to include the following:

- small towns, villages, and other populated places with fewer than 1000 people, according to the current census
- rural fringes of census metropolitan areas and census agglomerations that may contain estate lots, as well as agricultural, undeveloped, and non-developable lands
- agricultural lands
- remote and wilderness areas

The third element of rural life is the presence of a rural ideology and culture—that is, the values and beliefs rural residents hold about their community, the interaction between people and nature and with other people in the community, and the links between the economic unit and the extended family (Keating 2008).

Most research about older people has focused on residents of large urban communities. Approximately 19 per cent of older Canadians live in rural communities. Of these, fewer than 3 per cent actually live on a farm (Turcott and Schellenberg 2007). Across Canada, the proportion of those 65 and older living beyond the influence of or accessibility to metropolitan centres is highest in the Northwest Territories (77 per cent), Newfoundland and Labrador (55 per cent), Saskatchewan (47 per cent), New Brunswick (43 per cent), and Nova Scotia (40 per cent); and lowest in British Columbia (15 per cent) and Ontario (9 per cent) (Turcotte and Schellenberg 2007).

In some villages and towns, as many as 20 to 25 per cent of the residents may be over 65 years of age. Some rural communities have aged because many of the young people have left to seek work and a different lifestyle in cities. Other communities have aged because of the in-migration from urban areas of older retirees who seek an alternative lifestyle and a lower cost of living.

Older residents of rural communities are disadvantaged in some ways compared to their urban counterparts. These disadvantages include lower incomes, little if any public transportation; inadequate housing options; and fewer leisure, social, and health services because of a lower tax base and the closure of small hospitals (Keating 2008; Keating et al. 2011). Older people in rural areas who do not drive or who are no longer able to drive are isolated and dependent on others for transportation. However, there are also advantages to living in a rural community, such as proximity to inexpensive, locally grown food and the support of long-time friends and neighbours.

Those who have lived their entire lives in rural settings are part of a unique subculture characterized by a strong sense of community and feelings of independence, and a willingness to help others and to accept help from them. When formal services are needed but not available, older people often move from the rural community to a larger town or city, which can be traumatic, especially for lifelong rural residents. Thus, expanded policies and programs for older rural residents are needed so that they can "age in place." Highlight 8.1 juxtaposes some of the unique challenges faced by both new and long-term older adults living in rural communities.

Aging in Urban Communities

In cities and towns across Canada in 2011, the proportion of the population aged 65 and over varies as follows, from low to high (rounded): Calgary (10 per cent), Toronto (13 per cent), Halifax (13 per cent), Vancouver–Lower Mainland (14 per cent), Regina (14 per cent), Ottawa (14 per cent), Montreal (16 per cent), and Victoria (20 per cent). In total, almost one-third of all seniors in Canada reside in Vancouver, Toronto, or Montreal (calculated from CANSIM table: www12.statcan.gc.ca/census-recensement/2011/dp-pd/tbt-tt/Rp-eng). And there is considerable variation in the rate at which cities and towns are aging depending on **migration** patterns

Highlight 8.1
Life in Rural Canada for New and Long-Term Older Residents

In-migrants

Mr and Mrs P moved from Ottawa to the small town of Annapolis Royal, Nova Scotia, to enjoy an active outdoor life in retirement. Many older adults live in this scenic area. Some, like the Ps, were "new" transplants from the city with no family nearby; some are people who grew up here and chose to return after retirement; and many have always lived in the area, working in farming, fishing, or the lumber industry. Since her husband's death, Mrs P finds it difficult to maintain a three-bedroom house and large yard alone. Although she drives, has many friends, and is involved in several community and church groups, she feels somewhat isolated from her children and grandchildren in Ontario and Alberta. Moving back to a large city would be difficult; she would miss the friendliness and close community ties of Annapolis Royal, the view of the river and mountains, and the many varieties of birds that come to her feeder.

Lifelong Residents

Mr and Mrs A have lived on the family farm for more than 50 years since inheriting the land from Mr A's father. Both were born in the local village; they attended school together and married at the age of 20. Now in their 70s, with three children living in three different metropolitan areas in other provinces, Mr and Mrs A depend on the assistance of neighbours to harvest grain crops and for farm maintenance and animal care. Two years ago, Mr A was hospitalized for two months in an urban centre more than 100 km from the farm. Mrs A found this period stressful, and they are now searching for a way to sell the farm and move to an apartment in a nearby town. Their major concerns are whether it can be sold, whether the sale will generate sufficient income, and whether they will have sufficient income for Mrs A to survive on her own should Mr A die in the next few years.

Source: Minutes of the meeting of the National Advisory Council on Aging, Bethesda, Maryland. 1993. *Expression* 9 (1): 2. Ottawa: NACA.

and the aging patterns of those living in those cities.

Since 1991, more adults 65 and over have lived in the suburbs than in the central core of Canadian cities. Many of these older residents are "over-housed" in "empty nests," and an increasing number are widows who live alone in houses that are now 30 to 50 years old. As in rural areas, those who live in the suburbs are likely to need a car for shopping, leisure, and medical appointments.

However, some older people continue to live in the central core of cities because they cannot afford to rent or buy in newer areas. Some of these older residents are forced to move because of urban renewal projects or increases in taxes or in the cost of heating and repairs. If they must move, the proportion of older people living in the central core decreases through the process of **gentrification**—inner-city houses are purchased, renovated, or demolished, and a new, more expensive house is built on the lot. The composition of these neighbourhoods changes because new residents tend to be younger, well-educated professionals, many of whom are dual-income, childless couples. At the same time, rents in the area increase, forcing older residents living on fixed incomes to move elsewhere. This pattern has also occurred in many smaller cities and towns.

In stable neighbourhoods, especially low-income areas, there is a high degree of homogeneity with respect to age, race or ethnicity, and class. This homogeneity fosters the development of a network of neighbours who provide mutual support and assistance in later life. But when a neighbourhood experiences a rapid turnover in homeowners, or when homes are purchased by members of a different age, SES, or ethnic or racial group, heterogeneity increases and a sense of community may be lost. Consequently, in the later years, an older person who ages in place may live in a non-supportive, gentrified environment.

The Proclivity to Age in Place

Older people who are able to live independently have three general choices in where to live: remain in the house or apartment where they have lived for many years; move to another living unit in the same neighbourhood or community; or migrate to another community in a different part of the province or country.

For a variety of reasons, older people, especially in urban areas, strive to live in the family home unless forced to move late in life. Over time, our home represents a defined, personal place that provides independence, security, a sense of belonging, and a repository of family history and memories (Golant 2003; Rowles and Chaudhury 2005; Chaudhury 2008). People establish ties to the place, the people, and the physical setting of the neighbourhood or community. Aging in place allows older people to form and maintain a sense of identity and autonomy that institutionalized living does not permit or often encourage. When older people are faced with declining personal abilities or a deteriorating neighbourhood or home, they engage in psychological adaptation to convince themselves and others that they can remain in their current environment. This psychological adaptation may involve gradually accepting or denying health-related disabilities or difficulties, developing innovative strategies to cope with an environment that is becoming more challenging, changing expectations about what constitutes an ideal or adequate environment, denying the loss of competence to fully cope with the environment, or believing that with a short time left to live, a change in housing is not worth the effort (Wister 1989).

Living in a familiar environment becomes more difficult if a person is less able to walk or drive, is unable to perform the activities of daily living, has difficulty maintaining the interior or exterior of the home, or is afraid of crime in the area, or if there is a lack of services available to ensure a safe and healthy life. However, family, neighbours, friends, or service agencies may be able to alleviate these challenges. In situations where independent living is no longer an option, decisions must be made about a change in housing or in living arrangements. Relocation has the potential to make the residential environment more suitable to the needs and preferences of older adults.

An Ecological Model of Aging: Person–Environment Interaction

To explain the links between aging individuals and their environment, researchers have proposed a number of theories and models.[2] These theoretical perspectives focus either on the "meaning" that an environment evokes in an older person (i.e., whether it is satisfying because of feelings of attachment and memories and contributes to a desire to age in place) or on how individual competencies and environmental factors interact to foster adaptation in later life. These latter theories argue that individuals either change their personal environment or adjust to it through adaptive behaviour that maximizes the "fit," or congruence, between their personal needs and the demands of a specific environment in order to maximize their well-being. However, incongruence and discontent can result from major personal changes: a housing move, a sudden decline in health, a personal crisis such as divorce or widowhood, or the inability to drive or to manage tasks around the home. When there is deviation from some ideal balance between personal needs or abilities and the environment, a change in personal needs and/or the environment is necessary to restore congruence and well-being.

Environmental Press and Individual Competence

Lawton and his associates (Lawton and Nahemow 1973; Lawton 1980; Lawton et al. 1982) developed an "ecological model of adaptation and aging" that includes the macro-environment (the community where older people live) and the micro-environment (the housing where they spend most of their time). This model is based on the premise that adaptation involves the interaction of *individual competence* and *environmental press*. Individual competence includes health, sensorimotor functioning, perception, and cognitive skills, and it is measured by observable behaviour that reflects the presence of these states and abilities. Environmental press includes an assessment of five types of environments in later life (Lawton 1980, 17–18) that can create different demands, or "presses," for older people:

- the personal environment, including significant others, such as a spouse, children, and friends
- the group environment, which provides social norms and reference groups
- the supra-personal environment, or the average characteristics of individuals in the immediate neighbourhood (that is, similarities or differences in age, income, race, and ethnicity)
- the social environment, which includes cultural values, political events, and economic cycles
- the objective physical environment, whether it be small (one room) or large (a metropolitan or regional area)

In addition to the objective environment, the subjective or perceived environment is also important for successful adaptation in later life. These subjective experiences influence behaviour in addition to, and independently of, the "objective" environment. For example, an older person who feels that the porch stairs are becoming "too long or steep" and therefore avoids using them may reduce his or her daily interaction with others in the neighbourhood. Another older person, however, may be unwilling or unable to perceive that the stairs are dangerous, given his or her personal ability. In this situation, the stairs may increase the risk of a fall, which could lead to hospitalization, death, or the need to move to another type of housing unit.

The Ecological Model of Aging
The ecological model of aging (Figure 8.1) illustrates that the level of individual competence can vary from low to high, while the degree of environmental press can range from weak

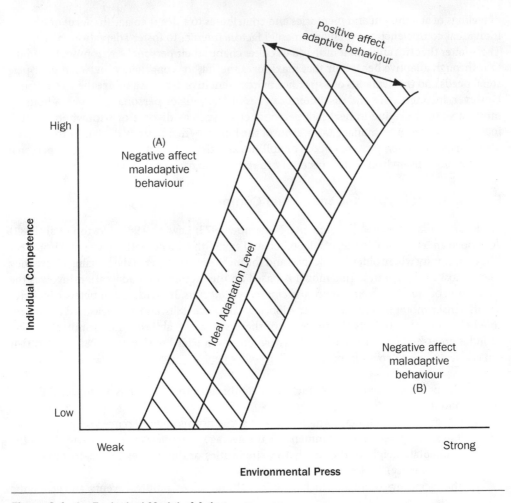

Figure 8.1 An Ecological Model of Aging

Source: Adapted from Lawton and Nahemow (1973).

to strong. The outcome of the interaction between competence and environment influences adaptive behaviour and affect (emotional or mental state); the slope represents ideal behavioural adaptation and positive affect. The slightly fan-shaped curve indicates that as the level of competence increases, the ability to tolerate higher levels of environmental press increases (this is termed the docility hypothesis). The less competent an individual, the more the environment influences adaptation and quality of life. Point A, which represents maladaptive behaviour and negative affect, can be illustrated by a situation in which highly competent people experience sensory deprivation (solitary confinement). Point B represents a low level of competence and strong environmental press. This situation also leads to maladaptive behaviour and negative affect and can be illustrated, in the extreme, by an elderly homeless person in a northern region who spends the winter trying to survive while living on the street.

Individual competence and environmental press are influenced by individual differences in needs and by the extent to which environments vary in their ability to satisfy these needs.

When competence and press are balanced, there is congruence and a positive mental state. A lack of balance suggests person–environment incongruence and a negative mental state. Since individual competence generally declines with age, a reduced capacity to cope with environmental demands may occur.

A major criticism of the ecological model of aging is that it assumes that people are passive and do not try to meet their needs or preferences through the use of environmental resources, or agency. The model has been criticized, as well, for not taking into account a person's familiarity with his or her current environment or a willingness to take behavioural risks in his or her environments (Wister 1989).

Environmental Proactivity

In response to criticism, Lawton (1990) introduced the concept of environmental proactivity. In this process, older people actively adapt to or change their physical or social environment before the environment creates pressure for change. How they do that depends on their personal, social, and economic resources to reduce "press." Environmental decisions are often made after a crisis, such as an illness, a fall, economic hardship, or the loss of a spouse. In reality, however, the wish to "age in place" often overrides any rational decisions concerning housing in later life.

Multilevel P–E Model of Aging

Cvitkovich and Wister (2001, 2002) argued that a life course perspective must be incorporated within the person–environment (P–E) model of aging, since the timing, duration, and sequencing of person–environment transactions and thresholds vary across the life course, particularly in later life. Their multi-level P–E model of aging involves an individual's subjective perception of the relative importance of three environmental domains: structural resources (e.g., housing, the neighbourhood, the community); social support (i.e., from family, friends, neighbours); and service support (i.e., from home care, community agencies, health services). Tested against three other P–E models, the multi-level model, which places more emphasis on the subjective interpretations, increases the prediction of well-being among a group of frail elderly persons.

Residential Normalcy

Golant (2011b) has offered a theoretical model of residential normalcy to explain residential stability or moves and the complex processes involved in those decisions (2011b, 193):

> The model equates individual-environment "residential normalcy" with older persons having favorable or positive emotion-based residential experiences that have relevance to them. Older persons are theorized as being in their residential comfort zones when they experience overall pleasurable, hassle-free, and memorable feelings about where they live; and in their residential mastery zones when they occupy places in which they feel competent and in control. When older persons are out of either (or both) of these experiential zones, they are expected to initiate accommodative and/or assimilative forms of coping to achieve residential normalcy. The former are mind strategies by which they change their residential goals or assessments, mollify their negative emotional experiences, or engage in denial behaviors; the latter are action strategies, by which they change their activities or modify their residential settings. Moving to a new address is the most studied and prominent assimilative coping strategy, but also the one that requires the most strenuous adaptive efforts.

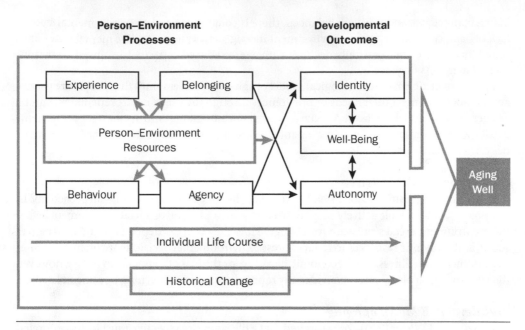

Figure 8.2 Conceptual Framework: Interplay of Belonging and Agency, Aging Well, and the Environment

Source: Adapted from Wahl et al. (2012). *The Gerontologist*, 52: 306–16 (Published by Oxford Journals). http://gerontologist.oxfordjournals.org/content/52/3/306/F1.large.jpg

This model weaves together the proactive, emotional, and adaptive processes that older people can use when evaluating their living environments. The model also helps us to understand why some older adults age in place even though professionals evaluate their housing environment in more negative terms. This leads us into a discussion of key environmental challenges that need to be recognized and addressed in program and policy debates and actions.

An Integrative Framework of Aging

An integrative framework of aging well within a person–environment interchange has been introduced by Wahl et al. (2012). This framework also connects the principal elements of many of the models presented above. It combines agency (proactivity), belonging, and person–environment resources with life-course changes and experiences to understand developmental outcomes—identity, well-being, and autonomy—and, ultimately, aging well. Figure 8.2 presents this model.

Coping with the Environment: Challenges and Adaptations

As people age, they may need assistance in order to carry out the essential **activities of daily living (ADLs)**, such as bathing, eating, using the toilet, and walking about the home. They may receive assistance from others, or they may need to use mechanical aids: a cane, a walker, a wheelchair, a riding chair for stairs, a chair and grab bars in a bathtub or shower, or a raised toilet seat with grab bars. Similarly, older people may lose their ability to perform **instrumental**

activities of daily living (IADLs), such as maintaining a house, preparing meals, and shopping or banking because of difficulty in walking or standing. As well, they may suffer from cognitive impairment, and they may be unable or unwilling to drive. In such cases, older people need help if they are to continue living in their home.[3]

This section discusses five environmental challenges facing older people: (1) the risk of falls and injuries; (2) the loss of private transportation; (3) crimes against older adults and the fear of crime among older people; (4) technology as a means of helping older people live in a safe and familiar environment; and (5) homelessness among older citizens.

Falls and Injuries: Risk Factors and Prevention

Falls and injuries (which may result in an acute injury or permanent disability) among older adults are a costly public-health problem and a major reason why older people lose their independence, move into sheltered housing or institutions, or visit emergency rooms in hospitals (Morley 2002; Public Health Agency of Canada 2010). Older people suffer burns from cooking, knife cuts from preparing food, muscle and joint injuries as a result of overexertion, poisoning from improper medication, and injuries resulting from falls. The definition and meanings of a fall can vary among older persons, their caregivers, and researchers, but the most common definition is when an individual inadvertently comes to rest on the ground or floor (Peel 2011; Speechley 2011).

Among older people, falls are the leading cause of both fatal and nonfatal unintentional injuries (Scott 2005; Peel 2011). Indeed, approximately one in three older adults falls once per year, or about 1.5 million seniors, and about one-quarter to one-half of those experience multiple falls (Public Health Agency of Canada 2010; Speechley 2011). While under-reporting of falls is likely, attempts are being made to educate professionals and the public to improve incident reporting (Peel 2011).

While most falls do not produce injury, between 10 and 15 per cent result in a serious injury, with the most common being hip and other bone fractures (Peel 2011). Falling is associated with reduced motor functioning and vision, with increased dependence and premature nursing home admission, and with death (Kenny 2005). For those aged 70 and older, more than 87 per cent of injuries resulting in hospitalization are caused by falls, and 75 per cent of these injuries lead to death (Health Canada 2002c). Women are more likely to fall than men, and falls are more common in long-term-care facilities, likely due to residents' frailty levels. The estimated annual direct and indirect cost to the health-care system of fall-related injuries to older adults is nearly $1 billion (NACA 2006).

Falls occur about equally inside and outside of the home. At home, people fall on stairs, when getting in and out of bed or chairs, in bathtubs and showers, on slippery floors, when dressing, and when suddenly changing direction while walking. Outside the home, they fall on uneven ground, at curbs when crossing streets, in malls when they are jostled or on escalators. A single fall may not cause a broken wrist, arm, leg, or hip, but repeated falls increase the risk of serious injury. And fear of falling leads to inactivity and social isolation.

There are three types of risk factors related to falls and injuries among older people: (1) personal, (2) home, and (3) community. The main personal risk factors are loss of strength, flexibility, and balance; being female; poverty; limited vision, cognitive impairment, or physical illness (strokes or Parkinson's disease); lack of concentration; unsuitable medication; impaired mobility because of problems with the feet, ankles, knees, or hips (Speechley et al. 2005; Menz et al. 2006; Martin 2011; Speechley 2011); living alone; drinking alcohol; and haste (when crossing a street or performing some task). Risk factors in the home environment include poor lighting; steep and slippery stairs; slippery floors; the absence of grab bars in bathtubs and showers; loose rugs; and high cupboards that require the person to reach. Community risk factors include high curbs; sidewalks with cracks and raised sections; traffic lights that allow only a short time for pedestrians to cross; snow or ice on walkways; inadequate lighting; and slippery or high stairs in public transit vehicles and buildings. Many of these risk factors are associated with one another by means of complex causal chains. For instance, some factors such as aging or being female are associated with factors such as balance and gait. Indeed, Speechley (2011) contends that understanding the large number of identified risk factors associated with falling may be advanced by considering balance and gait as the primary factor through which other factors combine to produce falls.

Preventive measures can reduce the incidence and seriousness of falls (Martin 2011; Speechley 2011).[4] At the personal level, these measures include exercising to improve balance, gait, strength, and flexibility; using an assistive device, such as a cane or walker; moving slowly when changing position from lying or sitting to standing; reducing alcohol consumption; using safe, well-fitting footwear and clothing, perhaps with plastic hip protectors or foam pads; and avoiding medications that have such side effects as loss of balance or judgment. In the home, interventions and adaptations include installing grab bars and railings; using ramps instead of stairs; installing padded flooring; using brighter lights and movement-sensor lights for nighttime; installing alarm and monitoring systems; using portable cordless telephones so that the person does not have to rush to the phone; and keeping traffic areas clear of obstructions.

Private and Public Transportation

Mobility is a key factor in maintaining one's quality of life and is essential to maintaining independence in later life (Flaherty et al. 2003; Tuokko et al. 2007). Yet the prevalence of reported problems with transportation among those 75 and over may be as high as 33 per cent among women and 10 per cent among men (Dupuis et al. 2007). As an elderly woman stated, "independence is power . . . to move around when you want to" (Finlayson and Kaufert 2002, 82). Accessible and affordable transportation enables older people to remain independent, obtain the goods and services they need, do volunteer work, engage in social activity, and fulfill obligations in later life. Yet access to and personal availability of transportation declines with age. Those who are most likely to have reduced access to private or public transportation in later life are widows, those in poor health, those over 80 years of age, rural residents, and those with low incomes. Those without access to a car or public transportation are less likely to go out of the home (Turcotte 2006), and those who relinquish their driver's licence, especially men, have a higher risk of depression (Satariano et al. 2004; Raglund et al. 2005) (see Highlight 8.2).

Older people who no longer drive or who have never driven (some women in current older cohorts) have three transportation alternatives: (1) be driven by volunteers, friends, or children; (2) take taxis or public transportation; or (3) use specialized transit services that provide door-to-door service. Rural residents who are unable to drive are even more likely than urban residents to be housebound and dependent. Where public transportation exists in urban or suburban areas, routes needed by older people may not be available or convenient, or the fare may be too expensive, even if reduced fares are available for "senior citizens" (Tuokko et al. 2007). In addition, a fear of crime on the subway and physical barriers (large crowds, high steps onto a bus) may discourage older adults from using public transit. Partly for those reasons, many communities have established "dial-a-ride" programs with door-to-door service.

Highlight 8.2
The Meaning of Loss of Transportation

"I can drive to see my old friends because I still have my licence. But I am afraid I may not be allowed to keep it. There is no local bus, and there are no shops or amenities nearby." (An 82-year-old widow living in a housing complex for seniors)

"When my driver's licence was revoked, it was a terrible loss of independence. I just don't have the money to spend on taxis and am too frail to use public transportation. My friends get tired of taking me where I need to go." (An 89-year-old widow living alone in her home)

"I had to give up driving eight years ago. I'm very frail now, and things have gotten worse since I fractured my hip last year. I can get into a car fairly well, but riding on city streets is very rough on my back. Any sudden stops and starts are very painful. Buses are impossible because of my back pain and the height of the steps." (A 92-year-old living alone in her apartment)

Source: Adapted from Statistics Canada. 1996. "Growing Old in Canada," Catalogue no. 96-321-MPE. Ottawa: 22 December. 1991 Census Monograph Series.

The Older Driver

In recent years, increasing attention has been directed to the habits of and risks associated with older drivers (Munro 2000; Bedard et al. 2002; Klavora and Heslegrave 2002; NACA 2003; Adler and Rottunda 2006; Rudman et al. 2006; Satariano 2007; Dickerson et al. 2007; Caragata et al. 2009; Nasvadi and Wister 2009). This has, in part, been the result of newspaper reports of serious accidents involving older adults, coupled with population aging. According to Turcotte (2006), 71 per cent of those aged 65 and over have access to a household vehicle as a driver. But gender differences are large in that among those aged 75 to 84, 83 per cent of the men but only 45 per cent of the women drive. Over 85 years of age, the difference is 66 per cent for men versus 33 per cent for women. This gender gap will narrow dramatically as the baby boomers age, since most women in this generation have always had driving and car-ownership patterns similar to those of men. Currently, just 40 per cent of those 65 and over drive three or more times a week, and distances driven tend to be, on average, 11 to 17 kilometres a day (NACA 2003). For the average number of kilometres driven, older drivers have more accidents than any other age group (Munro 2000). Indeed, Transport Canada (White 2007) found that Canadians over the age of 65 account for just 15 per cent of auto fatalities but that drivers over 75 cause more accidents per kilometre driven than their 16-year-old grandchildren. Possible causes include reduced vision, especially at night; poor hearing; dementia; side effects of medication (drowsiness); slower response time; shorter attention span; and an inability to make quick decisions. Yet because they drive comparatively little, the risk older drivers pose to traffic safety is much lower than that of other drivers (especially those under 25), even though older drivers are likelier to cause an accident when they do drive (Rand Institute for Civil Justice 2007).

How to ensure that older drivers are competent is a difficult task for families, for physicians (who are now liable if an elderly patient in their practice with dementia or stroke symptoms is at fault in an accident), and for public policy–makers. Older persons seldom volunteer to stop driving (Raglund et al. 2004), but they often engage in some regulation of their driving behaviours, such as not driving at night or staying off busy highways (Donorfio 2008). However, self-regulation does not necessarily reduce crash risk (Ross et al. 2009). Family members should ride with older relatives or follow them while they are driving to assess their driving ability. If there is concern, they should consult with the doctor or local police and ask them to take action.

From a public-policy perspective, this issue is a classic case of whether policies should be based on age or on competence. General approaches are to identify problem drivers and de-license them, use a graduated or restricted licence system that would not allow them to drive at night or on certain highways, require older drivers to take retraining, require annual vision and motor performance testing, and increase the use of such aids as wider mirrors, pedal extensions, booster seats, and visual enhancement systems. A recent BC study showed that restricted licenses among older drivers reduced crash risk (Nasvadi and Wister 2009). However, there are many unresolved issues concerning any attempt to monitor or control older drivers: (1) How do we balance the rights of individuals to remain independent and to drive against the need to ensure public safety? (2) Who is responsible for de-licensing: the government, the family, the police, or the physician? (3) What tests and criteria are fair and accurate when older drivers are tested (medical and visual exams, motor skills and reaction time tests, written tests, simulated tests, on-road tests)? In some jurisdictions, these issues have become highly political, with "seniors" groups lobbying against restrictions on elderly drivers. Others argue for a system of self-regulation for older drivers (Rudman et al. 2006). As a sign that older drivers are seen as becoming a serious public issue, a senior driver website has been created in the United States to provide information to families, older drivers, and policy-makers and to post the latest research and resources about older drivers (www.seniordrivers.org).

Victimization and Fear of Crime among Older Adults

Interest in the incidence of crime against older citizens has been stimulated by news reports of assaults or fraud involving older people and by the number who report that they have fears about being victimized, either in their home or in the community. In some cases, this fear may be so great that they become prisoners in their homes, afraid to walk in their neighbourhood during the day or night. This real or imagined unsafe environment reduces mobility and social interaction, thereby lowering the quality of life of older people.

Victimization of Older Adults

Many crime statistics do not accurately reflect either how many crimes are perpetrated against older people, or the victims' attributes. Older victims are sometimes referred to as "hidden victims" because they are less likely than younger people to report crimes—for fear of retaliation, for fear that their children or friends will think they are no longer able to take care of themselves, or from a reluctance to admit that they were exploited by a fraudulent investment scheme. To illustrate, in 2005, only about 51 per cent of violent crimes against seniors were reported to the police (Ogrodnik 2007).

When compared to crimes inflicted on members of all other age groups, the prevalence rates of crimes against older persons, based on official statistics, are lower, especially for violent crimes, such as homicide, rape, or assault with robbery. The 2004 *General Social Survey* and the 2005 *Uniform Crime Reporting Survey* (Ogrodnik 2007) reported that only 10 per cent of those aged 65 and older were victimized during the preceding 12 months, compared to 31 per cent of those under 65. Moreover, the rate of violent victimization (homicide, sexual assault, or assault with robbery) was 12 self-reported incidents for every 1000 older adults, about 4 times and 20 times less than for those 55 to 64 and 15 to 24, respectively. In 2005, there were 49 homicides involving older adults (25 men and 24 women), which represented 7 per cent of all homicides in Canada that year. Men are more likely to be victims of violent crimes, and 50 per cent of the violence against all seniors is committed by a family member (an adult child [35 per cent] or spouse [31 per cent]), a friend, or an acquaintance.[5] With respect to theft of personal property, there were 22 incidents per 1000 seniors in 2005, compared to 51 and 165 incidents for the 55 to 64 and 15 to 24 groups, respectively. However, even though these crime rates are low in relative terms, it is alarming that older adults are virtually invisible in government justice research and criminological literature (Hayman 2011).

How can these patterns of victimization be explained? The likelihood of personal victimization is related to environment and lifestyle. First, older people are victimized less than younger people because they are not as exposed to risk since they are less likely to go out at night; because they avoid high-crime environments (entertainment districts in large cities or poorly lit areas); and because the lifestyles of younger people expose them more frequently to environments or situations conducive to crime. Second, older people who experience a higher risk of victimization are often those who are more socially disadvantaged. Their chance of being assaulted increases if they live in or near neighbourhoods with high crime rates, if they live alone, and if they are dependent on walking or on public transportation rather than travelling by car. Third, persons who are marginalized with respect to income, ethnicity, or community have fewer resources linked to human and social capital that insulate people from exposure to crime.

Older citizens are often victims of fraud (Donahue 2001; Cohen 2006; Ogrodnik 2007), which may be conducted by mail, the Internet, telemarketing, or door-to-door salespeople. Fraud against older people involves credit cards, bank accounts, donations to fake charities, assuming a new mortgage on a mortgage-free home, contracting for unneeded home repairs, and even friendships or love affairs in which younger people gain the affections of vulnerable octogenarians and acquire money or property that might otherwise be left to adult children. The most common form of fraud is the awarding of fake prizes, typically through the Internet or mail (Cohen 2006). According to PhoneBusters, Canada's anti-fraud call centre, between 1996 and 2003, 84 per cent of the total dollar loss through telemarketing or prize and lottery scams was experienced by victims over 60 (Ogrodnik 2007). Being a victim of larceny, property loss, or a fraudulent crime is traumatic for older persons, partly because the loss often represents a larger percentage of their financial resources than it would for a younger person. Such crimes also generate fear and anxiety about the security of their environment.

To reduce crime against older people, educational, social support, and safety programs are being developed. These include special police units in neighbourhoods where there is a high percentage of middle- and low-income older residents; voluntary escort services to and from the home; dial-a-bus services; home security systems; support services for victims; and public education about crime in later life. For instance, a "senior Busters" program involves volunteers over the age of 50 assisting senior victims of telemarketing fraud by providing them with advice and emotional support, including how and to whom fraud should be reported (Ogrodnik 2007). There are also elder abuse centres in most major cities that maintain a crisis phone line, with some also providing temporary shelter.

Fear of Victimization

One indirect result of greater publicity about crime against older people and the creation of special support systems to prevent or discourage crime is increased fear. Although older people are victimized less than other age groups, in some studies a large number of respondents (as many as 50 per cent) express fear that they may be victimized and say that fear of crime is one of their most serious personal problems.

Fear is generally reported more frequently by older women who are poor or live alone in high-crime neighbourhoods, or in subsidized age-integrated or racially/ethnically integrated housing complexes.[6] Fear is higher among those who have been victimized or know someone who has been victimized, who are physically disabled, or who use public transportation. The characteristics of the neighbourhood environment also influence the incidence and level of fear—if street lights are not very bright, if there are few pedestrians or little or no police or security surveillance, or if young people congregate there. These areas should be targeted to improve perceptions and the actual safety of older adults. Fear of crime is another example of how declining personal competence and an environment that is or appears to be dangerous can interact to influence the quality of life in the later years.

Technology in Later Life[7]

Assistive Devices and Enabling Technology

Various devices maintain or increase functional capabilities among people with impaired vision or hearing or who have difficulty walking. Other devices provide assistance with personal care, homemaking, and leisure activities. The primary purpose of these devices is to enhance independence, safety, and function; increase the quality of life and active aging; and reduce health and social-support costs to the individual and to society (Health Canada 2002b; Cutler 2006; Scialfa and Fernie 2006; Sixsmith 2006; Sixsmith and Gutman 2013). Freedman et al. (2006) found that the use of technology in the home can reduce by 50 per cent the number of older people who become dependent on personal care.

Mechanical and technological aids for the home include non-slip floors, walkers, chairs for bathtubs or showers, raised seats for furniture and toilets, L-shaped door handles, grab bars, personal emergency response systems, telephones and books with large print, kitchen utensils with larger handles, talking books and specialized computer software, hearing aids, motion-activated lights and security systems, and wheelchair-accessible vans, entrances, and doorways. These aids contribute to a safer and more functional environment, especially for those living alone, and enable older people to remain living in their home (Chappell 1994; Zimmer and Chappell 1999; CAG 2000; NACA 2001; Charness and Schaie 2004; Cutler 2006). "Smart-home systems" assist and monitor older people with cognitive decline, difficulty in walking, and declining health. Sensors placed in clothing or jewellery or installed into furniture, ceilings, floors, or walls to collect and report data can be programmed to prevent the person from entering a kitchen or bathroom alone, from wandering inside or outside, or from stepping onto stairs (Sixsmith and Johnson 2004). These devices can also be used to measure changes in health status over time, and they highlight the potential of information and communication technologies to assist older people to age in place (Sixsmith and Sixsmith 2008; Sixsmith and Gutman 2013).

Aids also reduce caregiver stress and provide some relief to a spouse who may not be able to constantly monitor his or her partner's safety, movement, or health or lift a partner who falls or has difficulty standing up from a lying or sitting position. Such devices facilitate mobility in the home and community and enable older people to improve their quality of life and sense of self-worth and autonomy (Sixsmith 2006). While some technologies are not introduced until a person's health and coping problems emerge, others are part of most adults' normal daily living: banking machines; cell and portable phones with voice mail and caller ID; and the Internet for email, shopping, banking, stock trading, and information retrieval.

However, not all older people are able or willing to use the new technology. Some are "frightened" or insecure about using technology, while others are ambivalent, especially toward information technology (IT). The rate of adoption and mastery of new technology varies both across and within cultures and by education, health status, and work experience with IT (Charness and Czaja 2005). This adoption lag within the older population needs to be reduced so that inequities in access to available services and opportunities are minimized for older adults (Scialfa and Fernie 2006). In this sense, there is an age-based (as well as a socio-economic) "digital divide" across the population: between those who have access to and use technology to help them adapt to their environment and those who do not (Selwyn 2004; Charness and Czaja 2005). The introduction of more technology into rural Canada could reduce some of the isolation of rural living for older people (NACA 2001).

Nonetheless, older people's increasing use of the Internet indicates a willingness to adopt new technology. Each year, more older adults are using it to communicate with friends and relatives, for dating, for everyday activities such as banking and grocery shopping, for entertainment, for voting during elections, for online support groups and advice (about caregiving, widowhood), and for health (Friedman et al. 2006), travel, government, and leisure information. (The Public Health Agency of Canada website provides information to older adults on health matters: www .publichealth.gc.ca.) Newspaper headlines such as "Cyber Granny," "Surfing Seniors," or "Wired and Retired" are much less likely to be sensationalized with more widespread Internet use among older people, including at seniors' centres, libraries, and "Internet cafés." Most studies indicate that older adults, if motivated, can learn to use computers but are often slower in acquiring the skills and therefore may require more support and assistance (Charness and Czaja 2005).

Although the availability of technological aids is increasing, cost, lack of knowledge about their availability, unwillingness to adopt an unfamiliar technology, and the perceived stigma of using certain assistive devices limit their widespread use. Moreover, a debate has emerged as to whether impersonal technology or personal help is most appropriate for providing assistance to older people.

The Homeless Elderly

Although they are invisible to most members of a community, a growing number of older people live and sleep in public shelters or in streets, parks, subways, or abandoned buildings, especially in large cities (McDonald et al. 2007). Homelessness among older people is often a continuation of a lifestyle begun in youth or adulthood. But for a smaller number, homelessness is a new living arrangement triggered by relatively recent financial, health, or personal trauma that caused the person to leave his or her permanent residence (Ploeg et al. 2008; Crane and Warnes 2010). Reasons for this new state in life include the onset of personal problems (financial losses, death of a close relative who had provided support and supervision); long-term poverty and marginalization; disputes with other tenants or neighbours that resulted in eviction; alcohol, drug or gambling addictions; or recent physical or cognitive impairments. These personal troubles are compounded if there are insufficient welfare policies and programs in the community or if there is a lack of sufficient subsidized housing.

Most older homeless people are men, but the number of homeless women is growing, especially women who have been physically or sexually abused, are mentally ill, have substance abuse problems, or have been abandoned by partners or family. Other factors that contribute to homelessness in middle or later life are being discharged from a penitentiary or mental institution, lacking close family ties, and enduring lifelong poverty. Older, long-standing homeless people are often under the age of 65 since life expectancy for them is much lower than it is for most of their age cohort. For public-health services, older homeless people use outpatient services for substance abuse, chronic illness, and musculoskeletal conditions, and in-patient services for mental illnesses (Nakonezny and Ojeda 2005). Some formerly homeless people over 65 years of age have become wards of the state and are no longer living on the streets.

There is a small but growing number of studies of homeless older people (e.g., Cohen 1999; Crane 1999; CMHC, 2000a; Crane et al. 2005; McDonald et al. 2007; Ploeg et al. 2008; Crane and Warnes 2010). While we do not know exactly how many homeless elderly people there are in Canada because surveys are fraught with many limitations, estimates range from 14 to 28 per cent among persons aged 50 and over (they are often considered to be "older adults" due to higher mortality and morbidity among this population) (Stergiopoulos and Herrmann 2003). Absolute numbers will likely increase as the older population grows, especially if social support programs for older homeless people are not developed (Ploeg et al. 2008). The number of homeless women with a history of severe mental illness and substance abuse is increasing, and many report some form of physical or sexual abuse in childhood that prompted them to leave their home and family at an early age. Others reported being on the streets because of family or marital breakdowns. More than half reported being the victim of recent assaults "on the street" or being in a coed shelter or drop-in centre. Thus, gender-segregated shelters are essential, because many women avoid shelters or low-cost hotels for fear of rape or other assaults. These women seek shelter in more visible public spaces, such as storefronts, which they consider safer.

Members of this vulnerable group pose a challenge for the social-welfare system, which faces large annual increases in the number of homeless youth who must be served and protected. Homeless youth often receive priority in terms of facilities, programs, and policies. And the lifelong experience of poverty, mental illness, and marginalization makes it difficult for older homeless people to adjust to traditional long-term-care institutions. Many meet an early death and are often buried as "unknown" paupers. Furthermore, homeless elderly people are difficult to reach with social services. Many are transients who live from day to day or week to week in single-room-occupancy hotels (SROs) in poor, high-crime sections of a city. Here, they may develop an informal social-support system consisting of the hotel's staff and fellow residents. To serve this unique subculture of older people, structural risk factors (poverty, lack of housing, poor access to mental health services, etc.) must be eliminated. Ploeg et al. (2008) state that the provision of a coordinated, seamless service network with accessible low-cost housing, income support, and community health and support services is needed. For some, learned helplessness has become a way of life, characterized by living in a dependent and marginalized condition over extended periods of time. But job training and help with finding a low-skill job can alter the behaviour of some older homeless people.

Living Arrangements in Later Life

Throughout the life course, marriage, divorce, widowhood, poor health, poverty, or never having been married interact to influence who we live with. In later life, options include living in a kinship unit (with a spouse, adult children, a grandchild, siblings, or other relatives); living alone; living with unrelated persons, often in some type of group setting; or living in an institution.

The majority of older Canadians who are not in an institution either live with a family member, usually a spouse, or live alone (Turcotte and Schellenberg 2007; Connidis 2010). Table 8.1 illustrates the living arrangements of older Canadians as reported in the 2011 census. More men aged 65 and over tend to be in partnered arrangements than women (72.1 per cent compared to 43.8 per cent). Living alone is considerably more common for women aged 65+ (31.5 per cent compared to 16 per cent) and for those aged 85+ (36.6 per cent compared to 21.7 per cent). Rates of institutionalization are almost twice as high for older women than for older men 65 and over (10.1 per cent compared to only 5.3 per cent); and one-and-a-half times higher for older women aged 85 and over compared to their male counterparts (35.2 per cent compared to 22.6 per cent). Older women are also more likely to live with children, relatives, or non-relatives (see Table 8.1).

In Canada, values and preferences that are often linked to ethnicity are important factors affecting living arrangements. Kaida et al. (2009) found that elderly persons who hold familial cultural values (e.g., Italian, Chinese, South Asian, and East Asian) are more likely to live with kin than those embracing individualistic values emphasizing privacy and independence (e.g., British, German, Dutch). Most three-generation households are headed by immigrants, most of whom are from Asia, where both a cultural tradition of extended family living and economic necessity still prevail (Gee and Mitchell 2003). Chinese Canadians between the ages of 55 and 59 are nearly twice as likely to live with adult children, and those aged 80 to 85 are nearly four times as likely to live with children as are non-Asian people of the same age (Pacey 2002, 21–3).

At the structural level, decreasing fertility rates, more childless marriages, increased divorce rates and declining remarriage rates, more never-married women, and a growth in apartment, condo, and townhome housing options shape living arrangement opportunities and choices. At the personal level, more older adults have sufficient wealth to live alone and to buy assistance and services as needed, and more value privacy and autonomy. As well, most widowed people prefer to remain in their family home and familiar neighbourhood (Pacey 2002; Connidis 2010). In 2011, 24.6 per cent of the population aged 65 and over lived alone

Table 8.1   The Living Arrangements of Older Canadians (Percentages)

	With Spouse or Partner*	With Children/ Relatives/ Non-relatives	Alone		Institution	
	65+	65+	65+	85+	65+	85+
Women	43.8	14.6	31.5	36.6	10.1	35.2
Men	72.1	6.6	16.0	21.7	5.3	22.6

*Includes same-sex partners

Source: Data for this table from Figure 1, Statistics Canada. 2012. Living Arrangements of Seniors. Retrieved 8 October 2012 (www12.statcan.gc.ca/census-recensement/2011/as-sa/98-312-x/98-312-x2011003_4-eng.cfm).

(more than 1.2 million), with more women in this situation than men (see Table 8.1). Men are more likely to remarry, live with a woman, or live with a family member (Connidis 2010). Rates of living alone, especially for older women, have declined over the last decade, likely due to the fact that men are living longer and due to increased co-residence arrangements. Older women without much income are much more likely to live with an adult child (Pacey 2002). For older women who never married or were divorced or widowed in mid-life, living alone or living with an unrelated person represents a lifestyle adopted long before the onset of later life.

The next section examines the many types of housing available to older Canadians—from private homes to long-term-care geriatric settings.

Housing Alternatives in Later Life

Today, many older people are looking for more housing options from the public and private sectors. Initiatives to meet the demands have also been stimulated by the impending needs of members of the large baby boom generation who have already begun to move into their retirement years.

Independent Housing

The location and type of housing environment influences the social life and well-being of older people and determines what services are available for them in later life. Housing for older adults can be categorized and assessed along three intersecting dimensions: from independent to dependent, from age-integrated to age-segregated, and from low to high quality. More than 90 per cent of older Canadians live in private households for most of their later years. Of these, more than 60 per cent live in detached houses; 28 per cent, in apartments; 10 per cent, in semi-detached houses or townhouses; and 1 per cent, in mobile homes (Health Canada 2002a, 17; Clark 2005). About two-thirds of older Canadians own their home, and most of these homes are mortgage-free. Approximately one-quarter of those over 65 rent housing, and about half of that number live alone. For retirees who rent, the proportion of total income allocated to rent is higher than it is for renters in other age groups (Health Canada 2002a, 17). A small minority of older Canadians opt to live in age-segregated retirement communities, usually in temperate climates in southern Ontario or British Columbia. Thus, the majority of older Canadians are homeowners who age in place in the family home.

The home is a major asset, which helps retired or widowed owners to live on a reduced income. However, it can also be a liability because of increased operating costs because a high percentage of the owner's income is required for maintenance or because with declining health, a person is unable to maintain the house and garden. More than 75 per cent of houses owned by older Canadians appear to meet or exceed Canada's housing standards. This means "that their housing was in adequate condition, requiring no major repairs; suitable in size to meet their needs; and affordable, consuming less than 30 per cent of their total before-tax household income" (CMHC 2002; Health Canada 2002a, 17). However, approximately 17 per cent of senior households do not meet housing affordability, adequacy, and suitability criteria set out by the Canadian Mortgage and Housing Corporation (CMHC 2005; Weeks and LeBlanc 2010). The cost of housing is more of a burden for those who rent, those who live in large cities, those who are women who live alone, those who are over age 85, or those who are members of a visible minority group or a recent immigrant (i.e., the more vulnerable). For older women with a small

Highlight 8.3
Subsidized Housing Units for Low-Income Seniors: The Case of BC

- Households are deemed to be in "core need" if older adults pay more than 30 per cent of their income on housing.
- Older unattached women comprise the group in greatest need of core housing.
- Wait lists for subsidized one-bedroom or bachelor units can be as long as five years.
- Low-income seniors in subsidized rental housing units pay between $350 and $500 per month (30 per cent of income).
- In BC about 21,000 low-income seniors live in independent social housing.
- Some units are in assisted or supported environments, but have higher costs (see next section).
- A joint federal-BC government initiative costing $125 million has been underway since 2009 to build 1300 new affordable housing units for seniors in mainly small communities.

or declining pension, staying in the family home may become financially difficult. Although poverty rates have declined over the past decade for seniors, there are many at-risk groups, including older women living alone; certain immigrant groups; homeless elders; and those who have been marginalized (see Chapter 10). Highlight 8.3 provides an example of subsidized housing units for older adults living in BC.

People prefer to remain in the family home in their later years because the dwelling is a symbol of independence; a repository of family history, artifacts, and memories; a familiar and supportive social and physical environment; and a link to a valued "community" (Golant 1984; Rowles and Chaudhury 2005). Before a move from the family home is initiated—which can be stressful whether voluntary or not—the home can be renovated to make it safer and more accessible.[8] In addition, home-care workers can help with household chores, bathing and other personal care, and therapy; and a Meals on Wheels program can ensure that the older person is receiving a nutritious diet. Even though objective measures may suggest that a home is no longer safe, suitable, or accessible, many older people subjectively assess their situation differently and report being "satisfied" or "well-accommodated" in their place of residence. The next section introduces the concept of "supportive housing," which provides varying degrees of assisted living.

Supportive Housing

Supportive living is a form of housing that combines shelter, usually in the form of rented units, with a variety of services (congregate meals, security, housecleaning, and personal care) as needed (Spencer 2004). This type of housing arrangement may include independent living communities, assisted living, congregate housing,[9] and retirement homes. Sometimes, however, the type of arrangement available depends on provincial or state legislation (CHMC 2000b; Carder 2002; NACA 2002; Golant and Hyde 2008). Supportive living may be privately or publicly funded. Registered publicly funded units allow for low-income seniors to receive a subsidy for the costs of living in the residence after contributing 70 per cent of their after-tax income to the shelter cost (Spencer 2004).

In supportive housing, meals, housekeeping, and social and recreational programs are provided by qualified staff or through a home-care program. Residents can furnish their suites with their own possessions and can lock their doors, but they also have access to common areas (a dining hall, library, fitness room, spa, and social activity rooms). Residents are not viewed as "patients," as they are in nursing homes, and they are more involved in decisions about their "home" through a resident council and periodic consultations. This type of housing preserves the older person's autonomy, freedom of choice, privacy, and dignity in a home-like environment (Carder 2002; Golant and Hyde 2008). Most rooms are equipped with emergency call buttons. Additional services—laundry, personal care, massage, hairdressing—are available for a fee. Some facilities include a special floor for those with a cognitive or physical impairment who require 24-hour care and supervision but are not bedridden. Many of these facilities are privately funded and can be expensive (between $3000 and $4000 a month). Others are subsidized by the government, but waiting lists and careful screening for admission often delay a needed or desired move. It is interesting that research suggests that use of the health-care system declines once individuals move to supportive housing arrangements, such as assisted living, possibly due to the support received on site (McGrail et al. 2013).

With the aging of the baby boomers, CMHC (2000b) estimates that by 2031, there will be about four million people over 75 and about one million over 85 in Canada needing a variety of housing options. Many of these oldest Canadians will have activity limitations—CMHC estimates that 50 per cent of the 74 to 84 age group and 75 per cent of those 85 and over will have difficulty performing one or more of the activities of daily living. To meet the demand, a range of supportive housing options are required for low- as well as high-income citizens, which should be located in neighbourhoods close to where the person lived most of his or her adult life. As well, consumer protection mechanisms regarding contracts, billing for add-on services, staff-resident relations, and residents' rights and obligations must be developed and enforced (NACA 2002).

In recent years, the private sector has built multi-level housing and assistance options on a single site. These integrated facilities provide a continuum of housing, supervision, care, and assistance. At the most independent end of the housing continuum are self-contained apartments or condos where residents live independently of others in the complex, unless they decide to participate in some of the communal meals and social activities provided to the retirement home residents. Connected to the apartment or condo building is a retirement home where all meals are provided, as are a range of services and programs. The third element of the interconnected complex is a nursing home to which residents can be moved, when necessary, to receive long-term nursing care, including a locked floor for those with Alzheimer's disease, who are liable to wander. This type of complex enables a married couple to live in the same facility, even though one person is totally independent and lives in a condo unit, while the more dependent person with dementia typically lives in the adjacent nursing home.

Other forms of housing provide support through informal sources. The "accessory" apartment, either in the home of a child or attached to it, enables an older person to retain some privacy but to benefit, at the same time, from security and unobtrusive supervision. Another

Highlight 8.4
Home-Sharing in Later Life

An Age-Integrated Arrangement

By sharing his or her home with a university student or a young adult in the labour force, an older person acquires income, companionship, and security and receives assistance with household tasks. This living arrangement is a way to use housing stock more effectively, especially in university communities where housing is in short supply. The younger person spends less money on housing, contributes to the community, and, hopefully, learns about life from the wisdom and experience of an older person. And one or both may become "confidants" for the other in matters of personal and private concern.

An Age-Segregated Arrangement

Faced with living alone in a large house or being forced to move out of the family home, single older people, especially women, acquire a "housemate" of about the same age. This form of shared housing is a way to reduce costs, to be sociable and active, and to remain in safe and familiar surroundings. In some cases, tenants provide companionship or services in exchange for lodging rather than paying rent. The housemate may be a sibling or an old friend, but more often he or she is a stranger. With careful screening and selection, a friendship may evolve from the tenant–landlady arrangement.

---

version is a garden suite[10] or a "granny flat"—a self-contained cottage-like unit, consisting of one bedroom, a kitchen, a bathroom, and a living room, that is built on the property of an adult child or other relative. In the United States, these units are known as ECHO housing (for elder cottage housing opportunity). Originally conceived in Australia, they are more common in rural and suburban areas as the smaller lots that are common in many cities make such dwellings unfeasible. This type of housing enhances grandparent–grandchild relationships, minimizes travel time for family visiting, reduces guilt on the part of an adult child for "abandoning" a parent, and provides a temporary facility that is wheelchair-accessible and meets other specific needs created by physical disabilities.

Another type of "informal" supportive housing is home-sharing, in which a relative or tenant may move into the home of an older single person. Highlight 8.4 describes an age-integrated and an age-segregated home-sharing arrangement.

Some communities have agencies to facilitate home-sharing.[11] These agencies function like a matchmaking or dating service, and some offer mediation and monitoring services to help a housemate relationship grow and survive.

Dependent Living: Institutionalized Living in Later Life

With the passage in 1957 of the federal Hospital Insurance and Diagnostic Services Act, provinces were required to provide coverage for chronic and convalescent care. As a result, long-term-care facilities (also called residential care) for frail older people increased significantly in numbers and were established by provincial governments, by charitable and religious organizations, and by for-profit entrepreneurs. Since the 1970s, community support for independent living in the community has resulted in larger numbers of older adults remaining out of institutions until they have very limiting physical and/or mental-health problems. This means that, today, institutions care for individuals with more complex health needs than in the past (Hirdes et al. 2011).

Some of the major issues (Kane and Kane 2005; Stone 2006; Hirdes et al. 2011) concerning long-term care (LTC) include the following:

- determining the best level of care and improving services for residents with highly complex care needs
- enhancing residents' quality of life and survival rates
- meeting the needs of an ethnically and linguistically diverse older population
- designing institutions to facilitate autonomy, privacy, meaning, social interaction, and dignity in the later years of life
- defining "levels of care" with respect to the placement of individuals and the funding of institutions for the type of services they offer
- developing and maintaining minimum standards of care through voluntary or mandatory accreditation and/or licensing by the government
- deciding who pays for housing and services—the individual and/or the society—and in what proportions
- improving training and working conditions to retain employees and improve staff morale in retirement and nursing homes, where low wages are common in a very profitable industry

Since long-term-care facilities are not funded under the Canada Health Act, there are different services, funding levels, and definitions in each province. For example, the same level of care may be provided in a variety of facilities but with different names (Berta et al. 2005; Keays et al. 2009). Indeed, according to Statistics Canada (2011), there were 2216 residential-care facilities (homes for the aged, nursing homes, and lodges with four or more beds funded, licensed, or approved by provincial departments) providing care for the aged in Canada. These provided long-term care for 205,442 older adults. In 2011, approximately 10.1 per cent of women and 5.3 per cent of men 65 and over and 35.2 per cent of women and 22.6 per cent of men 85 and over lived in some type of institutionalized setting (see Table 8.1).

Decisions about who should or must be admitted to publicly funded long-term-care institutions are difficult. To provide objective assessments of relative need before admission to a facility, to monitor the changes in personal needs, and to assess the quality of care in an institution, since the mid-1990s most provinces have adopted a series of what have been termed interRAI assessments (Hirdes et al. 1999b, 2001, 2011; Warren 2000). The interRAI assessment instruments employ standardized methodologies to assess complex populations across home care, continuing care, and long-term-care environments (Hirdes et al. 2011). A series of RAIs are used in Canada: the Resident Assessment Instrument (RAI 2.0) for use in long-term-care facilities; the RAI-Home Care Instrument (RAI-HC) for assessing home-care needs; the RAI-Mental Health Assessment; the interRAI Contact Assessment; the interRAI Community Health Assessment; and the interRAI Palliative Care. These instruments have been shown to be highly reliable, valid, and useful in assessing both the needs and the quality of continuing and long-term care (Hirdes et al. 2011). In some provinces, RAIs are mandated by provincial legislation, whereas other provinces only recommend their use. The application of these standardized assessment tools provide vital information to address the long-term-care issues highlighted above.

Quality of Care

Nursing homes are subsidized and regulated by the provincial and territorial governments, whereas retirement homes operated by the private sector are not regulated. Consequently, inspection standards vary greatly, and the quality of living and care can range from "excellent" to "atrocious" in terms of sanitation, use of medication, nutrition, and the qualifications of and treatment by staff (Kane and Kane 2005; Schultz 2005; Keays et al. 2009). Occasionally, the media carry stories about physical or psychological neglect or abuse of residents, epidemic infections, unsanitary conditions, overmedication, or theft by staff. For this reason, government regulations are expanding to ensure that residents are not neglected, especially with respect to personal cleanliness; that their right to privacy and some control over their own lives are respected; and that an adequate staff-to-resident ratio is present at all hours of the day. Also, many jurisdictions require institutions to establish residents' councils that will provide feedback to the operators of those institutions. In reality, however, many of these councils are controlled by the staff of these same institutions; thus, some jurisdictions appoint ombudspersons and draft "bills of rights" to protect residents of long-term-care facilities.

The definition and measurement of quality in long-term-care institutions is a contentious issue,[12] and many factors and perspectives must be taken into account.[13] Staff, residents, and family members may have quite different opinions about the need for autonomy and privacy, about personal and public space, and about the quality and variety of food. Other issues include the scheduling of meals and bathing, who lives with whom and where in the facility, who can visit a resident and when, whether mobility and activity are permitted and encouraged to enhance self-esteem and self-care, and whether restraints are used to "control" residents (Hirdes et al. 1999a, 2011). Some of these quality issues are environmental—the arrangement of furniture, the provision of public space to encourage interaction with other residents, and the use of assistive devices (to transfer residents in and out of bed or to monitor or facilitate movement around the facility). For instance, the quality of, and access to, wheelchairs have been shown to enable mobility, connectedness, and staff assistance among residents of long-term-care facilities (Mortenson et al. in press). Other issues of quality can be addressed by staff training, to improve attitudes, procedures and care, and by regular consultation with residents and their families. Highlight 8.5 illustrates how one government (Ontario) seeks to improve the quality of life for residents of long-term facilities, while Highlight 8.6 identifies some unique long-term-care facilities that provide a high quality of life for residents.

Living and Working in a Long-Term-Care Facility

Moving in the later years from independent, private living to any type of institutional housing represents a major change in a person's life. Most people have difficulty adjusting to the lack of privacy, the reduction in personal and physical space, the regimented, monotonous daily routine, the "institutional" food, and the impersonal custodial care. Entering an institution is quite stressful, especially if the move is involuntary. The loss of one's home or apartment entails a loss of personal possessions, and it symbolizes vulnerability and frailty, loss of independence, and perhaps the imminence of death. For example, consider the thoughts of a 94-year-old widow who moved into a nursing home because she lost her balance and fell frequently:

Highlight 8.5
Principles and Regulations to Improve the Quality of Life in Long-Term-Care Facilities in Ontario

Residents of long-term-care (LTC) homes, and their families, need to be assured that they live with dignity and in safety, security, comfort, and cleanliness. There are 758 government-funded and regulated LTC homes in Ontario (Statistics Canada 2011). The following include a number of principles and regulations that the Ontario LTC system is attempting to put into practice through legislation:

- ensuring a fair and equitable process for gaining access to LTC homes that preserves the client's right to choice and maintains the requirement for consent on admission to any LTC home
- promoting zero tolerance of abuse and neglect of LTC residents whereby any alleged, suspected, or observed occurrence of abuse or neglect must be reported
- an enhanced Bill of Rights that entitles residents to privacy when meeting with a spouse or another person and to participation in the life of the LTC home
- whistle-blowing protection for staff, residents, and volunteers who report abuse and neglect
- requiring that a registered nurse be on duty in the LTC home 24 hours a day, seven days a week
- requiring residents' councils and encouraging family councils
- establishing an Office of the LTC Homes Resident and Family Advisor to provide information and assist residents, their families, and others
- restricting the use of restraints to limited circumstances where it is absolutely necessary and only with appropriate safeguards
- defining licence terms for LTC homes of up to 25 years, with the right to revoke a licence for noncompliance

Adapted from various documents and press releases by the Ontario Ministry of Health and Long-Term Care, 2004 to 2007. See www.health.gov.on.ca.

I'm a bump on a log. I'm absolutely useless. I'm just sitting here, a menace, you might say, worthless. . . . I'm not able to contribute to anything. I hope I don't live the rest of the year out because there's no point in it. There would just be more worry and more trouble for my son and his wife . . . they come every week no matter how busy they are. . . . But that is a burden to other people. There's nothing to look forward to. All you've got is your memories to look back on. (Gubrium 1993, 57)

In contrast, consider the observations of a granddaughter after her 80-year-old grandmother moved into an "assisted living" facility:

. . . before the stroke my grandmother was accustomed to living alone . . . this move forced her to cry often and claim, "Do you know what it is like to lose your freedom at my age?" . . . then she found a "crush" at her new home; a widower who lost his wife

Highlight 8.6
Exemplars of High-Quality, Innovative Care in Long-Term-Care Facilities

Montreal: Résidence Yvon-Brunet

This facility stresses that each resident is a full person, with the same rights and preferences they had before entering long-term care. The residence is considered a "home" and is a place to maintain interest in life, not just to maintain life. They have developed a "Charter of Rights and Freedoms of the Elderly" that includes 31 rights held sacred in the home, and they have a living environment advisor to ensure the rights are respected and invoked. The advisor also ensures that quality of life is stressed over staff routines and that resident rights are reflected in all decisions. Residents arise when they choose and have breakfast food choices. They can be present when rooms are cleaned, they have their own room key, and the facility includes a "Main Street" with a daycare, bakery, cafe, convenience store, tavern, travel agency, and bank.

Vancouver: Simon K.Y. Lee Seniors Care Home

In this facility for Chinese residents only, their own language and cultural traditions are employed by staff. Multi-level care is provided so that once living there, they can age in place. This facility adheres to the "Eden Alternative," which stresses that the facility must be seen as a habitat for human beings rather than for the frail and very old and that a self-identity and activity must be fostered, even among persons with dementia. Residents are offered as much control over decisions affecting them as possible, and a variety of programs are designed for persons with physical and mental limitations.

Toronto: Baycrest Centre

This facility is often labelled as the "gold standard" in Canada and throughout the world for its focus on research, combined with a high level of multi-level care wherein residents live in small, home-like units. Baycrest is a pioneer in caring for and conducting research on older adults with strokes or dementia. The main floor has a neighbourhood feeling with a courtyard, stores, restaurants, and an activity centre. They also have a daycare program for seniors living in the community.

Adapted from Minutes of the meeting of the National Advisory Council on Aging, Bethesda, Maryland. Exemplars of High Quality, Innovative Care in Long-Term Care Facilities', from NACA. 'The Changing Face of Long-Term Care', *Expression* 18 (4): 4–5.

20 years ago invited her to sit at breakfast with him and to go for coffee. As well, she has met some great ladies and all they do is joke together like sorority girls . . . "I'm living the college days I missed out on." One day she said to me, "If I had stayed in my own house alone after the stroke, I would never have had so many laughs." Recently, I joked that her love life is better than mine, and she responded, "You never know what can happen, even tomorrow. Things you'd never expect." (Adapted from Belluz 2007)

The stress of moving to an institution can be reduced if the older person is prepared in advance by touring the facility and if the family maintains contact and monitors the quality of care received and resident's specific needs after the move. It is easier to adjust if the person receives social support from friends and relatives, has moved voluntarily before any crisis or emergency, and is given some control over his or her daily life in the institution. Many new residents become more active after moving in and experience an improvement in their psychological, social, and physical well-being.

Adjustment is also easier if the person plays a part in designing a familiar interior environment rather than having to accept an impersonal institutionalized setting. Residents should be encouraged to bring items from their own homes to personalize their living area. As well, environmental stimulation should be provided throughout the institution (soothing colours, background music, and colour codes, signs, and symbols to identify floors and corridors). For those with dementia, meaningful activity, social interactions, and what has been called "personhood" should be provided. In other words, the staff must understand the residents' subjective experiences, their interactional environment, and their socio-cultural context (Chaudhury 2003; 2008; O'Connor et al. 2007). Some institutions provide an illuminated "memory box" outside each room for displaying personal objects meaningful to the resident. These boxes not only provide an identity for residents but also help them find their room. Highlight 8.7 describes "life" in a nursing home from the perspective of a sensitive, dedicated, and caring employee.

Ethical Issues in Long-Term-Care Facilities

A number of ethical dilemmas confront family and care workers when caring for frail and vulnerable older adults. The dominant framework of bioethics is "principlism"—that is, the use of commonly held principles (autonomy, justice, dignity, privacy) and ethical rules (obligation to reveal the truth) that guide what we "ought" to do when making decisions about or for others (Moody 2005). Principlism can fail to guide us when there are family, social, or cultural differences in what is considered an ethical practice or standard. For example, a contentious issue in long-term-care facilities is whether restraints should be used to protect residents from self-harm (Capezuti et al. 2008). Often, it is argued, these devices are used to make life easier for staff. However, it is the dignity of the person and the competing values of autonomy versus safety that must be at the core of any debate or decision as to whether chemical (sedatives) or physical restraints should be used to prevent wandering, falls, or aggressive behaviour. Physical restraints, such as bed rails, straps, or confining chairs, are used to restrict movement. These restraints may cause physical pain, may violate the individual's moral right to freedom of movement, and may cause humiliation and anger. If the person is mentally competent, informed consent is required for the use of restraints. As well, chemical restraints may add to a resident's existing confusion, fears, and anxiety.

A person may be declared "mentally incompetent" if he or she is unable to manage personal financial affairs, to understand information regarding personal or medical care, to judge the suitability of a recommended medical treatment, or to make a decision about personal or financial matters. An individual can be declared mentally incompetent only by a court after application by a spouse, child, or caregiver. A guardian is appointed who assumes legal responsibility for all decisions affecting the resident. A decision can be appealed, or it can be reviewed and reversed in the future. If a judge subsequently finds that a guardian is not performing his or her responsibilities adequately, a new guardian or a public trustee may be appointed to assume responsibility for an older person's welfare.

Highlight 8.7
Life in a Nursing Home: A Care Worker's Perspective

I have just finished my shift at the nursing home. I see Mrs M offering to feed her roommate, who is no longer able to feed herself. I see a kiss on the cheek offered to H, who wants to go home. "This is your home," we say, and often the crying stops. And D, with her infectious chuckle, is stripping for me as I wash her and put her to bed. She plays peek-a-boo with the covers as I say good-night. I know that if I try to relate these images to my family and friends, I will be met with uncomfortable silences, even groans. The fact is that nursing homes bring to mind images of suffering and death.

This is about the life in a nursing home, not the dying. As long as we exist, we live, and our final years are as precious as any other time. When we meet old people, we tend to see only that they are old. It is familiarity that reveals the residents' individuality. Mrs L is 95 and quite alert. Her table is filled with pictures of her youth, provided by her daughter, who visits almost every evening. At bedtime, Mrs L explains to me that she is getting married in the morning and must be up early. She is very verbal and occasionally bursts into tears and can't explain why.

There is a fine line between those who require supervision and those who can live more or less independently. Establishing the appropriate relationship with the residents is part of our task. When I go to assist W to bed, she is generally jovial and warm. I change her diaper and then offer to put on her pajamas. "I do myself," says W firmly. She is supporting herself with her arms on her wheelchair. I am so afraid she will fall. I open her drawer to get her pajamas. "No, no, I do myself!" she says, louder. I watch quietly for a few moments as she examines her clothes, then decide to leave. I check back in a few minutes and find her in the bathroom, brushing her teeth. "She manages," I think to myself, with wonder.

But there are behavioural problems as well. How do you manage D, who hates to be washed, kicks, spits, and scratches? Some nights we can skip washing him, but eventually he will begin to smell. In order to wash him, we often need three caregivers—two to hold his arms and prevent injury to the third. None of us are comfortable with this work, which is against his will.

Most of the women who work here are gentle and polite, intelligent and hard-working. They muster discretion and kindness with family members, creativity and patience with irrational behaviour. In these regards, my co-workers are a constant source of inspiration to me.

On my break, my mind returns to the nursing home where I trained. My first impression was that it was dark, with a pervasive smell of "oldness" and unanswered calls for help. Now I wonder at how those impressions have evaporated. Warmth and familiarity have replaced the darkness. I have not tried to paint a cheery picture of the nursing home. There are many problems: stress-related tempers, suspicious family members, unrealistic regulations—the nursing home is not a playground. But becoming familiar with it, and the many paths of aging, has enriched my life.

"Life in a Nursing Home—A Care Worker's Perspective," by Gail Landau, *The Globe and Mail* (22 September 1998, p. A24).

Changing Places: Local Moves and Migration in Later Life

Aging in place is the most common living pattern in later life. Only about 9 per cent of older Canadians move or migrate more than 200 kilometres from where they lived before they retired, and of those who move, 75 per cent move within 50 kilometres of their former residence (Lin 2005). The primary reasons for a move include for better adaptation to recent health limitations; to be closer to family; to live in a better neighbourhood; or to gain access to more social and leisure services (Moore and Rosenberg 1997). Future older cohorts, however, may be more mobile. Many baby boomers have moved often during their lives, they will be more affluent and less disabled than previous older cohorts, and more later-life housing options will be available to them.

Retiring, becoming widowed, or experiencing a significant change in health status often result in a reappraisal of living arrangements and lifestyle. Such a reappraisal can lead to a voluntary and rational (at least at the time) decision either to age in place or to move, locally or a long distance away (Golant 2011b). However, some older people who would like to move find themselves "involuntary stayers" (Moore and Rosenberg 1997). These individuals do not have the financial resources or sufficiently good health to move; they may also not be free to move because their adult children or very elderly parents live in their community or because they need a degree of personal care and support. Others adapt psychologically to their changing circumstances and prefer just to accept current conditions rather than to actively decide on an abrupt change. In general, moving in later life is influenced and shaped by earlier experiences of moving (frequency, distance, adjustment), by current emotional ties to the neighbourhood or community, by the location of key family members, by personal and spousal health, and by financial resources.

The decision to move can create emotional and cognitive stress among older adults faced with leaving a familiar home they may have occupied for decades. Any such move usually requires that they dispose of some of their personal possessions, especially if they are moving to a retirement home or apartment (Golant 2011b). Their possessions (furniture, art, photos, dishes, books, tools) have personal and emotional meanings and memories for them, and it is a difficult decision if they must give away the items or sell them (Ekerdt and Sergeant 2006).

Migration

Migration involves a move across jurisdictional boundaries to another county, province, or country, either seasonally or permanently. The major pattern of migration for older Canadian "snowbirds" tends to be a seasonal path[14] (November to March) to the southern United States or Mexico (Smith and House 2006). Such movement raises a number of issues, including spending patterns outside of Canada, pension money flowing out of the country, and the cost of supporting snowbirds when they return home (Northcott and Petruik 2011). Some affluent Canadians, however, not only go south in the winter but also migrate in the summer to a cottage or summer home outside an urban area after a short spring or fall stay in a "permanent" residence.[15]

In Canada, most permanent interprovincial migration among the older population is westward, although there is a small amount of return migration from Ontario to an Atlantic province. Between 1996 and 2001, only 1.2 per cent of all seniors moved permanently across provincial boundaries. As a result of migration patterns, there is a concentration of the elderly population in British Columbia (especially Vancouver Island and the Okanagan Valley), Alberta, and Ontario (especially in smaller cities and in the Niagara region). The arrival or departure of large numbers of older people significantly changes the economic resources of and the infrastructure demands on the community. Some communities, for the sake of economic development, actively encourage older people to migrate there (Smith and House 2006). Many older migrants are affluent married couples who contribute significant economic benefits to the receiving community by purchasing goods and services and by paying rent or property taxes (Northcott and Petruik 2011). The "home" or "sending" community, however, loses a significant amount of revenue for up to six months a year as a result of seasonal migration. Studies have shown that seasonal migration usually ends or is reduced as health or financial resources decline (Northcott and Petruik 2011). In this scenario, the original home community or region is a two-time loser—it loses the spending income of lifelong residents when they migrate seasonally during their healthy, affluent retirement years, and it must absorb the high costs of health care, social services, and institutionalization when the migrants return as partially or totally dependent residents.

In addition to migration within a continent, later-life international migration is increasing. Longino and Bradley (2006) identify two types of international migrants. International "assistance" migration is motivated by the onset of a moderate disability or increasing negative life circumstances (poverty, civil unrest, lack of social or health services) that persuades an older single parent or couple to join a child who already lives in another country. Or they might accompany their adult children who migrate as refugees or immigrants. For some older persons, these moves create depression, a sense of isolation, and intergenerational conflict that may result in a return migration to their more comfortable home community (see Highlight 2.7, p. 59). International "amenity" migration by healthy, independent older persons is motivated by a wish to live in a better climate or in a place where the cost of living is lower—for example, migrating from Canada to Mexico or a Caribbean island, from northern Europe or the UK to southern Europe or North Africa.

Summary

The lived environment and geographical location influence well-being and the quality of life in the later years. Where one lives and with whom are valued highly by older people. Older adults prefer to age "in place" in the family home in a familiar neighbourhood and community. Increasingly, however, older people are healthier and more mobile, and hence, either permanent or seasonal migrations are increasing. But as health declines and disabilities increase, independence and autonomy are weakened, and an older person may move, voluntarily or involuntarily, to more suitable housing if he or she is unable to drive, is liable to fall, is unwilling or unable to use assistive devices, is afraid of crime, or has difficulty walking. The availability of a variety of housing choices enables older people to live in a suitable, accessible, affordable, safe, and satisfying environment. A range of options reduces the burden on the family and also reduces the high cost of hospital stays and long-term-care facilities. In short, a prime goal of community leaders should be to ensure that older people live in suitable and affordable housing in their community, not in an institution.

For Reflection, Debate, or Action

1. Use the ecological model of aging (Figure 8.1) to identify some elements of environmental press that could present adaptation difficulties for older people in your community.
2. Assess the housing alternatives available for older adults in your community, and identify the type and amount of housing stock that will be needed in order to meet

the needs of two or three different generations of older people in 2030 when the entire baby boom generation has retired.

3. Make a list of emerging technological developments and social changes, and indicate whether, and why, they will have an impact on the aging process or on older people, today and in the future.

4. Debate the pros and cons of whether there should be mandatory driving tests and de-licensing for older adults. If you advocate de-licensing, what criteria should be used to ensure that assessments and decisions are fair and objective?

5. Visit a retirement home and a nursing home in your community (with permission), and identify the different levels of care and services provided. Determine to what extent residents are involved in decisions and to what extent RAI instruments are used for admission and for ongoing care decisions.

Notes

1. Age-friendly community developments have proliferated in the last decade. They aim to improve older adults' quality of life by providing policies and programs that enhance older adults' physical and social environment. A special issue of the journal *Generations* (Issue 2 [Summer], Vol. 33, 2009) covers many of these dimensions. Also, see Menec et al.'s (2011) article on conceptualizing age-friendly communities in the *Canadian Journal on Aging*.

2. Theories about aging and the environment can be found in Gubrium 1973; Windley and Scheidt 1980; Kahana 1982; Lawton et al. 1982; Golant 1984; Scheidt and Windley 1985, 1998; Cvitkovich and Wister 2001, 2002; Wahl and Weisman 2003; Wahl et al. 2004; Richard et al. 2005; Scheidt and Windley 2006; Golant 2011a, 2011b.

3. Chapter 12 discusses sources and types of social support to assist with ADLs and IADLs. Here, the emphasis is on adaptations to the environment through the use of mechanical or technological devices or through alterations to the physical environment.

4. See Health Canada 2002c; Robson et al. 2003; Martin 2011; Speechley 2011; Health Canada publications such as *Seniors and Aging—Preventing Falls Around Your Home* (www.hc-sc.gc.ca/hl-vs/alt_formats/pacrb-dgapcr/pdf/iyh-vsv/life-vie/fp-pc-eng.pdf).

5. Elder abuse is discussed in Chapter 12.

6. This statistic may partially reflect the fact that men are less likely to admit to being afraid. There are also more women than men in the older population.

7. The *International Journal of Technology and Aging* provides information about older adults' use of technology in a variety of residential, work, and leisure settings. Other references include Burdick and Kwon 2004; Charness and Schaie 2004; Fisk et al. 2004; Pew and van Hemel 2004; Cutler 2006; *Generations* 2006 (special issue) 30 (2); Sixsmith and Sixsmith 2008; Public Health Agency of Canada 2010.

8. CMHC, the federal housing agency, provides financial assistance up to $2500 to help low-income homeowners and landlords pay for home adaptations to extend the time older people can live independently in their home or a rented house or apartment.

This program, Home Adaptations for Seniors' Independence, includes an assessment manual and provides funds to install handrails, grab bars, walk-in showers, bath and stair lifts, wheelchair ramps, and widened doorways for wheelchair access (see www.cmhc-schl.gc.ca).

9. Congregate housing provides a semi-independent living arrangement where each individual or couple has an apartment or a room with a bathroom. Congregate housing provides services that include one to three meals a day, laundry and maid service, private transportation, security service, minor health care, and recreational programs. The congregate concept usually means that residents eat at the same time in a common dining room. Recent developments in this area are described in journals such as *Assisted Living Today, Provider, Contemporary Long Term Care*, and *Journal of Housing for the Elderly*.

10. See www.cmhc-schl.gc.ca/en/co/renoho/refash/refash_026.cfm for a description, floor plan, legislation, and financing options for Garden Suites in Canada. This site also provides CMHC publications about housing programs for older people. The National Association of Home Builders Research Centre (www.nahbrc.org) gives examples of unique housing design features for older people, such as those shown in the Life Wise Home demonstration project (click on "Seniors Housing").

11. In the United States, the National Council on Aging (NCOA) operates the National Shared Housing Resources Center, which runs home-sharing programs across the US (www.ncoa.org/get-involved/funding-sustainability/12-sources-articles/source-2-homesharing.html).

12. Many facilities are operated as private enterprises, and the owners seldom permit outsiders or researchers to study the facility or its residents. As a result, many studies on this topic involve nonprofit institutions or, less frequently, those where the residents are affluent, are in better health, and pay high fees.

13. The outcome of an evaluation of the quality of care provided by an institution depends on whether the evaluation includes the views of residents, their relatives, a staff member, and/or a government inspector. The most thorough type of evaluation considers the views of all stakeholders. Evaluations may include the amount of personal space; degree of privacy; safety of the physical structure; type, availability, and quality of health and medical care; degree of emotional interest in and concern for residents on the part of staff; the availability and variety of social, recreational, and therapeutic programs; the variety and nutritional quality of food; and the policies of the institution concerning visitors, sex, alcohol, and tobacco (see Hirdes et al. 2004, 2011; Arling et al. 2005; Castle and Lowe 2005; Keays et al. 2009).

14. Canadians who winter in the United States stay less than six months in order to meet the requirements of Canadian tax laws and to remain eligible for health insurance.

15. For a discussion of migration by older people, see Moore and Rosenberg 1997; Walters 2002; Statistics Canada 2003a, 2003b; Hayward 2004; Moore and Pacey 2004; Longino and Warnes 2005; Longino and Bradley 2006; Smith and House 2006; and Northcott and Petruik 2011.

Part III

Aging, Social Institutions, and Public Policy

Life is like riding a bicycle. To keep your balance you must keep moving.

— Albert Einstein

The understanding of both individual and population aging requires an examination of social institutions and public policy, which provide value orientations, norms, rights and regulations, and a structure for interaction in our daily lives. There are three general types of social institutions. The first type, socializing institutions—i.e., the *family*, the *peer group*, and the *educational system*—normally have the greatest influence from childhood to early adulthood. During adulthood, the family continues to be an important institution in which relationships change as we adopt new roles. Families are also a potential source of social support and care in later life. The second type of social institutions are regulative institutions, which include the economic, legal, and political systems. During adulthood, the economic system influences when we work, our work history (our employability), and our earnings and savings over the life course. Changes in labour force policies and practices influence the nature of work and, along with public policies, the time when we must or could retire. As well, regulative institutions may disadvantage some members of the labour force, such as women, the working class, ethnic groups, and older workers. Cultural institutions are the third type of social institutions and include the mass media, religion, voluntary associations, the arts, and sport. These provide a milieu for social participation during a person's leisure time across the life course.

Part 3 examines social relationships across the life course and the effect of transitions on individuals in the family, at work, in retirement, and during their leisure time. As well, this part discusses public policies for an aging population, elder abuse, and end-of-life issues faced by those dying and by their immediate caregivers. Involvement in family, the labour force, and leisure settings creates opportunities for or barriers to social interaction and influences our quality of life in the middle and later years. Transitions such as parenting, the empty nest, divorce, unemployment, retirement, or widowhood have the potential to either cause personal crises or create opportunities for personal growth. How an individual adjusts to these transitions is influenced by socio-demographic characteristics, past history, and the amount of social support available, especially from within the family.

Chapter 9 examines aging in the context of family interaction and intimate ties, such as relations between generations and within the same generation; marital satisfaction; and the effect of divorce, the empty nest, retirement, and widowhood on the individual and the family. Diversity in family types, ties, and relationships (never-married, gay or lesbian couples, or childless couples) is no longer unusual.

Chapter 10 reviews the effect of employment history on social interaction and lifestyles in later life and examines the process of retirement and the economic status of retired people and their dependents. Workers are becoming older, and some of these older employees experience discrimination in the workforce. Similarly, women have experienced discrimination in work opportunities and wages. Thus, special attention is directed to gender issues in the workforce and in retirement, including the feminization of poverty.

Chapter 11 describes the structure and size of social networks and diverse patterns of social participation in later life. Older adults are involved in such diverse "leisure" activities as religion, politics, education, the media, voluntary associations, tourism, crime, and gambling. But with increased life expectancy, filling one's time in a meaningful way is a personal trouble for some, especially those who were work-oriented for most of their adult life.

Older people need social support and care within the home and community if they are to delay or avoid a move to an institution. Chapter 12 focuses on issues, services, policies, and practices concerning the support and care of older adults who experience physical and cognitive changes or the onset of acute or chronic diseases. Topics include self-care; informal and formal support that helps with personal care and the instrumental activities of daily living and also offers emotional support; the responsibility, stress, and burden of being an informal or formal caregiver; and intervention and public-policy issues facing family caregivers, practitioners, and society. These issues involve the relative caregiving responsibility of the family and the state; the coordination of informal and formal support to prevent gaps in needed services; elder abuse; and principles for designing public policies for an aging population, especially concerning home care, community services, and health care. As more people live longer and as more women, the traditional providers of home care, are committed to work careers and otherwise less available to care for their aging relatives, greater attention needs to be directed to such end-of-life issues as home care, integrated health care, palliative care, power of attorney, advance directives, assisted suicide, and euthanasia.

9 Family Ties, Relationships, and Transitions

In every conceivable manner, the family is a link to our past, a bridge to our future.

— Alex Haley, author of *Roots: The Saga of an American Family*

Focal Points and Key Facts

- What influence does a major change in family composition or structure have on intergenerational relationships and in the provision of care in later life?

- Why are more grandparents raising young grandchildren?

- If one is single, childless, gay, or lesbian, to what extent, and why, do these situations influence family relations and support across the life course?

- Is marital satisfaction across the life course represented by a straight or a curved line?

- Why are widowhood and divorce so influential in the lifestyle and quality of life of older women?

- To what extent, and under what circumstances, do older adults date, cohabit, or remarry?

- In 2007, approximately 2.7 million Canadians aged 45 and over provided caregiving assistance, of whom about one-quarter also provided care to children living at home (Cranswick and Dosman 2008).

- More than 80 per cent of older people have at least one living child of their own, and some have stepchildren through common-law relationships or remarriage.

- Among those aged 65 and over, about 80 per cent of women and 75 per cent of men are grandparents. In 2011, more than half a million grandparents lived in the same household as one or more of their grandchildren, with 75,185 responsible for raising one or more grandchildren.

- Marital status data from the 2011 census shows that about 55.5 per cent of Canadian older adults are married; 3.4 per cent live in common-law relationships; 26.2 per cent are widowed; 7.7 per cent are divorced; 5.2 per cent have never been married; and about 1.5 per cent are childless.

- The 2011 census found that there were 64,575 same-sex couples of any age, an increase of 42 per cent from 2006, and that of these couples, about one-third were legally married (Bill C-38 legalized same-sex marriages federally in 2005) and the remaining were living common-law.

Introduction

The family influences our lives from birth to old age in profound and fundamental ways. While there is no singular definition of "the family" due to its diversity and ideological underpinnings, Mitchell (2012, 11) states that the term "families" can be "used in a fairly broad sense to refer to a group of people who have intimate or close social relationships and a shared history." Families provide stability, emotional and helping support, and financial assistance; age-integrated social interaction; socialization concerning values, morals, and life skills; and legal rights and obligations. Some individuals report having a positive and supportive family experience over the course of their lives whereas others experience significant tension and conflict. Indeed, most individuals experience a combination, falling somewhere between the extremes (Connidis 2010; Mitchell 2012). Families provide a structure in which we experience many life transitions, including marriage, raising children, the empty nest, divorce, widowhood, and remarriage. We have already learned about intergenerational family conflict and transfers (see Chapter 6) and about household composition and living arrangements in a family context (see Chapter 8). Later, we will see how the family interacts with work and retirement (Chapter 10), with social participation (Chapter 11), with caregiving and social support for frail and dependent parents as well as elder abuse (Chapter 12), and with issues such as guardianship and end-of-life decisions (Chapter 12).

Many books on aging discuss "family" in the context of intergenerational conflict, the problems and burdens of caring for frail parents, or the unique and stressful situation of those in the "sandwich" generation. Yes, family stress and conflict can result in domestic abuse and violence against children, spouses, and elderly parents. Yes, children and a spouse may be abandoned. Yes, divorce occurs in many families. And, yes, caring for an aging parent and a child at the same time can be stressful and burdensome, especially if the caregiver also holds a full-time job. But as Rosenthal (2000, 45) noted, there is more to family life than caregiving and dependency, and we need to examine both positive and negative aspects of family life over the life course. This contention is reinforced by Matthews' (2002) study of adult siblings who, for the most part, reported that caring for and assisting their parents was not a burden. There is a big difference between providing varying amounts of assistance to aging parents, versus assuming responsibility for full-time custodial care of elderly parents. Rather, helping parents can be seen as an extension of normal family interaction with a combination of sacrifices and rewards.

The "sandwich" generation is part myth, part fact—that is, there are relatively few middle-aged women who are employed full-time, have a child at home, and have an aging parent who needs daily help, supervision, and care. Analysis of the 2007 General Social Survey shows that about 3.5 million Canadians between the ages of 45 and 64 had children under 25 living at home. Of these, about 417,000 (12 per cent) reported providing some type of informal long-term care to an aging relative, friend, co-worker, or neighbour, with 84 per cent of these "sandwich" persons being involved in paid work as well. Of the 417,000 persons, 36 per cent cared for two seniors, while 7 per cent cared for three seniors. The caregiving was a near even split between men (49 per cent) and women (51 per cent). Yet the percentage of persons experiencing a "sandwiched" caregiving situation at any time in their life would be somewhat higher. Surprisingly, 95 per cent of the "sandwiched" persons reported that they were satisfied with their life in general. Yet when asked about the consequences of being "sandwiched," they reported such outcomes as having to reduce or change work hours; refusing a promotion or job offer; receiving a reduced income; feeling stressed and frustrated; experiencing a changing social life or cancelling vacation plans; and experiencing a change in sleep patterns and quality. Of course, the reported outcomes likely depend on both the intensity and the type of care that is provided. In Chapter 12, we discuss possible types of support for these sandwiched individuals. As for the future, Williams (2005) suggests that the associated stress and the number of sandwiched persons may grow when the boomer generation requires care because of their large numbers, increased life expectancy, lower fertility rates (fewer adult children to provide care), and delayed and later marriages by their children, who will be more likely to have children of their own at home by that time. As well, there may be more sandwiched Canadians in their sixties caring for elderly parents who experience a "cluttered" nest when their adult children return home, sometimes with grandchildren (Mitchell 2012).

This chapter discusses continuity, changes, and diversity in family structures and networks; the type, frequency, meaning, and quality of relationships; and the timing, sequencing, and duration of family-related transitions throughout life. Families are viewed as social networks that vary in structure, size, and gender composition. Consequently, more emphasis is placed on understanding the quality and meaning of family relationships and interaction than on the frequency or quantity of interaction across the life course (Matthews 2002). This emphasis on relationships enables us to understand more fully who does what, with whom, and for whom and whether the amount of assistance and interaction is considered fair by people who are caring for grandchildren, frail parents, or grandparents.

The Concept of Family

At one time, **family** meant a social group in which membership was determined by blood or marriage ties (termed "kinship"). Often, only a married couple with children, together with any of the couples' surviving parents, was included. Family-life trajectories were thought to be relatively constant and common: after marrying, an adult child moved from the family of orientation to a family of procreation, raised children, experienced the "empty nest" when children left home as young adults, and later became a grandparent and likely a widow or widower in later life. However, over the course of the twentieth century, considerable change and diversity emerged in the structure, transitions, and generational relations within kinship groups.[1]

Discontinuities and irregularities in the traditional family life course have resulted in a social reconstruction of the family. Family structures and relationships are more fluid and diverse due to divorce, single parenting, permanent family conflict, remarriage, childlessness, never-marrying, engaging in serial or long-standing common-law or cohabiting partnerships (whether same-sex or opposite-sex), and the return of adult children to live in the family home (because of educational pursuits, unemployment, divorce, illness, or preference) (Mitchell 2006). Thus, we use the term *family* in this broad sense whereas *kinship* refers to lineage through blood or marriage, although there is some overlap in the two concepts.

Rather than live in the same home as their adult children, most older people prefer "intimacy at a distance"—that is, living independently yet being close enough to visit. Even when health or financial losses force older people to leave their family home, they still prefer some form of independent living. In contrast, older members of some ethnic groups prefer to live with their children, or they do so because they have no choice due to financial or health reasons. Highlight 9.1 illustrates "intimacy at a distance" and why five older persons in Ottawa selected an independent life in a seniors' residence rather than live with one of their children.

In addition to family relationships, informal family-like relationships emerge with neighbours or friends over time. Some of these relationships evolve to a level where a friend or neighbour is almost like a relative. These people, known as **fictive kin** (MacRae 1992), become a core part of the social network of older adults, particularly for those who are unmarried, widowed, childless, gay or lesbian, or estranged from their children or whose children live far away and communicate infrequently or perhaps not at all. Women tend to form and value such relationships more than men, especially if they are divorced or widowed.

As a legal term, *family* defines certain rights and obligations for those who are related biologically or through marriage or adoption, including health and pension benefits, survivor benefits, and inheritance rights, such as access to a share of accumulated family wealth after being divorced or widowed. In contrast, those in a same or opposite-sex cohabiting partnership seldom have legal rights. For instance, they may not be allowed to visit a partner in the intensive care ward of a hospital or to make decisions about treatment, even though they may be closer to the patient than a more distant blood relative (Fox 2009).

Highlight 9.1
Intimacy at a Distance: The Choice of Independent Living in a Seniors' Residence

A.T.: When my doctor advised me that I shouldn't be living alone, my daughter was willing to have me move in with her, but I prefer the independence we have here.

V.S.: My son lives in Toronto, and he used to worry about me, but now he knows that someone looks in on me every day. I looked after my mother-in-law for 14 years, and I decided that no one was going to go through that with me.

W.C.: My family felt I shouldn't be living alone. My daughter has been very supportive, and I wouldn't want to have to get along without her—we speak on the telephone every day. She no longer worries because she knows we're well taken care of here.

V.W.: I lived with my granddaughter and her husband, and that would have worked out except that I began to feel isolated because they were away at work all day. We didn't live close to public transportation, and I began to feel I couldn't get out, especially in winter. I decided to move here because I'm the kind of person who likes to have other people around.

Source: Minutes of the meeting of the National Advisory Council on Aging, Bethesda, Maryland. 1986. 'The way it is: All in the family'. *Expression 3* (1): 3..

Social definitions of a family have evolved over the years. Statistics Canada (2002) defines a *census* family as follows:

> [A] married couple (with or without children of either or both spouses), a couple living common-law (with or without children of either or both partners), or a lone parent of any marital status, with at least one child living in the same dwelling. A couple living common-law may be of the opposite or same sex. "Children" in a census family include grandchildren living with their grandparent(s) but with no parent present.
>
> An *economic* family, on the other hand, is "a group of two or more persons who are related to each other by blood, marriage, common-law or adoption, and who live in the same dwelling." (Fox 2009)

Clearly, family and kinship units are social and ideological constructions, not just products of biology. Therefore, more inclusive definitions (e.g., same-sex partnerships) are being developed for collecting census data, for establishing legal rights, and for conceptualizing research and policies about family units across the life course (Mitchell 2012). As the next sections illustrate, there is more diversity in family structures and relationships today than in the early or middle years of the twentieth century.

Changing Family and Kinship Structures

The life-course perspective enables us to examine change and stability in the structure, transitions, and relations within family units across time. Continuity and change in family or kinship (lineage) structures and relationships across the life course influence who provides companionship and care in the later years. To understand and describe these structures across the life course, Hagestad (2003, 142) stated that we need the following information:

- the number of generations and the fertility rates and timing of births in each generation
- the relative age difference between and within each generation (age-condensed or age-gapped [see below])
- the gender composition of each generation
- the number of single, never-married individuals in each generation
- marital patterns resulting from divorce, widowhood, remarriage, and cohabitation

There are many myths and misconceptions about the structure of Canadian families over time, in particular the view that multi-generational families were common in the past (Mitchell 2012). In fact, during the first half of the previous century, multi-generational families were not common because of lower life expectancies (about 49 years in 1901, rising to 69 years in 1951). Grandparents seldom survived to see their grandchildren marry or have children. However, as health improved and longevity increased, family structures became longer, and at least one member (usually a woman) in the oldest generation often lived into his or her eighties. Then, after the baby boom, fertility rates declined, and each generation became narrower. As well, more women entered the labour force, more men and women delayed marriage, and more divorces occurred. Consequently, average age at marriage and age when a first child was born shifted to the later twenties or thirties. As well, more women did not marry, and more couples did not have children. Some couples married, had children, and then divorced; often, one or both partners remarried, thereby creating another branch to an existing kinship system. All of these changes have had an impact on the size and shape of the kinship structure (individuals related by blood or marriage).

In recent decades, five major changes in family and kinship structures have occurred (Hagestad 2003). First, the kinship system has become longer (at least three and perhaps four generations), with more vertical ties and intergenerational relationships, resulting in more complex family relationships. For example, at different stages in life, a married woman might be a daughter, a sister, a granddaughter, a wife, a daughter-in-law, an aunt, a mother, a mother-in-law, a grandmother, a great-grandmother, or a widow. Today, with single-parent households, childless couples, divorce, and remarriage in all generations, the same woman, once separated or divorced, may also be an ex-wife, a single parent, a stepmother, or a step-grandmother.

A second change in kinship structures is a shift from an "age-condensed" structure to an "age-gapped" structure in some extended families. In an age-condensed structure, successive generations in a family have children at an early age (21 and under), leading to a narrow age difference (often about 20 years) between children, their parents, and their grandparents. Delayed child-bearing over several generations (childbirth when the mother is 30 or over), however, creates "age-gapped" structures, with a gap between each generation of about 30 years. This structure is most likely in families where women are highly educated and have full-time careers. To illustrate, in Canada at the present time, the average age at which a woman gives birth is 29.5 years, leading to an age-gapped kinship structure (Mitchell 2012).

A third structural change is the emergence of truncated families in which a specific family lineage eventually disappears when the youngest generation is childless by choice or by chance. A fourth emerging change is the increased number of reconstituted or blended families as a result of remarriage following divorce or widowhood. This family structure creates a complex set of family relationships. For example, a child may have four, six, or eight sets of grandparents (for children, a dream in terms of birthday gifts; for parents, a nightmare in terms of visiting!). In this vein, the caption for a Herman cartoon (*The Globe and Mail*, 24 November 1983) had a schoolchild asking a teacher, "Which parent do you want to sign: my natural father, my stepfather, my mother's third husband, my birth mother, or my natural fathers' fourth wife who lives with us?" Thus, while there may be fewer biological grandchildren, there are more grandparents (Connidis 2010; Mitchell 2012). However, some grandparents (and aunts or uncles) are abandoned or isolated when the biological parents of a child divorce and remarry or when a custodial parent moves to another community.

The fifth emerging trend in kinship structures is the propensity for older adults to cohabit as partners (often considered as common-law in Canada after living together for at least one year) (Connidis 2010). This family pattern has increased the level of complexity of family life and relationships. For instance, non-married or previously married older adults choosing to live together, but not marry, create family links that are sometimes undefined (such as those defined as stepmother or stepfather), which can cause difficulties in family relationships concerning inheritance or caregiving should one member become ill or require long-term care.

Today, few people reach the later stages of life with no surviving kin.[2] The oldest surviving members of kinship systems are located in many types of family structures, including the following:

- a married male with a wife, one or more married children, one or more siblings, and many grandchildren
- a never-married woman with or without surviving siblings and perhaps with a few distant relatives
- a very elderly widow with no surviving children or siblings but with some grandchildren and perhaps great-grandchildren
- an elderly man cohabiting with an older or a younger woman
- two widowed siblings living together

Factors Influencing Family Relationships

Connidis (2010, 22) identified four dimensions of family relationships central to intimate ties and to relationships among and within generations in later life:

1. The number of relatives available and the nature of their relationship to the older person (spouse, child, sibling, grandchild)
2. The past and present patterns of contact and interaction (how many and how frequent) between older persons and available kin
3. The quality of family relationships across the life course, ranging from a supportive and emotional caring relationship (parent to infant, or adult child to parent) to an abusive or neglectful relationship

4.   The types of communication, assistance, and support given and received among members of different generations and in what direction the exchange flows

Gender, class, race, and ethnicity influence family relationships across the life course (McMullin 2010; Moen 2012). These elements create diversity in family-based norms, beliefs, and values, and they have the potential to create either barriers or opportunities for kin relationships. For example, gender, class, race, and ethnicity influence whether aging parents and adult children live in the same household or nearby; the amount and type of emotional, instrumental and financial support that is exchanged; and whether daughters and daughters-in-law work or care for elderly parents. The frequency and quality of interaction with parents, in-laws, and other relatives is stronger among women; indeed, mother–daughter ties are more robust and more intimate than son–parent ties. And widows generally have more contact with their children than do older married or divorced women.

Kinship interaction is often facilitated and promoted by one or two members of the extended family, usually women, who take on the role of **kin keeper** (Rosenthal 1985; Spitze and Logan 1989). This person ensures that members of the family keep in touch with one another, reminds people about birthdays, coordinates the care of a sick or aging family member, and keeps in touch with various relatives by telephone, letter, email, or visits. Much of this responsibility within the extended family is assumed by a grandmother, an older daughter, or a daughter-in-law. The kin keeper often serves as a confidant or caregiver for aging parents or other family members, thereby providing care, emotional support, and advice within the extended family. One outcome of a divorce in the middle or oldest generation is that a kin keeper may disappear for some members of the kinship unit, thereby leading to decreased interaction between family members within and across generations.

The importance of gender in later-life family relationships is partially related to the fact that women are more involved in expressive than in instrumental relationships at all stages of life (see chapters 11 and 12 on caregiving). Although sons act as caregivers in the absence of daughters, they tend to provide less personal care. Aging parents without a daughter may be at a disadvantage in the later years when they need assistance. For example, parents may receive financial aid from a son to hire a homemaker or nurse, or help with transportation or heavy work around the house, but they are less likely to receive personal care (such as help with dressing, bathing, shopping, or feeding), care management, and medical treatment, which a daughter might provide (Fast et al. 2010). The contributions of men in aging families is seldom studied. Matthews (2002), whose work is a notable exception, argues strongly that men must be included in research on family ties and family relationships, which is beginning to take place in the caregiving, grandparenthood, and widowhood literature, as we will observe in this chapter. With some men becoming more involved in family responsibilities throughout the life course, they likely will assume increased responsibilities for the monitoring and care of aging parents.

Social class also affects the frequency and nature of intergenerational relationships. Regular face-to-face visits are more common among those in the lower classes because of greater geographic proximity, in part as a result of less career mobility. Members of the higher social classes keep in contact more by phone and email and offer financial rather than instrumental assistance to their aging parents.

Racial and ethnic background influences family relationships across the life course. Most studies of ethnic or racial-minority families have found that there is greater obligation and dependence on kinship ties than in mainstream society for social relationships, housing, personal care, and financial support, especially in the later years. Perhaps because of minority-group status and unique cultural values, a closely knit extended family—rather than friends or social organizations—serves as the primary resource for assistance and support. But this dependence on family creates a stressful paradox for older members, especially those who are widowed. Elderly parents in immigrant families are well integrated into the kin network, often living in a child's household. But they often report feeling lonely, isolated, and bored in this type of living arrangement (Treas and Mazumdar 2002). Many are dependent on kin for emotional, social, and financial support, and some report that they are just servants for their children and grandchildren. If they do not speak English or French and if they live in non-ethnic, suburban communities, with no contact with age peers from their cultural group, the family may be their only social contact (see Highlight 2.8, page 61). However, as cultural values are weakened across generations through acculturation and assimilation, the primary resource for older people changes from the family to friends or social agencies in the ethnic or racial community (Wong et al. 2005; Shemirani and O'Connor 2006). To create effective policies, both the cultural heritage and the degree of assimilation of various ethnic groups into the host society must be understood.

Family Ties and Relationships

Marriage generally constitutes the most intimate and enduring family tie across the life course. However, not all adults in middle and later life are involved in a marital relationship. Rather, they may engage in serial or long-term monogamous ties that involve cohabiting in a hetero-sexual or homosexual relationship. Others live alone, with or without an intimate relationship with another person. The diversity of intimate family or family-like relationships requires that we examine various types of partnerships across the life course.

Marital Status and Marital Relationships

Marital status influences much of adult social life and is related to living arrangements, health, support, and general well-being (Connidis 2006, 2010, 56–9; Mitchell 2012). As shown in Table 9.1, in 2011 about 55.5 per cent of older adults reported living as a couple: 70.2 per cent of men 65 and over and only 43.8 per cent of women (Statistics Canada 2012a). This sex difference is even more pronounced among those 80 and over (62.1 per cent compared to 22.0 per cent).

The family network for married people is generally larger, even if there are no children, than for those who never married or who live common-law. More than 75 per cent of adults 75 years of age and over have at least one living child, and about 80 per cent are grandparents. Because of increased life expectancy, more grandparents, especially grandmothers, have adult grandchildren in their thirties or forties, which increases the likelihood they are or will become great-grandparents.

Marital Satisfaction in Later Life
Marital satisfaction in the later years is related to how close one feels to the spouse as a confidant and as a source of emotional support and to how much agreement there is in the partnership about marital closeness (Tower and Krasner 2006). Retirement as a life tran-sition can free people from work roles, responsibilities, and stresses and thereby provide increased opportunities for more companionship and marital satisfaction—or the transition

Table 9.1 Population 65+ and 80+, by Marital Status (%) and Sex, Canada, 2011

Category	Both Sexes		Males		Females	
	65+	80+	65+	80+	65+	80+
Married	55.5	36.9	70.2	62.1	43.8	22.0
Common-law*	3.4	1.2	4.7	2.1	2.3	0.9
Never Married**	5.2	5.3	5.0	4.6	5.4	5.8
Separated	2.0	1.3	2.2	1.9	1.8	0.6
Divorced	7.7	3.8	6.6	3.4	8.6	4.1
Widowed	26.2	51.5	11.1	25.9	38.2	66.5
TOTAL	100% (4,945,055)	100% (1,347,580)	100% (2,198,770)	100% (499,385)	100% (2,746,285)	100% (848,200)

Total numbers shown in parentheses.

* Common-law includes persons in other non-married categories who identified as living common-law in the 2011 Census.

** Never-married does not include common-law.

Source: Statistics Canada. 2012. *2011 Census of Population*. Catalogue no. 98-312-XCB2011041. Ottawa: Statistics Canada. (Calculated from CANSIM tables by authors.)

can lead to tension and conflict in the relationship. Among the current cohort of elderly people, high levels of marital satisfaction are generally reported more by men than by women. Connidis (2010, 67–9) found that marital satisfaction increases with age and that those who are more satisfied with their marriage enjoy better mental health and well-being. Conversely, those in a conflicted marriage may experience depression and lower levels of physical and mental health.

While cycles of satisfaction and dissatisfaction are likely to occur in any marriage, two general but different patterns of satisfaction are reported across the life course[3] (see Figure 9.1). First, there may be a gradual decline in marital satisfaction through all stages of the marriage (pattern A) that may or may not lead to separation or divorce. The second, alternative pattern, with variations in the slope reflecting the time at which changes begin (B1, B2, B3), is curvilinear. These two patterns are supported by both anecdotal reports and research findings (Rosenthal and Gladstone 1994). There is continuing debate as to whether satisfaction is actually higher in the later years than it is during the early years before children are born. This hypothetical pattern is represented by the extension upward (dotted lines) of the three curvilinear paths. Curve B1 suggests that the low point occurs when children are adolescents; B2 suggests that it occurs after the last child leaves home (the empty nest); and B3 suggests that it occurs just before or after the husband retires or when one partner becomes very ill.

In a detailed discussion of whether reported improvements in marital satisfaction across the life course are "real," Connidis (2010, 67–9) argued that satisfaction may be reported to increase because people adapt and are less critical and more accepting of a partner's faults as they age. Or the change may be due to cohort or period differences in the meaning of what constitutes a successful or "good" marriage (Glenn 1998). Indeed, among younger cohorts,

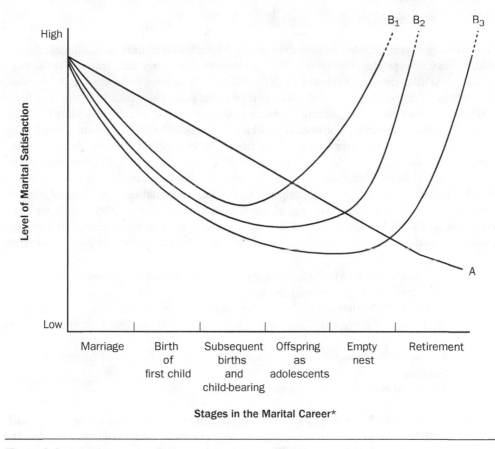

Figure 9.1 Four General Patterns of Marital Satisfaction over the Life Course

*Includes common-law relationships

divorce rates have increased, and although older couples are more likely to remain married, there is no evidence of an improvement in marital quality in the later years of long marriages (Glenn 1998). Moreover, the number of divorces after the age of 60 is increasing, often at the time that one or both partners retire (Brown and Lin 2012).

When one of the partners becomes cognitively or physically impaired, a form of "separation" occurs when that partner moves to a long-term-care institution. The partner who continues to live in the community is viewed as a "married widow or widower." That person may experience guilt, anger, sadness, resentment, and self-pity, all of which are tempered by feelings of relief from burdensome caregiving responsibilities. He or she recognizes that marriage and companionship are over, and yet he or she must continue to be a partner by caregiving (Gladstone 1995). Increasingly, after a period of years living alone, married widows or widowers are forming intimate or quasi-intimate relationships before their spouse dies. Or, after the death of a partner and a brief mourning period, they may begin a new relationship.

Sibling Relationships

Like marriage or common-law relationships, sibling interaction is an intra-generational relationship, unless it involves step-siblings, in which case there may be an age difference of 10 to 20 years between two different sibling cohorts. With increasing divorce rates and reconstituted families, there are more step-siblings and half-siblings than in the past. More than 80 per cent of older adults have at least one sibling, although for women over 80 years of age, the possibility of having a surviving sibling, especially a brother, is less likely. Sibling relationships represent a long-lasting family bond, with a shared genetic and cultural heritage from early childhood to death, and usually last longer than any other family tie (Connidis 2005, 2010). However, with lower fertility rates and more one-child families, there are fewer siblings in absolute numbers. Sibling relationships in later life are important for companionship and for mutual emotional and instrumental support. Yet with few exceptions (Matthews and Heidorn 1998; Campbell et al. 1999; Matthews 2002; Walker et al. 2005; Connidis 2010, 225–40), we know very little about relationships involving sisters and brothers across the life course. Sibling relationships can follow four possible patterns:

1. Frequent interaction in the family home during childhood and adolescence, then little or no interaction after leaving home
2. Frequent interaction in childhood continuing throughout the life course if they are "best friends," especially along a sister–sister or brother–brother link, and if spouses get along well
3. A slow drifting apart during adulthood after entering the labour force and getting married
4. A renewal of contact and closeness in later life

Until the death of one or both parents, siblings often maintain indirect contact with each other through the parents and by attending annual or periodic family celebrations. After the death of a parent, particularly a mother who may have been the kin keeper, sibling communication and interaction often increases, thereby renewing the relationship. However, contact is unlikely to be renewed for more than practical reasons if the relationship was characterized by rivalry and conflict in the past, or if distance or health prohibits regular visiting. In general, siblings who are close throughout early life tend to remain close in later life.

Sibling relationships in the later years are influenced by many factors, such as gender, marital status, age differences, and relationships with other family members, including parental caregiving responsibilities. Ties are stronger between sisters than between brothers or between a sister and a brother. However, just as most studies of widowhood and retirement involve women and men, respectively, very few studies of sibling ties in middle or later life examine ties between brothers. Most of what we know about brothers in sibling relationships is derived from studies of their involvement in the monitoring and care of elderly parents (see chapters 11 and 12). Cultural values and historical practices influence the quantity and quality of sibling relationships among members of some racial or ethnic groups. Within cultural groups that place a high value on family solidarity and mutual assistance, sibling links are more likely to be strong and continue throughout life and to increase in later life if one of the siblings becomes widowed or experiences a decline in health or financial status.

Siblings, especially if unattached, may be the only source of support for each other in the later years. Older widowed or never-married sisters sometimes create a common household in the later years to provide each other with social, emotional, and economic support. Although only a minority of siblings report that they receive support from a brother or sister, many report that their siblings are an available source during a crisis, especially if they live nearby (Connidis 2010). With families becoming smaller and with greater geographical mobility, siblings may be less readily available in the future. Highlight 9.2 relates some thoughts about sibling relationships in later life.

Highlight 9.2
Sibling Relationships in Later Life

Sibling relationships are sometimes rediscovered and reconstructed in middle or later life (Matthews 2002; Connidis 2010). Matthews (2002, 5) notes that just as adults continue to be seen as "children" by their parents, they continue to be considered brothers and sisters by their siblings. Connidis (2010, 225–6) adds that marriage creates siblings-in-law and that through divorce and reconstituted families, adults acquire half-siblings or step-siblings. Thus, in some families, there are many siblings or quasi-siblings with whom elderly people could connect. The following comments illustrate different themes at the heart of sibling relationships in later life.

Drifting Apart and Coming Together

When we were younger, we were all quite close. . . . And then, for some reason we drifted apart . . . we had very little in common. . . . But starting again 10, 12 years ago, we've really got back pretty much the relationship we had when we were kids. (Connidis 2010, 233)

If you develop relationships in the community and you're very involved with your family, you don't have much time for siblings. But then, after your children grow up, you probably think of your siblings more because you are fond of each other, and you want to maintain that relationship. (Connidis 2010, 234)

The Sharing of Intimate Moments

Many widows and retired sisters end up living together again with the same kind of intimacy as they shared in childhood. At the end of her life, as at the beginning, a sister may be privy to the small, personal details about the other—her eating, sleeping, and washing habits—to which possibly no other person, except a long-term sexual partner, ever has access. (McConville 1985, 56)

You don't mind having them (siblings) know what you've gone through. This is something (a divorce) that you need to talk about inside the family. (Connidis 2001, 228)

Sharing Parent Care

We probably drew closest together during the time we looked after our elderly mother. . . . We did it together. It was a joint decision. (Connidis 2010, 249)

Too much falls to me (a sister with four brothers). I don't think any of them are doing their fair share. Money doesn't take the place of giving of themselves. . . . All the work is left to me . . . but I have learned to accept it. (Matthews 2002, 178)

My brother and I are both available. . . . I organize it. I ask him to do things for Mom. He and I both do what we can to help her. He makes every effort to take half the responsibility. (Matthews 2002, 184)

Relationships between Older Parents and Their Adult Children

Most older people (more than 80 per cent) have at least one living child of their own, and they may have acquired stepchildren through remarriage. The 2011 census found the following:

- There were 1.6 million single-parent families, with 80 per cent headed by women.
- More than 1.5 million children were living in a single-parent household.
- Forty-five per cent of adults 20 to 29 years of age lived with their parents, and 57 per cent of these adults were men (Statistics Canada 2012b).

These demographic facts, combined with increased geographical mobility for both children and parents and increased labour force participation by women, have contributed to changes in the relations between parents and adult children in recent decades. In some cases, divorce, single-parenting, reconstituted marriages, and geographical mobility weaken or eliminate parent–child relations. In other cases, a relationship is strengthened because a transition (the birth of grandchildren) creates closer parent–child bonds; provides increased assistance and support, including co-residence; or creates larger family networks in reconstituted families when two sets of parents and additional sets of grandparents may be available.

Across the life course, a parent-child dyad is a relationship bound by ties of proximity, affection, legal responsibilities and rights, and moral responsibilities. The relationship is built on emotional bonding, communication, reciprocity of exchange, and interdependence of the two generations (Giarrusso et al. 2005). As children pass through adolescence and the early adulthood years, sources of conflict and tension revolve around the communication (or lack of) and interaction styles of parents (reported most by children); the habits and lifestyle choices of children (reported most by parents); child-rearing practices and values; work habits and orientations; household standards and maintenance; and differing perspectives on political, religious, or other ideological issues (Clarke et al. 1999; Mitchell 2012). Most of these intergenerational tensions, as we saw in Chapter 6, are temporary and do not lead to lifelong conflict or estrangement between parents and children. Moreover, strong relations in childhood persist through adulthood, even if frequency of contact diminishes because of geographical distance or a child's marriage and/or career.

Increasingly, adult child and older parent relationships are marked by both positive and negative components (Connidis and McMullin 2002; Pillemar and Suitor 2004; Mitchell 2006, 2012). To illustrate, Spitze and Gallant (2004) noted that older parents reveal strong desires for both autonomy and connection with their adult children that lead to ambivalence about receiving assistance from children. To deal with ambivalent feelings, older persons adopt strategies such as minimizing the help they receive, ignoring or resisting a child's attempt to control or help, and seeking others, rather than their own children, as confidants.

With increasing longevity and the likelihood of family crises increasing with each successive generation, the incidence of family stress or conflict may increase. Nevertheless, the prevailing evidence suggests that the relationship between older people and their adult children is not usually characterized by conflict and that most elderly people are not abandoned by or alienated from their children.

Crises, such as an acute illness, the death of one parent, a move to a long-term-care facility, financial difficulties, or divorce, increase parent–adult child interactions. A divorced person's relationship with his or her parents and grandparents can either become closer or more distant.

A divorced child may become dependent on his or her parents for emotional and financial support and for help in looking after children. Divorce also has negative, long-lasting effects on parent–child relations, especially for a biological father who is divorced when his children are young. If the mother has custody, birth fathers, voluntarily or involuntarily, may eventually lose contact with their children. Hence, a potential source of assistance and care from a daughter-in-law or grandchildren in later life is lost.

Adult children represent the predominant monitoring system and source of physical, emotional, and financial support for elderly parents. The parent–child dyad is a two-way reciprocal support network and a small mutual-aid system. Throughout life, these reciprocal relations involve giving and receiving love, social and instrumental support, and financial assistance in the form of cash or property. A past history of receiving or giving wealth, care, knowledge, or other resources across generations builds a reservoir of debt or tradition that is, or should be, continued into later life (Connidis 2004). In later life, however, an adult child becomes more of a giver than a receiver. Thus, over the life course, reciprocity and interdependence emerge among linked lives in a kinship structure (Hagestad 2003). The direction, frequency, type, and amount of exchange depends on personal needs and on opportunities to interact with and assist others in the family unit.

Most reciprocity involves unequal and variable transfers across the life course, and different points of view often emerge about the amount, direction, equity, or appropriateness of the transfers. Most of the flow is from parent to child, although in later life the balance shifts as children give more emotional and instrumental aid to parents and parents report receiving more help (Stone et al. 1998). However, until their death, and at death through a will, parents who have wealth continue to pass it on to their children or grandchildren.

Four main issues concerning relationships between older parents and adult children have been emphasized in recent years:

1. The amount of contact and the quality of interaction while an aging parent is independent, healthy, and mobile (Connidis 2010, 144–52)
2. The type and amount of exchanges provided by aging parents to adult children who experience a crisis or traumatic event, such as a divorce, the death of a child, or a child with a serious illness; unemployment; or widowhood in early or middle adulthood (Ganong and Coleman 1998; Connidis 2010, 169–77, 204–14)
3. The amount and quality of support provided to cognitively or physically frail parents who require increasing levels of physical, emotional, or financial assistance in the later years (see Chapter 12)
4. The shocking finding that while it is not common, family members, rather than care workers, are the most frequent perpetrators of elder abuse, fraud, or neglect (see Chapter 12)

Most older parents, especially after the age of 80, have one child living nearby, and most have contact at least once a week by telephone, email, letter, or a visit with at least one child. Approximately three-quarters of adult children engage in frequent contact with their elderly mother or father. If a daughter is employed full-time, there is less face-to-face contact. Parents with a strong religious affiliation, those from traditional ethnic backgrounds, and working-class parents tend to have more frequent contact with adult children.

If an adult child has an elderly divorced parent, the amount of help provided and the sense of obligation to help are influenced by the amount and quality of contact they have had over the years with the divorced, non-custodial parent and the needs of the adult child's own nuclear family (Ganong and Coleman 1998). Connidis (2010, 204–14) reports the following:

- Divorced parents, especially fathers, have less contact than married parents with their adult children.
- Divorced mothers receive more assistance and support from their children than do divorced fathers.
- Divorced parents generally provide less financial aid and support to their adult children.

If an adult child divorces, it is a distressing experience for most parents, especially if they were unaware of problems in the marital relationship. Most parents offer emotional, economic, and social support to a divorced child and to any grandchildren (see next section). But the divorce of an adult child requires renegotiating the parent–adult child relationship, especially if co-residency and/or grandchildren are involved.

Grandparent–Grandchild Relationships

At birth, about two-thirds of children have four living grandparents (including step-grandparents), and by 30 years of age, approximately 75 per cent still have at least one grandparent (Connidis 2001, 167; Connidis 2010, 188). The 2011 census reported that of the 13,320,615 private households in Canada, 413,490 (3.1 per cent) were either multi-generational with a grandparent present (2.7 per cent) or skip-generation households (0.4 per cent) (Statistics Canada 2012b). A skip-generation household is one in which there is one or more grandparents but no middle-generation (Milan and Hamm 2003). Of the 362,600 multi-generational households, about 60 per cent of the middle-generation had children. While multi-generational households are increasing in Canada, largely due to immigration patterns, their numbers are still relatively small. In skip-generation households, about half involve a single grandparent providing care for at least one grandchild.

Older people in the future will have fewer biological grandchildren than they do now, or none at all. However, step-grandchildren are acquired when a divorced or widowed child remarries or when an older widow or divorced person remarries or lives common-law. In contrast, with more common-law relationships, never-married children, and childless adult children, some older people never become grandparents. Moreover, face-to-face grandparent–grandchild interaction is less frequent than it was in the past because the grandparents and their adult children live at greater distances from each other, because grandparents with an active lifestyle are often not available, or because some grandparents have little or no access to their grandchildren after an adult child divorces. However, new communication technologies and social media, such as email, webcams, Facebook, Twitter, etc., provide opportunities for family members to be connected to one another.

Grandparents provide kinship continuity and contribute to the preservation and perpetuation of family rituals and history. The age at which one becomes a grandparent varies by class, education, and the age at which children marry. With delayed marriage and child-bearing in age-gapped families, some people may not become grandparents until after they retire, if at all. However, in age-condensed families, people often become grandparents in their late thirties or early forties.

Grandparenting roles have undergone significant changes compared to a generation ago. Individuals live longer, and keeping in touch with grandchildren has become easier. In addition, grandparents have more financial and social support resources to share (Kemp 2003; Uhlenberg 2004; Mitchell 2012). Most grandparenting is performed by a grandmother, who tends to have more contact (as a kin keeper) with adult children and their children (Reitzes and Mutran 2004). However, grandmothers in their fifties and sixties who work have less time to look after their grandchildren. And, once retired, many grandparents prefer to allocate more time to travel, volunteer work, or dating if they are widowed, rather than to taking care of grandchildren. Also, grandfathers appear to be becoming more involved with grandchildren as gender roles become more blurred (see below). Mueller et al. (2002) argue that there is more to the grandparent–grandchild relationship than how often they see each other. The quality of the relationship is what matters, and therefore measuring frequency of contact is less useful for understanding the relationship, especially since contact with young grandchildren is mediated through the parents. Mueller et al. (2002) found that intimacy, helping behaviour, instrumental acts, and being involved as an authority figure are important indicators of the meaning and quality of the relationship.

The degree to which grandparents interact with their grandchildren and consider the relationship important is influenced by how far apart they live, by their lifestyle and whether they are employed, by the number of sets of grandchildren they have, and by the age of the grandchildren. The relationship tends to be close from birth to the teenage years and then weakens as grandchildren become busy with their friends, education, career, and marriage. If a grandparent has been highly involved in child care during the pre-teen years, the relationship often continues to be quite close into the later years of life.

Kemp (2005), in a study of the relationships among adult grandchildren and grandparents, found that both groups viewed the other positively and considered the ties to be meaningful and to involve friendship, mutual trust, and shared confidences. Based on this study, Kemp (2005) suggested that the relationship grows more profound and meaningful as both generations age, as revealed in some of the following statements by her study participants:

- "I think that you get parent-like feedback without parent-like scrutiny or judgment . . . you'll get the kind of advice you would get from a parent, but it will be less biased in terms of judging you." (Grandson, 24)
- "You get a sense of history. . . . And then, as you learn more about your parents, where they came from, you can appreciate maybe why they are stubborn about some things or where they get some of their ideas." (Granddaughter, 32)
- "My grandmother, she's opened up and told me so much about herself . . . horrible and good things, and what she's been through . . . in some ways our relationship includes an element of friendship as well. When you're a kid, it's not at a stage where you could have that type of relationship." (Granddaughter, 27)
- "She knows if she tells me something in confidence it'll never go any further. And I know the same with her . . . it will never go any further." (Grandmother, 69)
- "They are my grandparents and they're like my best friends . . . It's not like, 'Oh, I have to go to my grandma's for dinner.' It's like, 'Oh, I'm going to go and sit down with my grandparents and chat with them. And I like it.'" (Granddaughter, 21)

Maternal grandparents are generally more involved with their grandchildren, and these ties are often closer, more meaningful, and more satisfying than those with paternal grandparents (Chan and Elder 2000; Rosenthal and Gladstone 2000). This stronger maternal tie is related to the fact that the mother–daughter tie is usually stronger than the parent–son tie and is often reflected in a stronger grandmother–granddaughter relationship, especially on the matrilineal side of the family. Mann (2007) contends that the role of grandfathers has been significantly underestimated and under-researched, in part due to a dominant feminist perspective. The author states that understanding grandfatherhood requires a masculinity-age identity lens to uncover the different ways in which grandfathers interact with grandchildren. For instance, grandfathers have been shown to adopt caring, support, and mentoring roles that appear to develop in mid-life.

The divorce of an adult child can change relationships with grandchildren. Usually, the daughter gains child custody, and the maternal grandparents often become more involved through support and financial assistance. In contrast, paternal grandparents are more likely to have less contact, or perhaps none, with their grandchildren, especially if the custodial parent moves to another community or remarries and a new set of step-grandparents assume the grandparenting role. Grandparents may have to acquire legal visitation rights through the courts if they are not allowed to see their grandchildren after a divorce. Some jurisdictions now guarantee grandparent access to grandchildren through civil laws pertaining to separation and divorce. Under Canada's Divorce Act, grandparents have the right to apply for access to or custody of grandchildren after the biological parents divorce. But if the grandchildren's parent is abusive, is incarcerated, or dies, legal access to or custody of grandchildren becomes more complex and varies greatly among the provinces. Consequently, volunteer organizations, such as GRAND (Grandparents Requesting Access and Dignity) in Ontario, have been formed to help grandparents who are denied access to their grandchildren.

If one or both grandparents move to a residential-care facility, the relationship with their grandchildren often changes. In many cases, active grandparenting ceases when the older person enters a nursing home. To compensate for this loss or for the unavailability of a grandparent at any time after a grandchild's birth, foster grandparent programs have been established. For active elderly people living in the community or in retirement homes, having a foster grandchild enhances self-esteem and morale, decreases feelings of loneliness and isolation, and creates an emotional bond and an extended family that benefits both the youngest and oldest generation. Similarly, some daycare centres have been located within or adjacent to retirement or nursing homes to create companionship for both preschool children and older people. Through intergenerational programs, elderly volunteers teach or play with preschoolers, acting as surrogate teachers or grandparents or simply as older friends and confidants.

Relationships between grandparents and grandchildren have been examined primarily from the grandparents' perspective. However, studies examining the experiences of grandchildren reveal that children who interact with grandparents view the relationship as "warm and close"; they have fewer prejudices about elderly people and growing old; and over time, they view their grandparents less as babysitters and gift-givers and more as companions and confidants. However, in three-generation immigrant families in which the first or second generation immigrated to Canada, grandchildren and grandparents may have had different experiences of acculturation and assimilation, and that can negatively affect the relationship.

Grandfamilies: Grandparents Raising Grandchildren

There is an important difference between grandparents looking after their grandchildren while a parent works or goes on vacation and grandparents being responsible for raising one or more grandchildren in a "skipped generation" household (see above). "Grandfamily" households (where a grandparent replaces biological parents) are increasing because of family crises (e.g., substance abuse problems, incarceration, or mental illness), more divorces, and increased reporting of child abuse and neglect (Goodman 2007). This is especially common in Sub-Sahara Africa, where mortality due to the spread of AIDS has resulted in many skipped or grandfamily households.

Within the North American context, grandparents raising children often view themselves more as a parent involved in education and discipline and as an authority figure than as a grandparent who can indulge and entertain the child. Many in this situation regret the loss of the typical grandparent role, as well as the time they would like to have for the grandchildren of other sons or daughters (Connidis 2010, 196–200).[4] In addition, the fight for legal custody can be costly and may create conflict between the grandparents seeking custody and one or both of the biological parents or other relatives. But legal custody is essential, since in some jurisdictions the absence of legal guardianship means denial of access to social services and even the right to attend the neighbourhood school. And legal custody facilitates claiming grandchildren as eligible dependents for income-tax purposes.

The entry of a grandchild into a grandparent's household can create stress and uncertainty for older people. It changes their retirement plans and reduces their retirement savings;[5] it interferes with their customary leisure and social activities; and it can harm the caregiver's health and lower marital satisfaction. The relationship with the biological parent or parents can be stressful, especially if they periodically and randomly reappear and begin acting as parents again. Many grandparents worry about the future of the infant or child should their health fail and they can no longer continue as the primary caregiver.

Common-Law Relationships

In the 2011 census, about 16.7 per cent of all Canadian couples and 31.5 per cent of all couples in Quebec reported that they were living common-law (Statistics Canada 2012b). Proportionately, more men than women seek and enter such relationships, in part because of a greater prevalence of male same-sex couples. They are also more common in younger age cohorts, often as a precursor to marriage, but sometimes these relationships are never converted to a legal marriage (Milan 2003). For others, a common-law relationship develops after separation, divorce, or widowhood (Brown et al. 2006). Among such relationships that begin earlier in life and persist into later life, the partnership and kin network is very similar to that of married couples. Many of these relationships produce children (16.3 per cent of children younger than 14 live with common-law parents), and grandparents are as involved as they are in families in which the parents are married. As shown in Table 9.1, the number of common-law relationships in later life is quite low at present (3.4 per cent of all older adults in 2011). But the number has been increasing and will likely continue to do so as more adults enter the later years having lived in one or more common-law relationship in earlier stages of life. Common-law relationships tend to be less permanent than marriages, and the partners do not have as much protection under law as married couples do. Therefore, the partners often sign agreements concerning wealth and property rights, guardianship rights for children, and inheritance. Such contracts are especially important for ensuring that a woman in this type of relationship has economic security in later life.

Gay and Lesbian Common-Law Partnerships
As Allen (2005) noted, sexual orientation across the life course, and especially in later life, tends to receive less attention than racial or ethnic diversity. The 2011 Canadian census asked respondents to identify whether they were living in a same-sex partnership and, if so, whether

they were legally married. While possibly under-reported, 64,575 reported being in a same-sex union. Of these, 21,015 indicated that they were married, a threefold increase since 2006, mainly because same-sex marriages became legal in Canada in 2005. In 2011, 6.2 per cent of all spouses or common-law partners were same-sex (Statistics Canada 2012b). At present, we do not know the actual number of such partnerships among older adults, but we do know that there is under-reporting by those over age 60 (O'Brien and Goldberg 2000; de Vries 2007; Connidis 2010, 73–6, 142–4, 238–9; Mitchell 2012). The traditional kin network available to older gays and lesbians is generally small, and the composition depends very much on their personal history.[6] Some have children from a failed heterosexual marriage, through adoption of a child as an individual or as a couple, or, for lesbian couples, through artificial insemination of one partner. Hence, children may be available for companionship and support throughout the middle and later years of life.

The family ties of older gay and lesbian adults with their family of origin is an under-studied topic (Kimmel and Lundy Martin 2002; Cruz 2003; Connidis 2003a; Mitchell 2012). Available research suggests that gay and lesbian adults are often estranged from or rejected by family members and may have little or no family support in later life. In fact, many enter later life with a legacy of stigmatization, marginalization, and discrimination (Allen 2005; de Vries 2007). This marginalized status requires negotiation by *all* family members and is illustrated by Laird, who is a mother, a grandmother, and a partner of a lesbian. Speaking of her own life experience, she notes the following:

> Ours is not an unusual story. Lesbians and gays come from families and are connected to these original families. . . . Most of us are not cut off from our families—not forever rejected, isolated, disinherited. We are daughters and sons, siblings, aunts and uncles, parents and grandparents. Like everyone else, most of us have continuing but complicated relationships with our families. We participate in negotiating the changing meanings, rituals, values, and connections that define kinship. (Laird 1996, 90)

Those who are rejected by family members often create a "surrogate" family that involves a network of gay, lesbian, and heterosexual friends. But whether and to what extent this network can provide the necessary personal assistance and care in later life, as a family would, is not known. As well, some are cut off from receiving family inheritances, which may mean that they lack financial resources to pay for private care in later life.

Among some older gays and lesbians, but especially among gay men because of AIDS, access to medical care, home care, and community social services can be fraught with discrimination in terms of unequal access to services and perhaps a lower quality of service because of care-worker attitudes. Partners also have limited legal rights, often due to the denial of marriage rights, and may experience constraints to accessing employer drug and health benefit plans, to medical and financial records, or to visitation rights in hospitals (Claes and Moore 2001; Brotman et al. 2003, 2007; de Vries 2007). Indeed, most medical record forms assume all clients are heterosexual and include such questions as "Are you married, and who is next-of-kin?" A lifelong partner may be denied an inheritance or the right to participate in a hospital discharge or end-of-life decision normally made by family. Similarly, gays and lesbians may experience verbal harassment from hospital staff, or the staff may be unwilling to touch, bathe, or treat gay men or lesbians in a hospital or nursing home. To meet the needs for supportive housing in later life and less discriminatory treatment in medical care and social services, social support groups have been created, and some retirement and nursing homes are being constructed for the expanding population of elderly gays and lesbians, but mostly in large urban areas.

Never-Married Older Persons

In the 2011 census, about 5.2 per cent of men and women over 65 reported that they have never been married (and do not live common-law). In absolute numbers, the population of ever-single older adults is likely to increase in the next 20 years. Although it is commonly assumed that an older person who never married is childless and without a history of intimate relationships, this may not be the situation for all single people in later life. Increasingly, some are single mothers or fathers through child-bearing or adoption.

In later life, most adults who never married report that they are not lonely or socially isolated because they have developed friendships with non-relatives, fictive kin, or extended family. They are used to living alone and being independent, although many do live with another person in a household. Many have siblings. Some, however, do regret not having children (Connidis 2010, 99). If they need assistance in later life, they may have few surviving family members to provide instrumental or social support (Wu and Pollard 1998; Pudrovska et al. 2006). Connidis (2010, 99–106) notes that older never-married women are likely to be highly educated and to have earned a pension and achieved economic independence. They do not perceive being single as a stigma because their identity as a single person was defined and accepted much earlier in life. In contrast, many older single men have little education and are less financially secure than married men of the same age. Late in life, older never-married persons who lose their independence because of cognitive or physical impairments may be institutionalized sooner than necessary because of the lack of immediate family support.

Childless Older Persons

Childlessness is not restricted to those who do not form long-term unions. Married and common-law couples may also be childless, whether by choice or not. About 14 per cent of the elderly population is childless (Connidis 2010), but this percentage will likely increase because of later marriages and individuals choosing not to have children. Those who cohabit in serial relationships are more likely to be childless than those who married or formed permanent, long-standing common-law relationships.

In general, childless older persons report high levels of well-being, are as socially active in their communities as elderly persons with children, and have adequate support networks, albeit with fewer "backup providers" than those with children (Connidis and McMullin 1996, 1999; Wu and Pollard 1998; Zhang and Hayward 2001; Dykstra and Hagestad 2007).[7] However, childless, unmarried older men report more loneliness than do women who are childless (Zhang and Hayward 2001; Dykstra and Hagestad 2007). In later life, those without children often receive support from family or friends, but once over 85, they are less likely to have someone close who can provide personal care, especially if they are widowed and in poor health. Consequently, the risk of being admitted to a long-term-care facility is higher among childless elderly women.

Increasingly, as new cohorts emerge, there is less stigma attached to being childless, even for married couples. Moreover, some speak of themselves as being "child-free" (www.childfree .net) rather than "childless," which implies that they are missing something they want. Those who call themselves "child-free," on the other hand, report that they made a conscious decision not to have children (Stobert and Kemeny 2003).

Among older people, three commonly reported advantages of being childless are having (1) fewer worries and problems, (2) more financial wealth, and (3) greater freedom. Three disadvantages are (1) lack of companionship, (2) lack of support and care, and (3) missed experiences and thus feeling incomplete (most likely to be reported by women) (Connidis and McMullin 1999). To conclude this section, Connidis (2001, 165) cogently noted the following:

> Clearly, it is not necessary to have children to have a satisfying old age. But, for those who wanted to have children and could not, a sense of regret about being childless continues into later life and lowers subjective well-being. In short, neither having children nor remaining childless guarantees happiness in later life.

Life Transitions in a Family Context

Family life changes when individuals and couples experience transitions across the life course. Major family transitions include cohabiting with an intimate partner, marriage, birth of a child or grandchild, an empty nest when adult children leave home, a refilled nest when adult children return to live in the family home, divorce, widowhood, retirement, and remarriage. These events can have both positive and negative outcomes for those who are directly involved, for other family members, and for the quality of family relationships. These transitions illustrate how lives within the extended family are linked and interdependent. In the following sections, the effect of some major family transitions on individuals and family members are examined. The effect on the family of two other major transitions is discussed in later chapters—retirement in Chapter 10 and deteriorating health and the need for family support and care in Chapter 12.

The Empty and Refilled Nest

When the last child leaves home, formal child-rearing is thought to be completed, and parents are described as living in an **empty nest**. For parents, the transition is often gradual because most have more than one child and all of the children rarely leave home at the same time. Generally, sons leave the family home later than daughters. With smaller families and increased longevity, parents can expect to live in the empty nest stage for a much longer time than their parents did.

The empty nest is less common outside North America. Because of a housing shortage in many countries, single children remain at home until they marry, and living on one's own or with roommates is much less common. In many developing countries, in parts of Europe, and especially in Asia, where filial piety remains a revered family value, it is common for one child, even if married, to form a household with his or her parents. While there is a similar trend for parents in some ethnic groups in Canada, recent transformations in family structure are also altering the empty nest experience for ethnic families. As well, the empty nest experience is different across ethnic groups. Mitchell and Lovegreen (2009) found that mid-life persons of Indo (South-Asian) descent, for example, report more negative feelings associated with this family transition than those of Chinese, Southern European, and British descent ethnic groups. The authors suggest that this pattern reflects rapid social change, a loss of social and economic support, and a reduction in community connectedness experienced among Indos.

The empty nest stage brings relief from domestic chores associated with child-rearing, a reduction in financial and parenting responsibilities, and the potential to begin living a different lifestyle. Some have suggested that the transition represents a loss of the "mothering" role and that women become depressed and bored because their main responsibility and source of life satisfaction is gone. Others argue that the transition brings enhanced freedom, especially for women, to pursue new opportunities outside the home through full- or part-time employment, volunteer work, a hobby, or attending university (Mitchell 2012).

For most parents, the transition to the empty nest stage is a positive experience. After the children leave home, a marriage may improve because a couple has more time for leisure interests and for each other. Conversely, an empty nest also has the potential to magnify existing marital tensions or dissatisfactions. In an unhappy marriage, divorce is considered more feasible at this stage because it is no longer necessary to "stay together for the sake of the children." Some of these post–empty nest separations or divorces, especially in the middle class, are initiated by women who seek a higher-quality relationship or who wish to have more freedom to pursue their own occupational or educational goals.

In recent years, there has been an increasing number of both "crowded" nests (Boyd and Norris 1999)—in which children continue to live in the family home into their thirties, sometimes with a "partner"—and "refilled" nests, in which "boomerang" children return home after an assumed permanent departure (Mitchell and Gee 1996; Mitchell 2000, 2006, 2012; Turcotte 2006). Due to a "delayed emptying" or "refilling" of the parental nest, 44 per cent of 20- to 29-year-olds live in the parental home, and 57 per cent of these adult children are men.

Despite the oft-cited phrase "you can't go home again," many adult children do return to the family nest in early or middle adulthood, often after a personal crisis or challenge. In the 2001 census, about one-quarter of 20- to 34-year-olds who had left home reported that they had returned for four months or more (Turcotte 2006). Reasons for the return include financial difficulties, unemployment, underemployment or the unexpected loss of a job, the ending of a common-law relationship, a divorce or early widowhood, or the ill-health of the adult child or a parent that necessitates daily caregiving.

Living longer with one's parents before leaving home or returning to live at home is more common among some ethnic groups (those from Asian backgrounds leave latest), among parents and children who for financial reasons need to pool their resources, among those who are close to their mother, and among those who complete university with a large debt. Living with parents at age 20 or 30 occurs as well when unemployment rises, when the cost of housing escalates, especially in urban centres, and when apartments are in short supply. To illustrate, Turcotte (2006) reported that among adult children 20 to 34 years of age in 2001, only 17 per cent were living with parents in rural areas, whereas the proportion was much higher in large metropolitan centres, such as Vancouver (41 per cent), Toronto (39 per cent), and Montreal (28 per cent). Most accounts of these living arrangements, both by parents and by the adult child, suggest that the relationship is positive and harmonious (Mitchell 2006). The parents receive instrumental help and companionship from the child, and they experience gratification in helping a child live comfortably, safely, and economically. Some parents, however, find that a refilling of the nest is stressful because their privacy and freedom disappear, especially if grandchildren also move into the house. They may also be forced to assume unexpected financial responsibilities at a time when they were allocating more of their income to leisure or retirement savings.

The media and some social scientists have suggested that "boomerang kids" and those who delay leaving home represent a family crisis or a social problem and that these young people are immature, unable to assume independence, or lazy. In reality, most relationships fostered by these living arrangements are not conflicted or stressful, although mothers are generally happier with the situation than fathers (Mitchell 2000, 2006, 2012).

Divorce in Middle and Later Life

The transition out of a marriage can occur at any age, and such transitions can have long-standing implications for the individuals concerned and for their family (Connidis 2010, 118–23, 204–14; Connidis 2003b). Divorce usually occurs earlier rather than later in life, although divorces among those 60 and over are increasing. According to the 2011 census, 7.7 per cent of all older adults (and only 3.8 per cent of those 80+) reported being divorced, with the percentage being slightly higher among women (see Table 9.1).

With longer life expectancy, "till death do us part" may no longer be sacrosanct or unquestioningly observed, especially among older women. To illustrate, Bair (2007) reported septuagenarian and octogenarian divorcees abandon marriages for the following reasons:

- "I could not go on living the same old life, in the same old rut with the same old boring person."
- "I don't know how many years of life I have left; I just know I don't want to live with him."
- "People change and forget to tell each other . . . people just grow apart."

Do these views represent a cultural shift and a major attitudinal shift about marriage in later life? And will this trend increase when members of the "boomer" generation enter their later years? Older adults become divorced to reduce stress and boredom, to improve their physical and mental health, because their interests and values have become too divergent, or because retirement triggers conflict and a desire for different lifestyles. With 20 or 30 years to live after retirement, one or both members may no longer wish to continue an unhappy or unsatisfying relationship. Divorce in later life has both positive and negative consequences for the divorcing partners (Chipperfield and Havens 2001; Jenkins 2003; Connidis 2010). A divorce is especially traumatic for a man when it is initiated by his wife at or about the time he retires because he loses two sources of companionship and social support at the same time. Increasingly, because of the mandatory sharing of accumulated marital assets (including savings, property, and pensions) in divorce settlements, older women are less disadvantaged financially by a divorce than they were in the past. This is especially true if they have had a career and are entitled to their own pension plus a share of their former husband's pension if their assets are lower.

Widowhood in Later Life

Approximately 26.2 per cent of older adults reported their married status as "widowed" in the 2011 census (38.2 per cent for women and 11.1 per cent for men) (see Table 9.1). Rates of widowhood have been declining over the past several decades because of longer life expectancies, and more divorced and single older persons (Connidis 2010; Martin-Matthews 2011). Among those 80+, 66.5 per cent of women compared to only 25.9 per cent of men are divorced. Becoming and being widowed in later life is primarily a gendered experience. For many if not most older married women, it is an "expectable life transition" because of gender differences in life expectancy and the tendency of women to marry men older than they are. For many women, widowhood is often preceded by periods of caregiving and the institutionalization of a partner. Most studies of widowhood have concentrated on how widows adjust to a change in their financial situation and on their social and psychological adaptation to living on their own.[8]

A widow's financial situation is most likely to change if she is ineligible for health care or pension benefits earned by her husband. The losses are compounded if she did not generate her own personal savings and private or public pension benefits while employed in the labour force. McDonald (1997) refers to retired widows as the "invisible poor" because they often lose financial benefits if they outlive their husband. Whereas the public retirement income system is designed to provide an adequate income for married couples, it often fails to support widows to an adequate level, especially if they were poor before they were widowed. Some widows leave the family home because they cannot afford property taxes, utility costs, or essential home repairs. Others have difficulty in learning how to manage and make decisions about financial matters because their husband "did all the financial work."

In continuing or establishing new social relationships, widows generally fare better than widowers, although research into widowers is in its infancy (see next section). Widows usually have a peer group of other women, including those already widowed, who provide social and emotional support and serve as confidants. But they often lose social connections associated with the husband's workplace or relationships involving "couple" activities. As well, widows become closer to their children, especially their daughters, after losing their husband. In contrast, widowers seldom have close confidants or a large group of friends; they have fewer emotional ties to their family; and they are generally less willing to share personal thoughts or needs with a confidant or family member. Men, however, are more likely to date, cohabit, or remarry after a period of bereavement, although this pattern is changing, especially in retirement homes and communities where more women are seeking male companionship.

These gender differences in financial status and social involvement will narrow in the future—more older women will have participated in the labour force and accumulated savings, property, and pensions; they will be more independent and better able to make decisions; they will have greater financial knowledge and a higher level of education; and they will experience more liberal norms concerning dating, cohabiting, and remarriage in the later years.

The diversity in widowhood experiences is likely to increase, given the cultural heterogeneity of older people in general, and the very different individual and social contexts of the aging baby boomers. Martin-Matthews (2011) makes the case for more prospective studies that follow the same individuals over time to improve our understanding of their experiences as they move through unique life courses.

Adapting to Single Life

Widowhood, like divorce, involves more than grieving and adapting to being single again. The process may begin with caring for a frail partner and the consequent realization, if not acceptance, that the partner is likely to die in the relatively near future. Then, following death, the process involves mourning and bereavement (see Chapter 12), negotiating a new identity as a "single" person, and learning new tasks and responsibilities. For both men and women, the process also involves a renegotiation of relationships: with children and grandchildren; with other married couples; and with single and married persons of the opposite sex. If a woman's identity has been closely linked to her husband's status and occupation, she may have difficulty changing from this identity to that of a single person. A woman must engage in identity work to determine "who she is now, given who she was" while attempting to rebuild her sense of self, her life, and her social world[9] (van den Hoonaard 2001; Chambers 2005). In same- or opposite-sex common-law unions, surviving partners experience much the same grieving process, but rebuilding an identity, renegotiating relationships, and not having legal rights make the process somewhat different and often more difficult. The widowhood experiences of older men have begun to receive attention in recognition of their unique experiences tied to their masculinity (van den Hoonaard 2010). While in the past they were often depicted in negative terms (i.e., as helpless and desolate), it is becoming apparent that older widowers adapt to this new role in diverse and often positive ways, albeit not as well as women in many cases.

For widows and widowers, the mourning and adjustment period can last for a year or more. This period is characterized by shock, depression, and anger. Loneliness and lack of companionship are frequently expressed feelings in the early stages of being on one's own, as noted in the following thoughts of widows (Martin-Matthews 1991, 18):

- "It's the loneliness. No one else takes the place of your spouse. There is no one to share with." (Widowed for 7 years)
- "Even though I have a great family, I find loneliness hard to bear, especially on weekends and holidays." (Widowed for 18 years)

In addition to losing a partner, a widow or widower often loses married friends, who continue to socialize as "couples." Sometimes a widow's friends "drop" her because they consider her less interesting or pleasant than her husband and the couple was the basis of the relationship, or because a widow continues to mourn and thus is not a pleasant social companion. In other cases, a widow herself fails to keep in touch with her friends and views the world as belonging to couples. Some widows believe that it is not possible or feasible to attend social events as a single person. Phrases such as "a fifth wheel," "the third person," "an outsider," or "the odd person out" express these feelings of discomfort that restrict social interaction. Moreover, some widows believe that their married female friends think widows are a threat to their marriage. Thus, widowed older individuals often see themselves as marginalized, isolated, and having lower status (van den Hoonaard 2001).

In rural areas, elderly widows experience loneliness and isolation if their children have moved away from the region. In addition, they may live far from health, leisure, and social services. Lack of public transportation and living at a great distance from social facilities create barriers that inhibit the reconstruction of an active life. In small towns, however, a place of worship often becomes an important centre for a widow's social involvement (van den Hoonaard 2001, Chapter 8).

There are few formal rituals or community resources in modern societies to help widowed persons adapt to a new identity and to single life. For elderly widows, however, "widow-to-widow" programs provide emotional support and knowledge. These programs include widowed volunteers, who visit recently bereaved persons; telephone help lines for information and assistance; group sessions to discuss common problems; and public education to inform the widowed person about available services and resources, including written materials on living alone, on employment, and on financial and legal matters. For some widows, a sudden requirement to become self-sufficient and live independently is viewed as a challenge and an opportunity for growth. Women who expected or permitted their husbands to perform most tasks and to make all major decisions often experience freedom and acquire confidence when they assume these responsibilities.

Programs to assist widowers are less effective because there are fewer widowers available to provide support and because men are more reluctant to discuss their feelings with a confidant. Although men usually need less assistance in coping with financial and legal matters after their wife's death, they are more likely to need help with homemaking (cooking meals, doing the laundry, cleaning the house) and with keeping in touch with their family (Connidis 2010). This pattern may change as new widowers bring different masculinity experiences to that role.

Once widowed, people often face decisions about where and how to live as a single person and whether to seek employment. The decision to work is usually based on economic necessity, age, employment status at widowhood, and the psychological need for a new focus in life and a new social network. Most older widows, at least initially, decide to live alone in their homes and to maintain intimacy with their children at a distance. However, if a widow is poor, frail, less educated, and has strong ethnic and cultural ties, she is more likely to share a household with a relative. A recent trend is for elderly widowed siblings, especially sisters, to reunite and form a household or, if they are not living together, to spend more social time together (Connidis 2010).

Dating, Cohabitation, and Remarriage in Later Life

A majority of older men have partners, whereas the majority of older women do not. This gendered difference in later-life partnerships is partly due to the fact that women live longer and fewer eligible men are available. As well, an increasing number of older widows report that they enjoy the freedom and independence of being single. Common reasons cited for not becoming intimately involved following widowhood include respect for the former partner; a feeling that the previous marriage was "perfect"; a belief that it is not proper to remarry; lack of support from children; possible loss of spousal pension benefits; not wanting to "nurse" another frail partner; and a desire for freedom and independence to live a different lifestyle.

Given that the number of unattached older men and women is growing, an increasing number consider it socially acceptable to "date," cohabit, or remarry. This is much more common among those who are divorced than among those who are widowed, and it is five times more likely to occur for men than for women (Connidis 2010, 124–9). As well, more older men than older women report being interested in a new marriage. Indeed, as many as 20 per cent of widowers over 65 cohabit or remarry within five years, compared to about 6 per cent of widows. Reasons cited for creating new partnerships include a need for companionship and intimacy, for love and sexual attraction, to share financial resources (on the assumption that two can live more cheaply and efficiently than one), and for security, safety, and comfort (a man acquires a homemaker as well as a companion). Highlight 9.3 describes how a 72-year-old widower's life was suddenly enriched by falling in love.

A decision to date, cohabit, or remarry is not easy for older divorced or widowed people. Nevertheless, an increasing number of elderly people are actively seeking new relationships by attending singles clubs or senior citizen centres, by using introduction or dating agencies, or by placing personal ads in local newspapers, in magazines for retired people, or on the Internet (see Highlight 9.4).

For many single seniors, there is trepidation and anxiety connected to the "dating scene" if they have not dated in many years. Consequently, dating sites for seniors often provide advice and information (see Highlight 9.5).

Highlight 9.3
Later-Life Romance

It is strange to be 72 and in love again. What kind of craziness is this? Just a few months ago, I was living alone and perfectly happy. Well, maybe not perfectly happy. My wife had died a couple of years before, and I had settled in Victoria, expecting to spend the rest of my life appreciating the beauty of the place, feasting on the arts, reading the great books, and generally wandering in the land of the mind.

But that turned out to be not so easy. When one has been half of a long union that suddenly ends, there is confusion about what was hers, what is mine, and what were the compromises that made it work for so long. When the sharp pain of grief receded into kind remembrance, I was surprised and a little chagrined to find it replaced with an exhilaration I had not experienced since the day I left home to go to college. I could do as I pleased and go where I liked and make decisions unhampered by the restraints imposed by a relationship, however loving and caring it might have been.

At some point, the sense of exhilaration left me, but I had the good sense to realize that losing a spouse after so many years is a life-changing episode, like adolescence, but deeper and more fundamental. I needed time and solitude to regain a sense of perspective, and the way I chose to heal was to drive alone across the country. If I learned anything on that trip it was that I can be my own best friend—in fact, maybe I have to be before I can be a friend to anyone else.

Yet how one hates to think of oneself as being alone. All the arts in the world do not take the place of a warm human relationship, and though I felt healed and to some extent content, I still hoped that in some miraculous way I could again drink from that enchanted cup we call love.

Then, mysteriously, at exactly the right time, she appeared. Well, to tell you the truth, there was nothing mysterious about it. A woman I once worked with telephoned from Vancouver. "I'm coming to Victoria, and I was wondering if we could have dinner?" she asked. "Do you mind if I bring along a friend?" she asked. "I'd like to see her too, and that will be my only chance to do that." "The more the merrier," I said. As it turns out, she fed the same line to Jill, who also responded positively, and the future became inevitable for both of us. I sat beside her that evening, and though not many words passed directly between us, I recognized in her a quality of happiness and adjustment to everything about her—to the beauty of the day, to the dark and to the sunlight, to the ordeal of meeting strangers. But there was something more—a chemistry, something as mysterious as true love always is.

In everyone's life there will come a moment of decision, of opportunity, when a second will decide the fate of that person for all remaining time. My moment came the next morning. I called her and like a stammering teenager made plans for another date. And after that, another and another and another. I did not know that life could once again hold such happiness.

When life has less length, it seems to have more depth and more beauty; the colours are brighter, the air purer, the view cleaner, and the love sweeter.

Source: Adapted and reprinted with permission of the author, Maurice Walford, and *The Globe and Mail* (10 October 2002, p. A26).

Other places where new relationships in later life begin are through friendship networks, religious or other organizations, cruise ships, funerals of friends, supermarkets and laundromats, retirement communities, adult recreation centres, or nursing homes (see Highlight 9.6).

Highlight 9.4
Dating Sites for Older Adults

An increasing number of unattached older adults seek an active social life. Rather than relying on friends or relatives to make introductions, some older people place advertisements, like the following, in the personal column of a newspaper, in magazines for older adults, or increasingly on the Internet. These sites specifically serve seniors and entail filling out some personal information and desirable characteristics of the person one seeks. Some examples of sites, and the content of a few ads are listed below:

- Be2: www.be2.ca
- Compatible Introductions: www.compatible-introductions.ca/en/
- Dating for Seniors: www.datingforseniors.com
- Senior Friend Finder: www.seniorfriendfinder.com
- Senior People Meet: www.seniorpeoplemeet.com
- "Male, 68 years old, seeking female companionship, 55–70 years old. I enjoy bowling, cards, home-cooked meals, quiet walks and times."
- "Would like to meet an honest, sincere widower, 65–70 years. Good sense of humour, social drinker, with car. PS: A way to a man's heart is through his stomach. My cooking includes garlic and onions."
- "Widower, 63, good health, financially secure, owns modern home on country acreage. I would like to meet a lady, 55–65, interested in country living, animals, and some travel."

Cohabiting is becoming more prevalent among older adults, perhaps because of earlier life experiences and fewer social constraints that discourage cohabitation. Some of these arrangements are permanent, some are seasonal (while "down south" as a snowbird); some are long-distance and periodic (one partner lives in Germany, the other in Canada); and some involve independent living by each partner, with overnight visits on weekends or certain nights of the week. This latter arrangement is also common among younger adults between the ages of 20 and 29. Brown et al. (2006) estimate that approximately 4 per cent of the US population over the age of 50 are in cohabiting relationships. This is likely higher in Canada (especially Quebec), where cohabitation is more common and accepted as an alternative partnership arrangement. This arrangement enables each partner to maintain some independence and privacy while enjoying the benefits of an intimate relationship.

Most older adults who remarry consider the marriage successful. Success is often dependent on both partners having a high level of motivation to remarry, the support of adult children and friends, and higher levels of education and health. Most older brides and some older grooms report that they never intended or expected to remarry. Some men remarry because they have difficulty adjusting to widowhood and prefer not to live alone. Older widowers often have little experience with domestic responsibilities, and they remarry to have someone take care of them. For older widows, the need for companionship, financial support, and intimacy, especially if adult children are not close, are motivating factors. Cohabitation rather than marriage occurs if a widow will lose the pension benefits of her deceased husband when she remarries or if her adult children discourage her from remarrying.

Highlight 9.5
Resolving First-Date Anxiety by Seniors

A first date is one of the most nerve-wracking aspects of dating at any age. If you are 50+ and just starting to date again after a few years or a few decades, however, the uncertainty about where to go, what to wear, and what to talk about can seem almost insurmountable.

Before the first date, you wonder whether your date will like you, whether you'll like him or her, and how much dating etiquette has changed since the last time you were out there.

While there are no absolutes when it comes to senior dating, there are a few tried and true strategies that may help calm your nerves and increase your chances for a successful first date:

- One purpose of every first date is to decide whether you want a second one. With that in mind, plan a first date that encourages conversation and helps you get to know each other, and avoid activities like movies and plays that leave you sitting silently in the dark.
- Tailor your first date to include a common interest, hobby, or shared value, which may help you establish an immediate connection around something that has meaning for both of you.
- If you plan to have a meal on your first date, make it lunch and combine it with some fun activity so you have more things to talk about while you eat. Dinner sometimes implies more intimacy than you may be ready for on a first date, and having the whole date depend on two near-strangers sitting across from each other and making conversation can create a lot of pressure.
- If the whole idea of senior dating makes you nervous, consider making your first date a group date with friends, or participating in a group activity such as a wine tasting or charity auction.
- Be smart, be safe, and have an exit strategy. On most first dates you're going out with someone you don't know well, so stick to public places and tell someone you trust who you are meeting and where you will be. If you start to feel uneasy about the person you are with, then leave.
- Don't put all your eggs in this first date basket. If the person doesn't turn out to be Prince (or Princess) Charming, so what? You met a new person, practiced your conversation skills, and learned more about what you want (and don't want) in a partner.

Whether you're 16 or 65, the best way to enjoy a first date is to keep an open mind, focus on the things you have in common, and make your primary goal to simply have a good time.

Adult children oppose a remarriage if they believe it represents a loss of respect and love for the deceased partner or if they fear they will lose their inheritance when their surviving parent dies. Others fear that if their mother remarries, she will become a nurse and a housemaid for

Highlight 9.6
Extended-Care Love: Nursing Homes as a Social Context for New Relationships

The Older Generation

John, age 89, and Adrienne, age 93, met at a "seniors" residence and decided to marry, since they were spending most of their time together in the residence. He had been widowed once, she had been married twice before. Friends and family blew bubbles at the "newlyweds" as they walked to a reception with cans and a sign, "Just Married," tied to each of their walkers. Commenting on the age difference, the new groom stated, "It doesn't bother me falling in love with an older woman. I stayed with my first wife for more than 50 years. I think, at our age, it may be a little less than 50 years this time, but you never know. I'm pretty easy to get along with."

The Middle-Aged Generation

This couple, in their 40s, did not meet at a singles bar, at work, or at a social event with age peers. Rather, they met while taking their mothers for a wheelchair ride on a sunny day in May. Their mothers had lived on the same floor in a continuing care facility for six years, but it was three years before their children met. Ironically, both children were divorced, worked in the same industry, and knew many of the same people in their field. Yet they had never met until they began bumping into each other while visiting and caring for their mothers. After about two years of dating, the couple were married in a synagogue next to the centre, and they invited staff, other residents, and their families to the ceremony and reception. As the bride noted, "I can truly say it's a blessing that my mother is here, because if not, I would never have met the man for me."

Centenarian Love

Many residents who move into a nursing home see the move as a symbol that their lives are ending or almost over. But for Fred, who entered the nursing home at 101 years of age in March, and Ida, who moved in at age 88 in May, the summer brought a whirlwind romance, a six-day engagement, and a September wedding. Both spend their days in wheelchairs, and Ida has been blind for 10 years. She had been a widow for 30 years, and never had a child, but does have many nephews and nieces. He was married to his first wife for 60 years. He remarried within six months of becoming a widower, but his second wife died two years before he moved into the nursing home. He has three sons, eight grandchildren, 14 great-grandchildren, and two great-great-grandchildren. For both it was love at first meeting. Says Ida, "I can't believe I met someone so nice and fell in love at my age. He is so caring and loving." Fred declares, "She had an awfully nice voice, and I found her pretty attractive and pretty nice." The courtship involved eating dinner together and sitting in the sun holding hands, sharing stories about their past. As for their wedding night, Ida thinks they will "just cuddle" in their new shared apartment.

Source: Adapted from news stories in *The Record*, 20 and 25 September 2000. Reprinted with permission from *The Record* of Kitchener, Waterloo, and Cambridge, Ontario.

another man, who will eventually become ill and disabled and then die. On the other hand, some adult children recognize that a remarriage reduces some of their responsibilities for looking after or helping their parent, since he or she no longer lives alone (Connidis 2010).

Remarriage or cohabitation is viewed, increasingly (but not by everyone) as a socially acceptable and viable alternative to living alone. For residents of a retirement or nursing home, however, cohabitation or remarriage is usually more difficult, often because the staff and the policies of the institution do not encourage, support, or permit such arrangements.

Summary

The extended family is an essential element of social life and social support throughout the life course. Relationships within and across generations are influenced by common transitions, such as marriage, common-law cohabitation, divorce, the empty nest when children move out, the refilled nest by boomerang children and/or grandchildren, widowhood, and declining health in later life. The structure, definition, and meaning of family as a social construct is evolving as family structures and relationships change across the life course, including in later life. More research is needed about those who never married, gay and lesbian family members, those who are childless or child-free, sibling ties in adulthood, grandparenthood, and the many combinations of step and step-like relatives following divorce, widowhood, remarriage, or subsequent cohabitation relationships. With changing social norms, more older adults are dating, cohabiting, or remarrying, including those who live in retirement or nursing homes. An analysis of family relationships illustrates the gendered nature of family experiences, and the need to apply feminism and masculinity theoretical frameworks to understand the unique experiences of older adults. Mother-daughter-granddaughter ties are the strongest; women function as the kin keepers and confidants in most families; divorced or widowed women are more likely to experience economic hardship and to have fewer chances or options or desire to remarry; and women in a divorce settlement usually gain custody of children and the accompanying lifelong responsibility for their welfare as a single parent.

For Reflection, Debate, or Action

1. Identify those whom you consider your "family," and indicate how frequently you have contact with each member. What are the purposes of this contact, and where does it take place?

2. Identify the kin keeper in your family. Interview that person to learn about their experiences and how they define their responsibilities. Why does the person, and you, think that she (or he), rather than another member of the family, has become the kin keeper?

3. What are the social norms and barriers that impede dating, cohabitation, or remarriage in later life? How can the barriers be reduced or eliminated so that more older adults can participate if they choose to do so? Why might dating be a pleasant or unpleasant experience for older people? Are these reasons any different from those that apply to younger people?

4. There are few Canadian studies about common-law relationships in later life. Design a study to gain an understanding of the meaning and interaction patterns of common-law relationships for older adults (review the sections on methods and theory in Chapter 5).

5. Are there any fictive kin in your family network? If so, what support do they provide and to whom?

Notes

1. The structure of kinship systems is discussed by Blieszner and Hilkevitch Bedford, 1995; Bowen et al. 2000; Price et al. 2000; Hareven 2001; Phillipson et al. 2001; Matthews 2002; Bengtson et al. 2004; Connidis 2004, 2010; Lowenstein 2005; Haber 2006; Matthews and Sun 2006; Mitchell 2006, 2012; and Fox 2009.

2. Among older institutionalized residents, many do not have any relatives to look after them, and it is this situation that increases the likelihood that they will move into a residential care facility.

3. Most cross-sectional studies suggest that the relationship is between age and marital satisfaction. However, the degree of satisfaction may reflect, as well, the number of years a couple has been married and the stages in the marriage that have been completed. Unfortunately, longitudinal studies on this relationship have not been completed.

4. Discussions of grandparents raising grandchildren can be found in Cox 1999; Minkler 1999; Hayslip et al. 2000; Fuller-Thomson and Minkler 2001, 2003; Climo et al. 2002; Hill 2002; Milan and Hamm 2003; Harper 2005; Hayslip and Kaminski 2005; Fuller-Thomson 2005; Musil et al. 2006; Goodman 2007; and Connidis 2010, 196–200.

5. To assist poor older couples who are responsible for raising grandchildren, the city of Boston created GrandFamilies House—a supportive housing unit with 26 apartments and a social-work infrastructure to enable grandchildren to grow and mature in a safe and supportive environment.

6. Sources of information about gay and lesbian aging include Connidis 2003a, 2010; Heidt and deVries 2004; Allen 2005; Claasen 2005; Clunis et al. 2005; Kimmel et al. 2006; Richard and Brown 2006; Cohler and Hostetler 2006; Brotman et al. 2007; de Vries 2007; Mitchell 2012; and such websites as www.primetimersww.org/chapters. htm; http://gaynorfolk-net.norfolk.on.ca/gay-seniors; and http://gayseniors.com.

7. For cross-national research on childlessness, see the special issues of the *Journal of Family Issues*, "Multiple meanings of childlessness in late life: Findings for seven societies," part 1, 28 (10) and part 2, 28 (11).

8. For a discussion of widowhood (primarily adaptation by widows), see Lopata 1987a, 1987b; Martin-Matthews 1987, 1991; van den Hoonaard 2001, 2010; Hungerford 2001; Hurd and Macdonald 2001; Jenkins 2003; Chambers 2005; and Connidis 2010, 108–18.

9. Martin-Matthews (1991), Hurd and Macdonald (2001), van den Hoonaard (2001), and Chambers (2005), employing qualitative studies, present the "voices" of widows at various stages in the process of losing their identity as a wife and accepting their identity as a single and widowed person.

10 Work, Retirement, and Economic Security

Don't simply retire from something; have something to retire to.

— Harry Emerson Fosdick

Focal Points and Key Facts

- Are older workers less efficient, productive, reliable, or creative than younger workers?

- Why is the Canadian labour force aging and shrinking in size?

- Is there age-based discrimination in the hiring, promotion, or retraining of older workers and in the salary and benefits they are offered?

- Will there be enough workers to ensure a productive society once the baby boomers retire?

- Is retirement being delayed due to economic uncertainties, including inadequate pension resources?

- Are flexible, innovative retirement policies and practices needed to sustain the needs of the workforce and to maintain the viability of both the Canada Pension Plan and private pension plans?

- What is an "adequate" income in later life?

- To what extent is poverty a reality in later life, especially among women? Is the "feminization of poverty" fact or fiction?

- Does our pension system (private and government) require an overhaul, and if so, should there be a shift in relative responsibility for income security in later life? (This is the private trouble or public responsibility debate.)

- It is projected that by 2021, 25 per cent of the labour force will be 45 to 54 years of age and that one in seven workers will be 55 to 64 years of age.

- The average age at retirement for men and women is about 62 years; should older people be encouraged to continue working and why?

- More older adults continue to work. After 65 years of age, about 8 per cent of older women and 16.5 per cent of older men are in the Canadian labour force.

- Over the next 20 to 30 years, a retirement wave will evolve as 9.5 million baby boomers become eligible to retire.

- Starting in 2023, the age of eligibility for Old Age Security benefits will gradually increase to age 67 from age 65, with the full transition completed by 2029.

- In 2011, about 7 per cent of those aged 65 and over lived below the poverty line, but the range varied from about 3 per cent for couples to 5 per cent for single men and 9 per cent for single women.

Introduction

The timing and pattern of transitions into and out of the workforce, the meaning of work, the nature of careers, and the degree of economic security in later life resulting from a particular work history have all changed in recent decades (Ekerdt 2010). Currently, the degree of global economic uncertainty is at an all-time high and is having a ripple effect on the above issues. These changes, at both the individual and the societal level, influence work life, the retirement process, the amount of individual economic security in later life, and a society's productive capacity. These social transformations may result in the following patterns:

- More retirees have a great degree of economic security because of enhanced public retirement benefits.
- There are more frequent and rapid shifts in the economy, leading to job losses, company mergers, downsizing, the outsourcing of work to other countries where labour is cheap, and fluctuations in retirement and pension plan investments.
- There is increased individualization of the work life: individuals, not just employers, make decisions concerning entry into and exit from the workforce based on personal interests, ambitions, and abilities to seek a "work–life balance."
- There is increased education and labour-force participation among women.
- Gender relations are changing at home and at work: men are more involved in family responsibilities because of two-career couples; women are more involved in management and leadership positions at work.
- Increasingly, lives are linked across generations and institutions (McMullin 2005, 2010; Mitchell 2006): entry to the workforce is delayed because of educational pursuits or a weak economy; family events or decisions are arranged around careers or work demands; women postpone entering the labour force or leave it early to care for children, grandchildren, or elderly parents.
- A knowledge-based economy with increased technology reduces the physical labour in jobs, necessitates retraining, stimulates organizational change, and requires fewer workers with more specialized skills (Chan et al. 2001; Marshall and Taylor 2005).
- Work–retirement transitions are becoming more fluid and complex. Retirement is no longer, for many, a predictable event that occurs on or about the 65th birthday.
- There is a cultural shift in attitudes toward active aging and the possibility of optimizing employment opportunities for an aging labour force and for aging individuals who wish to continue working in later life.

This chapter examines the links between the work history and meaning of work among older workers, the process of retiring from the workforce, and the influence of work history and the timing of retirement for economic security in later life. Particular attention is directed to gender differences in work opportunities and patterns and the effect of these differences on the economic situation of older women. Throughout, the use of a life-course perspective reminds us that jobs and careers can change; that the meaning and importance of work in our daily lives can change because of family responsibilities, leisure interests, health, or the challenge of the job itself; that retirement pathways from the workforce are increasingly heterogeneous, complex, and prolonged; and that agency is an important element in decisions about work and careers at transition points. Transition points arise when a person is offered a promotion that requires moving to a new city or extensive travel; when a company downsizes and eliminates positions without warning or offers incentives for early retirement; when a personal or family crisis (an illness, death, divorce, or accident) requires time away from work or results in early retirement or a return to work; or when rapid technological change necessitates retraining if one is to remain employed.

Older Workers in the Pre-retirement Years

Today, issues pertaining to pre-retirement include both structural and individual processes:

- What is the effect on older workers of a changing work environment where there is downsizing, contracting out, offshore manufacturing, and employment in small companies without unions, pensions, or contracts to protect workers?

- Are older workers discriminated against in the workforce?
- Are older workers as productive and reliable as younger workers? Can they adapt to change and be retrained?
- Will there be a labour shortage once the baby-boom generation retires in the next 20 years, and will older workers need to be retained in the labour force?
- How do older workers survive in a linked global economy and in a knowledge-based economy where information technology (IT) skills are essential?
- Does a downturn in the economy force older people to work longer and delay retirement?
- What is the influence of work history (periods of unemployment or part-time work and "bridge" jobs) on retirement decisions and on economic security in later life?

Changing Patterns of Work across the Life Course

For much of the twentieth century, the traditional age-segregated pattern of the life course (education, work, and then retirement) was considered normative and ideal. After completing formal education (high school or university), a young man was expected to enter the labour force and to work continuously throughout his life. Women, on the other hand, after completing their education, were expected to marry and raise children or, if unmarried, to work full-time, although part-time work was acceptable for a married woman after her children were of a certain age. Once employed, most of one's career was spent with the same company, out of loyalty and to maximize one's salary and pension benefits. Then, at age 65, unless declining health or disability required an earlier exit, an individual retired, if eligible, with full public and/or private pension benefits.

Since the 1980s, however, working life in the developed countries has been and continues to be restructured (Marshall et al. 2001a; Marshall and Taylor 2005; McMullin 2005; Cooke 2006; Ekerdt 2010; McDonald and Donahue 2011). Young people are spending more years acquiring an education, and many earn a graduate degree or a specialized post-baccalaureate diploma. Thus, many enter the workforce at a later age than their parents did. Moreover, because of economic conditions early in the twenty-first century, younger workers may be unemployed or underemployed for a few years after completing their education. Hence, the transition to a working life is delayed further.

Once a person enters the labour force, working life may include periods of unemployment, voluntary or involuntary job changes, and, perhaps, a voluntary or forced early retirement. In some occupations, because of a long period of education, late entry to the workforce, and early retirement, some workers spend only about 50 per cent of their lifespan at work compared to their parents or grandparents, who spent 65 to 70 per cent of their lifespan at work. Additionally, approximately 38 per cent of the population is employed in "non-standard work," covering part-time and intermittent work that can create employment insecurity, low earnings, and limited or no access to employer-sponsored pension benefits (McDonald and Donahue 2011, 402).

The Meaning of Work

Despite the changing nature of work lives, work remains a central life focus, even though its meaning and importance ebb and flow across the life course. Work also has the potential to influence life satisfaction or dissatisfaction, although this varies by the type of job. For example, employees in high-prestige decision-making positions and those in the professions generally report high levels of job satisfaction. In contrast, workers engaged in repetitive manual labour are more likely to report lower levels of job satisfaction and less commitment to the job. This dissatisfaction and lack of commitment may result from a low income, the unchallenging nature of the job, impersonal or conflict-driven employee–employer relations, and lack of advancement opportunities. In addition, those at the lower occupational levels are more concerned throughout their work careers with job security, income, and friendships with colleagues than with the meaning and satisfaction they derive from the job. Regardless of the nature of the work, workers with a continuous and stable work history generally enjoy work more, and face retirement with a more positive attitude, than those who experience unstable work histories or chronic unemployment.

Mid-Life Career Changes

Some occupations encourage or require a mid-life career change. After a specified number of years of employment combined with age, for example, those who work as teachers, members of the armed forces, public servants, and unionized blue-collar workers (among other occupations) are eligible in their mid- to late-fifties to retire with full pension benefits and to pursue other employment options. This creates opportunities to hire and promote younger people. Other mid-life career changes result from being laid off through downsizing or restructuring, from the onset of a disability that requires a change in occupation, and from age-related retirement requirements (e.g., for partners in many law and accounting firms, who must retire at age 60 or 62).[1] In general, work trajectories have become less permanent and more complex because of growth in the size of companies, mechanization and technology, and increased competition linked to globalization.

A Changing (and Greying) Labour Force

The labour force is both aging and becoming more highly educated. In 2011, workers aged 55 or older made up 17.5 per cent of the total labour force, compared to 15.3 per cent in 2006. Furthermore, in 2011, 66 per cent of men and 51 per cent of women in the 55 to 64 age group were in the labour force (Statistics Canada 2012). Also, the median age of the workforce rose from 39.5 years in 2001 to 41.2 years in 2006 and to over 42 years in 2011. The percentage of those 65 and over in the labour force also rose, from about 9 per cent in 2001 to 11.9 per cent in 2011 (Statistics Canada 2012). This pattern will increase if the baby boomers choose to work longer than previous cohorts (Turcotte and Schellenberg 2007; Carrière and Galarneau 2011). At the same time, the Canadian labour force is shrinking in size because there are fewer younger workers as a result of lower fertility rates. Another change is that in today's linked global economy, more work is performed "offshore."

While there was a clear trend toward early retirement in the 1980s and 1990s (in part due to downsizing), there appears to have been a reversal in this pattern since the late 1990s (Wannell 2007; Carrière and Galarneau 2011; McDonald and Donahue 2011). The average age at retirement in 2006 was 61.5 years (Marshall and Ferrao 2007).Those most likely to work beyond 65 are men; those with more education, especially advanced degrees; self-employed persons; those employed in farming, sales, and accounting sectors; and those in specific occupations, such as judges, family doctors, legislators, and religious leaders (Duchesne 2002). The large baby boomer cohorts moving through retirement transition points will have a large impact on the labour market, on pension systems, and on the economy. For instance, if baby boomers continue to work longer, this may significantly reduce the demand placed on pension systems (Brown 2011). Highlight 10.1 provides a summary of findings about employment and retirement trends among older adults.

Both the private and public sectors need to address the changing age structure of the labour force, both in general and in specific occupations and industries. Canadians are experiencing longer work lives, but they are also experiencing longer periods of retirement because of longer life expectancies. This has created policy concerns since the large birth cohorts comprising the baby boomers are moving into the retirement phase. The meltdown of the financial markets in 2008 and the subsequent global recession exposed a number of weaknesses in pension plans, such as the underfunding of corporate pension plans and the need to restructure C/QPP (McDonald and Donahue 2011). While the proportion of workers in registered or employment programs provided by companies or the public sector have diminished and a shift has occurred from defined-benefit plans to defined-contribution plans, the proportion of workers with private pension plans (e.g., RRSPs) has grown. This means that individuals have relatively more responsibility for economic security in retirement and will likely do so in the future.

At the societal level, encouraging older workers to extend their work lives clearly has a number of benefits (NSC 2011). And since the skills of older persons are underused, greater work flexibility over the life course would be beneficial (Hicks 2003; McDonald and Donahue 2011). The projected shortfalls in labour supply over the next few decades could be offset by recruiting and attracting highly skilled immigrants for specific occupations; by recruiting,

---

Highlight 10.1
Is Delayed Retirement a New Trend?

- The employment rate for persons aged 55 and over reversed in the mid-1990s—declining from 1976 until the mid-1990s, and rising until 2010.
- While average age of retirement has remained relatively stable over the past two decades, and declined in the prior two decades, a more accurate method of estimation is to calculate average expected working life, similar to life expectancy calculations. This is because "average age" of retirement is a crude measure that is influenced by the large baby boomer cohorts transitioning from work to retirement, and is more sensitive to early versus late retirements.
- Employed 50-year-old men can expect to work for approximately 16 more years whereas women of that age can expect to work an additional 15 years.
- There is a significant increase in delayed retirement since the mid-1990s and an even longer expected work period than observed in the 1970s.
- Despite a small drop in the average work week for those aged 55 and over, there has still been a significant increase (87 per cent) in annual hours worked since 1997.
- Delayed retirement will increase economic sustainability in the face of population aging and will reduce population pressures on pension systems.

Source: Adapted from Carrière and Galarneau 2011. "Delayed retirement: A new trend?" *Perspectives on Labour and Income*, Winter, Catalogue 75-001-X. Ottawa: Statistics Canada.

training, or retraining younger and older workers for specific jobs; or by restructuring pension plans (Policy Research Initiative 2005; Cooke 2006; Hardy 2006; Government of Canada 2007). Marshall and Taylor (2005) noted that the idea of "active aging," which has emerged in Europe and Canada, includes a work component. To achieve this objective of active aging via work, the European Union established some guidelines, including the following:

- Improve the skills, motivation, and mobility of older workers.
- Promote lifelong learning.
- Adapt workplaces to workforce aging.
- Facilitate access to more suitable and flexible forms of work for aging workers.
- Remove age-discriminatory attitudes, policies, and practices.

Women and Work Histories

Education is an important precursor to labour force and employment patterns. Participation in university education has increased for both men and women over the last several decades, but has risen faster for women. The participation rate for men aged 18 to 24 was 21 per cent in 2005–6 and 28 per cent for women of that age during the same time period. Women often outnumber male students in typically male-dominated professional schools, such as business, medicine, pharmacy, and law.

The participation rate of women in the labour force has also risen dramatically in the past few decades, with more than 70 per cent of all Canadian women working part-time or full-time outside the home. The percentage of women working beyond age 65 has typically been very low but is increasing: the rate was 6.7 per cent in 2009, and it may rise further (McDonald and Donahue 2011). Many women are employed in what are often considered traditional "female" occupations: clerical, sales or service, teaching, and nursing. However, with increased education, about 20 per cent of women entered 25 nontraditional (previously "male") occupations between the 1970s and 1990s, with more than 80 per cent entering occupations classified as management, professional, or sales. Between 1990 and today, women have made inroads into most male-dominated occupations, with few exceptions. On average, however, women in these nontraditional occupations earn less than their male co-workers. In effect, many occupations are becoming either more gender-neutral or gender-integrated, and some that were previously dominated by men, such as opticians, optometrists and bartenders, are now dominated by women.

In recent years, more research[2] has been devoted to issues concerning labour force participation by women, the meaning of work for women, gender-based inequities in opportunity, the discontinuous pattern of work for women and its impact on economic security, and the balancing of family and work responsibilities, especially in two-career families. This research has shown that the life-course pathway for women at work is neither orderly nor neatly segmented into education, work, and retirement. Rather, career paths for women are closely embedded in and linked to family and work responsibilities (Moen and Han 2001; McDonald and Donahue 2011; Moen 2012). Moreover, as Moen contends, women's work careers are often sacrificed in order to provide care for family members or to enhance a spouse's career. Recently, research has examined work-specific health risks for older women, such as job stress, discrimination, physical hazards, and the "double burden" of paid work and family caring responsibilities (Payne and Doyle 2010).

Cultural norms, structural inequities, historical events, and personal biographies (involving a partner, raising children, and caring for parents) influence the meaning of work and the career path for women more than for men. Thus, whereas studies of men's involvement in work or careers focus almost exclusively on the work domain, to understand women's involvement in work, we must look as well at their family situation across the life course. Although more childless and never-married women pursue continuous and successful lifelong careers, most women still acquire or assume family responsibilities or experience life transitions that significantly influence their work history—marriage, children, divorce, an empty nest, widowhood, and parent or grandchild care (McDaniel 2002; Moen 2012). Many transitions into and out of the labour force are influenced by these family transition events. Consequently, some mid- and later-life work transitions for women represent a response to earlier unfulfilled life goals once a woman has fewer family responsibilities after her children leave home or if she becomes divorced or widowed.

The meaning of work and the opportunities for work vary for women in different birth cohorts. Mothers of the baby boomers were less likely to separate work and family experiences and responsibilities. Women in this cohort generally married and then followed one of three work patterns: family-oriented and never employed, even part-time; work-oriented but took time off from work to look after their children or elderly parents; or continuous work, especially by those with higher levels of education or who were divorced or widowed early in life (Pienta et al. 1994).

In contrast, female baby boomers are "a generation at work," with between 70 and 80 per cent being employed (Galarneau 1994). The first wave (born between 1946 and 1955) entered the labour force when many employment opportunities were available. If married, they gave birth to a first child relatively later in life, but many remained childless. The second wave (born between 1956 and 1965) joined the labour force earlier and entered occupations with a higher status (the professions, managerial positions, science, medicine, and engineering), primarily because of their high educational attainment but combined with more opportunities as a result of affirmative action and pay equity policies and less gender discrimination in hiring and promotion.

Recent cohorts of women entering the labour force have encountered less discrimination in the workplace than previous cohorts. As Bernard et al. (1995, 59) noted, the rules, norms, and outcomes of work have traditionally been "socially constructed and give males an advantage over females." But as social gains are earned, gendered ageism and discrimination in the workplace are decreasing somewhat, at least in some sectors of the economy. Consequently, younger cohorts of women experience a "convergence" model of work in which their work experiences across the life course are more similar to those of men. At the same time, some younger male peers are assuming a "convergence" model of family involvement in which there is more sharing of parenting and housework. This more equitable division of family labour has facilitated, to some extent, more gender-equitable opportunities in the labour force, although gender differences remain more pronounced among those in the lower social strata, who have fewer work options (Tremblay 2001; Moen 2012).

A number of individual factors influence the frequency and pattern of labour force participation by women in the middle and later years of life. Marital status has the most profound effect. Women who are single, separated, divorced, or widowed are more likely to work, to work full-time, and to work later in life. The health of women and caregiving responsibilities also play an important role in a woman's decision to participate in the labour force or not. And as we will learn in Chapter 12, women are more likely to leave the labour force if they are required to care for a frail parent. At the societal level, women are more involved in the labour force because of legislation that prohibits or discourages income and occupational discrimination, because of the greater availability of daycare centres, and because of recognition that women can be successful in occupations previously assumed to be the exclusive domain of men.

Who Are These Older Workers?

"Older workers" are defined by most government agencies as those over 45 years of age.[3] Consequently, this category now includes the entire baby boom generation, most of whom are still in the workforce. Yet with higher levels of education, improved health, and fewer strenuous jobs in most industries (because of automation and new technology), there is no longer a biological or social basis for those in their forties and fifties to be considered "older workers" or for age 65 to remain as the retirement age.

While mandatory retirement has been virtually eliminated in Canada (the exception being New Brunswick), this has not eliminated age discrimination in the workforce. Age discrimination is manifested in stereotypical negative views of older workers held by employers and younger workers, in fewer opportunities for older workers to be trained or retrained, in fewer older workers being hired or promoted in open competitions, and in restructuring strategies that force older workers to accept an early retirement package. Once out of work, unemployed older workers take longer to find another job, receive a lower salary and fewer benefits than they did in their previous position, or find a new job that is only a contract position or temporary or seasonal work. Some of these unemployed older workers eventually abandon the search for work and "slide" into retirement without ever returning to the labour force (Marshall and Clarke 1996; Underhill et al. 1997). Ageism in the workforce marginalizes older workers and increases their feelings of powerlessness. On the basis of a study of older garment workers in Montreal, McMullin and Marshall (2001, 114–21) concluded that ageism represents the "intersection of structured age relations and individual actions. . . . Individuals act within the structure of age relations to both reinforce and challenge it [ageism]."

The Capacity and Performance of Older Workers

Discrimination in the workforce is based on employers' belief that older workers are less productive, lack physical strength, are slow to learn, have slower reaction times, are forgetful, are afraid of new technology, fear change, are less motivated, and are resistant to re-education or retraining. There is also a view held by some, and which may increase with the elimination of mandatory retirement, that older workers should step aside so that younger people can enter the workforce (Underhill et al. 1997, 32–4; Prager 2002; Ekerdt 2010).

Most studies find that productivity does not decline with age, assuming average health and motivation. The amount and rate of any decline in physical or cognitive ability is highly variable. Where there is some decline, it is often compensated for by experience or adaptation. Adaptation varies among individuals at any age and is influenced by such factors as economic necessity, health, family demands, retraining opportunities and support, and the physical demands of the tasks. In short, there are individual differences in work-related skills and motivation among *both* younger and older workers.

Work performance at any age is influenced by knowledge, experience, abilities, and personal factors unrelated to work, such as health, marital stress, and alcohol or drug use. Moreover, the stereotypes about older workers are not based on reliable objective measures of productivity, performance, or potential. Some of these views are based on the subjective ratings of performance by supervisors, who may have negative attitudes toward older workers. Stereotypes are often a function of the age of the evaluator: younger evaluators may assess older workers less favourably ("they are less productive or creative than my age peers"), while older evaluators may evaluate older workers more favourably ("older people like myself are loyal, efficient, and experienced workers").

However, attitudes about and toward older workers on the part of managers and human resources personnel are changing. As Marshall (2001a) noted, such attitudes will continue to change and improve as the workforce continues to age, as successive cohorts enter the older-worker category (45 and over) with more education and technical and IT skills, and if the demand for labour creates the need to retain or recruit older workers. In summary, discrimination against older workers is probably due less to personal abilities and chronological age and more to the state of the economy, the need for certain types of labour, and the cost of hiring, training, and employing more expensive older workers. Highlight 10.2 describes an older woman who has committed her senior years to community service.

Highlight 10.2
"Hurricane" Hazel McCallion—Canada's 90-Year-Old Mayor

She was first elected to lead Mississauga, ON, in 1978 at age 57 and has served continuously since then. McCallion was a rookie mayor when Mississauga suffered its worst-ever disaster: a Canadian Pacific freight train derailed with tankers of hazardous chemicals catching fire and exploding, forcing about 240,000 residents to flee their homes in November 1979. Despite spraining her ankle early in the disaster, McCallion kept hobbling to update briefings. Her handling of the situation won the rookie mayor the confidence of her city's voters, something she has never lost.

"You don't find very many female mayors, especially of a city as large as Mississauga, and you certainly don't find many mayors who have stuck around 32 years," said one Mississauga resident.

"There's good reason why Hazel doesn't need to actively campaign: she's very visible, she's very well liked and she's very much appreciated for her performance."

Born Hazel Journeaux in Port Daniel, Que., in 1921, her father owned a fishing and canning company. Her mother was a homemaker and ran the family farm. After high school she attended business secretarial school in Quebec City and Montreal. After working in Montreal, she was transferred by the Kellogg company to Toronto. She met and married her husband, Sam McCallion, and they had three children.

As another example of her grass roots involvement, Mayor McCallion was hailed as a hero in 2006 during a police standoff involving a distraught man who was threatening to kill himself. The five-hour standoff came to a peaceful end when McCallion appeared and demanded the man stand down so police, paramedics and fire personnel could attend to more important matters.

Source: Adapted from The Canadian Press, Monday 25 October 2010. http://toronto.ctv.ca/servlet/an/local/CTVNews/20101025/hazel-election-101025/20101025/

Interventions to Retain or Recruit Older Workers

Employers have proposed various actions to increase older workers' ability to perform effectively until retirement or to recruit retirees if and when labour shortages emerge as the baby boomers retire in large numbers, especially shortages in specific occupations or sectors (Hardy 2006; NSC 2011, 2013). Some of these proposals specifically target older workers at risk due to their economic and social position in society, or due to disability or other health limitations. The suggestions include the following:

- Raise awareness of employers and human resource departments about the specific needs of older workers, including "at risk" older workers.
- Implement job counselling and move employees to a new job that is better suited to their abilities.
- Redesign jobs, workplaces, or equipment to make the work less difficult and the worker more efficient.
- Develop innovative training strategies adapted to the age of the worker.
- Introduce alternative forms of work, including working at home, flex-time, job-sharing, longer vacations, seasonal work, or contract work to encourage older workers to remain employed.
- Accommodate workers with discontinuous work histories (in particular, women and older workers) by offering more flexible pension and health benefits.
- Accommodate older employees who have parental responsibilities through flexible hours and providing such benefits as paid time off for caregiving or subsidizing home-care workers.
- Encourage and support sharing information, tools, and resources relating to the development and implementation of policies and practices that engage "at risk" older workers in the labour force. For example, Web-based approaches could be cost-effective and reach key stakeholders and audiences.
- Develop employer assistance programs targeted to older workers to help them cope with age-onset transitions (e.g. health, balancing work and family caregiving responsibilities, retirement and lifelong learning) and stay engaged in the workforce.

Older workers should be enabled and encouraged to extend their working lives to benefit themselves, their families, and society. Not all older persons will want to continue in or return to the labour force, but for those who do, especially for financial reasons, opportunities should be provided by the public and private sectors.

The Process of Retirement

Retirement emerged as a social institution with the establishment of social security payments in welfare states,[4] the growth of industrialization and unions that won the right to a pension and retirement, and the increased importance attached to leisure and consumption in daily life.[5]

At the institutional level, retirement is shaped by social and economic factors across time and at specific periods in history. Government legislation and employer pension plans provide incentives or requirements to retire at specific ages (Klassen and Gillin 1999; Henretta 2003). Retirement will continue to be shaped by the political, economic, and social forces operating throughout an individual's life. Indeed, your retirement and economic status in later life will not be determined solely by your working life, your biography, or your lifetime earnings and savings. Rather, your later life will be influenced by factors beyond your individual control, such as global and national economic crises; **inflation** and unemployment rates; fertility rates, which influence the dependency ratio; the national debt; public and private-sector policies concerning retirement and pensions; the degree of gender inequality in work and career opportunities, wages, and pensions; and immigration policies that affect the size and composition of the labour force.

In recent years, transitions from work to retirement have become blurred, in what has been termed the new retirement (McDonald and Donahue 2011), as individuals strive to balance individual choice and needs with available resources and opportunities.[6] Some retire fully; others become part of the "contingent workforce" (Ekerdt 2010), working casually or seasonally through short-term contracts or consulting (sometimes called bridge retirement). Others may start their own business. Primarily, those with higher levels of education, greater savings, and some managerial experience are more likely to succeed in this type of contingent work. More often, the decision is "forced" when firms offer early retirement incentive packages, either through a collective agreement or when the economy weakens and the labour force must be reduced. For some, the economic benefits of accepting an early retirement package are preferable to refusing the package and later being laid off as a result of downsizing. A more common type of forced or "involuntary retirement" happens after a person of any age is "laid off" or "fired," a pattern that has been on the increase recently (Wang and Shultz 2010). Park (2011) reports that while a sizeable minority of older adults continue to work out of necessity, financially secure and higher income older adults are more likely to remain employed than those who are not secure or have lower incomes.

The Concept of Retirement

In addition to being an important economic institution, retirement is an event, a process, and an increasingly lengthy and complex stage in life. There is considerable diversity in how and when working life ends, if it ever ends. Consequently, it is much more difficult to determine the percentage of people who are retired and to arrive at a clear definition of *retired*. Some older adults are refusing to retire if given a choice, while others retire but then return to work full- or part-time for a salary or as a volunteer. Retirement is one of the best examples of the constant interaction between the processes of individual and population aging. It is yet another example of how individual biographies intersect with institutional requirements and benefits. Highlight 10.3 lists the many individual and societal-level factors influencing retirement decisions and lifestyles.

Attitudes about and Preparation for Retirement

Most studies find that before the transition to retirement, more than 80 per cent of older respondents report favourable attitudes toward it. Generally, such positive attitudes are associated with good health, high income, a high level of education, and a high degree of support concerning the approaching event from significant others in the family and from peers at work (Ekerdt 2000). When it comes to retirement planning and preparedness, McDonald and Donahue (2011) contend that it is the most vulnerable (women, those who are poor, recent immigrants, etc.) who are least ready for this transition.

For those holding negative attitudes toward retirement, these attitudes are based on a fear of financial difficulties in retirement, on a high degree of interest in and satisfaction with

Highlight 10.3
Individual and Societal Factors Influencing Retirement Decisions and Lifestyles

Individual Factors

- work history (regular versus irregular, full-time versus part-time)
- partner's work history and age
- economic status (earnings, savings, investments, entitlement to public and private pensions)
- health status (perceived, objective)
- leisure interests and experiences
- informal support (family, friends)
- attitudes toward retirement
- personal factors:
  - age
  - sex
  - social class
  - education
  - race or ethnicity
  - marital status

Societal Factors

- labour force requirements (past, present, and future re: unemployment benefits)
- economic history (periods of inflation, recessions, amount of government debt)
- leisure opportunities (government programs and services)
- formal support (subsidized housing, transportation, home care
- legislation and policies for retirement and social security (mandatory versus voluntary, availability of private and public pensions, vesting, portability)
- fertility, mortality, and immigration rates
- life expectancy
- disability-free life expectancy
- sex ratio
- dependency ratio

work, or on work being the major or only life interest. These individuals view retirement as an unwanted crisis that must be postponed or avoided. Thus, a person's attitudes toward work or retirement influence the timing of retirement. Highlight 10.4 illustrates three types of pre-retirement images (positive, ambivalent/uncertain, and negative) expressed by 50- to 60-year-old professionals.

To help people adjust to retirement, some employers or entrepreneurs in the local community offer pre-retirement programs. These programs range from a brief conversation about retirement benefits between the retiree and a human resources officer during the last week of work to comprehensive educational programs that begin a number of months or years before the retirement date. The more comprehensive programs involve discussions about finances,

Highlight 10.4
Images of Retirement among 50- to 60-Year-Old Professionals

Positive Images

"I'm 59 and pretty much committed to the idea of retirement at 63. I want to try new experiences. In retrospect it's what I've done all along, trying this and then that . . . not out of a feeling of frustration but more curiosity. I've always had the exploring urge. I'm interested in getting involved more in world government in an active way rather than just passive support."

"I pick up the newspaper every day and see a couple of guys in their early fifties have died. So, you say to yourself, wouldn't it be a lousy thing to work all this time and never get to travel or read the books [you want to]? And it would be wonderful to finally have the time to sit down [and do what you want]. When you're 30, life stretches out forever."

Uncertain or Ambivalent Images

"Barring unforeseen events, I'll continue what I'm doing, adding variety where I can and building in what you may call retirement activities. I've toyed with the idea—don't tell my wife—of an art gallery, where I could bring in money. I became interested in business when I started my practice and realized how much of a business it is."

"When I think about it [retirement], I think that I'm not prepared for it. I'm a little bit concerned about it. If I can work until 70, I will work, assuming that one still has one's marbles. For me work is really very important. . . . I guess the time to think about retirement would be about five years before you do it. [But] I can't imagine ever giving up work."

Negative Images

"I was surprised to see how many retired people I knew who would come back and talk about it. They all appeared to be happy, but when you asked them, all they did was play golf down in Florida with the same people all the time. I couldn't think of anything more appalling than that at 60 years of age. I made up my mind that I wasn't going to get myself into that trap. I wasn't frightened in any way of death, but of retirement. What the hell would I do?"

"I get shivers thinking about not working. I'd hate to sit in a park. I just can't think of getting to that point. Retirement is death. As I see retirement, I don't see it as a happy time at all."

health, post-retirement employment options, leisure opportunities, and community resources. Whether these programs are effective and lead to a successful retirement remains to be confirmed, especially since they tend to ignore individual differences in health, finances, and past lifestyle.

The End of Mandatory Retirement in Canada

The choice of 65 as the age for mandatory retirement in Canada goes back many decades to a time when life expectancy was much lower. Today, however, when average life expectancy is about 80 and the workforce is aging, it is not surprising that mandatory retirement at 65 has been deemed unconstitutional for most jobs (except where physical ability is a prerequisite, such as firefighting) and in most provinces (not yet in New Brunswick). Legislation has supported mandatory retirement as recently as the early 1990s, however. In the 1990 Supreme Court of Canada decision involving a group of professors and physicians who argued that mandatory retirement violated their rights under the Canadian Charter of Rights, arguments against mandatory retirement included examples of great achievements by gifted and productive older people. After much debate, the court upheld mandatory retirement. Those in favour argued that there was no stigma attached to being retired at age 65, that for those employed in a public institution such as a university or hospital, any infringement of equal rights is justified under section 1 of the Charter as a "reasonable limit" in a democratic society, and that mandatory retirement treats everyone the same over a period of time. Since that time, mandatory retirement has been made illegal; however, even where mandatory retirement has been eliminated, subtle forms of age-based discrimination remain in places of employment (Ibbott et al. 2006).

Adjustment to Retirement

Individual adaptive strategies after retirement involve developing replacement roles and activities, adjusting to a perceived loss of identity and self-worth, adapting to new income and spending patterns, and re-establishing social relationships. If the retirement process involves an unstable exit via a series of "bridge" jobs or chronic unemployment after a stable career, there can be adverse effects on health (Marshall et al. 2001b; Drentea 2002; Schellenberg et al. 2005; McDonald and Donahue 2011). And if the health of one or both partners declines and caregiving is the major retirement activity, health may decline further and stress in the partnership may occur. Similarly, if partners spend more time together following retirement and have few common interests or activities, the relationship may become more stressful than it was before retirement. This is often a precipitating factor in later-life divorces.

Most research finds that more than 70 per cent of respondents have few problems in adjusting to retirement. The transition is easier and more satisfying for those with good health and wealth, for those who have a harmonious marriage and support from a partner and family, for those who continue to participate in social activities, for those with a positive attitude toward leisure, and for those with positive attitudes toward retirement. Those who do not adjust well to retirement either return to the workforce or remain dissatisfied, and they often experience a decline in physical or mental health.

Women and the Retirement Process

Just as the study of widowhood among men has been neglected, so, too, has the effect of retirement on women. As McDonald (2002) noted, because women were invisible in the workplace, they were invisible during the development of legislation and in the early research about retirement.[7] A traditional view held by legislators was that a woman's welfare in later life was tied to her legal male partner or to her children. At first, researchers (mainly men) were concerned primarily with how wives (common-law couples were seldom studied) reacted to their partner's retirement, how retirement affected the marital relationship, and how the husband's adjustment could be facilitated by his wife. However, retirement is no longer a male-only process, and, consequently, there is a need to study within-gender retirement issues rather than comparing women to men (Price 2000).

When the work history of women was characterized by discontinuous or random employment, retirement was considered a "foreign" concept for women. They did not work long enough to accumulate pension rights or to "talk about" retirement in the traditional sense that applied to men who were in the labour force throughout adulthood. But with higher participation rates by women in the labour force contributing to greater diversity in work experience, the retirement process for women must be re-examined to be fully understood, especially given the employment history of baby boomer women, many of whom will retire late in life after a full career.[8]

Compared with men, women generally reach retirement "with fewer financial resources, less preparation for retirement, and a different work and family history" (McDonald and Wanner 1990, 94). Many women enter and leave the workforce because of the gendered division of family responsibility for child-rearing or caring for parents or to follow a partner whose job required him to move to another city. Moreover, women are less likely to work full-time, they are usually paid less than men, they are more likely to be employed in low-skill service positions, and they are less likely to have a pension (McDonald and Donahue 2011).

Some women have less attachment to the workforce and, perhaps, they have a broader interpretation of the meaning of retirement. They may feel this way because of the discontinuous nature of their work history, their greater involvement in part-time or less career-oriented work, their greater economic dependence on a partner, and their responsibility for domestic labour, which continues in retirement. If women do return to the labour force full-time in their forties or fifties, they are more likely to retire early. Indeed, feminist scholars such as Calasanti (1993, 143) argue that women do not "retire" from the labour force. Rather, they "merely acquire more freedom to schedule domestic work during normal 'working' hours rather than restricting these responsibilities to evenings and weekends."

For women, the timing and process of retirement is closely linked to family responsibilities, which affect the timing and context of retirement transitions. Some studies have found that women are less likely than men to make plans for retirement or to pick a specific time in advance (Marshall 1995). The factors influencing both the timing of retirement and women's adjustment to retirement include a change in marital status (being divorced or widowed), which results in a later retirement; the retirement of a partner, which may lead to an early retirement, as does the unexpected need to care for an elderly parent, an adult child, or a grandchild; and restructuring at the place of employment, which may lead to earlier retirement. Consequently, women often have less choice than men as to when and how they retire. It is much more likely that women retire at the same time as a partner rather than vice versa, although if a partner is much older, a woman may retire later to fulfill her career ambitions or to continue building pension credits.

Evidence concerning women's adjustment to retirement is contradictory. Some studies have found that retired older women are not as well-adjusted as working older women, although both groups are more satisfied than homemakers who have not worked. Other studies report that there are no gender differences in overall well-being after retirement or in attitudes toward retirement. Some argue that women adapt to retirement more easily because work was not a central role in their life, they are used to living without paid work, and they continue to perform domestic work and fulfill family responsibilities whether they "work" or not (Bernard et al. 1995). Women may spend 20 or more years in retirement. But they do so, in general, after a much shorter work history involving lower wages and few, if any, pension benefits. Women may require a longer period of adjustment, especially if they hold negative attitudes toward retirement and if they retire involuntarily.

Economic Security in Later Life

To live independently, with dignity, and at an acceptable or adequate standard of living, individuals and society jointly strive to ensure the economic security of all citizens. Despite the claims that retirees are a "drain" on the economic system, it is estimated (Galt 2007) that older workers between 60 and 79 contribute more than $2.2 billion each year in tax payments on their employment income and that they perform the equivalent of more than $3.1 billion in volunteer work annually (calculated by the number of hours multiplied by the average minimum wage). Economic security can be achieved through both economic production (employment) and social support programs (pensions, health care, transportation and housing subsidies, community/home-care support). The meaning or level of economic security varies according to how individuals and governments define *adequate income*, *poverty*, or *insecurity*. The economic status of older persons, in Canada and globally, ranges from extremely wealthy to very poor. In much of the world, especially developing countries, the economic status of older people is similar to that experienced earlier in life—namely, they continue to live in poverty or near poverty (England 2001, 2002). It is estimated that only about 15 per cent of the world's population has access to a formal system of retirement income support (Schulz and Borowski 2006). In comparison to the Organisation for Economic Co-operation and Development (OECD) countries (34 European countries plus Canada and the US), Brown (2011) contends that retirement income among older adults in Canada has increased over time and is better than in most OECD countries.

Economic *in*security is created by uncertainty about one's financial future. A person's standard of living may be lowered by the loss of a job, a divorce, the death of a spouse (particularly for women), the onset of a disability, deteriorating health, or an unexpected retirement. Societal changes such as high inflation, the collapse of a stock market, decreased fertility rates, or a shift in government policies pertaining to pensions, social security,[9] or medical care in the later years also have a significant impact on economic status in later life (Brown 1991, 3–6).

The provision of economic security in later life was designed to shift responsibility from the individual to the state. In Canada, the Pension Act of 1918 provided assistance for war veterans only. The first supposedly universal pension plan, introduced in 1927 (the Old Age Pension Act), paid $20 a month at age 70 and beyond (at a time when few reached or lived beyond this age). However, it was not truly a universal plan, since a means test determined whether an older person needed the $20. This test was imposed because it was still expected that adult children would support their elderly parents, and the financial situation of adult children was included as part of the means test for their parents. It was not until 1952 that a truly universal Old Age Security (OAS) system was introduced, which paid $40 per month to all Canadians over 65 years of age. The OAS system was enhanced in 1966 by the Canada Pension and Quebec Pension Plans (CPP/ QPP); in 1967, by the need-based Guaranteed Income Supplement (GIS); and in 1975, by the Spousal Allowance (SPA) for low-income or widowed partners (ages 60 to 64) of OAS recipients.

These programs represent a social contract between the state and all citizens. A contract is also created between generations by which income is redistributed from workers to the retired and from younger to older adults. This redistribution is a "pay as you go" system in which each generation contributes a portion of its earnings and taxes to support or subsidize members of older cohorts. As long as enough workers are employed on a regular basis to meet the projected payments to those who receive them, the system remains in equilibrium. But as we saw in earlier discussions about apocalyptic demography, if unemployment shrinks the labour force, if life expectancy increases, and if older workers retire before age 65, pension systems might run short of funds. Hence, if the apocalyptic argument holds in the extreme, the economic and social security systems could become bankrupt. However, an increase in CPP contributions by workers and tax "clawbacks" from wealthier older persons, or a later age of retirement, or a later age criterion for receiving pensions, or slightly higher productivity would all counteract the demands on the system by the large baby boom cohort (Brown 2011). In reality, it is the private company pension plans that are in more danger today, given their stock market losses since 1998. Moreover, some large companies have declared bankruptcy, and both current and former employees have lost their pension entitlements.

The following sections examine Canada's economic retirement system, the economic status of older persons, and issues related to the retirement income of individuals, including the feminization of poverty. Important challenges we will face in the next 20 to 30 years include the following:

- an overall decrease in the size of the available labour force
- a longer work life as more years of work are needed to maintain sufficient income replacement in retirement
- an ever-changing mix of philosophy, policy, and practice (defined benefits versus defined contributions in private plans; the relative balance of private versus public pensions to provide adequate income), and legislation concerning the relative responsibility of the state and the individual to provide an adequate retirement income. (Should benefits be taxed or not? Should registered retirement savings plan [RRSP] annual contribution limits be increased?)

These issues are a classic example of the debate as to whether private or public responsibility should be invoked and in what proportion.

As a personal note of caution, once you enter the labour force, pay attention to pension plan issues and changes within your place of employment and at the government level so that, late in life, you do not find that your public and/or private plan does not provide the level of economic security you had expected.

The Retirement Income System in Canada

Economic security in later life is both a private trouble and a public issue (Holden and Hatcher 2006). The considerable diversity in economic status among older people is related to education, work history, gender, marital history, consumption and savings patterns over the life course, whether they were renters or homeowners, employment status in the retirement years, and whether they are eligible for some or all of the government income programs (see Highlight 10.5).

At best, income security systems ensure that most citizens receive an adequate replacement income after they retire so that they do not experience economic hardship. Most pension systems are designed to replace between 70 and 90 per cent of a person's pre-retirement income. While most Canadians reach this level, one-fifth of Canadians (especially in the bottom income level) do not (Mintz 2009). This level is thought to be sufficient because retirees have lower

Highlight 10.5
The Diversity of Economic Status in Later Life

Mr and Mrs A

Mr A, now 63, took early retirement at age 61 from his position as vice-president at a food company. A large private pension, CPP benefits, and numerous investments and savings provide Mr and Mrs A with a combined annual income of more than $120,000. Owners of a cottage and a condominium, they winter in the southern United States in an affluent retirement community. Mr A makes frequent trips back to Canada as a consultant to various food companies.

Mrs B

Widowed for more than 10 years, Mrs B, at age 70, receives small CPP, OAS, and GIS benefits, plus a provincial income supplement. Her deceased husband, who worked for more than 40 years as a garage mechanic, never contributed to a private pension plan. Mrs B worked periodically throughout her life but spent most of her earnings on mortgage payments or home improvements. While she has some Canada Savings Bonds and owns her home, her annual income seldom exceeds $25,000. With rising property taxes and home maintenance costs, she may be forced to sell her home, and use the proceeds from the sale to survive.

Mr and Mrs C

Mr C, now 62, was forced to retire at age 58 because of a severe back problem. He receives a disability pension and a much-reduced private pension because of his forced early retirement. Mrs C earns the minimum wage working as a waitress five evenings a week. Their combined income from investments, savings, social security benefits, and earnings is $35,000.

Mr D

Mr D, a 68-year-old widower, immigrated to Canada 11 years ago to live with his son. Before he was forced to retire last year because of ill-health, Mr D had worked as an unskilled labourer in the construction industry. He is not eligible to receive full OAS benefits because he lived in Canada for only eight years before age 65. His monthly income is less than $500, which he gives to his son in return for housing and care. He has no other source of income and is financially dependent on his son and daughter-in-law.

expenses since they spend less on clothes, they no longer pay union dues, and they have less need for transportation; because they no longer contribute to government or employer pension plans or RRSPs; because their homes are usually mortgage-free; because they receive income-based or age-based tax breaks; and because they may be eligible for discounts and subsidies (free drugs, reduced fares on public transportation, and low-income housing).

An income security system cannot eliminate income inequality in later life, but it can reduce inequality, at least among some retirees (Myles 2000; Prus 2000, 2003). At present, beneficiaries of the Canada/Quebec Pension Plan can expect, according to assumptions inherent in the system, to receive only about 25 per cent of their average pre-retirement wage. Thus, most retired Canadians are dependent on additional levels of public or personal support. The system is more generous to those at or near the bottom of the socio-economic scale. However, as we will learn later, there are still many older people who live in or near poverty—unattached older women, especially widows; those with less education, who probably had intermittent work histories with low wages; immigrants and Aboriginal people; and those with chronic health problems (NSC 2009).

Canada's retirement support system has three levels, representing a mix of government and individual responsibility for ensuring an adequate income in later life (Oderkirk 1996a, 1996b; National Council of Welfare 1999; Denton et al. 2000; Baker et al. 2001; McDonald 2002; Turcotte and Schellenberg 2007; Brown 2011, 394–5). The first level includes three public-sector programs: Old Age Security (OAS), Guaranteed Income Supplement (GIS), and the Allowance (known as the Spousal Allowance [SPA] before common-law partners, including same-sex partners, were eligible for OAS and CPP benefits). Individuals must apply for these benefits. It has been estimated that about 3 per cent of those eligible for the GIS do not receive this benefit because they do not apply or do not know how or when to reapply because of language or literacy barriers (Statistics Canada 2006). Currently, about 4.2 million Canadians receive the OAS benefit, and some 1.7 million of them also receive the GIS.

The second level, also government-based, is the Canada Pension Plan or, for residents of Quebec, the Quebec Pension Plan.

The third level includes *private* pensions and individual savings and investments. These elements require long-term planning and discipline if they are to ensure a secure financial future. Only about 40 per cent of Canadian workers are covered by a private (employer) pension plan. There are two types of employer pension plans: *defined benefits* (DB) in which a specific, guaranteed monthly benefit is paid upon retirement according to a formula based on average earnings in the last three to five years of employment, plus years of service with the employer; and *defined contributions* (DC), in which the benefit paid after retirement varies by the amount contributed by the individual and the employer and the investment return on the contributions in the fund. In a DB plan, the risk is assumed by the employer, and all retirees are assured of a specific and known amount of income per month. A DB plan provides long-standing and higher-paid employees with much larger monthly retirement payments than those who were employed for shorter periods and/or had lower incomes. In a DC plan, also known as a money purchase plan, the individual assumes most of the risk. The value of the fund at the time of retirement varies, and for that reason, different people receive pension payments of different amounts, depending on how long they contributed, when they retired, the payment options selected, and the investment success of the plan. In some ways, a DC plan is like a lottery in that the payment is unknown until funds must be withdrawn. In recent years, most new plans and many established plans have been created or restructured in the DC format, since they are less expensive for employers (Brown 2011). It also forces more of the retirement income responsibility on the individual. The company that manages the DC plan can contribute less than the employee or an equal amount, according to negotiated agreements. The major problems with a DC plan are as follows: more decisions about investing must be made by the individual, who may have limited financial knowledge; if it is adopted in a large private company, too much of the fund may be invested in company stock and may be lost should the company ever declare bankruptcy; and it entails high administrative costs that must be borne by the employee (Schultz and Borowski 2006; Brown 2011).

In private plans, to which both the employee and the employer make regular contributions, all accumulated benefits are protected if workers are fired, if they resign, or if they retire early.

An increasing number of private pension plans are *portable*—contributions can be transferred to a plan in another company. This ensures that retirement benefits will be similar to those that would have been paid had the person not changed employers. Similarly, most plans provide for *vesting*—those who are fired or who quit before they retire receive all or part of the benefits they have earned before leaving the organization, including the employer contributions. Normally, an individual must remain at least two years with an employer before vesting occurs. Most private plans also include survivor benefits so that a partner is protected in the event of the employee's death. Increasingly, plans will provide reduced benefits for those who retire before the age at which they would be eligible for a full pension.

The third level of the system also includes individual savings, including the Tax-Free Savings Account (TFSA) which began in 2009, and investments such as stocks, bonds, mutual funds (some of which can be held in tax-protected RRSPs), and real estate. Even if a person is self-employed, works for an employer without a pension plan, or is not eligible for an employer's plan (as is the case for most part-time workers), he or she can contribute to a Registered Retirement Savings Plan according to regulations established by the Canada Revenue Agency (www.cra-arc.gc.ca).

Income from the third level during retirement is highly dependent on the amount of wealth accumulated. Those with higher levels of education and earnings are generally able to accumulate more wealth for the retirement years. While investments in RRSPs have risen over the past several decades, the economic downturn has significantly decreased the value of these investments. Equity in a home or other property is another important component of personal wealth and economic security in later life. Property can be sold, if necessary, often at a large profit, to generate cash for survival in later life. Capital gains on the principal residence are not taxed. Increasingly, for many recent and future retirees, an inheritance from deceased parents, together with an intergenerational transfer of wealth and property before their death, contributes greatly to retirement wealth. Highlight 10.6 summarizes details about public and private retirement programs.

Pension Issues and Pension Reforms

Periodically, because of changing political or philosophical ideologies or the onset of potential or real economic crises, debate arises concerning the viability of the public retirement system. Most debates are economically driven and revolve around the appropriate mix of state (public) versus individual (private) responsibility for supporting retired people, the need for retrenchment (reduced coverage) by the welfare state, how to sustain the system, or how to find revenue for other social problems—poverty among children, high youth unemployment, crime, escalating costs of health care, or the low standard of living of disadvantaged groups such as Aboriginal people. Specific triggering events for these debates include the following:

- excessive government debts and deficits
- inflation, which increases the cost of living and requires indexed plans to increase monthly payments
- a decrease in total annual C/QPP contributions because of an increase in the number of people who retire early or high unemployment among younger workers who do not contribute to the system
- demographic projections that argue that the C/QPP system will become bankrupt
- significant declines in the value of the stock market over an extended period of time

Highlight 10.6
Canada's Retirement Income System*

Old Age Security (OAS)

- It is paid monthly starting at age 65, but a portion (a "clawback") is repaid to the government if annual income exceeds a specified threshold, which is linked to inflation (about $70,954 in 2013).
- About 5 per cent of recipients receive reduced OAS payments, while about 2 per cent lose the entire amount once their net income exceeds $114,793.
- The maximum payable per month was about $550 in 2013.
- The amount of a person's pension is determined by how long he or she has lived in Canada, according to the following rules: A person who has lived in Canada, after reaching age 18, for periods that total at least 40 years, may qualify for a full OAS pension. A person who has not lived in Canada for 40 years after age 18 may still qualify for a full pension if, on July 1, 1977, he or she was 25 years of age or over and
  – lived in Canada on July 1, 1977 or
  – had lived in Canada before July 1, 1977, after reaching age 18 or
  – possessed a valid immigration visa on July 1, 1977
- The amount of the OAS payment is adjusted every three months according to the Consumer Price Index.
- Canadians residing outside Canada are eligible if they lived a minimum of 20 years in Canada.
- Benefits can still be received if a person is employed after age 65.
- The Canadian government announced in 2012 that the age of eligibility for OAS benefits will gradually increase to 67 from 65, with a six-year phase-in plan that begins in 2023 and ends in 2029. The government also promised an increase in benefits at that time.

Guaranteed Income Supplement (GIS)

- It was designed to assist low-income elderly people.
- A non-taxable monthly payment is based on the income of an individual, plus that of his or her spouse or common-law partner. If combined income (not including OAS) exceeds $22,032 (the 2013 limit), an individual or a couple is not eligible to receive the GIS.
- In 2013, the monthly payment was $746 for a single person, $494 for the spouse of a pensioner, and $746 for the spouse of a non-pensioner.

The Allowance

- A monthly, non-taxable allowance (about $1044 per month in 2013) is paid between the ages of 60 and 64 to low-income spouses or common-law partners of OAS pensioners and ($1169) to widowed persons aged 60 to 64 if their income does not exceed a set limit (about $30 864 in 2013).
- At age 65, recipients are eligible to receive OAS payments.

Canada/Quebec Pension Plan (C/QPP)

- A compulsory insurance plan funded equally by contributions from the employer and the employee; self-employed people pay both the employer and the employee shares. Contributions are tax-deductible.

Continued

- A "pay-as-you-go" plan in which the current contributions of employed workers pay for the pensions of those who are retired.
- The C/QPP is designed to replace about 25 per cent of pre-retirement earnings.
- It pays a monthly but reduced pension to retired people aged 60 to 64, a full pension if they do not begin receiving it until age 65, or an enhanced pension if payment does not begin until after 65 and up to 70 years of age.
- Drop-out periods (up to 15 per cent of the years between ages 18 and 65) for people with no or low earnings (owing to disability, maternity or child-rearing leave, or unemployment) are excluded in the calculation of pensionable earnings.
- Payments are taxable.
- Benefits are indexed every January to reflect the annual cost of living—the maximum payment in 2013 was about $1012 per month.
- Benefits must be shared with a divorced spouse.
- A disability benefit ($1213 per month in 2013) is paid to those under 65 who have CPP credits but cannot work.
- A lump-sum death benefit ($2500) is paid to a deceased contributor's estate.
- The Q/CPP provides survivor benefits to a partner regardless of age and to dependent children. Survivors 65 and over received $608 per month in 2013 if they were not receiving any CPP benefits of their own and a lesser amount if they were receiving some benefits. However, no survivor benefit is paid to those 65 and over if they receive the maximum CPP benefit on their own behalf.
- As of March 31, 2013, the CPP fund had a value of $183.3 billion invested to pay the future pensions of Canadians (see www.cppib.ca).
- Based on current contributions and projected investment returns, the CPP is expected to remain sustainable for at least another 75 years (CARP 2007).

Private Pension Plans (Registered Retirement Plans [RRPs] and RRSPs)

- Individual retirement savings plans permit a maximum annual contribution to an RRP and/or an RRSP of $24,270 for the 2013 taxation year, which is tax-deductible.
- After two years of employment, benefits in an RRP are "locked in" and can be used only for retirement income.
- Any early withdrawals from an RRSP are taxable.
- By the end of the year in which a person turns 71, RRSPs must be converted to an annuity or a Registered Retirement Investment Fund (RRIF), and taxes must be paid on all withdrawals.
- Upon death, pension benefits under an RRP continue for a designated partner (usually the partner at the time of retirement), although not all private pension plans consider a same-sex partner an eligible beneficiary.

*For current payment rates and regulations of Canada's public income security system, see www.hrsdc.gc.ca/eng/retirement/index.shtml.

To maintain or enhance the economic viability of a public pension system, four options are available (McDonald 1997a):

1. Increase revenues by raising individual and employer C/QPP contributions, levying special taxes, or transferring more general government revenue to pension funds.
2. Decrease benefits by changing eligibility requirements, charging penalties or reducing the incentives for early retirement, eliminating partial indexing of pensions, raising the mandatory retirement age to delay payment and shorten the period for which benefits are paid and eliminating some benefits, such as the death benefit or the Allowance.
3. Shift the burden of financing pensions to individuals or to private pension plans by increasing the tax advantages of RRSPs.
4. Lower the dependency ratio by reducing unemployment rates through job creation and retraining; increase the labour force participation rate of older workers to delay or reduce the payment of pension benefits; provide a larger pension for those who remain longer in the labour force; eliminate discrimination in the hiring of and in the amount of wages paid to older workers; create incentives to increase fertility rates so that more workers are available in the future; or raise immigration rates among young adults who will work in sectors where workers are needed.

To make the C/QPP system more sustainable, it has been argued that the retirement age should increase to about 70 years and/or gradually raise the age of eligibility for benefits (the United States is gradually raising the age to 67). Brown (2011) argues that a modest increase in the normal retirement age coupled with a modest increase in workforce productivity would result in a sustainable economic security system in Canada, given population aging and increasing life expectancy. Similarly, Chen (1994) proposes that for each one-year gain in average life expectancy, normal retirement age should be extended by about nine months. If average life expectancy continues to increase as projected, the mandatory retirement age in 2025 and 2060 should be 71 years, eight months, and 73 years, one month, respectively (Chen 1994). To support this approach to sustainability, Myles (2002, 325) noted that "a small increase in the average retirement age has a greater impact on retirement costs than large cuts in retirement benefits."

Highlight 10.7, based on an article in *The Economist*, argues that the retirement age must be increased or else pension systems will collapse. Note that this US-based article came out before the announcement by the Canadian government in 2012 that it will increase the eligibility age for the Old Age Security pension from age 65 to age 67 beginning in 2023, with a graduated phase-in that ends in 2029. As you read Highlight 10.7, think about how older workers are sometimes viewed as a burden to workforce productivity, and how they are sometimes viewed as the answer to workforce shortages and pension system sustainability by increasing their average work life through policy reform.

Others argue that raising the retirement age would have an adverse effect on those with disabilities and in poor health. As well, those at the lower ends of the educational, occupational, and income scales would have a difficult time obtaining jobs or keeping them late in life. On the other side of the argument, enabling older people to work longer would encourage active and healthy aging, contribute to longer periods of independence for the individual, and reduce payment burdens for the government (Walker 2000). Working longer, whether in paid labour or volunteer work, contributes to a nation's productivity.

The emergence of "young pensioners" (persons choosing to draw on their CPP/QPP pensions before age 65) is also contributing to concerns about the viability of pension plans; however, given a pattern of longer work life, early retirement will likely decline (Wannell 2007).

Highlight 10.7
70 or Bust!

Current plans to increase the retirement age are not bold enough. Demography and declining investment returns are conspiring to keep people working for more years than they expected. Governments, to deal with ageing problems, have announced increases in the official retirement age [which would affect eligibility to certain pensions] to hold down the costs of state pensions while encouraging workers to stay in their jobs or get new ones.

Since 1971 the life expectancy of the average 65-year-old in the rich world has improved by four to five years. By 2050, forecasts suggest, a further three years will be added. Until now, people have converted the extra lifespan into leisure time. Declining fertility rates imply that by 2050 there will be just 2.6 American workers supporting each pensioner. The young will be shoring up pensions systems which are riddled with problems. Some governments are planning increases in the eligibility age for certain public pensions. America is heading for 67, Britain for 68. Working longer has great advantages. The employee gets more years of wages; the government receives more taxes and pays out less in benefits; and the economy grows faster as more people work for longer. Older workers are a neglected consumer market.

Raising the official retirement age for eligibility of pensions is only part of the solution, since many workers retire before the official age. For that to happen, working practices and attitudes need to change. Western managers worry too much about the quality of older workers. The public sector pension problem is sharpest in American states. The deficits in their pension funds may amount to $3 trillion. Private-sector workers face a different problem. The demise of final-salary pensions leaves them facing two big risks: that falling markets will undermine their retirement planning, and that they will outlive their savings. Thus, governments feel they should encourage workers to save more. And the basic state pension should be high enough to give those unlucky elderly with insufficient savings a decent income, without penalising those who have been thrifty. It is argued that this is the least people deserve in return for toiling until they are 70.

Source: Adapted from *The Economist*, Editorial. 2011. Vol. 398, Issue 8728, p. 13.

Many of these young pensioners earn about 66 per cent of their pre-retirement income the year after they retire. Moreover, about 50 per cent of young pensioners earn a salary the year after they begin receiving their pension, but most of this work is part-time or intermittent since only about 30 per cent report earning at least $5000 beyond their pension income.

The Economic Status of Older Canadians

The economic status of Canadians has been improving over time, whether we examine income replacement ratios, poverty rates, or actual income (Whitehouse 2009; Brown 2011). One reference point is to compare income replacement against the average income level in a country, and to compare Canada against other countries. Canada's figure is close to 90 per cent (meaning that retirement incomes are 90 per cent of the average income, or just below), which is at the high end of OECD countries (Brown 2011). The financial well-being of retired people is also improving because of public and private pension reforms, greater incentives to save and invest, increased in-kind transfers and tax benefits for retirees, increased participation in private pension plans, especially by women, and greater financial planning earlier in life (Denton et al. 2004; Cutler 2005; Kemp et al. 2006; Mintz 2009; Brown 2011).

Yet attaining economic security for older adults is a highly complex policy and practice. For instance, Cutler (2005), in arguing for more research in the emerging subfield of financial gerontology, noted that today the *accumulation* stage of wealth starts later and ends earlier while the *expenditure* stage starts earlier and lasts longer. In fact, you will have fewer years to accumulate wealth that must last longer because of increased life expectancy and uncertain inflationary periods that may strike during your retirement years. Three major factors influencing the amount of accumulated wealth and income in later life are education, work history, and marital history.[10] Possible sources of wealth and income for older adults include the following:

- savings and investments (cash, RRSPs, stocks, mutual funds, and bonds)
- private pensions
- home and other property
- family transfers (inheritances and gifts)
- social security (OAS and GIS)
- C/QPP payments
- tax benefits and "senior" subsidies
- earnings from full- or part-time work

The contributions from each source vary by gender, although the gaps are decreasing as more women have a history of regular labour force participation, increased savings, and greater eligibility for private and C/QPP pension benefits. However, marital status and duration are important factors in the economic status of older women. If women remain married, they have a better chance of financial well-being in retirement (Yabiku 2000; McDonald and Donahue 2011), especially if they have participated in the labour force and contribute a second pension to a retired couple's income. Being widowed or divorced has a negative effect on retirement financial well-being for both men and women but especially for women. McDonald and Robb (2004) found that separated and divorced women, versus never-married or widowed women, are the poorest of all unattached women in Canada.

Economic status is a vivid example of the heterogeneity within the older population, ranging from the very affluent to those living in poverty, including the homeless (see Chapter 8). The family wealth of households headed by someone 65 years of age and older is increasing. It is important when assessing older adults' financial situation to include wealth, not just income. While older families have lower average incomes than younger families, few older adults have debt (see Highlight 10.8 later in the chapter). Still, many older individuals and couples report a fear of financial uncertainty as they enter the retirement years. Uncertainty is created by whether they can or will continue to work; how long they will live, and how long they will remain in good health; whether inflation will increase the cost of living, especially if retirement payments are not indexed to inflation; whether sufficient survivor benefits will be available to a spouse; and how long they can live "rent-free" in the family home. The definition of an "adequate" income is based on both objective indicators and subjective perceptions, by an individual and by others. Assessments of adequacy have seldom identified a standard to which "adequate" can be compared. But in comparison to earlier cohorts, current retirees receive more benefits from private pension plans and social security payments, as well as greater tax concessions and in-kind benefits. Although objective indicators, such as annual income, provide information about the relative economic status of retired cohorts, subjective responses to a lower income must also be assessed, especially when considering the relationship between economic status and well-being. Subjective perceptions of financial "adequacy" by an individual or couple may be more relevant than an evaluation of objective economic indicators by outsiders. Individuals are aware of their own needs and resources, and some are able to accept a satisfactory, albeit lower, standard of living in retirement.

The perceived adequacy of financial resources in retirement is usually based on a comparison with the individual's past lifestyle and with age peers among his or her friends and family circle. Thus, definitions of economic situations in retirement are based more on perceptions about relative deprivation than on actual disposable income. Despite reduced incomes, and even when there are objective indicators of poverty, many retirees report that their economic situation is satisfactory. Even in the face of objective evidence that they are close to or below the poverty line, women, especially unattached women, report more positive evaluations of their economic status than do men. This is why Ballantyne and Marshall (2001) argue that subjective evaluations of income adequacy should not be included in any discussion of social policies for income redistribution. If subjective rather than objective evaluations are used, it is too easy for governments to argue that retirees are satisfied and do not need subsidized economic support.

Many older people report that their basic need for goods and services decreases with age. But changes vary by cohort and gender, and they may involve a more restricted life (moving to a smaller home, spending less on clothing and entertainment, selling a car) or buying less food or less nutritious food. With a reduced income in later life, older adults must allocate a higher proportion of all their expenditures to food, shelter, and household maintenance. Turcotte and Schellenberg (2007) reported that among adults aged 65 and over, expenditures on accommodation, transportation, and food accounted for about 66 per cent of each consumption dollar.

Older Consumers

With older people making up a large proportion of the population, it is not surprising that the business sector has sought to increase this group's spending patterns. Each cohort entering retirement has, in general, more discretionary income and more savings than the preceding cohort (Brown 2011). Spending by retired boomers will increase further because they have had a history of being spenders and consumers of products. Not only will they be wealthier, but they will be healthier and have more time, in years, in which to spend money on leisure and consumer goods. An awareness of increased affluence and health among older adults has led to increased advertising and to the marketing of products for the "maturity" or "grey" market.[11] For example, the average age of Harley Davidson motorcycle owners is about 52!

Older consumers, through focus groups and surveys, are consulted about the design and delivery of goods and services they might purchase, especially with respect to ease of use, the labels on the products (size of print, clarity of instructions), taste, and the nutritional content of food (low in fat, salt, and sugar). Advertisements stress active and healthy lifestyles (travel, cycling, yoga), and they depict active, attractive older role models. Women, especially, demand clothing that is attractive and fashionable. The retiring baby boomer cohorts will attract even greater attention by advertisers and companies seeking to sell their products to this emerging consumer group.

Older Women: The Feminization of Poverty

As noted earlier, the work histories of many women are intermittent or discontinuous. Women enter and leave the labour force more frequently than men, often to provide child or elder care. They are also more likely to work part-time and to retire before they are 65. Moreover, many women in the labour force occupy low-prestige, low-income positions; they seldom seek or receive an opportunity to advance to high-status, high-paying positions; and they are less likely to be eligible for private pension plans unless they work full-time for many years. Women are also more likely to convert pension benefits earned early in life into cash when they change jobs or leave the labour force (Hardy and Shuey 2000). Throughout their working lives, women generally earn less than men,[12] save less, invest less, and own less property. However, the economic situation of older women is improving with each successive cohort that reaches age 65. This improvement is due to higher education levels, longer periods in full-time jobs, less wage discrimination, increased pension eligibility, more equitable distribution of assets upon dissolution of a marriage (including rights to a portion of the spouse's pension), greater participation in better-paid professional positions, and greater numbers of childless and never-married career-oriented women (Rosenthal et al. 2000; Brown 2011). Indeed, the economic situation of baby boomer women is better than that of their mothers.

However, there are still large numbers of older women who are at risk of living in poverty for part or all of their later life. This gender gap in later life, labelled the "feminization of poverty," can apply at earlier stages of life as well, especially for women who are single parents. Most elderly women who are poor are not likely in this situation because they created their own poverty but because society creates gender-based inequalities that have economic consequences, creating a cumulative disadvantage over the life course (O'Rand 2006; McMullin 2010). Women reach later life with fewer economic resources because, if married, they are economically tied to their husband's wealth; because they lose economic capital if they are divorced; and because they have not been employed full-time throughout most of their working life. In short, the feminization of poverty in later life is an accumulated life-course economic disadvantage. It occurs because of social responsibilities for child-rearing and parent care, the gendered division of labour-force hiring and promotion, wage inequity (unequal pay for equal work), and a dependence on small old age security payments if they are not eligible for public or private pensions. As Neysmith (1984) summarizes, "older women are like perennial plants—the roots of their poverty develop early in life and come to fruition when they are old."

Specific subgroups of older women are known as the "hidden" or "invisible" poor (McDonald 1997b, 2002; McMullin 2010). In addition to the lifelong systemic barriers they face, some women are disadvantaged because of their ethnic or cultural background, the dissolution of a marriage or common-law relationship, financial abuse, or living alone. Some widows are not eligible for survivor benefits, or, if they remarry, they may lose accrued pension benefits from a previous marriage. Older women who were divorced earlier in life are likely to be economically disadvantaged, especially if they were fully responsible for raising children and if they were divorced when pensions were not considered family assets to be shared in a divorce settlement, as they are at present in most jurisdictions. Davies and Denton (2003) found that women who were separated or divorced at age 45 or older were more likely to be poor later in life than either married women or men who divorced or separated in middle or later life. This poverty is accounted for by gender inequalities in the family, and in legal, labour force, and retirement systems. However, some of these later-life negative economic impacts can be offset by remarriage, by a high level of education, and by labour-force experience before the separation.

Poverty is also more likely among widowed or divorced older women who live alone. They may be "overhoused" in a family home that is expensive to maintain, or they may not be able to afford housing alternatives because most of their income is derived from OAS and GIS payments (Moore and Rosenberg 1997; McDonald et al. 2000; Smith et al. 2000; McDonald and Donahue 2011). However, never-married women, especially if well-educated, do not tend to fall into this poverty group, since they are more likely to have had lifelong employment. These women are less dependent on government transfers and are more likely to have investments and savings, including real estate.

Other groups of highly disadvantaged older women are Aboriginals, recent immigrants, and those living in retirement or nursing homes (McMullin 2010). Members of these groups are seldom included in research studies about poverty in later life. For example, immigrant women may have no official Canadian labour-force experience and are therefore not eligible for C/QPP pension benefits, or if they arrive in Canada late in life as part of a family reunification plan, they are not eligible for full OAS or GIS benefits. Similarly, if they outlive their husbands, they may not inherit a pension because their husbands may have had a short and irregular work history with few, if any, public pension benefits and no private pension. Brotman (1998) found, for example, that poverty rates in Canada among black, Chinese, Aboriginal, and Greek women over age 65 were at least 5 per cent higher than the national average for older women. And if women from these groups lived alone, they were even more disadvantaged.

Another category of women who may experience poverty in later life are those who remain homemakers throughout their adult life. These women are not eligible to receive public pensions (C/QPP); however, they are eligible, on the basis of need, for OAS and GIS payments. Many argue that the responsibilities of permanent homemakers constitute unpaid labour and therefore they should be eligible for increased social security payments in recognition of their labour in the home (Chappell and Funk 2011). It has also been argued that women who spend their adult lives raising children should be eligible for full Canada Pension Plan benefits because of their contribution to society.[13] Some even argue that benefits to married older women should be financed by their husband during his working years, by higher contributions from all workers, or by funds from general tax revenues.

However, others have argued that homemakers should not be eligible for special considerations if this places an economic burden on current workers or if it increases the national debt. Proponents of this view claim that women who remain permanently at home do so voluntarily, often because they feel they do not need to work for economic reasons. Proposals for reducing the feminization of poverty in later life have focused on changing employment and salary conditions early in life so that employed women who take maternity leave or parent care leave will not lose their jobs or experience reduced pension benefits or loss of seniority. And increasingly, employers are providing daycare or flexible hours to facilitate child-rearing or parent care for women engaged in full-time employment.

In terms of pension reform, some proposed solutions to enhance benefits for women include the following:

- provisions to allow women to accumulate pension credits when they are absent from the labour force to look after their children or parents
- C/QPP pension eligibility for part-time workers
- continuation of pension benefits to a surviving spouse, regardless of later marital or economic status
- a requirement that private pension plans be offered by all employers, regardless of the size of the company
- unisex tables for the calculation of retirement contributions and benefits

- mandatory coverage in private plans for all permanent part-time employees on a pror-ated basis

Clearly, many lifelong economic issues must be addressed to enhance the economic status of the rapidly growing population of older women, especially those who are widowed or divorced and live beyond 80 years of age.

Poverty in Later Life: Fact or Fiction?

Since the 1960s, the real income of seniors has risen substantially (and rates of poverty have dropped) in both absolute and relative terms compared to non-elderly persons (Baker and Gunderson 2005). Whitehouse (2009) concluded that the poverty rate among seniors in Canada was the fifth lowest among the OECD countries. But despite economic gains in recent decades, income inequalities persist among older people.[14]

What is the poverty line in Canada? Before we can determine who is living near or in poverty, at any age, we need a commonly accepted measure (Giles 2004). The use of different measures results in different estimates of the number of people living in poverty and, hence, it is difficult to compare individual or family poverty across time or place. As well, there are different philosophies or policies as to what constitutes poverty, and this means that it is difficult to administer welfare programs fairly. The most common and oldest measure of relative poverty in Canada (in use since 1968) is Statistics Canada's low income cut-offs (LICOs). This measure, which is adjusted annually according to the consumer price index, is based on patterns of family expenditures for food, clothing, and shelter for a given community size and family size. It is not an absolute measure of poverty but, rather, a relative measure of how individuals or subgroups of the population compare at a given time; it identifies those who are less well-off than the average for their family size and within their geographical region (Fellegi 1997; Giles 2004).

A number of years ago, older people were often the largest group in the low-income category. More recently, lone-parent families headed by women tend to be the largest group. LICOs identify the pre-tax or post-tax income below which families or unattached individuals spend 20 per cent more of their income than the average Canadian family on food, shelter, and clothing (Baker and Gunderson 2005). To illustrate, in 2011 it was calculated that Canadians spend an average of 43 per cent of their after-tax income on food, shelter, and clothing. Therefore, for 2012, the LICO drawn by Statistics Canada represents the point at which 63 per cent of income (43 per cent plus 20 per cent) is spent on these necessities, a proportion that is then adjusted for family size and geographical region.

As an absolute measure, however, the LICO has some limitations, and, according to Statistics Canada policy, is not to be considered a measure of poverty. For one thing, the LICO can be calculated based on either *before-tax* or *after-tax* income. The before-tax measure can lead to overestimates of the incidence of poverty.[15] Hence, the after-tax LICO reflects the actual disposable income that is available to purchase the necessities of food, shelter, and clothing. Some studies of seniors have shown that the percentage who fall below the LICO before taxes is about twice the percentage of those who are below the LICO after taxes (Turcotte and Schellenberg 2007). Others argue that the LICO is misleading because it establishes a very low income level for indicating poverty. This means that a large number of people are above the line and, objectively, appear to be in a good financial position while in reality they are not. For example, why should a person or couple that is $1 or $10 above the arbitrary LICO line not be classified as "poor"? In fact, a large percentage may live near the poverty line, especially if they cannot access some social or economic programs (see below). Table 10.1 illustrates the 2010 after-tax and before-tax LICOs for family units of one to three persons living in rural or urban areas. For all seniors, on average, about 7 per cent live under the after-tax LICO.

Another common measure of poverty is the low income measure (LIM) generated by Statistics Canada since the early 1990s. This is a much simpler measure that draws the low-income line at 50 per cent of the median family or single income in Canada, after tax and transfers. This measure is adjusted for family size, and is a common definition of "relative poverty" (Giles 2004). This measure, which reflects an *inability* to pay for groceries, rent, and transit fares, is used to compare year-over-year changes in Canada and to compare poverty levels in Canada with those in other countries (Baker and Gunderson 2005). The LIM poverty rate among the elderly in Canada dropped significantly between the 1970s (approximately 35 per cent) and the mid-1990s (3 per cent) but has risen again to about 7 per cent in 2011. Citing tables from the Luxemborg Income Study, Veall (2007) noted that Canada has few seniors below the LIM compared to the US (25 per cent), Australia (23 per cent), the United Kingdom

Table 10.1 After-Tax Low Income Cut-Offs (LICOs) for 2010 by Family Size* and Type and Size of Community

Place of Residence	Size of Family Unit	After-Tax Level ($)
Rural	1	12,271
	2	14,936
	3	18,598
Population < 30,000	1	14,044
	2	17,094
	3	21,283
Population 30,000 to 99,999	1	15,666
	2	19,069
	3	23,744
Population 100,000 to 499,999	1	15,865
	2	19,308
	3	24,043
Population 500,000+	1	18,759
	2	22,831
	3	28,430

*Additional data for family sizes between 4 and 7+ can be found in the source below.

Source: Adapted from Statistics Canada 2011. Current LICOs can be found on the Statistics Canada website (www. statcan.gc.ca/pub/75f0002m/2012002/tbl/tbl01-eng.htm).

(20 per cent), Germany (10 per cent), and Sweden (8 per cent). Only the Netherlands (2 per cent) had a rate below that of Canada. Who are the 7 per cent living below the LIM in Canada? Veall (2007) found that those in this category were disproportionately immigrants, especially recent arrivals; those who were widowed or divorced, especially women; and those who were supporting a dependent adult child or grandchildren.

A third measure has been developed by Human Resources Development Canada. Its "market basket" measure of poverty, in which the poverty line is based on the income needed to purchase basic goods and services in the basket, is calculated for a typical family of four (two parents, a 13-year-old son, and a 9-year-old daughter) in 48 geographical areas and can be adjusted to create measures for other family types and sizes (Giles 2004). This *absolute* measure of poverty identifies families whose disposable income—total income minus taxes, payroll deductions, support payments, and child care, and out-of-pocket medical expenses—does not enable them to purchase a basket of basic goods and services consisting of food, clothing and footwear, shelter, transportation, and other goods and services, including furniture, telephone service, and postage stamps. Being able to pay for this basket of goods represents the minimum standard for decent living in Canada. This measure generates a higher reported poverty rate in most communities than does the LICO measure.

What Is the Economic Status of Older People in Canada?

The good news is that far fewer older women now fall into the low-income category. This improvement has resulted from increased benefits in the OAS and GIS programs and from more women being eligible for C/QPP and private pension plans. However, OAS and GIS payments are often insufficient—if they are the sole source of income—to allow seniors, especially if they live alone, to rise above the LIM or LICO levels for their region. This is particularly the case for seniors living in large urban areas, where the cost of living is high and increasing faster than the general rate of inflation.

Factors that reduce the likelihood of poverty in later life include high levels of education, good health, living as a couple, being male, and having a history of full-time employment. To illustrate, Moore and Rosenberg (1997, 45–6) found that women living alone are seven times more susceptible to poverty than men living with spouses, that each year of formal education reduces the likelihood of poverty, and that full-time employment reduces the odds by 70 per cent and part-time employment by 33 per cent relative to those not in the labour force.

The overall improvement in economic security among seniors and baby boomers has led some to argue that these groups are "greedy" and over-advantaged, and that younger generations are suffering as a result. Highlight 10.8 addresses the debate.

Summary

In the early decades of the twenty-first century, the meaning of work and retirement and the economic status of older Canadians continue to change. For instance, the pattern of work across the life course is changing as many older workers have been caught in the middle of a shift from a traditional model of a working life to an emerging model. In the traditional model, people spent most of their life working for the same company and doing much the same type of work. In contrast, the emerging model involves lifelong learning and retraining for many serial jobs that may be held in a variety of companies or while self-employed. Moreover, new

Highlight 10.8
Intergenerational Conflict and Economic Security: A Rising Debate

An increasing number of articles in newspapers and journals have (e.g., Foot and Venne 2005; Kershaw 2011) made the argument that older generations have benefited economically since the 1970s at the expense of the current younger generations. The declines in poverty rates among older people have been pitted against substantial increases in average housing prices, cost of living, and higher educational costs, with fewer work opportunities for younger generations. Some consider that the economic situation of young families is the result of "a silent generational crisis." The contention is that young people are not voting or shaping policy development that would help them (improved private and public funding for parental leave, child care, and flex work time); therefore, they are at the mercy of the large baby boom generation and seniors, who are influencing public policy to benefit themselves. Furthermore, these authors state that baby boomers have enjoyed economic prosperity during their life while leaving a legacy of a quadrupled national debt and that seniors have selfishly created an expensive health-care system for treating end-of-life diseases (benefiting seniors).

In contrast, many authors (e.g., Gee and Gutman 2000; Ploeg et al. 2003; Chappell and Hollander 2011), based on research and existing policies and practice, argue against the perspective of intergeneration conflict over a limited pot of resources. There are several Scandinavian countries with higher rates of population aging than Canada, as well as aging boomers, yet many have incorporated the exact policies listed earlier that assist young families. Furthermore, research in gerontology (see Chapter 7) has established that rising health-care costs are primarily the result of a more expensive system, not population aging per se. And while health reform is needed to improve efficiencies in the face of population aging, our health-care system benefits everyone. High costs of living facing young families are mainly due to escalating housing prices and low employment opportunities due to a deteriorating global economic situation, not generational greed or competition.

An analysis of the relationship between population aging, economic and social development, and related policies since the 1970s is highly complex. This requires a consideration of globalization, consumerism, and other economic and system-level analysis tied to individuals and families experiencing these conditions over their life courses. Post-secondary education levels have doubled over the same time period (at a cost of increased taxes to the older cohorts), changes that may be seen as benefiting more recent younger generations. Many boomers are delaying retirement because their pensions have been eroded while others retire early to care for their aging parents—these generations are highly diverse in terms of economic security.

A generational conflict approach merely pits one generation against another, and oversimplifies multi-faceted aging processes. It promotes ageist attitudes and overlooks the plethora of contributions that older adults and boomers have made in the past, and will continue to do at present and in the future (e.g., intergenerational transfers, unpaid caregiving, volunteerism). Such an approach also downplays the fact that families link generations; for instance, considerable wealth is transferred from one generation to the next in terms of family inheritance, gifts, and loans.

Young families face more difficult economic times than recent prior generations, but to attribute the cause to the values, attitudes, or behaviours of the older generation is erroneous. We do not have to take away from one generation to improve the lives of another; but we do require social change and policy reform that benefits all (see policy discussion in Chapter 12, p. 403).

work options that permit more flexibility and more choice as to where and when one works are being introduced.

The definition and timing of retirement are changing for both men and women. Some retire before 65 (voluntarily or involuntarily) while others continue to work for a number of years after 65. Such decisions are influenced by personal work histories, by accumulated savings, by government and employer regulations, and by the relative meaning and importance of work and leisure to an individual. Despite the increased options, few workers engage in much formal retirement planning, and we know very little about the retirement process as experienced by women with a variety of work histories. Older workers today have more skills and potential to keep working, and they should not be subject to forced retirement or unemployment on the basis of age. Indeed, given the greying of the labour force as fewer younger workers are available and more older workers opt for early retirement, mechanisms to retain or recruit older workers are likely to be needed before the baby boom is fully retired by about 2030.

Women comprise a larger percentage of the labour force as more gender-equitable opportunities to participate have emerged. They are acquiring higher levels of education in more diverse fields, and employers are introducing policies that make it easier for women to move into and out of the labour force as family needs dictate.

It is the responsibility of both the retired individual and the state to ensure that an "adequate" income is available until death. This income must also protect a partner after the death of the primary or sole wage earner in a marital or common-law relationship. The economic status of older Canadians has improved over recent decades, and it ranges from extreme affluence to poverty, especially among elderly widows who are not eligible for survivors' benefits in private pension plans. Economic security in later life is more strongly related to education, employment type and history, private pensions, personal savings and investments, and intergenerational transfers than to public security systems (receiving payments from the OAS, GIS, and C/QPP). Although the "feminization of poverty" has been less prevalent in recent years, it is still a reality for many older widowed or divorced women, especially those who were not long-standing members of the workforce earlier in life. To provide more economic security for Canadians in the future, pension reforms are periodically debated and introduced, but major changes are slowly or seldom enacted.

For Reflection, Debate, or Action

1. Develop an argument for or against the proposition that women should receive a salary, plus accumulated C/QPP benefits, for each year they spend out of the labour force caring for their children or parent.
2. If you were to start your own business in the next few years, what policies would you adopt concerning older workers and such issues as recruitment, retention, remuneration, benefits, and retirement (including mandatory retirement)?
3. Write a letter to the editor of a local paper arguing why society should adhere to the position that the public pension eligibility age for full benefits should be raised beyond age 65 to some later age.
4. Discuss whether and to what extent seniors are the reason why the current generation of young adults are struggling economically.

5. To ensure that Canada's social security system is viable and solvent when you and your parents retire, develop an argument or a policy to indicate which of the following measures you would implement and why: raise the eligibility age for benefits, reduce benefits, increase revenues, encourage more private savings, or other options.

6. Interview women in the workforce, as well as those who have retired, to determine ways in which they have experienced or observed gender differences at work and in retirement.

7. Debate whether the "feminization of poverty" is primarily a public issue, a private trouble, or both.

Notes

1. From the perspective of a society or an organization, these career changes represent an economic cost or loss in that the investment in training an individual for his or her career has been lost. Some companies have responded to these work history changes by creating more work output demands to increase productivity (see McDonald and Donahue 2011).

2. Labour force participation by women is discussed in Gee and Kimball 1987; Nishio and Lank 1987; McDonald and Wanner 1990; McDonald and Chen 1994; McDonald 1997a; Anisef and Axelrod 2001; Moen and Han 2001; Tremblay 2001; Davies and Denton 2003; McMullin 2005; Marshall and Ferrao 2007; McDonald and Donahue 2011; and Moen 2012.

3. For information about older workers, see Salthouse and Maurer 1996; Mutran et al. 1997; Walker 2000; Czaja 2001; Marshall et al. 2001a; McMullen and Marshall 2001; Henretta 2003; Marshall and Taylor 2005; Hardy 2006; Government of Canada 2007; Statistics Canada publishes (in print or web format) *Perspectives on Labour and Income* (www.statcan.gc.ca/pub/75-001-x/75-001-x2012003-eng.htm) every month.

4. Retirement as a public policy was first introduced in Germany in 1889 when Otto von Bismarck established the first pension act as an "insurance against invalidity and old age." German workers were permitted to leave the labour force at 70 years of age with a modest amount of guaranteed economic support. However, since few individuals lived to the age of 70 to reap this benefit, the age criterion was later lowered to 65.

5. For a historical analysis of retirement and retirement policies, see Myles 1989, 2000, 2002; McDonald and Wanner 1990, 17–38; Snell 1996; McDonald 2002; Gillin et al. 2005; and McDonald and Donahue 2011.

6. For a discussion of decision-making, see Henkens 1999; Szinovacz and DeVinney 2002; Pienta and Hayward 2002; Henretta 2003; Schellenberg and Silver 2004; Szinovacz and Davey 2005; and Raymo and Sweeney 2006.

7. McDonald (2002) presents a detailed history and analysis of retirement concerning women in Canada.

8. The retirement process for women has been discussed by Arber and Ginn 1995; Bernard et al. 1995; Price 2000; McDonald 2002; Pienta and Hayward 2002; Berger and Denton 2004; and McDonald and Donahue 2011.

9. In Canada, social security comprises all subsidized hospital, drug, and medical plans; government subsidies for housing, transportation, and home care; a retirement income system that includes a basic benefit and a guaranteed income supplement

and an allowance (all based on total income), and a public pension plan. See www.canadabenefits.gc.ca and a Statistics Canada CD-ROM published annually, titled "Canada's Retirement Income Programs" (catalogue no. 74-57-XCB).

10. For a discussion of factors influencing income and wealth in later life, see McDonald and Robb 2004; Cutler 2005; NACA 2005; Holden and Hatcher 2006; Schulz and Borowski 2006; Denton and Boos 2007; Brown 2011.

11. Most advertising and products directed toward older adults involve leisure and travel; retirement housing; drugs, cosmetics, and health care; clothing; products for easier living; financial services; education; food; and specialized magazines for older people.

12. In 2010, average earnings for Canadian women were $28,315 compared with $40,000 for men.

13. The pension plan operated by the province of Quebec gives special consideration to women during the years they drop out of the labour force to raise children. Quebec family law requires mandatory pension-sharing for spouses to recognize the time that women spend out of the labour force. The CPP also provides some credit for women who opt out of the labour force to raise children.

14. For a historical and comparative overview of the evolution of and reduction in poverty among seniors in Canada, see Osberg 2001; Bernard and Li 2006; Milligan 2007; Mintz 2009; Whitehouse 2009; and Brown 2011.

15. As you read media or research articles about LICOs, note carefully whether the annual level is reported in pre- or post-tax dollars. Those who want to emphasize the extent of poverty usually use the higher pre-tax dollar figures.

11 Social Participation, Social Connectedness, and Leisure in Later Life

We make a living by what we get, but we make a life by what we give.

— Winston Churchill

Focal Points and Key Facts

- In what way do social networks influence social participation in later life?
- What is the relationship between social participation in later life and a higher quality of life?
- To what extent, and why, are older adults involved in volunteer work, education, tourism, gambling, crime, politics, religion, and the mass media?
- The social network of older Canadians primarily includes immediate family (45 per cent), friends and extended family (30 per cent), and neighbours (15 per cent).
- What are the meanings and forms of "leisure" in later life?
- About 40 to 50 per cent of older adults are engaged in formal volunteer activities.
- More than 100,000 older Canadians are enrolled in some type of educational program, including a few who are pursuing a PhD degree.
- Among those aged 65 and older, an estimated 2 per cent have a moderate to severe gambling-related health or financial problem, and there is likely considerable under-reporting of such cases.
- About 1 per cent of Canadians accused of a Criminal Code offence are 65 years of age and older, but the number is increasing among older men, especially for violent crimes.

Introduction

Older adults are increasingly contributing to society in diverse and often hidden ways through such activities as volunteer work, caregiving, and civic engagement (Fast et al. 2006a). Contrary to popular belief, very few older people live in isolation or report being lonely. Rather, their social participation and engagement resemble that of the earlier years, although the type, location, or intensity of involvement may increase or decrease as health, interests, or opportunities change. An active social life integrates individuals into a family or community, helps to create and maintain a social identity, and stimulates cognitive abilities and emotional feelings (Fast et al. 2006b; Cutler et al. 2011). At the same time, managing daily affairs and being socially active demonstrate self-sufficiency and independence. One type of social participation is "civic engagement," which involves a range of activities intended to support or improve one's community or country. As Cutler at el. (2011, 222) noted, "Civic engagement encompasses volunteering on behalf of formal organizations, including schools, churches, hospitals, and non-profit organizations; political participation; as well as informal acts such as helping friends, neighbours, and relatives."

Civic engagement, like the broader concept of social participation, benefits the individual in terms of activity and integration; the person or people who are being helped; and society at large by giving back to it and shaping its future. Whether a person is involved in a solitary or group activity, participation provides meaning and purpose to the life of engaged individuals. However, we should not assume that all individuals want or should be socially engaged or that those who are not engaged are to blame, given that there are opportunity barriers across gender, socio-economic status (SES), health status, and age (Rozanova et al. 2012). The possible outcomes of social participation include a perceived higher quality of life, positive aging, a sense of belonging to a community, better physical and mental health, and an improvement in well-being, especially for people who live alone, are widowed, have little family contact, and have an illness or declining functional abilities that require social support (Fast et al. 2006a; Thomas 2009; NSC 2010; Theurer and Wister 2010; Chappell and Funk 2011; Cutler et al. 2011; Rozanova et al. 2012). Social engagement in later life involves adapting to changing lifestyles across the life course and to social changes. In recent decades, older adults have had to adapt in the following ways:

- attaching less importance to work, with new meanings and greater importance being connected to leisure—the constant search for a work–life balance
- shifting from a medical and disease treatment model of health to a health promotion and prevention model, which stresses the importance of "active living" or "active aging" as the ideal lifestyle (Windsor et al. 2004)
- adjusting to technological forms of communication (e.g., cellphones, computers, social media)
- placing increased importance on participating in social networks to enhance health, well-being, and social integration into a community (Krause 2006a; Cornwell et al. 2009)

Activity has become a major feature of social participation in old age and is embedded within lifestyles during retirement, including obligatory activities like activities of daily living; physical, cognitive, and social activities; leisure activities; and productive activities (work, caregiving, and volunteering). The World Health Organization has adopted the term "active aging" as an ideal objective for middle-aged and older adults. This ideal lifestyle involves optimizing opportunities for health, social participation, and security in order to enhance the quality of life as people age (World Health Organization 2002). Aging actively—and well—involves finding meaning and purpose in how time is spent, especially in the retirement years. One's lifestyle reflects personal preferences and decisions (agency), modes of living, and social status whereby differences in personal, social, and structural circumstances yield different lifestyles (Hendricks and Hatch 2006). Figure 11.1 presents components of a personal resource model that conceptualizes "lifestyle."

Being active means living a fulfilling life, and in later life it means remaining healthy and connected. Katz (2000, 142–3), however, cautioned that sometimes activity in later life is pursued only to "manage" or control everyday life or to demonstrate competence and an "active" image. This over-management, or over-activity, by oneself or by others, has inspired resistance on the part of some older persons through anti-activity attitudes or activities! Most retired adults want to be active, but many struggle with the meaning and form of activity. They want to make choices and not have activities imposed on their daily lifestyle. The following comments (Katz 2000, 144–6) express the views of older people about being "busy," being "over-organized," and "needing to be free" to make choices:

"At first I thought I have to keep going—got to make a contribution—make sure your life is worthwhile. And now I still have to struggle with days when I feel I'm not doing anything. . . . If you live in these places (retirement communities) and don't participate you are pressured into taking part. . . . It isn't that I want to be nonactive, though, it is that I want to be able to choose."

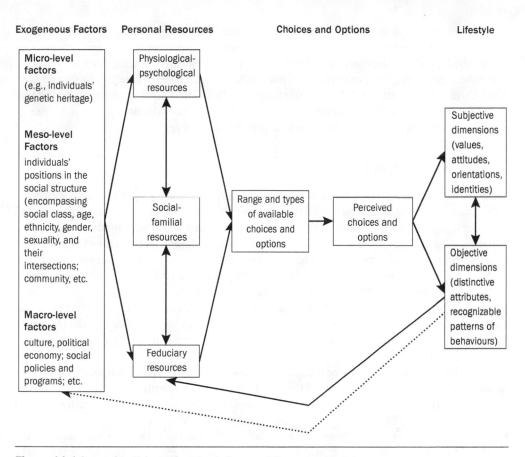

Figure 11.1 Conceptualizing Lifestyle: A Personal Resource Model

Source: Hendricks and Hatch (2006, 313). Copyright © Elsevier 2005.

"You have no idea—exercise—it's just like you were back at school, as if you're such imbeciles you couldn't think of a thing to do yourself. . . . Inside this body, that may look like it's aging to you, is still a fourteen year old screaming to get out."

"You have to decide what a 'senior citizen' is. Do you want to be told what to do, when you should go and play golf, when to join a group, or do you want to do things because you enjoy them? For example, in senior citizen retirement homes, your meals are planned for you and your company is planned for you. You see it right here too, that is, what we could call a senior citizen or active retired 'lifestyle.' I think some people need this retirement lifestyle because they are insecure. They want their meals planned, they want to be told what to do. This is a good, comfortable way of life, but it's not for everybody."

In short, active living in later life should provide satisfaction or contentment, should be chosen freely, and should not be "busy" work. Older people should not be pressured to participate, nor should they be over-organized in socially constructed ideal "senior" activities.

Sooner or later, many older adults experience events or transitions that restrict or eliminate past activities or types of social involvement. These include retirement, illness, widowhood, loss of mobility, a reduced income, some level of cognitive impairment, caring for a frail spouse, fear of falling, fear of crime, or a move to a nursing home or long-term care facility (Strain et al. 2002; Yardley and Smith 2002; Moody and Sasser 2012). In all of these situations, a reasonable level of activity and social interaction can continue through the selection of new activities or the adaptation of specific activities to fit with present abilities and needs.[1]

Social Networks

Throughout life, social relations occur through a variety of **social networks** involving individuals, groups, and organizations. Social networks are important because they are fundamental to understanding changes and adaptations to social support, social participation, and leisure activities over the life course. Social networks are typically described in terms of type (family, friendship, work, etc.), size (number in the network), heterogeneity (diversity of members), and density (the degree to which individuals or groups in a network interact with each other). Networks include those with whom we do not live but with whom we maintain personal relations, and they usually involve a relatively permanent core group (the immediate and extended family) and more transitory extended groups (friends, co-workers, neighbours). The transitory component expands and contracts in size and composition as we enter and leave different social worlds across the life course.

The networks for older people tend to shrink due to transitions such as retirement, widowhood, migration, etc.; however, overall they tend to be large, kin-centred, and dense (Cornwell et al. 2009). Turcotte and Schellenberg (2007) found that the network of Canadian seniors is generally comprised of about 45 per cent immediate family, 30 per cent friends and extended family, and 15 per cent neighbours. The size and composition of these networks vary by ethnicity, gender, education, income, health, occupation, place of residence (urban versus rural), size and proximity of extended family, employment status, and marital status. The membership and composition of a network represents those who are potentially available for interaction and support but does not indicate the sense of obligation, the degree of interaction or support, or the quality of relationships. These social support elements will be examined in detail in Chapter 12. Highlight 11.1 illustrates how the presence or absence of a partner in later life influences involvement in a network.

Stage in life and personal changes, rather than chronological age per se, change the size, composition, or density of a social network over the life course. Normally, the size, density, and heterogeneity of our social networks can be represented by a curvilinear line across the lifespan: the network is small, thin, and homogeneous during infancy and early childhood when it consists mainly of the family, and it grows into a larger, more heterogeneous, and denser network as we move through adolescence and into adulthood (as a result of going to school, working, marrying, and raising children). It decreases to a smaller, less heterogeneous, and less dense network as we move through the later years of life and experience widowhood, retirement, the death of friends, or a decline in health.

Our social world consists of an expanding and contracting circle of nodes that may include individuals, groups, and formal organizations. These nodes are linked into a network by informal social bonds or by formal relations. A network fosters processes of social interaction, emotional and social support, and social integration (Thomese et al. 2005). Networks also provide social capital (emotional or material) that is acquired through exchanges and relationships among

Highlight 11.1
Partner Status and Personal Networks

The type and degree of involvement in social networks is influenced by whether we have a partner or not. All four cases below involve people from the same class background, of about the same age (mid-seventies), and in good health.

Mr and Mrs A

Married for 55 years, they live in the same home they have owned for 40 years. Many of their friends are also long-time residents of the neighbourhood. Hence, most of their socializing is with neighbours. Mrs A belongs to a Monday-evening church group and works as a volunteer two mornings a week at an elementary school. Mr A works part-time as a school crossing guard and plays cards and golf regularly with a group of friends. Mr and Mrs A belong to a bridge club, and at least once a month they entertain other couples in their home. Their three children live within 30 kilometres, and each Sunday they have dinner with one of the children and their family. Mr and Mrs A have independent social lives but share many couple activities as well. As a result, they both have a number of high-quality ties that provide emotional support, companionship, and confidants. Should one of them experience a significant loss of health, a large network of informal support would be available to provide assistance.

Mrs B

Widowed for five years, Mrs B was never employed and thus lacks a work-related network of friends. Her only child, a son, lives in another province, and contact with him is limited to random telephone calls and a visit every two or three years. Since the death of her husband, she has lost contact with most of their "couple" friends, many of whom had worked with her husband. Since she is unable to drive, a volunteer from the church takes her shopping and to complete errands once or twice a week. Other than casual contact with neighbours in her apartment building and a few phone calls each day, she has little interaction with family, friends, or neighbours. She may encounter difficulties if her health fails because she lacks a network and hence a support system.

Mr C

Never married, he has lived in an apartment throughout his adult life. His only relative is an older sister living in a nursing home. He has never been part of a neighbourhood network. Throughout his career, he travelled extensively and spent most of his holidays travelling to pursue his major life interest, photography. He has never attended church or belonged to voluntary associations. Not having a large pension, and having spent much of his earnings on travel, he no longer owns a car. Hence, he is spending more and more time in his apartment, and he lacks a network to provide emotional, physical, or social support. Mr C's lack of participation in a social network may create hardships in his later years.

Ms D

One of the few women to graduate from an engineering program in Canada during the 1930s, Ms D never married, although she has a large active network of former colleagues. In addition, she has two older sisters and six nephews and nieces, who have always viewed her as an older sister and a friend. She has frequent contact with each relative by telephone or through face-to-face visits. Seven years ago, Ms D was hospitalized and required a long convalescence. During this period, relatives and friends, coordinated by a niece, took turns providing care and support. Hence, it is likely that Ms D will have an extensive network of support should she have a health crisis in the future that requires long-term support or care.

individuals within different networks. This capital can be mobilized if and when it is needed in later life to enhance well-being, mental and physical health, and a sense of belonging (or social integration) (Turcotte and Schellenberg 2007; Theurer and Wister 2010; Chappell and Funk 2010).

Across the life course, network relationships vary in durability, quality, intensity, frequency of interaction, purpose, and reciprocity (i.e., directional flow). While social networks shrink over the life course for most people, a core group of family and friends remains that is relatively stable in size and degree of intimacy for most older adults. Antonucci (1990) refers to this core group as a "convoy of support," which surrounds the individual and is available across the life course in times of need.

The presence of a convoy does not, however, guarantee that interaction will occur, that support is available, or that all ties will be supportive (Lachman 2003; Antonucci et al. 2006). Indeed, some relationships within the core can become stressful, abusive, or even life-threatening when neglect or abuse occurs (see Chapter 12). The membership and the nature of relationships in a specific convoy change at different stages in the life course, but many strong intimate bonds persist. Women tend to be more involved in kinship networks (as "kin keepers") while men are more involved in friendship or work-related networks. Not surprisingly, women, especially if employed or active in voluntary organizations, have large and diverse networks and a more permanent, intimate, and confiding convoy; unmarried men have the smallest and least intimate networks and therefore in later life have fewer sources of informal support.

Adults with higher social status generally have larger, more widespread networks consisting of family, friends, and colleagues whereas those from a lower-class background have smaller networks, mainly involving family and neighbours. Similarly, persons with specific racial, religious, ethnic, or cultural backgrounds, especially if they are recent immigrants, are linked to a homogeneous network primarily composed of their family and members of the same religious or cultural group in the neighbourhood, at a place of worship, or at an ethnic club (Gaudet 2007; Jackson et al. 2011). If most members of a racial or ethnic group have limited access to network resources, this could have a negative effect on their health outcomes over their life course. The density and size of a network also varies by living arrangements: whether in an urban or rural setting; whether age-segregated or age-integrated; and whether in a single-family home, a multi-household building, or a retirement or nursing home.

Most elderly adults are not isolated, disengaged, alienated, or abandoned. Rather, networks of varying sizes, with relationships of varying strengths and quality, are available for social interaction and social support. These networks provide companionship, knowledge, a confidant,[2] emotional support, help with minor personal or home-care needs, and assistance during acute or chronic illnesses. Not surprisingly, older persons prefer to rely on adult children and friends for interaction and for assistance with basic needs. As dependence increases, the need for more specialized support and caregiving increases. This caregiving network grows to include both informal ties with primary groups (family, friends, neighbours) and links with formal organizations (social welfare agencies, home-care workers, nursing homes, respite care facilities). To provide suitable and adequate assistance, all parts of the support network must be integrated and coordinated. Each person should have different skills or resources to assist and support an older person so that gaps in service or support do not emerge in a caregiving network (see Chapter 12).

Loneliness and Social Isolation in Later Life: Myth or Fact?

Loneliness is sometimes assumed to be a common experience among older adults and is often reported as one of the main problems in later life. But is loneliness a universal and inevitable experience? The answer, like so many social processes associated with aging, is that it depends on a number of personal and structural determinants. Consequently, loneliness, like many other characteristics found among the older population, reflects heterogeneity and change over time. Some adults are lonely throughout the life course; others have never been lonely. Some become and remain lonely after experiencing certain life events (widowhood, institutionalized living), or due to being socially excluded from society through ageism; others recover from periods of loneliness.

Loneliness is often associated with social isolation and/or exclusion, but the cause-effect directional relationship, if any, is not at all clear. Loneliness represents a subjective evaluation characterized by the unpleasant feeling of lacking relationships or missing a certain level of quality communication in one's contact with other people (Gierveld and Havens 2004, 110). There appear to be two types of loneliness: emotional, when an intimate partner or a friend is absent; and social, when a broad network of friends is not present. Loneliness is more likely to be reported by women, especially recent widows; by those not engaged with other family members; by those in poor physical or mental health; by those living alone or in an institutionalized setting; by those living in a deteriorating physical environment (e.g., a crime-ridden neighbourhood); by those living in communities where there are few social services; and by those aged 85 and older (Havens et al. 2004; Wenger and Burholt 2004; Perlman 2004; Gierveld and Dykstra 2008; Chappell and Funk 2011). **Social isolation** represents an *objective* evaluation of the situation people face when they perceive that their network of social relationships is small, or has decreased significantly, and that they lack relationships with other people (Gierveld and Havens 2004, 110).

Loneliness is one possible outcome of perceived social isolation, but socially isolated persons are not necessarily lonely, and lonely persons are not necessarily socially isolated. Some people, even if they are embedded in a social network, may prefer to be alone and opt for privacy. Moreover, more supportive cultural and social norms about living alone and being independent in later life have changed the subjective perception of loneliness. As Perlman (2004, 186) concluded,

> . . . loneliness occurs in all, or virtually all, cultures. Nevertheless, I suspect loneliness is significantly influenced by cultural factors . . . they shape loneliness's prevalence, intensity, and antecedents; perhaps even culture shapes the very nature of the phenomenon itself. In this sense, loneliness is not universal; it is culture bound.

Social Participation in Later Life

Interaction with others in later life is highly correlated with reported well-being, happiness, and life satisfaction. This does not mean that older people do not or should not engage in solitary activities, such as reading, watching television, or knitting. But it does imply that a mixture of group and solitary activities creates a balanced life that enhances well-being and both physical and mental health in the later years. During later life, however, a number of individual and societal constraints reduce social involvement or change leisure pursuits. At the *individual* level, such constraints include the following:

- declining health and energy
- loss of interest in specific activities

- lack of a partner owing to illness, death, or divorce
- a decline in financial resources and a loss of discretionary income
- changes in the leisure interests or health of a spouse
- an inability to drive or to use public transportation

At the *societal* level, constraints are imposed on older adults under the following circumstances:

- when information about leisure opportunities is not widely disseminated
- when local or regional norms and cultural values discourage the involvement of older adults in specific activities, such as formal education, sports, or drama
- when there are no programs or facilities, such as senior citizen centres, especially in rural and inner-city areas
- when public transportation is inaccessible or unavailable
- when government cutbacks limit age-friendly initiatives, such as green spaces
- when expensive leisure pursuits are not subsidized
- when a deteriorating and unsafe neighbourhood induces a fear of crime or a fear of falling so that older adults stay at home
- when myths or negative stereotypes in the media promote the idea that older adults are not capable of or interested in studying and learning, becoming computer-literate, becoming physically fit, or dating

Social activities provide an environment and a structure in which social networks can be maintained or created, thus enhancing a sense of self-worth. To understand more fully the meaning and the use of social activities in later life, we need to examine the ways in which various forms of social participation contribute to life satisfaction and to a higher quality of life. It is more informative to determine whether there has been a change in the meaning of an activity to a person over time rather than whether there has been an hourly, daily, or weekly decrease or increase in participation. The following sections identify and discuss various forms of social participation that are of interest to older adults.

Volunteerism and Participation in Voluntary Associations

Proponents of apocalyptic demography often hold the view that older people do not make an economic contribution to society and are therefore a burden to society. A more positive and realistic view argues that older people represent an untapped resource for society. Many people over 60 remain engaged in productive activities into later life through voluntary involvement in organizations and community groups[3] or through informal contributions in the form of caregiving, social support, and donating money to family, friends, or neighbours. Because of this voluntary, unpaid activity, retirees in Canada are increasingly viewed by society as productive citizens who make a valuable social and economic contribution outside the paid labour force (Gottlieb 2002; Fast et al. 2006a, 2006b; Martinson and Minkler 2006; Statistics Canada 2006; Morrow-Howell and Freedman 2007; Turcotte and Schellenberg 2007; Gottlieb and Gillespie 2008; National Seniors Council 2010; Cutler et al. 2011).

If not for volunteers, much of this unpaid help would have to be purchased by others in society or funded by the state. This is particularly true of caregiving, since most (80 per cent) of the assistance provided in later life comes from family and friends (see Chapter 12), including from older adults (Fast et al. 2006a; Chappell and Funk 2011). Other contributions provided by older adults include mentoring and counselling, providing leadership in community service organizations, volunteering in political parties and in religious organizations, and performing a variety of tasks or services related to one's skill and experience (e.g., fundraising, home repairs, preparing tax returns, tutoring).

Various surveys have sought to quantify (by hours or dollars) the contribution of older people to Canadian society. Turcotte and Schellenberg (2007) report the following in recent years:

- Of those 65 to 74 years of age, 39 per cent volunteer, and each volunteer contributes an average of 250 hours of volunteer work per year.
- Seniors account for about 17 per cent of all formal volunteer hours, yet they represent only about 12 per cent of the population.
- Three million retirees spend five billion hours each year on productive activities (paid and volunteer work), which represents a contribution to the Canadian economy of about $60 *billion*.
- About 22 per cent of seniors are members of a religious group while 16 per cent, especially men, are members of service or fraternal groups.

Other studies have found that among older adults, more volunteer labour is contributed by married people than by single people, by those who are more highly educated, and by those who have had a history of volunteer work. Li (2007) found that for widows, voluntary participation following bereavement helped to offset the negative impact of widowhood on well-being in later life. Butrica et al. (2009) showed that having a spouse volunteer increases the likelihood of engaging in that activity oneself. Unfortunately, for some older adults the opportunity to volunteer is restricted by structural or social circumstances (e.g., living in a rural or remote area, suffering from poor health, or lacking transportation) unique to their situation (Martinson and Minkler 2006; Cutler et al. 2011).

Membership in voluntary associations tends to be curvilinear[4] across the life course (curve C in Figure 11.2, which appears near the end of this chapter), with peak involvement occurring within about 10 years of retirement (Cutler and Hendricks 2000). Indeed, many "young" senior volunteers assist "older" seniors or work with children in intergenerational activities, such as mentoring, teaching, or coaching. However, volunteering does not cease for many older adults even after they move into a retirement home. Therefore, many baby boomers are likely to continue volunteer work in later life, and more women will continue to volunteer after they retire because early life involvement as a volunteer often continues into later-life involvement. Highlight 11.2 illustrates how older people contribute to society by volunteering their services.

But not all volunteer experiences in later life are positive. In a study of 19 not-for-profit agencies using older volunteers to serve older clients, Gottlieb (2002) discovered three issues of concern to older volunteers: (1) clients are becoming more difficult to serve, more demanding, more needy, and more dependent; (2) volunteers are increasingly concerned about their safety and well-being; and (3) as a consequence of the first two issues, which make volunteering less appealing, there is high turnover, and volunteers are in short supply for this expanding service sector. In addition, older volunteers, like those of any age, can experience burnout due to an ever increasing demand for more and more of their unpaid time. Thus, as more older people demonstrate that they want to lead full and active lives, volunteer agencies may find it to their

Highlight 11.2
Volunteers in Later Life

Anne

Anne, a 76-year-old volunteer, works a 10-hour shift each weekday at a local hospital. She meets incoming patients scheduled for surgery, takes them to the surgical room, and comforts those who are frightened and alone. At other times she delivers flowers to patients. For the last 10 years she has never missed a day. She volunteers year round and must take two buses to reach the hospital. When winter weather delays the bus, she takes a cab at her own expense in order to arrive on time.

(Adapted from an article in the *Kitchener-Waterloo Record*, 17 February 1997, pp. B1, B2.)

Prue

Since completing a course on peer counselling, Prue has been an active volunteer for 16 years. She spends 15 hours a week as a senior citizen counsellor in Victoria, BC. Five years into her new career, she recognized the need for a home-delivery service for seniors and the disabled. After approaching grocery stores in the community, she launched Sendial, a program in which volunteers deliver groceries to those who cannot shop at the stores. Prue also helped set up a Students/Seniors Work Assistance Program (SWAP). This employment project, run in cooperation with the University of Victoria Employment Centre, enables students to earn money by helping older adults with home maintenance or with transportation.

(Adapted and reprinted with permission from the University of Victoria Centre on Aging *Bulletin* 5 (1) (1997), pp. 6–7.)

Bill

A 75-year-old retired businessman, Bill had always wanted to teach. Confined to a wheelchair, he now works two mornings a week at an elementary school, helping students to speak, write, and read in order to improve their literacy. He has also donated $25,000 to the school's literacy program. In addition, Bill has become a friend, counsellor, and storyteller, relating historical events in the community.

(Adapted and reprinted with permission from *Board's Eye View*, North York Board of Education, June 1990.)

advantage to actively recruit them as volunteers and make a greater effort to accommodate their interests, skills, safety, and personal schedules. Tax credits and/or reimbursement for expenses would also help in attracting and retaining high-quality volunteers.

Why do people volunteer, and what are some of the outcomes for the individual and society (Van Willigen 2000; Gottlieb and Gillespie 2008; Butrica et al. 2009; Theurer and Wister 2010)? In general, people volunteer their time for the following reasons:

- to meet people, expand their network, and avoid social isolation and loneliness
- to be productive and contribute to society
- to assist other generations

- to share their knowledge, experience, wisdom, and skills
- to advance a personal interest or cause
- to fill time, keep active, improve health, and build a sense of purpose in daily life
- to develop or maintain an identity, self-esteem, and well-being
- to engage in an active and healthy lifestyle
- to demonstrate independence
- to acquire new skills
- to gain entry to a full- or part-time job
- to play a leadership role
- to interact with younger people, especially those who have similar interests

Volunteering has been shown to increase subjective well-being, in part due to greater availability of social support from friends and family, relative to non-volunteers (Theurer and Wister 2010; Pilkington et al. 2012). From the perspective of a society or organization, volunteerism builds social responsibility; promotes social cohesion, integration, and assimilation (in the case of ethnic associations); builds social capital in a community or an organization; creates a sense of community and belonging; provides social services (in the case of service and fraternal groups); and fosters social change (in the case of political activist groups or labour unions). Indeed, many voluntary groups are organized as advisory or advocacy groups to promote the specific interests and needs of older adults or retirees—for example, the National Seniors Council (NSC) and Canadian Association of Retired Persons' (CARP). Others provide home care or serve as drivers for Meals on Wheels programs to help older people remain in their own home when their mobility and independence decline.

A unique age-based type of voluntary organization for older adults involves the "senior citizen" or "older adult" centres found in many communities. These centres, usually funded by municipal governments or religious organizations, depend heavily on volunteers to offer programs and services. Despite their widespread presence, a majority of older adults do not become involved in these centres, either by choice or because they are not aware of them (Strain 2001). Those most likely to participate regularly are women and rural residents, as well as those who are in good health, live alone, have easy access to transportation, have always been "joiners," have higher levels of education, identify strongly with the neighbourhood, community, or religious sponsor, or are not afraid of crime or of falling en route to or from the centre. Non-users say they are unaware of a centre or its programs, too busy, or not interested in an "old folks" club.

In many cases, those who would benefit the most from attending such a centre—people who are lonely and isolated—do not participate. For older adults who do participate regularly in these clubs or centres, they provide information, educational services, friendship groups and support networks, and a sense of identity. As well, centres may provide meals, vision, hearing, and dental clinics, counselling, and informal health and safety monitoring by staff and fellow members.

Political Participation

Civic engagement in the political process is another form of active and productive aging (Burr et al. 2002; Walker 2006; Wilson and Simson 2006; Gottlieb and Gillespie 2008; Cutler et al. 2011). As the older population has increased in size, and with each cohort that enters later life being better educated, more older adults report being involved as voters, as political candidates, as members of political organizations, and as political activists. While there is a general curvi-linear relationship between age and civic activity, especially for voting behaviour, decreased involvement in later life is less pronounced today than it was 20 or 30 years ago. Much of the increased involvement among older people is accounted for by a significant increase in political interest and political activity among women.

Changes in political interest or attitudes across the life course are due to a combination of maturational changes, cohort effects, and period effects. For example, although cross-sectional studies suggest that older people as a group are more conservative than other age cohorts, this does not imply that they become more conservative with age. Rather, they were politically socialized at a period in history when conservatism prevailed. They also appear more conservative relative to younger cohorts because of dramatic changes in social values over a 20- or 30-year period characterized by the women's movement, political activism by youth, and the emergence of new political ideas and parties (e.g., the Green Party).

Individual priorities attached to specific political issues vary by stage in life. Generally, younger people are more concerned with issues such as tuition fees, unemployment, the environment, child-care support, women's rights, abortion, and gay rights. Older age cohorts tend to be more concerned with inflation, health care, pension benefits, and taxes. Often, these different political agendas are reflected in voting behaviour. Whether the political views of younger cohorts persist or change across the life course remains to be confirmed by longitudinal studies. Period effects also influence age-related differences in political orientations or participation patterns. A war, a depression, high unemployment, a global recession, or a political scandal can dramatically change political beliefs, involvement, attitudes, and voting choices for members of specific age cohorts at a specific period in history. Sometimes these period effects persist throughout the life course; at other times they dissipate as history evolves.

There are notable regional and social class variations with respect to political matters. For example, the values and lifestyles of those who live in the Atlantic provinces are traditionally more conservative than those of people living in provinces such as Ontario. This regional variation is partly related to prevailing subcultural norms and values, which in turn are related to the geographical distance from the centres of political and economic power in Canada. Regional differences are also related, however, to differences in average ages and levels of educational attainment, to ethnic composition, and to isolation and rural living, which can restrict access to information.

Political participation requires a commitment of time, money, and skills. Turcotte and Schellenberg (2007) note that participation by older adults can be passive, which involves following the news and current affairs and searching for information on a daily basis, or active, which includes voting, joining a political party and attending party meetings, serving on committees or as an elected or appointed public official, and politically motivated, such as signing a petition, writing letters to politicians or newspapers, or participating in protests (e.g., the Occupy Movement). Most of this active voluntary participation occurs at the local level, at least initially. But most involvement is expressed through voting, and politicians recognize the size of the potential voting block that older adults represent. For example, people over 65 constituted approximately 17 per cent of all eligible Canadian voters in 2010, but this will increase dramatically to 25 per cent by 2030.

Generally, participation in voting by older people is high because they are long-time residents of a community, have a history with and an understanding of issues, and may have a long-standing identification with a particular political party. There is little evidence that older people vote as a block, primarily because they are a very heterogeneous group that usually lacks a common opinion or agenda on most issues. Nevertheless, by their sheer numbers they represent an implied electoral force that could swing an election if they voted in concert. But at present, at least beyond local issues, voting behaviour is not strongly related to either "old age" policy issues or "age-based" interests.

People over 60 or 65 are eligible to hold political office. In fact, often older citizens are elected because of their perceived stability and experience and because they serve as a symbol of wisdom. In the future, older people are more likely to hold public office because an increasingly larger proportion of the electorate will be their age peers and because they will enter later life with more understanding and interest in the political process than earlier older age cohorts; this is especially the case for women and members of immigrant groups.

Rather than seeking political office, however, increasing numbers of older citizens who feel marginalized or isolated in the political domain are becoming political activists, either individually or collectively. That is, they engage in "self-advocacy" when governments ignore their interests or shift resources to other age groups, and when they perceive that they lack access to formal channels through which they could exert political pressure (Cutler et al. 2011). Moreover, under the guise of generational equity or the influence of apocalyptic demography, politicians may not view older people as the "deserving poor" and begin to question the costs associated with population aging in terms of public pensions tied to inflation, long-term care, health care, social services, and housing (Walker 2006, 342). If older people feel ignored or discriminated against by politicians, they are more likely to engage in activist behaviour (demonstrations, lobbying, disrupting political speeches, withholding taxes). The creation of age-based interest groups is increasing in Canada but has yet to reach the stage that it has in the Netherlands, where age-based interest groups have evolved into the 50PLUS and Union 55+ parties. In recent elections, these parties have won as many as 7 seats in a 150-member Dutch parliament but currently only hold 1 of 75 seats in the Senate.

Age-based interest groups for older adults are created to generate visibility, to pool resources, and to lobby politicians on issues of concern, such as health care, housing, pensions, and transportation. The American Association of Retired Persons (AARP) is one of the world's largest and most developed age-based interest groups with over 35 million readers of their magazine (see www.aarp.org/). In Canada we have a similar but much smaller organization (about 300,000 members) called the Canadian Association of Retired Persons' (CARP: see www.carp.ca). Most of these groups use researchers and marketing experts to develop factual and logical documents and to prepare effective advertisements or arguments on an issue. They also employ skilled lobbyists who generate media attention, mobilize seniors as necessary, and meet regularly with politicians and their staff to establish or keep an issue on the public agenda. Increasingly, these groups insist that they be consulted regularly, that they be given the right to contribute to royal commissions and other public inquiries, and that they be included on standing or ad hoc committees or as panelists at public meetings.

Religious Participation

Religious affiliation, spirituality, and degree of religious involvement can influence life satisfaction, the quality of life, and both physical and mental health in later life (Atchley 2009; Corsentino et al. 2009; Idler et al. 2009; Whitehead and Bergeman 2011; Rote et al. 2013).[5] Much of this influence is based on the beliefs of a particular religion and whether a person values these beliefs sufficiently for them to affect or control the way he or she lives (Krause and Bastida 2011). Organized religion provides some members of the older population with a sense of meaning and security, a readily available social and support group, and a sense of community that fosters social integration. Rote et al. (2013) show that religious attendance increases social integration and thereby decreases feelings of loneliness among older adults. Spirituality may assist, as well, in helping older people to cope with grief, changing personal situations, or death.[6]

Religion also influences attitudes toward and beliefs about the status of older people. For example, in North America, some religious groups (Jews, Mennonites, Hutterites, and the Amish) believe that high-quality care for older members is an obligation that must be met by the family or the religious community rather than by the state. Thus, they provide religious-based nursing homes and hospice care, in-home support services, and opportunities for religious observance for home-bound and hospitalized older persons. The members of three of these religious groups usually live in rural settings, often as a subculture outside mainstream society. But each religion has its own beliefs and values about the veneration of old age, with Eastern religions generally emphasizing respect for the elderly to a much greater extent than Western religions (Idler 2006).

For recently arrived elderly immigrants and refugees, religious organizations and institutions help to integrate them into life in Canada. Temples, mosques, synagogues, and churches serve as centres for social, spiritual, and leisure activities, and they provide a range of social welfare, social support, health care, psychological, and financial services that may not be available in mainstream society. These religious institutions may build "seniors" centres or housing for older members of the religious group, often in co-operation with linguistically or culturally based ethnic organizations or with settlement or social service agencies. The involvement of religious organizations makes it easier for elderly newcomers to use social and health services than it would be if they were fully dependent on mainstream agencies.

Religious involvement is a form of voluntary behaviour, and at least four patterns of religious participation, usually measured by attendance at organized services, are possible:

1. An increase from childhood to early adulthood, then stable across the life course
2. Cyclical, random attendance, often related to stage in family life[7]
3. A decrease after middle age
4. Regardless of the pattern earlier in life, an increase in the later years

Most studies find that attendance at religious services remains stable across the life course or that there is a temporary or permanent withdrawal in the middle and later years. Religion is an important element in the life of older age cohorts, who usually report stronger religious beliefs than younger age cohorts (Idler 2006). Turcotte and Schellenberg (2007) found that in 2003, 50 per cent of those aged 65 and over reported attending a religious service at least once per month, with 10 per cent reporting no religious involvement. Interestingly, they found that this reported lack of involvement varied considerably by region—from a low of 2 per cent in Quebec and 5 per cent in the Atlantic provinces, to 9 per cent in the Prairie provinces, 10 per cent in Ontario, and 26 per cent in British Columbia.

Religion and spirituality are positively related to health, well-being, and social support in later life (Kirby et al. 2004; Krause 2006b; Atchley 2009; Corsentino et al. 2009; Whitehead and Bergeman 2011; Rote et al. 2013). Older people who are more involved in and committed to their faith and those who exhibit higher levels of spirituality enjoy better physical and mental health than those who are not as religious or spiritual. This tends to be heightened for those dealing with serious health and illness challenges (Idler et al. 2009; Krause and Bastida 2011). However, the causal mechanism behind this relationship is unknown. One explanation is that religious settings create social ties that provide social and emotional support that may buffer the effects of illness stressors (Krause 2006b; Krause and Bastida 2011; Whitehead and Bergeman 2011). Kirby et al. (2004) suggest that spirituality is a resource in maintaining psychological well-being and that the use of this resource is more significant for those with greater levels of frailty. As well, religious commitment and beliefs may encourage a person to avoid unhealthy practices, such as smoking, drinking, using recreational drugs, and eating certain types of food, and may lead to optimism and a positive mental attitude.

As with other forms of social participation, we must distinguish between aging, cohort, and period effects with respect to religious activity. We must also identify the directionality of relationships between religion, religiosity, and spirituality and such outcomes as health and well-being, given that these may influence each other. In addition, religious attendance and religiosity are not the same.

More recent studies have adopted a multi-dimensional concept of religious involvement and have attempted to understand how people derive meaning in life through religion and spirituality (Atchley 2008, 2009). This model incorporates the degree of public participation in religious services, the strength of religious attitudes and beliefs, and the degree of private participation (watching religious services on television, reading, or praying). Recent studies support the finding that religious participation does not end in later life but that there is a decrease in public participation and a compensating increase in private worship. Moreover, those who are more socially active in general are more active in public, organized religious activities; older women are more involved in religious activity than men; members of certain racial and ethnic groups are more involved; and geographical/cultural variations tend to be found among and within countries.

Media Consumption

The media (newspapers, the Internet, radio, and television) are designed to reach a large and diverse audience. As an influential social institution, the media entertain, inform, promote social integration, and perpetuate cultural norms and beliefs. In addition, the media provide people with indirect contact with the social world and may help to prevent loneliness and social isolation among older adults.

As people age, they often read fewer books and newspapers. They also attend fewer films because of financial constraints, declining vision, or loss of interest in the content. However, television viewing increases, especially among women, the less educated, and those with lower incomes. Television is the medium that older adults select most often for entertainment and information.

Although it is still debated whether media consumption is a substitution or a compensation for a lack of face-to-face interpersonal relations, television does provide surrogate companionship for some older people. It also provides a structured daily schedule for older adults, whose mealtimes, activities of daily living, and bedtime are regulated or scheduled to some extent by the television programs they watch.

The use of television or radio to deliver educational programs to older adults is increasing. As more older people use computers and mobile devices, Internet use will also increase (Rogers and Fisk 2010). Cable television, pay-TV, and the Internet have the potential to provide learning experiences, intellectual stimulation, and social and commercial services for adults of all ages. Indeed, television and Internet shopping may serve the needs of housebound older people in the future. As for "social media," no studies as of 2013 have specifically examined the use of Facebook, Twitter, etc., by older adults.

Lifelong Learning

In a knowledge-based economy, lifelong learning has become essential in the workforce because of rapid technological and social change. Lifelong learning also helps to prevent social isolation in the community and may help to increase a nation's productivity if people engage in paid or volunteer work with upgraded skills and knowledge. It also increases life satisfaction and enhances subjective health (Simone and Cesena 2010). But learning has also become a major leisure activity during adulthood, especially as the level of formal education rises for each new cohort. Moreover, while older cohorts have lower literacy rates than younger age groups, the literacy rate of each cohort reaching age 65 is higher than that of the preceding cohorts.[8] While it is difficult to assess the literacy factor in many developing countries due to lack of data, in some developing countries only 10 to 14 per cent of the women and 34 to 41 per cent of the men in the 60+ age group can read and write.

Those with low literacy skills and a low level of education tend to watch more television and to read fewer magazines, books, and newspapers. The more literate and educated are exposed to more information and understand it better, including information about health practices and healthy lifestyles (Roberts and Fawcett 2003; Wister et al. 2010). This greater knowledge often translates into better health (see Chapter 7), resulting in lower mortality rates and better cognitive functioning in later life.

No longer is education completed by late adolescence or early adulthood. Each year, more than 100,000 older Canadians enrol in some type of educational program, and the number of older households with access to the Internet increases annually. For some older adults, learning also fosters age-integrated relationships.

Although it was once thought that older people lacked the ability to learn, recent evidence suggests that given the opportunity, encouragement, and enough time, an older person can acquire new skills and knowledge through formal and informal educational programs (see Chapter 3). Education for older adults has not been a high priority of the formal education system, but a shift in values and beliefs about lifelong learning and recognition that retirees constitute an untapped "market" has led to an increase in the number and type of educational opportunities available in later life. Programs are provided, as well, to enhance knowledge or increase literacy rates, especially among elderly recent immigrants. Today, many older adults actively seek educational experiences to acquire cultural and intellectual enrichment, to earn a degree, to enhance their social life, or to foster social integration and a higher quality of life (Simone and Cesena 2010; Goulding 2012). Highlight 11.3 illustrates the later-life educational achievements of an intellectually active retiree.

Changing social norms and new forms of delivery enable adults to pursue higher education in the home through audiotapes, television, or the Internet, in off-campus centres in the community, and on college or university campuses. Older students who participate in these programs are more likely to be members of the upper and middle classes, to have completed their early schooling in North America, to be in good health, and to have access to transportation. Highlight 11.4 illustrates educational programs developed specifically for older adults.

Highlight 11.3
A Student at 80

Born in the early 1920s, W.T. left high school at 14 years of age during the Depression to help pay taxes on the family farm. He finished high school by correspondence courses while serving in the army from 1942 to 1946. "In my mind, I had never quit the idea of learning," he said. "I can't imagine how dull life would be without it."

Retiring as a draftsman in 1986 after a 32-year career, he pursued a general BA, graduating in 1993. Then, he continued and earned an honours BA in geography in 1999. He credits his wife with igniting his passion for the environment, and following her death he enrolled in a master's program in environmental studies. At the age of 80, he wrote and successfully defended a 200-page thesis on river basin ecosystems to earn his third degree. During his time as a graduate student, people would say, "You'll be 80 years old when you finish." But he always responded, "How old will I be if I don't do it?"

During his university career, he studied with young students, they borrowed his lecture notes, they went for coffee after class, and they made jokes about his age— "You're 80 and just graduating? You must be a slow learner." And he, in return, says, "They helped me more than I helped them. It (university) put me around people who were filled with enthusiasm and life. They're going to make the world better, and I assure you they will." At the age of 82, in September 2003, W.T. began a PhD program in geography, graduating in 2010. Learning is truly a lifelong pursuit for this older Canadian.

Source: Adapted from B. Aggerholm. 2002. "Never Too Late to Learn," *The Record*, 6 July. Reprinted with permission from *The Record* of Kitchener, Waterloo, and Cambridge, Ontario.

Travel and Tourism

With improved health and a lifetime of pursuing leisure beyond the home, an increasing number of older adults are embracing travel and tourism as forms of social participation in later life. Whether a trip is part of an organized tour or undertaken independently, and whether the purpose is culture, adventure tourism, education, camping, photography, biking, or simply pleasure and relaxation (at spas, at beach resorts, and on cruise ships), older adults travel widely. To illustrate, the "grey nomad" leisure lifestyle in Australia enables adults over 50 to spend three or more months per year "on the road" living in a camper or converted bus (Onyx and Leonard 2007). Unlike "snowbirds" in North America who remain in one place during their southern sojourn, the grey nomads are constantly on the move, covering many kilometres, including travel to remote areas of the outback, regardless of the risks involved in being alone as they pursue this lifestyle.

The travel industry organizes tours specifically designed to meet older adults' interests and needs, including more opportunities and better accommodations for the older single person who travels alone or as part of a group tour. The frequency and diversity of travel experiences for older adults will increase as well-educated, healthy, and affluent baby boomers, with a history of travel for work and leisure, enter retirement seeking personal challenges, novelty, education, social relationships, and escape. Already, older travellers, especially women, constitute the fastest-growing segment of the travel industry.

Highlight 11.4
Education as Leisure in the Later Years

Many older adults are returning to formal or informal education. Some of the educational programs are offered by seniors who volunteer to share a specific skill or type of expertise; some are offered by professors or other professionals through distance education (by means of the Internet, audiotapes, or television); and others offer experiential learning opportunities.

Road Scholar/Exploritas/Elderhostel (www.roadscholar.org/)

Elderhostel was established in 1975 as a not-for-profit organization in the United States, and in Canada in 1980, providing adventures in lifelong learning. It underwent a name change to Exploritas in 2009, followed by a second change to the umbrella organization Road Scholar in 2010. Today, it provides over 8000 learning programs originating from North America and targeting 90 countries around the globe. The program typically offers one- to four-week learning experiences, with accommodations that may consist of shared rooms in university residences, single rooms in luxury hotels and conference centres, cabins on trains or ships, mountain chalets, jungle lodges, or cabins in remote regions. Each class normally runs for 90 minutes a day, and classes are scheduled to allow participants (who must be at least 55) to enrol in up to three courses per session. There are no grades, exams, or homework, and many courses range from $1000 to $2000 per week (depending on destination) for registration, accommodation, meals, classes, and extracurricular activities, including field trips. For those who cannot afford the full tuition, scholarships are available to offset some of the cost.

Road Scholar's mission is to offer programs that involve intergenerational interaction; the humanities and social sciences; the development of individual skills; the pursuit of active outdoor adventures; discovery through travel; service learning and activities; adventures on ships; and special courses that meet women's interests and needs. More adventurous and affluent older adults can take courses in Africa, Europe, China, India, and South America, and in recognition of "active" aging, Road Scholar offers canoe trips, cycling, mountain treks, caving, and camping. This innovative learning experience provides intellectual activity for both active and disabled older adults who want to expand their horizons and develop new interests. Some describe Road Scholar as a global university that offers experiential learning adventures on a worldwide as well as local campus.

Universities of the Third Age and Senior Colleges

Universities of the "Third Age," first established in France in 1973 (United Nations 1992), and "senior colleges," created in Japan in 1969, offer educational programs designed for older adults. Their purpose is to encourage and support lifelong learning, to improve the quality of life for older citizens, to involve older people in activities that are beneficial to the community, to train volunteer leaders for the community, and to conduct research about aging and older adults. The programs offered include physical activity and health knowledge, cultural and intellectual activities, tourism, the learning and preservation of cultural traditions, and retirement preparation and adjustment.

One growing area of travel and leisure among many older adults is RVing—living and travelling in a recreational vehicle (RV). This form of leisure involves travel and social engagement in many forms. Highlight 11.5 provides a description of this leisure activity and demonstrates how community formation may occur even among persons who are mobile.

University and College Programs

Some universities and colleges offer special programs for middle-aged and older people. Examples include the Wilfrid Laurier University Association for Lifelong Learning, which offers six-week courses three terms a year; the McGill Institute for Learning in Retirement, which conducts about 30 self-directed study groups a year; and the Simon Fraser University Seniors Program, which offers a variety of credit and non-credit courses.

The University of California at Los Angeles (UCLA) offers a program known as the Perpetual Learning and Teaching Organization (PLATO) that utilizes retired and semi-retired professionals to share their knowledge on a variety of topics (see www.honors .ucla.edu/plato.html). This program is unique: there are no classes, teachers, or exams—only study groups, topic coordinators, and learning for learning's sake. Each member leads a one-week session, usually on a topic not related to his or her life experience or expertise: lawyers lead groups on literature; pharmacists, on philosophy; engineers, on art. Informal rules ban any discussion of personal health, wealth, or family matters. But they do allow a few fourth-year honours students from UCLA to attend sessions, thereby fostering intergenerational learning and relationships. Online lifelong learning has also increased in popularity for persons of all ages. For instance, Coursera (www.coursera .org/) is an educational technology company that offers open online courses on a variety of topics.

Retirement Community Programs

In the United States, land developers are building retirement communities near or on land owned by universities (see www.kah.kendal.org; www.ithaca.edu/longview; www .retirement.org/davis). These communities, which have informal and formal links to the campus, appeal to older people who value and pursue lifelong education. Many of the residents are retired alumni, faculty, and staff. This environment also promotes intergenerational contact with students. Many links between the community and the campus are fostered, including the following:

- Residents interact with students in university classes, at cultural events, in health-care services, and at athletic events.
- Students are employed or volunteer in the retirement dining hall or leisure centre.
- Residents have access to research experts and programs in a gerontology centre on campus.
- Faculty and students give lectures or musical concerts at the retirement community.
- Residents serve as volunteers or paid part-time workers during university athletic, cultural, or conference events.
- Residents participate in faculty and student research projects.

Gambling: A Leisure Activity or a Hidden Problem?

In 2006, gambling revenue in Canada (net of prizes) from government-operated lotteries, lottery tickets, race tracks, and casinos exceeded $14.5 billion, yielding $10.6 billion in profit. Of

Highlight 11.5
RVing Seniors and Building Community around Leisure

Many RVers prefer to travel independently, following their own schedule. Others choose to spend at least some time traveling together or meeting periodically at a common RV destination to see old friends and share experiences and information. This may include structured parks where RVers stay put for a period of time in an RV community or unstructured RV parks where RVers stay for a brief stay as part of a travel plan.

Social life in established parks is often structured in terms of leisure activities. Parks where most residents rent for a month or more usually employ an activity director. In non-commercial parks, volunteers often hold an equivalent position. The activity director is responsible for organizing activities with wide appeal. Dances, communal meals, parties, trips to local attractions, exercise or other classes are favorites. Bingo and poker nights are also popular, as is dining out in inexpensive local restaurants. Pizza parlors are favorite choices. If there is a pool and a qualified instructor, the activity director schedules regular "swimmercize" classes. An activity director may also arrange special events such as a diesel maintenance seminar, a crafts show and sale, or a seminar where anthropologists discuss their research project about RV participants. The activity director or park manager also invites newcomers to help with weekly clean-up chores. Travelers staying for a week or more often become volunteers in the host community's senior center, schools, or other community or public services. In this way, RVers develop a community built around leisure activities and social engagement.

Source: Excerpts from Counts and Counts. (2001). *Over the Next Hill: An Ethnography of RVing Seniors in North America*, Second Edition. Toronto: Broadview Press.

the profit, $7.4 billion enriched government finances, and $3.2 billion was directed to charities (Jones 2007). These amounts may be underestimates, however, because Statistics Canada does not collect data about charitable and First Nations gaming (Canadian Gaming Association 2008).Gambling is heavily promoted by governments, which use their share of the revenues to fund health care, build schools, train elite and Olympic athletics, and support charities, including those serving seniors. Casinos have become resort-like: they are leisure destinations that not only involve gambling but also offer concerts and gourmet restaurants.

Gambling as a form of social participation is increasingly popular among the older population, whether at bingo halls or casinos (Hope and Havir 2002; Muggeridge 2002; Zaranek and Chapleski 2005; NACA 2006; Jones 2007; Community Links 2010; Tirachaimongkol et al. 2010). O'Brien Cousins et al. (2002) found that about 16 per cent of Albertans 65 and over played bingo regularly because it was less expensive than going to a casino. Most of these participants were women, some of whom had health problems, low incomes, and little education. Many lived alone and played bingo to "fill time" and enjoy a social outing in a safe place. Across Canada, NACA (2006) reported that 68 per cent of seniors are engaged in some type of gambling activity, which may involve bingo, horse races, sport lotteries, lottery tickets, casinos, or even playing the stock market for "fun" (as "day traders").

For many older adults, gambling is an enjoyable, non-serious leisure activity. It offers social interaction with others, an escape from boredom or loneliness, excitement and suspense, a safe way to "be bad," and harmless entertainment in a socially acceptable setting (Hagen et al.

2005). Currently, a visit to any casino in Canada, especially during the day or early evening, illustrates quite dramatically how many retirees are engaged in gambling, whether they are fully mobile or use a cane, a walker, or a wheelchair. Retirees represent big business for the travel industry and casinos. A growing number of older adults are delivered regularly by bus as part of daily outings organized by tour companies linked to seniors clubs or retirement homes or by casinos that offer free transportation, and perhaps a free lunch (Higgins 2005; Parekh and Morano 2009; Community Links 2010). Nobody really knows how much older adults spend at casinos—it may range from $25 to hundreds of dollars per visit. But the *Lethbridge Herald* (2003) did report that video lottery terminals and casino gambling are partially to blame for about 15 per cent of the bankruptcies among seniors in Alberta.

Evidence is mounting that more older people are becoming addicted to gambling, although they are the least likely of all age groups to become addicted and to need counselling or treatment and are more likely to quit (Parekh and Morano 2009; Martin et al 2011). NACA (2006) reported that among Canadians 60 and over, an estimated 2.1 per cent have moderate to severe gambling-related health or financial problems. In reality, as with all types of addictive behaviour, those afflicted are not aware that they have a problem, or if they are, they deny it or fail to seek help because they are embarrassed or do not wish to be labelled as a chronic or addicted gambler. In short, gambling addictions among the older population are a "hidden" issue, and the prevalence is probably highly under-reported (Zaranek and Lichtenberg 2008). This type of addiction may start as a periodic social activity for fun that becomes a major activity, a habit, and a secret that can lead to loss of control and an addiction crisis (NACA 2006). As to why older adults are susceptible to a gambling addiction, the theories include loneliness and boredom, cognitive impairment, too easy access (lottery tickets for sale in stores, organized seniors' trips to casinos), too much discretionary time and wealth, too little wealth, or the presence of other addictions (alcoholism, smoking).

Call centres for those with gambling problems report that they receive more calls from older adults with an apparent gambling problem or from friends or relatives who worry about gambling by a parent or friend. Most calls express concern about financial losses by someone on a fixed income or about dramatic changes in social behaviour or relationships. As an indirect indication that the number of cases is increasing or that it is becoming a more serious social problem, manuals, guides, and educational workshops have been developed to provide family and social service personnel with advice or information on programs to prevent, reduce, or ameliorate this addictive behaviour among members of the older population (Centre for Addiction and Mental Health 2006; Lemay et al. 2006; Parekh and Morano 2009; Community Links 2010). Tirachaimongkol et al. (2010) further state that protecting older adults from late-life problem gambling entails helping them to become being meaningfully engaged in old age, to feel appreciated and respected, and to reduce factors that may diminish older adults' enjoyment and outlook on life.

Asocial Behaviour: Older Criminals

Until the 1980s, criminologists did not consider that older age had an impact on offending. Since that time, attention has been given to two principle types of older criminals: those who offend in old age, and those who have grown older while incarcerated. The number of criminal offences committed by older people is increasing, although the number of arrests and convictions is quite low.[9] Only about 1 per cent of all persons accused of a Criminal Code offence are 65 years of age or over. Of these cases, about 40 per cent are for violent offences, including sexual assault; 42 per cent, for property offences, such as thefts; and the remaining 18 per cent, for minor offences, such as disturbing the peace or impaired driving. A conviction occurs in less than 60 per cent of the cases since older criminals tend to be treated leniently by the courts: they are placed on probation or receive a fine or reduced sentence unless the crime involved violence or a firearm (Steffensmeir and Motivans 2000). In Canada's federal prisons, about 12 per cent of the population is over 60 years of age (Simard 2000; Public Safety Canada 2011), but this includes a preponderance of prisoners who have aged in place, rather than entered prison as an older adult. Indeed, only 3.1 per cent of the population in federal prisons is aged 60 and over at age of admission; however, there has been an increase in the proportion of males who are aged 60 and over at time of admission between 2001 and 2011: from 1.9 per cent to 3.2 per cent (Public Safety Canada 2011).

It is unclear whether an increase in crimes by older men is due to the growth in the size of the older population, to habitual criminals living longer, to an increase in the number of older people who commit their first crime in later life, or to an increase in the number of older persons who are charged by the police if they are apprehended. Accurate statistics about criminal acts by older people are difficult to obtain since victims may not press charges and the police may not arrest the accused if a crime, such as shoplifting or drunkenness in a public space, is a first-time offence. Moreover, except for those charged with violent crimes (or drunk driving), the judicial system is unlikely to incarcerate older people convicted of crimes. For instance, it is more common for older prisoners to undergo community supervision than younger ones, including parole or halfway supervision.

Most offences committed by older men include drunkenness and driving while intoxicated. However, the number of sexual assaults and physical assaults against partners (or roommates in a nursing home) by older men is increasing, perhaps because of the stress of caregiving, or because of alcohol, side effects of drugs, cognitive impairment, psychiatric problems, or lifelong marital violence. "Mercy" killings of a frail, impaired partner to end his or her suffering are not common, but they do occur in later life, as do "murder-suicide" attempts or occurrences when one or both partners can no longer cope with their current situation.

Among older women, the most frequent crime is shoplifting: the theft of food, clothing, or other basic necessities. One explanation is economic hardship as a result of living on an ever-decreasing income. For example, an elderly woman caught stealing dog food reported that she did not have a dog. She thought it was less risky to steal dog food because it was cheaper than meat. Similarly, an 82-year-old man, arrested after a string of bank robberies using stolen bicycles, reported that he needed to supplement his meagre income to survive. Older women offenders in the federal prison system tend to be serving time for their first offence (80 per cent) compared to younger offenders, and tend to exhibit fewer needs with respect to substance abuse, employment, and attitude, while also showing greater potential for reintegration (Greiner and Allenby 2010).

In addition to theft motivated by need, crimes by elderly "delinquents" also occur. This type of crime is motivated by boredom or a need for excitement. For example, an 80-year-old bald man was accused of stealing a hairbrush and an 82-year-old woman of stealing birth control pills. Other possible explanations for petty crimes in later life are a reaction to stress associated with transitions and losses, seeking attention because of feelings of marginality or loss of prestige in society, the side effects of prescription drugs, cognitive impairment, or increased alcohol consumption. Most elderly "delinquents" receive a warning, are placed on probation, must enter an educational program designed to prevent recurrences, or are required to do voluntary work in the community.

Leisure and Aging: Conceptual and Methodological Issues

Changes occur in the relative balance among family, work, and leisure activities in our daily lives at different points in the life course. Hence, the way we use time for obligatory or discretionary activities varies. Individuals select leisure activities to fit their personal identity (how they define themselves) and their social identity (how they believe they are defined by others). We develop a "core" of leisure pursuits that persist throughout our lives, entailing solitary and/or group activities. These core pursuits may include such interests as the mass media, volunteering, cultural activities, tourism, and sports. Then, we pursue other activities that suit the needs or desires of our personal and social identity and our abilities and interests at specific stages in life. These latter activities change as roles, self-definitions, interests, occupations, competencies, relationships, and opportunities change.

Like many other aspects of social life, opportunities for leisure vary by income, gender, education, social class, ethnicity, health, employment, and marital status. Hence, as in other domains of our social and working lives, there is inequality in leisure. Structural constraints (gender, socio-economic status, place of residence) or lack of personal resources mean that some adults are not able to spend their leisure time as they might wish. This can result in a lack of congruence between actual and desired use of leisure time.

Leisure, as an expressive rather than an instrumental domain of daily life, has profound meaning for those who do not find their identity in the world of work (Thomas and Venne 2002; Hendricks and Cutler 2003). Indeed, leisure has been associated with higher levels of self-esteem and well-being in older adults (Hsu 2010). Leisure, as well, is a domain of everyday life that illustrates the importance and potential of agency and autonomy and the reality and possibility of shifting priorities and interests over time (Hendricks and Cutler 2003, 123).

With longer lives and changing lifestyles, there is greater diversity in leisure pursuits, and new forms of leisure are emerging. As the baby boomers age, there will undoubtedly be even greater variety in the types of leisure activities that older persons engage in. There are both individual-level changes over time in agency, abilities, and interests as well as changes at the societal level in the structure and allocation of leisure opportunities, such as education, facilities, and programs. Thus, we are more likely today to see people from a lower-class background playing golf or enjoying fine art, women engaged in a wider array of leisure activities outside the home, and adults in their eighties who travel throughout the world and engage in physical activity.

Increasingly, leisure activities for older people, especially women, take place outside the family in public and private facilities. Shopping malls, seniors' centres, parks, and other recreational facilities are places where older adults engage in a social life in safe, public spaces. Often, these settings facilitate the creation of informal groups that meet voluntarily and regularly for casual conversation. To illustrate, the Red Hat Society is a social group for women that fosters a global and/or local support network of "sisters" in middle and later life (Yarnal 2006). Another example, based on a participant observation study of older adults who regularly met in a fast-food restaurant, shows that older people in this type of setting create non-obligatory, casual friendships involving a form of play, laughter, and conversation. Serious, personal matters are seldom, if ever, discussed. These group gatherings become an important part of the everyday routine in the lives of older persons. For many of the participants, the setting is more meaningful than a "seniors centre," which they consider a place for "old folks" (Cheang 2002).

Defining Leisure

Leisure is defined by the participants, at a specific stage or point in time, to meet their social, cognitive, and emotional needs; to help define themselves; and, perhaps, to provide intrinsic rewards. Many aspects of leisure are similar to those found in work. Both work and leisure, for example, have the potential to provide an individual with a sense of worth, identity, prestige, and status (Hsu 2010). Both involve a milieu where a person can establish and maintain social interactions, and they both provide an outlet for expressive and instrumental needs. The inability to agree on a definition of leisure persists because it is a multi-dimensional concept,[10] because activities have a variety of meanings or functions for an individual at different times in the life course,[11] because individuals can engage in more than one leisure activity at a time,[12] and because some activities fall into overlapping categories.[13] Furthermore, people may consider leisure to be a non-essential, voluntary, not-for-profit activity, or others may view it as "big business," for example, in the professional sport, travel, or entertainment industries.

The meaning of leisure for a given individual or social group is influenced, as well, by cultural or structural norms, values, experiences, and opportunities (Gibson and Singleton 2012). In fact, leisure as a concept is unknown to members of some cultures. Cultural and structural factors, unique to individuals or groups, sometimes differentiate leisure by age, gender, race, education, ethnicity, socio-economic status, religion, or place of residence. More specifically, the amount, type, or intensity of leisure that individuals pursue is influenced by the demands of a job, marital and family responsibilities, economic status, health, climate, access to transportation, quality of the neighbourhood, and prevailing social values concerning leisure.

Increasingly, more emphasis is placed on the quality rather than the quantity of leisure—both in general and with respect to particular leisure and social activities. Not only do leisure activities change over the life course, but the quality or meaning of a specific leisure experience also changes[14] (Gibson and Singleton 2012). For example, someone in early adulthood might view hiking primarily as a physical activity in which one hikes up and down a mountain trail as fast as possible to improve one's fitness. By middle adulthood, a person might view hiking as a means to escape the urban environment or the stress or boredom associated with work. Later in life, a person might hike up a mountain at a leisurely pace to find a setting for a hobby such as photography.

The Meaning and Use of Time

Time is a non-renewable resource that, once used or wasted, cannot be replaced. Thus, how we use time and the proportion of time we allocate to specific domains are important decisions that merit both personal reflection and scholarly inquiry. On the basis of time-budget surveys that measure the amount of time allocated to specific activities, we know that members of the lower class, compared to those in the middle and upper classes, are less future-oriented, are less punctual, and adhere less rigidly to time schedules. Yet those with lower incomes spend fewer hours per week at paid and unpaid work and report having more leisure hours per day, much of which is spent watching television (Williams 2002). Similarly, health status has a significant influence on the amount of time spent on a range of activities.

Time is a valued commodity and a central element in differentiating contemporary lifestyles. For example, the amount of "free" time influences whether and when an event will happen, the duration and sequence of events, and when, how, and to what extent we play a variety of social and leisure roles. Over a 24-hour period, daily lives are generally structured into three domains: obligatory activities, social or family activities, and leisure activities (Altergott 1988b). The amount of time allocated to each domain is influenced by individual values and preferences, the obligatory roles we must perform, social and economic constraints and opportunities, and the demands of others (children, partners, employers, and aging parents) for our time. Thus, at different stages in life, we perceive and use time in different ways, and we have more or less discretionary time at some stages than at others (Alwin et al. 2006). As well, time use in later life varies from country to country (Gauthier and Smeeding 2003).

When we do not have enough time for obligatory activities—i.e., work, family, or household responsibilities—we sacrifice our leisure, sleep, and social activities. Statistics Canada (2010) reports that in 2010, more Canadians 55 to 74 years of age were engaged in work, were working later in life, and were spending less time on leisure than had been revealed in earlier surveys of older adults. Women have less free time than men and spend less time on paid work and more time on unpaid work (Statistics Canada 2010). To illustrate, the 2010 General Social Survey shows that Canadian women over 15 years of age spend approximately 4.25 hours a day on household work, compared to about 3 hours for men; and Canadian women spend twice as much time on child care than men do (Statistics Canada 2010).

Retirement, unemployment, living alone, or illness in later life force people to cope with unstructured time after a lifetime in which most of their daily life was structured around work and family obligations. In later life, there is more discretionary time and less time may be needed for obligatory activities, assuming health and mobility remain constant. In 2010, those aged 65 to 74 spent on average approximately 7.5 hours per day on leisure (Statistics Canada 2010). Contrary to conventional wisdom, the "problem" of retirement is often not the amount of free time but rather an inability to decide how to use that free time. As Zuzanek and Box (1988, 179) state, "Having more free time does not automatically translate into greater happiness. Being able to fill this time with activities and to structure it in a meaningful and diversified way does! Acquiring a satisfying lifestyle in retirement presupposes the ability to structure one's time."

Time is a cultural product that may or may not be viewed as a scarce resource at specific moments or stages in life. The clock and a calendar provide some degree of order, routine, and structure to our lives. However, time is regarded in different ways by different individuals and at different stages in life. Despite the alleged increase in discretionary time because of a shorter work week, some people feel that they never have enough time, and they employ others to clean, cook, or shop for them. Others "multi-task" by conducting business or social matters during meals, or by reading newspapers or work reports while watching television. In addition, many stores are open 24 hours a day, and Internet shopping is available to fit alternative work and leisure lifestyles. For some, time becomes a scarce commodity because of a need to pursue further education in a knowledge-based economy, "moonlighting" at a second job, longer commuting time on congested roads, the conflicting schedules of dual-career couples, or caregiving for an elderly parent or a dependent child.

Generational differences exist within the same ethnic group in the time allocated to specific activities, and people with smaller social networks (those who are single, widowed, divorced, retired, or childless) often report having more discretionary time. Moreover, the nature of an activity influences how, when, and whether time is allocated to the activity. For example, consider the ease of watching television or working on a hobby at home compared with having to reserve a tennis court for a weekly noon-hour game of doubles and then finding three other players of comparable ability to play each week at the designated time and place.

In the later years of life, some people feel that time passes quickly; for others, it passes slowly. If time is wasted, or if a person is unable to use discretionary time in a meaningful way, time drags and boredom results. Boredom, a self-induced state, occurs when there is an excess of discretionary time or an inability to manage time. Others say that time "flies" and that they haven't enough of it. In reality, these people do not have less time than others. Rather, they are more socially involved, and their daily or weekly calendars are filled with meaningful activities.

Leisure Activities in the Early and Middle Years

The type of activities that people pursue during leisure time and the meaning and function of these activities vary across the life course. Throughout life's journey, we acquire a repertoire of leisure skills and activities that we pursue regularly, such as music, sports, or reading. Activities that remain part of the repertoire across the life course are those in which we display some competence and those that provide meaning or satisfaction in our daily lives.

At different stages in life, individual activities change as a result of shifts in preferences, individual or societal constraints, abilities, and health. But consistency in the leisure repertoire generally prevails (Agahi et al. 2006). For example, a lifelong opera fan may attend fewer operas as he or she ages but may spend as much or more time listening to opera on radio or CDs. But a long-time opera fan is unlikely to become a consumer of country music in later life.

Descriptive studies regularly report the frequency or type of leisure activities at a particular stage in life, at a particular chronological age, or at a particular time. Although some general patterns across the life course can be identified from these cross-sectional studies, longitudinal studies are lacking, so it is not possible to explain patterns observed across the life course—whether these patterns are due to aging, to cohort, or to period effects. For example, some leisure pursuits, such as skateboarding or certain forms of dance, are fads that one age cohort but not others may adopt for a period of time; in other words, they are a cohort effect. Or people in several different age cohorts may pursue an activity, such as watching "reality" television shows, at the same time, but then abandon the activity, which is a period effect. People may abandon other pursuits in middle or later life because of normal aging effects, such as loss of health or physical or cognitive changes.

Adopting a specific leisure activity early in life often significantly influences leisure involvement throughout life. For example, those who were pre-adolescents, adolescents, and young adults in the 1980s and 1990s were exposed to the "fitness boom" and the beginning of the health promotion movement. Consequently, many adopted some type of daily physical activity. These cohorts will likely engage in higher levels of physical activity than earlier or later cohorts at all subsequent stages in their life course. That is why many predict very "active" lifestyles among the retired baby boomers.

Although we cannot identify a single leisure pattern across the life course, some general patterns can be described. Figure 11.2 illustrates a variety of possible patterns of leisure involvement across the life course. The curves represent hypothetical patterns of leisure involvement in sport (A), visiting (B), membership in a political party (C), reading for pleasure (D), travel (E), or home-centred activities (F). These patterns may hold for specific individuals or birth cohorts; they may reflect the pattern for a given activity (reading); or they may apply to six different individuals or six different age cohorts for the same leisure activity. In reality, involvement is not as orderly as these smooth curves suggest. Peaks and

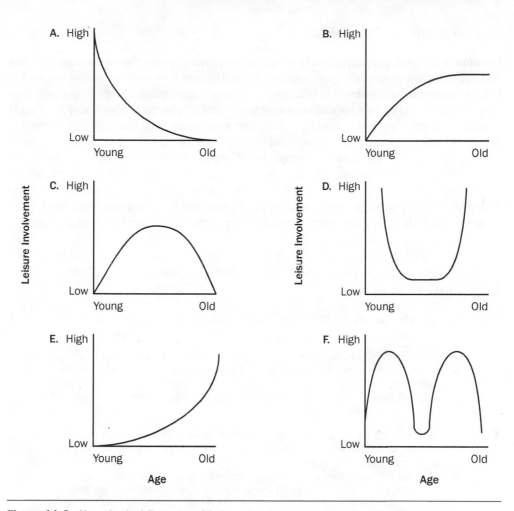

Figure 11.2 Hypothetical Patterns of Leisure Involvement across the Life Course

valleys in involvement occur at various stages in the life course because of institutional, cultural, or individual constraints.

Many patterns of leisure involvement are possible in the early and middle years of adulthood. Individual differences in these patterns are related to social class and type of occupation, to local or regional variations in opportunity and values, to variations in the events in an individual family life course, and to variations by gender, race, and ethnicity. For this reason, chronological age is a weak predictor of leisure or social participation patterns across the life course, especially for age-integrated activities. For example, among 24-year-olds, some attend university, others are employed full-time in the labour force, others are unemployed and looking for work; some are members of the upper socio-economic stratum, others are from the lower stratum; some are married, others are not; and some are parents. Similarly, the leisure patterns of women within any one age category varies depending on social class, marital status, presence and age of children, education, employment status, and past leisure experiences and interests.

Leisure Activities in Later Life

For most older adults, engaging in leisure activities represents an attempt to use their time in a meaningful way, to shape their identity in later life, and to contribute to their families and society (e.g., by taking grandchildren on holidays or by volunteering). Because of agency and conscious decisions about the meaning of and identity derived from leisure, the quality (more so than the quantity) of these processes is considered more important in later life. This reflects the view that new leisure pursuits can be initiated and that participation should be a high-quality experience throughout later life, even after older people move into a retirement home or a long-term care facility. Highlight 11.6 illustrates how agency can influence the leisure lifestyles of older adults.

Changing leisure lifestyles reflect the interaction of social structural and historical events with personal biographies or histories. Over time, leisure has become a more significant component of later life. Leisure experiences earlier in life are cumulative and exert an influence on

---

Highlight 11.6
Agency in Later Life: We Have Choices

One negative aspect of aging is internalizing the myth that after 65, you are expected to opt out of life and turn into a vegetable of your choice. The only part of this myth that is salvageable is "choice." We do not become a different species at 65, and in fact, aging can bring freedom to explore and do things for the first time. Examples of new beginnings after 65 abound in everyday life:

- Ann, an 80-plus retired nurse, recently embarked on a new pursuit as a very successful sculptor. She also finds time to serve as president of a major seniors' organization.
- Al, a retired pharmacist, is fighting hard as a volunteer activist to preserve Canada's medicare system. At the same time, he is the main caregiver for his wife, who suffers from Alzheimer's disease—a responsibility he never imagined he could cope with, but he does.
- Bernice spent her life as a homemaker looking after her children and husband—and making the best chocolate cookies on the block. At the age of 75, she discovered the Senior Olympics. Her trophies are the pride of the whole family.
- Bertie retired from her seamstress job at 66, after 50 years, to look after her grandson so that her daughter, a single mother, could work. Sharing in the raising of the child, and spending so much time with him, energizes her. She no longer lives alone and is doing what she's always wanted to do—be a homemaker.
- Louis's dream of being a playwright came true for him when, at the age of 75, his first script was produced by a local seniors' drama group. He is working on his second play and acting in other productions. A lifelong desire that had to be put aside in order to support his parents and then his own family is now being fulfilled.

Source: "Agency in Later Life: We Have Choices," from Gleberzon and Cutler, "Dispelling the Myths of Aging", *Aging, Health and Society: News and Views*.

leisure choices and opportunities in later life. For the most part, there is continuity in individual leisure patterns. But changes in the frequency, type, intensity, and location of leisure are increasingly likely and possible in later life. Many older adults renew their participation in activities that they may have dropped years before or take up new activities that they did not have access to, did not know about, or could not afford earlier in life (McGuire et al. 1999; Victorino and Gauthier 2005; Gibson and Singleton 2012).

The stereotypical images of leisure pursuits in later life as sedentary and passive are being cast aside by "senior" role models, male and female, who volunteer, travel, attend university to earn degrees, and engage in such competitive sports as marathon races, hockey, windsurfing, skiing, and weightlifting. These new images fit with the known physical and cognitive capacity and potential of older adults and with the idea that leisure activities, especially outside the home, provide an opportunity for social relations.

Summary

Most older adults strive to achieve an active, healthy lifestyle, and to increase levels of social interaction and engagement. By engaging in social interaction across a range of diverse activities, people create a leisure lifestyle in later life that provides benefits to both themselves and society. Increasingly, older people are pursuing meaningful leisure experiences that add quality and "life to years." An active lifestyle is possible because more activities and opportunities are available outside the home in many social settings, although barriers such as access and cost may prevent some older adults from fully participating. There are also many changes in the types of activities in which older people engage as they transition through their elder years, and in the preferences reflected by those individuals over time. This is especially true for women, who are becoming involved in more forms of leisure and in more leisure outside the home.

However, older adults' contributions to caregiving, volunteerism, and civic engagement are often underestimated in society. With increases in discretionary income, and as the baby boom generation retires over the next 30 years, a large amount of time and money will be spent on activities that promote and develop the well-being, health, and quality of life of older people. Yet being active and busy is not enough to guarantee a higher quality of life or happiness. Rather, activities must be freely chosen and must provide personal meaning and satisfaction. The meaning of leisure and of specific activities changes and varies across the life course because of aging, cohort, or period effects. Older adults can become involved in a variety of social activities, in particular, volunteering, political organizations, physical activities, travel, formal education, and gambling.

For Reflection, Debate, or Action

1. Visit local coffee shops or other public places, such as parks and shopping malls, and observe whether groups of older adults meet regularly at certain times for informal conversation. Note whether there are any common socio-demographic characteristics of the members of the informal group and whether there are any obvious leaders. As well, observe how many "seniors" visit or "hang out" in the setting on their own.
2. Interview retired men and women in your community who are volunteers, and find out where and how they volunteer, how frequently, and why. Ask them to describe any disadvantages of being a volunteer.

3. To understand how older people spend their time, select three to five older adults of different ages, and ask them to keep a time-use diary for a week, recording every activity they are engaged in for every half-hour of a 24-hour day. Analyze how these older adults are socially, cognitively, and physically involved in leisure or work pursuits.

4. On the basis of media coverage in recent months, identify emerging political issues that should be of interest to older Canadians.

5. Visit a local senior centre to determine the programs and activities that are available. Which activities are the most popular among men and among women? Then visit a local community centre not targeting seniors, and compare activities and characteristics of the clients with those you observed at the senior centre.

Notes

1. For programs and policies concerning activities for older adults, see the journal *Activities, Adaptation & Aging*.

2. A confidant is not necessarily a close friend or blood relative. Service or voluntary personnel, such as doormen, hairdressers, housekeepers, bartenders, mail carriers, or social workers can play this role so that an older person has regular social contact with someone with whom they can share concerns, news, or ideas.

3. Many terms are used to define this type of voluntary social participation: *voluntary activity, civic engagement, volunteerism, volunteer work, voluntary action, voluntary behaviour*.

4. The curvilinear pattern may reflect cohort effects rather than aging effects since older cohorts, at present, are generally less educated and may have had fewer opportunities to join associations.

5. For a discussion of religiosity in later life, see Atchley 1997, 2008, 2009; Gatz and Smyer 2001; Fletcher 2004; Schaie et al. 2004; MacKinlay 2005; Marcoen 2005; Idler 2006; Krause 2006b; Idler et al. 2009; Whitehead and Bergeman 2011; and Rote et al., 2013. Also see the Special Issue of *Generations*, 32 (2), 2008.

6. While most research has focused on the positive aspects of religion, Pargament (1997) suggests that there can also be a "dark side" to the relationship between religion and coping in later life in that it may create an overdependence that generates false or unrealistic hope for a cure or for a healthier future.

7. One pattern for families is a peaking of religious participation when the children are attending Sunday school and a decline when they leave home; another is a decline from 18 to 35 years of age and then an increase until the later years, when it decreases again as general social involvement declines because of ill health or difficulty getting around.

8. The International Adult Literacy Survey identifies three dimensions of literacy that should be measured: (1) prose (ability to understand and use information from texts); (2) document (ability to locate and use information from documents); and (3) quantitative (ability to perform everyday arithmetic to balance a chequebook or calculate tips).

9. Criminal offences by older adults are described in Rothman and Dunlop 2000; Simard 2000; Statistics Canada 2001; Aday 2003; Wahidin and Cain 2006; Greiner and Allenby 2010; and Public Safety Canada 2011.

10. Some of the common dimensions are expressive/instrumental, free choice/constrained involvement, low involvement/high involvement, active/passive, individual/group, home-centred/community-centred, institutionalized/non-institutionalized, inexpensive/expensive, mass culture/high culture, creative/non-creative, spontaneous/planned, structured/unstructured, work/non-work, and physical/non-physical. Each dimension represents a continuum, not a dichotomous "either/or" scale, and there is overlapping among the dimensions.

11. For example, people may read as a leisure activity to increase their knowledge or intellectual capacity, to learn a skill, to study for a degree, or to fill free time.

12. For example, people can listen to music while reading, watch television while visiting someone, or read a newspaper while watching television.

13. An example of an activity in an overlapping category is television viewing. The activity can be categorized as educational or recreational or as a solitary or group activity, depending on the situation in which it takes place. Similarly, cooking, gardening, or other household activities can be viewed as either work or leisure.

14. Some events that can change leisure patterns or choices are marriage, the birth of a child, a promotion at work, unemployment, an empty nest, entrance of the partner into the labour force, retirement, death of a partner, looking after an ill partner, divorce, acquiring a new partner in later life, and personal illness.

12 End of the Life Course: Social Support, Dying Well, and Public Policy

. . . as long as we can love each other, and remember the feeling of love we had, we can die without ever really going away. All the love you created is still there. All the memories are still there. You live—in the hearts of everyone you have touched and nurtured while you were here. . . . Death ends a life, not a relationship.

— Morrie Schwartz, in Albom 1997, p. 174

Focal Points and Key Facts

- To what extent should the family versus the public or private sector provide care to older adults living in the community?

- To what extent, and how, do caregiving responsibilities influence the work, family, and leisure life of caregivers?

- Can an integrated continuum-of-care system be designed to ensure that the assistance and services needed by older adults are delivered at the right time and in the right place (the home, community, or institution)?

- Globally, in the coming decades, there may be as many as two to four times the number of older persons needing care than there are people to provide care.

- More than two million Canadians provide informal care or support to an older adult who is a family member or a close friend, with about 6 per cent of these two million caregivers being 75 years of age or older themselves.

- Approximately 18 per cent of Canadians 15 years of age and older provide *unpaid* personal care, visiting, or errands to seniors; 21 per cent are women, 16 per cent are men. This amounts to over 25.6 million hours of unpaid assistance or care to seniors who are relatives or neighbours.

- Why, and in what form, does elder abuse or neglect occur within families, and what are the precipitating factors?

- It is estimated that between 4 and 6 per cent of elderly people around the world experience some form of abuse in their home. In Canada, approximately 4 to 10 per cent of older persons experience abuse or neglect.

- How do we, as individuals and as a society, ensure a "good" death with dignity and choice?

Introduction

This chapter addresses the final transitions in the life course—the last chapter in life. As people age, they become more aware of the need for assistance and support in order to function in daily life, whether at home or in an institutionalized setting. They also become more susceptible to abuse and neglect by those charged with the responsibility of caring for them as they become more dependent and frail. And they begin to contemplate death and try to deal with dying a good death, with as little suffering for themselves and their loved ones as possible. From a societal perspective, public policy to serve the needs and interests of older adults is essential and must be developed to ensure security and equity in the delivery of services to our oldest citizens. These individual and societal matters are addressed as we focus on the end of the life course.

In an ideal world, a continuum of informal and formal care and support would enable older people to age in the family home for as long as possible; to live in their home after being discharged from a hospital; and to receive help with activities of daily living (ADLs) and instrumental activities of daily living (IADLs) as their strength, mobility, cognitive functioning, or health declines. This continuum includes the following:

- informal assistance provided by family, friends, or neighbours with shopping, shovelling snow, daily monitoring, cooking, bathing, banking, or transportation
- formal care by paid employees who visit or live in the family home to help with meals, bathing, therapy, and mobility
- twenty-four-hour care in institutions (retirement homes, nursing homes, and long-term geriatric-care facilities)

To ensure independent living in the community for as long as possible when health and functional abilities begin to decline, a "partnership" needs to be created to provide care and assistance (Strain and Blandford 2003). Each person's situation is unique, and therefore partnerships involve varying contributions by the following:

- the individual through self-care
- the family through informal assistance
- the state through formal home and community services
- volunteer organizations such as Meals on Wheels, volunteer driving
- the health-care system (physicians, therapists, hospitals)
- the private sector (agencies that supply homecare workers or specialized equipment)

An integrated continuum-of-care model includes a wide range of formal/paid services along the continuum of care that are matched to individual needs as they change. This requires case management, accurate assessment of needs, and funding from a number of sources (see Chapter 7, as well as "Coordinating Services: Toward an Integrated Continuum of Care," later in this chapter).

Changing demographic and social trends—longer life expectancy, lower fertility rates, more childless marriages, higher divorce rates, more single adults, increased geographical mobility of children, more labour force participation by middle-aged women—often mean that people are less able to look after or even help their aging relatives directly (Chappell and Funk 2012). Consequently, the following questions arise:

- Who should provide care?
- What type of care and how much should be provided in the family home and by whom?
- Who should pay for home care?
- What interventions are needed to help both the care recipients and caregivers?

Help in making such decisions can be found in various service agencies, and educational programs are available for the older person and for adult children who serve as primary caregivers or case managers.[1]

Family Responsibility for Elder Care

The type and level of family responsibility for caregiving is not a recent issue. In Canada, the "filial responsibility" laws of the 1920s and 1930s appeared in a number of provinces and emphasized the family's responsibility for supporting dependent elderly parents. By law, adult children who were capable of doing so were required to support parents who were unable to maintain themselves. Any dependent parents could, with the written consent of a crown attorney, summon one or more of their children before a magistrate, who could order support payments of up to $20 weekly, depending on the children's means and circumstances. Action on the parents' behalf could also be initiated by a designated public official or charitable institution (Snell 1996, 78–9). Before proceeding to court action, officials would notify an adult child and appeal to him or her to keep his or her parent off the charity roll, thereby avoiding the stigma of social welfare and poverty for the family. Consequently, the legislation was seldom used to prosecute a family member. In reality, "there is no evidence that the laws actually increased the level of support from adult children" (Snell 1996, 98).

Today, all provinces have laws requiring adult children to assume some responsibility for the support and care of elderly parents. A child is only liable when the parent is dependent on the child by reason of age, infirmity, or economic circumstances. Yet most care received by older adults is provided by family sources. For instance, approximately 70 to 80 per cent of care for frail elders originates from the family (Fast et al. 2010). The amount of support given to an elderly parent or family member is closely related to the sense of obligation and affection built throughout family history. Where intergenerational relations are strong, family assistance is more likely. Mitchell (2003) found that even in families with a strong ethnic identity, and therefore perhaps a greater culturally based obligation to care for parents, the most important predictor of who would share a home with an elderly parent was the quality of the adult child's relationship with his or her parent. However, the type and the quality of assistance, and the degree of perceived responsibility, will vary if a caregiver is divorced, is employed, or lives at a distance.

Patterns of assistance are also affected by the availability and ability of potential caregivers, and available support systems for the helper (Sims-Gould and Martin-Matthews 2007). For example, parents in their eighties may have adult children who are in their sixties and need assistance themselves. In this situation, other relatives or public or private agencies may have to assume responsibility for the oldest generation. Keefe et al. (2007) concluded that the continued focus on the family to meet the needs of older Canadians is not sustainable because of the growing number of older persons and the decreasing number of children available. Consequently, they argue that new public policies and respite care services for family caregivers must be developed.

Public Responsibility for Elder Care

While most families maintain that they hold strong responsibilities for their aging family members, they also utilize formal services, especially when family members require high levels of care (Guberman et al. 2006). As older adults become more dependent, they may have to rely more on formal support provided by government or private sector programs. In a welfare state such as Canada, different levels of government develop public policies in response to lobbying by interest groups and to perceived public needs. Creating policies inevitably requires that spending choices be made, for example, between building schools and building long-term-care facilities, or among building roads, improving health care, or creating social welfare programs. In recent years, various jurisdictions have debated where older frail adults should receive care—in a general or convalescent hospital, in a retirement home, in their own home or that of a family member, or in a long-term-care facility. These debates are framed by costs, the availability of beds in institutional settings, the allocation of responsibility for care, the avoidance of duplication of services and resources, and the principles of equity and accessibility (Patsios and Davey 2005; Chappell 2011).

Governments develop public policy in a context of either conflict or co-operation among local, regional, provincial, and federal government agencies. Policies are shaped, as well, by the current government's political philosophy and by the current or anticipated economic climate. Hence, governments often sacrifice long-term planning for short-term political gain. Policy-making becomes even more complex when public policies must be coordinated with those in the private sector, especially in such areas as pensions, housing, and home care for older adults. In these cases, it must be determined who is responsible for what actions or programs and to what extent. Even more important, public policy for an aging population must be integrated with changing family values and family dynamics, especially concerning health and home care.

A recurring debate centres on the extent to which elder care is a private trouble or a public issue, on how the responsibility for care should be shared, and on who will pay (Ward-Griffin and Marshall 2003; Guberman et al. 2006; Chappell 2011). Ideally, informal and formal care are linked processes, not dichotomous responsibilities. Therefore, they require renegotiated responsibilities as the older person's needs change. Both salaried care workers and unpaid family members must contribute to ensure that an aging parent receives complete, high-quality care when it is needed. As an aside, note that older Canadians are not the major recipients of social support, as is commonly believed. Rather, those 25 to 54 years of age receive more public support, especially related to child care (Turcotte and Schellenberg 2006).

Social Support and Caregiving in an Aging Society

Social support involves a variety of activities and services. It may entail emotional support, helping with transportation to appointments or social events, rehabilitation and caregiving assistance to maintain independence in the home and community, during convalescence from an acute illness or surgery, or long-term care for the highly dependent older person. The ideal support system involves different sources, formal and informal, providing a combination of emotional, psychological, and instrumental help when and where it is needed.

Social support is a major factor in achieving a balanced person–environment fit in later life. Many people over 65 are themselves part of a support system for partners, siblings, friends, or neighbours. Indeed, more than 80 per cent of the support received by older persons comes from family members, primarily a spouse or adult children (Fast et al. 2004; Chappell and Funk 2011). With increasing support from the family and the community, the "warehousing" of frail older persons in long-term-care institutions is less likely today than it was in the past (Cranswick 2003). The 2011 census found that among those aged 65 and over, less than 10 per cent of women and about 5 per cent of men lived in long-term-care institutions. But for those aged 85 and over, the proportion increases to about 35 per cent for women and 23 per cent for men.

Among those aged 65 and over who live in the community, about one-third of women and one-fifth of men receive care because of a long-term health problem. At age 85 and above, the levels rise to two-thirds for women and about half for men. When elderly parents are hospitalized for an acute or chronic illness or when they are living in a retirement home or long-term-care facility, most receive help from adult children or grandchildren. This assistance may include companionship or personal care, such as feeding, shaving, and bathing. In effect, a family member serves as a case manager to provide a link between the informal and the formal systems on behalf of an elderly parent. This process involves serving as a facilitator, mediator, advocate, and adviser and acting as a buffer against the formal bureaucracy of a government or institution.

The need for social support becomes most apparent when an older person begins to suffer from memory loss, Alzheimer's disease (AD), or other dementias that lead to functional disabilities, behavioural problems, and increasing dependence on another person (often the spouse). The prevalence of these cognitive impairments and disease states increases with age (also see Chapter 7). It is estimated that Alzheimer's disease and other forms of dementia affect 8 per cent of those aged 65 and over (almost 400,000 Canadians) and that the proportion rises to 33 per cent for those 85 years and over (Hébert et al. 2003). Almost half of these older adults live at home with family support. But if this support was not available, the demand for long-term-care facilities would increase by 34 per cent (Hébert et al. 2003). The sections that follow discuss models of social support, informal social support, and the stress and burden of caregiving. But first, there are two caveats:

1. The research literature and journalistic reports use many terms to discuss social support in general. These include "assistance," "caregiving," "elder care," "home care," "community care," "monitoring," "care management," and "case management." They all represent a form of social support and often are used interchangeably. However, "assistance" and "caregiving" are different. Assistance involves more casual help, including periodic help to others, whereas caregiving involves a regular commitment to help a person with some specific health or personal-care need. Assistance may not be requested or required, and the recipient may not even view the help as a "support" activity. In contrast, caregiving is required and is requested either by the older person or by a physician or a family member. Similarly, "monitoring" is an informal way to keep an eye on an older person's safety, health, and ability to function, whereas "care or case management" is a formal process carried out regularly by a family member or by professional care workers. Home care and community care, which provide support outside an institution, involve providing services in the home or taking an older person to a community-based facility for a program or service.

2. Although many instances of social support involve assistance and care for those with cognitive impairment or dementias, or multiple chronic illnesses, social support exchanges may take many forms. Support ranges from spouses helping each other with household or personal activities to regular visits to the home by professional care workers who provide therapy, bathing, nursing care, counselling, or home repairs. As well, essential emotional support can be provided on an ongoing manner, or during stress or crises in later life.

Social Support: Reciprocity and Obligation

Social support and the exchange of gifts, assistance, and money usually flow in two directions between aging individuals and others in their social network. Within the family, physical, emotional, economic, and social resources are exchanged, depending on the needs and the stage in life. Serial, or one-way, exchanges of resources generally involve a downward flow of assistance from the older generation to a younger generation because of a sense of responsibility and affection. They typically flow in the other direction (upward) because of health-care needs. Reciprocal exchange, or a two-way flow, is most common between the members of the middle and oldest generations. This process of exchange usually involves services (baby-sitting, giving advice, shopping, and household maintenance); gifts of money or goods; or companionship through visits, telephone calls, or while helping an older person with an ADL or IADL. Reciprocity continues in later life as children spend more time helping and monitoring their parents. For many children, this support to aging parents is a privilege, an obligation, and a right. These feelings vary according to the personal history of a specific relationship (whether or not it has been amiable and rewarding) and to cultural beliefs based on ethnicity, class, race, or gender. There also tends to be more support if more time has been spent on shared activities with the parents and if the parents have provided financial support to adult children (Silverstein et al. 2002).

In families, reciprocity is often viewed within the context of a life course; that is, a shift in the flow of support may equalize earlier imbalances. The amount and type of support given and received is influenced by physical and mental health, skills and knowledge, opportunities, geographical proximity, and love and motivation on the part of both the giver and the receiver. For some older adults, a child's offer of assistance is interpreted as a disruption of the balance of exchange. If an older person's resources are diminished or devalued, dependence is perceived in the exchange relationship. If reciprocity is not possible, this can lower the self-esteem and morale of the older person, who may refuse to accept help from members of the informal network. This is more likely to happen in relationships with friends and neighbours than in kinship relations. Even in the later years, parent–child relationships are based on reciprocity, with emotional and financial support being the most common type of exchange and older parents still trying to give something in return (Keefe and Fancey 2002).

Informal Social Support

Informal support is provided in the home or community by family, friends, neighbours, or volunteers. Even when elderly persons have no family, fictive or quasi-kin often substitute for blood relatives. For elderly women living alone, these fictive kin play instrumental and emotional roles in later life that would normally be played by family members. These activities and services help to maintain independence, self-esteem, and an acceptable quality of life. Such assistance may involve companionship; providing information; helping with housework, transportation, and shopping; or helping with moderate levels of personal care (dressing, bathing, feeding) during recuperation from an acute illness or surgery or as health and functional ability fluctuate or deteriorate. Informal support may also involve monitoring the quality of care and assisting with personal care in a long-term-care institution. In these facilities, family members, through shared experiences, frequent contact, and the building of trust, form relationships with staff who care for their dependent parent.

Most support is a family matter,[2] and only in difficult personal situations is a formal support system invoked. An estimated 70 to 80 per cent of care provided to older adults in private households is delivered by informal caregivers who are an essential and often invisible part of the health-care system (Hébert et al. 2001; Carrière et al. 2002; Rosenthal and Ansello 2007; Chappell and Funk 2011). However, the percentage receiving this informal support decreases to about 40 per cent for those aged 85 and older. And if a person lives alone, the formal system delivers about 64 per cent of the care (Turcotte and Schellenberg 2006). Of the informal caregivers, more than 50 per cent are adult children (Health Canada 2002). Cranswick (2003) found that in 2002, more than two million people aged 45 to 64 were providing informal care to almost 2.3 million adults over 65 years of age. About 6 per cent of these two million caregivers were 75 or over themselves. Thus, older adults give as well as receive care.

Informal support has a subjective and an objective component (Chappell and Funk 2011). The *subjective* component involves the quality (i.e., access to people one can trust, able to share intimacies with, and able confide in), meaning (the importance or value of contact with kin and friends for well-being), and satisfaction with the support that is received. The *objective* component refers to the quantity of relationships (number of available kin, friends, and neighbours), the availability of assistance when needed, and the degree to which the available support is used (the amount, frequency, and intensity of interaction).

Friends and neighbours are a significant source of informal support for older adults, and these helping relationships are based on mutual choice and need rather than on lifelong family obligations. However, the non-family support network becomes smaller once declining health reduces social interaction and mobility outside the home and when more intimate care is needed (bathing). A network is also reduced when friends die, move away, or experience declining health themselves.

Sources of Informal Support: The Caregivers

Although family support is evident throughout adult life, parents are monitored more closely as they reach their later years, and adult children show more concern about a parent's health, safety, and ability to complete ADLs and IADLs in the home. When we speak of "family" caregivers, we usually mean a daughter or daughter-in-law. Thus, much informal support is a gendered process—daughters or daughters-in-law tend to be the primary caregivers, and elderly women, especially widows and divorcees, tend to be the recipients of more social support than men (Fast 2010). These patterns evolve due to the following reasons:

- Women are more likely to be comfortable with both giving and receiving in expressive, nurturing relationships.
- Mother-daughter relationships are stronger and more intimate.
- Women are more likely to live close to members of the family and therefore to visit often.

However, as more women join the labour force, the level and type of available support changes. Increasingly, working women become case managers, and in addition to providing some direct help (shopping, home care, emotional support, and transportation), they purchase other home and personal care services from home care and nursing agencies. The gendered nature of caregiving, where it exists,[3] is due to gender role expectations and to the preference of care recipients, especially women, to be helped by a daughter because of the personal nature of care. Men report that they "expect" to receive care from their partner whereas women "feel guilty" when their partner takes care of them (Davidson et al. 2000; Connidis 2010). There is also a gender difference among siblings in how and what care should be provided to parents. Whereas daughters are more likely to take the initiative in providing care and provide more services, sons wait to be asked for assistance and then tend to provide financial assistance to buy services (Matthews 2002). Women are more likely to be the primary or sole caregiver to a parent, whereas sons may be part of a team if there are other siblings, or a son may "manage" a team of informal and formal caregivers. Grandchildren, as young adults, often serve as a secondary level of support to help with the care and monitoring of a grandparent.

Increasingly, however, more men are involved as primary caregivers[4] (Fast 2010) because gender roles are changing, more women are employed full-time and are therefore less available as full-time caregivers, and married men are living longer and assuming a caregiving role for their partner. Sons are becoming more involved as caregivers if they are an only child or the nearest child and because there is a growing cultural expectation that men should accept some of the family responsibilities formerly borne solely by women.

Where one lives also influences caregiving. Those who live in rural communities, for example, generally receive more help from community members, perhaps more than from relatives who may live far away. Thus, rural caregivers, who generally have fewer formal support services in the community, provide more informal care and report more stress than urban caregivers (Skinner and Rosenberg 2002; Keating 2008).

The giving (and receiving) of social support in the later years is influenced as well by the cultural beliefs, practices, and values of a specific ethnic, religious, or racial group (Wu and Hart 2002; Brotman 2003; Lai 2007). More assistance is offered within cultural groups in which older people are highly respected and valued, assistance and care are believed to be private family matters, and elderly people are not eligible for government assistance. Family assistance is also greater when the older person does not speak English or French and therefore is less able to use formal support systems or to understand diagnoses or medical instructions, and when older members of an ethnic group have not been culturally or structurally assimilated into mainstream society. Moreover, members of small ethnic minority groups are less likely to have access to interpreters or culturally sensitive services (Brotman 2003). The high levels of help given to older relatives among ethnic groups is partly due, as well, to the fact that many older immigrants, for financial reasons, live in the same household as their adult children (Keefe et al. 2000).

Among Canada's Aboriginal people, older adults are highly dependent on the economic and emotional support of both the extended family and others in the community (Wister and Moore 1997). The provision of informal support is a traditional part of respect for elders and is usually provided by wives or daughters who return to the community. Many older people in these communities need care because of chronic health problems, poor nutrition, and substance abuse (Cooke et al. 2008; Wilson et al. 2010, 2011). Because they tend to live in small or isolated communities, few formal services are available, which increases the pressure on their relatives and neighbours to provide high levels of support (Buchignani and Armstrong-Esther 1999). Even when government support services and medical services do exist, Aboriginal people tend to make less use of them because of cultural beliefs or past practices.

Outcomes of Informal Support

For older people, an informal support network has the potential to prevent or alleviate stress and to help them make decisions, live independently, and recuperate from an acute illness or adapt to a chronic illness. Supportive family, friends, and neighbours can enhance or maintain physical or mental health and contribute to higher levels of well-being and life satisfaction. Among older adults who live alone, isolation and loneliness can be alleviated by an informal network of supportive friends and acquaintances.

The presence of a spouse, adult child, other relative, friend, or neighbour does not, however, guarantee that assistance will be provided or that it will be of high quality. Rather, the social and physical environment of the elderly person, and the personal characteristics of both the potential caregivers and recipients, must be considered when one is assessing the resources of an informal support network. Of particular importance is the elderly person's degree of frailty or dependency, the caregiver's proximity and his or her social, ethnic, health, and employment background, especially if the caregiver is not a member of the immediate family. It is also important that a caregiver have or acquire sufficient knowledge to be effective as a caregiver, especially for older people with severe dementia, a stroke, or Parkinson's disease.

But not all assistance is beneficial. Although the caregiver may have the best intentions, the recipient may see things quite differently. For example, older persons may resent the loss of privacy that results from increasing levels of personal care—they may feel they are being overprotected and losing personal control, and they may resent being treated like a child in a demeaning manner. If different formal-care workers visit the home, an older person may not trust them, may regard them as unwanted strangers in their home, or may view their work as unnecessary or shoddy (Aronson 2002). Moreover, if the level of interaction with caregivers fails to meet needs or expectations, or if a primary caregiver experiences a crucial life transition (a job promotion, failing health), an older person may feel neglected, deprived, and isolated.

The Prevalence and Costs (Hidden and Unhidden) of Caregiving

Based on analyses of the 2002 and 2007 General Social Surveys, the proportion of persons aged 45 or over who are caregivers increased from 19.5 to 28.9 per cent, with about 56.5 per cent being women compared to 43.5 per cent men (Fast et al. 2010). It has also been estimated that family/friend caregivers provide 70 to 80 per cent of care to persons with a chronic health problem or disability at an estimated value of $25 to 26 billion annually (Fast et al. 2010).

The emotional, psychological, and financial costs of informal caregiving are difficult to estimate and are often hidden from the public (Fast et al. 1997; Zukewich 2003). The financial costs for a caregiver may be considerable, especially if the parent is impoverished and must be supported by his or her children. These costs include loss of wages for time away from work, transportation to and from the recipient's home, long-distance telephone calls, home renovations, drugs and other medical supplies, and food. The cost of caregiving can create financial hardship for a caregiver who strives to keep a parent out of a residential institution (see "Assisting Caregivers," later in the chapter).

Informal care has other costs. First, a caregiver may lose the freedom to enjoy leisure time with his or her family and friends. Second, after a period of time, the caregiver's health may suffer due to loss of sleep, anxiety, feelings of guilt, and a general failure to pay attention to his or her own nutrition and health practices owing to the demands of caregiving and a lack of time (Pearlin et al. 2001). Some caregivers provide 40 to 60 hours a month or more of informal assistance. Third, the time that women spend out of the labour force because of caregiving leads to lost career opportunities, lower salaries, and smaller pensions (Gignac et al. 1996; Keating et al. 1999). Fourth, if caregivers are employed, their employer loses out as a result of absenteeism and loss of productivity on the part of the employee as a result of phone calls with parents, worry, and early departure or late arrival. In addition, there is great job turnover on the part of employees who help with elderly parents and greater use of employee assistance programs that provide information and counselling. A Special Issue of the *Canadian Journal on Aging*, "Hidden Costs/Invisible Contributions of Caregiving" (Supplement, 2007) elaborates on these issues.

Caregiver Stress and Burden

Adult children and others report many benefits of being a caregiver—the satisfaction of helping others, repaying a debt for past assistance and support, preventing or postponing institutionalization, and increased intimacy with a parent (Keating et al. 1999; Chappell and Funk 2011;

Health Council of Canada 2012). However, many caregivers feel the burden as the length of time in the role grows and as the demands of caregiving increase (Pearlin et al. 1996; Joseph and Hallman 1996; Rosenthal and Ansello 2007; Martin-Matthews and Phillips 2008; CIHI 2010; Connidis 2010; del Pino-Casado et al. 2011). Indeed, CIHI (2010) reports that one in six people providing informal care to seniors experiences distress. The most burdensome cases involve caring for a person with dementia because of behavioural problems, such as wandering, sleep disturbances, agitation, verbal or physical attacks on the caregiver, incontinence, and paranoia, as well as cases involving memory, understanding, and decision-making problems (Hawranik 2002; CIHI 2010). The burden is greatest if the caregiver lives with the older person 24 hours a day. Double-duty caregiving occurs when a person provides care duties in a work role, such as nursing, concurrent with caregiving for an older parent (Ward-Griffin 2004; Ward-Griffin et al. 2011). This can result in compassion fatigue (Ward-Griffin et al. 2011).

Even formal home-care workers experience considerable stress as a result of shift work, injuries, pain from lifting or being attacked by a client, verbal harassment, and long hours with low pay (Denton et al. 1999, 2007; Martin-Matthews and Sims-Gould 2010). Most studies find that between 10 and 20 per cent of formal and informal caregivers report that they are experiencing a significant burden. However, under-reporting is likely, especially by family members. The more serious cases may have been transferred to a long-term-care facility, and in many cases, the burden is random and cyclical rather than constant. Caregiving stress involves fatigue, anxiety, and guilt as to whether the person is being properly cared for, as well as low morale and a sense of being alone, helpless, and isolated while providing care. These feelings and reactions are sometimes called the subjective components of burden (Keating et al. 1999; del Pino-Casado et al. 2011). The objective components of burden, which are more visible, include the following:

- demands that cause changes in lifestyle
- a loss of sleep
- a change in employment status (quitting work or beginning to work part-time)
- financial difficulties because of increased expenses and loss of income
- physical or mental-health problems (sore knees or back from lifting, increased alcohol consumption, depression)
- a loss of friends and leisure time as a result of having no vacation time or days off
- a deteriorating personal relationship with the older person or with others (a spouse or sibling) in the immediate family (Keating et al. 1999)

In these situations, caregivers become hidden victims in the social support system if they do not receive education and assistance from the formal support system (Fast et al. 2010). In extreme cases, primary caregivers simultaneously play the role of nurse, homemaker, social worker, psychologist, and chauffeur—often in addition to their "normal" responsibilities at work and in their own home (Martin-Matthews and Phillips 2008). To assist primary caregivers, social intervention services and programs are being introduced in some communities (see "Assisting Caregivers," later in the chapter).

Spousal Stress and Burden

Caregiving is especially stressful when an elderly person is caring for his or her cognitively impaired spouse. CIHI (2010) found that distress was twice as likely among spousal caregivers as among other family members. The 24-hour-a-day duties represent a significant problem. These difficulties are compounded by the loss of a partner in an emotional sense, by physical difficulties in coping with some of the necessary tasks, by anxiety about financial matters, by deterioration in the caregiver's own physical health, and by depression or loneliness. Often, spousal care is not adequate compared with what would be available in an institution. But sometimes the caregiving spouse decides against transferring a dependent spouse to an institution, even if he or she no longer wishes to be a burden to the spouse or family. Highlight 12.1 presents a case study illustrating the burden of caring for a spouse, while Highlight 12.2 illustrates some of the difficulties that adult children who care for an aging parent experience.

Highlight 12.1
The Burden of Spousal Care

Robert is 68 years old and takes care of Fran, 66, who has cancer and is bedridden. Before Fran's illness, the couple followed a tranquil routine. "In the evenings we watched TV together. I can hardly remember any arguments between us." Despite Fran's presence, Robert often speaks for her. When she does try to say something, he interrupts her and completes the sentence. At night he sleeps lightly, since Fran constantly needs his assistance, and even a small sigh is enough to get him out of bed.

He no longer sees his friends and says his state of mind is deteriorating: "It's nerve-wracking to be together all the time and not see other faces. I want to go out but I can't leave her. Like in a prison, I'm with her and she's with me all the time." He feels helpless but says he has no regrets about devoting himself to his wife. When reminded about the option of institutionalization, he rejects the idea outright: "Never. Even at home she suffers more than enough. She doesn't deserve having more troubles. No. I couldn't do it."

Sources: Adapted from Navon and Weinblatt 1996. Reprinted by permission of the *Journal of Aging Studies* (JAI Press).

Highlight 12.2
The Burden of Parent Care

The following statement depicts the extent to which stress, fear, guilt, and bizarre behaviour can occur in a caregiving relationship.

When it became apparent that my mother could no longer live by herself, two choices were available: move her to a nursing home or move her into our home. I decided to care for her in my home. I thought it would work. I was unprepared to meet her need for medical care. Her emotional outbursts and demands made me feel like a child again, and my husband grew more distant as I was consumed by the demands of caregiving. In about three years, it became a question of my marriage and sanity versus institutionalized care for my mother. It has taken me a long time to resolve the guilt of this decision, especially when I visit and see her empty life. The full responsibility and "wear and tear" have fallen on me. My sister, who lives 10 miles away, contributes nothing but telephone calls to me—to see how "her" mother is doing! She never asks how I am doing or if she can help in any way.

Adult Children's Stress and Burden

The level of stress and burden experienced by an adult child caring for a parent is related to the unique interaction of a number of factors:

- the type and degree of impairment in terms of functional ability and behavioural problems
- the caregiver's personality and self-perceived ability to play the role
- the availability and use of educational and training programs and self-help groups
- the availability of social support from both outside and within the family
- the availability of financial support
- other work/family demands
- the older person's personality and demands
- the quality of the lifelong relationship between the adult child and the elderly parent
- the presence of competing demands or problems in the caregiver's life, such as a career, children, his or her health, alcoholism, or unemployment

Formal Social Support

Formal support is provided to dependent and frail adults by public and private agencies in the home or in an institution by trained volunteers or professional health- and social-care workers. Public sector programs are created by laws, policies, or regulations across different levels of government. Private sector programs fill a service gap when public services or facilities are inequitable, inaccessible, dysfunctional, or nonexistent, or when an elderly person's family members are unable to meet the elderly person's needs. The support system can be described as a series of concentric circles surrounding an older person at the core. While the elements of the informal system are generally more intimate and accessible, the formal system is more impersonal and bureaucratic and may be difficult to use, even if it is available.

Formal support includes a range of health care and social services provided by government agencies, not-for-profit voluntary organizations, or private businesses. The aim is to provide a safety net through such services as community-based and in-home programs, adult daycare centres, respite care, retirement homes, nursing homes, and long-term chronic care institutions. Ideally, formal support should involve a coordinated system so that all needs are met and so that no one is neglected or overlooked. Historically,[5] public funds have been allocated to long-term institutional housing. (Institutionalized housing and care, part of the continuum of formal care services in later life, is discussed in Chapter 8; in this section, the emphasis is on formal support provided through home care and community-based programs.) Since the 1970s, there has been a gradual social movement toward de-institutionalizing all special groups—physically and mentally disabled people of all ages, elderly people, and criminals. Not surprisingly, the rising cost[6] of caring for an expanding aging population has forced the state to shift more responsibility for the care of frail and dependent older adults to individuals and families or to the private sector. However, to help families assume more responsibility, governments and employers have introduced services for caregivers, as well as for elderly care recipients. These programs are designed to support and complement the services provided by informal family caregivers. Highlight 12.3 lists formal services provided in some communities.

Highlight 12.3
Formal Support Services for an Aging Population

Home-Based

- visiting and monitoring those who live alone
- Meals on wheels
- daily or 24-hour telephone contact
- personal support workers (also called community health workers, home-care aides)—for personal care, cleaning, meal preparation
- counselling
- home maintenance and renovation
- palliative care
- equipment and supplies (walkers, canes, bed poles, raised chairs)
- professional visits—nurses, therapists, social workers

Community-Based

- information and referral services and assessments
- outreach programs to locate elderly people at risk in their home
- training and educating caregivers
- self-help support groups (for those caring for someone with Alzheimer's disease or Parkinson's disease)
- daycare
- respite care
- transportation (subsidized dial-a-bus, wheelchair access vans or buses, or taxi services for appointments)

Employer-Based

- parental leave policies
- employee assistance programs, including education, advice, and support for employees caring for an aging parent
- flextime
- teleworking (working at home), full- or part-time

The Use of Formal Services

The use of formal services by older adults is quite low, with the main users being frail couples living in their home; those who live alone, especially women; those over 75 years of age with poor self-reported health; and those who have used home care previously (CIHI 2011). There are several possible reasons for not using community services:

- a lack of knowledge about the availability of formal services or how to use them
- a desire to remain independent or dependent on a spouse, child, or friend
- a denial that services are needed
- a fear of having strangers in the home
- subtle discrimination against members of ethnic groups who speak and read only their own language

- user fees, which may be too expensive
- a lack of services in rural or remote communities
- a cultural tradition of accepting help only from family
- a shortage of personnel with proper certification and training and high staff turnover as a result of stress and low wages
- cognitive or behavioural problems that are beyond the service level available
- a shortage of volunteers to deliver services (telephone companions or drivers for Meals on Wheels programs)
- bureaucratic barriers, such as eligibility tests for need
- a lack of need if a person is being looked after satisfactorily by the family or can afford private care services

Levels of use are determined, as well, by a given program's or agency's rules and regulations. Are services available to all citizens who reach a certain age, therefore representing a universal program (such as health care)? Or is access limited to those who can demonstrate need (such as poverty or the unavailability of children to help)? These issues are revisited in the "Public Policy" section of this chapter.

Home-Care Services

The home-care or community-care system was established in Canada in the early 1990s to relieve overburdened hospitals and long-term-care facilities, as well as overburdened or untrained informal caregivers. If people who were ill, disabled, or dying could be cared for at home, governments would save money, more beds would be available in hospitals for the treatment of acute illness, and older people could remain in a familiar and comfortable environment. The demand for home-care programs has increased in recent years as hospitals are closed or downsized, especially in small and rural communities.

In 2003, 15 per cent of seniors reported receiving some level of home-care services from private or public agencies, with 9 per cent receiving formal care; 4 per cent, informal care; and 2 per cent, a combination of both informal and formal care. The characteristics of home-care clients include women over the age of 85; seniors with chronic conditions; seniors with high levels of assessed complex needs; seniors who experience pain and/or depression; and seniors who are at risk of falls (Health Council of Canada 2012). The percentage receiving any type of home care was estimated at 8 per cent for those 65 to 74 years of age and 42 per cent for those 85 and older. However, seniors used less government-funded home-care services in 2003 than in 1999 (8.9 per cent versus 11.5 per cent). It is not possible to explain this decreased use: did they require less home care, or did they use more private sector services or family help, perhaps because government-funded services were unknown, unavailable, or inaccessible?

Health Canada defines home care as "an array of services enabling Canadians, incapacitated with a disability or a chronic health problem, in whole or in part, to live at home, often with the effect of preventing, delaying or substituting for long-term care or acute care alternatives" (Health Council of Canada 2012). Home care includes the provision of services by professional care workers, nurses, social workers, and therapists and the provision of programs for the care recipient (e.g., stimulation and activity programs for people with Alzheimer's disease or exercise programs for people who have had a stroke) and for the caregiver (e.g., adult daycare programs or long-term respite care). Each situation is unique and therefore requires an assessment of the older person's functional capacity and health, the safety of the home, the informal support available, and how to coordinate the delivery of all support services before implementing a home-care program.

Programs include a blend of health, social, and non-medical support services to the client and his or her caregiver (Keefe 2002; Shapiro 2002; Canadian Home Care Association 2004; Penning et al. 2006; Health Council of Canada 2012). From the individual's perspective, there are both therapeutic and compensatory goals. The therapeutic goal, for example, may be to help the older person recover from an accident or illness or to prevent further deterioration from a medical or disease condition. The compensatory goal may be to promote comfortable and meaningful daily living despite the onset of dependence created by disabilities or frailties (Feldman 1999). From society's perspective, the goals include efficiency, cost effectiveness, and equity in access.

Because home care is an effective and necessary part of the health-care system, advocates argue that a national home-care system should be included in the Canada Health Act (CARP 2001; Shapiro 2002; Hollander et al. 2007; Hollander et al. 2009). As with long-term care, home care is a provincial, regional, or municipal service, and consequently there is considerable variation in cost, availability, content, quality, accessibility, and eligibility. Analyses of the standardized Resident Assessment Instrument for Home Care (RAI-HC) data in Canada show that average home-care costs are approximately $300 per week for clients expected to live less than six months and approximately $150 per week for all others, although large discrepancies exist across provinces (Health Council of Canada 2012). Some jurisdictions charge user fees, have residence requirements (how long one has lived in the province, region, or municipality), set limits on the number of service hours per week or on the maximum amount that can be spent on one individual, or require some services to be delivered by the private sector (Shapiro 2002). Another criticism of current home-care systems is that they are primarily funded as short-term post-hospital care, which raises issues of access, availability, equity, and sustainability. Private services, which are very expensive (as much as $1500 a week or more depending on the services provided), have emerged since publicly funded home-care programs may have restrictions on the type of services provided in terms of quality or quantity.

Social Intervention Strategies and Issues

Strategies must be developed to ensure that a minimum level of care is provided when needed, that there is equal access to home care, and that information and assistance is provided to informal caregivers. The number and the variety of services available in any given community depend on the tax revenues available, the quality of leadership, and the priorities of politicians and city or regional staff. This section introduces intervention strategies, as well as some issues related to intervention approaches.

Assisting Caregivers

There is considerable debate about whether and how family caregivers should be assisted. One approach argues that a family should assume full responsibility for the care of aging parents and that the government should assist only those who have no living relatives. Extreme proponents of this view argue that if family members are unable to cope with caring for a frail parent, they must reimburse the government for the cost of institutionalization. Another approach assumes that while most families do as much as they can to care for frail parents, caregivers become overburdened at some point. Hence, assistance is needed so that a family can avoid, for as long as possible, moving a parent to a long-term-care facility. Adherents of this approach argue that the government has a responsibility to assist the primary caregivers of frail adults (Keefe and Rajinovich 2007; Health Council of Canada 2012).

The quality of home-care service provided by family members, volunteers, or salaried home-care workers varies greatly. Those caring for a frail elderly person, especially one with dementia, may work in isolation, lack training and information about the disease or its behavioural manifestations, have little or no time off, have round-the-clock responsibility, and seldom if ever receive any support or feedback. Moreover, for many paid home-care workers, wages are low, benefits are minimal, training is inadequate, there is little opportunity for career advancement, and they often serve several clients a day in many parts of a city or region. Keefe and Fancey (1997) found that paid caregivers in Nova Scotia spent 31 to 40 hours a week on care and received an average compensation of only $88 a week (much less than the minimum wage). Some argue that low payment to caregivers may increase the incidence of elder abuse (see below). Yet the working conditions for home-care workers are seldom considered in the design or implementation of policies, even though there is a clear need to reduce the high level of job turnover as a result of stress, poor wages, and low job satisfaction (Denton et al. 2007).

There are three general methods of helping both older people and their primary caregivers. First, to relieve the caregiver's stress and improve the quality of care for the recipient, programs should provide educational, emotional, and social support for the caregiver (Hébert et al. 2003; CIHI 2010). Such programs include individual or group education about the specific disease state or about palliative care, skills training so that health and personal care needs can be met in the home, and mutual-help support groups (for caregivers of Alzheimer's patients). To illustrate, Stewart et al. (2006) designed a telephone support intervention program in which experienced family caregivers provided weekly telephone support to new family caregivers of seniors suffering from Alzheimer's disease or a stroke. Many of the new caregivers did not have a support network and were coping in isolation until the intervention was introduced. Three types of support were provided over the telephone: (1) *information* about the disease or illness, about available resources, and about caring practices and strategies specific to the disease or illness; (2) *affirmation* that what they were experiencing is common and not unique to their situation; and (3) *emotional support* through listening, raising spirits, empathizing, and giving the person an opportunity to vent. The perceived outcomes of this telephone intervention were increased confidence, knowledge, and competence; decreased caregiver burden and loneliness; greater satisfaction with playing the role of caregiver; and better coping.

A second type of assistance consists of financial incentives or reimbursements for the caregiver through tax credits or a subsidy to offset lost income or to purchase needed services (Keefe and Rajnovich 2007). Working women could use this financial assistance to purchase daytime personal care for an elderly parent (Quebec offers $600 a year for respite services). Sometimes, payments are provided directly to the care recipient, who purchases whatever services are needed and from whomever they wish. Whether such financial assistance should go to the older person or to the primary caregiver, and who should decide, continues to be a policy debate. In Nova Scotia, the Home Life Support program compensates family caregivers of frail elderly people; caregivers must have a family income that is under or near the poverty line to be eligible for the program.

A third source of assistance involves private or publicly supported care (with or without a subsidy/user fee) provided within or outside the home. Some of these programs include the provision of assistive devices or home maintenance services, such as mobility and health monitoring devices; transportation; congregate or communal housing; or personal in-home health care, such as bathing, nursing, and therapy. Adult day programs provide older people with social and physical stimulation and their caregivers with respite. They offer a variety of social and therapeutic programs, usually for at least three days a week. Sometimes these programs take place in a nursing home, which may discourage some people from attending if they do not want to be associated with the "stigma" of being frail (Weeks and Roberto 2002).

Respite care provides temporary supervision or care by professionals so that a primary caregiver can take a daily, weekend, or vacation break from the routine, responsibility, and burden of caregiving. The older person remains in his or her home, and a care worker moves in. Or she or he is moved to a retirement or nursing home as a short-term visitor or stays at an adult daycare centre or a hospital as an outpatient for a short period.

Ideally, respite care is used before any family crisis arises. Respite care is underused, however, perhaps because people may not know it exists. Or they may worry about the quality of care, it may be too difficult to transport a parent to the respite site, or the older person's emotional and behavioural problems may bar him or her from being accepted into the program. For caregivers, the temporary relief gives them an opportunity to look after other responsibilities, to interact with friends and others in similar situations (through support groups), and to have a complete physical and mental break from caregiving and the care recipient (Weeks and Roberto 2002).

Coordinating Services: Toward an Integrated Continuum of Care

In addition to care and assistance from informal caregivers, older people and their caregivers may receive help from voluntary and nongovernmental organizations (NGOs), employers, and a variety of government-sponsored services. The volunteer sector includes programs such as home nursing offered by the Victorian Order of Nurses, widow-to-widow support networks, adult recreation centres, and self-help or mutual-support groups that provide emotional support and/or skills to primary caregivers. Some employers offer flextime or periods of family leave for an employee who is an elderly person's primary caregiver. However, family leave for parental care is not universally available because a number of issues remain to be resolved: Is the leave paid or unpaid? If paid, who is responsible for payment, the government or the employer? Who is eligible and for how long? These cost-related issues are an obstacle to innovative programs through which employers could provide support to primary caregivers.

Since the 1970s, many provinces and some communities have created integrated care models or systems (also called an integrated continuum of care) to a varying extent (Chappell and Hollander 2011a) (see the section in Chapter 7, "Integrated Models of Care Delivery"). This system has a single entry point, which is initiated through an in-home or in-hospital assessment by a multidisciplinary team consisting of a social worker, a nurse, a home-care manager, and a doctor. Then, after the assessment and a discussion with the older person and his or her family caregivers, recommendations are made about the best location and sources of care, including a broad range of services, such as home care and home support services, supportive housing, residential care, and geriatric assessment (Chappell and Hollander 2011b). Once an initial decision has been made about needs and care, the team performs regular assessments, ideally under the leadership of the same case manager (Hollander and Prince 2008).

An integrated continuum of care model, designed to meet the changing needs of older adults, connects home, community, and residential care services so that a person can be transferred seamlessly, as needed, from one level to the next (Hollander et al. 2007, 2009; Hollander and Prince 2008; Chappell and Hollander 2011a, 2011b; Hébert 2011). This necessitates coordination and complex funding mechanisms that connect various levels of government (e.g., community, health, and housing). There have also been proposals for long-term-care insurance as a funding mechanism in Canada (Hébert 2011). An integrated care system can prolong independent living and delay or prevent premature admission to or a long-term stay in an acute or chronic care hospital or nursing home. Moreover, integrated care has been shown to be less expensive than more fragmented models of care (Hollander et al. 2009; Chappell and Hollander 2011a). The Senior Citizens Department of the Niagara Region in Ontario defined a continuum of care as

> a range of planned, organized, financed and co-ordinated support programs and living options, which are based on an assessment of individual needs such as preventive health, life enrichment, health promotion and wellness that promote overall well-being and independence as long as possible. As well, it should include support programs and living options that enhance the quality of life and support the independence and needs of the community-based older person and family caregivers. A range of institutional settings recognizes that there are varying degrees of physical and mental frailty. (CMHC 1990, 19)

Highlight 12.4 illustrates two contrasting ways in which an older person can enter such a system.

A long-standing policy debate has centred on whether the formal system should be a substitute for or a complement to informal support (Chappell 2011). The substitution hypothesis argues that the public sector must provide a formal safety net when families are unavailable, unable, or unwilling to help; when older adults are isolated or abandoned; or when informal caregivers can no longer provide adequate support. In contrast, the complementarity hypothesis argues that a coordinated system of informal support (by the family) and formal support (by government or the private sector) is essential to enhance the quality of life of both older people and their caregivers (Ward-Griffin 2002; Ward-Griffin and Marshall 2003; Hollander and Prince 2008). Evidence suggests that the most successful formal system is complementary, since it provides a continuum of assistance and care to meet the diverse and ever-changing needs of both the elderly person and his or her caregivers.

Elder Abuse and Neglect: A Hidden Problem

Elder abuse was first exposed in the late 1980s when incidents of "granny bashing" were reported in the media and when gerontologists began to study the prevalence and causes of abuse and neglect.[7] At first, this problem was viewed almost exclusively as a North American issue because of the many newspaper and television reports. However, in the intervening years, cases of elder abuse and/or neglect have been documented in most countries, including the developing nations (Daichman 2005; McDonald 2011). Like child and spousal abuse, abuse and neglect of older people is difficult to identify and confirm. Non-reporting and under-reporting by victims occurs if they are unaware that certain behaviour is abusive, if they fear reprisal or loss of care from caregivers or abusers, or if they do not know where to report the abuse. Others fear that disclosing abuse will be seen as a sign of incompetence and frailty. In most cases, abused and

Highlight 12.4
Entrance to a Continuum of Care System: Two Examples

Mrs S

Mrs S initially contacted the Senior Citizens Department six months after her husband's death because she found home maintenance chores difficult. She thought she would have to move to an apartment. A community worker from the Senior Citizens Department arranged for a home-care worker to assist Mrs S with the chores she was unable to do.

A year later, Mrs S suffered a stroke. After her hospitalization, she moved to the home of her daughter. Her daughter and son-in-law both worked outside the home full-time, and Mrs S found herself lonely and lacking the stimulation to be as active as her doctor recommended. She called the community worker, who suggested participation in a day program at the home for the aged nearest to where Mrs S lives. She has attended the program twice a week for 18 months. Her attendance at the day program provides her with priority for admission to the home should it be necessary in the future, but she says, "It's not time yet."

Mrs T

Mrs T had been in hospital for several months due to poor nutrition and inadequate management of her diabetic condition. She was admitted to a home for the aged, directly from the hospital.

Although Mrs T found it difficult to adjust to the home, in time she grew accustomed to the group living situation. With proper attention to her nutritional and medical needs, her physical and emotional condition improved. Mrs T then expressed a desire to move back to the community.

The home's social worker, admissions counsellor, and director of care worked together assisting her to make arrangements for community living. The admissions counsellor helped Mrs T make arrangements for an apartment and for attending the day program two days a week. The director of care and the social worker met with Mrs T and her son to assure them of priority readmission to the home for the aged if that became necessary. Following discharge, the social worker kept in touch with Mrs T regarding services and her transition back into the community.

Mrs T lived safely in her apartment for two years. When further medical difficulties arose, she was readmitted to the first appropriate bed and is now very content in the home, having enjoyed two additional years in the community.

abusive people are family members and/or caregivers, although one of the fastest-growing types is financial abuse, especially telephone, mail, and Internet fraud (Rabiner et al. 2006; Fitzwater and Puchta 2010). Abuse can occur behind closed doors in nursing and retirement homes or in a family home, where it tends to be viewed as a private family matter, even though some forms of abuse are criminal acts. Usually, suspecting neighbours are unwilling to intervene in family troubles, or formal care workers fail to build a case to support their observations.

Older dependent adults are potentially vulnerable to abuse and neglect in institutions, which includes, for women, the risk of sexual abuse (Teaster and Roberto 2004). However, emerging regulations and laws are reducing these risks and provide increased protection for residents. To prevent abuse, there is more supervision and training of employees and mandatory reporting of suspected cases of mistreatment by staff, as well as new guardianship and adult-protection laws concerning the use of restraints and residents' rights.[8] Moreover, most jurisdictions employ an ombudsperson to investigate complaints of abuse in nursing homes or long-term-care institutions.

Definitions of Abuse and Neglect

There is no single definition of **elder abuse** and neglect, although there is agreement that the major types of elder abuse include physical, psychological, financial, and sexual abuse (McDonald 2011). What is considered abusive in one family may be considered normal in another because of past practices or because of cultural or religious beliefs and practices. To illustrate, Chinese cultural values about aging and the care of the elderly consider abuse as disrespectful behaviour, and therefore the isolation or marginalization of Chinese elders in any form is considered abusive behaviour (Tam and Neysmith 2006).

In general, three types of instruments have been used to measure or identify abuse or neglect: interviews with older people by professional care workers to identify victims; classification schemes to indicate types of abuse (Wilber and McNeilly 2001; Fulmer et al. 2005); and survey instruments with lists of abusive behaviour to identify incidents of abuse or attitudes as to whether such behaviour is abusive and, if so, how prevalent (Stones and Bédard 2003, Appendix; Laumann et al. 2008). The Elder Abuse Survey Tool (EAST), designed by Stones and Bédard (2003), lists 96 behaviours that constitute mistreatment in a situation where a person lives with or is supervised by a person in a position of trust and 15 that might take place when older people live in an institution.

Elder abuse occurs in situations in which a frail, dependent person is assisted or cared for by a person in a position of trust, such as a relative, friend, or employee of an institution where the person lives; however, abuse may be reciprocal in nature, for instance, among spouses with a history of conflict. Abuse represents a conscious or unconscious act that violates the trust and moral obligation to care for and protect a vulnerable, dependent person. Acts of abuse include varying degrees of the following:

- *physical abuse*: the use of physical force, punishment, physical restraint, coercion, personal attacks, or rough handling that leads to physical pain, bruises, abrasions, dislocations, fractures, burns, or, in extreme cases, death[9]
- *Sexual abuse*: non-consensual sexual contact of any kind
- *emotional or psychological abuse*: yelling, verbal threats, insults, or humiliation; blackmail; lack of attention or withholding affection; isolation by confinement to a chair, bed, or room
- *medical abuse*: withholding food or medicine, not seeking medical assistance, over- or under-administering prescribed drugs
- *financial or material abuse*: telephone, mail, or internet fraud; stealing money or possessions; cashing and keeping pension cheques; and dishonest use of an elderly person's money or property
- *legal abuse*: any violation of human rights and freedoms; forced changes in a will; denial of access to public services, such as home care, nursing, and therapeutic services

- *abandonment*: desertion by a person who had legal, physical custody or a moral responsibility to care for an older person

Elder neglect, which may be intentional or unintentional, is the failure or refusal to perform necessary caregiving or monitoring responsibilities for an older adult, especially one who is cognitively or physically impaired. Lack of knowledge about how to care for an Alzheimer's patient or about community support services can lead to unintentional neglect that has serious consequences for the dependent elderly person. Neglect on the part of a caregiver to meet the physical, psychological, or emotional needs of an older person is often a precursor to abandonment. An interesting legal issue involves who, among potential primary caregivers, might be considered negligent or neglectful in their responsibilities to an elderly parent, who, in turn, is considered a legally independent adult. Highlight 12.5 illustrates some tragic case histories of elder abuse and neglect.

Older adults may engage in self-neglect or self-abuse that threatens their own safety and health, especially when they are not monitored or visited regularly by family, friends, or care workers. **Self-neglect** is the failure to provide oneself with the necessities to ensure physical and mental health and a safe environment—food, clean clothing, regular bathing, shelter, medication, or social interaction. Self-neglect may involve **self-abuse**, such as malnutrition or drug or alcohol abuse, which results in physical or mental injury. This type of abuse is "hidden" and is often undetected unless a care worker or emergency department personnel are called to the home. For some, self-abuse is a continuation of behaviour exhibited in early and middle adulthood, especially if the person is socially isolated. For others, this behaviour begins after they retire, are widowed, or are diagnosed with a chronic or terminal illness and become depressed or isolated. In addition to abuse and neglect, older adults are often victims of fraud—telephone sales, donations to charities (real or fabricated), unneeded home repairs, and Internet scams (Fitzwater and Puchta 2010).[10] Fraud is often under-reported because of embarrassment and a lack of information about who committed the fraud.

The Prevalence of Abuse and Neglect

Prevalence statistics are derived from cross-sectional studies that identify the proportion of incidents or cases of abuse that have been experienced by or observed in members of a particular age (in this case, 65 and over) or gender or among those who live at home or in a retirement or nursing home. These statistics identify the approximate extent of the problem by type and location (nationally, regionally, or locally) and by gender of the victim and perpetrator.

It is difficult to determine the number and type of elder abuse and neglect cases in a given community or setting (McDonald 2011). Studies are limited and often not comparable because they are based on small and non-representative samples (since the respondents are volunteers); they use different definitions and measures of abuse; and respondents may not be able to remember or be willing to report incidents, or reported cases cannot be confirmed. In most jurisdictions, the police do not include a victim's age in crime reports, nor are specific crimes labelled as "elder abuse." Moreover, abuse and neglect in an institutional setting is often "covered up" and seldom reported by co-workers who may have observed or suspect a person is abusing a resident.

Most population-based studies suggest that between 4 and 10 per cent of elderly people have experienced some form of abuse in the home, although rates vary based on the country,

Highlight 12.5
Elder Abuse and Neglect: Tragic Family Scenarios

Financial Abuse, Alcoholism, and Neglect

An alcoholic in his fifties, Fred moved in with his elderly mother after he lost his job. She receives a large pension and has other sources of income but is physically and cognitively impaired. Fred cashed her cheques and went on drinking binges, often leaving her alone for days. During one of these bouts, a concerned neighbour found Fred's mother lying on the living-room floor in a disoriented, malnourished, dehydrated, and unclean state.

Marital Discord and Spousal Abuse

After a long and tension-filled marriage, John became bedridden and incontinent. His wife, obliged to care for him 24 hours a day, began to withhold drugs and food and slapped him and screamed at him whenever he demanded attention and care. When he was unexpectedly visited at home by a physician, bruises were discovered on his face and arms, and he was moved to a long-term-care institution.

Psychological Abuse

An elderly woman, no longer able to maintain the family home yet unwilling to move, invited a single niece to share her home in return for help with the housekeeping. For two years, the relationship appeared to be mutually beneficial, but increasingly the niece began to insult her aunt and threatened that she would leave if she did not receive large sums of money on a regular basis. The niece began to assume that it was her home—she decided which television programs were watched, when they went to bed and ate meals, when and whether they went out, and how the aunt's money was spent. Moreover, the niece only talked to the aunt when it was essential, withdrew all signs of affection, and encouraged the aunt to spend more and more time in her bedroom. In reality, the aunt had become a prisoner in her own home with no meaningful social interaction.

Frustration and Stress

Charged with the killing of his 84-year-old wife, the defendant argued that he was no longer able to care for his mentally and physically frail wife, whose sight, hearing, and cognitive abilities had deteriorated rapidly. He stated that he could no longer tolerate her suffering, his own stress, or the frustration of dealing with the social welfare system. Despite repeated calls to the local social service office for assistance, he reported that "no one wanted to look after us. We were condemned to die like two dogs." After receiving a suspended sentence, he was admitted to a nursing home, which is what he had wanted for his wife all along.

type of abuse, and reporting method (see McDonald 2011 for a review). In the US, a large prevalence study showed that 9 per cent of respondents reported verbal abuse; 3.5 per cent reported financial abuse; and 0.2 per cent reported physical abuse, although these were the only types included in the survey (Laumann et al. 2008). Self-reports of abuse are likely underestimates because of a fear of reprisals when reporting abuse in surveys. Fitzwater and Puchta (2010) also contend that financial abuse is on the rise in the US, and likely in other countries, and yet there are numerous gaps in our knowledge as well as barriers to addressing the problem (Rabiner et al. 2006).

In Canada as of 2011, the Canadian Network for the Prevention of Elder Abuse (www .cnpea.ca) reported that "most Canadian research finds that between 4 and 10 per cent of older adults experience one or more forms of abuse or neglect at some point in their later years from someone they trust or rely on." Yon et al. (2013) reported that the prevalence rates of elder spousal abuse for older adults ranged from 6.9 per cent for emotional/financial abuse to 1.0 per cent for physical/sexual abuse. While the overall rate of violence is higher among older men than older women, senior women are more likely abused by a family member, whereas senior men tend to be victimized by a stranger or acquaintance (Statistics Canada 2011). Within institutions, incidents of physical and psychological abuse by staff are likely much higher, but they are seldom reported by the abused person or by others. Abuse or neglect within institutions is more likely to occur where care standards are low, where staff are poorly trained and overworked, where the physical environment is deficient for both staff and residents, where policies with regard to care favour the interests of the institution rather than the resident, and where there is no policy or procedure to protect a "whistleblower." Organizational theory may help to understand the connections among predictors of institutional abuse by focusing attention on the norms, culture, and practices embedded in large complex organizations of this type and their influence on resident treatment (McDonald 2011).

Explanations for Abuse and Neglect

Most abuse and neglect occurs in family settings by someone in a position of trust who is known to the victim. The most vulnerable older people include women; seniors who are frail, cognitively impaired, or physically disabled; and those who live with the perpetrator. Early explanations for abuse were based on a situational-stress model. It was argued that caring for a dependent elderly person, especially one who is cognitively impaired and prone to behavioural problems, leads to significant stress for the caregiver, who reacts by engaging in abuse or negligence. More recently, the focus is more on family relations, personal characteristics, and lifestyle factors unique to the relationship between the caregiver and the care recipient. For example, abuse and violence can occur in both directions, especially if an older person is cognitively impaired or there has been a history of conflict between two people. It has been suggested that a life-course perspective applied to elder abuse places abuse in the context of life histories and integrates contextual factors (e.g., one's ethnic community, or living arrangement); individual action and social contexts (e.g., family relationship quality); and structural contexts (such as changing policy and normative environments) (McDonald 2011).

A life-course approach emphasizes timing and sequencing of events embedded in the aging process, linked lives, and agency. Thus, some incidents of spousal elder abuse are a continuation of lifelong spousal abuse, whereas other cases appear as new forms of abuse unique to old age, for instance, an adult child "pays back" an abusive parent and uses physical force, verbal abuse, or neglect to control the parent (Yon et al. 2013). Abuse or neglect may be due, as well, to cognitive, emotional, or behavioural problems, such as substance abuse or mental-health disorders, on the part of the perpetrator.

Highlight 12.6 provides a list of factors that have been shown to increase the risk of community-based elder abuse in multiple studies, and those that have been shown to increase risk in a limited number of studies or with contradictory support.

Highlight 12.6
Elder Abuse Risk Factors

Factors Shown to Increase Risk of Elder Abuse in Multiple Studies

- shared living situation
- social isolation and poor social networks
- the presence of dementia (for physical abuse)
- the presence of functional disability of the victim
- mental illness of the perpetrator, mainly depression
- hostility of the perpetrator
- alcohol or substance abuse by the perpetrator
- history of abuse throughout life course
- disability level of the victim
- perpetrator dependency on the abused older adult

Possible Risk Factors with Limited or Contradictory Support

- being female
- higher propensity of a spouse being a perpetrator versus other family members
- large age gap between spouses
- perceptions of high neighbourhood crime
- high medication use by the victim
- personality characteristics of the victim, such as aggressiveness
- visible minority status

Source: Adapted from McDonald 2011 and Yon et al. 2013.

Preventing Abuse and Neglect

A variety of intervention strategies have been proposed to increase prevention and to protect victims of elder abuse.[11] One more area includes educating and training health- and social-care professionals, members of the legal and law-enforcement communities, older adults, family members, and the public about how to identify and report abuse and about where to obtain help. Another includes building crisis shelters for abused older adults, especially women. Other researchers recommend creating assessment, screening, and intervention programs; providing legal advice; forming local peer counselling and support groups; initiating changes to the legal code; and educating and empowering older adults to act for themselves and to advocate for their own interests, including how and where to report abuse by family or care workers (NSC 2007; Ploeg et al. 2009; Gutman and Spencer 2010). Thus far, few intervention studies have significantly reduced elder abuse (Ploeg et al. 2009).

Different types of abuse and different situations require different interventions. Intervention involves identifying high-risk elders and caregivers and providing social assistance, enacting legislation to protect the rights of elderly people, enforcing and prosecuting violations of criminal and civil law, and requiring professionals to report any suspected cases of abuse or neglect (Ploeg et al. 2009; Gutman and Spencer 2010). Specific policies or programs include the following:

- educating seniors and their family about abuse, neglect, and fraud
- providing social, financial, and health resources directly to an elderly person, who then purchases services from whomever he or she chooses
- offering financial support to caregivers, who purchase services such as nursing care and transportation from trained professionals, thereby alleviating some of the burden
- providing professional case managers with the right to make decisions about who should be the primary caregiver and how total care should be managed
- training police officers to deal exclusively with the problem of elder abuse, fraud, or neglect
- establishing a seniors' abuse telephone line (Au Coin 2003, 27)

In Manitoba, after this service was established in 1999, more than 300 calls were received from seniors between April 1999 and March 2002. The majority of these calls concerned emotional or financial abuse.

Barriers to Intervention

Conflicting ethics in a profession can prevent identification and intervention (McDonald et al. 1995; McDonald 2011). For example, there may be disagreement about what information can be revealed and to whom, as well as about who should or can be the target of an intervention (i.e., the abuser or the victim?). Moreover, legislation varies among jurisdictions as to how abuse is defined, what investigative powers are given to the authorities, whether a person who reports an abusive situation (the "whistleblower") is protected from identification and retaliation, and whether due process and legal representation are assured for the victims. Similarly, there may be turf wars or policy gaps in the provision of education and services among a particular jurisdiction's social services, health care, and legal entities.

Traditional intervention strategies are less successful in multicultural settings, where cultural or ethnic differences in values, traditions, beliefs, and language make it difficult for an outside professional worker to intervene. Both the victim and the abuser may not understand that the abusive behaviour violates the values or laws of mainstream Canadian society. Where power and control is based on a patriarchal system, elderly women may consider verbal, physical, or material abuse by a spouse or son to be normal. As well, abuse is more likely to be hidden and to continue if members of an ethnic group make little or no use of social and health-care services.

End of the Life Course:
Dying Well, with Support and Dignity

Our last chapter in the life course is concerned with facing and coping with death and managing the process of dying with dignity and with as little pain and suffering as possible. Very few people die suddenly from a stroke, heart attack, or accident. Rather, most older people die over a period of time that may range from a few months to a few years. Dying, like birth, marriage, or retirement, is a life-course transition. As more older people suffer from a degenerative chronic illness or live longer with frailty, more are being kept alive through the use of technology and medication and thus have a longer dying trajectory requiring more decisions (Seale 2005). Consequently, at some point, individuals and their family may raise questions about the quality of life. Living and dying well requires open communication about death, emotional support, informed choice about treatment, as much personal control as possible, and the maintenance of personal dignity (Fisher et al. 2000).

Dying is primarily a later-life event; people aged 65 and over account for about 80 per cent of all deaths in Canada every year. In addition to concerns about the quality of care and how to provide care as death approaches, the following questions are being debated:

- Where should end-of-life care be provided: in a hospital, at home, or in special facilities?
- When should there be a transition from "cure" (living well) to "care" (dying well), and who should make such decisions and on what basis?
- Do individuals have the right to die when, how, and where they choose?
- Who has a legal and moral responsibility to make decisions for an incapacitated dying person to ensure a good death?
- Should euthanasia and assisted suicide be legalized?
- How can the last chapter in the life course be completed with dignity and as much personal control as possible?[12]

Wilson et al. (2008) have concluded that a best-practice end-of-life care model needs to have the following components: (a) universality, (b) care coordination, (c) assured access to a broad range of basic and advanced end-of-life services, and (d) provision of care regardless of care setting.

The Social Context of Death and Dying

Most people die over a period of time, in a social setting. This setting involves interactions, positive and negative, with family, friends, and health and social-service workers. Just as many older people prefer to age in place at home, many also prefer to die at home.

In reality, however, most older people end their life journey in a hospital or long-term-care facility, a process that is very expensive for the state and often for the individual and the family. Many hospital beds are occupied by older people who are dying. Wilson (2002, 391) estimated that if 71 per cent of the expected 225,000 deaths in 2002 took place in an acute-care hospital after an average stay of 21 days or longer, then every hospital bed in Canada would be used at least one month a year for end-of-life care. Motiwala et al. (2006) examined the place of death of almost 59,000 persons aged 66 and older who died in 2001 or 2002 in Ontario. They found that almost 80 per cent of the deaths occurred in an institutional setting (49 per cent in a hospital; 30.5 per cent in a long-term-care facility) and 20 per cent in their home (50 per cent of whom were receiving care and 50 per cent were not). If cancer was the cause of death, there was a greater likelihood of dying at home with care; if dementia was the major cause, they were more likely to die in a long-term-care facility; and if death was from a major acute illness (heart attack, stroke), death was most likely in a hospital. The authors noted that the percentages for where death occurred in Ontario were similar to those in other provinces.

Statistics like the ones above are used to argue for more end-of-life care at home or in long-term-care facilities. Consequently, new models and practices for end-of-life care are being proposed. The proposals include palliative care in other than primary health-care facilities, support groups for family and paid caregivers, and sensitivity in the type of care provided to account for cultural and religious diversity in the beliefs and practices associated with dying and death. These proposals try to account for diversity in the meaning and alleviation of pain, in who has the right to make health-care decisions, in practices such as withdrawing or withholding treatment, and in the cultural and religious systems and values of both the dying person and the family, which may differ from those of the health-care team (Niemeyer and Werth 2005).

Dying, as a social process, involves the individual who is striving for a good exit and a dignified death, professional health- and social-care workers, and family and friends who provide support, make decisions, and begin to mourn the impending loss of a loved one. Dying and death is a family experience. Family members are involved in caregiving; in making decisions about health care, financial matters, and the care and support of the other parent; and in arranging a funeral. Such responsibilities have the potential to create either conflict or harmony among siblings (Matthews 2002).

Today, more than in the past, older adults understand and are ready to talk about the process of dying. They express concerns about pain, losing self-control, becoming a burden to others and to society, and wanting to control when, where, and how they die. With increased longevity and more chronic illness, many people fear that they will spend their last days, months, or years living in a totally dependent, painful, confused, or comatose state. If this happens, communication and social relationships will cease, and they question the social value of continuing to live. These concerns are magnified if dying is prolonged through the use of medical technology and when options for a quicker death are known and perhaps available but not employed.

Regardless of whether an individual dies in an institution or at home, an increasing number of older adults express a wish to experience a "good exit or death" for themselves and their survivors, especially a spouse. They do not want to be neglected or abandoned, yet they do not want to become a burden to others. Consequently, an increasing number of people state, through advance directives, how they would like to die, and more people are planning their own funerals and how they wish to be remembered and honoured after they die. This planning consists of organizing their personal matters, reflecting on their life and perhaps writing their own obituary, and discussing what kind of medical care they want when they are dying and whether they want to die at home or in an institution.

Advance Directives: Protecting Dependent Older People

A major issue in end-of-life care is the need to protect the legal rights of older people who are unable to make decisions about living or dying.[13] Today, more people are employing advance directives to protect their autonomy and right to choose how they want to die. Based on interviews with 96 terminally ill elders, Schroepfer (2006) identifies six possible frames of mind that dying persons may hold toward death:

1. Neither ready for nor accepting death
2. Not ready but accepting
3. Ready and accepting
4. Ready, accepting, and wishing death would occur
5. Considering a hastened death but no plan in place
6. Considering a hastened death, with a specific expressed plan or wish

The frame adopted depends on a number of socio-demographic factors (gender, education, race, marital status, religion, region), psychological factors (preferences, unfinished business to be completed, fear of dying, loneliness, feelings of dependency, lack of hope), medical factors (pain at present or fear of suffering in the near future), social relationships with the family (quality, quantity), and spiritual beliefs and needs (Garrett et al. 2008).

Many older persons express their preferences in advance about treatments (such as the use of life-support systems, tube feeding, and resuscitation) and about how and when to die. Others, however, express only general preferences that define goals and values and thereby allow surrogate decision-makers some leeway (or uncertainty) in interpreting and acting on their behalf. This approach can result in the surrogate misunderstanding or misinterpreting the person's preferences (Hawkins et al. 2005). Without a written document (sometimes termed a living will) expressing an individual's wishes, determining who can make such decisions becomes a legal and ethical issue. These decisions are particularly complex if a person is comatose or mentally incapacitated and his or her wishes were not previously known. While a verbal expression of personal wishes might provide a clue, it has no legal status.

Advance directives written by lawyers are legal documents about preferences for medical and personal care if at any time in the future persons cannot speak for themselves. Thus, they enable incapacitated people to control their destiny. These documents can be amended or revoked at any time as long as the person remains mentally competent. Family doctors should have a copy in the patient's file because adult children may not be present or able to make a decision if one is needed.

Power of Attorney

Older adults are protected to the greatest degree if they assign **power of attorney** to someone they trust who can make decisions on their behalf if the need arises. A "durable" power of attorney authorizes an agent (usually the spouse or one or more children) to act on behalf of an individual with regard to financial matters. A "medical" or "health care" power of attorney authorizes an agent to make decisions about medical care for a person who is incapable of making such decisions.

A power of attorney allows more decisions by someone else than is possible with a living will. For example, a living will is of little use in determining where a severely impaired AD patient should live, whether an investment portfolio should be restructured or sold, what doctors should be visited, or what treatments should be attempted at end of life. Questionnaires are available that can help to ensure that most situations that may arise have been included in the power of attorney.[14]

Guardianship

In the absence of living wills or "durable" or "medical" powers of attorney, a court order assigning guardianship to one or more people (or to the Public Guardian) may be necessary if an older person without relatives is unable to make decisions about personal care or financial matters. Or guardianship may be necessary if a family member with power of attorney is accused by others of not acting in the individual's best interests.

The Right to Die: Assisted Suicide and Euthanasia

In primitive societies, communities often had formal or informal customs about when and how older members died if they were ill or no longer able to contribute or keep up as a nomadic tribe changed location. Older people might be abandoned or killed, or they might leave the group on their own to enter the next world. Today, end-of-life issues are being raised by advocacy groups and enlightened older adults, who seek the right to die with dignity at a time and place of their choosing. **Assisted suicide** and **euthanasia** are hotly debated topics, and many complex legal, ethical, medical, religious, and philosophical arguments have been made for or against such procedures.[15] In Canada, euthanasia and assisted suicide are illegal,[16] at present, but they have been legalized in other places, notably Belgium, the Netherlands, Switzerland, and Oregon.

In ancient Greece, *euthanasia* meant a "good death." Today, people are discussing the merits and advantages of a "good" versus a "bad" death and whether an individual, or his or her delegate, has the right to choose the time and manner of death. Such a decision is taken to improve the quality of death when quality of life is lost because of pain or being bedridden, comatose, or mentally incapacitated. *Passive* euthanasia allows death to occur by withdrawing treatment, such as drugs or life support, while providing medication to relieve pain. Or the family or health-care workers may ignore a patient's refusal to eat or take medication. *Active* euthanasia on the part of the person involved causes death by refusing to continue treatment, by requesting discharge from a hospital to die at home, or by overdosing on drugs, usually by lethal injection.

Assisted suicide is active euthanasia with the assistance of a physician who provides drugs and/or advice so that a patient can end his or her own life. Labelled as either a compassionate act or legalized murder, depending on one's views, euthanasia has been legally possible in Oregon since the passage of the Death with Dignity Act in 1997. This legislation contains rigid guidelines for all parties involved in the decision and act. After its passage, the Supreme Court of the United States ruled that physician-assisted suicide for terminally ill patients is not a constitutional right. Since then, there have been test cases in other states every few years. Opponents argue that there is an important difference between refusing life-sustaining medical treatment and obtaining a lethal dose of medication. Other opponents argue that dying patients are not receiving the care they need, and if good palliative care were available, physician-assisted suicide would no longer be wanted. In one study, 63 per cent of 379 palliative-care cancer patients from across Canada believed that assisted death should be legalized, and 40 per cent said they would consider requesting physician-assisted suicide if their situation deteriorated (Wilson et al. 2007).

In the Netherlands, more than 3000 cases of euthanasia took place each year for more than 25 years, all illegal but without sanctions. However, in April 2001, euthanasia was legalized in the Netherlands, as long as the person or their delegate consults at least two physicians and both attest that no reasonable alternatives are available to improve the quality of life. Many residents of the Netherlands carry "euthanasia" passports, which request assistance with suicide if specified medical conditions arise. It is estimated that 6 to 10 per cent of people with advanced cancer pursue this option.

The practice of euthanasia raises many difficult moral and ethical questions:

- Should euthanasia or assisted suicide be available to anyone at any time or only for those in certain age groups?
- Should it be available only for a terminal illness and only when the quality of life deteriorates beyond a defined point?
- Should it be used only for physical and not for mental illnesses?
- Who should be involved in the decision to end a life: the individual, the family, a guardian, a physician, a religious figure?

In Canada, we have begun to observe a shift toward legalization of assisted suicide but not without considerable opposition. In June 2012, a BC Supreme Court judge ruled that Canada's law against physician-assisted suicide is unconstitutional, thus opening the way for assisted suicide in BC. However, that judgment is being challenged by the Supreme Court of Canada, as shown in Highlight 12.7.

Highlight 12.7
Assisted Suicide Debate Heats Up in Canada

Call it what you will—assisted suicide, euthanasia or therapeutic homicide—it is an issue that politicians are reluctant to engage in, but one that is not going away. Last month, a BC Supreme Court judge ruled that Canada's ban on assisted suicide is unconstitutional on grounds that it violates two sections of the Charter of Rights concerning the right to equality, and the right to life, liberty and security of the person. The ruling did not strike down the law, but ordered Ottawa to amend the Criminal Code provisions that make it an offence to counsel or assist someone to commit suicide. It did, however, extend an exemption for a plaintiff in the case, a 64-year-old BC woman suffering from Lou Gehrig's disease (or ALS), to die with a doctor's assistance.

Justice Minister Rob Nicholson announced that the federal government will appeal all aspects of the decision, including the exemption granted the plaintiff. This is as it should be, because the issue of assisted suicide should be decided not on the judicial, but on the political level. But rather than merely appealing the ruling, the government should promote a national conversation on assisted dying, possibly by way of a royal commission, and thereafter a free vote in Parliament on whether to maintain the law as it is or to change it. It is a profoundly difficult choice in that both advocates and opponents have compelling arguments.

On the one side are those who maintain that terminally ill people in the grip of unending excruciating pain should have the right to "die with dignity" should they so choose and have recourse to medical assistance in the process. On the other are those who warn of embarking on a "slippery slope" that would see people who could live longer with proper palliative care opt to die because they feel they are a burden on their families and caregivers, or they feel pressured by family members who consider them to be that.

In Quebec, a National Assembly committee came up with a set of guidelines that might inform federal legislators in reconsidering the law. These were drawn from jurisdictions where assisted dying has been legalized, including Belgium, the Netherlands, Switzerland and three US states. The proposals include provisions that would require requests for assisted dying to be made in writing. People making the requests would have to be terminally ill and in constant physical or psychological suffering. The proposals also call for two doctors to approve the procedure and for it be carried out in a clinical setting, with family members having no part in it.

It is true that the Supreme Court ruled against assisted suicide in 1993 by a 5–4 margin in the landmark case of Sue Rodriguez, also an ALS sufferer. It is also true that a majority of the House of Commons voted against decriminalization in 2010 when it was proposed in a private member's bill. But more recently, an editorial in the *Canadian Medical Association Journal* called for a national debate on the issue and a political resolution. A national poll in December 2011 found that two-thirds of Canadians favour changing the law to enable assisted dying.

The pressure mounts on lawmakers to come to grips with the issue. Failing that, physician-assisted suicide is likely to proliferate in any case, but in a "back-street, or private clinic, hush-hush kind of way," as a senior editor of the *CMA Journal* put it. In that light, the sooner federal legislators grasp this nettle, the better.

Source: Adapted from "Assisted suicide debate is due," *The Vancouver Sun*, 19 July 2012.

Palliative Care

Palliative care, sometimes called hospice care, is designed for those with a terminal illness who need relief from pain and other symptoms, such as loss of appetite, nausea, incontinence, and breathing difficulties. The goal is to improve the quality not the quantity of life through physical, social, emotional, and spiritual support for the dying person; as well as provide education, training, and support for their caregivers (Gott and Ingleton 2011; Parliamentary Committee on Palliative and Compassionate Care 2011). Such care is available in a limited way in acute-care hospitals as well as in nursing homes, in the person's home, or in hospices, which are separate buildings used only for this purpose.[17] To date, most palliative care facilities are dedicated to those dying of cancer or AIDS, and little space is available for older people with dementia or chronic degenerative disease. Yet these diseases are on the increase, leading many to argue that palliative care units are underfunded.

The **hospice movement** was founded in 1967 in London, England, by Dame Cicely Saunders. The first hospice in Canada was established in 1975 at the Royal Victoria Hospital in Montreal, but at present there are few hospices in Canada. Globally, half of all countries have no formal end-of-life care services, and where they do exist, only 15 per cent are integrated into the health-care system, with the remainder being localized and access being variable (International Observatory on End of Life Care 2007).

The hospice movement is a philosophy as much as it is a facility. It represents a "death with dignity" approach to caring and provides an array of services when further hospital treatment is no longer possible for those with a terminal illness. Services and education are provided to the dying person's family. No aggressive life-saving devices or procedures are used, but efforts are made to alleviate the patient's pain. Volunteers provide help with nursing and homemaking chores as well as emotional support. They also provide information and understanding through discussions about death with both the dying person and his or her immediate family. Volunteers are an essential component of an integrated, interdisciplinary palliative-care team (McKee 2007; Parliamentary Committee on Palliative and Compassionate Care 2011). Often, the hospice program is linked with widow-to-widow support programs that help women adapt to life without a spouse. A 2004 survey indicated that about 90 per cent of Canadians wish to remain in their own homes during the final stages of life (Canadian Hospice Palliative Care Association 2004).

A major difficulty with palliative care is that it is unclear who should cover the cost of medication, care workers, and medical supplies and equipment if care is provided outside a hospital. In long-term-care settings, only some of these costs are fully absorbed by the facility. At the federal level, the Romanow Commission (2002) recommended that the Canada Health Act be expanded to include palliative home-care services in the last six months of life. But to date, the only significant federal initiatives have been the Veterans Affairs Palliative Care Program for at-home care and the Compassionate Care Leave Benefit, implemented as part of the Employment Insurance Act in 2004. This latter benefit permits up to six weeks of paid leave to qualified persons who need to leave work to provide care and support to a gravely ill family member who is at risk of dying within six months.

Death, Bereavement, and Cultural Rituals

The meaning of death is socially constructed in different cultural contexts, as is the coping by family and friends through bereavement and the rituals associated with burial and with honouring and remembering deceased relatives and friends.

Death

Social values, beliefs, and practices concerning death and dying are changing. There is more open discussion about and acceptance of death, more advance directives are written, more palliative care is provided, more decisions are being made not to delay or impede death, and there is more emphasis on managing a "good and dignified death." As well, support is growing for the right to die through assisted suicide, for death ceremonies and rituals that are viewed as a celebration of life, and for cremation rather than burial in a casket and large plot.[18]

Just as there are individual differences in the way people live, so, too, are there differences in beliefs and practices concerning death. First, there are individual differences in coping skills, cognitive competence, understanding and acceptance of death, the will to live, and pain tolerance. Second, the type and amount of emotional support given to a dying person by his or her family influences whether he or she dies well and with dignity. And third, there are socio-cultural differences in how members of social groups manage the dying process and in how they honour deceased persons. Death rituals change as new ways of thinking about death are introduced into a society, subculture, or religion. Often, religious and cultural beliefs and practices interact or coexist, as in the case of Catholicism and Hispanic culture. Such interactions have a direct influence on bereavement practices, on whether and how end-of-life decisions are made or not made (Braun et al. 2001; Leichtentritt and Rettig 2001; Leming and Dickinson 2011), and on the type of ceremony to honour and bury a relative.

Bereavement: Mourning and Grief Management

Bereavement is the objective state of having lost a significant other and of coping with a death. Consequently, grief in the days following a death can be expressed through shock, numbness, vulnerability, and depression. A grief response involves expressing feelings for a deceased person, as well as recognizing the social loss and vacuum created by his or her death. A partner is left alone, and a child becomes an orphan when the last parent dies. The grief period raises thoughts and questions about the reality of death and the meaning of life, and it offers a period in which to reflect and to learn about the self and others.

The mourning period involves short-term decisions about religious and cultural rituals (a public or private service, a funeral or a memorial service, internment in a casket or cremation, flowers or charitable donations, a small reception or a wake) and about personal behaviour (what to wear for a service, the amount of social interaction and with whom). Mourning is both an individual and a cultural matter. This period is somewhat easier if the deceased openly discussed his or her wishes with partners and family and if pre-planned funeral arrangements were made, including payment for a plot and a casket or urn, the format of the service, and even the writing of an obituary.

Grief management can be a long process for survivors, especially for an intimate elderly partner, and for women in general, who seem to disproportionately bear the burden of a loss among family and friends (Williams et al. 2006; Leming and Dickinson 2011). Even if a partner was severely ill for months or years and some anticipatory grieving occurred before the death, the grieving process often endures for six to twelve months or more after the death. A surviving spouse may experience loneliness, depression, and an inability to function. As much as possible, protracted and intense grief should be avoided and eliminated because in the extreme it can lead to heart disease, alcohol or drug abuse, or suicide (Neimeyer and Werth 2005). Bereavement groups (hospice volunteers and widow-to-widow volunteers) can create a sense of community with and provide support from others who understand or who have experienced a similar loss of a loved one.

Death Rituals and Ceremonies

Death rituals and ceremonies are managed by the funeral home industry[19] because regardless of the type of funeral, a funeral home must be involved. The cost of a funeral for the service, an administration fee, and a casket or urn, plus a burial plot, can range from about $3000 to more than $20,000. If a death is sudden, and services and a plot have not been pre-purchased, emotionally vulnerable survivors may not make rational decisions about the purchase of funeral services.

Obituaries are cultural artifacts, and they range from serious, short, factual statements about the person and his or her survivors to lengthy narratives about lifetime achievements and interests. Obituaries are part of the grieving process and help to define the individual and his or her place in the world.[20] Long obituaries may be written as a public eulogy. With those left behind and personal wishes in mind, the following paragraph is part of a recent obituary for one of the author's friends:

> Barbara did not wish to have a formal funeral service, opting instead for a singular departure from this world. She once commented that she would rather people take those few hours that would otherwise be spent at her funeral and do something meaningful with them—a walk in the woods, a game with kids, a conversation with an old friend or loved one. She knew that every single hour in life is precious, and she was adamant that her own death would not take up even a few of them from those of us left behind.

Highlight 12.8 is an obituary written as a final public statement to family, friends, and colleagues.

Eulogies, delivered at funerals and memorial services by a friend or relative, are a public expression of what and how much a deceased person has meant to those who knew the person well and of their contributions to the world. Similarly, gravestones can record the thoughts of the deceased or their loved ones in a permanent way—although less common today, with more people being cremated and memorialized with just a small plaque on the ground. They can express a person's values and uniqueness beyond basic chronological facts. A walk through a cemetery, especially those with markers from earlier centuries, reveals such thoughts and reflections. To illustrate, a grave marker in the original cemetery in Aspen, Colorado, offered this reflective thought by a deceased person: "To enter the highlands of the mind, into the mountains I must go."

Public Policy for an Aging Population

Public policies represent distant forces that can have a positive or negative impact on individual lives, especially in the interconnected domains of education, work, family, economic security, and health care across the life course (Settersten 2003). They have the potential to facilitate or constrain human development and independence across the life course. For most of the twentieth century, public policies were designed for a young society, and policies for older people were a secondary consideration, except for economic security. This approach illustrates how a "cultural or structural lag" exists in policy-making. This cultural lag can be pronounced in countries like Canada that have an open-door immigration policy and hence an ethnically diverse society. In such countries, public policy needs to account for this diversity to meet the needs of all citizens and to avoid conflict when politically active minority groups focus on policy gaps that lead to discrimination or to unequal access to benefits or services (Torres-Gil 2005).

Today, population aging and changing social values require that public policies meet the needs of all citizens in an aging society, regardless of age.[21] Consequently, a life-course approach

Highlight 12.8
A Self-Written Obituary

John Ross Cuthbert (29 August 1952–24 November 1999)

My Friends

Forgive me for leaving the party early. I have chosen not to have a standard funeral or a formal viewing because these would not be happy events—and I insist on leaving this world the same way I have tried to live in it—with smiles, joy, and goodwill.

My death is sad but not tragic because I have had a rich life. I have laughed, cried, loved and been loved, enjoyed the company of friends, and lived life to the fullest extent that I could. I have lived longer than expected and survived against the odds to find romance, love, and above all, to witness the birth and development of my two little miracles—Brittany and Yardley. Who would have believed it possible 30 years ago?

I have treasured the many and varied friends I have had at my side throughout my journey. There are no words to express my gratitude, to repay you for all the love and comradeship, the support given so freely—no words to even say a proper "thanks" just for being a friend. I will miss you. But I have had yet another gift lately—the time to visit, call, or talk to as many of my friends and family as possible. Let these happy contacts serve as my goodbyes to you all.

My family will be saying goodbye to me privately on the Scarborough Bluffs—one of our favourite places to be together, to walk and find peace. Please remember me in a similar fashion. Remember the good times, the laughs we had, the special times we all shared. No greater tribute could I request.

I leave asking but one last favour. Cathy, Brittany, and Yardley will be beyond my protection, and I will be unable to supply the hugs and kisses that they all need. Please remember them and love them as you would your own family—they will need good friends at every step of their life's journey.

My love to you all—may you walk life's journey in good health, with friends at your side and a smile on your face.

Ross Cuthbert
November 1999

Source: *The Globe and Mail*, Obituaries, November 1999.

to social policy is being advocated to prevent intergenerational conflict and to recognize that increasingly, the traditional view of a life course with three distinct stages (education, work, retirement) is no longer the societal norm. Rather, the three stages overlap, and citizens have the right and the opportunity to learn and work at any age, including well past the age of 65. For example, in Sweden and Finland, social policies are, by law, "age-neutral" and encourage people to remain active as they age. The policies integrate employment programs, continuous learning programs, and a reformed pension system that does not penalize people for working beyond age 65.

The Public Policy Context in Canada

In a welfare state like Canada, fully funded or subsidized government programs are designed to enhance well-being, to provide a safety net for citizens, and to ensure financial security, health care, and social assistance for all citizens. These programs aim to enhance the welfare of both the individual and the state. Public policy consists of a set of laws, regulations, services, support systems, and programs that result from the decisions made by one or more of the federal, provincial, regional, or local governments. Some programs, such as the Canada Pension Plan, are designed and delivered at the federal level only. Some, such as the health-care system under the Canada Health Act and federal and provincial regulations, are delivered across two levels. Many are addressed by several levels of government in different but often uncoordinated ways, as is the case with home care, transportation, and housing. And some programs, such as education, are partially funded at one level (federal) and delivered at another (provincial).

The issue of who is responsible for the welfare of older adults is complicated by the multi-level structure of government in Canada (federal, provincial, regional, and local). The British North America Act (1867, renamed in 1982 to the Constitution Act) gave the federal government jurisdiction over social matters and economic security (public pensions) but left other, related responsibilities to the provinces. However, the provinces could not afford to offer all necessary services and became dependent on the federal government for transfer payments to pay for health care, education, social welfare, and transportation. When the federal debt and deficits grow, transfer payments to the provinces are reduced. One outcome of reduced federal transfer payments is that the quality of and accessibility to health care, higher education, and community social services that are delivered by the provinces is reduced. And, in turn, the provinces reduce transfer payments to regional and municipal governments—a process known as "downloading" fiscal responsibility to a lower level of government and to the individual, who must now pay for a service that might previously have been provided by a government agency. This process represents a "retrenchment" of the welfare state.

Seldom, if ever, is one agency responsible for the needs of older adults. To illustrate, at the federal level, programs for seniors are provided by at least six major departments: Human Resources and Skills Development Canada (pensions, income security, the New Horizons for Seniors program, and lifelong learning and training for older workers, as well as publication of the *Guide to Government Services for Seniors*); the Public Health Agency of Canada, Division of Aging and Seniors (promotion of active living, mental health and fall-prevention programs, emergency planning); Health Canada, First Nations and Inuit Health (home and community care services, delivery of dental, vision, mental health, and pharmaceutical services); Aboriginal Affairs and Northern Development Canada (adult care program to provide in-home, institutional, and foster care); Veterans Affairs Canada (health and home care, caregiver support, disability pensions, a prescription drug plan, and income support for veterans and their dependent survivors); and the Canada Mortgage and Housing Corporation (research and information on seniors' housing, renovation programs to accommodate disabilities). Similar multi-departmental responsibilities exist at the provincial, territorial, regional, and municipal levels.

Uncertainty over jurisdictional responsibility inhibits cohesive policy-making, fosters a lack of coordination among agencies, and creates gaps in the ideal continuum of services (MacAdam 2008). Hence, the seamless delivery of needed services and programs may not occur. For example, ideological conflict can occur between a health ministry, which seeks to cure and care for elderly people (often in hospitals or long-term-care institutions), and a social service ministry, which seeks to provide services that will keep elderly people living in the community. Therefore, the needs of specific groups may be neglected because one level believes that another level of government should be responsible, or services may be duplicated or uncoordinated.

Public policy on issues of aging is a shared responsibility of the state, the individual, and the family, as well as some private sectors. As early as 1991, the National Advisory Council on Aging (NACA 1991) argued for a national aging policy in which all levels of government would work with the private sector to coordinate, harmonize, and standardize services for aging Canadians. The same argument is made today in lobbying efforts to enhance health care, home care (a "hot" policy issue), and drug benefits for older adults.

Developing policies inevitably involves making choices: Who is responsible? Who is eligible and for how long? Which policy domain is most urgent? Who will deliver the programs? The process occurs in a context of conflict and co-operation for scarce resources among different levels of government, in the presence of disagreements about whether programs should be universal or need-based, in debates about what need is greater (a school or a long-term-care facility), and under the pressure of many competing demands from different interest groups. As well, policies are shaped by—or not introduced at all because of—the political ideology of the party in power and the existing or anticipated economic climate.

Policy Issues for an Aging Population

Reactive versus Proactive Policies

Many policies are developed in response to a problem, such as poverty or lack of access to appropriate care and are, therefore, reactive policies. However, the goal of policies should be to delay or prevent the problems from arising in the first place; in other words, they should be proactive. For example, home renovation subsidies can help to prevent falls and institutionalization, and spousal benefits can protect common-law and same-sex partners from poverty. In the past, many public policies were based on the assumption that elderly people became dependent on others in society. It was alleged that this dependence occurred because of inevitable, deteriorating biological or cognitive changes and because of financial dependence following retirement. Moreover, since the older population was assumed to be homogeneous, eligibility for assistance was determined by age rather than by need. More recent policies are designed to provide a variety of services to a heterogeneous older population.

Equity in Delivery

Services and programs provided under a policy should not create or perpetuate social inequality or produce negative unanticipated consequences. Policies must accommodate gender, marital, ethnic, regional, class, urban-rural, and other personal differences among both the recipients and those who provide care and services. Given the sex ratio of the older population, social policies must not ignore the special needs of older women, especially those who live alone (Brewer 2001; Connidis 2010). Yet many policies foster rather than redress gender inequalities and thereby disadvantage women, both as care providers and care recipients. Similarly, members of some religious or ethnic groups are ignored in health, social, or economic policies.

Policies should address the needs of older people who are most at risk because of their personal circumstances. What is needed are "inclusive" policies that take into account risk factors that are often related (e.g., being a divorced woman and poverty), emerging situations (e.g., benefits for gay and lesbian partners), and diverse geographical settings where older people may live (e.g., rural as opposed to urban or an Aboriginal community in a remote northern region) (Settersten 2003). Although not typically performed, analyses of existing or proposed policies should assess the relative costs and benefits of implementing the policy and examine the intended and unintended consequences of the policy for an older population.

Fiscal Responsibility and Entitlement

The apocalyptic view of public policy argues that population aging means we can no longer finance all the health, social, and economic benefits that older adults need. Thus, public policies are often shaped by the desire to reduce public expenditures rather than meet individual needs: taxes are increased; user fees are introduced; benefits like OAS and GIS are "clawed back" from those with higher incomes; and programs with universal entitlements are converted to need-based programs. As Gee (1995, 17) critically noted, "demographic change has become wedded to economic troubles." Consequently, the social contract between the government and older Canadians is being revised. Increasingly, universal benefits, or an automatic entitlement, are not provided to all older adults who attain a specified age (usually 65). Rather, policies include a mix of universal and need-based benefits, social insurance, and increased individual responsibility to pay some or all of the cost for a benefit or service (Hudson 1997; Béland and Shapiro 1995; Feldman 2003; Breda and Schoenmaekers 2006; Chappell 2011).

In the income-security domain, McDonald (1997) labelled this new approach the residual model of social welfare, which emphasizes a shift from full entitlement to "social insurance" (adequate and continuous income for everyone during retirement) to partial "social assistance" (subsistence income provided only to "needy" retirees). Settersten (2003) argues that an age-based entitlement to benefits stigmatizes older adults and increases the possibility of ageism and intergenerational conflict. Yet at the same time, he notes how difficult it is to measure and define need, as we learned in Chapter 10 with respect to defining poverty and eligibility for economic assistance.

Proponents of universal systems of support argue that they promote equity and enhance the dignity of all citizens because a means test for eligibility is not required. In contrast, proponents of need-based support argue that not all older adults need assistance from the government and that such programs become considerably less expensive when the size of the eligible group is limited to those who demonstrate need.

Who Is Responsible for Support?

Underlying the development of public policies for an aging population is the long-standing debate about whether the needs of older people should be viewed as a "private trouble" of the individual or a "public issue" facing society. This debate is fuelled when the following questions about economic and social security are raised:

- Should the public provide universal and complete pensions, or should individuals, through the private sector, be responsible for building their own pension benefits?
- Should the family or the state be responsible for the care and welfare of older citizens?
- Do older adults have the right, because of their past contributions, to be cared for in the later years?
- Should expensive health-care services, such as heart transplants and hip replacements, MRI diagnoses, pacemakers, and kidney dialyses, be rationed or restricted on the basis of age rather than need?
- Should scarce resources be reallocated to the elderly in the interest of social justice? For example, should we reduce public financial support for schools and universities to provide more universal programs and facilities for baby boom retirees?

Rather than an "either-or" solution, ideally there should be programs and services that meet needs along a continuum from "individualism" (personal responsibility) to "collectivism" (public responsibility). Moreover, public policies for older adults should integrate the respon-sibilities and contributions of individuals and families with those of the public and private sectors, especially with respect to housing, health care, and home care. Because there are many diverse family structures, public policies must serve older people and their caregivers within all types of family structures and living arrangements.

Privatization of Services

An emerging issue in health and home care is whether services that were previously the respon-sibility of the public sector should be privatized. Since many older adults do not need or use most public services, advocates of privatization argue that if certain programs or services were privatized, it would ease the public financial burden. In this process, some or all of the responsibility for health and social services would be transferred to charities, private founda-tions, religious or ethnic groups, or the for-profit sector. Privatization of services for older adults involves nursing homes, personal and home-care services, and expensive diagnostic and health-care procedures, some of which are elective. For governments, privatization is a way to reduce spending and demonstrate fiscal restraint to the voting public. However, researchers and the public are asking whether or not private services are more efficient, whether access to services will be restricted to those who can afford them (a two-tiered system), and whether a lower quality of care may result if public services are discontinued or if the required standards of care are unenforceable or are reduced so that a private entrepreneur can generate a profit.

Principles of Public Policy–Making to Serve an Aging Population

To enhance well-being and independence, to ensure comprehensive coverage and full access to the benefits provided by policies, to contain costs, and to meet the diverse needs of an aging population, policy-makers should be guided by fundamental principles and core values. Those values and principles help to eliminate discriminatory practices against older people, and they ensure older adults' autonomy, independence, safety, security, dignity, self-esteem, privacy, and right to choose. Policies and programs for older adults are often most effective if they are as follows:

1. Not exclusively based on age as a criterion for access or eligibility—age as the sole cri-terion ignores the heterogeneity of the older population in terms of abilities, interests, and needs.
2. Developed by following need assessments and research reviews that facilitate evi-dence-based decision-making.
3. Inclusive and provide equitable benefits to all—ask who is included and excluded: are the needs of the frail elderly and special groups (Aboriginal people, recent immigrants, and the homeless) being met?
4. Based on sharing through user fees—costs can be covered through full or partial subsidies and by co-payments from the private and public sectors and the individual.
5. Client-centred—direct or indirect payments can be paid to the client or the caregiver.
6. Coordinated and integrated so that there are no gaps between the informal and formal support systems—has jurisdictional responsibility been established or negotiated to prevent gaps in the system and to ensure the seamless delivery of services?
7. Based on collaboration and co-operation between ministries or agencies at all levels of government.

8. Protective of legal and human rights whether an older person is living in the community or in an institution.

9. Designed to ensure that a minimum standard of living is maintained throughout later life for all older citizens—policies and programs must serve the needs of aging persons more than those of the state.

10. Evaluated and revised, as necessary—a schedule is established for evaluating and, if necessary, revising or rescinding the policy if it is not meeting its objectives.

11. Flexible—allowing for access to benefits on a temporary or permanent basis and providing minimum or maximum amounts of support as needs change.

12. Sustainable—ensuring services will continue during economic downturns and following changes in governments.

Summary

Most individuals, regardless of age, are never totally isolated from others. Rather, an individual's social world evolves to provide possible sources of informal or formal assistance and support. This network consists of the individual, his or her family, friends, and neighbours, and ultimately formal care workers. Informal support, provided mainly by the family, especially daughters, is available to older adults who have lived in an extended family system. This system involves reciprocal exchange relationships in which older adults are helped in later life by adult children who have been supported and assisted by their parents throughout their lives.

For family caregivers, there are hidden financial, emotional, and health costs that add to the burden of caring for a frail or demented parent over a long period of time. Sometimes caregiving leads to elder abuse or neglect in the family, although in some cases abuse stems from cultural traditions or lifelong habits. Some of the burden borne by caregivers can be relieved by respite care and education programs, such as an Alzheimer's support group. Eventually, in most cases, informal support is supplemented or replaced by services in the formal support system, such as home-care workers provided by the public or private sector.

Today, there is more open discussion and acceptance of death among older people, and more individuals are expressing their wishes about health care and death through advance directives and powers of attorney. There is more emphasis on "dying a good death" with as little pain and suffering as possible and with less emotional and financial burden for family members. Palliative care in non-hospital settings is increasing, but more facilities, family-based approaches, volunteers, and trained personnel are needed.

Public policies to support older adults are necessary but difficult to design because of the heterogeneous needs and characteristics of older adults. Key policy areas that require attention in an aging society include the assurance of economic security and health care in later life; the elimination of age, gender, religious, regional, or ethnic discrimination and inequity in services and policies; the provision of high-quality and effective home care and long-term care; and the preservation of the dignity and human rights of older people, including the right to full participation in their social world. These policies must protect the human rights of older people and ensure that there is equity in the delivery of services, that all responsible jurisdictions coordinate their services to eliminate gaps in the system, and that the family, the state, and the private sector provide integrated and coordinated quality assistance and care for older people.

For Reflection, Debate, or Action

1. If an older member of your family needed assistance and ongoing care, who would be available and why? If nobody is likely to be available, explain why and how you as a case manager would ensure that the person received complete assistance and care.

2. Should supporting older relatives in later life be a private or a public responsibility? How would you allocate, and in what areas, proportionate responsibility?

3. Interview a caregiver in your family or in the community to identify sources of stress and the burdens associated with caring for an older adult. See if they are aware of various formal and community supports.

4. In your neighbourhood, you meet a 69-year-old widow who has recently moved to Canada from Jamaica to live with her daughter. She reports that she is lonely, feels useless, and receives little social or emotional support at home. What local services would enable this woman to expand her social network and become involved with age peers in the community?

5. On the basis of your reading, social philosophy, and political views, debate with a friend the following contrasting views about the intent or content of public policies designed for older people. Should programs be
   - need-based or universal?
   - based on user-pay or fully or partially subsidized?
   - the responsibility of the local, regional, provincial, or federal government and in what proportions?
   - funded by a subsidy or grant to the older person so that he or she can buy services or by a grant to a volunteer caregiver for the purchase of services or as compensation for lost income?

6. Visit a nursing home, a palliative-care facility, or an adult day centre to observe and learn about emerging thoughts and practices concerning dying and death. You may require ethics approval from your university prior to the visit.

7. Develop an argument, pro or con, as to why governments should or should not legalize assisted suicide. In your argument, address the questions raised in the last paragraph of the section on euthanasia and assisted suicide. Should this legislation, if approved, apply only to people of a certain age?

Notes

1. See Mindszenthy and Gordon 2002; Government of Canada 2003; Stobert and Cranswick 2004; Cranswick and Thomas 2005; and Keefe et al. 2007.

2. Informal social support by family members is discussed in Keating et al. 1999; Martin-Matthews 2000; Henderson 2002; Matthews 2002; Mindszenthy and Gordon 2002; Fast et al. 2004; Raina et al. 2004; Burr et al. 2005; Patsios and Davey 2005; Keefe et al. 2007; Connidis 2010; Chappell and Funk 2011; and CIHI 2011.

3. Gender differences in caregiving are discussed in Harris and Long 1999; Kramer and Lambert 1999; Campbell and Martin-Matthews 2000; Dupuis and Norris 2001; Matthews 2002; Ward-Griffin and Marshall 2003; Fast et al. 2004; Rosenthal and Ansello 2007; Connidis 2010; and Chappell and Funk 2011.

4. Gender differences in the quality and quantity of support tend to disappear as the aging parent becomes more frail and dependent and as adult children must make more decisions.

5. Forbes et al. (1987, 2–14) chronicle the history of institutional care from early Christian and medieval periods to the present era; Gee and Boyce (1988) and Montigny (1997) discuss how legislation (from before 1918 to the 1980s) contributed directly and indirectly to the development of health and social services for older Canadians; Snell (1990, 1996) examines the history of filial responsibility laws in Canada; Keating et al. (1999) analyze the context, content, and consequences of elder care in the late 1990s; Alexander (2002) describes the history of long-term care in Canada; and NACA (2006) provides a *Report Card on Seniors in Canada*.

6. The estimated saving for the government is somewhere between $5000 and $10,000 per person, per year, if an older person is provided with informal and formal care services and remains in his or her home, even at the palliative care stage (within one to six months of a projected death from a terminal illness). The presence of a spouse of an elderly person with a long-term illness significantly reduces the amount of publicly funded care that would have been provided (Hayward et al. 2004).

7. For information about elder abuse, see Podnieks et al. 1990; McDonald et al. 1991; Decalmer and Glendenning 1993; Maclean 1995; McDonald and Wigdor 1995; Carp 2000; McDonald and Collins 2000; Wilber and McNeilly 2001; World Health Organization 2002; Dauvergne 2003; Stones and Bédard 2003; Au Coin 2003; Weeks et al. 2004; Dyer 2005; Fulmer et al. 2005; Mellor and Brownell 2006; the National Citizens' Coalition for Nursing Home Reform 2007; National Seniors Council 2007; Ploeg et al. 2009; Gutman and Spencer 2010; Fitzwater and Puchta 2010; McDonald 2011; Yon et al. 2013; the Canadian Network for the Prevention of Elder Abuse (www.cnpea.ca); provincial elder abuse networks (www.onpea.org, www.bcceas.ca, www.rqcaa.org, and www.albertaelderabuse.ca); and the *Journal of Elder Abuse and Neglect*.

8. There are three types of adult-protection legislation in Canada. In the first type, in the Atlantic provinces, personnel are assigned to investigate suspected cases of abuse. The legislation gives them the legal power to investigate and intervene and may require the mandatory reporting of suspected cases of senior abuse. The second type, found in Ontario, includes adult-protection provisions in legislation pertaining to adult guardianship. Allegations that an older person is unable to manage his or her property or personal care, is being abused, or is in danger of being abused must be investigated, but no services are provided to the victim. The third type of legislation, found in British Columbia, provides for intervention in cases of abuse, neglect, or self-neglect and provides community-based service networks to help seniors (Au Coin 2003, 28).

9. In March 2007, in what is considered to be the first case of death resulting from elder abuse in Canada, a 55-year-old son was convicted of manslaughter and given a seven-year sentence for beating and abandoning his 78-year-old mother, who was afflicted with Alzheimer's disease (*The Globe and Mail*, 21 March 2007, p. A13).

10. In Ontario, fraud is the number-one crime against older adults. In 1999, seniors lost $3.5 million to telephone fraud, and the Ontario Provincial Police reported that 85 per cent of consumers who lost more than $5000 to fraud were seniors (Au Coin 2003, 27). Fitzwater and Puchta (2010) contend that financial abuse is on the rise.

11. The National Film Board of Canada has produced two films in its The Elderly at Risk series: *Mr Nobody*, which is concerned with self-neglect, and *A House Divided*, which

examines caregiver stress and elder abuse. And each year, either as a specially designated day in June (Elder Abuse Awareness Day) or as part of Seniors Month (June),
prevention and awareness messages about elder abuse and neglect are disseminated
to the public (see www.cnpea.ca and www.onpea.org).

12. For discussions about death and dying, see Albom 1997; Johnson 1999; Auger 2000;
Lawton 2000, 2001; Northcott and Wilson 2001; Kuhl 2002; Ross et al. 2002; Wilson
2002; Bryant 2003; Hayslip and Peveto 2005; Neimeyer and Werth 2005; Seale 2005;
Garrett et al. 2008; Wilson et al. 2008; Leming and Dickinson 2011; and such journals
as *Death Studies, Journal of Palliative Care,* and *Omega: Journal of Death and Dying.*

13. Most of this debate and possible actions, beyond the philosophical, moral, and ethical
aspects, centre on government legislation. Recent reports, books, and articles that
discuss legal matters and aging in Canada and the provinces should be consulted
for a more detailed discussion than is possible in this section. Laws may be changed,
and they often vary across federal and provincial jurisdictions, especially in relation
to Quebec, where the civil code prevails as opposed to common law. In Quebec, the
principles of powers of attorney are called "mandates."

14. A useful book that provides such a questionnaire is *Let Me Decide* (Molloy et al. 1996).

15. Right-to-die issues, pro and con, are discussed by Weir (1997); Braun et al. (2000);
Brogden (2001); Snyder and Caplan (2001); Foley and Hendin (2002); Fisher et al.
(2000); Tulloch (2006); Parliamentary Committee on Palliative and Compassionate
Care (2011); and Yahnke (2003a, 2003b), who has reviewed videos and films about
end-of-life issues and decisions.

16. In Canada, aiding and abetting a suicide is a crime under the Criminal Code and
carries a maximum prison term of 14 years.

17. Information about palliative care can be found in Thomas et al. 2006, Parliamentary
Committee on Palliative and Compassionate Care 2011.

18. Dimensions and the meaning of death have been studied and taught by scholars in
anthropology, biology, chemistry, economics, business, health studies, nursing, medicine, sociology, psychology, philosophy, ethics, law, history, religious studies, social
work, and education.

19. Websites about the funeral home industry include www.funeralnet.com and www.drk
loss.com. Many funeral homes have websites on which they announce deaths, provide
information about death and dying, and give friends of the deceased an opportunity
to express condolences to the family through "electronic sympathy cards" (Roberts
2004). See also a special issue of *Generations* (summer 2004) for articles about funerals
and memorial practices.

20. Changes in obituaries over the years are captured in various anthologies of obituaries
that are available in public libraries.

21. For discussions of public policy for aging societies, see *The Public Policy and Aging
Report* (published by the Gerontological Society of America); the *Canadian Journal
on Aging; Canadian Public Policy;* Canadian Policy Research Network (now under
Carleton University); the Seniors' Policies and Programs Database (http://publications.
gc.ca/site/eng/276636/publication.html); *Policy Horizons* (Government of Canada
Knowledge Organization, www.horizons.gc.ca/eng/search/site/seniors); *A Quebec for
All Ages* (published by the government of Quebec, 2002); Estes et al. 2001; Settersten
2003; Hollander 2007; and Chappell 2011.

Appendix: Study Resources

Internet and World Wide Web Sources

Note: Website addresses change. Those listed were correct as of March 2013. If an address is not accessible, consult your instructor or use a search engine to locate the current address. In addition to the sites listed below, other sites are listed in the text and/or endnotes of many chapters.

Demographic and Statistical Data

CANADA

Canadian Social Research Links: www.canadiansocialresearch.net/index.htm
Statistics Canada: www.statcan.gc.ca/start-debut-eng.html
Statistics Canada: 2006 Census—Portrait of the Canadian Population:
www12.statcan.gc.ca/census-recensement/2006/as-sa/97-550/index-eng.cfm
Statistics Canada: 2011 Census: www12.statcan.gc.ca/census-recensement/index-eng.cfm
Statistics Canada: Proportion of foreign-born population [1994–2001 censuses]:
www.statcan.gc.ca/tables-tableaux/sum-som/l01/cst01/demo47a-eng.htm
Statistics Canada: Report on the demographic situation in Canada (an annual report,
    The Daily): www.statcan.gc.ca/ads-annonces/91-209-x/index-eng.htm

UNITED STATES

International demographic statistics [University of Colorado/Boulder] (US):
    http://ucblibraries.colorado.edu/govpubs/lan/international.htm
National Archive of Computerized Data on Aging (NACDA) (US): www.icpsr.umich.edu/NACDA
Population Reference Bureau (US): www.prb.org
US Census Bureau: www.census.gov
US Census Bureau: 2010 Census: http://2010.census.gov/2010census/#
US Census Bureau: International Data Base (Global demographic statistics):
    www.census.gov/population/international/
US Census Bureau: 2012 Statistical Abstract: www.census.gov/compendia/statab/

UN

United Nations: Population projections: www.unpopulation.org

Electronic Journals and Databases*

American Association of Retired Persons (AARP) Research: www.aarp.org/research/
CSA Sociological Abstracts: www.csa.com/factsheets/socioabs-set-c.php
Demographic Research [Max Planck Institute]: www.demographic-research.org
Journals on Aging [Rutgers University]: http://crab.rutgers.edu/~deppen/journals.htm

SAGE Publications: www.sagepub.com
SAGE KE Science of aging knowledge environment: http://sageke.sciencemag.org/
United Nations: Official Documents and Databases: www.un.org/databases/index.html
WebMD: www.webmd.com

* Several databases need to be accessed through a university library system in order to obtain the full text of journal articles. There are over 100 electronically accessible journals in aging/gerontology.

Newsletters about Aging

Center for Demography of Health and Aging, University of Wisconsin–Madison, *Current Awareness in Aging Report* (weekly report): www.ssc.wisc.edu/cdha/pubs/caar.html
CIHR E-newsletters: www.cihr-irsc.gc.ca/e/26998.html
National Academy on Aging Society, *Public Policy and Aging E-Newsletter:* www.agingsociety.org/agingsociety/publications/public_policy/PPAR_ENewsletter.html
Premium Publishing Corp, *Help's Here* (Resources for Seniors and Caregivers): www.helpshere.com

Bibliographic Sources

CANADA

Institut Universitaire de Gériatrie de Montréal: www.iugm.qc.ca
McMaster University, Faculty of Health Sciences: www.fhs.mcmaster.ca/main/index.html
McMaster University, Social and Economic Dimensions of an Aging Population (SEDAP): http://socserv.socsci.mcmaster.ca/sedap
Simon Fraser University Gerontology Research Centre (GRC): www.sfu.ca/grc/
University of Alberta, Research on Aging, Policies and Practice (RAPP): www.hecol.ualberta.ca/rapp
University of Manitoba, Centre on Aging: www.umanitoba.ca/centres/aging/
University of Manitoba, J.W. Crane Library: http://libguides.lib.umanitoba.ca/deerlodge
University of Western Ontario Aging and Information Technology in the Workplace: www.wane.ca

UNITED STATES

Institute of Gerontology, Wayne State University (US): www.iog.wayne.edu/index.php
University of California, Resource Center on Aging (US): http://garnet.berkeley.edu/~aging
University of North Carolina (UNC) Institute on Aging (IOA) (US): www.aging.unc.edu
University of North Carolina Agelib Digital Library (more resources) (US): www.uncioa.org/agelib/index.asp

Aging Organizations, Associations, and Networks

CANADA

Active Living Coalition for Older Adults (ALCOA): www.alcoa.ca
Alberta Association on Gerontology (AAG): www.aagweb.ca

Alzheimer Society (Canada): www.alzheimer.ca

Association québécoise de gerontology: www.aqg-quebec.org/fr/accueil.aspx?sortcode=1

Canadian Association on Gerontology (CAGACG): www.cagacg.ca

Canadian Association on Gerontology, Student Connection (SC-CE):
    www.cagacg.ca/student-connection/

Canadian Caregiver Coalition (CCC-CCAN): www.ccc-ccan.ca

Canadian Coalition for Seniors' Mental Health (CCSMH): www.ccsmh.ca

Canadian Council on Social Development (CCSD): www.ccsd.ca

Canadian Healthcare Association: www.canadian-healthcare.org

Canadian Home Care Association (CHCA): www.cdnhomecare.ca

Canadian Hospice Palliative Care Association (CHCPA): www.chpca.net

Canadian Mental Health Association (CMHA): www.cmha.ca

Canadian Network for Third Age Learning (CATALIST), University of Regina:
    http://dev.www.uregina.ca/catalist/eindex.html

Canadian Women's Health Network (CWHN): www.cwhn.ca

Council on Aging of Ottawa: www.coaottawa.ca

Council on Aging of Ottawa—Champlain Elder Abuse Response Coalition (CEARC):
    www.coaottawa.ca/elder-abuse/index-en.html

Fifty-Plus (Canadian): www.50plus.com

National Seniors Council (Canada): www.seniorscouncil.gc.ca

Ontario Gerontology Association (OGA) (Canada): http://gerontario.org

Hospice Palliative Care Ontario (HPCO) (Canada): http://hpco.ca

UNITED STATES

American Association of Retired Persons (AARP): www.aarp.org

American Society on Aging (ASA): www.asaging.org

Association for Gerontology in Higher Education (AGHE): www.aghe.org

Caregiver Media Group (US): www.caregiver.com

Caregiving.com (US): www.caregiving.com

ElderCare Online (US): www.ec-online.net

Family Caregiver Alliance (FCA) (US): www.caregiver.org

Gerontological Society of America (GSA) (US): www.geron.org

International Longevity Center (ILC), Columbia University, Mailman School of Public Health
    (US): www.mailman.columbia.edu/academic-departments/centers
    /international-longevity-center

National Academy on an Aging Society (US): www.agingsociety.org/agingsociety

National Association of Professional Geriatric Care Managers (NAPGCM) (US):
    www.caremanager.org

National Council on Aging (NCOA) (US): www.ncoa.org

National Hospice and Palliative Care Organization (NHPCO) (US): www.nhpco.org

INTERNATIONAL

International Association of Gerontology (IAGG): www.iagg.info

International Federation on Ageing (IFA): www.ifa-fiv.org

Long Term Care Planning Network (LTCPN) www.ltcplanningnetwork.com

UN

United Nations (UN): www.un.org
World Health Organization (WHO): www.who.int

Government Resources

CANADA

Aboriginal Affairs and Northern Development Canada: www.aadnc-aandc.gc.ca
CanadaBenefits: www.canadabenefits.gc.ca
Canada Mortgage and Housing Corporation (CMHC): www.cmhc-schl.gc.ca
Canada Mortgage and Housing Corporation (CMHC)—Home Adaptations for Seniors'
    Independence (HASI): www.cmhc-schl.gc.ca/en/co/prfinas/prfinas_004.cfm
Canada Revenue Agency: www.cra-arc.gc.ca
Canadian Institutes of Health Research (CIHR), Institute of Aging (IA):
    www.cihr-irsc.gc.ca/e/8671.html
Canadian Network for the Prevention of Elder Abuse (CNPEA): www.cnpea.ca
Government of Canada portal: www.canada.gc.ca
Health Canada: www.hc-sc.gc.ca
Health Canada, First Nations and Inuit Health: www.hc-sc.gc.ca/fniah-spnia/index-eng.php
Health Canada, Safety and Injuries: www.hc-sc.gc.ca/hl-vs/securit/index_e.html
Health Canada, Seniors: www.hc-sc.gc.ca/hl-vs/seniors-aines/index-eng.php
Healthy Canadians portal: www.healthycanadians.gc.ca
Human Resources and Skills Development Canada (HRSDC) (Public pension plan):
    www.hrdc-drhc.gc.ca
Human Resources and Skills Development Canada (HRSDC), New Horizons for Seniors
    Program (NHSP): www.hrsdc.gc.ca/eng/community_partnerships/seniors/index.shtml
Ontario eHealth: www.ehealthontario.ca (search: seniors)
Ontario Ministry of Health and Long-Term Care: www.health.gov.on.ca
Ontario Ministry of Health and Long-Term Care, Press Releases (2008–12):
    www.health.gov.on.ca/en/news/release/
Ontario Seniors' Info: www.seniorsinfo.ca
Ontario Seniors' Secretariat: www.seniors.gov.on.ca/en/index.php
Seniors Canada: www.seniors.gc.ca/h.4m.2@.jsp?lang=eng
Policy Horizons Canada (Government of Canada Policy Research Initiative):
    www.horizons.gc.ca
Service Canada (Government of Canada Services portal): www.servicecanada.gc.ca
Veterans Affairs Canada: www.veterans.gc.ca

UNITED STATES

Administration on Aging (AOA) (US): www.aoa.gov
National Institutes of Health (NIH) (US): www.nih.gov
National Institutes of Health (NIH), National Institute on Aging (NIA) (US):
    www.nia.nih.gov

Aging Policy and Research

CANADA

Canadian Foundation for Healthcare Improvement (CFHI): www.cfhi-fcass.ca
Canadian Policy Research Networks (CPRN): www.cprn.org
Canadian Social Research Links: www.canadiansocialresearch.net
Institute for Research on Public Policy (IRPP) (Canada): www.irpp.org

UNITED STATES

American Association of Retired Persons (AARP) (US): www.aarp.org
National Association of Home Builders (NAHB) (US): www.nahb.org
National Association of Home Builders (NAHB) NAHB Research Center (US):
    www.nahbrc.org
RAND Corp. (US): www.rand.org
SeniorDriving.AAA.com (US): http://seniordriving.aaa.com

INTERNATIONAL

HelpAge: www. helpage.org
ESA Research Network on Ageing in Europe (RN1): www.ageing-in-europe.org

Selected Programs and Projects on Aging

CANADA

Canadian Longitudinal Study on Aging: www.uofaweb.ualberta.ca/hcic
Hidden Cost/Invisible Contributions of Caregiving: www.uofaweb.ualberta.ca/hcic
McMaster University, Social and Economic Dimensions of an Aging Population (SEDAP):
    http://socserv.socsci.mcmaster.ca/sedap
National Initiative for the Care of the Elderly (NICE): www.nicenet.ca
Population Change and Lifecourse—Strategic Knowledge Cluster: http://sociology.uwo.ca/
    cluster/en/
Workforce Aging in the New Economy (WANE): www.aging.unc.edu/programs/wane/index.
    html

INTERNATIONAL

International Institute for Applied Systems Analysis (IIASA): www.iiasa.ac.at

UN

Ageing: Social Policy and Development Division: http://social.un.org/index/Ageing.aspx

Other Sources on Specific Aging Topics

CANADA

Alcohol and Seniors: www.agingincanada.ca
Coalition for Active Living (CAL): www.activeliving.ca
Creative Retirement Manitoba: www.crm.mb.ca
Lakehead University/Government of Ontario, The Successful Aging Project (Cdn): www.successfulaging.ca/
Public Health Agency of Canada—Physical Activity Tips for Older Adults (65 years and older): www.phac-aspc.gc.ca/hp-ps/hl-mvs/pa-ap/08paap-eng.php

UNITED STATES

AgeWork (jobs in aging), Gerontological Society of America (GSA) (US): http://agework.com
American Academy of Anti-Aging Medicine (A4M) (US): www.a4minfo.net
First Step to Active Health: www.firststeptoactivehealth.com
Global Aging Quiz—University of North Carolina (UNC) Institute on Aging (IOA) (US): www.aging.unc.edu/infocenter/resources2/globalagingquiz.html
Gray Panthers (US): www.graypanthers.org
Living to 100 Life Expectancy Calculator: www.Livingto100.com
McGraw-Hill Higher Education (MHHE) (US)—Sociology Internet Guide: www.mhhe.com/socscience/sociology/guide/
National Center on Senior Transportation (NCST) (US): www.seniortransportation.net
Northwestern Mutual Life Insurance Longevity Game (US): www.northwesternmutual.com/learning-center/the-longevity-game.aspx
Road Scholar educational adventures (US): www.roadscholar.org
Senior resource.com: Resources, retirement communities, and planning (US): www.seniorresource.com
Senior Women Web (US): www.seniorwomen.com
SeniorNet (US): www.seniornet.org

INTERNATIONAL

Asian MetaCenter: www.populationasia.org
ElderWeb: www.elderweb.com
ILC-Japan: International Longevity Center-Japan: http://longevity.ilcjapan.org/
University of Amsterdam, Social Science Information System: www.sociosite.net/index.php
World Bank: www.worldbank.org

UN

UN Economic and Social Development: www.un.org/en/development/index.shtml
UN Women, the United Nations Entity for Gender Equality and the Empowerment of Women: www.un-instraw.org

Glossary

Aboriginal people The original or indigenous inhabitants of Canada, which normally includes three general categories of people, as defined by the government of Canada: Status Indians, Métis, and Inuit.

Acculturation A process in which individuals from one cultural group, through contact with another cultural group, learn and internalize the cultural traits of the other group.

Active life expectancy The number of years an individual can expect to live free of serious disability.

Activities of daily living (ADLs) Basic personal and necessary activities of daily living, such as getting in and out of bed or a chair, dressing, grooming, toileting, and eating.

Age cohort A group of individuals born in the same year (for example, 2008) or within the same period of time (for example, a five- or ten-year period).

Age discrimination The unequal treatment of someone because of their age. This can be preferential but differential treatment, by age, or exclusion from some right on the basis of one's age. It often arises where ageism is present. In some jurisdictions, age discrimination, such as mandatory retirement at age 65, is prohibited by law.

Age grading The process in which age determines social location, roles, norms, and interpersonal relationships.

Age identity Shaped by social observations and interactions with others, people define themselves through speech, dress, behaviour, and thoughts as being younger or older than others.

Age strata Age groups used in a classification system in which individuals are grouped according to chronological age (for example, 10–19, 20–39, 40–59, 60–9, 70–9, 80+).

Age structures Social dimensions of age that affect individuals and society.

Ageism Discriminatory attitudes or actions toward others on the basis of negative perceptions or beliefs about the actual or perceived chronological age of an individual or group.

Agency A process in which individuals construct and shape their biographies across the life course and determine their personal experience of aging (within a unique class, race, or gender structure) by acting or choosing, as opposed to letting events or situations happen to them without being proactive or reactive.

Assimilation A process by which an individual or group becomes more like the dominant group in such cultural elements as language, dress, values, and identity.

Assisted suicide The provision of drugs and/or advice so that a patient can end his or her own life.

Attitudes Learned positive or negative evaluations and responses (verbal or behavioural) toward persons (others or oneself) or situations that are relatively persistent and consistent and that include an emotional component.

Baby boom The large birth cohorts comprising those born in Canada between 1946 and 1965.

Beliefs Socially constructed and shared views that influence the perceptions and behaviour of people.

Biological aging The rate and incidence of biological changes in the muscular, skeletal, reproductive, neural, sensory, and cardiovascular systems that influence the number of years a person is likely to live.

Cautiousness A generalized tendency to respond slowly or not at all to a stimulus or task, perhaps out of fear of making a mistake or in order to complete the task as successfully as possible.

Centenarians Persons ages 100 years or over.

Chronological age norms Expected patterns of behaviour that are based on the chronological age of individuals in a particular society or subculture. These rights and/or responsibilities are assigned or earned by reaching a specific age or stage in life.

Chronological aging The passage of calendar time from one birthday to the next.

Cohort Individuals born in a specific year (1990) or in a specific period of years (1990–5). (See also **generation**.)

Cohort analysis A comparative analysis of specific birth cohorts.

Cohort-centrism Interpretations or views of the world in which generalizations about a social phenomenon (e.g., the aging process or the status or behaviour of older people) are derived on the basis of studying only one age cohort.

Cohort flow A process in which a series of birth cohorts, varying in size and composition, succeed one another over time.

Comorbidity The condition of having more than one illness at a given time, typically connected to an index disease (e.g., persons with diabetes who have one or more other chronic conditions).

Community A geographical space defined by political, municipal, or national geographic boundaries; and/or a concentrated settlement of people with a group identity based on living and interacting with others in the neighbourhood, town, or region or in a religious and ethnic group.

Competence Adaptive behaviour that is demonstrated to varying degrees in a specific situation.

Compression of disability With increasing life expectancy, there is a tendency for the onset of disability (functional status) to occur closer to the end of life (see also **morbidity compression**).

Concept An abstract, generalized idea about an object or a phenomenon that provides a common meaning.

Conflict perspective A sociological view of the world in which society is seen as dynamic and changing, and conflict among groups is inevitable because one or more groups have more power, wealth, or authority than other groups. Change occurs through this conflict and is necessary so that all groups have an equal share of, or an equal chance to obtain, the valued resources.

Creativity The quantitative and qualitative productivity of an individual that is evaluated by others.

Critical perspective A sociological view of the world wherein the social structure fosters inequities (by gender, age, race, class, or ethnicity), which create disadvantages for some members of society that limit their life chances and lifestyles.

Crude birth rate The number of births per 1000 people during a one-year period.

Crude death rate The number of deaths per 1000 people during a one-year period.

Crystallized intelligence Based on education, experience, and acculturation, this type of intelligence involves vocabulary, verbal comprehension, and a numerical ability to solve problems.

Culture A set of shared symbols and their meanings that are passed on to subsequent generations within a society. Some cultural elements are language, dress, art, literature, music, laws, folklore, ceremonies, rituals, sports, and games.

Demographic transition A gradual process in which a society moves from having high rates of fertility and mortality to low rates of fertility and mortality. Populations begin to age when fertility declines and adult mortality rates decline.

Demography A field of study that examines changes in the fertility, mortality, and migration rates of a society and that makes projections pertaining to the future size and composition of the population.

Dependency ratio The number of non-workers who are supported directly or indirectly by members of the labour force.

Disability A physical or mental condition or a health problem that restricts an individual, partially or totally, in the ability to perform a physical, social, or cognitive activity in the manner or within the range considered normal for a human being.

Disability-free life expectancy A measure of the average number of years of life remaining without experiencing disability.

E-health A term used to describe the application and storage of information and communications technologies in the health sector.

Elder abuse A conscious or unconscious physical, psychological, or fraudulent act against a frail or dependent older person. This action may result in physical, psychological, or financial trauma for the older person.

Elder neglect The failure or refusal on the part of a caregiver to meet an older adult's physical or psychological needs.

Empty nest A state experienced by parents once the last child has moved out of the family home, thereby signalling the end of child-rearing.

Environment The sum of the various personal, group, social, and physical components that influence behaviour and life chances throughout the life cycle.

Epidemiological transition A process by which a nation's health improves as nutrition, personal health care, and public sanitation improve. During the transition, the leading causes of death shift from infectious, parasitic, acute, and epidemic illnesses to chronic and degenerative diseases, especially as the population ages.

Ethics An objective and reflective way of thinking about how we should debate and resolve moral or social issues, taking into account the best interests of all involved in the decision or its outcome.

Ethnic subculture A subgroup within a larger society in which members have a common ancestry and an identifiable culture, including customs, beliefs, language, dress, foods, or religion (for example, Cubans, Aboriginal people, East Indians, Italians, Portuguese).

Ethnocentrism A tendency for individuals or groups to consider their own culture as superior to others and as the ideal standard when evaluating the worth of those from other cultures, societies, or groups.

Euthanasia An active or passive action that is taken to end a life.

Family A kinship group in which members are determined by blood, marriage, or common-law ties.

Fertility rate The average number of births per woman through the "normal" child-bearing years from 14 to 49. The replacement level to maintain a consistent population is assumed to be 2.1 births per woman.

Fictive kin Informal, family-like relationship with a friend or neighbour in which the person is viewed almost as a blood relative. Such people often are a core part of the informal social network of older persons who lack legal kin or who do not have legal kin available for support and assistance.

Field-dependent Individuals who are more aware of their social environment, more people-oriented, and generally more conventional in their behaviour.

Field-independent Individuals who are more analytical, more internally directed, and less constrained in their behaviour by tradition and convention.

Filial piety A felt need, duty, or moral obligation to honour and care for one's parents in their middle and later years.

Fluid intelligence Based on the functioning of the nervous system, this type of intelligence involves incidental learning that is necessary for reasoning and problem-solving.

Formal support The provision of assistance and care by formal or voluntary associations in the private sector and by formal agencies in the public sector.

Frailty A disease state that is most common late in life, characterized by muscular weakness, fatigue and low energy, weight loss, slow or unsteady gait, and decreased physical and social activity.

Functional age How well an individual performs specific physical, cognitive, or social tasks at a given age, compared with age norms or the average performance for the task.

Gender The cultural definition of what it means to be male and female. Gender-related behaviour and attributes are linked to the social roles of men and women and to the cultural definitions of masculinity and femininity, which are learned and perpetuated within a culture or a subculture.

Gender relations The interaction of men and women based on the changing definitions and roles of what it means to be male or female in a particular social group.

Generation A unique group of people (for example, baby boomers), born during the same period, who have experienced and reacted similarly to significant social, political, or historical events that emerged at particular points in their life. These special events or factors have led members of the cohort to think and behave in ways that make them different from other generations.

Generational analysis A comparison of age cohorts outside the family structure.

Generational equity The perceived or actual fairness in the distribution of publicly funded resources and obligations across age groups and generations.

Generational unit Within a generation, a subgroup whose members demonstrate unique styles of thought, dress, and behaviour at a particular point in their life (for example, hippies, skinheads, rappers).

Generativity A process in mid-life to late-life wherein individuals become less concerned with the self and more concerned and involved with mentoring others and with contributing to various groups, organizations, or communities.

Gentrification The gradual resettlement and reconstruction of inner-city neighbourhoods by young to middle-aged affluent adults. As a result of this process, the elderly and other low-income groups are usually displaced.

Geriatrics A sub-specialty of medicine that focuses on the physical and mental diseases of later life and on the clinical treatment and care of elderly patients by specialized physicians.

Guardian A person lawfully invested by a court with the power to make some or all personal care decisions on behalf of a person who is mentally incapable of personal care.

Health According to the World Health Organization, a state of complete physical, mental, and social well-being and the capacity to perform activities of daily living and to function with some degree of independence; not merely the absence of disease.

Health literacy The ability to seek and understand health information.

Health transitions The changing states of health as individuals age. These occur because of the dynamic interplay among individual decisions, personal history, and social conditions.

Healthy-immigrant effect The tendency for life expectancy and general health to be higher for immigrants than for persons born in Canada and for this health differential to decline with duration in Canada.

Healthy lifestyles Clusters of health behaviours that influence the health risk faced by individuals as the result of life chances and choices and the social context in which these occur.

Hospice movement A philosophy that promotes "death with dignity" by providing care centres to assist those who are dying from a terminal illness, and to provide support to relatives and friends of the person who is dying.

Hypothesis A prediction about the relationship between two or more variables.

Instrumental activities of daily living (IADLs) Activities of daily living that demonstrate competence and independence, such as preparing meals, shopping, banking and managing finances, cleaning and maintaining a home, driving a car.

Impairment The loss of some physical or mental function.

Incidence The frequency of new occurrences during a specific period of time, usually one year.

Independent variable The antecedent variable that is hypothesized to explain the outcome of a relationship between two or more variables.

Individual aging The structural, physical, sensory, motor, cognitive, and behavioural changes within an individual over a period of years.

Inflation A large increase in the price of consumer goods and services that results in a loss of purchasing power, especially for those whose income remains fixed or whose income rises slower than inflation. Inflation is often measured by the size and the rate of increase in the Consumer Price Index.

Informal support The provision of care and assistance by members of the extended family, neighbours, and friends. This process may or may not involve an exchange of resources.

Intelligence A multi-level concept involving the ability to think logically, to conceptualize, and to reason.

Interpretive perspective A sociological view of the world in which individuals negotiate, define, interpret, and control their involvement in institutionalized social roles, thereby creating and controlling the social order.

Kin keeper A member of the extended family who takes responsibility for informing the family about others and for organizing and perpetuating family rituals.

Leisure Freely selected activities during the time not required for work or for mandatory personal or domestic responsibilities.

Life chances Variation in educational, occupational, and leisure opportunities in early and mid-life that are influenced by social structural attributes, such as gender, social class, religion, race, ethnicity, and place of residence.

Life course A social construct that reflects our personal biography across the time we live.

Life-course perspective A perspective that considers the timing and order of major life events and the dialectical interplay between biographies and population aging, as well as the interplay among the individual, age cohorts, and a changing social structure.

Life expectancy The average number of years of life remaining at a given age (for example, at birth, at age 65).

Lifespan The theoretical maximum number of years an individual can live.

Lifestyle Patterns of thought, behaviour, dress, work, and leisure pursuits that represent personal or group expressions of values, attitudes, orientations, identities, and norms. It represents the outcome of interaction among structural factors, personal resources, and agency (perceived choices and decisions).

Lineage effects A comparison of generations within extended families.

Loneliness A subjective feeling that one lacks personal relationships (emotional or social) and/or meaningful communication with significant others.

Marginalization UNESCO states that "marginalization occurs when people are systematically excluded from meaningful participation in economic, social, political, cultural and other forms of human activity in their communities and thus are denied the opportunity to fulfill themselves as human beings."

Median age The chronological age at which the population is divided into equal numbers of younger and older persons.

Medical iatrogenesis Illness that is induced through contact with the medical system (surgery, hospital-induced infections).

Mental health The ability to think, feel, and interact with others as we encounter challenges in daily life.

Mental illness A disorder of thinking, feeling, and acting that can range from a stressful disorder to an organic brain disease with severe disorientation and memory impairment. The causes of mental illness may be social, psychological, or physical.

Migration Movement by an individual or group from one geographic region to another.

Minimum Data Set Refers to standardized assessment tools used to evaluate health conditions of individuals requiring different types of care.

Minority group A group having subordinate status in the social, political, or economic sense rather than in the numerical sense. Such groups are blocked from full and equal participation in some or all phases of social life because of their age, gender, ethnicity, or race.

Modernization A shift from an agricultural to an industrialized economy or from a "traditional" primitive, rural social system to a "modern" industrialized, urban social system.

Morbidity A state of disease or chronic illness.

Morbidity compression Also known as compression of morbidity. The theory supporting the notion that as people live longer, there is a tendency for the onset of disease to occur closer to the end of life.

Mortality The incidence of death in a population during a period of time.

Multiple jeopardy The presence of several attributes (i.e., ethnicity, gender, and class) that raise the likelihood of marginalization and differential treatment.

Natural growth rate Population growth associated with only births and deaths.

Norm A commonly accepted formal or informal rule about how an individual or group is expected to act in a specific social situation.

Normative perspective A sociological view of the world in which it is assumed that individuals learn, internalize, and accept social rules and roles without question, thereby having little control over their lives.

Old-age dependency ratio The number of retired people supported by those in the labour force who are between 18 and 64 years of age.

Palliative care A type of care that seeks to improve the quality of life for a dying person by relieving his or her physical pain and psychosocial discomfort.

Personality The characteristic style of thought, feeling, and behaviour of an individual, as measured by multi-dimensional traits.

Personality trait A distinguishing characteristic or quality of the human personality (for example, passive, aggressive, extroverted, egocentric, emotional).

Personality type A characteristic way of thinking and behaving that tends to prevail in most or all social settings.

Population aging A demographic phenomenon in which, because of decreased fertility and longer life expectancy, an increasing percentage of the population is made up of older people.

Population displosion A process in which the composition of a population within a geographic region becomes more heterogeneous (for example, in terms of age, wealth, power, education).

Population explosion A demographic process that results in a large increase in the size of a population over a relatively short time (for example, the baby boom from the late 1940s to the mid-1960s).

Population implosion A demographic process in which the population becomes concentrated in urban areas.

Power of attorney A written document that gives someone the power to act on another's behalf in financial matters.

Presbycusis A progressive inability to hear higher-frequency sounds in music and speech.

Presbyopia A progressive loss of flexibility in the lens of the eye that decreases the ability to focus on objects at varying distances.

Prevalence The number of cases of a phenomenon in a population at a specified point in time, such as the number of cases of elder abuse per 1000 older persons.

Prolongevity A significant extension of average life expectancy or maximum lifespan.

Psychological aging Changes in learning ability, memory, creativity, and cognition across the life course, as well as changes in psychological states (moods, attitudes) as a result of personal losses (a job, a spouse) or stressors in one's life.

Public policy The outcome of a decision-making process that leads to laws, procedures, regulations, or programs that help individuals and society to cope with current issues or problems.

Racial subculture A subgroup within a larger society in which biological physical appearances, along with cultural commonalities, combine to define the boundaries of membership (for example, African Canadians, Aboriginal people).

Reaction time The period of time from the perception of a stimulus (such as a red light) and the initiation of an appropriate reaction (such as moving the foot from the accelerator to the brake).

Respite care A service available to caregivers that gives them relief from daily caregiving demands through a daily, weekly, or vacation break. Respite provides brief periods of temporary emotional, psychological, and social normality in a caregiver's life.

Retirement The process of withdrawal from the labour force, normally at or around 65 years of age.

Role A social definition of the behavioural patterns, rights, and responsibilities expected from those occupying a specific status position. These normative expectations serve as guidelines for behaviour in specific situations.

Self-abuse The outcome of a lifestyle in which an individual consumes excessive amounts of alcohol or drugs or ignores normal safety or nutrition practices, thereby placing himself or herself at risk.

Self-care The actions and decisions that an individual takes to maintain and improve health; to prevent, diagnose, and treat personal ill-health; and to use both informal support systems and formal medical services.

Self-concept A subset of personality relating to how we perceive and represent ourselves.

Self-efficacy The perceived confidence that one can accomplish a behavioural change or adopt a new behaviour; deemed an important precursor to making an actual shift in behaviour.

Self-neglect The failure of a person to provide himself or herself with the necessities for physical and mental health, including a safe environment.

Sex The reproductive, physiological, and sexual characteristics that differentiate females from males and influence some aspects of behaviour that are determined by genetic differences in abilities and capacities (e.g., strength, speed).

Sex ratio The number of males per 100 females in a population.

Social aging A process whereby social structures, social norms and values, and social institutions influence how we move across the life course and how we are influenced in our actions by social timetables and by our interactions with other age cohorts.

Social capital A major determinant of health that involves aspects of the community that facilitate mutual support, caring, self-esteem, sense of belonging, and enriched social relationships.

Social institution A cultural product that persists across generations to provide values, norms, beliefs, traditions, and a social structure.

Social determinants of health A number of changeable elements in a person's economic and social environment, including socio-economic status, living and working conditions, and social support from family, friends, and the community.

Social differentiation The separation and ranking of positions based on ascribed attributes (e.g., age, gender, class, ethnicity, race) or achieved roles (e.g., spouse, parent, employee).

Social isolation An objective self-perception that one's social network is small or decreasing and that one lacks social relations with other people.

Social network A set of formal and informal relationships that include a core group (the family) and a more transitory extended group (friends, co-workers, neighbours). The number and availability of members in the network varies at different stages across the life course.

Social phenomenon An observable fact or occurrence that appears in social life on a regular or patterned basis. Most social phenomena stem from the influence of one or more persons on another person or group. They represent patterns of behaviour, thoughts, or events that comprise the basic data and knowledge of sociology.

Social stratification The differential ranking or evaluation of persons in a society or group based on social attributes that are either ascribed (e.g., age, gender, class, race, ethnicity) or achieved (e.g., social class, education). This creates a social structure in which some people are considered superior to, or more worthy or valuable, than others.

Social structure Patterned relationships that differentially rank or distribute individuals according to socially evaluated characteristics (e.g., age, race, gender, social class, ethnicity, education, wealth).

Socialization A complex developmental process by which individuals learn and internalize (adopt) the norms, roles, language, beliefs, and values of a society or subgroup.

Status A culturally defined position in a society or a group that reflects ideas about what rights, responsibilities, and obligations are accorded to specific individuals. The status may be acquired (e.g., by means of education or wealth) or ascribed (because of race, sex, age).

Stereotypes A set of usually biased generalizations about a group that tends to portray an unfavourable and inaccurate image about a person or group who holds some of the observable characteristics (gender, age, race, religion, ethnicity).

Structural lag A period of social change in which social norms and social institutions fail to keep pace with changes in individuals' lives.

Subculture A set of unique and distinctive beliefs, norms, values, symbols, and ideologies that guide the thinking, behaviour, and lifestyles of a subset of the larger population.

Symbolic interactionism A sociological view of the world in which individuals are active participants in defining both the social situation and the self according to how they interpret and define a situation.

Technoplosion A rapid growth in the discovery and adoption of technological developments, which in turn has a significant impact on the work and leisure lifestyles of the population.

Theory A set of interrelated propositions that presents a tentative explanation for a phenomenon.

Values Cultural or subcultural ideas about the desirable goals and behaviour for members of a group. These internalized criteria are employed to judge the appropriateness or inappropriateness of individual and group actions.

Variable A concept (such as age) that has more than one value and to which numbers can be assigned to measure variation from one situation, individual, or group to another situation, individual, or group.

Wisdom An accumulated ability based on experience that enables an individual to adapt to changing situations and to make appropriate decisions.

References

Chapter 1
Aging as a Social Process

Albom, M. 1997. *Tuesdays with Morrie: An Old Man, a Young Man and Life's Greatest Lesson*. New York: Doubleday.

Alkema, G., and D. Alley. 2006. "Gerontology's future: An integrative model for disciplinary advancement." *The Gerontologist* 46 (5): 574–82.

Arber, S., and J. Ginn, Eds. 1995. *Connecting Gender and Aging: A Sociological Approach*. Philadelphia: Open University Press.

––––––. 2005. "Gender dimensions of the age shift." In M. Johnson, Ed., *The Cambridge Handbook of Age and Ageing*, 527–37. New York: Cambridge University Press.

Barfoot, J. 2010. *Exit Lines*. Toronto: Knopf Canada.

Barrett, A. 2003. "Socioeconomic status and age identity: The role of dimensions of health in the subjective construction of age." *Journal of Gerontology: Social Sciences* 58B (2): S101–9.

Bayer, K. 2005. "Cosmetic surgery and cosmetics: Redefining the appearance of age." *Generations* 29 (3): 13–18.

Bengtson, V., and A. Achenbaum, Eds. 1993. *The Changing Contract across the Generations*. New York: Aldine de Gruyter.

Berzlanovich, A., et al. 2005. "Do centenarians die healthy? An autopsy study." *Journal of Gerontology: Medical Sciences* 60A (7): 862–5.

Bialystok, E., and F. Craik, Eds. 2006. *Lifespan Cognition: Mechanisms of Change*. Don Mills, ON: Oxford University Press.

Biggs, S. 2005. "Beyond appearances: Perspectives on identity in later life and some implications for method." *Journal of Gerontology: Social Sciences* 60B (3): S118–28.

Binstock, R. 2003. "The war on anti-aging medicine." *The Gerontologist* 43 (1): 4–14.

Birren, J., and K.W. Schaie, Eds. 2006. *Handbook of the Psychology of Aging*. 6th ed. New York: Academic Press.

Blakeborough, D. 2008. "'Old people are useless': Representations of aging on *The Simpsons*." *Canadian Journal on Aging* 27 (1): 57–67.

Bodily, C. 1991. "I have no opinions, I'm 73 years old: Rethinking ageism." *Journal of Aging Studies* 5 (3): 245–64.

Bonnesen, J., and E. Burgess. 2004. "Senior moments: The acceptability of an ageist phrase." *Journal of Aging Studies* 18 (2): 17–27.

Booth, W., Ed. 1992. *The Art of Growing Older: Writers on Living and Aging*. Toronto: Poseidon Press.

Bowling, A. 2007. "Aspirations for older age in the 21st century: What is successful aging?" *International Journal of Aging and Human Development* 64 (3): 263–97.

Breda, J., and D. Schoenmaekers. 2006. "Age: A dubious criterion in legislation." *Ageing and Society* 26 (4): 529–47.

Butler, R. 1969. "Ageism: Another form of bigotry." *The Gerontologist* 9 (3): 243–6.

––––––. 2002. "Declaration of the Rights of Older Persons." *The Gerontologist* 42 (2): 152–3.

Bytheway, B. 2005a. "Ageism and age categorization." *Journal of Social Issues* 61 (2): 361–74.

––––––. 2005b. "Ageism." In M. Johnson, Ed., *The Cambridge Handbook of Age and Ageing*, 338–45. New York: Cambridge University Press.

Cantor, M. 2006. "No information about me without me: Technology, privacy and home monitoring." *Generations* 30 (2): 49–53.

Chappell, N., and M. Hollander. 2011. "An evidence-based policy prescription for an aging population." *Healthcare Papers* 11 (1): 8–19.

Cheal, D. 2003a. "Aging and demographic change in Canadian context." *Horizons* 6 (2): 21–3.

––––––, Ed. 2003b. *Aging and Demographic Change in Canadian Context*. Toronto: University of Toronto Press.

Clements, G. 2002. "Ethical and legal issues: A legal perspective." In M. Stephenson and E. Sawyer, Eds, *Continuing the Care: The Issues and Challenges for Long-Term Care*, 333–60. Ottawa: CHA Press.

Cohen, E. 2001. "The complex nature of ageism: What is it? Who does it? Who perceives it?" *The Gerontologist* 41 (5): 576–7.

Cole, T., and M. Holstein. 1996. "Ethics and aging." In R. Binstock and L. George, Eds, *Handbook of Aging and the Social Sciences*, 480–97. San Diego: Academic Press.

Connidis, I. 2010. *Family Ties and Aging*. 2nd edn. Thousand Oaks, CA: Pine Forge Press.

Cooper, B. 1984. *Over the Hill*. Freedom, CA: Crossing Press.

Craik, F.I.M., and E. Bialystok. 2006. "Cognition through the lifespan: Mechanisms of change." *Trends in Cognitive Sciences* 10 (3): 131–8.

Dannefer, D. 1999. "Neoteny, naturalization and other constituents of human development." In C. Ryff and V. Marshall, Eds, *The Self and Society in Aging Processes*, 67–93. New York: Springer.

——— . 2003. "Cumulative advantage/disadvantage and the life course: Cross-fertilizing age and social science theory." *Journal of Gerontology: Social Sciences* 58B (6): S327–37.

Dannefer, D., and P. Uhlenberg. 1999. "Paths of the life course: A typology." In V. Bengtson and W. Schaie, Eds, *Handbook of Theories of Aging*, 306–26. New York: Springer.

Dannefer, D., and R. Settersten Jr. 2010. "The study of the life course: Implications for Social Gerontology." In D. Dannefer and C. Phillipson, Eds, *The Sage Handbook of Social Gerontology* 3–19. Thousand Oaks, CA: Sage.

Davenport, J., et al. 2009. Aging in Atlantic Canada: Service-rich and service-poor communities. *Healthcare policy* 12 (1): e132–44.

Davis, N., and D. Friedrich. 2010. "Age stereotypes in middle-aged through old-old adults." *International Journal of Aging and Human Development* 70 (3): 199–212.

de Beauvoir, S. 1970. *The Coming of Age*. New York: W.W. Norton.

Denton, F., and B. Spencer. 2000. "Population aging and its economic costs: A survey of the issues and evidence." *Canadian Journal on Aging* 19 (1): 1–31.

——— . 2002. "Some demographic consequences of revising the definition of 'old age' to reflect future changes in life table probabilities." *Canadian Journal on Aging* 21 (3): 349–56.

Dychtwald, K. 1997. "Wake-up call: The 10 physical, social, spiritual, economic and political crises the boomers will face as they age in the 21st century." *Critical Issues in Aging* 1: 11–15.

Elder, G., and M. Johnson. 2003. "The life course and aging: Challenges, lessons and new directions." In R. Settersten, Ed., *Invitation to the Life Course: Toward a New Understanding of Later Life*, 49–81. New York: Baywood.

Ellis, S., and T. Morrison. 2005. "Stereotypes of ageing: Messages promoted by age-specific paper birthday cards available in Canada." *International Journal of Aging and Human Development* 61 (1): 57–73.

Estes, C. 2005. "Women, ageing and inequality: A feminist perspective." In M. Johnson, Ed., *The Cambridge Handbook of Age and Ageing*, 552–59. New York: Cambridge University Press.

Evans, R., et al. 2001. "Apocalypse no: Population aging and the future of health care systems." *Canadian Journal on Aging* 20 (supplement 1): 160–91.

Fast, J., et al. 2006. *Participation, Roles, and Contributions of Seniors*. Ottawa: Social Development Canada.

Featherstone, M., and M. Hepworth. 2005. "Images of ageing: Cultural representation of later life." In M. Johnson, Ed., *The Cambridge Handbook of Age and Ageing*, 354–62. New York: Cambridge University Press.

Federal/Provincial/Territorial Ministers Responsible for Seniors. 2009. Age-Friendly Rural and Remote Communities: A Guide. www.phac-aspc.gc.ca/seniors-aines/publications/public/healthy-sante/age_friendly_rural/index-eng.php.

Ferraro, K. 2006. "Gerontology's future: An integrative model for disciplinary advancement." *The Gerontologist* 46 (5): 571–3.

Fischer, D. 1977. *Growing Old in America*. London: Oxford University Press.

Fisher, A., and J. Morley. 2002. "Antiaging medicine: The good, the bad and the ugly." *Journal of Gerontology: Medical Sciences* 57A (10): M636–9.

Friedland, R., and L. Summer. 1999. *Demography Is Not Destiny*. Washington: National Academy on an Aging Society.

Gee, E. 2000. "Population and politics: Voodoo demography, population aging, and Canadian social policy." In E. Gee and G. Gutman, Eds, *The Overselling of Population Aging: Apocalyptic Demography, Intergenerational Challenges and Social Policy*, 5–25. Don Mills, ON: Oxford University Press.

Gee, E., and G. Gutman, Eds. 2000. *The Overselling of Population Aging: Apocalyptic Demography, Intergenerational Challenges and Social Policy*. Don Mills, ON: Oxford University Press.

Gee, E., and M. Kimball. 1987. *Women and Aging*. Toronto: Butterworths.

Giddens, A. 1984. *The Constitution of Society*. Cambridge: Polity.

Gotlieb, B., and Gillespie, A. 2008. "Volunteerism, health, and civic engagement among older adults." *Canadian Journal on Aging* 27 (4): 399–406.

Gruman, G. 2003. *A History of Ideas about the Prolongation of Life*. New York: Springer.

Hagestad, G., and P. Uhlenberg. 2005. "The social separation of old and young: A root of ageism." *Journal of Social Issues* 61 (2): 343–60.

Hareven, T. 2001. "Historical perspectives on aging and family relations." In R. Binstock and L. George, Eds, *Handbook of Aging and the Social Sciences*, 141–59. New York: Academic Press.

Harris, D., and P. Changas. 1994. "Revision of Palmore's Facts on Aging Quiz from a true-false to a multiple-choice format." *Educational Gerontology* 20 (6): 741–54.

Hébert, R. 2002. "Research on aging: Providing evidence for rescuing the Canadian health care system." *Canadian Journal on Aging* 21 (3): 343–7.

Hébert, R. 2011. "Public long-term care insurance: A way to ensure sustainable continuity of care for older people." *Healthcare Quarterly* 11 (1): 69–75.

Heinz, W., and V. Marshall, Eds. 2003. *Social Dynamics of the Life Course: Transitions, Institutions and Interrelations*. Hawthorne, NY: Aldine de Gruyter.

Hendricks, J. 2004. "Public policies and old age identity." *Journal of Aging Studies*, 18 (3): 245–60.

Hess, T. 2006. "Attitudes toward aging and their effects on behavior." In J. Birren and W. Scaie, Eds, *Handbook of the Psychology of Aging*, 379–406. San Diego: Academic Press.

Hicks, P. 2003. "The policy implications of aging: A transformation of national and international thinking." *Horizons* 6 (2): 12–16.

Hudson, R., Ed. 2004. "The pros and cons of anti-aging medicine." *Public Policy and Aging Report* 14 (2): 1–31.

Hurd, L. 1999. "'We're not old!': Older women's negotiation of aging and oldness." *Journal of Aging Studies* 13 (4): 419–39.

Johnson, T., Ed. 1999. *Handbook on Ethical Issues in Aging*. Westport, CT: Greenwood.

Jolanki, O., et al. 2000. "Old age as a choice and as a necessity: Two interpretive repertoires." *Journal of Aging Studies* 14 (4): 359–72.

Kapp, M. 2006. "Aging and the law." In R. Binstock and L George, Eds, *Handbook of Aging and the Social Sciences*, 419–35. San Diego: Academic Press.

Kaufman, S., et al. 2004. "Revisiting the biomedicalization of aging: Clinical trends and ethical challenges." *The Gerontologist* 44 (6):731–8.

Kaufman, G., and G. Elder. 2002. "Revisiting age identity: A research note." *Journal of Aging Studies* 16 (2): 169–76.

———. 2003. "Grandparenting and age identity." *Journal of Aging Studies* 17 (3): 269–82.

Keating, N., Ed. 2008. *Rural Ageing: A Good Place to Grow Old?* London, UK: Policy Press.

Kenyon, G., et al. 2001. *Narrative Gerontology: Theory, Research and Practice*. New York: Springer.

Kessler, E., et al. 2004. "The portrayal of older people in prime time television series: The match with gerontological evidence." *Ageing and Society* 24: 531–52.

Kimmel, M. 2000. *The Gendered Society*. New York: Oxford University Press.

Kinsella, K., and W. He. 2009. *An Aging World: 2008*. US Census Bureau, series P95/09-1. Washington: US Government Printing Office.

Kinsella, K., and D. Phillips. 2005. "Global aging: The challenge of success." *Population Bulletin* 60 (1): 1–44.

Land, K., and Y. Yang. 2006. "Morbidity, disability and mortality." In R. Binstock and L. George, Eds, *Handbook of Aging and the Social Sciences*, 41–58. San Diego: Academic Press.

Laurence, M. 1964. *The Stone Angel*. Toronto: McClelland and Stewart–Bantam.

Law Commission of Canada. 2004. *Does Age Matter? Law and Relationships between Generations*. Ottawa: Law Commission of Canada.

Layder, D. 1994. *Understanding Social Theory*. Thousand Oaks, CA: Sage.

Lee, M., et al. 2007. "Representations of older adults in television advertisements." *Journal of Aging Studies* 21 (1): 23–30.

Lin, M.-C., et al. 2004. "Representation of age identities in on-line discourse." *Journal of Aging Studies* 18 (2): 261–74.

Longhofer, J. 1994. "Nursing home utilization: A comparative study of the Hutterian Brethren, the old order Amish, and the Mennonites." *Journal of Aging Studies* 8(1): 95–120.

Longino, C. 2005. "The future of ageism: Baby boomers at the doorstep." *Generations* 29 (3): 79–83.

McDaniel, S. 1986. *Canada's Aging Population*. Toronto: Butterworths.

———. 2004. "Generationing gender: Justice and the division of welfare." *Journal of Aging Studies* 18 (1): 27–44.

McDonald, L., et al. 2000. "The economic consequences of unexpected early retirement. In B. Spencer and F. Denton, Eds, *Independence and Economic Security in Old Age*, 267–92. Vancouver: University of British Columbia Press.

McPherson, B. 1983. *Aging as a Social Process: An Introduction to Individual and Population Aging*. Toronto: Butterworths.

Marshall, V. 1980. *Aging in Canada: Social Perspectives*. Don Mills, ON: Fitzhenry and Whiteside.

———. 1994. "Social research on aging: Retrospect and prospect." In J. Frideres and C. Bruce (Eds.), *The Impact of an Aging Population on Society, 1-21*. Calgary: Faculty of Social Sciences.

———. 2000. "Agency, structure, and the life course in the era of reflexive modernization." Paper presented at the American Sociological Association annual meeting, August, Washington.

Marshall, V., and J. McMullin. 2010. "The life course perspective and public policy formation: Observations on the Canadian case." In G. Naegele (Ed.), *Social Life Course Policy*, 732–47. New York: Springer Verlag.

Martin-Matthews, A., et al. 1984. "The Facts on Aging Quiz: A Canadian validation and cross-cultural comparison." *Canadian Journal on Aging* 3 (4): 165–74.

Martin-Matthews, A., and F. Béland, Eds. 2001. *Canadian Journal on Aging* 20 (supplement 1).

Masoro, E., and S. Austad, Eds. 2006. *Handbook of the Biology of Aging.* 6th edn. San Diego: Academic Press.

Mehlman, M., et al. 2004. "Anti-aging medicine: Can consumers be better protected?" *The Gerontologist* 44 (3): 304–10.

Miller, D., et al. 2004. "Stereotypes of the elderly in US television commercials from the 1950s to the 1990s." *International Journal of Human Development* 58 (4): 315–40.

Miller, R., and R. Dodder. 1980. "A revision of Palmore's Facts on Aging Quiz." *The Gerontologist* 20 (6): 673–9.

Mills, C.W. 1959. *The Sociological Imagination.* Oxford: Oxford University Press.

Mitchell, B. 2003. "Life course theory." In J. Ponzetti, Ed., *The International Encyclopedia of Marriage and Family Relationships*, 2nd edn, 1051–5. New York: Macmillan Reference USA.

Moen, P. 2001. "The gendered life course." In R. Binstock and L. George, Eds, *Handbook of Aging and the Social Sciences*, 179–96. New York: Academic Press.

Moody, H. 1996. *Ethics in an Aging Society.* Baltimore, MD: Johns Hopkins University Press.

Morgan, J. 1996. *Ethical Issues in the Care of the Dying and Bereaved Aged.* Amityville, NY: Baywood.

Morgan, R., and S. David. 2002. "Human rights: A new language for aging advocacy." *The Gerontologist* 42 (4): 436–42.

Morrow-Howell, N. 2010. "Volunteering in later life: Research frontiers." *Journal of Gerontology: Social Sciences* 65B (4): B461–9.

Myles, J. 2002. "Back to Bismarck? The public policy implications of living longer." *Canadian Journal on Aging* 21 (3): 325–9.

NACA (National Advisory Council on Aging). 1993a. *Ethics and Aging.* Ottawa: NACA.

———. 1993b. *Expression* 9 (1): 2. Ottawa: NACA.

———. 2003. *Interim Report Card: Seniors in Canada, 2003.* Ottawa: NACA.

Nelson, T., Ed. 2002. *Ageism: Stereotyping and Prejudice against Older Persons.* Cambridge, MA: MIT Press.

———. 2005. "Ageism: Prejudice against our feared future self." *Journal of Social Issues* 61 (2): 207–21.

Olshansky, S.J., et al. 2002. "Position statement on human aging." *Journal of Gerontology: Biological Sciences* 57A (8): B292–7.

O'Rand, A. 1996. "The cumulative stratification of the life course." In R. Binstock and L. George, Eds, *Handbook of Aging and the Social Sciences*, 188–207. San Diego: Academic Press.

Palmore, E. 1977. "Facts on aging: A short quiz." *The Gerontologist* 17 (4): 315–20.

———. 1980. "The Facts on Aging Quiz: A review of findings." *The Gerontologist* 20 (6): 669–72.

———. 1981. *The Facts on Aging Quiz: A Handbook of Uses and Results.* New York: Springer.

———. 1988. *The Facts on Aging Quiz: A Handbook of Uses and Results.* New York: Springer.

———. 1990. *Ageism: Negative and Positive.* New York: Springer.

———. 2000. "Ageism in gerontological language." *The Gerontologist* 40 (6): 645.

———. 2001. "The ageism survey: First findings." *The Gerontologist* 41 (5): 572–5.

Palmore, E., et al., Eds. 2005. *Encyclopedia of Ageism.* Binghampton, NY: Haworth.

Pearlin, L. 2009. "The life course and the stress process: Some conceptual comparisons." *Journal of Gerontology: Social Sciences*, 65B (2): 207–15.

Population Reference Bureau. 2011. *The 2011 World Population Data Sheet.* Washington: Population Reference Bureau.

Pratt, H. 1976. *The Gray Lobby.* Chicago: University of Chicago Press.

Raina, P., et al. 2009. "The Canadian Longitudinal Study on Aging." *Canadian Journal on Aging* 28 (3): 221–9.

Randall, W., and G. Kenyon. 2004. "Time, story, and wisdom: Emerging theories in narrative gerontology." *Canadian Journal on Aging* 23 (4): 333–46.

Riley, J. 2001. *Rising Life Expectancy: A Global History.* New York: Cambridge University Press.

Robinson, T., et al. 2007. "The portrayal of older characters in Disney animated films." *Journal of Aging Studies* 21 (3): 203–13.

Rodriguez, L. 1992. "Susanna re-membered." *Canadian Woman Studies* 12 (2): 24–30.

Ross, M., et al. 2002. "End of life care: The experience of seniors and informal caregivers." *Canadian Journal on Aging* 21 (1): 137–46.

Rowe, G. 2003. "Fragments of lives: Enabling new policy directions through integrated life-course data." *Horizons* 6 (2): 7–11.

Rozanova, J., et al. 2006. "'Seniors' portrayals of intra-generational and inter-generational inequality in *The Globe and Mail*." *Canadian Journal on Aging* 25 (4): 373–86.

Settersten, R. 2005. "Linking the two ends of life: What gerontology can learn from childhood studies." *Journal of Gerontology: Social Sciences* 60B (4): S173–80.

———. 2002. "Declaration of the Rights of Older Persons." *The Gerontologist* 42 (2): 152–3.

Sheets, D., and E. Gallagher. 2013. "Aging in Canada: State of the art and science." *The Gerontologist* 53 (1): 1–8.

Smith, G. 1996. *Legal and Healthcare Ethics for the Elderly.* Washington: Taylor and Francis.

Smith, G., et al. 2000. "The effects of interpersonal and personal agency on perceived control and psychological well-being in adulthood." *The Gerontologist* 40 (4): 458–68.

Sontag, S. 1972. "The double standard of aging." *The Saturday Review of the Society* 1 (1): 29–38.

Statistics Canada. 2011. *Life Expectancy at Birth, by Sex and by Province.* CANSIM table 102-0512 and catalogue no. 84F-537-XIA. Ottawa: Statistics Canada. www.statcan.gc.ca/l01/cst01/health26-eng .htm, retrieved 28 December 2011.

Statistics Canada. 2012. *2011 Census of Population.* Catalogue no. 98-312-XCB2011041. Ottawa: Statistics Canada.

Timiras, P., Ed. 2002. *Physiological Basis of Aging and Geriatrics.* Boca Raton, FL: CRC Press.

Tollefsbol, T., Ed. 2010. *Epigenetics of Aging.* New York, NY: Springer.

Twigg, J. 2007. "Clothing, age, and the body: A critical review." *Ageing and Society* 27 (2): 285–305.

United Nations. 2007. *World Population Ageing, 2007.* New York: United Nations Department of Economic and Social Affairs, Population Division. www.un.org/esa/socdev/ageing/agewpop.htm.

US Census Bureau. 2012. *International Data Base, Regional Summaries,* Retrieved 23 August 2012.

Vincent, J. 2008. "The cultural construction of old age as a biological phenomenon: Science and anti-ageing technologies." *Journal of Ageing Studies* 22: 331–9.

Voyer, G. 1998. "What is ethical care?" *Canadian Journal on Aging* 17 (1): i–vii.

Westerof, G., and A. Barrett. 2005. "Age identity and subjective well-being: A comparison of the United States and Germany." *Journal of Gerontology: Social Sciences* 60B (3): S129–36.

Wister, A.V. 2011. "Population pressures, system-level inertia and healthy aging policy revisited: Commentary to 'an evidence-based policy prescription for an aging population.'" *Healthcare Papers* 11: 41–5.

Yahnke, R., and R. Eastman. 1995. *Literature and Gerontology: A Research Guide.* Westport, CT: Greenwood.

Chapter 2

Historical and Cultural Perspectives on Aging

Achenbaum, A. 1996. "Historical perspectives on aging." In R. Binstock and L. George, Eds, *Handbook of Aging and the Social Sciences*, 137–52. San Diego: Academic Press.

———.2010. "Past as prologue: Toward a global history of ageing." In D. Dannefer and C. Phillipson, Eds, *The Sage Handbook of Social Gerontology*: 20–32. Thousand Oaks, CA: Sage.

Albert, S., and M. Cattell. 1994. *Old Age in Global Perspective.* New York: G.K. Hall.

Amoss, P., and S. Harrell, Eds. 1981. *Other Ways of Growing Old: Anthropological Perspectives.* Stanford, CA: Stanford University Press.

Andersson, L., Ed. 2002. *Cultural Gerontology.* Westport, CT: Greenwood.

Angel, R., and J. Angel. 2006. "Diversity and aging in the United States." In R. Binstock and L. George, Eds, *Handbook of Aging and the Social Sciences*, 94–110. San Diego: Academic Press.

Baker, S., and V. Kirkness. 1994. *Khot-La-Cha: The Autobiography of Chief Simon Baker.* Vancouver: Douglas and McIntyre.

Bengtson, V., et al., Eds. 2000. *Aging in East and West: Families, States and the Elderly.* New York: Springer.

Bond, J., et al. 1987. "Familial support of the elderly in a rural Mennonite community." *Canadian Journal on Aging* 6 (1): 7–17.

Buchignani, N., and C. Armstrong-Esther. 1999. "Informal care and older Native Canadians." *Ageing and Society* 19 (1): 3–32.

Burgess, E., Ed. 1960. *Aging in Western Societies.* Chicago: University of Chicago Press.

Chappell, N., and K. Kusch. 2007. "The gendered nature of filial piety: A study among Chinese Canadians." *Journal of Cross-Cultural Gerontology* 22 (1): 29–45.

Cheung, C., and A. Kwan. 2009. "The erosion of filial piety by modernization in Chinese cities." *Ageing & Society* 29: 179–98.

Chui, T., et al. 2005. "Chinese Canadians: Enriching the cultural mosaic." *Canadian Social Trends* Spring: 24–32.

CIC. (2010). "Sponsoring your family: Eligible relatives—Who can apply?" www.cic.gc.ca/english /immigrate/sponsor/relativesapply-who.asp, 12 June.

Connidis, I. 2010. *Family Ties and Aging.* 2nd edn. Thousand Oaks, CA: Pine Forge Press.

Cooke, M., et al. 2008. "The changing well-being of older adult registered Indians: An analysis using the Registered Indian Human Development Index." *Canadian Journal on Aging* 27 (4): 385–97.

Cowgill, D. 1974a. "The aging of populations and societies." *The Annals of the American Academy of Political and Social Science* 415 (September): 1–18.

———. 1974b. "Aging and modernization: A revision of the theory." In J. Gubrium, Ed., *Late Life*:

Communities and Environmental Policy, 123–46. Springfield, IL: Charles C. Thomas.

———. 1986. *Aging around the World*. Belmont, CA: Wadsworth.

Cowgill, D., and L. Holmes. 1972. *Aging and Modernization*. New York: Appleton-Century-Crofts.

de Beauvoir, S. 1972. *The Coming of Age*. New York: Putnam.

Elliott, G., Ed. 1999. *Cross-Cultural Awareness in an Aging Society*. Hamilton, ON: Office of Gerontological Studies, McMaster University.

Finkelstein, S., D. Forbes, and C. Richmond. 2012. "Formal dementia care among First Nations in Southwestern Ontario." *Canadian Journal on Aging* 31 (3): 257–70.

Foner, N. 1984. *Ages in Conflict: A Cross-Cultural Perspective on Inequality between Old and Young*. New York: Columbia University Press.

Fry, C., Ed. 1980. *Aging in Culture and Society: Comparative Viewpoints and Strategies*. New York: Praeger.

———. 1985. "Culture, behavior and aging in comparative perspective." In J. Birren and W. Schaie, Eds, *Handbook of the Psychology of Aging*, 216–44. New York: Van Nostrand Reinhold.

———. 1988. "Theories of age and culture." In J. Birren and V. Bengtson, Eds, *Emergent Theories of Aging*, 447–81. New York: Springer.

———. 1996. "Age, aging and culture." In R. Binstock and L. George, Eds, *Handbook of Aging and the Social Sciences*, 117–36. San Diego: Academic Press.

———. 1999. "Anthropological theories of age and aging." In V. Bengtson and W. Schaie, Eds, *Handbook of Theories of Aging*, 271–86. New York: Springer.

———. 2010. "Social anthropology and ageing." In D. Dannefer and C. Phillipson, Eds, *The Sage Handbook of Social Gerontology* 48–60. Thousand Oaks, CA: Sage.

Gilleard, C. 2007. "Old age in Byzantine society." *Ageing & Society* 27: 623–42.

Gilleard, C. 2009. "Old age in the Dark Ages: The status of old age during the Middle Ages." *Ageing & Society* 29: 1065–84.

Goins, R., and S. Spencer. 2005. "Public health issues among older American Indians and Alaska Natives." *Generations*, 29 (2): 30–5.

Goins, R., et al. 2007. "Disability among older American Indians and Alaska natives: An Analysis of the 2000 Census Public Use Microdata Sample." *Gerontologist* 47 (5): 690–8.

Gutmann, D. 1976. "Alternatives to disengagement: The old men of the Highland Druze." In J. Gubrium, Ed., *Time, Roles and Self in Old Age*, 88–108. New York: Human Sciences Press.

Haber, C. 2006. "Old age through the lens of family history." In R. Binstock and L. George, Eds, *Handbook of Aging and the Social Sciences*, 59–75. San Diego: Academic Press.

Hashimoto, A., and C. Ikels. 2005. "Filial piety in changing Asian societies." In M. Johnson, Ed., *The Cambridge Handbook of Age and Ageing*, 437–42. New York: Cambridge University Press.

Havighurst, R., et al., Eds. 1969. *Adjustment to Retirement: A Cross-national Study*. Assen, The Netherlands: Van Gorcum.

Health and Welfare Canada. 1992. *Aboriginal Health in Canada*. Ottawa: Minister of Supply and Services.

Health Canada. 2002. *Canada's Aging Population: A Report*. Ottawa: Minister of Public Works and Government Services Canada.

Hendricks, J. 1982. "The elderly in society: Beyond modernization." *Social Science History* 6 (3): 321–45.

Herrera, E. 1994. "A mother's plea for independence." *The Moment* 21: 11. Toronto: Centre for Spanish-Speaking People.

Holmberg, A. 1969. *Nomads of the Long Bow*. Garden City, NY: Natural History Press.

Ikels, C., et al., Eds. 2004. *Filial Piety: Practices and Discourse in Contemporary East Asia*. Stanford, CA: Stanford University Press.

Ilels, C., and C. Beall. 2001. "Age, aging and anthropology." In R. Binstock and L. George, Eds, *Handbook of Aging and the Social Sciences*, 125–40. New York: Academic Press.

Indian and Northern Affairs Canada. 1995. *Highlights of Aboriginal Conditions, 1991, 1986*. Catalogue. no. R32-15411-1986E. Ottawa: Minister of Public Works and Government Services Canada.

Jervis, L., et al. 2002. "Need for, availability of, and barriers to the provision of long term care services for older American Indians." *Journal of Cross-Cultural Gerontology* 17: 295–311.

Katz, S. 2005. *Cultural Aging: Life Course, Lifestyle and Senior Worlds*. Peterborough, ON: Broadview.

Keith, J. 1982. *Old People as People: Social and Cultural Influences on Aging and Old Age*. Cambridge, MA: Winthrop.

———. 1985. "Age in anthropological research." In R. Binstock and E. Shanas, Eds, *Handbook of Aging and the Social Sciences*, 231–63. New York: Van Nostrand Reinhold.

———. 1990. "Age in social and cultural contexts: Anthropological perspectives." In R. Binstock and L. George, Eds, *Handbook of Aging and the Social Sciences*, 91–111. San Diego: Academic Press.

Keith, J., et al., Eds. 1994. *The Aging Experience: Diversity and Commonality across Cultures*. Thousand Oaks, CA: Sage.

Kobayashi, K. 2000. "The nature of support from adult Sansei (third generation) children to older Nisei (second generation) parents in Japanese Canadian families." *Journal of Cross-Cultural Gerontology* 15 (3): 185–205.

Kobayashi, K., and L. Funk. 2010. "Of the family tree: Congruence on filial obligation between older parents and adult children in Japanese Canadian families." *Canadian Journal on Aging* 29 (1): 85–96.

Koehn, S. 2009. "Negotiating candidacy: Ethnic minority seniors' access to care." *Ageing & Society* 29: 585–608.

Koehn, S., Spencer, C., & Hwang, E. 2010. "Promises, promises: Cultural and legal dimensions of sponsorship for immigrant seniors." In D. Durst, & M. MacLean, Eds, *Diversity and Aging among Immigrant Seniors in Canada: Changing Faces and Greying Temples,* 79–102. Calgary, AB: Detselig Enterprises Ltd.

Lai, D. 1988. *Chinatowns: Towns within Cities in Canada.* Vancouver: University of British Columbia Press.

Laslett, P. 1985. "Societal development and aging." In R. Binstock and E. Shanas, Eds, *Handbook of Aging and the Social Sciences,* 199–230. New York: Van Nostrand Reinhold.

Leviatan, U. 1999. "Contribution of social arrangements to the attainment of successful aging: The experience of the Israeli kibbutz." *Journal of Gerontology: Psychological Sciences* 54B (4): 205–13.

Maxwell, R., and P. Silverman. 1970. "Information and esteem: Cultural consideration in the treatment of the aged." *Aging and Human Development* 1 (4): 361–92.

Mehta, K. 1997. "Respect redefined: Focus group insights from Singapore." International *Journal of Aging and Human Development* 44 (3): 205–19.

Mitchell, B. 2012. *Family Matters: An Introduction to Family Sociology in Canada.* 2nd edn. Toronto: Canadian Scolars' Press Inc.

Mjelde-Mossey, L., and E. Walz. 2006. "Changing cultural and social environments: Implications for older East Asian women." *Journal of Women and Aging* 18 (1): 5–20.

NACA (National Advisory Council on Aging). 2005. *Seniors on the Margins: Seniors from Ethnocultural Minorities.* Ottawa: NACA.

NACDD (National Association of Chronic Disease Directors). 2010. Caregiving in Indian Country: Conversations with Family Caregivers. www.chronicdisease.org/i4a/pages/index.cfm?pageid=3838, 12 September.

Newhouse, D., and E. Peters, Eds. 2003. *Not Strangers in These Parts: Urban Aboriginal Peoples.* Ottawa: Policy Research Initiative.

Ng, A., et al. 2002. "Persistence and challenges of filial piety and informal support of older persons in a modern Chinese society: A case study in Tuen Mun, Hong Kong." *Journal of Aging Studies* 16 (2): 135–53.

Ogawa, N., and R. Retherford. 1993. "Care of the elderly in Japan: Changing norms and expectations." *Journal of Marriage and the Family* 55 (3): 585–97.

Ontario Advisory Council on Senior Citizens. 1993. *Denied Too Long: The Needs and Concerns of Seniors Living on First Nations Communities in Ontario.* Toronto: The Council.

Population Reference Bureau. 2011. *2011 World Population Data Sheet.* Washington: Population Reference Bureau.

Quadagno, J. 1982. *Aging in Early Industrial Society: Work, Family and Social Policy in Nineteenth Century England.* New York: Academic Press.

Quadagno, J., and J. Janzen. 1987. "Old age security and the family life course: A case study of nineteenth-century Mennonite immigrants to Kansas." *Journal of Aging Studies* 1 (1): 33–49.

Salari, S. 2002. "Invisible in aging research: Arab Americans, Middle Eastern immigrants and Muslims in the United States" *The Gerontologist* 42 (5): 580–8.

Schaie, W., and G. Elder, Eds. 2005. *Historical Influences on Lives and Aging.* New York: Springer.

Shanas, E., et al. 1968. *Old People in Three Industrial Societies.* New York: Atherton.

Shemirani, F., and D. O'Connor. 2006. "Aging in a foreign country: Voices of Iranian women aging in Canada." *Journal of Women and Aging* 18 (2): 73–90.

Shin, E., and J. Lee. 1989. "Convergence and divergence in the status of the aged: An analysis of cross-national and longitudinal variations in 32 selected countries." *Journal of Aging Studies* 3 (3): 263–78.

Simmons, L. 1945. *The Role of the Aged in Primitive Society.* New Haven, CT: Yale University Press.

———. 1952. "Social participation of the aged in different cultures." *The Annals of the American Academy of Political and Social Science* 279 (January): 43–51.

———. 1960. "Aging in preindustrial societies." In C. Tibbits, Ed., *Handbook of Social Gerontology,* 60–91. Chicago: University of Chicago Press.

Smith, A., and K. Kobayashi. 2002. "Making sense of Alzheimer's disease in an intergenerational context: The case of a Japanese Canadian Nisei (second-generation)-headed family." *Dementia: The International Journal of Social Research and Practice* 1 (2): 213–25.

Sokolovsky, J., Ed. 1997. *The Cultural Context of Aging: Worldwide Perspectives.* Westport, CT: Bergin and Garvey.

Statistics Canada. 2001. *Aboriginal Peoples in Canada.* Profile series catalogue. no. 85F0033MIE. Ottawa: Statistics Canada.

————. 2002. *How Healthy Are Canadians? A Summary 2002 Annual Report*. Catalogue no. 82-003-SIE. Ottawa: Statistics Canada.

————. 2003a. *Aboriginal Peoples Survey, 2001: Initial Findings: Well-Being of the Non-reserve Aboriginal Population*. Catalogue no. 89-589-XIE. Ottawa: Statistics Canada.

————. 2003b. *Aboriginal Peoples of Canada, 2001 Census*. Catalogue no. 94F00041XCB. Ottawa: Statistics Canada.

————. 2007. "2006 census: Immigration, citizenship, language, mobility and migration." *The Daily* 4 December. Ottawa: Statistics Canada.

————. 2008a. *Aboriginal Identity Population, 2006 Counts, Percentage Distribution, Percentage Change for Both Sexes, for Canada, Provinces and Territories, 20% Sample Data*. www12.statcan.ca/english/cennsus06/data/Aboriginal, 22 February.

————. 2008b. *Population by Age Groups, sex, and Aboriginal Identity Groups, 2006 Counts, for Canada, Provinces and Territories, 20% Sample Data*. www12.statcan.ca/english/census06/data/highlights/Aboriginal, 22 February.

————. 2012. *Immigrant languages in Canada*. www12.statcan.gc.ca/census-recensement/2011/as-sa/98-314-x/98-314-x2011003_3-eng.cfm, 29 November.

Stearns, P., Ed. 1982. *Old Age in Preindustrial Society*. New York: Holmes and Meier.

Stewart, M.J., et al. 2006. "Immigrant women family caregivers in Canada. Implications for policies and programmes in health and social sectors." Health and Social Care in the Community, 14 (4), 329–40.

Sung, K.-T. 2001. "Elder respect: Exploration of ideals and forms in East Asia." *Journal of Aging Studies* 15 (1): 13–26.

Takagi, E., and M. Silverstein. 2006. "Intergenerational coresidence of the Japanese elderly: Are cultural norms proactive or reactive?" *Research on Aging* 28 (4): 473–92.

Tsutsui, T., and N. Muramatsu. 2007. "Japan's universal long-term care system reform of 2005: Containing costs and realizing a vision." *Journal of the American Geriatrics Society* 55: 1458–63.

Turcotte, M., and G. Schellenberg. 2007. *A Portrait of Seniors in Canada*, 2006. Ottawa: Statistics Canada.

Vanderburgh, R. 1987. "Modernization and aging in the Anicinabe context." In V. Marshall, Ed., *Aging in Canada: Social Perspectives*, 100–10. Markham, ON: Fitzhenry and Whiteside.

White, J., et al., Eds. 2003. *Aboriginal Conditions: Research as a Foundation for Public Policy*. Vancouver: University of British Columbia Press.

Wilson, K., et al. 2010. "Aging and health: An examination of differences between older Aboriginal and non-Aboriginal people." *Canadian Journal on Aging* 29 (3): 369–82.

Wilson, K., et al. 2011. "Aboriginal peoples. Health and healing approaches: The effects of age and place on health." *Social Science and Medicine* 72: 355–64.

Wister, A.V., and C. Moore. 1998. "First Nations elders in Canada: Issues, problems and successes in health care policy." In A.V. Wister and G. Gutman, Eds, *Health Systems and Aging in Selected Pacific Rim Countries: Cultural Diversity and Change*, 103–24. Vancouver: Simon Fraser University, Gerontology Research Centre.

Yeo, G. 1993. "Ethnicity and nursing homes: Factors affecting use and successful components for culturally sensitive care." In C. Barresi and D. Stull, Eds, *Ethnic Elderly and Long-Term Care*, 161–77. New York: Springer.

Yoon, H., and J. Hendricks, Eds. 2006. *Handbook of Asian Aging*. Amityville, NY: Baywood.

Chapter 3

Individual Aging: Physical and Psychological Change across the Life Course

Abrams, L., et al. 2010. "Older adults' detection of misspellings during reading." *Journal of Gerontology: Psychological Sciences* 65B (6): 680–3.

Ackerman, P. 2008. "Knowledge and cognitive aging." In F. Craik and T. Salthouse, Eds, *Handbook of Aging and Cognition*, 445–89. New York, NY: Psychology Press.

Albert, M. 2008. "The neuropsychology of the development of Alzheimer's disease." In F. Craik and T. Salthouse, Eds, *Handbook of Aging and Cognition*, 97–132. New York, NY: Psychology Press.

Aldwin, C., et al. 2006. "Health, behavior and optimal aging: A life span developmental perspective." In J. Birren and W. Schaie, Eds, *Handbook of the Psychology of Aging*, 85–104. San Diego: Academic Press.

Arnold, A., et al. 2010. "Body weight dynamics and their association with physical function and mortality in older adults: The Cardiovascular Health Study." *Journal of Gerontology: Medical Sciences* 65A (1): 63–70.

Auyeung, A., et al. 2010. "Survival in older men may benefit from being slightly overweight and centrally obese—a 5-year follow-up study in 4,000 older adults using DXA." *Journal of Gerontology: Medical Sciences* 65A (1): 99–104.

Baker, J., et al. 2009. "Physical activity and successful aging in Canadian older adults." *Journal of Aging and Physical Activity* 17: 223–35.

Baltes, P., and Staudinger, U. 2000. "Wisdom: A metaheuristic (pragmatic) to orchestrate mind and virtue toward excellence." *American Psychologist* 55: 122–36.

Bauer, M., et al. 2009. "Catering to love, sex and intimacy in residential aged care: What information is provided to consumers?" *Sex and Disability* 27: 3–9.

Berrington de Gonzalez et al. 2010. "Body–mass index and mortality among 1.46 million white." *New England Journal of Medicine 363*: 2211–19.

Binstock, R., and J. Fishman 2010. "Social dimensions of anti-ageing science and medicine." In D. Dannefer and C. Phillipson, Eds, *The Sage Handbook of Social Gerontology* (pp. 472–82). Thousand Oaks, CA: Sage.

Birren, J., and W. Schaie, Eds. 2006. *Handbook of the Psychology of Aging.* San Diego: Academic Press.

Bischoff, H., et al. 2006. "The effect of undernutrition in the development of frailty in older persons." *Journal of Gerontology: Medical Sciences* 61A (6): 585–8.

Bortz, W. 2002. "A conceptual framework of frailty: A review." *Journal of Gerontology: Medical Sciences* 57A (5): M283–8.

Braver T., and R. West. 2008. "Working memory, executive control, and aging." In F. Craik and T. Salthouse, Eds, *Handbook of Aging and Cognition*, 311–72. New York, NY: Psychology Press.

Brugman, G. 2006. "Wisdom and aging." In J. Birren and W. Schaie, Eds, *Handbook of the Psychology of Aging*, 445–76. San Diego: Academic Press.

Carpenter, L., et al. 2006. "Sex after 40? Gender, ageism, and sexual partnering in midlife." *Journal of Aging Studies* 20 (2): 93–106.

Carstensen, L., et al. 2006. "Aging and the intersection of cognition, motivation, and emotion." In J. Birren and W. Schaie, Eds, *Handbook of the Psychology of Aging*, 343–62. San Diego: Academic Press.

Canadian Fitness & Lifestyle Research Institute (CFLRI). 2009. Physical activity levels of Canadians. Ottawa: Canadian Fitness & Lifestyle Research Institute.

Cavanaugh, J., and F. Blanchard-Fields. 2011. *Adult Development and Aging,* 6th Ed. Belmont, CA: Wadsworth.

Chapman, B., et al. 2006. "Personality and perceived health in older adults: The five factor model in primary care." *Journal of Gerontology: Psychological Sciences* 61B (6): 362–5.

Charness, N., Ed. 2007. "Cognitive interventions and aging." *Journal of Gerontology: Psychological Sciences* 62B (special issue): 5–96.

Clarke, L. 2006. "Older women and sexuality: Experiences in marital relationships across the life course." *Canadian Journal on Aging* 25 (2): 129–40.

Cohen, G. 2006. "Research on creativity and aging: The positive impact of the arts on health and fitness." *Generations* 30 (1): 7–15.

Craik, F., and T. Salthouse, Eds. 2008. The *Handbook of Aging and Cognition*, 3rd edn. New York, NY: Psychology Press.

Cusack, S., and W. Thompson. 2003. *Mental Fitness for Life: Seven Steps to Healthy Aging.* Toronto: Key Porter.

DeLamater, J., and S. Moorman. 2007. "Sexual behavior in later life." *Journal of Aging and Health* 19 (6): 921–45.

Erikson, E. 1985. *Childhood and Society.* Norton: New York.

Ferrucci, L., et al. 2006. "Frailty and the foolishness of Eos." *Journal of Gerontology: Medical Sciences* 61A (3): 260–1.

Ferrucci, L., and E. Simonsick. 2006. "A little exercise." *Journal of Gerontology: Medical Sciences* 61A (11): 1154–6.

Fozard, J., and S. Gordon-Salant. 2001. "Changes in vision and hearing with aging." In J. Birren and W. Schaie, Eds, *Handbook of the Psychology of Aging*, 241–66. San Diego: Academic Press.

Freiheit, E.A., et al. 2010. "Development of a frailty index for patients with coronary heart disease." *Journal of the American Geriatric Association* 58(8): 1526-31.

George, L. 1996. "Missing links: The case for a social psychology of the life course." *The Gerontologist* 36 (2): 248–55.

Giarrusso, R., et al. 2001. "The aging self in social contexts." In R. Binstock and L. George, Eds, *Handbook of Aging and the Social Sciences*, 295–312. San Diego: Academic Press.

Gillette-Guyonnet, S., et al. 2007. "IANA Task Force on nutrition and cognitive decline with aging." *Journal of Nutrition, Health and Aging 11* (2): 132–52.

Hagestad, G. 2006. "Should we be concerned about age segregation? Some theoretical and empirical explorations." *Research on Aging* 28 (6): 638–53.

Hansson, J., and B. Hagberg. 2005. "Determinant factors contributing to variations in memory performance in centenarians." *The International Journal of Aging and Human Development* 60 (1): 19–51.

Havighurst, R. 1969. "Research and development in social gerontology." *The Gerontologist* 9 (4): 1–90.

Hawley, K., et al. 2006. "Knowledge of memory aging in adulthood." *The International Journal of Aging and Human Development* 63 (4): 317–34.

Himes, C., Ed. 2004. "Obesity in later life." *Research on Aging* 26 (1; special issue): 3–176.

Hofer, S., and D. Alwin. Eds. 2008. *Handbook of Cognitive Aging: Interdisciplinary Perspectives.* Thousand Oaks, CA: Sage.

Hogan, D., et al. 1999. "Disease, disability and age in cognitively intact seniors: Results from the Canadian Study of Health and Aging." *Journal of Gerontology: Medical Sciences* 54A (2): M77–82.

Hoyer, W., and P. Verhaeghen. 2006. "Memory aging." In J. Birren and W. Schaie, Eds, *Handbook of the Psychology of Aging,* 209–32. San Diego: Academic Press.

Hultsch, D., et al. 2008. "Intraindividual variability, cognition, and aging." In F. Craik and T. Salthouse, Eds, *Handbook of Aging and Cognition,* 491–556. New York, NY: Psychology Press.

Jeste, D., et al. 2010. "Expert consensus on characteristics of wisdom: A Delphi method study." *The Gerontologist* 50(5): 668–80.

Katz, S., and B. Marshall. 2003. "New sex for old: Lifestyle, consumerism, and the ethics of aging well." *Journal of Aging Studies* 17 (1): 3–16.

Karunananthan, S., et al. 2009. "A multidisciplinary systematic literature review on frailty: Overview of the methodology used by the Canadian Initiative on Frailty and Aging." BMC Medical Research Methodology 12: 9–68.

Katz, S., and B. Marshall. 2003. "New sex for old: Lifestyle, consumerism, and the ethics of aging well." *Journal of Aging Studies* 17 (1): 3–16.

Kelley-Moore, J. 2010. "Disability and ageing: The social construction of causality." In D. Dannefer and C. Phillipson, Eds, *The Sage Handbook of Social Gerontology* 96–110. Thousand Oaks, CA: Sage.

Kempler, D. 2005. *Neurocognitive Disorders in Aging.* Thousand Oaks, CA: Sage.

Ketcham, C., and G. Stelmach. 2001. "Age-related declines in motor control." In J. Birren and W. Schaie, Eds, *Handbook of the Psychology of Aging,* 313–48. San Diego: Academic Press.

Kirkwood, T. 2005. "The biological science of human aging." In M. Johnson, Ed., *The Cambridge Handbook of Age and Ageing,* 72–81. New York: Cambridge University Press.

Kline, D., and C. Scialfa. 1996. "Visual and auditory aging." In J. Birren and W. Schaie, Eds, *Handbook of the Psychology of Aging,* 181–203. San Diego: Academic Press.

Kuh, D., et al., Eds. 2007. "Unconventional views of frailty." *Journal of Gerontology: Medical Sciences* 62A (7): M717–51.

Langer, N. 2009. "Late life love and intimacy. *Educational Gerontology* 35: 752–64.

Liu-Ambrose, T., et al. 2009. "Dual-task gait performance among community-dwelling senior women: The role of balance confidence and executive functions. *Journal of Gerontology: Medical Sciences* 64A (9): M975–82.

Magai, C. 2001. "Emotions over the life span." In J. Birren and W. Schaie, Eds, *Handbook of the Psychology of Aging,* 399–426. San Diego: Academic Press.

Margrain, T., and M. Boulton. 2005. "Sensory impairment." In M. Johnson, Ed., *The Cambridge Handbook of Age and Ageing,* 121–30. New York: Cambridge University Press.

Marsiske, M., and J. Margrett. 2006. "Everyday problem solving and decision making." In J. Birren and W. Schaie, Eds, *Handbook of the Psychology of Aging,* 315–42. San Diego: Academic Press.

Masoro, E., and S. Austad, Eds. 2001. *Handbook of the Biology of Aging.* San Diego: Academic Press.

———, Eds. 2006. *Handbook of the Biology of Aging.* San Diego: Academic Press.

McClearn, G., and G. Vogler. 2001. "The genetics of behavioral aging." In J. Birren and W. Schaie, Eds, *Handbook of the Psychology of Aging,* 109–31. San Diego: Academic Press.

McDaniel, M., et al. 2008. "New considerations in aging and memory: The glass may be half full." In F. Craik and T. Salthouse, Eds, *Handbook of Aging and Cognition,* 251–310. New York, NY: Psychology Press.

McGue, M., and W. Johnson 2008. "Genetics of cognitive aging." In F. Craik and T. Salthouse, Eds, *Handbook of Aging and Cognition,* 55–96. New York, NY: Psychology Press.

McLeish, J. 1976. *The Ulyssean Adult: Creativity in the Middle and Later Years.* New York: McGraw-Hill.

McMullin, J., and J. Cairney. 2004. "Self-esteem and the intersection of age, class and gender." *Journal of Aging Studies* 18 (1): 75–90.

Mitchell, B. 2012. *Family Matters: An Introduction to Family Sociology in Canada,* 2nd edn. Toronto: Canadian Scholars' Press.

Morley, J., et al. 2002. "Something about frailty." *Journal of Gerontology: Medical Sciences* 57A (11): M698–704.

Mroczek, D., et al. 2006. "Personality and aging." In J. Birren and W. Schaie, Eds, *Handbook of the Psychology of Aging,* 363–77. San Diego: Academic Press.

Mroczek, D., and T. Little, Eds. 2005. *Handbook of Personality Development.* Mahwah, NJ: Laurence Erlbaum.

Mroczek, D., and A. Spiro. 2003. "Modeling intra-individual change in personality traits: Findings from the normative aging study." *Journal of Gerontology: Psychological Sciences* 58B (3): P153–65.

Murdock, B. 1967. "Recent developments in short term memory." *Quarterly Journal of Experimental Psychology* 18 (3): 206–11.

Narushima, M. 2005. "Payback time: Community volunteering among older adults as a transformative mechanism." *Ageing and Society* 25 (4): 567–84.

Newell, K., et al. 2006. "Aging, complexity and motor performance." In J. Birren and W. Schaie, Eds, *Handbook of the Psychology of Aging*, 163–82. San Diego: Academic Press.

Newson, R., and E. Kemps. 2006. "The nature of subjective cognitive complaints of older adults." *International Journal of Aging and Human Development* 63 (2): 139–51.

Orpana, H.M., et al. 2010. "BMI and mortality: Results from a national longitudinal study of Canadian adults." *Obesity* 18: 214–18.

Phoenix, C., and Grant, B. 2009. "Expanding the agenda for research on the physically active aging body." *Journal of Aging and Physical Activity* 17: 362–79.

Prohaska, T., et al. 2006. "Physical activity, public health and aging: Critical issues and research priorities." *Journal of Gerontology: Social Sciences* 61B (5): S267–73.

Rejeski, W. J., et al. 2010. "The Lifstyle Interventions and Independence for Elders Pilot (LIFE-P): 2-Year follow-up." *Journal of Gerontology: Medical Sciences* 64A (4): 462–7.

Reynolds, S., et al. 2005. "The impact of obesity on active life expectancy in older American men and women." *The Gerontologist* 45 (4): 438–44.

Ruth, J.-E., and P. Coleman. 1996. "Personality and aging: Coping and management of the self in later life." In J. Birren and W. Schaie, Eds, *Handbook of the Psychology of Aging*, 308–22. San Diego: Academic Press.

Ryff, C., et al. 2001. "Personality and aging: Flourishing agendas and future challenges." In J. Birren and W. Schaie, Eds, *Handbook of the Psychology of Aging*, 477–99. San Diego: Academic Press.

Ryff, C., and V. Marshall, Eds. 1999. *The Self and Society in Aging Processes*. New York: Springer.

Schaie, W. 1996. "Intellectual development in adulthood." In J. Birren and W. Schaie, Eds, *Handbook of the Psychology of Aging*, 266–86. San Diego: Academic Press.

——. 2005. *Developmental Influences on Adult Intelligence: The Seattle Longitudinal Study*. New York: Oxford University Press.

Schieber, F. 2006. "Vision and aging." In J. Birren and W. Schaie, Eds, *Handbook of the Psychology of Aging*, 129–61. San Diego: Academic Press.

Shields, M., and L. Martel 2006. Healthy Living among Seniors. Health Reports Supplement, 8: 7–20. Statistics Canada, Catalogue 82-003.

Schumm, L.P., et al. 2009. "Assessment of sensory function in the National Social Life, Health, and Aging Project." *Journal of Gerontology: Social Sciences* 64B (3): i76–i85.

Small, B., et al. 2003. "Stability and change in adult personality over 6 years: Findings from the Victoria Longitudinal Study." *Journal of Gerontology: Psychological Sciences* 58B (3): P166–76.

Smetanin, P., et al. 2009. *Rising Tide: The Impact of Dementia in Canada 2008 to 2038*. Toronto: RiskAnalytica.

Spence, J., et al. 2001. *Compilation of Evidence of Effective Active Living Interventions: A Case Study Approach*. Report submitted to Health Canada on behalf of the Canadian Consortium of Health Promotion Research. Ottawa: Health Canada.

Statistics Canada. 2007. *Participation and Activity Limitation Survey (pals) 2006: Tables*. Catalogue no. 89-628-XIE. Ottawa: Statistics Canada.

Staudinger, U. 2005. "Personality and ageing." In M. Johnson, Ed., *The Cambridge Handbook of Age and Ageing*, 237–44. New York: Cambridge University Press.

Sternberg, R., and E. Grigorenko. 2005. "Intelligence and wisdom." In M. Johnson, Ed., *The Cambridge Handbook of Age and Ageing*, 209–15. New York: Cambridge University Press.

Sternberg, R., and T. Lubart. 2001. "Wisdom and creativity." In J. Birren and W. Schaie, Eds, *Handbook of the Psychology of Aging*, 500–22. San Diego: Academic Press.

Stones, M., and A. Kozma. 1996. "Activity, exercise and behavior." In J. Birren and W. Schaie, Eds, *Handbook of the Psychology of Aging*, 338–52. San Diego: Academic Press.

Terracciano, A., et al. 2006. "Longitudinal trajectories in Guilford-Zimmerman Temperament Survey data: Results from the Baltimore Longitudinal Study of Aging." *Journal of Gerontology: Psychological Sciences* 61B (2): P108–16.

Tiefer, L. 2001. "A new view of women's sexual problems: Why new? Why now?" *Journal of Sex Research* 38 (2): 89–96.

Tolman, J., et al. 2005. "Psychological adaptation to visual impairment and its relationship to depression affect in older adults with age-related macular degeneration." *The Gerontologist* 45 (6): 747–53.

Valliant, G. 2007. "Generativity: A Form of Unconditional Love." In S. Post, Ed., *Altruism and Health*, 219–29. New York: Oxford University Press.

Vares, T., et al. 2007. "Reconceptualizing cultural narratives of mature women's sexuality in the Viagra era." *Journal of Aging Studies* 21 (2): 153–64.

Vincent, J., et al. 2008. "The anti-aging enterprise: Science, knowledge and expertise." *Journal of Aging Studies* 22 (4): 291–4.

Wallhagen, M., et al. 2004. "Impact of self-assessed hearing loss on a spouse: A longitudinal analysis of couples." *Journal of Gerontology: Social Sciences* 59B (3): S190–6.

Webster's New World Dictionary. 1997.

Weiss, C., et al. 2010. "Relationships of cardiac, pulmonary, and muscle reserves and frailty to exercise capacity in older women." *Journal of Gerontology: Medical Sciences* 65A (3): 287–94.

WHO. 2005. *Preventing Chronic Disease: A Vital Investment*. WHO: Geneva, Switzerland.

Williamson, J., et al. 2010. "Changes in cognitive function in a randomized trial of physical activity: Results of the Lifestyle Interventions and Independence for Elders Pilot Study." *Journal of Gerontology: Medical Sciences* 64A (6): 688–94.

Willis, S., et al. 2006. "Long-term effects of cognitive training on everyday functional outcomes in older adults." *Journal of the American Medical Association* 296 (23): 2805–14.

Wister, A.V. 2005. *Baby Boomer Health Dynamics: How Are We Aging?* Toronto: University of Toronto Press.

Wolinsky, F., et al. 2009. "Does cognitive training improve internal locus of control among older adults?" *Journal of Gerontology: Psychological Sciences* 65B (5): 591–8.

Chapter 4

Population Aging: A Demographic and Geographic Perspective

AARP (American Association of Retired Persons). 2002. *Global Aging: Achieving Its Potential*. Washington: AARP.

Bloom, D., et al. 2010. *The Greying of Global Population and Its Macroeconomic Consequences*. The WDA—HSG Discussion Paper Series on Demographic Issues, University of St. Gallen: WDA Forum.

Carrière, Y., and D. Galarneau. 2011. "Delayed retirement: A new trend?" *Perspectives on Labour and Income, Winter, Catalogue. 75-001-X*. Ottawa: Statistics Canada.

Centre on Aging. 1996. *Manitoba Fact Book on Aging*. Winnipeg: Centre on Aging, University of Manitoba.

Chappell, N., and M. Hollander. 2011. "An evidence-based policy prescription for an aging population." *Healthcare Papers* 11 (1): 8–19.

Cheal, D. 2000. "Aging and demographic change." *Canadian Public Policy* 26 (supplement 2): S109–22.

———, Ed. 2003. *Aging and Demographic Change in the Canadian Context*. Toronto: University of Toronto Press.

CIHR. 2010. "Will you be there when I am old? How Canada's aging population will impact the health care system." CIHR Café Scientifique. www.cihr-irsc.gc.ca/e/42742.html, retrieved 15 August 2012.

Connidis, I. 2003. "The impact of demographic and social trends on informal support for older persons." In D. Cheal, Ed., *Aging and Demographic Change in the Canadian Context*, 105–32. Toronto: University of Toronto Press.

Dychtwald, K. 1997. "The 10 physical, social, spiritual, economic and political crises the boomers will face as they age in the 21st century." *Critical Issues in Aging* 1: 11–13.

Easterlin, R. 1996. *Growth Triumphant: The Twenty-First Century in Historical Perspective*. Ann Arbor: University of Michigan Press.

Elliot, G., et al. 1996. *Facts on Aging in Canada*. Hamilton, ON: Office of Gerontological Studies, McMaster University.

Foot, D., and D. Stoffman. 1998. *Boom, Bust and Echo 2000: Profiting from the Demographic Shift in the New Millennium*. Toronto: Macfarlane Walter and Ross.

Friedland, R., and L. Summer. 1999. *Demography Is Not Destiny*. Washington: National Academy on an Aging Society.

Gee, E., and G. Gutman, Eds. 2000. *The Overselling of Population Aging: Apocalyptic Demography, Intergenerational Challenges, and Social Policy*. Don Mills, ON: Oxford University Press.

George, M., et al. 2001. *Population Projections for Canada, Provinces and Territories, 2000–2026*. Catalogue no. 91-520-XPB. Ottawa: Statistics Canada, Demography Division.

Government of Canada. 2002. "Canada's aging population." Ottawa: Minister of Public Works and Government Services Canada. http://publications.gc.ca/collections/Collection/H39-608-2002E.pdf.

Graham, H. 2004. "Social determinants and their unequal distributions: Clarifying policy understandings." *Milbank Quarterly* 82 (1): 101–24.

Hayward, M., and Z. Zhang. 2001. "Demography of aging: A century of global change, 1950–2050." In R. Binstock and L. George, Eds, *Handbook of Aging and the Social Sciences*, 69–85. New York: Academic Press.

Health Canada. 2002. *Canada's Aging Population*. Ottawa: Minister of Public Works and Government Services.

Hogan, S., and J. Lise. 2003. "Life expectancy, health expectancy, and the life cycle." *Horizons* 6 (2): 17–20.

Jeune, B., and K. Christensen. 2005. "Biodemography and epidemiology of longevity." In M. Johnson, Ed., *The Cambridge Handbook of Age and Ageing*, 85–94. New York: Cambridge University Press.

Kalache, A., et al. 2005. "Global ageing: The demographic revolution in all cultures and societies." In M. Johnson, Ed., *The Cambridge Handbook of Age and Ageing*, 30–46. New York: Cambridge University Press.

Kinsella, K., and W. He. 2009. *An Aging World: 2008.* US Census Bureau, series P95/09-1. Washington: US Government Printing Office.

Kinsella, K., and D. Phillips. 2005. "Global ageing: The challenge of success." *Population Bulletin* 60 (1): 1–44.

Lascelles, E. 2004. "Bad news: You're getting older." *Canadian Business* 12 (27): 40.

Longino, C. 2005. "The future of ageism: Baby boomers at the doorstep." *Generations* (fall): 79–83.

Martin, G. 2011. "Demography and aging." In R. Binstock, L. George, S. Cutler, J. Hendricks and H. Schulz, Eds, *Handbook of Aging and the Social Science,* 7th edn, 33–45. New York: Oxford, UK: Elsevier.

Martin, L., et al. 2009. "Health and functioning among baby boomers approaching 60." *Journals of Gerontology: Social Sciences* 64B: 369–77.

McDaniel, S., and Rozanova, J. 2011. "Canada's aging population (1986)." *Canadian Journal on Aging* 30 (3): 511–21.

McKie, C. 1993. "Population aging: Baby boomers into the 21st century." *Canadian Social Trends* 29 (summer): 2–6.

Mitchell, B. 2006. *Boomerang Age: Transitions to Adulthood in Families.* Piscataway, NJ: Transaction.

Moore, E., et al. 2000. *Geographic Dimensions of Aging: The Canadian Experience*, 1991–1996. SEDAP Research Paper no. 23. Hamilton, ON: McMaster University. http://socserv2.mcmaster.ca/sedap.

Moore, E., and M. Rosenberg. 1997. *Growing Old in Canada: Demographic and Geographic Perspectives.* Ottawa: Statistics Canada.

Morgan, D. 1998. "Introduction: The aging baby boom." *Generations* 22 (1): 5–9.

Northcott, H. 1992. *Aging in Alberta: Rhetoric and Reality.* Calgary: Detselig.

Northcott, H., and P. Milliken. 1998. *Aging in British Columbia: Burden or Benefit?* Calgary: Detselig.

Northcott, H., and C. Petruik. 2011. "The geographic mobility of elderly Canadians." *Canadian Journal on Aging* 30 (3): 311–22.

O'Brien, S. 2012. *Fun Facts about the Senior Population: Demographics.* http://seniorliving. about.com/od/lawpolitics/a/senior_pop_demo. htm, retrieved 13 September 2012.

Oeppen, J., and J. Vaupel. 2002. "Enhanced and broken limits to life expectancy." *Science* 296 (10 May): 1029–31.

Olshansky, J., et al. 2001. "Prospects for human longevity." *Science* 291 (23 February): 1491–2.

Owram, D. 1996. *Born at the Right Time: A History of the Baby Boom Generation.* Toronto: University of Toronto Press.

Parker, M.G., and M. Thorslund. 2007. "Health trends in the elderly population: Getting better or getting worse?" *The Gerontologist* 47 (2): 150–8.

Peterson, P. 1999. *Gray Dawn.* New York: Crown.

Poon, L., et al. 2005. "Profiles of the oldest-old." In M. Johnson, Ed., *The Cambridge Handbook of Age and Ageing*, 346–53. New York: Cambridge University Press.

Population Reference Bureau. 1999. *World Population: More than Just Numbers.* Washington: Population Reference Bureau.

_____. 2006. *The 2006 World Population Data Sheet.* Washington: Population Reference Bureau.

_____. 2011. *The 2011 World Population Data Sheet.* Washington: Population Reference Bureau.

Pruchno, R., Ed. 2012. "Not your mother's old age: Baby boomers at age 65." *The Gerontologist* 52 (2): 149–52.

Riley, J. 2001. *Rising Life Expectancy: A Global History.* New York: Cambridge University Press.

Robine, J., et al. 2003. *Determining Health Expectancies.* New York: Wiley.

Rosenberg, M. 2000. "The effects of population ageing on the Canadian health care system." SEDAP Research Paper no. 14. Hamilton, ON: McMaster University. http://socserv2.mcmaster.ca/sedap.

Rozanova, J., et al. 2006. "Seniors and portrayals of intra-generational and inter-generational inequality in *The Globe and Mail*." *Canadian Journal on Aging* 25 (4): 373–86.

Statistics Canada. 2001. *Population Projections for Canada, Provinces, and Territories.* Catalogue no. 91-520, Ottawa: Statistics Canada.

_____. 2002a. *Profile of the Canadian Population by Age and Sex: Canada Ages.* Catalogue no. 96F0030 XIE2001002. Ottawa: Statistics Canada. www. statcan.ca.

_____. 2002b. *A Profile of Disability in Canada, 2001.* Catalogue no. 89-57-XIE. Ottawa: Statistics Canada.

_____. 2003. *The Daily,* 25 September.

_____. 2007. Tables produced by Statistics Canada, October 2007.

_____. 2010a. Participation and Activity Limitation Survey (Tables). www.statcan.gc.ca/pub/89-628-x/89-628-x2010015-eng.htm, retrieved 13 September 2012.

_____. 2010b. Dependency Ratio. www.statcan.gc.ca/pub/82-229-x/2009001/demo/dep-eng.htm, retrieved 14 September 2012.

_____. 2010c. Population Projections for Canada, Provinces, Territories, 2009–2036. www.statcan.gc.ca/pub/91-520-x/91-520-x2010001-eng.pdf, retrieved 14 September 2012.

_____ . 2011. *Life Expectancy at Birth , by Sex, by Province.* www.statcan.gc.ca/tables-tableaux/sum-som/l01/cst01/health26-eng.htm, retrieved 14 September 2012.

_____ . 2012a. *The Canadian Population Age and Sex.* www.statcan.gc.ca/bsolc/olc-cel/olc-cel?catno=98-311-XWE2011001&lang=eng, retrieved 30 August 2011.

_____ . 2012b. *Generations in Canada.* www12.statcan.gc.ca/census-recensement/2011/as-sa/98-311-x/98-311-x2011003_2-eng.cfm, retrieved 30 August 2011.

_____ . 2012c. *Centenarians in Canada.* www12.statcan.gc.ca/census-recensement/2011/as-sa/98-311-x/98-311-x2011003_1-eng.cfm, retrieved 30 August 2011.

Turcotte, M., and G. Schellenberg. 2007. *A Portrait of Seniors in Canada, 2006.* Ottawa: Statistics Canada.

United Nations. 2002a. *Population Ageing, 2002.* New York: United Nations, Department of Economic and Social Affairs, Population Division.

_____ . 2002b. *World Population Ageing, 1950–2002.* New York: United Nations, Department of Economic and Social Affairs, Population Division.

_____ . 2007a. *World Population Ageing, 2007.* New York: United Nations, Department of Economic and Social Affairs, Population Division.

_____ . 2007b. *World Population Prospects: The 2006 Revision.* New York: United Nations, Department of Economic and Social Affairs, Population Division.

US Census Bureau. 2012. *International Data Base, Regional Summaries.* Retrieved 23 August 2012.

Verbrugge, L. 1997. "A global disability indicator." *Journal of Aging Studies* 11 (4): 337–62.

Wister, A.V. 2005. *Baby Boomer Health Dynamics: How Are We Aging?* Toronto: University of Toronto Press.

Wister, A.V., et al. 2006. *Fact Book on Aging in British Columbia.* Vancouver: Simon Fraser University, Gerontology Research Centre.

Yi, Z., et al. 2003. "Gender differentials of the oldest old in China." *Research on Aging* 25 (1): 65–80.

Chapter 5

Theories and Research in Explaining and Understanding Aging Phenomena

Achenbaum, A. 2009. "A metahistorical perspective on theories of aging." In V. Bengtson, D. Gans, N. Putney, and M. Silverstein, Eds, *Handbook of Theories of Aging*, 25–38. New York: Springer.

Alkema, G., and D. Alley. 2006. "Gerontology's future: An integrative model for disciplinary advancement." *The Gerontologist* 46 (5): 574–82.

Arber, S., and J. Ginn, Eds. 1995. *Connecting Gender and Ageing: A Sociological Approach.* Philadelphia: Open University Press.

Atchley, R. 1971. *The Social Forces in Later Life.* Belmont, CA: Wadsworth.

_____ . 1989. "A continuity theory of normal aging." *The Gerontologist* 29 (2): 183–90.

Baars, J., et al. 2006. *Aging, Globalization and Inequality: The New Critical Gerontology.* Amityville, NY: Baywood.

Bass, S. 2009. "Toward an integrative theory of social gerontology." In V. Bengtson, D. Gans, N. Putney, and M. Silverstein, Eds, *Handbook of Theories of Aging*, 347–74. New York: Springer.

Bengtson, V., et al. 1996. "Paradoxes of families and aging." In R. Binstock and L. George, Eds, *Handbook of Aging and the Social Sciences*, 253–82. San Diego: Academic Press.

_____ . 1997. "Theory, explanation and a third generation of theoretical development in social gerontology." *Journal of Gerontology: Social Sciences* 52B (2): S72–88.

_____ . 1999. "Are theories of aging important? Models and explanations in gerontology at the turn of the century." In V. Bengtson and W. Schaie, Eds, *Handbook of Theories of Aging*, 3–20. New York: Springer.

_____ . 2005. "The problem of theory in gerontology today." In M. Johnson, Ed., *The Cambridge Handbook of Age and Ageing*, 3–20. New York: Cambridge University Press.

_____ . 2009. "Theories about age and aging." In V. Bengtson, D. Gans, N. Putney, and M. Silverstein, Eds, *Handbook of Theories of Aging*, 3–24. New York: Springer.

Bengtson, V., and W. Schaie, Eds. 1999. *Handbook of Theories of Aging.* New York: Springer.

Berger, P., and T. Luckmann. 1966. *The Social Construction of Reality.* Garden City, NY: Doubleday.

Biggs, S. 2001. "Toward critical narrativity: Stories of aging in contemporary social policy." *Journal of Aging Studies* 15 (4): 303–16.

Biggs, S. 2008. "Aging in a critical world: The search for generational intelligence." *Journal of Aging Studies* 22: 115–19.

Biggs, S., et al. Eds. 2003. *The Need for Theory: Critical Approaches to Social Gerontology.* Amityville, NY: Baywood.

Birren, J., et al., Eds. 1996. *Aging and Biography: Explorations in Adult Development.* New York: Springer.

Blieszner, R. 1993. "A socialist-feminist perspective on widowhood." *Journal of Aging Studies* 7 (2): 171–82.

Burgess, W. 1960. *Aging in Western Societies.* Chicago: University of Chicago Press.

Calasanti, T. 1992. "Theorizing about gender and aging: Beginning with women's voices." *The Gerontologist,* 32 (2): 280–2.

——. 1993. "Introduction: A socialist-feminist approach to aging." *Journal of Aging Studies,* 7 (2): 107–9.

——. 1996. "Incorporating diversity: Meaning, levels of research, and implications for theory." *The Gerontologist* 36 (1): 147–56.

——. 2003. "Theorizing age relations." In S. Biggs, A. Lowenstein, and J. Hendricks, Eds, *The Need for Theory: Critical Approaches to Social Gerontology,* 199–218. Amityville, NY: Baywood.

——. 2004a. "Feminist gerontology and old men." *Journal of Gerontology: Social Sciences* 59B (6): S305–14.

——, 2004b. "New directions in feminist gerontology." *Journal of Aging Studies* 18 (1): 1–121.

Calasanti, T. 2009. "Theorizing feminist gerontology, sexuality, and beyond: An intersectional approach." In V. Bengtson, D. Gans, N. Putney, and M. Silverstein, Eds, *Handbook of Theories of Aging,* 471–86. New York: Springer.

Calasanti, T., and M. Bowen. 2006. "Spousal caregiving and crossing gender boundaries: Maintaining gendered identities." *Journal of Aging Studies* 20: 253–63.

Calasanti, T., and A. Zajicek. 1993. "A socialist-feminist approach to aging: Embracing diversity." *Journal of Aging Studies* 7 (2): 117–31.

Campbell, R., and A. O'Rand. 1988. |"Settings and sequences: The heuristics of aging research." In J. Birren and V. Bengtson, Eds, *Emergent Theories of Aging,* 58–79. New York: Springer.

Chaudhury, H. 2003. "Quality of life and place-therapy." *Journal of Housing for the Elderly* 17 (1/2): 85–103.

Cobb, A., and S. Forbes. 2002. "Qualitative research: What does it have to offer to the gerontologist?" *Journal of Gerontology: Medical Sciences* 57A (4): M197–202.

Cole, T., et al., Eds. 1993. *Voices and Visions of Aging: Toward a Critical Gerontology.* New York: Springer.

——, Eds. 2000. *Handbook of the Humanities and Aging.* New York: Springer.

Cooley, C. 1902. *Human Nature and the Social Order.* New York: Scribner's.

Crabtree, B., and W. Miller, Eds. 1999. *Doing Qualitative Research.* Newbury Park, CA: Sage.

Cruikshank, P. 2003. *Learning To Be Old: Gender, Culture, and Aging.* Lanham, MD: Rowman and Littlefield.

Cumming, E. 1963. "Further thoughts on the theory of disengagement." *International Social Science Journal* 15 (3): 377–93.

Cumming, E., et al. 1960. "Disengagement: A tentative theory of aging." *Sociometry* 23 (1): 23–35.

Cumming, E., and W. Henry. 1961. *Growing Old: The Process of Disengagement.* New York: Basic Books.

Dannefer, D., et al. 2009. "Theorizing the life course: New twists in the Paths." In V. Bengtson, D. Gans, N. Putney, and M. Silverstein, Eds, *Handbook of Theories of Aging,* 389–412. New York: Springer.

Dawe, A. 1970. "The two sociologies." *British Journal of Sociology* 21 (2): 207–18.

Denzin, N., and Y. Lincoln, Eds. 2000. *The Handbook of Qualitative Research.* Thousand Oaks, CA: Sage.

Elder, G. 1999. *Children of the Great Depression: Social Change in Life Experience.* 25th anniversary edition. Chicago: University of Chicago Press.

Elder, G., and M. Johnson. 2003. "The life course and aging: Challenges, lessons and new directions." In R. Settersten, Ed., *Invitation to the Life Course: Toward New Understandings of Later Life,* 49–81. Amityville, NY: Baywood.

Estes, C. 1991. "The new political economy of aging: Introduction and critique." In M. Minkler and C. Estes, Eds, *Critical Perspectives on Aging: The Political and Moral Economy of Growing Old,* 19–36. Amityville, NY: Baywood.

——. 1999. "Critical gerontology and the new political economy of aging." In M. Minkler and C. Estes, Eds, *Critical Gerontology: Perspectives from Political and Moral Economy,* 17–35. Amityville, NY: Baywood.

——. 2004 "Social security, privatization and older women: A feminist political economy perspective." *Journal of Aging Studies* 18 (1): 9–26.

Estes, C., et al. 1996. "The political economy of aging." In R. Binstock and L. George, Eds, *Handbook of Aging and the Social Sciences,* 346–61. San Diego: Academic Press.

——, Eds. 2003. *Social Theory, Social Policy and Aging: A Critical Introduction.* London: Open University Press.

Etches, V., et al. 2006. "Measuring population health: A review of indicators." *Annual Review of Public Health* 27: 29–55.

Featherstone, M., and C. Wernick. 1995. *Images of Aging.* New York: Routledge.

Garner, J. 1999. *Fundamentals of Feminist Gerontology.* New York: Haworth.

Gee, E., and M. Kimball. 1987. *Women and Aging.* Toronto: Butterworths.

George, L. 1995. "The last half century of aging research and thoughts for the future." *Journal of Gerontology: Social Sciences* 50B (1): S1–3.

———. 1996. "Missing links: The case for a social psychology of the life course." *The Gerontologist* 36 (3): 248–55.

Giele, J., and G. Elder, Eds. 1999. *Methods of Life-Course Research: Qualitative and Quantitative Approaches*. Newbury Park, CA: Sage.

Goffman, E. 1959. *The Presentation of Self in Everyday Life*. New York: Doubleday.

Grant, B. 1999. "Physical activity and the meaning to self." Presented at the Fifth World Congress on Physical Activity, Aging and Sports, Orlando, FL, 10–14 August.

Grant, B., and S. O'Brien-Cousins 2001. "Aging and physical activity: The promise of qualitative research." *Journal of Aging and Physical Activity* 9 (3): 237–44.

Gubrium, J. 1993. *Speaking of Life: Horizons of Meaning for Nursing Home Residents*. New York: Aldine de Gruyter.

Gubrium, J., and J. Holstein. 1997. *The New Language of Qualitative Methods*. Oxford: Oxford University Press.

———. 1999. "Constructionist perspectives on aging." In V. Bengtson and W. Schaie, Eds, *Handbook of Theories of Aging*, 287–305. New York: Springer.

Hagestad, G. 1990. "Social perspectives on the life course." In R. Binstock and L. George, Eds, *Handbook of Aging and the Social Sciences*, 151–68. San Diego: Academic Press.

Hagestad, G., and D. Dannefer. 2001. "Concepts and theories of aging: Beyond microfication in social science approaches." In R. Binstock and L. George, Eds, *Handbook of Aging and the Social Sciences*, 3–21. New York: Academic Press.

Halliwell, J., and J. Lomas. 1999. Dimensions of Health Research: The Four CIHR Sectors- Perspectives and Synergies. Discussion Paper. SSHRC & CHSRF: Ottawa.

Hamilton, R. 1993. "Feminist theories." *Left History* 1 (1): 9–33.

Hare-Mustin, R., and J. Marecek. 1994. "Gender and the meaning of difference: Postmodernism and psychology." In A. Herrmann and A. Stewart, Eds, *Theorizing Feminism: Parallel Trends in the Humanities and Social Sciences*, 49–76. Boulder, CO: Westview.

Havighurst, R., and R. Albrecht. 1953. *Older People*. New York: Longmans, Green.

Hazan, H. 1994. *Old Age: Constructions and Deconstructions*. Cambridge: Cambridge University Press.

Heinz, W., and V. Marshall, Eds. 2003. *Social Dynamics of the Life Course: Transitions, Institutions, and Interrelations*. New York: Aldine De Gruyter.

Henry, W. 1964. "The theory of intrinsic disengagement." In P. Hansen, Ed., *Age with a Future*, 415–18. Philadelphia: F.A. Davis.

Hirdes, J., et al. 1999. "Integrated health information systems based on the rai/mds series of assessment instruments." *Healthcare Management Forum* 12 (4): 30–40.

Hirdes, J., and I. Carpenter. 1997. "Health outcomes among the frail elderly in communities and institutions: Use of the minimum data set (mds) to create effective linkages between research and policy." *Canadian Journal on Aging/Canadian Public Policy* (supplement): 53–69.

Hitlin, S., and G. Elder. 2007. "Time, self and the curiously abstract concept of agency." *Sociological Theory* 25 (2): 170–91.

Holstein, J., and J. Gubrium. 2000. *Constructing the Life Course*. Dix Hills, NY: General Hall.

Holstein, M., and M. Minkler. 2003. "Self, society and the new gerontology." *The Gerontologist* 43 (6): 787–96.

Johnson, C., and B. Baier. 1992. "Patterns of engagement and disengagement among the oldest old." *Journal of Aging Studies* 6 (4): 351–64.

Kail et al. 2009. "The political economy perspective on aging." In V. Bengtson, D. Gans, N. Putney, and M. Silverstein, Eds, *Handbook of Theories of Aging*, 555–72. New York: Springer.

Katz, S. 2003. "Critical gerontological theory: Intellectual fieldwork and nomadic life of ideas." In S. Biggs et al., Eds, *The Need for Theory: Critical Approaches to Social Gerontology*, 15–32. Amityville, NY: Baywood.

Kenyon, G., and W. Randall. 1999. "Introduction: Narrative gerontology." *Journal of Aging Studies* 13 (1): 1–5.

Kimmel, M. 2000. *The Gendered Society*. New York: Oxford University Press.

Krause, N. 2002. "A comprehensive strategy for developing closed-ended survey items for use in studies of older adults." *Journal of Gerontology: Social Sciences* 57B (5): S263–74.

Laws, G. 1995. "Understanding ageism: Lessons from feminism and postmodernism." *The Gerontologist* 35 (1): 112–18.

Layder, D. 1994. *Understanding Social Theory*. Thousand Oaks, CA: Sage.

Lincoln, Y., and E. Guba. 1985. *Naturalistic Inquiry*. Beverly Hills, CA: Sage.

Locher, J., et al. 2006. "Ethical issues involving research conducted with homebound older adults." *The Gerontologist* 46 (2): 160–4.

Longino, C., and J. Powell 2009. "Toward a phenomenology of aging." In V. Bengtson, D. Gans, N. Putney, and M. Silverstein, Eds, *Handbook of Theories of Aging*, 375–88. New York: Springer.

Lopata, H. 1995. "Feminist perspectives in social gerontology." In R. Bleiszner and V. Hilkevitch Bedford, Eds, *Handbook of Aging and the Family*, 114–31. Westport, CT: Greenwood.

Luborsky, M., and R. Rubinstein. 1995. "Sampling in qualitative research." *Research on Aging* 17 (1): 89–113.

Lynott, R., and P. Lynott. 1996. "Tracing the course of theoretical development in the sociology of aging." *The Gerontologist* 36 (6): 749–60.

MacQuarrie, M., and B. Keddy. 1992. "Women and aging: Directions for research." *Journal of Women and Aging* 4 (2): 21–32.

MacRae, H. 1990. "Older women and identity maintenance in later life." *Canadian Journal on Aging* 9 (3): 248–67.

Marshall, C., and G. Rossman. 1999. *Designing Qualitative Research*. Thousand Oaks, CA: Sage.

Marshall, V. 1996. "The state of theory in aging and the social sciences." In R. Binstock and L. George, Eds, *Handbook of Aging and the Social Sciences*, 12–30. San Diego: Academic Press.

———. 1999. "Analyzing social theories of aging." In V. Bengtson and W. Schaie, Eds, *Handbook of Theories of Aging*, 434–55. New York: Springer.

———. 2009. "Theory informing public policy: The life course perspective as a policy tool." In V. Bengtson, D. Gans, N. Putney, and M. Silverstein, Eds, *Handbook of Theories of Aging*, 573–94. New York: Springer.

Marshall, V., and P. Clarke. 2007. "Theories of aging: Social." In J. Birren, Ed., *Encyclopedia of Aging*, 2nd edn, 621–30. Amsterdam: Academic Press.

———. Forthcoming 2009. "Agency and social structure in aging and life course research." In D. Dannefer and C. Phillipson (Eds), *The Sage Handbook of Social Gerontology*. Newbury Park, CA: Sage.

Marshall, V., and M. Mueller. 2003. "Theoretical roots of the life course perspective." In W. Heinz and V. Marshall, Eds, *Social Dynamics of the Life Course: Sequences, Institutions and Interrelations*, 3–32. New York: Aldine de Gruyter.

Matthews, S. 2002. *Sisters and Brothers/Daughters and Sons: Meeting the Needs of Old Parents*. Bloomington, IN: Unlimited.

Maxwell, J.A. 2005. *Qualitative Research Design: An Interactive Approach*. 2nd edn. Thousand Oaks, CA: Sage.

McDaniel, S. 1989. "Women and aging: A sociological perspective." *Journal of Women and Aging* 1 (1–3): 47–67.

———. 2004. "Generationing gender: Justice and the division of welfare." In "New directions in feminist gerontology," special issue, *Journal of Aging Studies* 18 (1): 27–44.

McMullin, J. 1995. "Theorizing age and gender relations." In S. Arber and J. Ginn, Eds, *Connecting Gender and Ageing: A Sociological Approach*, 30–41. Philadelphia: Open University Press.

———. 2000. "Diversity and the state of sociological aging theory." *The Gerontologist* 40 (5): 517–30.

———. 2010. *Understanding Inequality: Intersections of Class, Age, Gender, Ethnicity and Race in Canada*, 2nd edn. Toronto: Oxford University Press.

McWilliam, C. 1997. "Using a participatory research process to make a difference in policy on aging." *Canadian Journal on Aging* 16 (supplement): 70–89.

Mendes de Leon, C. 2007. "Aging and the elapse of time: A comment on the analysis of change." *Journal of Gerontology: Social Sciences* 62B (3): S198–202.

Milligan, C., et al. 2005. "Digging deep: Using diary techniques to explore the place of health and well-being among older people." *Social Science and Medicine,* 61: 1882–92.

Mills, C.W. 1959. *The Sociological Imagination*. New York: Oxford University Press.

Minkler, M. 1996. "Critical perspectives on aging: New challenges for gerontology." *Ageing and Society* 16 (2): 467–87.

Minkler, M., and C. Estes, Eds. 1991. *Critical Perspectives on Aging: The Political and Moral Economy of Growing Old*. Amityville, NY: Baywood.

———, Eds. 1999. *Critical Gerontology: Perspectives from Political and Moral Economy*. Amityville, NY: Baywood.

Minkler, M., and M. Holstein. 2008. "From civil rights to . . . civil engagement? Concerns of two older critical gerontologists about a 'new social movement' and what it portends." *Journal of Aging Studies* 22: 196–204.

Mitchell, B. 2003. "Life course theory." In J. Ponzetti, Ed., *The International Encyclopedia of Marriage and Family Relationships*, 2nd edn, 1051–5. New York: Macmillan Reference USA.

———. 2006. *Boomerang Age: Transitions to Adulthood in Families*. Piscataway, NJ: Transaction.

———. 2012. *Family Matters: An Introduction to Family Sociology in Canada,* 2nd edn. Toronto: Canadian Scholars' Press.

Moen, P., and K. Chermack. 2005. "Gender disparities in health: Strategic selection, careers, and cycles of control." *Journal of Gerontology* 60B (special issue II): 99–108.

Moody, H. 1988. "Toward a critical gerontology: The contributions of the humanities to theories of aging." In J. Birren and V. Bengtson, Eds, *Emergent Theories of Aging*, 19–40. New York: Springer.

———. 1993. "Overview: What is critical gerontology and why is it important?" In T. Cole et al., Eds, *Voices and Visions: Toward a Critical Gerontology*, xv–xii. New York: Springer.

Munhall, P., and C. Boyd. 2000. *Nursing Research: A Qualitative Perspective*. New York: Jones and Bartlett.

Myles, J. 1989. *Old Age in the Welfare State: The Political Economy of Public Pensions*. 2nd edn. Lawrence: University of Kansas Press.

National Research Council. 2001. *Preparing for an Aging World: The Case for Cross-National Research*. Washington: National Academy Press.

Neysmith, S. 1995. "Feminist methodologies: A consideration of principles and practice for research in gerontology." *Canadian Journal on Aging* 14 (supplement 1): 100–18.

O'Rand, A. 2006. "Stratification and the life course: Life course capital, life course risks, and social inequality." In R. Binstock and L. George, Eds, *Handbook of Aging and the Social Sciences*, 145–62. San Diego: Academic Press.

Osmond, M., and B. Thorne. 1993. "Feminist theories: The social construction of gender in families and society." In P. Boss et al., Eds, *Sourcebook of Family Theories and Methods: A Contextual Approach*, 591–623. New York: Plenum.

Phillipson, C. 1998. *Reconstructing Old Age*. Thousand Oaks, CA: Sage.

———. 2003. "Globalization and the reconstruction of old age: New challenges for critical gerontology." In S. Biggs et al., Eds, *The Need for Theory: Critical Approaches to Social Gerontology*, 163–80. Amityville, NY: Baywood.

———. 2005. "The political economy of old age." In M. Johnson, Ed., *The Cambridge Handbook of Age and Ageing*, 502–9. New York: Cambridge University Press.

———. 2009. "Reconstructing theories of aging: The impact of globalization on critical gerontology." In V. Bengtson, D. Gans, N. Putney, and M. Silverstein, Eds, *Handbook of Theories of Aging*, 615–28. New York: Springer.

Phoenix, C., et al. 2010. "Narrative analysis in aging studies: A typology for consideration." *Journal of Aging Studies* 24: 1–11.

Pillemar, K., et al. 2003. "Finding the best ways to help: Opportunities and challenges of intervention research on aging." *The Gerontologist* 43 (special issue I): 5–8.

Powell, J. 2005. *Social Theory and Aging*. Lanham, MD: Rowman and Littlefield.

Powell, J., and A. Wahidin, Eds. 2006. *Foucault and Aging*. Hauppage, NY: Nova Science Publishers.

Quadagno, J., and J. Reid. 1999. "The political economy perspective in aging." In V. Bengtson and W. Schaie, Eds, *Handbook of Theories of Aging*, 344–58. New York: Springer.

Raina, P., et al. 2009. "The Canadian Longitudinal Study on Aging (CLSA)." *Canadian Journal on Aging* 28 (3): 221–29.

Randall, W., and G. Kenyon. 2004. "Time, story and wisdom: Emerging themes in narrative gerontology." *Canadian Journal on Aging* 23 (4): 333–46.

Ray, R. 1996. "A postmodern perspective on feminist gerontology." *The Gerontologist* 36 (5): 674–80.

———. 1998. "Introduction: Critical perspectives on the life story." *Journal of Aging Studies* 12 (2): 101–6.

Reason, P., and H. Bradbury, Eds. 2001. *Handbook of Action Research: Participative Inquiry and Practice*. Newbury Park, CA: Sage.

Reinharz, S. 1992. *Feminist Methods in Social Research*. New York: Oxford University Press.

Reitzes, D., et al. 1995. "Activities and self-esteem: Continuing the development of activity theory." *Research on Aging* 17 (3): 260–77.

Ries, N. 2010 "Canadian Institutes of Health Research—Institute of Aging: Profile ethics, health research, and Canada's aging population." *Canadian Journal on Aging* 29 (4): 577–80.

Riley, M. 1971. "Social gerontology and the age stratification of society." *The Gerontologist* 11 (1): 79–87.

———. 1973. "Aging and cohort succession: Interpretations and misinterpretations." *Public Opinion Quarterly* 37 (1): 35–49.

———. 1985. "Age strata in social systems." In R. Binstock and E. Shanas, Eds, *Handbook of Aging and the Social Sciences*, 369–411. New York: Van Nostrand Reinhold.

———. 1994. "Aging and society: Past, present, and future." *The Gerontologist* 34 (4): 436–46.

Riley, M., et al. 1972. "Elements in a model of age stratification." In M. Riley, et al., Eds, *Aging and Society, vol. 3: A Sociology of Age Stratification*, 3–26. New York: Russell Sage Foundation.

———. 1994. *Age and Structural Lag: Society's Failure to Provide Meaningful Opportunities in Work, Family and Leisure*. New York: Wiley.

———. 1999. "The aging and society paradigm." In V. Bengtson and W. Schaie, Eds, *Handbook of Theories of Aging*, 327–43. New York: Springer.

Rowles, G.D., and N.E. Schoenberg, Eds. 2002. *Qualitative Gerontology*. New York: Springer.

Rozanova, J., et al. 2006. "Seniors and portrayals of intra-generational and inter-generational inequality in *The Globe and Mail*." *Canadian Journal on Aging* 25 (4): 373–86.

Rubinstein, R.L. 2002. "The qualitative interview with older informants: Some key questions." In G.D.

Rowles and N.E. Schoenberg, Eds, *Qualitative Gerontology,* 137–53. New York: Springer.

Russell, C. 1999a. "Introduction: Perspectives on using qualitative research in aging studies." *Journal of Aging Studies* 13 (4): 365–8.

———. 1999b. "Interviewing vulnerable old people: Ethical and methodological implications of imagining our subjects." *Journal of Aging Studies* 13 (4): 403–18.

Salari, S. 2002. "Invisible in aging research: Arab Americans, Middle Eastern immigrants, and Muslims in the United States." *The Gerontologist* 42 (5): 580–8.

Schaie, W. 1965. "A general model for the study of developmental problems." *Psychological Bulletin* 64 (2): 92–107.

———. 1988. "The impact of research methodology on theory building in the developmental sciences." In J. Birren and V. Bengtson, Eds, *Emergent Theories of Aging,* 41–57. New York: Springer.

Scheidt, R., and P. Windley. 2006. "Environmental gerontology: Progress in the post-Lawton era." In J. Birren and W. Schaie, Eds, *Handbook of the Psychology of Aging,* 105–25. San Diego: Academic Press.

Schroots, J. 1995. "Psychological models of aging." *Canadian Journal on Aging* 14 (1): 44–66.

———. 1996. "The fractal structure of lives: Continuity and discontinuity in autobiography." In J. Birren et al., Eds, *Aging and Biography: Explorations in Adult Development,* 117–30. New York: Springer.

Settersten, R., Ed. 2003. *Invitation to the Life Course: Toward New Understandings of Later Life.* Amityville, NY: Baywood.

———. 2005. "Linking the two ends of life: What gerontologists can learn from childhood studies." *Journal of Gerontology: Social Sciences* 60B (4): S173–80.

———. 2006. "Aging and the life course." In R. Binstock and L. George, Eds, *Handbook of Aging and the Social Sciences,* 3–19. San Diego: Academic Press.

Sheets, D., and E. Gallagher. 2013. "Aging in Canada: State of the art and science." *The Gerontologist* 53 (1): 1–8.

Singer, B., and C. Ryff. 2001. "Person-centered methods for understanding aging: The integration of numbers and narratives." In R. Binstock and L. George, Eds, *Handbook of Aging and the Social Sciences,* 44–65. New York: Academic Press.

Stephenson, P., et al. 1999. "A methodological discourse on gender, independence, and frailty: Applied dimensions of identity construction in old age." *Journal of Aging Studies* 13 (4): 391–401.

Stoller, E. 1993. "Gender and the organization of lay health care: A socialist-feminist perspective." *Journal of Aging Studies* 7 (1): 151–70.

Thomas, W. 1931. "The definition of the situation." In W. Thomas, Ed., *The Unadjusted Girl,* 41–50. Boston: Little, Brown.

Thompson, E., Ed. 1994. *Older Men's Lives.* Thousand Oaks, CA: Sage.

Turner, J. 1982. *The Structure of Sociological Theory.* 3rd edn. Homewood, IL: Dorsey.

van den Hoonaard, D. 2010. *By Himself: The Older Man's Experience of Widowhood.* Toronto: University of Toronto Press.

Walker, A. 1999. "Public policy and theories of aging: Constructing and reconstructing old age." In V. Bengtson and W. Schaie, Eds, *Handbook of Theories of Aging,* 361–78. New York: Springer.

Weisman, G. 2003. "Creating places for people with dementia: An action research perspective." In W. Schaie et al., Eds, *Aging Independently: Living Arrangements and Mobility,* 162–73. New York: Springer.

Windsor, R., et al. 2004. *Evaluation of Health Promotion, Health Education, and Disease Prevention.* NY: McGraw Hill.

Wister, A.V., and D. Wanless. 2007. "A health profile and exploratory analysis of Canadian nonagenarians." *Canadian Journal on Aging* 26 (1): 1–18.

Wolinsky, F.D. 1993. "Age, period and cohort analyses of health-related behaviour." In K. Dean, Ed., *Population Health Research: Linking Theory and Methods,* 54–73. London: Sage.

Chapter 6

Social Structures, Social Inequality, and the Life Course

Adams, M. 1997. *Sex in the Snow: Canadian Social Values at the End of the Millennium.* Toronto: Viking.

Alwin, D. 2002. "Generations X, Y and Z: Are they changing America?" *Contexts* (fall/winter): 42–50.

Arber, S., et al. (Eds). 2004. *Gender and Aging: Changing Roles and Relationships.* Maidenhead, UK: Open University Press.

Arber, S., and J. Ginn, Eds. 1995. *Connecting Gender and Aging: A Sociological Approach.* Philadelphia: Open University Press.

———. 2005. "Gender dimensions of the age shift." In M. Johnson, Ed., *The Cambridge Handbook of Age and Ageing,* 527–37. New York: Cambridge University Press.

Barnard, R., et al. 1998. *Chips and Pop: Decoding the Nexus Generation*. Toronto: Malcolm Lester.

Bengtson, V., et al. 1990. "Families and aging: Diversity and heterogeneity." In R. Binstock and L. George, Eds, *Handbook of Aging and the Social Sciences*, 263–87. San Diego: Academic Press.

———. 1996. "Paradoxes of families and aging." In R. Binstock and L. George, Eds, *Handbook of Aging and the Social Sciences*, 253–82. San Diego: Academic Press.

Bengtson, V., and N. Cutler. 1976. "Generations and intergenerational relations: Perspectives on age groups and social change." In R. Binstock and E. Shanas, Eds, *Handbook of Aging and the Social Sciences*, 130–59. New York: Van Nostrand Reinhold.

Calasanti, T. 1999. "Feminism and gerontology: Not just for women." *Hallym International Journal of Aging* 1 (1): 44–55.

Calasanti, T. 2009. "Theorizing feminist gerontology, sexuality, and beyond: An intersectional approach." In V. Bengtson, D. Gans, N. Putney, and M. Silverstein, Eds, *Handbook of Theories of Aging*, 471–86. New York: Springer.

Calasanti, T., and K. Slevin. 2001. *Gender, Social Inequalities and Aging*. Walnut Creek, CA: AltaMira Press.

Cheung, C., and A. Kwan. 2009. "The erosion of filial piety by modernization in Chinese cities." *Ageing & Society* 29: 179–98.

Connidis, I. 2010. *Family Ties and Aging*, 2nd edn. Thousand Oaks, CA: Sage.

Coupland, D. 1992. *Generation X: Tales for an Accelerated Culture*. New York: St Martins Press.

Cremer, H., et al. 1994. "Public and private intergenerational transfers: Evidence and a simple model." In J. Ermisch and N. Ogawa, Eds, The Family, the State and the Market in Aging Societies, 216–31. Oxford, UK: Clarendon Press.

Cutler, S., and J. Hendricks. 2001. "Emerging social trends." In R. Binstock and L. George, Eds, *Handbook of Aging and the Social Sciences*, 462–80. New York: Academic Press.

Dannefer, D., et al. 2009. "Theorizing the life course: New twists in the Paths." In V. Bengtson, D. Gans, N. Putney, and M. Silverstein, Eds, *Handbook of Theories of Aging*, 389–412. New York: Springer.

Elder, G. 1999. *Children of the Great Depression: Social Change in Life Experience*. 25th anniversary edn. Chicago: University of Chicago Press.

Estes, C. 2005. "Women, ageing and inequality: A feminist perspective." In M. Johnson, Ed., *The Cambridge Handbook of Age and Ageing*, 552–9. New York: Cambridge University Press.

Ferraro, K. 2001. "Aging and role transitions." In R. Binstock and L. George, Eds, *Handbook of Aging and the Social Sciences*, 313–30. New York: Academic Press.

Ferraro, K., et al. 2009. "The political economy perspective on aging." In V. Bengtson, D. Gans, N. Putney, and M. Silverstein, Eds., *Handbook of Theories of Aging*, 413–34. New York: Springer.

Foner, A. 1996. "Age norms and the structure of consciousness: Some final comments." *The Gerontologist* 36 (2): 221–3.

———. 2000. "Age integration or age conflict as society ages?" *The Gerontologist* 40 (3): 272–6.

Foot, D., and D. Stoffman. 1998. *Boom, Bust and Echo 2000: Profiting from the Demographic Shift in the New Millennium*. Toronto: MacFarlane Walter and Ross.

Foot, D., and R. Venne. 2005. "Awakening to the intergenerational equity debate in Canada." *Journal of Canadian Studies* 39 (1): 5–21.

Fors, S., et al. 2009. "Childhood living conditions, socioeconomic position in adulthood, and cognition in later life: Exploring the associations." *Journal of Gerontology: Social Sciences* 64B(6): 750–7.

Gee, E. 1990. "Preferred timing of women's life events: A Canadian study." *International Journal of Aging and Human Development* 31 (4): 279–94.

———. 2000. "Population and politics: Voodoo demography, population aging, and Canadian social policy." In E. Gee and G. Gutman, Eds, *The Overselling of Population Aging: Apocalyptic Demography, Intergenerational Challenges and Social Policy*, 5–25. Don Mills, ON: Oxford University Press.

Gee, E., and M. Kimball. 1987. *Women and Aging*. Toronto: Butterworths.

Gray, J. 1992. *Men Are from Mars, Women Are from Venus: A Practical Guide for Improving Communication and Getting What You Want in Your Relationships*. New York: HarperCollins.

Guralnik, J., et al. 2006. "Childhood socioeconomic status predicts physical functioning a half century later." *Journal of Gerontology: Medical Sciences* 61A (7): 699–701.

Hamil-Luker, J., and P. Uhlenberg. 2002. "Later life education in the 1990s: Increasing involvement and continuing disparity." *Journal of Gerontology: Social Sciences* 57B (6): S324–31.

Hareven, T. 2001. "Historical perspectives on aging and family relations." In R. Binstock and L. George, Eds, *Handbook of Aging and the Social Sciences*, 141–59. New York: Academic Press.

Hatch, L. 2000. *Beyond Gender Differences: Adaptation to Aging in Life Course Perspective*. Amityville, NY: Baywood.

Hendricks, J. 1993. "Recognizing the relativity of gender in aging research." *Journal of Aging Studies* 7 (2): 111–16.

Holstein, M. 2010. "Ethics in old age: The second generation." In D. Dannefer and C. Phillipson, Eds, *The Sage Handbook of Social Gerontology* 630–40. Thousand Oaks, CA: Sage.

Hsu, H.-C., et al. 2002. "Age, period, and cohort effects on the attitude toward supporting parents in Taiwan." *The Gerontologist* 41 (6): 742–50.

Johnson, M. 2005. "The social construction of old age as a problem." In M. Johnson, Ed., *The Cambridge Handbook of Age and Ageing*, 653–71. New York: Cambridge University Press.

Kaida, L., and M. Boyd. 2011. "Poverty variations among the elderly: The roles of income security policies and family co-residence." *Canadian Journal on Aging* 30 (1): 83–100.

Kimmel, M. 2000. *The Gendered Society*. New York: Oxford University Press.

Koehn, S. 2009. "Negotiating candidacy: Ethnic minority seniors' access to care." *Ageing & Society* 29: 585–608.

Kohli, M. 2005. "Generational changes and generational equity." In M. Johnson, Ed., *The Cambridge Handbook of Age and Ageing*, 518–26. New York: Cambridge University Press.

——. 2006. "Aging and justice." In R. Binstock and L. George, Eds, *Handbook of Aging and the Social Sciences*, 456–78. San Diego: Academic Press.

Kotash, M. 2000. *The Next Canada: In Search of Our Future Nation*. Toronto: McClelland and Stewart.

——. 2004. *Does Age Matter? Law and Relationships between Generations*. Ottawa: Law Commission of Canada.

Kovaks, P., and J. Lee. 2010. "Developing a community-university partnership for intergenerational programming: Relationship building is key." *Journal of Intergenerational Relationships* 8 (4): 406–11.

Larkin, E., et al., Eds. 2005. *Intergenerational Relationships: Conversations on Practice and Research across Cultures*. Binghampton, NY: Haworth.

Longino, C., and J. Powell 2009. "Toward a phenomenology of aging." In V. Bengtson, D. Gans, N. Putney, and M. Silverstein, Eds, *Handbook of Theories of Aging*, 375–88. New York: Springer.

MacKenzie, S., et al. 2011. "The Meadows School Project: A unique intergenerational 'immersion' program." *Journal of Intergenerational Relationships* 9 (2): 207–12.

Mannheim, K. 1952. *Essays in the Sociology of Knowledge*. London: Routledge and Kegan Paul.

Marshall, V. 1983. "Generations, age groups and cohorts: Conceptual distinctions." *Canadian Journal on Aging* 2 (3): 51–62.

Marshall, V., and M. Mueller. 2003. "Theoretical roots of the life course perspective." In W. Heinz and V. Marshall, Eds, *Dynamics of the Life Course: Sequences, Institutions and Interrelations*, 3–32. New York: Aldine de Gruyter.

Martin-Matthews, A. 2000. "Intergenerational caregiving: How apocalyptic and dominant demographies frame the questions and shape the answers." In E. Gee and G. Gutman, Eds, *The Overselling of Population Aging*, 64–79. Don Mills, ON: Oxford University Press.

Matthews, S. 1979. *The Social World of Old Women: Management of Self-Identity*. Beverly Hills, CA: Sage.

McDaniel, S. 1997. "Intergenerational transfers, social solidarity, and social policy: Unanswered questions and policy challenges." *Canadian Journal on Aging* (supplement): 1–21.

——. 2000. "What did you ever do for me? Intergenerational linkages in a reconstructing Canada." In E. Gee and G. Gutman, Eds, *The Overselling of Population Aging*, 129–52. Don Mills, ON: Oxford University Press.

——. 2002. "Intergenerational interlinkages: Public, family and work." In D. Cheal, Ed., *Aging and Demographic Change in Canadian Context*, 22–71. Toronto: University of Toronto Press.

McMullin, J. 1995. "Theorizing age and gender relations." In S. Arber and J. Ginn, Eds, *Connecting Gender and Ageing: A Sociological Approach*, 30–41. Philadelphia: Open University Press.

——. 2000. "Diversity and the state of sociological aging theory." *The Gerontologist* 40 (5): 517–30.

——. 2004. *Understanding Inequality: Intersections of Class, Age, Gender, Ethnicity and Race in Canada*. Don Mills, ON: Oxford University Press.

——. 2010. *Understanding Inequality: Intersections of Class, Age, Gender, Ethnicity and Race in Canada*, 2nd edn. Don Mills, ON: Oxford University Press.

Mitchell, B. 2012. *Family Matters: An Introduction to Family Sociology in Canada*, 2nd edn. Toronto: Canadian Scholars' Press Inc.

Moen, P. 1996. "Gender, age and the life course." In R. Binstock and L. George, Eds, *Handbook of Aging and the Social Sciences*, 171–87. San Diego: Academic Press.

——. 2001. "The gendered life course." In R. Binstock and L. George, Eds, *Handbook of Aging and the Social Sciences*, 179–96. New York: Academic Press.

Moen, P., and D. Spencer. 2006. "Converging divergencies in age, gender, health and well-being: Strategic selection in the third age." In R. Binstock and L. George, Eds, *Handbook of Aging and the Social Sciences*, 127–44. San Diego: Academic Press.

Morgan, L., and S. Kunkel. 2011. *Aging, Society and the Life Course*. New York: Springer.

Nichols, B., and P. Leonard, Eds. 1994. *Gender, Aging and the State*. Montreal: Black Rose.

O'Rand, A.1996. "The cumulative stratification of the life course." In R. Binstock and L. George, Eds, *Handbook of Aging and the Social Sciences*, 188–207. San Diego: Academic Press.

———. 2001. "Stratification and the life course: The forms of life-course capital and their interrelationships." In R. Binstock and L. George, Eds, *Handbook of Aging and the Social Sciences*, 197–213. New York: Academic Press.

———. 2006. "Stratification and the life course: Life course capital, life course risks and social inequality." In R. Binstock and L. George, Eds, *Handbook of Aging and the Social Sciences*, 145–62. San Diego: Academic Press.

O'Rand, A., and J. Hamil-Luker. 2005. "Process of cumulative adversity: Childhood disadvantage and increased risk of heart attack across the life course." *Journals of Gerontology* 60B (special issue II): 117–24.

Ploeg, J., et al. 2003. "Helping to build and rebuild secure lives and futures: Intergenerational financial transfers from parents to adult children and grandchildren." SEDAP Research Paper no. 96. Hamilton, ON: McMaster University. http://socserv2.mcmaster.ca/sedap.

Price, S., et al., Eds. 2000. *Families across Time: A Life Course Perspective*. Los Angeles: Roxbury.

Pyke, K. 1996. "Class-based masculinities: The interdependence of gender, class and interpersonal power." *Gender and Society* 10 (5): 527–49.

Riley, M., et al. 1994. *Age and Structural Lag*. New York: John Wiley and Sons.

Riley, M., and J. Riley. 1994. "Structural lag: Past and future." In M. Riley et al., Eds, *Age and Structural Lag*, 15–36. New York: John Wiley and Sons.

———. 2000. "Age integration: Conceptual and historical background." *The Gerontologist* 40 (3): 266–70.

Settersten, R., and G. Hagestad. 1996a. "What's the latest? Cultural age deadlines for family transitions." *The Gerontologist* 36 (2): 178–88.

———. 1996b. "What's the latest? II: Cultural age deadlines for educational and work transitions." *The Gerontologist* 36 (5): 602–13.

Silverstein, M., Ed. 2005. "Focus on intergenerational relations across time and place." *Annual Review of Gerontology and Geriatrics* 24. New York: Springer.

———. 2006. "Intergenerational family transfers in social context." In R. Binstock and L. George, Eds, *Handbook of Aging and the Social Sciences*, 165–80. San Diego: Academic Press.

Simpson, Jeffrey. 1997. "A generation bequeaths a terrible mess to the next." *The Globe and Mail* 18 February: A14.

Sinnott, J., and K. Shifren. 2001. "Gender and aging: Gender differences and gender roles." In J. Birren and W. Schaie, Eds, *Handbook of the Psychology of Aging*, 454–76. New York: Academic Press.

Thau, R., and J. Heflin, Eds. 1997. *Generations Apart: Xers vs. Boomers vs. the Elderly*. Amherst, NY: Prometheus.

Thompson, E., Ed. 1994. *Older Men's Lives*. Thousand Oaks, CA: Sage.

Tindale, J., et al. 2002. "Catching up with diversity in intergenerational relationships." In D. Cheal, Ed., *Aging and Demographic Change in Canadian Context*, 223–44. Toronto: University of Toronto Press.

Uhlenberg, P. 2000. "Introduction: Why study age integration?" *The Gerontologist* 40 (3): 261–6.

Uhlenberg, P., and S. Miner. 1996. "Life course and aging: A cohort perspective." In R. Binstock and L. George, Eds, *Handbook of Aging and the Social Sciences*, 208–28. San Diego: Academic Press.

Valliant, G. 2007. "Generativity: A form of unconditional love " In S. Post, Ed., *Altruism and Health*, 219–29. New York: Oxford University Press.

van den Hoonaard, D., Ed. 2007. "Aging and masculinity." *Journal of Aging Studies* 21 (4): 277–368.

Ven, S., et al. 2011. "Gender and aging." In R. Settersten and J. Angel, Eds, *Handbook of Sociology of Aging*, 71–81. New York: Springer.

Walker, A. 2000. "Public policy and the construction of old age in Europe." *The Gerontologist* 40 (3): 304–8.

Williams, D., and C. Wilson. 2001. "Race, ethnicity and aging." In R. Binstock and L. George, Eds, *Handbook of Aging and the Social Sciences*, 160–78. New York: Academic Press.

Williamson, J., et al., Eds. 1999. *The Generational Equity Debate*. New York: Columbia University Press.

Wister, A.V. 2005. *Baby Boomer Dynamics: How Are We Aging?* Toronto: University of Toronto Press.

Worell, J., et al., Eds. 2000. *Encyclopedia of Women and Gender*, vols 1 and 2. New York: Academic Press.

Yeo, G. 1993. "Ethnicity and nursing homes: Factors affecting use and successful components for culturally sensitive care." In C. Barresi and D. Stull, Eds, *Ethnic Elderly and Long-Term Care*, 161–77. New York: Springer.

Zarit, S., and L. Pearlin, Eds. 2005. "Health inequalities across the life course." *Journal of Gerontology: Psychology and Social Sciences* 60B (special issue): 5–139.

Chapter 7
Health Status and Health-Care Transitions

Alexander, T. 2002. "The history and evolution of long-term care in Canada." In M. Stephenson and E. Sawyer, Eds, *Continuing the Care: The Issues and Challenges for Long-Term Care*, 1–55. Ottawa: CHA Press.

Allan, D., and D. Cloutier-Fisher. 2006. "Health service utilization among older adults in British Columbia: Making sense of geography." *Canadian Journal on Aging* 25 (2): 219–32.

Alzheimer Society of Canada. 2010. *Rising Tide: The Impact of Dementia on Canadian Society*. Toronto: Alzheimer Society of Canada.

American Council on Science and Health. 1999. *Environmental Tobacco Smoke: Health Risk or Health Hype?* New York: American Council of Science and Health.

Armstrong, P., and H. Armstrong. 2003. *Wasting Away: The Undermining of Canadian Health Care*. Don Mills, ON: Oxford University Press.

Ballantyne, P., et al. 2005. "Factors associated with medicine use and non-use by Ontario seniors." *Canadian Journal on Aging* 24 (4): 419–31.

Beeston, D. 2006. *Older People and Suicide*. Staffordshire, UK: Centre for Ageing and Mental Health, Staffordshire University.

Béland, F., et al. 2006. "Integrated services for frail elders (sipa): A trial of a model for Canada." *Canadian Journal on Aging* 25 (1): 24–42.

Berkman, L.F., and I. Kawachi. 2000. *Social Epidemiology*. New York: Oxford University Press.

Binkley, J.K., et al. 2000. "The relation between dietary change and rising obesity." *International Journal of Obesity* 24 (8): 1032–9.

Binstock, R., et al. 2006. "Anti-aging medicine and science: Social implications." In R. Binstock and L. George, Eds, *Handbook of Aging and the Social Sciences*, 436–55. San Diego: Academic Press.

Binstock, R., and L. George, Eds. 2006. *Handbook of Aging and the Social Sciences*. San Diego: Academic Press.

Black, C., et al. 1995. "Rising use of physician services by the elderly." *Canadian Journal on Aging* 14 (2): 225–44.

Blazer, D. 2003. "Depression in late life: Review and commentary." *Journal of Gerontology: Medical Sciences* 58A (3): M249–65.

British Columbia Ministry of Health Services. 2004. *Pharmacare Trends 2003*. www.hlth.gov.bc.ca/pharme/pharmacare trends 2003.pdf.

Buckley, N., et al. 2004. "Healthy aging at older ages: Are income and education important?" *Canadian Journal on Aging* 23 (supplement): S155–69.

Burke, M., et al. 1997. "Dementia among seniors." *Canadian Social Trends* 45 (summer): 24–7.

Butler, R. 2003. "Senility: The epidemic of the twenty-first century of longevity." Unpublished essay in the Imagining Longevity Series. New York: International Longevity Center. www.ilcusa.org.

———. 2008. *The Longevity Revolution: The Benefits and Challenges of Living a Long Life*. New York: Perseus Publishing.

Cain, M., et al. 2000. *Health E-people: The Online Consumer Experience: Five Year Forecast*. Written for the California Health Care Foundation. www.chcf.org/documents/ihealth/HealthEPeople.pdf.

Cairney, J. 2000. "Socio-economic status and self-rated health among older Canadians." *Canadian Journal on Aging* 19 (4): 456–78.

Canadian Coalition for Seniors' Mental Health. 2009. *Delirium in Older Adults: A Guide for Seniors and their Families*. Ottawa: Canadian Coalition for Seniors' Mental Health.

Canadian Public Health Association. 1997. *Health Impacts of Social and Economic Conditions: Implications for Public Policy*. Ottawa: Canadian Public Health Association.

Cataldo, J. 2003. "Smoking and aging: Clinical implications. Part I: Health consequences." *Journal of Gerontological Nursing* 29 (9): 15–20.

Chappell, N., and L. Funk. 2011. "Social support, caregiving and aging." *Canadian Journal on Aging* 30 (3): 355–70.

Chappell, N., and D. Lai. 1998. "Health care service use by Chinese seniors in British Columbia, Canada." *Journal of Cross-Cultural Gerontology* 13 (1): 21–37.

Chappell, N., and M. Hollander. 2011a. "An evidence-based policy prescription for an aging population." *Healthcare Papers* 11 (1): 8–19.

Chappell, N., and M. Hollander. 2011b. "The authors respond." *Healthcare Papers* 11 (1): 88–91.

Chappell, N., et al. 2008. *Aging in Contemporary Canada*, 2nd edn. Toronto: Pearson.

Chen, J., et al. 2002. "Unmet health care needs." *Canadian Social Trends* 67 (winter): 18–22.

Chipperfield, J. 1993. "Perceived barriers in coping with health problems." *Journal of Aging and Health* 5 (1): 123–39.

Chou, H.B., and A.V. Wister. 2005. "From cues to action: Information seeking and exercise self-care among older adults managing a chronic illness." *Canadian Journal on Aging* 24 (4): 395–408.

CIHI (Canadian Institute for Health Information). 2002. *Health Care in Canada*. Ottawa: CIHI.

———. 2003. *How Healthy Are Canadians, 2002?* Ottawa: CIHI.

———. 2004. *Improving the Health of Canadians*. Ottawa: CIHI.

———. 2005. *Exploring the 70/30 Split: How Canada's Health Care System is Financed*. http://secure. CIHI.ca/cihiweb/products/FundRep_EN.pdf.

———. 2007. *Drug Claims by Seniors: An Analysis Focusing on Potentially Inappropriate Medication Use, 2000–2006*. Ottawa: CIHI.

———. 2010. *Health Care in Canada, 2010*. http://secure.cihi.ca/cihiweb/products/ HCIC_2010_Web_e.pdf, retrieved 22 March 2011.

———. 2011a. *Health Care in Canada, 2011: A Focus on Seniors and Aging*. Ottawa: CIHI.

———. 2011b. *National Health Expenditure Trends,1975 to 2011*. www.cihi.ca/ cihi-ext-portal/internet/en/document/ spending+and+health+workforce/spending/ release_03nov11, retrieved 30 November 2012.

CIHR (Canadian Institutes of Health Research). 2005. *Investing in Canada's Future: CIHR's Blueprint for Health Research and Innovation*. www.cihr-irsc. gc.ca/about_cihr/organization.

Clarke, J. 2000. *Health, Illness and Medicine in Canada*. Don Mills, ON: Oxford University Press.

Coles, L.S. 2004. "Demography of human supercentenarians." *Journal of Gerontology: Biological Sciences* 59 (6): B579–86.

Colley, R., et al. 2011. "Physical activity of Canadian adults: Accelerometer results from the 2007 to 2009 Canadian Health Measures Survey." (Statistics Canada, Cat. 82-003). *Health Reports* 22 (1): 15–23.

Conn, D. 2002. "Mental health services and long-term care." In M. Stephenson and E. Sawyer, Eds, *Continuing the Care: The Issues and Challenges for Long-Term Care*, 143–61. Ottawa: CHA Press.

Crimmins, E. 2004. "Trends in the health of the elderly." *Annual Review of Public Health* 25: 79–98.

Crimmins, E., and Y. Saito. 2001. "Trends in life expectancy in the United States, 1970–1990: Gender, racial and educational differences." *Social Sciences and Medicine* 52: 1629–41.

Dannefer, D. 2003. "Cumulative advantage/disadvantage and the life course: Crossfertilizing age and social science theory." *Journals of Gerontology: Social Sciences* 58B (6): S327–37.

D'Arcy, C. 1998. "Health status of Canadians." In D. Coburn et al., Eds, *Health and Canadian Society: Sociological Perspectives*, 43–68. Toronto: University of Toronto Press.

DeBaggio, T. 2003. *Losing My Mind: An Intimate Look at Life with Alzheimer's*. New York: Free Press.

De Coster, C., et al. 2005. "Use of acute care hospitals by long-stay patients: Who, how much, and why?" *Canadian Journal on Aging* 24 (supplement): 97–106.

Epp, J. 1986. *Achieving Health for All: A Framework for Health Promotion*. Ottawa: Minister of National Health and Welfare.

Evans, R., et al. 2001. "Apocalypse no: Population aging and the future of health care systems." *Canadian Journal on Aging* 20 (supplement 1): 160–91.

Evert, J., et al. 2003. "Morbidity profiles of centenarians: Survivors, delayers and escapers." *Journals of Gerontology: Medical Sciences* 58A (3): 232–7.

Feder, J., et al. 2001. "The financing and organization of health care." In R. Binstock and L. George, Eds, *Handbook of Aging and the Social Sciences*, 387–405. San Diego: Academic Press.

Ferraro, K. 2006a. "Health and aging." In R. Binstock and L. George, Eds, *Handbook of Aging and the Social Sciences*, 238–56. San Diego: Academic Press.

———. 2006b. "The color of hospitalization over the adult life course: Cumulative disadvantage in blacks and whites?" *Journals of Gerontology: Social Sciences* 61B (6): S299–306.

Fick, D.M., et al. 2003. "Updating the Beers criteria for potentially inappropriate medication use in older adults." *Archives of Internal Medicine* 163 (22): 2716–24.

Fiske, A., and R. Jones. 2005. "Depression." In M. Johnson, Ed., *The Cambridge Handbook of Age and Ageing*, 245–51. Cambridge: Cambridge University Press.

Forbes, D., et al. 2006. "Rural and urban Canadians with dementia: Use of health care services." *Canadian Journal on Aging* 25 (3): 321–30.

Frank, J., and Mustard, J.F. 1991. *The Determinants of Health*. Toronto: Canadian Institute of Advanced Research.

Fries, J.F. 1983. "Compression of morbidity." *Milbank Memorial Fund Quarterly*, 61: 397–419.

———. 2003. "Measuring and monitoring success in compressing morbidity." *Annals of Internal Medicine* 139 (5) part 2: 455–9.

Gallant, M., et al. 2007. "Help or hindrance? How family and friends influence chronic illness self-management among older adults." *Research on Aging* 29 (5): 375–409.

Gee, E., et al. 2004. "Examining the 'healthy immigrant effect' in mid- to later life: Findings from the Canadian Community Health Survey." *Canadian Journal on Aging* 23 (supplement): S61–70.

Gee, E., and M. Kimball. 1987. *Women and Aging*. Toronto: Butterworths.

George, L. 2003. "What life-course perspectives offer the study of aging and health?" In R. Settersten, Ed., *Invitation to the Life Course: Toward New Understandings of Later Life*, 161–88. Amityville, NY: Baywood.

Gift, H., et al. 1997. "Conceptualizing oral health and quality of life." *Social Science and Medicine* 44 (5): 601–8.

Gilmour, H. 2007. "Physically active Canadians." (Statistics Canada, Cat. 82-003). *Health Reports* 18 (3): 45–65.

Gottlieb, B. 2000. "Self-help, mutual aid and support groups among older adults." *Canadian Journal on Aging* 19 (supplement 1): 58–74.

Green, R., et al. 2008. "Can Canadian seniors on public pensions afford a nutritional diet"? *Canadian Journal on Aging* 27 (1): 69–79.

Grootendorst, P., et al. 2003. "A review of the comprehensiveness of provincial drug coverage for Canadian seniors." *Canadian Journal on Aging* 22 (1): 33–44.

Gross, D., et al. 2004. "The growing pains of integrated health care for the elderly: Lessons from the expansion of pace." *Milbank Memorial Fund Quarterly* 82: 257–82.

Grossberg, G., and A. Desai. 2003. "Management of Alzheimer's disease." *Journal of Gerontology: Medical Sciences* 58A (4): 331–53.

Gruenewald, T.L., et al. 2006. "Combinations of biomarkers predictive of later life mortality." *Proceedings of the National Academy of Sciences* 103: 14158–63.

Gruman, G. 2003. *A History of Ideas about the Prolongation of Life*. New York: Springer.

Hamilton, N., and T. Bhatti. 1996. *Population Health Promotion: An Integrated Model of Population Health and Health Promotion*. Ottawa: Health Promotion Development Division.

Health Canada. 1999. *Canada's Health Care System*. Ottawa: Health Canada. www.hc.sc.gc.ca/medicare.

———. 2002. *The Social Determinants of Health: An Overview of the Implications for Policy and the Role of the Health Sector*. Ottawa: Health Canada.

———. 2006a. "Social capital and health: Maximizing the benefits." *Health Policy Research* 12 (September). Ottawa: Health Canada.

———. 2006b. *Health Care System: eHealth*. www.hc-sc.gc.ca/hcs-sss/ehealth-esante/index_e. html.

Healthy Aging and Wellness Working Group. 2006. *Healthy Aging in Canada: A New Vision, A Vital Investment from Evidence to Action*. Vancouver: BC Ministry of Health, Population Health and Wellness, Healthy Children, Women and Seniors Branch.

Hébert, R. 2011. "Public long-term care insurance: A way to ensure sustainable continuity of care for older people." *Healthcare Quarterly* 11(1): 69–75.

Hébert, R., et al. 2010. "Impact of PRISMA, a coordination-type integrated service delivery system for frail older people in Quebec (CANADA): A quasi-experimental design." *Journal of Gerontology: Social Sciences*, 65B (1): 107–18.

Herd, P., et al. 2011. "Health disparities among older adults: Life course influences and policy solutions." In R. Binstock, L. George, S. Cutler, J. Hendricks and H. Schulz, Eds, *Handbook of Aging and the Social Science*, 7th edn, 121–34. New York: Oxford, UK: Elsevier.

Himes, C. 2004. "Obesity in later life: An overview of the issues." *Research on Aging* 26 (1): 3–12.

Hogan, D., et al. 1999. "Disease, disability and age in cognitively intact seniors: Results from the Canadian Study of Health and Aging." *Journal of Gerontology: Medical Sciences*, 54A (2): M77–82.

———. 2003. "Models, definitions, and criteria of frailty." *Aging Clinical and Experimental Research* 15 (supplement 3): 3–29.

Hollander, M. 2007. *Thematic Scan of the Canadian and International Literature on Health System Responses to Aging Populations*. Ottawa: Health Canada, Home and Continuing Care.

Hollander, M., et al. 2007. "Providing care and support for an aging population: Briefing notes on key policy issues." *Healthcare Quarterly* 10 (3): 34–45.

———. 2009. "Increased value for money in the Canadian healthcare system: New findings and the case for integrated care for seniors." *Healthcare Quarterly* 12 (1): 38–47.

Hollander, M., and M. Prince. 2008. "Organizing healthcare delivery systems for persons with ongoing care needs and their families: A best practices framework." *Healthcare Quarterly* 11 (1): 42–52.

Holstein, M. 1997. "Alzheimer's disease and senile dementia, 1885–1920: An interpretive history of disease negotiation." *Journal of Aging Studies* 11 (1): 1–13.

House, J., et al. 2005. "Continuity and change in the social stratification of aging and health over the life course: Evidence from a nationally representative longitudinal study from 1986 to 2001/2002 (Americans' Changing Lives Study)." *Journal of Gerontology: Social Sciences* 60B (special issue II): 15–26.

Hu, F. 2003. "The Mediterranean diet and mortality: Olive oil and beyond." *New England Journal of Medicine* 348 (26): 2595–6.

Hu, F., et al. 2000. "Prospective study of major dietary patterns and risk of coronary heart disease in men." *American Journal of Clinical Nutrition* 72 (4): 912–21.

Hubert, H., et al. 2002. "Lifestyle habits and compression of morbidity." *Journal of Gerontology: Medical Sciences* 57A (6): M347–51.

Illich, I. 1977. *Limits to Medicine: Medical Nemesis: The Expropriation of Health.* New York: Penguin.

Jenkins, K. 2004. "Body-weight change and physical functioning among young old adults." *Journal of Aging and Health* 16 (2): 248–66.

Jeune, B. 2000. "What can we learn from centenarians?" In P. Martin et al., Eds, *Centenarians: Autonomy Versus Dependence in the Oldest Old,* 9–24. New York: Springer.

Johnson, M., Ed. 2005. *The Cambridge Handbook of Age and Ageing.* New York: Cambridge University Press.

Keating, N. 2005. "Introduction: Perspectives on healthy aging." *Canadian Journal on Aging* 24 (1): 3–4.

Keating, N., Ed. 2008. *Rural Ageing: A Good Place to Grow Old?* London, UK: Policy Press.

Keating, N., et al. 2011. "Aging in rural Canada." *Canadian Journal on Aging* 30 (3): 323–38.

Keefe, J., et al. 2012. *Disability and Support Networks of Older Canadians. Research Paper No. 3,* Population Change and Lifecourse Strategic Knowledge Cluster. London, ON: Population Studies Centre, UWO.

Kirby, M. 2002. *The Health of Canadians: The Federal Role.* Ottawa: The Senate.

Koehn, S. 2009. "Negotiating candidacy: Ethnic minority seniors' access to care." *Ageing & Society* 29: 585–608.

Koehn, S., et al. 2012. "Understanding Chinese-Canadian pathways to a diagnosis of dementia through a critical-Constructionist lens." *Journal of Aging Studies,* 26 (1): 44–54.

Koehn, S., et al. 2013. "Revealing the shape of knowledge using an intersectionality lens: Results of a scoping review on the health and health care of ethnocultural minority older adults."*Ageing and Society,* 33 (3): 437–64. doi: 10.1017/S0144686X12000013

Knight, B., et al. 2006. "Improving the mental health of older adults." In J. Birren and W. Shaie, Eds, *Handbook of the Psychology of Aging,* 407–24. New York: Academic Press.

Laditka, S., and J. Laditka. 2002. "Recent perspectives on active life expectancy for older women." In S. Laditka, Ed., *Health Expectations for Older Women: International Perspectives,* 163–84. New York: Haworth.

Lai, D., et al. 2007. "Relationships between culture and health status: A multi-site study of the older Chinese in Canada." *Canadian Journal on Aging* 26 (3): 171–84.

Lalonde, M. 1974. *A New Perspective on the Health of Canadians.* Ottawa: Information Canada.

Lees, F.D., et al. 2005. "Barriers to exercise behavior among older adults: A focus-group study." *Journal of Aging and Physical Activity* 13 (1): 23–33.

Legris, L., and M. Préville. 2003. "Les motifs du suicide gériatrique: Une étude explorative." *Canadian Journal on Aging* 22 (2): 197–205.

Légaré, J., and Y. Décarie. 2007. "Applying Statistics Canada LifePaths Microsimulations Model to project the health status of Canadian elderly." Paper presented at the International Microsimulation Association Conference, Vienna, 20 August 2007.

Li, L. 2005. "Trajectories of ADL disability among community-dwelling frail older persons." *Research on Aging* 27 (1): 56–79.

Lomas, J. 1998. "Social capital and health: Implications for public health and epidemiology." *Social Science and Medicine* 47 (9): 1181–8.

MacAdam, M. 2008. *Frameworks of Integrated Care for the Elderly: A Systematic Review.* Ottawa, ON: Canadian Policy Research Network.

MacCourt, P., et al. 2002. "CAG policy statement on issues in the delivery of mental health services to older adults." *Canadian Journal on Aging* 21 (2): 165–74.

MacEntee et al. 2011. *Summary of a Scoping Review and Research Synthesis on Financing and Regulating Oral Healthcare in Long-Term Care Facilities.* Vancouver, BC: UBC.

McDonald-Miszczak, L., et al. 2005. "Younger-old and older-old adults' recall of medication instructions." *Canadian Journal on Aging* 24 (4): 409–17.

McDonald-Miszczak, L., and Wister, A.V. 2005. "Predicting self-care behaviors among older adults coping with arthritis: A cross-sectional and one year longitudinal comparative analysis." *Journal of Aging and Health* 17 (6): 836–57.

McMullin, J. 2010. *Understanding Inequality: Intersections of Class, Age, Gender, Ethnicity and Race in Canada,* 2nd edn. Don Mills, ON: Oxford University Press.

Maddigan, S., et al. 2003. "Predictors of older adults' capacity for medication management in a self-medication program." *Journal of Aging and Health* 15 (2): 332–52.

Makomaski Illing, E., and M. Kaiserman. 2004. "Mortality attributable to tobacco use in Canada and its regions, 1998." *Canadian Journal of Public Health* 95 (1): 38–44.

Malatesta, V., Ed. 2007. "The need to address older women's mental health issues." *Journal of Women and Aging* 19 (1/2): 1–196.

Manton. K. 2008. "Recent declines in chronic disability in the elderly population: Risk factors and future dynamics." *Annual Review of Public Health* 29: 91–113.

Manton, K., et al. 2006. "Change in chronic disability from 1982 to 2004/2005 as a measure of long-term changes in function and health in the U.S. elderly population." *Proceedings of the National Academy of Sciences* 103 (48): 18374–9.

Manuel, D., and S. Schultz. 2001. *Adding Years to Life and Life to Years: Life and Health Expectancy in Ontario*. Toronto: Institute for Clinical Evaluation Sciences.

Martin, L., et al. 2009. "Health and functioning among baby boomers approaching 60." *Journals of Gerontology: Social Sciences* 64B: 369–77.

Martin-Matthews, A. 2002. *Seniors' Health*. Ottawa: Health Canada Synthesis Series. www.hc-sc.gc.ca/htf-fass.

Matthews, F., et al. 2013. "A two-decade comparison of prevalence of dementia in individuals aged 65 years and older from three geographical areas of England: Results of the Cognitive Function and Ageing Study I and II." *The Lancet*, 16 July 2013. http://dx.doi.org/10.1016/S0140-6736(13)61570-6.

Matthews, S. 2002. *Sisters and Brothers/Daughters and Sons: Meeting the Needs of Old Parents*. Bloomington, IN: Unlimited.

Maxwell, C., and K. Oakley. 1998. Editorial: "Older women's health issues." *Canadian Journal on Aging* 17 (2): i–ix.

Menec, V., et al. 1999. "Self-perceptions of health: A prospective analysis of mortality, control and health." *Journal of Gerontology: Psychological Science* 54B (2): P85–93.

———. 2005. "Trends in the health status of older Manitobans, 1985–1999." *Canadian Journal on Aging* 24 (supplement 1): 5–14.

Mitchell, L., et al. 2006. "Indicators of home care use in urban and rural settings." *Canadian Journal on Aging* 26 (3): 275–80.

Moore, E., and M. Rosenberg. 1997. *Growing Old in Canada*. Toronto: Nelson.

Mor, V. 2005. "The compression of morbidity hypothesis: A review of research and prospects for the future." *Journal of the American Geriatrics Society* 53 (9: supplement 1): S308–9.

Morley, J., and J. Flaherty. 2002. Editorial: "Putting the 'home' back in nursing home." *Journal of Gerontology: Medical Sciences* 57 (7): M419–21.

Morrongiello, B., and B. Gottlieb. 2000. "Self-care among older adults." *Canadian Journal on Aging* 19 (supplement 1): 32–57.

National Geographic. 2005. "Secrets to Longevity." www7.nationalgeographic.com/ngm/0511/feature1/index.html.

Newbold, K., and J. Filice. 2006. "Health status of older immigrants to Canada." *Canadian Journal on Aging* 25 (3): 305–19.

Newsom, J., et al. 2004. "Health behaviors in a representative sample of older Canadians: Prevalences, reported change, motivation to change, and perceived barriers." *The Gerontologist* 44 (2): 193–205.

Newsom, J., et al. 2012. "Health behavior change following chronic illness in middle and later life." *Journals of Gerontology: Psychological Sciences* 667 (3): 279–88.

O'Rand, A., and J. Hamil-Luker. 2005. "Process of cumulative adversity: Childhood disadvantage and increased risk of heart attack across the life course." *Journals of Gerontology: Social Sciences* 60B (special issue II): 117–24.

Ory, M., et al. 2011. "Contextualizing rurality for family and community health research." *Family and Community Health*. 34 (2): 90–92.

Parker, M.G., et al. 2005. "Health changes among Swedish oldest old: Prevalence rates from 1992 and 2002 show increasing health problems." *Journal of Gerontology: Medical Sciences* 60A (10): 1351–5.

Parker, M.G., and M. Thorslund. 2007. "Health trends in the elderly population: Getting better or getting worse?" *The Gerontologist* 47 (2): 150–8.

Perez, C. 2002. "Health status and health behaviour among immigrants." *Health Reports* 13. Catalogue no. 82-003. Ottawa: Statistics Canada.

Perls, T. 2012. "What Centenarians Tell Us About Aging." Keynote presentation at the 41st Annual Scientific and Educational Meeting of the Canadian Association on Gerontology, Vancouver, BC, 18–20 October 2012.

Perls, T., et al. 2002. "The genetics of exceptional human longevity." *Journal of the American Geriatrics Society* 50: 359–68.

Poulin, M. 2001. "Validation of an exceptional male longevity area in Sardinia." Paper presented at the 17th Congress of the International Association of Gerontology, Vancouver, 1–6 July.

Préville, M., et al. 2009. "Use of mental health services for psychological distress symptoms among older adults." *Canadian Journal on Aging* 28 (1): 51–61.

Pringle, D. 1998. *Aging and the Health Care System: Am I in the Right Queue?* Forum Collection. Ottawa: National Advisory Council on Aging.

Prohaska, T., et al. 2006. "Physical activity, public health, and aging: Critical issues and research priorities." *Journal of Gerontology: Social Sciences* 61B (5): S267–73.

Prus, S. 2004. "A life course perspective on the relationship between socio-economic status and health: Testing the divergence hypothesis." *Canadian Journal on Aging* 23 (supplement): S145–53.

———. 2007. "Age, SES, and health: A population level analysis of health inequalities over the lifecourse." *Sociology of Health & Illness* 29 (2): 275–96.

———. 2011. "Comparing social determinants of self-rated health across the United States and Canada." *Social Science & Medicine* 73 (1): 50–59.

Public Health Agency of Canada. 2010. *The Chief Public Health Officer's Report on the State of Public Health in Canada 2010: Growing Older—Adding Years to Life*. Ottawa: Public Health Agency of Canada.

Quadagno, J., et al. 2005. "Health policy and old age: An international review." In M. Johnson, Ed. *The Cambridge Handbook of Age and Ageing*, 605–12. Cambridge: Cambridge University Press.

Robine, J., et al. 1998. "Examination of the causes and mechanisms of the increase in disability-free life expectancy." *Journal of Aging and Health* 10 (2): 171–91.

Romanow Commission. 2002. *Building on Values: The Future of Health Care in Canada*. Ottawa: Royal Commission on the Future of Health Care in Canada.

Roos et al. 1993. "Living longer but doing worse: Assessing health status in elderly persons at two points in Manitoba, Canada, 1971 and 1983. *Social Science and Medicine* 36 (3): 273–82.

Rosenstock, I. 1974. "Historical origins of the health beliefs model." *Health Education Monographs* 2: 328–35.

Saunders, L., et al. 2001. "Trends in the utilization of health services by seniors in Alberta." *Canadian Journal on Aging* 20 (4): 493–516.

Segall, A., and C. Fries. 2011. *Pursuing Health and Wellness*. Don Mills, ON: Oxford.

Shaw, M., et al. 1999. *The Widening Gap: Health Inequalities and Policy in Britain*. Bristol, UK: Policy Press.

Sheets, D., and E. Gallagher. 2012. "Aging in Canada: State of the art and science." The Gerontologist, Advanced Access, 29 November 2012.

Standing Senate Committee on Social Affairs, Science and Technology. 2004. Mental Health, Mental Illness and Addiction: An Overview of Policies and Programs in Canada. Ottawa: The Standing Senate Committee on Social Affairs, Science and Technology.

Statistics Canada. 1999a. "Health among older adults." *Health Reports* 11 (3): 47–61, catalogue no. 82-003.

———. 1999b. "Health in mid-life." *Health Reports* 11 (3): 35–46, catalogue no. 82-003.

———. 2001. *Health Indicators*. Ottawa: Statistics Canada.

———. 2002a. *A Profile of Disability in Canada, 2001*. Ottawa: Statistics Canada.

———. 2002b. *How Healthy Are Canadians? A Summary of the 2002 Annual Report*. Catalogue no. 82-003-SIE. Ottawa: Statistics Canada.

———. 2003. *Canadian Community Health Survey*. Ottawa: Statistics Canada.

———. 2006. *Leisure-Time Physical Activity, by Age Group and Sex, Household Population Aged 12 and over, Canada, 2003*. www.statcan.ca/english/freepub/82-221-XIE/tables/htlm.

———. 2007. "Participation and activity limitation survey, 2006." *The Daily*, Statistics Canada, 3 December.

———. 2012. Health Indicator Profile, Annual Estimates, by Age Group and Sex, Canada, Provinces, Territories, Health Regions. CANSIM Tables. www5.statcan.gc.ca/cansim/a26.

Stephenson, M., and E. Sawyer, Eds. 2002. *Continuing the Care: The Issues and Challenges for Long-Term Care*. Ottawa: Canadian Healthcare Association Press.

Stessman, J., et al. 2005. "Strategies to enhance longevity and independent function: The Jerusalem Longitudinal Study." *Mechanisms of Ageing and Development* 126 (2): 327–31.

Stone, S.D. 2003. "Disability, dependence, and old age: Problematic constructions." *Canadian Journal on Aging* 22 (1): 59–67.

Sudha, S., and E. Mutran, Eds. 2001. "Age and health in a multiethnic society; ii: Health care issues." *Research on Aging* 23 (1): 3–126.

Tamblyn, R. 2000. Editorial: "Canadian Association on Gerontology policy statement: Seniors and prescription drugs." *Canadian Journal on Aging* 19 (1): vii–xiv.

Tamblyn, R., and R. Perreault. 2000. "Prescription drug use and seniors." *Canadian Journal on Aging* 19 (supplement 1): 143–75.

Tierney, M., and J. Charles. 2002. "The care and treatment of people with dementia and cognitive impairment." In NACA, *Mental Health and Aging*, 97–113. Ottawa: National Advisory Council on Aging.

Tjam, E., and J. Hirdes. 2002. "Health, psycho-social and cultural determinants of medication use by Chinese-Canadian older persons." *Canadian Journal on Aging* 21 (1): 63–73.

Tourigny, A., et al. 2004. "Quasi-experimental study of the effectiveness of an integrated service delivery network for the frail elderly." *Canadian Journal on Aging* 23 (3): 231–46.

Urster, J., Eds. 2008. *Research Tends in Nutrition for the Middle Aged and Elderly*. New York: Nova Science Publishers.

Vaupel, J.W., and Jeune, B. 1995. "The emergence and proliferation of centenarians." In B. Jeune and J.W. Vaupel, Eds, *Exceptional Longevity: From Prehistory to Present*, 186–204. Odense, Denmark: Odense University Press.

Votova, K., and A.V. Wister. 2007. "Complementary and alternative medicine use among older adults: The role of health belief structures." *Gerontology* 53 (1): 21–7.

Wanless, D., et al., 2010. "Social determinants of health for older women in Canada: Does rural/urban location matter?" *Canadian Journal of Aging*, 29(2): 233–47.

Wilkins, R., et al., 2001. "Health expectancy by neighbourhood income in urban Canada, using census disability data for 1996." Paper presented at reves 13, Vancouver, June.

Wister, A.V. 2003. "It's never too late: Healthy lifestyles and aging." *Canadian Journal on Aging* 22 (2): 149–50.

——. 2005. *Baby Boomer Health Dynamics: How Are We Aging?* Toronto: University of Toronto Press.

——. 2009. "We Still Have a Long Way to Go: Patterns of Health and Healthy Lifestyles Across the Generations." Keynote Address: 19th John Friesen Conference: Staying Active, Staying Healthy: Aging Well in Contemporary Society,Vancouver, BC, 23–24 April 2009.

——. 2011. "Population pressures, system-level inertia and healthy aging policy revisited." *Healthcare Papers* 11 (1): 8–19.

Wister, A.V., and Z. Romeder. 2002. "The chronic illness context in exercise self-care among older adults: A longitudinal analysis." *Canadian Journal on Aging* 21 (4): 521–34.

Wister, A.V., and D. Wanless. 2007. "A health profile and exploratory analysis of Canadian nonagenarians." *Canadian Journal on Aging* 26 (1): 1–18.

Wister, A.V., et al. 2010. "Life-long educational practices and resources in enabling health literacy among older adults." *Journal of Aging and Health,* 22: 827–54.

Wolf, D., et al. 2007. "Trends in rates of onset of and recovery from disability at older ages: 1982–1994." *Journal of Gerontology: Social Sciences* 62B (1): S3–10.

Wolfson, C., et al. 1993. "Adult children's perceptions of their responsibility to provide care for dependent elderly parents." *The Gerontologist* 33 (3): 315–23.

Woods, B. 2005. "Dementia." In M. Johnson, Ed., *The Cambridge Handbook of Age and Ageing,* 252–60. Cambridge: Cambridge University Press.

Zarit, S.H., et al. 2004. "Pain perceptions of the oldest old: A longitudinal study." *The Gerontologist* 44 (4): 459–68.

Chapter 8

The Lived Environment: Community and Housing Alternatives in Later Life

Adler, G., and S. Rottunda. 2006. "Older adults' perspective on driving cessation." *Journal of Aging Studies* 20 (3): 227–35.

Arling, G., et al. 2005. "Future development of nursing home quality indicators." *The Gerontologist* 45 (2): 147–56.

Bedard, M., et al. 2002. "Traffic-related fatalities among older drivers and passengers: Past and future trends." *The Gerontologist* 41 (6): 751–6.

Belluz, J. 2007. "Decline feared, yet love blooms." *The Globe and Mail* 16 February: A18.

Berta, W., et al. 2005. "Observations on institutional long-term care in Ontario: 1996–2002." *Canadian Journal on Aging* 24 (1): 71–84.

Burdick, D., and S. Kwon, Eds. 2004. *Geron-technology: Research and Practice in Technology and Aging.* New York: Springer.

CAG (Canadian Association on Gerontology). 2000. *Policy Statement on Assistive Devices for Seniors.* Ottawa: CAG.

Capezuti, L., et al., Eds. 2008. *Evidence-based Geriatric Nursing Protocols for Best Practice.* New York: Springer.

Caragata, G., et al. 2009. "Fit to drive: A pilot study to improve the physical fitness of older drivers." *Activities, Adaptation and Aging* 33 (4): 240–55.

Carder, P. 2002. "The social world of assisted living." *Journal of Aging Studies* 16 (1): 1–18.

Castle, N., and T. Lowe. 2005. "Report cards and nursing homes." *The Gerontologist* 45 (1): 48–67.

Chappell, N. 1994. "Technology and aging." In V. Marshall and B. McPherson, Eds, *Aging: Canadian Perspectives,* 83–96. Peterborough, ON: Broadview.

Charles, C., and C. Schalm. 1992a. "Alberta's resident classification system for long-term care facilities. Part I: Conceptual and methodological development." *Canadian Journal on Aging* 11 (3): 219–32.

——. 1992b. "Alberta's resident classification system for long-term care facilities. Part II: First-year results and policy implications." *Canadian Journal on Aging* 11 (3): 233–48.

Charness, N., and S. Czaja. 2005. "Adaptation to new technologies." In M. Johnson, Ed., *The Cambridge Handbook on Age and Ageing,* 662–9. New York: Cambridge University Press.

Charness, N., and W. Schaie, Eds. 2004. *Impact of Technology on Successful Aging.* New York: Springer.

Chaudhury, H. 2003. "Quality of life and place therapy." *Journal of Housing for the Elderly* 17 (1/2): 85–106.

Chaudhury, H. 2008. *Remembering Home: Rediscovering the Self in Dementia.* Baltimore: Johns Hopkins University Press.

Chaudhury, H., and A. Mahmood. 2008. "Immigrants' residential experience in North America: An overlooked area in environmental design research." *The Journal of Architectural and Planning Research* 25 (1): 1–5.

Clarke, W. 2005. "What do seniors spend on housing?" *Canadian Social Trends* 78 (autumn): 2–7.

CMHC (Canadian Mortgage and Housing Corporation). 2000a. *Women on the Rough Edge: A Decade of Change for Long-Term Homeless Women.* Research Highlights no. 54. Ottawa: CMHC.

————. 2000b. *Supportive Housing for Seniors.* Research Highlights no. 56. Ottawa: cmhc.

————. 2002. *Seniors' Housing Conditions.* Research Highlights no. 78. Ottawa: cmhc.

————. 2005. 2001 Census Housing Series: Issue 9 Revisited. The Housing Conditions of Canada's Seniors. Socio-economic Series 05-006. Ottawa: Canada.

Cohen, C. 1999. "Aging and homelessness." *The Gerontologist* 39 (1): 5–14.

Cohen, C. 2006. "Consumer fraud and the elderly." *Journal of Gerontological Social Work* 46 (3/4): 12–25.

Connidis, I. 2010. *Family Ties and Aging,* 2nd edn. Thousand Oaks, CA: Pine Forge Press.

Crane, M. 1999. *Understanding Older Homeless People.* Philadelphia: Open University Press.

Crane, M., et al. 2005. "The causes of homelessness in later life: Findings from a 3-nation study." *Journal of Gerontology: Social Sciences* 60B (3): S152–9.

Crane, M., and A. Warnes. 2010. "Homelessness among older people and service responses." *Reviews in Clinical Gerontology* 20: 354–63.

Cutler, S. 2006. "Technological change and aging." In R. Binstock and L. George, Eds, *Handbook of Aging and the Social Sciences,* 257–76. San Diego: Academic Press.

Cvitkovich, Y., and A.V. Wister. 2001. "Comparison of four person-environment fit models applied to older adults." *Journal of Housing for the Elderly* 14 (1, 2): 1–25.

————. 2002. "Bringing in the life course: A modification to Lawton's ecological model of aging." *Hallym International Journal of Aging* 4 (1): 15–29.

Dickerson, A., et al. 2007. "Transportation and aging: A research agenda for advancing safe mobility." *The Gerontologist* 47 (5): 578–90.

Donahue, P. 2001. *Fraud in Ethnocultural Seniors' Communities.* SEDAP Research Paper no. 37. Hamilton, ON: McMaster University. http://socserv2.mcmaster.ca/sedap.

Donorfio, L., et al. 2008. "A qualitative study of self-regulation behaviors among older drivers." *Journal of Aging and Social Policy* 20 (3): 323–39.

du Plessis, V., et al. 2001. "Definitions of rural." *Rural and Small Town Canada Analysis Bulletin.* Vol. 3, no. 3. Cat no. 21-006-XIE. www.statcan.gc.ca/pub/21-006-x/21-006-x2001003-eng.pdf, retrieved 19 December 2011.

Dupuis, J., et al. 2007. "Gender and transportation access among community-dwelling seniors." *Canadian Journal on Aging* 26 (2): 149–58.

Ekerdt, D., and J. Sergeant. 2006. "Family things: Attending the household disbandment of older adults." *Journal of Aging Studies* 20 (3): 193–205.

Finlayson, M., and J. Kaufert. 2002. "Older women's community mobility: A qualitative exploration." *Canadian Journal on Aging* 21 (1): 75–84.

Fisk, A., et al. 2004. *Designing for Older Adults: Principles and Creative Human Factors Approaches.* London: Taylor and Francis.

Flaherty, J., et al. 2003. "A consensus statement on nonemergent medical transportation services for older persons." *Journal of Gerontology: Medical Sciences* 58 (9): 826–31.

Freedman, V., et al. 2006. "Trends in the use of assistive technology: Personal care for late-life disability, 1992–2001." *The Gerontologist* 46 (1): 124–7.

Friedman, D.B., et al. 2006. "Health literacy and the world wide web: Comparing the readability of leading incident cancers on the Internet." *Medical Informatics and the Internet in Medicine* 31 (1): 67–87.

Gee, E., and B. Mitchell 2003. "One roof: Exploring multi-generational households in Canada." In M. Lynn, Ed., *Voices: Essays on Canadian Families,* 2nd edn, 291–311. Scarborough, ON: Thomson Nelson.

Generations. 2006. 30 (2).

Golant, S. 1984. *A Place to Grow Old: The Meaning of Environment in Old Age.* New York: Columbia University Press.

Golant, S. 2003. "Conceptualizing time and space in environmental gerontology: A pair of old issues deserving new thought." *The Gerontologist* 43(5): 638–48.

Golant, S. 2011a. "The changing residential environments of older people." In R. Binstock, L. George, S. Cutler, J. Hendricks and H. Schulz, Eds, *Handbook of Aging and the Social Science,* 7th edn., 207–20. New York: Oxford, UK: Elsevier.

Golant, S. 2011b. "The quest for residential normalcy by older adults: Relocation but one pathway." *Journal of Aging Studies* 25: 193–205.

Golant, S., and J. Hyde, Eds. 2008. *The Assisted Living Residence: A Vision for the Future.* Baltimore: Johns Hopkins University Press.

Gubrium, J. 1973. *The Myth of the Golden Years: A Socio-environmental Theory of Aging.* Springfield, IL: Charles C. Thomas.

————. 1993. *Speaking of Life: Horizons of Meaning for Nursing Home Residents.* Hawthorne, NY: Aldine de Gruyter.

Hayman, S. 2011. "Older people in Canada: Their victimization and fear of crime." *Canadian Journal on Aging* 30 (3): 423–36.

Hayward, L. 2004. "Mid-life patterns and residential mobility of older men." *Canadian Journal on Aging* 23 (1): 73–90.

Health Canada. 2002a. *Canada's Aging Population.* Ottawa: Minister of Public Works and Government Services Canada.

———. 2002b. *Go for It! A Guide to Choosing and Using Assistive Devices*. Ottawa: Minister of Public Works and Government Services Canada.

———. 2002c. *Healthy Aging: Prevention of Unintentional Injuries among Seniors*. Ottawa: Health Canada.

Herd, P., et al. 2011. "Health disparities among older adults: Life course influences and policy solutions." In R. Binstock, L. George, S. Cutler, J. Hendricks and H. Schulz, Eds, *Handbook of Aging and the Social Science,* 7th edn., 121–34. New York: Oxford, UK: Elsevier.

Hirdes, J., et al. 1999a. "International and regional variations in restraint use: Implications for selecting benchmarks." *Canadian Journal on Quality in Health Care* 15 (2): 19–23.

———. 1999b. "Integrated health information systems based on the rai/mds series of assessment instruments." *Healthcare Management Forum* 12 (4): 30–40.

———. 2001. "Development of the Resident Assessment Instrument—Mental Health (rai-mh)." *Hospital Quarterly* 4 (2): 44–51.

———. 2004. "Home care quality indicators (HCQ's) based on the mds-hc." *The Gerontologist* 44 (5): 665–79.

———. 2011. "Beyond the 'iron lungs of Gerontology': Using evidence to shape the future of nursing homes in Canada." *Canadian Journal on Aging* 30 (3): 371–90.

Kahana, E. 1982. "A congruence model of person-environment interaction." In P. Lawton et al., Eds, *Aging and the Environment: Theoretical Approaches*, 97–121. New York: Springer.

Kaida, L., et al. 2009. "Cultural preferences and economic constraints: The living arrangements of elderly Canadians." *Canadian Journal on Aging* 28 (4): 303–13.

Kane, R., and R. Kane. 2005. "Long-term care." In M. Johnson, Ed., *The Cambridge Handbook of Age and Ageing*, 638–46. New York: Cambridge University Press.

Keating, N., Ed. 2008. *Rural Ageing: A Good Place to Grow Old?* London, UK: Policy Press.

Keating, N., et al. 2011. "Aging in rural Canada." *Canadian Journal on Aging* 30 (3): 323–38.

Keays, S., et al. 2009. "Characteristics of administrators and quality of care in long term care facilities." *Journal of Housing for the Elderly* 23 (3): 243–60.

Kenny, R. 2005. "Mobility and falls." In M. Johnson, Ed., *The Cambridge Handbook of Age and Ageing*, 131–40. New York: Cambridge University Press.

Klavora, P., and R. Heslegrave. 2002. "Senior drivers: An overview of problems and intervention strategies." *Journal of Aging and Physical Activity* 10 (3): 322–35.

Lawton, P. 1980. *Environment and Aging*. Monterey, CA: Brooks/Cole.

———. 1990. "Residential environment and self-directedness among older people." *American Psychologist* 45 (5): 638–40.

Lawton, P., et al., Eds. 1982. *Aging and the Environment: Theoretical Approaches*. New York: Springer.

Lawton, P., and L. Nahemow. 1973. "Ecology and the aging process." In C. Eisdorfer and P. Lawton, Eds, *The Psychology of Adult Development and Aging*, 619–74. Washington: American Psychological Association.

Lin, J. 2005. "The housing transitions of seniors." *Canadian Social Trends* 79 (winter): 22–6.

Longino, C., and D. Bradley. 2006. "Internal and international migration." In R. Binstock and L. George, Eds, *Handbook of Aging and the Social Sciences*, 76–93. San Diego: Academic Press.

Longino, C., and A. Warnes. 2005. "Migration and older people." In M. Johnson, Ed., *The Cambridge Handbook of Age and Ageing*, 538–45. New York: Cambridge University Press.

MacLean, M., and J. Klein. 2002. "Accessibility to long-term care: The myth versus reality." In M. Stephenson and E. Sawyer, Eds, *Continuing the Care: The Issues and Challenges for Long-Term Care*, 71–86. Ottawa: CHA Press.

Mahmood, A., et al. 2008. "The housing and community characteristics of South Asian immigrant older adults in Greater Vancouver." *The Journal of Architectural and Planning Research* 25 (1): 54–75.

Martin, F. 2011. "Falls risk factors: Assessment and management to prevent falls and fractures." *Canadian Journal on Aging* 30 (1): 33–44.

McDonald, L., et al. 2007. "Living on the margins: Older homeless adults in Toronto." *Journal of Gerontological Social Work* 49: 19–46.

McGrail, K., et al. 2013. "Health care system use in assisted living: A time series analysis." *Canadian Journal on Aging* 32(2): 173–83.

Menec, V., et al. 2011. "Conceptualizing age-friendly communities." *Canadian Journal on Aging* 30 (3): 479–93.

Menz, H., et al. 2006. "Foot and ankle risk factors for falls in older people: A prospective study." *Journal of Gerontology: Medical Sciences* 61A (8): M866–70.

Moody, H. 2005. "Ethical dilemmas in old age care." In M. Johnson, Ed., *The Cambridge Handbook of Age and Ageing*, 583–7. New York: Cambridge University Press.

Moore, E., and M. Pacey. 2004. "Geographic dimensions of aging in Canada, 1991–2001." *Canadian Journal on Aging* 23 (supplement): S5–21.

Moore, E., and M. Rosenberg. 1997. *Growing Old in Canada: Demographic and Geographic Perspectives*. Ottawa: Statistics Canada.

Morley, J. 2002. "A fall is a major event in the life of an older person." *Journal of Gerontology: Medical Sciences* 57A (8): M492–5.

Mortenson, B., et al. In press. "Grey spaces: The wheeled fields of residential care." *Sociology of Health and Illness* 34 (3).

Munro, M. 2000. "The driver is Miss Daisy." *National Post* 19 April: A17.

NACA (National Advisory Council on Aging). 2001. *Seniors and Technology*. Ottawa: NACA.

———. 2002. *The NACA Position on Supportive Housing for Seniors*. Position Paper no. 22. Ottawa: NACA.

———. 2003. "Let's get moving." *Expression* 16 (1): 4–8.

———. 2005. "The changing face of long-term care." *Expression* 18 (4): 4–6.

———. 2006. *Seniors in Canada: 2006 Report Card*. Ottawa: NACA. www.naca.ca/rc2006/pdf/rc2006_e. pdf.

Nakonezny, P., and M. Ojeda. 2005. "Health services utilization between older and younger homeless adults." *The Gerontologist* 45 (2): 249–54.

Nasvadi, G., and A.V. Wister. 2009. "Do restricted driver's licenses lower crash risk among older drivers? A survival analysis of insurance data from British Columbia." *The Gerontologist*, 49 (4): 474–84.

Northcott, H., and C. Petruik. 2011. "The geographic mobility of elderly Canadians." *Canadian Journal on Aging* 30 (3): 311–22.

Nyman, S. 2011. "Psychosocial issues in engaging older people with physical activity interventions for the prevention of falls." *Canadian Journal on Aging* 30 (1): 45–55.

O'Connor, D., et al. 2007. "Personhood in dementia care: Developing a research agenda for broadening the vision." *Dementia: The International Journal of Social Research and Practice* 6 (1): 121–42.

Ogrodnik, L. 2007. "Seniors as victims of crime, 2004 and 2005." Ottawa: Canadian Centre for Justice Statistics Profile Series, Statistics Canada (85F0033MIE-No.014).

Pacey, M. 2002. *Living Alone and Living with Children: The Living Arrangements of Canadian and Chinese-Canadian Seniors*. SEDAP Research Paper no. 74. Hamilton, ON: McMaster University. http:// socserv2.mcmaster.ca/sedap.

Peel, N. 2011. "Epidemiology of falls in older age." *Canadian Journal on Aging* 30 (1): 7–19.

Pew, R., and S. van Hemel, Eds. 2004. *Technology for Adaptive Aging*. Washington: National Academy of Sciences.

Ploeg, J., et al. 2008. "A case study of a Canadian homelessness intervention programme for elderly people." *Health and Social Care in the Community* 16 (6): 593–605.

Public Health Agency of Canada. 2010. *The Chief Public Health Officer's Report on the State of Public Health in Canada 2010: Growing Older—Adding Years to Life*. Ottawa: Public Health Agency of Canada.

Raglund, D., et al. 2004. "Reasons given by older people for limitation or avoidance of driving." *The Gerontologist* 44 (2): 237–44.

———. 2005. "Driving cessation and increased depressive symptoms." *Journal of Gerontology: Medical Sciences* 60A (3): M399–403.

Rand Institute for Civil Justice. 2007. *What Risks Do Older Drivers Pose for Traffic Safety?* Santa Monica, CA: Rand Corporation.

Richard, L., et al. 2005. "The quality of life of older adults living in an urban environment: Professional and lay perspectives." *Canadian Journal on Aging* 24 (1): 19–30.

Robert, S. 2002. "Community context and aging: Future research issues." *Research on Aging* 24 (6): 579–99.

Robson, E., et al. 2003. "Steady as you go (SAYGO): A falls-prevention program for seniors living in the community." *Canadian Journal on Aging* 22 (2): 207–16.

Ross, L., et al. 2009. "Do older drivers at-risk for crashes modify their driving over time"? *Journal of Gerontology: Psychological Sciences* 64B (2): 163–70.

Rowles, G., and Chaudhury, H., Eds. 2005. *Home and Identity in Later Life: International Perspectives*. New York: Springer.

Rudman, D., et al. 2006. "Holding on and letting go: The perspectives of pre-seniors and seniors on driving self-regulation in later life." *Canadian Journal on Aging* 25 (1): 65–76.

Satariano, W. 2007. "Driving and the promotion of safe mobility in older populations." *Journal of Gerontology: Medical Sciences* 62A (10): M1111–12.

Satariano, W., et al. 2004. "Problems with vision associated with limitations or avoidance of driving in older populations." *Journal of Gerontology: Social Sciences* 59B (5): S281–6.

Scheidt, R., and P. Windley. 1985. "The ecology of aging." In J. Birren and W. Schaie, Eds, *Handbook of the Psychology of Aging*, 245–58. New York: Van Nostrand Reinhold.

———, Eds. 1998. *Environment and Aging Theory: A Focus on Housing*. Westport, CT: Greenwood.

———. 2006. "Environmental gerontology: Progress in the post-Lawton era." In J. Birren and W. Schaie, Eds, *Handbook of the Psychology of Aging*, 105–25. San Diego: Academic Press.

Schulz, R., Ed. 2005. "Dementia care and quality of life in assisted living and nursing homes." *The Gerontologist* 45 (special issue): 5–145.

Scott, V., et al. 2005. *Hospitalizations due to Falls among Canadians Age 65 and Over: Report on the Seniors' Falls in Canada*. Ottawa: Minister of Public Works and Government Services Canada.

Scialfa, C., and G. Fernie. 2006. "Adaptive technology." In J. Birren and W. Schaie, Eds, *Handbook of the Psychology of Aging*, 425–41. San Diego: Academic Press.

Selwyn, N. 2004. "The information aged: A qualitative study of older adults' use of information and communication technology." *Journal of Aging Studies* 18 (4): 369–84.

Sixsmith, A. 2006. "New technologies to support independent living and quality of life for people with dementia." *Alzheimer's Care Quarterly* 7 (3): 194–202.

Sixsmith, A., and G. Gutman. 2013. Eds. Technologies for Active Aging. New York: Springer.

Sixsmith, A., and N. Johnson. 2004. "A smart sensor to detect falls of the elderly." ieee *Pervasive Computing* 3 (2): 42–7.

Sixsmith A., and J. Sixsmith. 2008. "Ageing in place in the United Kingdom." *Ageing International*. 32 (3): 219–35.

Smith, S., and M. House. 2006. "Snowbirds, sunbirds and stayers: Seasonal migration of elderly adults in Florida." *Journal of Gerontology: Social Sciences* 61B (5): S232–9.

Snell, J. 1996. *The Citizen's Wage: The State and the Elderly in Canada, 1900–1951*. Toronto: University of Toronto Press.

Speechley, M. 2011. "Unintentional falls in older adults: A methodological historical review." *Canadian Journal on Aging* 30 (1): 21–32.

Speechley, M., et al. 2005. "Risk factors for falling among community-dwelling veterans and their caregivers." *Canadian Journal on Aging* 24 (3): 261–74.

Spencer, C. 2004. "Assisted living in British Columbia's 'new era.'" *Seniors Housing Update* 13: 1–8.

Statistics Canada. 2002. *Profile of Canadian Families and Households: Diversification Continues*. Catalogue no. 96F0030XIE2001003. 22 October. Ottawa: Statistics Canada.

———. 2003a. "Net migrants and net migration rates by age group, provinces and territories, 1996–2001. www12.statcan.ca/english/census01/products/analytic/companion, retrieved 10 October 2006.

———. 2003b. "International migration for census metropolitan areas by age groups, 1996–2001. www12.statcan.ca/english/census01/products/analytic/companion/mob/tables/migage, retrieved 21 November 2007.

———. 2003c. *2001 Census Dictionary*. Catalogue no. 92-378-XIE. Ottawa: Statistics Canada.

———. 2004. *Mapping the Socioeconomic Diversity of Rural Canada*. Catalogue no. 21-006-XIE. Ottawa: Statistics Canada.

———. 2011. *Residential Care Facilities*. Catalogue no. 83-237-X. Ottawa: Ministry of Industry.

———. 2012. *Living Arrangements of Seniors*. www12.statcan.gc.ca/census-recensement/2011/as-sa/98-312-x/98-312-x2011003_4-eng.cfm, retrieved 8 October 2012.

Stergiopolous, V., and N. Herrmann. 2003. "Old and homeless: A review and survey of older adults who use shelters in an urban setting." *Canadian Journal of Psychiatry* 48: 374–80.

Stolee, P., et al. 2009. "Risk factors for hip fractures in older home care clients." *Journal of Gerontology: Medical Sciences* 64 (3): M403–10.

Stone, R. 2006. "Emerging issues in long-term care." In R. Binstock and L. George, Eds, *Handbook of Aging and the Social Sciences*, 397–418. San Diego: Academic Press.

Tuokko, H., et al. 2007. *The Older and Wiser Rider: An Examination of Transportation for Older Drivers. Prepared for the Capital Regional District Traffic Safety Commission and BC Transit*. Victoria: Centre on Aging, University of Victoria.

Turcotte, M. 2006. "Seniors' access to transportation." *Canadian Social Trends* (December): 43–50.

Turcotte, M., and G. Schellenberg. 2007. *A Portrait of Seniors in Canada, 2006*. Ottawa: Statistics Canada.

Wahl, H., et al., Eds. 2004. "Aging in context: Sociophysical environments." *Annual Review of Gerontology and Geriatrics* 23. New York: Springer.

Wahl, H., and G. Weisman. 2003. "Environmental gerontology at the beginning of the new millennium: Reflections on its historical, empirical, and theoretical development." *The Gerontologist* 43 (5): 616–27.

Wahl, H., et al. 2012. "Aging well and the environment: Toward an integrative model and research agenda for the future." *The Gerontologist* 52 (3): 306–16.

Walters, W. 2002. "Place characteristics and later-life migration." *Research on Aging* 24 (2): 243–77.

Ward-Griffin, C., et al. 2004. "Falls and fear of falling among community-dwelling seniors: The dynamic tension between exercising precaution and striving for independence." *Canadian Journal on Aging* 23 (4): 307–18.

Warren, S. 2000. Editorial: "Resident assessment instruments: Their use for health care planning and research." *Canadian Journal on Aging* 19 (supplement 2): i–xv.

Weeks, L., and K. LeBlanc 2010. "Housing concerns of vulnerable older Canadians." *Canadian Journal on Aging* 29 (3): 333–47.

White, P. 2007. "Wrestling the wheel from seniors a tough task." *The Globe and Mail* 27 August.

Windley, P., and R. Scheidt. 1980. "Person environment dialectics: Implications for component functioning in old age." In L. Poon, Ed., *Aging in the 1980s*, 407–23. Washington: American Psychological Association.

Wister, A.V. 1989. "Environmental adaptation among persons in their later life." *Research on Aging* 11 (3): 267–91.

———. 2005. "The built environment, health and longevity: Multilevel salutogenic and pathogenic pathways." *Journal of Housing for the Elderly* 19 (2): 49–70.

Zimmer, Z., and N. Chappell. 1999. "Receptivity to new technology among older adults." *Disability and Rehabilitation* 21 (5/6): 222–30.

Chapter 9
Family Ties, Relationships, and Transitions

Allen, K. 2005. "Gay and lesbian elders." In M. Johnson, Ed., *The Cambridge Handbook of Age and Ageing*, 482–9. New York: Cambridge University Press.

Bair, D. 2007. *Calling It Quits: Later-Life Divorce and Starting Over*. New York: Random House.

Bengtson, V., et al., Eds. 2004. *Sourcebook of Family Theory and Research*. Thousand Oaks, CA: Sage.

Blieszner, R., and V. Hilkevitch Bedford, Eds. 1995. *Handbook of Aging and the Family*. Westport, CT: Greenwood.

Bowen, G., et al. 2000. "Families in the context of communities across time." In S. Price, et al., Eds, *Families across Time: A Life Course Perspective*, 117–28. Los Angeles: Roxbury.

Boyd, M., and D. Norris. 1999. "The crowded nest: Young adults at home." *Canadian Social Trends* 52 (Spring): 2–5.

Brotman, S., et al. 2003. "The health and social service needs of gay and lesbian elders and their families in Canada." *The Gerontologist* 43 (2): 192–202.

———. 2007. "Coming out to care: Caregivers of gay and lesbian seniors in Canada." *The Gerontologist* 47 (4): 490–503.

Brown, S., and I. Lin. 2012. "The gray divorce revolution: Rising divorce among middle-aged and older adults, 1990–2010." *Journal of Gerontology: Social Sciences* 67B (6): S731–41.

Brown, S., et al. 2006. "Cohabitation among older adults: A national portrait." *Journal of Gerontology: Social Sciences* 61B (2): S71–9.

Campbell, L., et al. 1999. "Sibling ties in later life: A social network analysis." *Journal of Family Issues* 20 (1): 114–48.

Chalmers, L., and A. Milan. 2005. "Marital satisfaction during the retirement years." *Canadian Social Trends* 76 (spring): 14–17.

Chambers, P. 2005. *Older Widows and the Life Course: Multiple Narratives and Hidden Lives*. Burlington, VT: Ashgate.

Chan, C., and G. Elder. 2000. "Matrilineal advantage in grandchild-grandparent relations." *The Gerontologist* 40 (2): 179–90.

Chipperfield, J., and B. Havens. 2001. "Gender differences in the relationship between marital status transitions and life satisfaction in later life." *Journal of Gerontology: Psychological Sciences* 56B (3): P176–86.

Claasen, C. 2005. *Whistling Women: A Study of the Lives of Older Lesbians*. Binghampton, NY: Haworth.

Claes, J., and W. Moore. 2001. "Caring for gay and lesbian elderly." In L. Olson, Ed., *Age through Ethnic Lenses: Caring for the Elderly in a Multicultural Society*, 217–29. New York: Rowman and Littlefield.

Clarke, E., et al. 1999. "Types of conflicts and tensions between older parents and adult children." *The Gerontologist* 39 (3): 261–70.

Climo, J., et al. 2002. "Using the double bind to interpret the experience of custodial grandparents." *Journal of Aging Studies* 16 (1): 19–35.

Clunis, M., et al. 2005. *Lives of Lesbian Elders: Looking Back, Looking Forward*. Binghampton, NY: Haworth.

Cohler, B., and A. Hostetler. 2006. "Gay lives in the Third Age." In J. James and P. Wink, Eds, *Annual Review of Gerontology and Geriatrics* 26: 263–80. New York: Springer.

Connidis, I. 2001. *Family Ties and Aging*. Thousand Oaks, CA: Sage.

———. 2003a. "Bringing outsiders in: Gay and lesbian family ties over the life course." In S. Arber et al., Eds, *Gender and Ageing: New Directions*, 79–94. Buckingham, UK: Open University Press.

———. 2003b. "Divorce and union dissolution: Reverberations over three generations." *Canadian Journal on Aging* 22 (4): 353–68.

———. 2004. "Stability and change in childhood and parenting: Observations across three generations." In M. Silverstein, Ed., *Annual Review of Gerontology and Geriatrics* 24: 98–119. New York: Springer.

———. 2005. 'sibling ties across time: The middle and later years." In M. Johnson, Ed., *The Cambridge Handbook of Age and Ageing*, 429–36. New York: Cambridge University Press.

———. 2006. "Intimate relationships: Learning from later life experience." In T. Calasanti and K. Slevin, Eds, *Age Matters: Realigning Feminist Thinking*, 123–53. New York: Routledge.

———. 2010. *Family Ties and Aging*, 2nd edn. Thousand Oaks, CA: Pine Forge Press.

Connidis, I., and J. McMullin. 1996. "Reasons for and perceptions of childlessness among older persons: The impact of marital status and gender." *Journal of Aging Studies* 10 (2): 205–22.

———. 1999. "Permanent childlessness: Perceived advantages and disadvantages among older persons." *Canadian Journal on Aging* 18 (4): 447–65.

———. 2002. "Sociological ambivalence and family ties: A critical perspective." *Journal of Marriage and the Family* 64 (3): 558–67.

Cox, C., Ed. 1999. *To Grandmother's House We Go and Stay: Perspectives on Custodial Grandparents.* New York: Springer.

Cranswick, K., and D. Dosman. 2008. Eldercare: What we know today. *Canadian Social Trends,* Cat. 11-008, No. 86, 48–56.

Cruz, J. 2003. *Sociological Analysis of Aging: The Gay Male Perspective.* Binghampton, NY: Haworth.

de Vries, B. 2007. "LGBT couples in later life: A study in diversity." *Generations* 31 (3): 18–23.

Dykstra, P., and G. Hagestad. 2007. "Childlessness and parenthood in two centuries: Different roads, different maps." *Journal of Family Issues* 28 (11): 1518–32.

Fast, J., et al. 2010. "Gender differences in family/friend caregiving in Canada." *Research on Aging Policies and Practices.* December Issue: 1–4. Edmonton: University of Alberta.

Fox, B., Ed. 2009. *Family Patterns, Gender Relations,* 3rd edn. Don Mills, ON: Oxford University Press.

Fox, B., and M. Luxton. 2001. "Conceptualizing family." In B. Fox, Ed., *Family Patterns, Gender Relations,* 22–33. Don Mills, ON: Oxford University Press.

Fuller-Thomson, E. 2005. "Canadian First Nations grandparents raising grandchildren: A portrait in resilience." *International Journal of Aging and Human Development* 60 (4): 331–42.

Fuller-Thomson, E., and M. Minkler. 2001. "American grandparents providing extensive child care to their grandchildren: Prevalence and profile." *The Gerontologist* 41 (2): 201–9.

———. 2003. "Housing issues and realities facing grandparent caregivers who are renters." *The Gerontologist* 43 (1): 92–8.

Ganong, L., and M. Coleman. 1998. "Attitudes regarding filial responsibilities to help elderly divorced parents and stepparents." *Journal of Aging Studies* 12 (3): 271–90.

Giarrusso, R., et al. 2005. "Ageing parents and adult children: New perspectives on inter-generational relationships." In M. Johnson, Ed, *The Cambridge Handbook of Age and Ageing,* 413–21. New York: Cambridge University Press.

Gladstone, J. 1995. "The marital perceptions of elderly persons living or having a spouse living in a long-term care institution in Canada." *The Gerontologist* 35 (1): 52–60.

Glenn, N. 1998. "The course of marital success and failure in five American 10-year marriage cohorts." *Journal of Marriage and the Family* 60 (6): 569–76.

Goodman, C. 2007. "Intergenerational triads in skipped generation grandfamilies." *Journal of Aging and Human Development* 65 (3): 231–58.

Haber, C. 2006. "Old age through the lens of family history." In R. Binstock and L. George, Eds, *Handbook of Aging and the Social Sciences,* 59–75. San Diego: Academic Press.

Hagestad, G. 2003. "Interdependent lives and relationships in changing times: A life-course view of families and aging." In R. Settersten, Ed., *Invitation to the Life Course: Toward New Understandings of Later Life,* 135–59. Amityville, NY: Baywood.

Hareven, T. 2001. "Historical perspectives on aging and family relations." In R. Binstock and L. George, Eds, *Handbook of Aging and the Social Sciences,* 141–59. New York: Academic Press.

Harper, S. 2005. "Grandparenthood." In M. Johnson, Ed., *The Cambridge Handbook of Age and Ageing,* 422–8. New York: Cambridge University Press.

Hayslip, B., et al., Eds. 2000. *Grandparents Raising Grandchildren.* New York: Springer.

Hayslip, B., and P. Kaminski. 2005. "Grandparents raising their grandchildren: A review of the literature and suggestions for practice." *The Gerontologist* 45 (2): 262–9.

Heidt, G., and B. deVries, Eds. 2004. *Gay and Lesbian Aging: Research and Future Directions.* New York: Springer.

Hill, T. 2002. "Social structure and family law: The underlying factors of grandparent legislation." *Journal of Aging Studies* 16 (3): 259–78.

Hungerford, T. 2001. "The economic consequences of widowhood on elderly women in the United States and Germany." *The Gerontologist* 41 (1): 103–10.

Hurd, M., and M. Macdonald. 2001. *Beyond Coping: Widows Reinventing Their Lives.* Halifax: Pear Press.

Jenkins, C., Ed. 2003. *Widows and Divorcees in Later Life: On Their Own Again.* Binghampton, NY: Haworth.

Kemp, C. 2003. "The social and demographic contours of contemporary grandparenthood: Mapping patterns in Canada and the United States." *Journal of Comparative Family Studies* 34 (2): 187–212.

———. 2005. "Dimensions of grandparent-adult grandchild relationships: From family ties to intergenerational friendships." *Canadian Journal on Aging* 24 (2): 161–78.

Kimmel, D., et al., Eds. 2006. *Lesbian, Gay, Bisexual and Transgender Aging: Research and Clinical Perspectives.* New York: Columbia University Press.

Kimmel, D., and D. Lundy Martin, Eds. 2002. *Midlife and Aging in Gay America*. Binghampton, NY: Haworth.

Laird, J. 1996. "Invisible ties: Lesbians and their families of origin." In J. Laird and R. Green, Eds, *Lesbians and Gays in Couples and Families: A Handbook for Therapists*, 89–122. San Francisco: Jossey-Bass.

Lopata, H., Ed. 1987a. *Widows. Volume 1, The Middle East, Asia and the Pacific*. Durham, NC: Duke University Press.

———, Ed. 1987b. *Widows. Vol. II, North America*. Durham, NC: Duke University Press.

Lowenstein, A. 2005. "Global ageing and challenges to families." In M. Johnson, Ed., *The Cambridge Handbook of Age and Ageing*, 403–12. New York: Cambridge University Press.

MacRae, H. 1992. "Fictive kin as a component of the social networks of older people." *Research on Aging* 14 (2): 226–47.

Mann, R. 2007. "Out of the shadows? Grandfatherhood, age and masculinities." *Journal of Aging Studies* 21 (2): 281–91.

Martin-Matthews, A. 1987. "Widowhood as an expectable life event." In V. Marshall, Ed., *Aging in Canada: Social Perspectives*, 343–66. Markham, ON: Fitzhenry and Whiteside.

———. 1991. *Widowhood in Later Life*. Toronto: Butterworths.

———. 2011. "Revisiting widowhood in later life: Changes in patterns and profiles, advances in research and understanding." *Canadian Journal on Aging* 30 (3): 339–54.

Martin-Matthews, A., et al. 2001. *Age-Gapped and Age-Condensed Lineages: Patterns of Intergenerational Age Structure among Canadian Families*. SEDAP Research Paper no. 56. Hamilton, ON: McMaster University. www.socserv2. mcmaster.ca/sedap.

Matthews, S. 2002. *Sisters and Brothers/Daughters and Sons: Meeting the Needs of Old Parents*. Bloomington, IN: Unlimited.

Matthews, S., and J. Heidorn. 1998. "Meeting filial responsibilities in brothers-only sibling groups." *Journal of Gerontology: Social Sciences* 53B (5): S278–86.

Matthews, S., and R. Sun. 2006. "Incidence of four-generation family lineages: Is timing of fertility or mortality a better explanation?" *Journal of Gerontology: Social Sciences* 61B (2): S99–106.

McConville, B. 1985. *Sisters: Love and Conflict within the Lifelong Bond*. London: Pan Books.

McDonald, L. 1997. "The invisible poor: Canada's retired widows." *Canadian Journal on Aging* 16 (3): 553–83.

McMullin, J. 2010. *Understanding Inequality: Intersections of Class, Age, Gender, Ethnicity and Race in Canada*, 2nd edn. Don Mills, ON: Oxford University Press.

Milan, A. 2003. "Would you live common-law?" *Canadian Social Trends* 70 (autumn): 2–6.

Milan, A., and B. Hamm. 2003. "Across the generations: Grandparents and grandchildren." *Canadian Social Trends* 71 (winter): 2–7.

Minkler, M. 1999. "Intergenerational households headed by grandparents: Contexts, realities and implications for policy." *Journal of Aging Studies* 13 (2): 199–218.

Mitchell, B. 2000. "The refilled 'nest': Debunking the myth of families in crisis." In E. Gee and G. Gutman, Eds, *The Overselling of Population Aging*, 80–99. Don Mills, ON: Oxford University Press.

———. 2006. *The Boomerang Age: Transitions to Adulthood in Families*. Piscataway, NJ: Aldine-Transaction Publishers.

———. 2012. *Family Matters: An Introduction to Family Sociology in Canada*, 2nd edn. Toronto: Canadian Scholars' Press.

Mitchell, B., and E. Gee. 1996. "Boomerang kids and midlife parental marital satisfaction." *Family Relations* 45 (6): 442–8.

Mitchell, B., and L. Lovegreen. 2009. "The empty nest syndrome in midlife families: A multi-method exploration of parental gender differences and cultural dynamics. *Journal of Family Issues* 30 (12): 1654–70.

Moen, P. 2012. "Still a Gendered Life Course? Work and Family in a Changing World." Keynote presentation at the 41st Annual Scientific and Educational Meeting of the Canadian Association on Gerontology, Vancouver, BC, 18–20 October 2012.

Mueller, M., et al. 2002. "Variations in grandparenting." *Research on Aging* 24 (3): 360–88.

Musil, C., et al. 2006. "Grandmothers, caregiving, and family functioning." *Journal of Gerontology: Social Sciences* 61B (2): S89–98.

NACA (National Advisory Council on Aging). 1986. "The way it is: All in the family." *Expression* 3 (1): 3.

O'Brien, C.-A., and A. Goldberg. 2000. "Lesbian and gay men inside and outside families." In N. Mandell and A. Duffy, Eds, *Canadian Families: Diversity, Conflict and Change*, 115–45. Toronto: Harcourt Brace.

Phillipson, C., et al. 2001. *The Family and Community Life of Older People*. London: Routledge.

Pillemer, K., and J. Suitor. 2004. "Ambivalence and the study of intergenerational relations." In M. Silverstein and W. Schaie, Eds, *Annual Review of Gerontology and Geriatrics* 24: 3–28. New York: Springer.

Price, S., et al., Eds. 2000. *Families across Time: A Life Course Perspective*. Los Angeles: Roxbury.

Pudrovska, T., et al. 2006. "Strains of singlehood in later life: Do race and gender matter?" *Journal of Gerontology: Social Sciences* 61B (6): S315–22.

Reitzes, D., and E. Mutran. 2004. "Grandparenthood:

Factors influencing frequency of grandparent-grand-child contact and grandparent satisfaction." *Journal of Gerontology: Social Sciences* 59B (1): S9–16.

Richard, C., and A. Brown. 2006. "Configurations of informal social support among older lesbians." *Journal of Women and Aging* 18 (4): 49–65.

Rosenthal, C. 1985. "Kinkeeping in the familial division of labor." *Journal of Marriage and the Family* 47 (4): 965–74.

———. 2000. "Aging families: Have current changes and challenges been 'oversold'?" In E. Gee and G. Gutman, Eds, *The Overselling of Population Aging*, 45–63. Don Mills, ON: Oxford University Press.

Rosenthal, C., and J. Gladstone. 1994. "Family relationships and support in later life." In V. Marshall and B. McPherson, Eds, *Aging: Canadian Perspectives*, 158–74. Peterborough, ON: Broadview.

———. 2000. *Grandparenthood in Canada*. Ottawa: Vanier Institute of the Family.

Shemirani, F., and D. O'Connor. 2006. "Aging in a foreign country: Voices of Iranian women aging in Canada." *Journal of Women and Aging* 18 (2): 73–90.

Spitze, G., and M. Gallant. 2004. "The bitter with the sweet: Older adults' strategies for handling ambivalence in relations with their adult children." *Research on Aging* 26 (4): 387–412.

Spitze, G., and J. Logan. 1989. "Gender differences in family support: Is there a payoff?" *The Gerontologist* 29 (1): 108–13.

Statistics Canada. 2002. *General Social Survey, Cycle 15: Family History*. Catalogue no. 89-575-XIE. Ottawa: Statistics Canada.

Statistics Canada. 2008. *Legal Marital Status, Common-law Status, Age Groups and Sex for the Population 15 years of Age and Over, for Canada, Provinces, and Territories, 100% Sample Data*. Cat. No. 97-552-X2006007. www12.statcan.ca/english/census06/data/topics, retrieved 22 February 2008.

———. 2012a. *2011 Census of Population*. Catalogue no. 98-312-XCB2011041. Ottawa: Statistics Canada.

———. 2012b. *Portrait of Families and Living Arrangements in Canada*. Catalogue no. 98-312-X2011001. Ottawa: Statistics Canada.

Stobert, S., and A. Kemeny. 2003. "Childfree by choice."

Canadian Social Trends 69 (summer): 7–10.

Stone, L., et al. 1998. *Parent-Child Exchanges of Supports and Intergenerational Equity*. Catalogue no. 89-557-XPE. Ottawa: Statistics Canada.

Tower, R., and M. Krasner. 2006. "Marital closeness, autonomy, mastery, and depressive symptoms in a US Internet sample." *Personal Relationships* 13 (4): 429–49.

Treas, J., and S. Mazumdar. 2002. "Older people in America's immigrant families: Dilemmas of dependence, integration, and isolation." *Journal of Aging Studies* 16 (3): 243–58.

Turcotte, M. 2006. "Parents with children living at home." *Canadian Social Trends* 80 (spring): 2–9.

Uhlenberg, P. 2004. "Historical forces shaping grandparent-grandchild relationships: Demography and beyond." In M. Silverstein and W. Schaie, Eds, *Annual Review of Gerontology and Geriatrics* 24: 77–97. New York: Springer.

van den Hoonaard, D. 1999. "No regrets: Widows' stories about the last days of their husbands' lives." *Journal of Aging Studies* 13 (1): 59–72.

———. 2001. *The Widowed Self: The Older Woman's Journey through Widowhood*. Waterloo, ON: Wilfrid Laurier University Press.

———. 2010. *By Himself: The Older Man's Experience of Widowhood*. Toronto: University of Toronto Press.

Walker, A., et al. 2005. "Theorizing and studying sibling ties in adulthood." In V. Bengtson et al., Eds, *Sourcebook of Family Theory and Research*, 167–81. Thousand Oaks, CA: Sage.

Williams, C. 2005. "The sandwich generation." *Canadian Social Trends* 77 (summer): 16–21.

Wong, S., et al. 2005. "The changing meaning of family support among older Chinese and Korean immigrants." *Journal of Gerontology: Social Science* 61B (1): S4–9.

Wu, Z., and M. Pollard. 1998. "Social support among unmarried childless elderly persons." *Journal of Gerontology: Social Sciences* 53B (6): S324–35.

Zhang, Z., and M. Hayward. 2001. "Childlessness and the psychological well-being of older persons." *Journal of Gerontology: Social Sciences* 56B (5): S311–20.

Chapter 10

Work, Retirement, and Economic Security

Anisef, P., and P. Axelrod. 2001. "Baby boomers in transition: Life-course experiences of the Class of '73." In V. Marshall et al., Eds, *Restructuring Work and the Life Course*, 473–88. Toronto: University of Toronto Press.

Arber, S., and J. Ginn. 1995. "Choice and constraint in the retirement of older married women." In S. Arber and J. Ginn, Eds, *Connecting Gender and Ageing: A Sociological Approach*, 69–86. Philadelphia: Open University Press.

Baker, M., et al. 2001. *The Retirement Incentive Effects of Canada's Income Security Programs.* SEDAP Research Paper no. 65. Hamilton, ON: McMaster University. http://socserv2.mcmaster.ca/sedap.

Baker, M., and M. Gunderson. 2005. "Seniors' income adequacy." Expert Roundtable on Seniors, 19–20 January. Ottawa: Social Development Canada.

Ballantyne, P., and V. Marshall. 2001. "Subjective income security of (middle) aging and elderly Canadians." *Canadian Journal on Aging* 20 (2): 151–73.

Berger, E., and M. Denton. 2004. "The interplay between women's life course work patterns and financial planning for later life." *Canadian Journal on Aging* 23 (supplement): S99–113.

Bernard, A., and C. Li. 2006. *Death of a Spouse: The Impact on Income for Senior Men and Women.* Ottawa: Statistics Canada.

Bernard, M., et al. 1995. "Gendered work, gendered retirement." In S. Arber and J. Ginn, Eds, *Connecting Gender and Ageing: A Sociological Approach,* 56–68. Philadelphia: Open University Press.

Brotman, S. 1998. "The incidence of poverty among seniors in Canada: Exploring the impact of gender, ethnicity and race." *Canadian Journal on Aging* 17 (2): 166–85.

Brown, R. 1991. *Economic Security in an Aging Population.* Toronto: Butterworths.

Brown, R. 2011. "Economic security in an aging Canadian population." *Canadian Journal on Aging* 30 (3): 391–9.

Calasanti, T. 1993. "Bringing in diversity: Toward an inclusive theory of retirement." *Journal of Aging Studies* 7 (2): 133–50.

CARP (Canada's Association for the Fifty-Plus). 2007. "The truth about CPP." CARP *Magazine* (August): 9.

Carrière, Y., and D. Galarneau. 2011. "Delayed retirement: A new trend?" *Perspectives on Labour and Income, Winter,* Catalogue 75-001-X. Ottawa: Statistics Canada.

Chan, D., et al. 2001. "Linking technology, work, and the life course: Findings from the Nova case study." In V. Marshall et al., Eds, *Restructuring Work and the Life Course,* 270–87. Toronto: University of Toronto Press.

Chappell, N., and L. Funk. 2011. "Social support, caregiving and aging." *Canadian Journal on Aging* 30 (3): 355–70.

Chappell, N., and M. Hollander. 2011. "An evidence-based policy prescription for an aging population." *Healthcare Papers* 11 (1): 8–19.

Chen, Y.-P. 1994. "Equivalent retirement ages and their implications for social security and Medicare financing." *The Gerontologist* 36 (6): 731–5.

Cooke, M. 2006. "Policy changes and the labour force participation of older workers: Evidence from six countries." *Canadian Journal on Aging* 25 (4): 387–400.

Cutler, N. 2005. "Wealth, health and aging: The multiple modern complexities of financial gerontology." In M. Johnson, Ed., *The Cambridge Handbook of Age and Ageing,* 588–96. New York: Cambridge University Press.

Czaja, S. 2001. "Technological change and the older worker." In J. Birren and W. Schaie, Eds, *Handbook of the Psychology of Aging,* 547–68. San Diego: Academic Press.

Davies, S., and M. Denton. 2003. "The economic well-being of older women who become divorced or separated in mid and later life." *Canadian Journal on Aging* 21 (4): 477–93.

Denton, F., et al., Eds. 2000. *Independence and Economic Security in Old Age.* Vancouver: University of British Columbia Press.

Denton, M., et al. 2004. "Reflexive planning for later life." *Canadian Journal on Aging* 23 (supplement): S71–82.

Denton, M., and L. Boos. 2007. "The gender wealth gap: Structural and material constraints and implications for later life." *Journal of Women and Aging* 19 (3/4): 105–20.

Drentea, P. 2002. "Retirement and mental health." *Journal of Aging and Health* 14 (2): 167–94.

Duchesne, D. 2002. "Seniors at work." *Perspectives on Labour and Income* 3 (5): 5–16. Catalogue no. 75-001-XIE. Ottawa: Statistics Canada.

Ekerdt, D. 2010. "Frontiers of research on work and retirement." *Journal of Gerontology: Social Sciences* 65B (1): 69–80.

Ekerdt, D., et al. 2000. "The normative anticipation of retirement by older workers." *Research on Aging* 22 (1): 3–22.

England, R. 2001. *The Fiscal Challenge of an Aging Industrial World.* Washington: Center for Strategic and International Studies.

————. 2002. *The Macroeconomic Impact of Global Aging: A New Era of Economic Frailty.* Washington: Center for Strategic and International Studies.

Fellegi, I. 1997. *On Poverty and Low Income.* Ottawa: Statistics Canada.

Foot, D., and R. Venne. 2005. "Awakening to the inter-generational equity debate in Canada." *Journal of Canadian Studies* 39 (1): 5–21.

Galarneau, D. 1994. *Female Baby Boomers: A Generation at Work.* Ottawa: Statistics Canada.

Galt, V. 2007. "Older workers a drain? Not a chance, study finds." *The Globe and Mail* 23 May: B5.

Gee, E., and G. Gutman, Eds. 2000. *The Overselling of Population Aging: Apocalyptic Demography, Intergenerational Challenges and Social Policy.* Don Mills, ON: Oxford University Press.

Gee, E., and M. Kimball. 1987. *Women and Aging.* Toronto: Butterworths.

Giles, P. 2004. *Low Income Measurement in Canada.* Catalogue no. 75F0002MIE-no.011. Ottawa: Statistics Canada.

Gillin, C., et al., Eds. 2005. *Time's Up! Mandatory Retirement in Canada.* Toronto: James Lorimer.

Government of Canada. 2007. "Population at 2017: The many dimensions of population aging." *Horizons* 9 (4): 1–53.

Hardy, M. 2006. "Older workers." In R. Binstock and L. George, Eds, *Handbook of Aging and the Social Sciences*, 201–18. San Diego: Academic Press.

Hardy, M., and K. Shuey. 2000. "Pension decisions in a changing economy: Gender, structure, and choice." *Journal of Gerontology: Social Sciences* 55B (5): S271–7.

Heinz, W. 2001. "Work and the life course: A cosmopolitan-local perspective." In V. Marshall et al., Eds, *Restructuring Work and the Life Course*, 3–22. Toronto: University of Toronto Press.

Henkens, K. 1999. "Retirement intentions and spousal support: A multi-actor approach." *Journal of Gerontology: Social Sciences* 54B (2): S63–73.

Henretta, J. 2003. "The life course perspective on work and retirement." In R. Settersten, Ed., Invitation to the Life Course: Toward New Understandings of Later Life, 85–105. Amityville, NY: Baywood.

Hicks, P. 2003. "New policy research on population aging and life-course flexibility." *Horizons* 6 (2): 3–6.

Holden, K., and C. Hatcher. 2006. "Economic status of the aged." In R. Binstock and L. George, Eds, *Handbook of Aging and the Social Sciences*, 219–37. San Diego: Academic Press.

Ibbot, P., et al. 2006. "Probing the future of mandatory retirement in Canada." *Canadian Journal on Aging* 25 (2): 161–78.

Karp, D. 1989. "The social construction of retirement among professionals 50–60 years old." *The Gerontologist* 29 (6): 750–60.

Kemp, C., et al. 2006. "Financial planning for later life: Subjective understandings of catalysts and constraints." *Journal of Aging Studies* 19 (3): 273–90.

Kershaw, P. 2011. "Struggles of the next generation." *The Vancouver Sun*, 26 September.

Klassen, T., and C. Gillin. 1999. "The heavy hand of the law: The Canadian Supreme Court and mandatory retirement." *Canadian Journal on Aging* 18 (2): 259–76.

Marshall, K., and V. Ferrao. 2007. "Participation of older workers, 2006." *Perspectives on Labour and Income* 8 (8): 5–11. Catalogue no. 75-001-XIE. Ottawa: Statistics Canada.

Marshall, V. 1995. "Rethinking retirement: Issues for the twenty-first century." In E. Gee and G. Gutman, Eds, *Rethinking Retirement*, 31–50. Vancouver: Gerontology Research Centre, Simon Fraser University.

Marshall, V., et al., Eds. 2001a. *Restructuring Work and the Life Course.* Toronto: University of Toronto Press.

———. 2001b. "Instability in the retirement transition: Effects on health and well-being in a Canadian study." *Research on Aging* 23 (4): 379–409.

Marshall, V., and P. Clarke. 1996. *Facilitating the Transition from Employment to Retirement.* Ottawa: National Forum on Health.

Marshall, V., and P. Taylor. 2005. "Restructuring the life course: Work and retirement." In M. Johnson, Ed., *The Cambridge Handbook of Age and Ageing*, 572–82. New York: Cambridge University Press.

McDaniel, S. 2002. "Women's changing relations to the state and citizenship: Caring and intergenerational relations in globalizing Western democracies." *Canadian Review of Sociology and Anthropology* 39 (2): 1–26.

McDonald, L. 1997a. "The link between social research and social policy options: Reverse retirement as a case in point." *Canadian Journal on Aging/Canadian Public Policy* (spring: supplement): 90–113.

———. 1997b. "The invisible poor: Canada's retired widows." *Canadian Journal on Aging* 16 (3): 553–83.

———. 2002. "The invisible retirement of women." SEDAP Research Paper no. 69. Hamilton, ON: McMaster University. http://socserve2.mcmaster.ca/sedap.

McDonald, L., et al. 2000. "The poverty of retired widows." In F. Denton et al., Eds, *Independence and Economic Security in Old Age*, 328–44. Vancouver: University of British Columbia Press.

McDonald, L., and M. Chen. 1994. "The youth freeze and the retirement bulge: Older workers and the impending labour shortage." In V. Marshall and B. McPherson, Eds, *Aging: Canadian Perspectives*, 113–39. Peterborough, ON: Broadview.

McDonald, L., and P. Donahue. 2011. "Retirement lost?" *Canadian Journal on Aging* 30 (3): 401–22.

McDonald, L., and L. Robb. 2004. "The economic legacy of divorce and separation for women in old age." *Canadian Journal on Aging* 23 (supplement): S83–97.

McDonald, L., and R. Wanner. 1990. *Retirement in Canada.* Toronto: Butterworths.

McMullin, J. 2005. "Patterns of paid and unpaid work: The influence of power, social context, and family background." *Canadian Journal on Aging* 24 (3): 225–36.

McMullin, J. 2010. *Understanding Inequality: Intersections of Class, Age, Gender, Ethnicity and Race in Canada*, 2nd edn. Don Mills, ON: Oxford University Press.

McMullin, J., and V. Marshall. 2001. "Ageism, age relations and garment industry work in Montreal." *The Gerontologist* 41 (1): 111–22.

Milligan, K. 2007. "The evolution of elderly poverty in Canada." SEDAP *Research Paper* no. 170. Hamilton, ON: McMaster University.

Mintz, J. 2009. *Summary report on retirement income adequacy research*. Ottawa, ON: Dept. of Finance.

Mitchell, B. 2006. *Boomerang Age: Transitions to Adulthood in Families*. Piscataway, NJ: Transaction.

Moen, P. 2012. "Still a Gendered Life Course? Work and Family in a Changing World." Keynote presentation at the 41st Annual Scientific and Educational Meeting of the Canadian Association on Gerontology, Vancouver, BC, 18–20 October 2012.

Moen, P., and S.-K. Han. 2001. "Reframing careers: Work, family and gender." In V. Marshall et al., Eds, *Restructuring Work and the Life Course*, 424–45. Toronto: University of Toronto Press.

Moore, E., and M. Rosenberg. 1997. *Growing Old in Canada*. Toronto: Nelson.

Mutran, E., et al. 1997. "Self-esteem and subjective responses to work among mature workers: Similarities and differences by gender." *Journal of Gerontology: Social Sciences* 52B (2): S89–96.

Myles, J. 1989. *Old Age in the Welfare State: The Political Economy of Public Pensions*. Lawrence: University Press of Kansas.

———. 2000. "The maturation of Canada's retirement income system: Income levels, income inequality and low income among older persons." *Canadian Journal on Aging* 19 (3): 287–316.

———. 2002. "Back to Bismarck? The public policy implications of living longer." *Canadian Journal on Aging* 21 (3): 325–9.

NACA (National Advisory Council on Aging). 2005. *Seniors on the Margin: Aging in Poverty*. Ottawa: NACA.

———. 2006. *Seniors in Canada: 2006 Report Card*. Ottawa: NACA.

National Council of Welfare. 1999. *A Pension Primer*. Catalogue no. 68-49/1999E. Ottawa: Minister of Public Works and Government Services Canada.

National Seniors Council (NSC). 2009. *Report of the National Seniors Council on Low Income Among Seniors*. Ottawa: Minister of Human Resources and Skills Development, and the Minister of the State (Seniors).

National Seniors Council (NSC). 2011. *Labour Force Participation of Seniors and Near Seniors, and Intergenerational Relations*. Ottawa: Minister of Human Resources and Skills Development, and the Minister of the State (Seniors).

National Seniors Council (NSC). 2013. *Older Workers at Risk of Withdrawing from the Labour Force or Becoming Unemployed: Employers' views on how to retain and attract older workers*. Ottawa: Minister of Human Resources and Skills Development, and the Minister of the State (Seniors).

Neysmith, S. 1984. "Poverty in old age: Can pension reform meet the needs of women?" *Canadian Woman Studies* 5: 17–21.

Nishio, H., and H. Lank. 1987. "Patterns of labour participation of older female workers." In V. Marshall, Ed. *Aging in Canada: Social Perspectives*, 228–44. Markham, ON: Fitzhenry and Whiteside.

Oderkirk, J. 1996a. "Old Age Security: An overview." *Canadian Social Trends* 40 (spring): 2–7.

———. 1996b. "Canada and Quebec Pension Plans." *Canadian Social Trends* 40 (spring): 8–15.

O'Rand, A. 2006. "Stratification and the life course: Life course capital, life course risks, and social inequality." In R. Binstock and L. George, Eds, *Handbook of Aging and the Social Sciences*, 145–62. San Diego: Academic Press.

Osberg, L. 2001. "Poverty among senior citizens: A Canadian success story." In P. Grady and A. Sharpe, Eds, *The State of Economics in Canada: Festschrift in Honour of David Slater*, 151–82. Ottawa and Kingston: Centre for the Study of Living Standards and the John Deutsch Institute.

Park, J. 2011. "Retirement, health and employment among those 55 plus." *Perspectives on Labour and Income* (spring). Catalogue no. 75-001-XIE. Ottawa: Statistics Canada.

Payne, S., and L. Doyle. 2010. "Older women, work and health." *Occupational Medicine* 60(3): 172–77.

Pienta, A., et al. 1994. "Women's labour force participation in later life: The effects of early work and family experiences." *Journal of Gerontology: Social Sciences* 49B (5): S231–9.

Pienta, A., and M. Hayward. 2002. "Who expects to continue working after age 62? The retirement plans of couples." *Journal of Gerontology: Social Sciences* 57B (4): S199–208.

Ploeg, J., et al. 2003. "Helping to build and rebuild secure lives and futures: Intergenerational financial transfers from parents to adult children and grandchildren." SEDAP Research Paper no. 96. Hamilton, ON: McMaster University. http://socserv2.mcmaster.ca/sedap.

Policy Research Initiative. 2005. *Encouraging Choice in Work and Retirement: Project Report*. Ottawa: Policy Research Institute.

Prager, J. 2002. "Aging and productivity: What do we know?" In D. Cheal, Ed., *Aging and Demographic Change in Canadian Context*, 133–89. Toronto: University of Toronto Press.

Price, C. 2000. "Women and retirement: Relinquishing professional identity." *Journal of Aging Studies* 14 (1): 81–101.

Prus, S. 2000. "Income inequality as a Canadian cohort ages: An analysis of the later life course." *Research on Aging* 22 (3): 211–37.

———. 2003. "Changes in income within a cohort over the later life course: Evidence for income status convergence." *Canadian Journal on Aging* 21 (4): 475–504.

Raymo, J., and M. Sweeney. 2006. "Work-family conflict and retirement preferences." *Journal of Gerontology: Social Sciences* 61B (3): S161–9.

Rosenthal, C., et al. 2000. "Changes in work and family over the life course: Implications for economic security of today's and tomorrow's older women." In F. Denton et al., Eds, *Independence and Economic Security in Old Age*, 85–111. Vancouver: University of British Columbia Press.

Salthouse, T., and T. Maurer. 1996. "Aging, job performance, and career development." In J. Birren and W. Schaie, Eds, *Handbook of the Psychology of Aging*, 353–64. San Diego: Academic Press.

Schellenberg, G., et al. 2005. "What makes retirement enjoyable?" *Canadian Social Trends* 78 (autumn): 12–14.

Schellenberg, G., and C. Silver. 2004. "You can't always get what you want: Retirement preferences and experiences." *Canadian Social Trends* 75 (winter): 2–7.

Schulz, J. 2001. *The Economics of Aging*. Westport, CT: Auburn House.

Schulz, J., and A. Borowski. 2006. "Economic security in retirement: Reshaping the public-private pension mix." In R. Binstock and L. George, Eds, *Handbook of Aging and the Social Sciences*, 360–79. San Diego: Academic Press.

Smith, R., et al. 2000. "The independence and economic security of older women living alone." In F. Denton et al., Eds, *Independence and Economic Security in Old Age*, 293–327. Vancouver: University of British Columbia Press.

Snell, J. 1996. *The Citizen's Wage: The State and the Elderly in Canada, 1900–1951*. Toronto: University of Toronto Press.

Statistics Canada. 2004. "More seniors at work." *Perspectives on Labour and Income* 5 (2): 5–17. Ottawa: Statistics Canada.

———. 2006. *Income in Canada, 2004*. Catalogue no. 75-202-XIE. Ottawa: Statistics Canada.

———. 2011. *Low Income Cut-Offs after tax*. Catalogue no. 75F0002 MIE. Ottawa: Statistics Canada.

———. 2012. *Labour force Characteristics by Age and Sex*. www.statcan.gc.ca/tables-tableaux/sum-som/l01/cst01/labor20a-eng.htm, retrieved 18 October 2012.

Szinovacz, M., and A. Davey. 2005. "Predictors of perceptions of involuntary retirement." *The Gerontologist* 45 (1): 36–47.

Szinovacz, M., and S. DeViney. 2002. "Marital characteristics and retirement decisions." *Research on Aging* 22 (5): 470–98.

Tremblay, D.-G. 2001. "Polarization of working time and gender differences: Reconciling family and work by reducing working time of men and women." In V. Marshall et al., Eds, *Restructuring Work and the Life Course*, 123–41. Toronto: University of Toronto Press.

Turcotte, M., and G. Schellenberg. 2007. *A Portrait of Seniors in Canada*. Ottawa: Statistics Canada.

Underhill, S., et al. 1997. *Options 45+: hrcc Survey Final Report*. Ottawa: One Voice.

Veall, M. 2007. "Which Canadian seniors are below the low-income measure? QSEP *Research Report* no. 414. Hamilton, ON: McMaster University. http://socserve.mcmaster.ca/qsep.

Walker, A. 2000. "Towards active ageing in Europe." *Hallym International Journal of Aging* 2 (1): 49–60.

Wang, M., and K. Shutz. 2010. "Employee retirement: A review and recommendations for future investigation." *Journal of Management* 36 (1): 172–206.

Wannell, T. 2007. "Young pensioners." *Perspectives on Labour and Income* 8 (2): 5–14. Catalogue no. 75-001-XIE. Ottawa: Statistics Canada.

Whitehouse, E. 2009. *Canada's retirement-income provision: An international perspective*. Ottawa, ON: Dept. of Finance.

Yabiku, S. 2000. "Family history and pensions: The relationships between marriage, divorce, children, and private pension coverage." *Journal of Aging Studies* 14 (3): 293–312.

Chapter 11

Social Participation, Social Connectedness, and Leisure in Later Life

Aday, R. 2003. *Aging Prisoners: Crisis in American Corrections*. Westport, CT: Praeger.

Agahi, N., et al. 2006. "Continuity of leisure participation from middle age to old age." *Journal of Gerontology: Social Sciences* 61B (6): S34–46.

Altergott, K. 1988a. "Daily life in later life: Concepts and methods for inquiry." In K. Altergott, Ed., *Daily Life in Later Life: Comparative Perspectives*, 11–22. Newbury Park, CA: Sage.

———. 1988b. *Daily Life in Later Life: Comparative Perspectives*. Newbury Park, CA: Sage.

Alwin, D., et al. 2006. "Modeling the effects of time: Integrating demographic and developmental perspectives." In R. Binstock and L. George, Eds, *Handbook of Aging and the Social Sciences*, 20–38. San Diego: Academic Press.

Antonucci, T. 1990. "Social support and social relationships." In R. Binstock and L. George, Eds, *Handbook of Aging and the Social Sciences*, 205–26. New York: Academic Press.

Antonucci, T., et al. 2006. "Social relations in the third age: Assessing strengths and challenges using the convoy model." In J. Boone James and P. Wink, Eds, *Annual Review of Gerontology and Geriatrics* 26: 193–209. New York: Springer.

Atchley, R. 1997. "The subjective importance of being religious and its effect on health and morale 14 years later." *Journal of Aging Studies* 11 (2): 131–42.

———. 2008. "Spirituality, meaning, and the experience of aging. Generations 32 (2): 12–16.

———. 2009. *Spirituality and Aging*. Baltimore, MD: Johns Hopkins University Press.

Burr, J., et al. 2002. "Productive aging and civic participation." *Journal of Aging Studies* 16 (1): 87–105.

Butrica, B., et al. 2009. "Volunteer dynamics of older Americans" *Journal of Gerontology: Social Sciences* 64B (5): 644–55.

Canadian Gaming Association. 2008. *A Caution Regarding Recent Statistics Canada Gambling Data*. Ottawa: Canadian Gaming Association's Economic Impacts of the Canada Gaming Industry Study.

Centre for Addiction and Mental Health. 2006. *Responding to Older Adults with Substance Use, Mental Health and Gambling Challenges: A Guide for Workers and Volunteers*. Toronto: Centre for Addiction and Mental Health.

Chappell, N., 2002. *Volunteering and Healthy Aging: What We Know*. Ottawa: Health Canada.

Chappell, N. and L. Funk. 2010. "Social capital: Does it add to the health inequalities debate?" *Social Indicators Research* 99 (3): 357–73.

Chappell, N. and L. Funk. 2011. "Social support, caregiving and aging." *Canadian Journal on Aging* 30 (3): 355–70.

Cheang, M. 2002. "Older adults' frequent visits to a fast-food restaurant: Nonobligatory social interaction and the significance of play in a 'third place.'" *Journal of Aging Studies* 16 (3): 303–21.

Community Links 2010. *Seniors Gambling: A Hidden Problem? A Report on the Seniors and Gambling Project*. Nova Scotia: Nova Scotia Gambling Foundation.

Corsentino, E., et al. 2009. "Religious attendance reduces cognitive decline among older women with high levels of depressive symptoms." *Journal of Gerontology: Biological and Medical Sciences* 64A (12): 1283–9.

Cornwell, B., et al. 2009. "Social networks in the NSHAP study: Rationale, measurement, and preliminary findings." *Journal of Gerontology: Social Sciences* 64B (SI): i47–55.

Counts, D., and Counts, D. 2001. *Over the Next Hill: An Ethnography of RVing Seniors in North America,* 2nd edn. Toronto: Broadview Press.

Cutler, S., et al. 2011. "Civic engagement and aging." In R.Binstock, L. George, S. Cutler, J. Hendricks and H. Schulz, Eds, *Handbook of Aging and the Social Science*, 7th edn., 221–33. New York: Oxford, UK: Elsevier.

Cutler, S., and J. Hendricks. 2000. "Age differences in voluntary association memberships: Fact or artifact?" *Journal of Gerontology: Social Sciences* 55B (2): S98–107.

Fast, J., et al. 2006a. "Participation, roles and contributions of seniors." Expert Roundtable on Seniors Report. Ottawa: Social Development Canada.

———. 2006b. "Productive activity in later life: Stability and change across three decades." *Research on Aging* 28 (6): 691–712.

Finlay, D. 2000. "Elderly offenders: Getting by with a little help from their friends." *Let's Talk: Public Perceptions and Corrections* 25 (2): 5–7.

Fletcher, S. 2004. "Religion and life meaning: Differentiation between religious beliefs and religious community in constructing life meaning." *Journal of Aging Studies* 18 (2): 171–85.

Gatz, M., and M. Smyer. 2001. "Mental health and aging at the millennium." In J. Birren and W. Schaie, Eds, *Handbook of the Psychology of Aging*, 523–44. San Diego: Academic Press.

Gauthier, A., and T. Smeeding. 2003. "Time use at older ages: Cross-national differences." *Research on Aging* 25 (3): 247–74.

Gibson, and J. Singleton. Eds. 2012. *Leisure and Aging: Theory and Practice*. Champaign, IL: Human Kinetics.

Gierveld, J., and B. Havens. 2004. "Cross-national comparisons of social isolation and loneliness: Introduction and overview." *Canadian Journal on Aging* 23 (2): 109–13.

Gierveld, J., and P. Dykstra. 2008. "Virtue is its own reward? Support-giving in the family and loneliness in middle and old age. *Ageing and Society,* 28, 271–87.

Gleberzon, B., and J. Cutler. 2002. "Dispelling the myths of aging." *Aging, Health and Society: News and Views* 8 (1): 3. Hamilton, ON: Program in Gerontology, McMaster University.

Gottlieb, B. 2002. "Older volunteers: A precious resource under pressure." *Canadian Journal on Aging* 21 (1): 5–9.

Gottlieb, B., and A. Gillespie. 2008. "Volunteerism, health and civic engagement among older adults." *Canadian Journal on Aging* 27 (4): 399–406.

Goulding, A. 2012. "Lifelong learning for people aged 64+ within the contemporary art gallery context. *Educational Gerontology*, 38 (4): 215–27.

Greiner, L., and K. Allenby. 2010. *A Descriptive Profile of Older Women Offenders*. Ottawa: Correctional Services of Canada.

Hagen, B., et al. 2005. "Stacking the odds: A phenomenological study of non-problem gambling in later life." *Canadian Journal on Aging* 24 (4): 433–42.

Havens, B., et al. 2004. "Social isolation and loneliness: Differences between older rural and urban Manitobans." *Canadian Journal on Aging* 23 (2): 129–40.

Hendricks, J., and S. Cutler. 2003. "Leisure in life-course perspective." In R. Settersten, Ed., *Invitation to the Life Course: Toward New Understandings of Later Life*, 107–34. Amityville, NY: Baywood.

Hendricks, J., and L. Hatch. 2006. "Lifestyle and aging." In R. Binstock and L. George, Eds, *Handbook of Aging and the Social Sciences*, 301–19. San Diego: Academic Press.

Higgins, J. 2005. "Explaining the politics and policy surrounding senior center gambling activities." *Journal of Aging Studies* 19 (1): 85–107.

Hope, J., and L. Havir. 2002. "You bet they're having fun! Older Americans and casino gambling." *Journal of Aging Studies* 16 (2): 177–97.

Hsu, C. 2010. "Physical and leisure activity, social support, self-esteem and depression among community-based older adults in Taiwan." *United States Sports Academy*. Dissertation. 145 pages; 3437342.

Idler, E. 2006. "Religion and aging." In R. Binstock and L. George, Eds, *Handbook of Aging and the Social Sciences*, 277–300. San Diego: Academic Press.

Idler, E., et al. 2009. "Religion and the quality of life in the last year of life." *Journal of Gerontology: Social Sciences* 64B (4): 528–37.

Jackson, J., et al. 2011. "Racial and ethnic influences over the life course." In R.Binstock, L. George, S. Cutler, J. Hendricks and H. Schulz, Eds, Handbook of Aging and the Social Science, 7th edn., 91–103. New York: Oxford, UK: Elsevier.

Jones, A. 2007. "Canadians spent $14.5 billion in gambling in 2006, study finds." *The Globe and Mail* 27 April: A5

Katz, S. 2000. "Busy bodies: Activity, aging and the management of everyday life." *Journal of Aging Studies* 14 (2): 135–52.

Kirby, S., et al. 2004. "Spirituality and well-being in frail and nonfrail adults." *Journal of Gerontology: Psychological Sciences* 59 (B): P123–9.

Krause, N. 2006a. "Social relationships in late life." In R. Binstock and L. George, Eds, *Handbook of Aging and the Social Sciences*, 181–200. San Diego: Academic Press.

———. 2006b. "Religion and health in late life." In J. Birren and W. Schaie, Eds, *Handbook of the Psychology of Aging*, 499–518. San Diego: Academic Press.

Krause, N., and E. Bastida 2011. "Religion, suffering, and self-rated health among older Mexican Americans." *Journal of Gerontology: Psychological Sciences and Social Sciences* 66B (2): 207–16.

Lachman, M. 2003. "Negative interactions in close relationships: Introduction to a special section." *Journal of Gerontology: Psychological Sciences* 58B (2): P69.

Lemay, A., et al. 2006. *Betting on Older Adults: A Problem Gambling Prevention Clinical Manual for Service Providers*. Sault Ste. Marie, ON: Sault Area Hospital, St Joseph's Care Group, and Centretown Community Health Centre.

Lethbridge Herald. 2003. "More seniors declaring bankruptcy." 25 February: A1.

Li, Y. 2007. "Recovering from spousal bereavement in later life: Does volunteer participation play a role?" *Journal of Gerontology: Social Sciences* 62B (4): S257–66.

MacKinlay, E., Ed. 2005. *Spirituality in Later Life*. Binghampton, NY: Haworth.

Marcoen, A. 2005. "Religion, spirituality and older people." In M. Johnson, Ed., *The Cambridge Handbook of Age and Ageing*, 363–70. New York: Cambridge University Press.

Martin, F., et al. 2011. "A longitudinal study: Casino gambling attitudes, motivations, and gambling patterns among urban elders." *Journal of Gambling Studies* 27: 287–97.

Martinson, M., and M. Minkler. 2006. "Civic engagement and older adults: A critical perspective." *The Gerontologist* 46 (3): 318–24.

Moody, H., and J. Sasser. 2012. *Aging: Concepts and Controversies*, 7th edn. Thousand Oaks, CA: Sage.

Morrow-Howell, N., and M. Freedman, Eds. 2007. "Civic engagement in later life." *Generations* 30 (4).

Muggeridge, P. 2002. "Government greed for gaming revenue may be hurting us all." *Fifty Plus* (August): 14–20.

NACA (National Advisory Council on Aging). 2006. "Seniors and addictions: A bad gamble." *Expression* 19 (4): 1–8.

National Seniors Council (NSC). 2010. *National Seniors Council on Volunteering Among Seniors and Positive and Active Aging*. Ottawa: Minister of Human Resources and Skills Development, and the Minister of the State (Seniors).

O'Brien Cousins, S., et al. 2002. *High Quality Aging or Gambling with Health? The Lifestyles of*

Elders Who Play Bingo: Report for the Alberta Gaming Research Institute. Edmonton: University of Alberta, Faculty of Physical Education and Recreation.

Onyx, J., and R. Leonard. 2007. "The grey nomad phenomenon: Changing the script of aging." *International Journal of Aging and Human Development* 64 (4): 381–98.

Parekh, R., & Morano, C. 2009. "Senior gambling: Risk or reward?" *Journal of Gerontological Social Work* 52: 686–94.

Pargament, K. 1997. *The Psychology of Religion and Coping: Theory, Research and Practice.* New York: Guilford.

Perlman, D. 2004. "European and Canadian studies of loneliness among seniors." *Canadian Journal on Aging* 23 (2): 181–8.

Pilkington, P., et al. 2012. "Volunteering and subjective well-being in mid-life and older adults: The role of subjective social networks." *Journal of Gerontology: Social Sciences* 67B (2): 249–60.

Public Safety Canada. 2011. *Corrections and Conditional Release Statistical Overview, Annual Report 2011: Building a Safe and Resilient Canada.* Ottawa: Public Safety Canada.

Roberts, P., and G. Fawcett. 2003. *At Risk: A Socioeconomic Analysis of Health and Literacy among Seniors.* Catalogue no. 89F010XIE. Ottawa: Statistics Canada.

Rogers, W., and A. Fisk. 2010. "Toward a psychological science of advanced technology design in older adults." *Journal of Gerontology: Psychological Sciences and Social Sciences* 65B (6): 645–53.

Rote, S., et al. 2013. "Religious attendance and loneliness in later life." *The Gerontologist* 53 (1): 39–50.

Rothman, M., and B. Dunlop, Eds. 2000. *Elders, Crime and the Criminal Justice System: Myth, Perception and Reality in the 21st Century.* New York: Springer.

Rozanova, J., et al. 2012. "Unequal social engagement for older adults: Constraints on choice." *Canadian Journal on Aging* 31 (1): 25–36.

Schaie, W., et al., Eds. 2004. *Religious Influences on Health and Well-Being in the Elderly.* New York: Springer.

Simard, P. 2000. "Are the senior years really the golden years for offenders?" *Let's Talk: Public Perceptions and Corrections* 25 (2): 4–5.

Simone, P., and J. Cesena. 2010. "Student demographics, satisfaction and cognitive demand in two lifelong learning programs. Educational Gerontology 36 (5): 425–34.

Statistics Canada. 2001. *The 2001 National Survey of Giving, Volunteering and Participating.* Catalogue no. 71-542-XPE. Ottawa: Statistics Canada.

———. 2006. "Aging well: Time use patterns of older Canadians." *General Social Survey on Time Use: Cycle 19, 2005.* Catalogue no. 89-622-XIE. Ottawa: Statistics Canada.

———. 2010. *The General Social Survey—2010 Overview of the Time Use of Canadians.* Catalogue no. 89-647-X. Ottawa: Statistics Canada.

Steffensmeier, D., and M. Motivans. 2000. "Older men and older women in the arms of criminal law: Offending patterns and sentencing outcomes." *Journal of Gerontology: Social Sciences* 55B (3): S141–51.

Strain, L. 2001. "Senior centres: Who participates?" *Canadian Journal on Aging* 20 (4): 471–91.

Strain, L., et al. 2002. "Continuing and ceasing leisure activities in later life: A longitudinal study." *The Gerontologist* 42 (2): 217–23.

Theurer, K., and A.V. Wister. 2010. "Altruistic behavior and social capital as predictors of well-being among older Canadians." *Ageing and Society* 30: 157–81.

Thomas, P. 2009. "Is it better to give than to receive? Social support and the well-being of older adults." *Journal of Gerontology: Social Sciences* 65B (3): 351–7.

Thomas, M., and R. Venne. 2002. "Work and leisure: A question of balance." In D. Cheal, Ed., *Aging and Demographic Change in Canadian Context,* 190–222. Toronto: University of Toronto Press.

Thomese, F., et al. 2005. "Network dynamics in later life." In M. Johnson, Ed., *The Cambridge Handbook of Age and Ageing,* 463–8. New York: Cambridge University Press.

Tirachaimongkol et al. 2010. "Pathways to problem gamblers of seniors." *Journal of Gerontological Social Work* 53 (6): 531–46.

Turcotte, M., and G. Schellenberg. 2007. *A Portrait of Seniors in Canada.* Ottawa: Statistics Canada.

United Nations. 1992. "The Third Age University." *Bulletin on Ageing* 3: 5–7.

Van Willigen, M. 2000. "Differential benefits of volunteering across the life course." *Journal of Gerontology: Social Sciences* 55B (5): S308–18.

Victorino, C., and A. Gauthier. 2005. "Are Canadian seniors becoming more active? Empirical evidence based on time-use data." *Canadian Journal on Aging* 24 (1): 45–56.

Wahidin, A., and M. Cain, Eds. 2006. *Aging, Crime and Society.* Portland, OR: Willan Publishing.

Walker, A. 2006. "Aging and politics: An international perspective." In R. Binstock and L. George, Eds, *Handbook of Aging and the Social Sciences,* 339–59. San Diego: Academic Press.

Wenger, C., and V. Burholt. 2004. "Changes in levels of social isolation and loneliness among older people in a rural area: A twenty-year longitudinal study." *Canadian Journal on Aging* 23 (2): 115–27.

Whitehead, B., and C. Bergeman. 2011. "Coping with daily stress: Differential role of spiritual experience on daily positive and negative affect." *Journal of Gerontology: Psychological and Social Sciences.* doi: 10.1093/geronb/gbr136. First published online: 22 December 2011.

Williams, C. 2002. "Time or money? How high and low income Canadians spend their time." *Canadian Social Trends* 65 (summer): 7–11.

Wilson, L., and S. Simson, Eds. 2006. *Civic Engagement and the Baby Boomer Generation: Research, Policy and Practice Perspectives.* Binghampton, NY: Haworth.

Windsor, R., et al. 2004. *Evaluation of Health Promotion, Health Education, and Disease Prevention.* NY: McGraw Hill.

Wister, A.V., et al. 2010 "Life-long educational practices and resources in enabling health literacy among older adults." *Journal of Aging and Health* 22: 827–54.

World Health Organization. 2002. *Active Ageing: A Policy Framework.* New York: United Nations.

Yardley, L., and H. Smith. 2002. "A prospective study of the relationship between feared consequences of falling and avoidance of activity in community-living older people." *The Gerontologist* 42 (1): 17–23.

Yarnal, C. 2006. "The Red Hat Society: Exploring the role of play, liminality and communitas in older women's lives." *Journal of Women and Aging* 18 (3): 51–73.

Zaranek, R., and E. Chapleski. 2005. "Casino gambling among urban elders: Just another social activity." *Journal of Gerontology: Social Sciences* 60B (2): S74–81.

Zaranek, R., and P. Lichtenberg. 2008. "Urban elders and casino gambling: Are they at risk of a gambling problem?" *Journal of Aging Studies,* 22 (1), 12–23.

Zuzanek, J., and S. Box. 1988. "Life course and the daily lives of older adults in Canada." In K. Altergott, Ed., *Daily Life in Later Life: Comparative Perspectives,* 147–85. Newbury Park, CA: Sage.

Chapter 12

End of the Life Course: Social Support, Dying Well, and Public Policy

Albom, M. 1997. *Tuesdays with Morrie.* New York: Broadway Books.

Alexander, T. 2002. "The history and evolution of long-term care in Canada." In M. Stephenson and E. Sawyer, Eds, *Continuing the Care: The Issues and Challenges for Long-Term Care,* 1–55. Ottawa: CHA Press.

Angus, D., et al. 1995. *Sustainable Health Care for Canada.* Ottawa: University of Ottawa Economic Projects.

Aronson, J. 2002. "Frail and disabled users of home care: Confident consumers or disentitled citizens." *Canadian Journal on Aging* 21 (1): 11–25.

Au Coin, K. 2003. "Family violence against older adults." In H. Johnson and K. Au Coin, Eds, *Family Violence in Canada: A Statistical Profile, 2003,* 21–32. Catalogue no. 85-224-XIE. Ottawa: Statistics Canada.

Auger, J. 2000. *Social Perspectives on Death and Dying.* Halifax: Fernwood.

Béland, F., and E. Shapiro, Eds. 1995. "Policy issues in care for the elderly in Canada." *Canadian Journal on Aging* 14 (2): 153–8.

Braun, K., et al., Eds. 2000. *Cultural Issues in End-of-Life Decision Making.* Thousand Oaks, CA: Sage.

———. 2001. "Support for physician-assisted suicide: Exploring the impact of ethnicity and attitudes toward planning for death." *The Gerontologist* 41 (1): 51–60.

Breda, J., and D. Schoenmaekers. 2006. "Age: A dubious criterion in legislation." *Ageing and Society* 26 (4): 529–47.

Brewer, L. 2001. "Gender socialization and the cultural construction of elder caregivers." *Journal of Aging Studies* 15 (3): 217–35.

Brogden, M. 2001. *Geronticide: Killing the Elderly.* Philadelphia: Jessica Kingsley.

Brotman, S. 2003. "The limits of multiculturalism in elder care services." *Journal of Aging Studies* 17 (2): 209–29.

Bryant, C., Ed. 2003. *Handbook of Death and Dying.* Thousand Oaks, CA: Sage.

Buchignani, N., and C. Armstrong-Esther. 1999. "Informal care and older Native Canadians." *Ageing and Society* 19 (1): 3–32.

Burr, J., et al. 2005. "Caregiving and volunteering: Are private and public helping behaviors linked?" *Journal of Gerontology: Social Sciences* 60B (5): S247–56.

Campbell, L., and A. Martin-Matthews. 2000. "Caring sons: Exploring men's involvement in filial care." *Canadian Journal on Aging* 19 (1): 57–79.

Canadian Home Care Association. 2004. *Portraits of Home Care: A Picture of Progress and Innovation.* Ottawa: Canadian Home Care Association.

Canadian Hospice Palliative Care Association. 2004. *Fact Sheet.* Ottawa: Canadian Hospice Palliative Care Association.

CARP (Canada's Association for the Fifty-Plus). 2001. *CARP's Report Card on Home Care in Canada, 2000.* Toronto: CARP.

Carp, F. 2000. *Elder Abuse in the Family: An Interdisciplinary Model for Research*. New York: Springer.

Carrière, Y., et al. 2002. "Changing demographic trends and use of home care services." In *Report on the Demographic Situation in Canada*, 137–59. Catalogue no. 91-209-XPE. Ottawa: Statistics Canada.

Chappell, N. 2011. *Population Aging and the Evolving Care Needs of Older Canadians: An Overview of the Policy Challenges*. IRPP Study, No. 21, October 2011.

Chappell, N., and L. Funk. 2011. "Social support, caregiving and aging." *Canadian Journal on Aging* 30 (3): 355–70.

Chappell, N., and M. Hollander. 2011a. "An evidence-based policy prescription for an aging population." *Healthcare Papers* 11 (1): 8–19.

Chappell, N., and M. Hollander. 2011b. "The authors respond." *Healthcare Papers* 11 (1): 88–91.

CIHI (Canadian Institute for Health Information). 2010. Supporting Informal Caregivers—The Heart of Home Care. Ottawa: CIHI.

CIHI (Canadian Institute for Health Information). 2011. *Health Care in Canada, 2011: A Focus on Seniors and Aging*. Ottawa: CIHI.

CMHC (Canadian Mortgage and Housing Corporation). 1990. *The Senior Citizens' Department of the Regional Municipality of Niagara, Ontario, and Its Continuum of Care Model: A Case Study*. Ottawa: CMHC.

Connidis, I. 2010. *Family Ties and Aging*, 2nd edn. Thousand Oaks, CA: Pine Forge Press.

Cooke, M., et al. 2008. "The changing well-being of older adult registered Indians: An analysis using the Registered Indian Human Development Index." *Canadian Journal on Aging* 27 (4): 385–97.

Cranswick, K. 2003. *General Social Survey, Cycle 16: Caring for an Aging Society*. Catalogue no. 89-582-XIE. Ottawa: Statistics Canada.

Cranswick, K., and D. Thomas. 2005. "Elder care and the complexities of social networks." *Canadian Social Trends* 75 (summer): 10–15.

Daichman, L. 2005. "Elder abuse in developing nations." In M. Johnson, Ed., *The Cambridge Handbook of Age and Ageing*, 323–31. New York: Cambridge University Press.

Dauvergne, M. 2003. "Family violence against seniors." *Canadian Social Trends* 68 (spring): 10–14.

Davidson, K., et al. 2000. "Gendered meanings of care work within late life marital relationships." *Canadian Journal on Aging* 19 (4): 536–53.

Decalmer, P., and F. Glendenning, Eds. 1993. *The Mistreatment of Elderly People*. Newbury Park, CA: Sage

del-Pino-Casado, R., et al. 2011. "Coping and subjective burden in caregivers of older relatives: A systematic review." *Journal of Advanced Nursing* 67 (11): 2311–22.

Denton, M., et al. 1999. "Occupational health issues among employees of home care agencies." *Canadian Journal on Aging* 18 (2): 154–81.

———, et al. 2007. "Market-modelled home care: Impact on job satisfaction and propensity to leave." *Canadian Public Policy*, XXXIII (supplement): 81–99.

Dilworth-Anderson, P., et al. 2002. "Issues of race, ethnicity, and culture in caregiving research: A 20-year review (1980–2000)." *The Gerontologist* 42 (2): 237–72.

Dupuis, S., and J. Norris. 2001. "The roles of adult daughters in long-term care facilities: Alternative role manifestations." *Journal of Aging Studies* 15 (1): 27–54.

Dyer, C. 2005. "Neglect assessment in elderly persons." *Journal of Gerontology: Medical Sciences* 60A (8): M1000–1.

Estes, C., et al. 2001. *Social Policy and Aging: A Critical Perspective*. Thousand Oaks, CA: Sage.

Fast, J., et al. 1997. *Conceptualizing and Operationalizing the Costs of Informal Elder Care*. Edmonton: Department of Human Ecology, University of Alberta.

———. 2004. "Characteristics of family/friend care networks of frail seniors." *Canadian Journal on Aging* 23 (1): 5–19.

———. 2010. "Gender differences in family/friend caregiving in Canada." *Research on Aging Policies and Practices*. December Issue: 1–4. Edmonton: University of Alberta.

Feldman, P. 1999. "Doing more with less: Advancing the conceptual underpinnings of home-based care." *Journal of Aging and Health* 11 (3): 261–76.

———, Ed. 2003. "Special issue: From philosophy to practice: Selected issues in financing and co-ordinating long-term care." *Journal of Aging and Health* 15 (1): 5–291.

Fisher, R., et al., Eds. 2000. *A Guide to End-of-Life Care for Seniors*. Ottawa: Population Health Directorate, Health Canada.

Fitzwater, E., and C. Puchta. 2010. "Guest editorial: Elder abuse and financial exploitation: Unlawful and just plain awful!" *Journal of Gerontological Nursing* 36 (12): 3–5.

Foley, K., and H. Hendin, Eds. 2002. *The Case against Assisted Suicide: For the Right to End-of-Life Care*. Baltimore, MD: Johns Hopkins University Press.

Forbes, W., et al. 1987. *Institutionalization of the Elderly in Canada*. Toronto: Butterworths.

Fulmer, T., et al. 2005. "Dyadic vulnerability and risk profiling for elder neglect." *The Gerontologist* 45 (4): 525–34.

Garrett, D., et al. 2008. "End-of-life care: Findings from the Canadian Study of Health and Aging."

Canadian Journal on Aging 27 (1): 11–21.

Gaudet, S. 2007. "Social participation through the life course: Theoretical and empirical tool for social policy development." *Horizons* 9 (3): 3–8.

Gee, E. 1995. "Population aging: A contested terrain of social policy." In E. Gee and G. Gutman, Eds, *Rethinking Retirement*, 13–29. Vancouver: Simon Fraser University, Gerontology Research Centre.

Gee, E., and M. Boyce. 1988. "Veterans and veterans legislation in Canada: An historical overview." *Canadian Journal on Aging* 7 (3): 204–17.

Gignac, M., et al. 1996. "The impact of caregiving on employment: A mediational model of work-family conflict." *Canadian Journal on Aging* 15 (4): 525–42.

Government of Canada. 2003. *Services for Seniors*. Ottawa: Minister of Public Works.

Government of Quebec. 2002. *A Quebec for All Ages*. Quebec City: Province of Quebe. www.bnquebec.ca.

Gott, M., and C. Ingleton. Eds. 2011. *Living with Ageing and Dying: Palliative and End of Life Care for Older People*. Oxford University Press.

Guberman, N., et al. 2006 "Families' values and attitudes regarding responsibility for the frail elderly." *Journal of Aging and Social Policy* 18 (3 & 4): 59–78.

Gutman, G., and C. Spencer, C., Eds. (2010). *Aging, Ageism and Abuse: Moving from Awareness to Action*. Burlington, MA: Elsevier.

Harris, P., and S. Long. 1999. "Husbands and sons in the United States and Japan: Cultural expectations and caregiving experiences." *Journal of Aging Studies* 13 (3): 241–67.

Hawkins, N., et al. 2005. "Micromanaging death: Process preferences, values and goals in end-of-life medical decision-making." *The Gerontologist* 45 (1): 107–17.

Hawranik, P. 2002. "In home service use by caregivers and their elders: Does cognitive status make a difference?" *Canadian Journal on Aging* 21 (2): 257–71.

Hayslip, B., and C. Peveto. 2005. *Cultural Changes in Attitudes toward Death, Dying and Bereavement*. New York: Springer.

Hayward, L., et al. 2004. "Publicly-funded and family-friend care in the case of long-term illness: The role of the spouse." *Canadian Journal on Aging* 23 (supplement): 539–48.

Health Canada. 2002. *Canada's Aging Population*. Ottawa: Health Canada.

Health Council of Canada. 2012. *Seniors in Need, Caregivers in Distress: What Are the Home Care Priorities for Seniors in Canada?* Toronto: Health Council of Canada.

Hébert, R. 2011. "Public long-term care insurance: A way to ensure sustainable continuity of care for older people." *Healthcare Quarterly* 11 (1): 69–75.

Hébert, R., et al. 2001. "Resources and costs associated with disabilities of elderly people living at home and in institutions." *Canadian Journal on Aging* 20 (1): 1–21.

———. 2003. "Efficacy of a psychoeducative group program for caregivers of demented persons living at home: A randomized controlled trial." *Journal of Gerontology: Social Sciences* 58B (1): S58–67.

Henderson, K. 2002. "Informal caregivers." In J. Stephenson and E. Sawyer, Eds, *Continuing the Care: The Issues and Challenges for Long-Term Care*, 267–90. Ottawa: CHA Press.

Hollander, M., et al. 2007. "Providing care and support for an aging population: Briefing notes on key policy issues." *Healthcare Quarterly* 10 (3): 34–45.

Hollander, M., et al. 2009. "Increased value for money in the Canadian healthcare system: New findings and the case for integrated care for seniors." *Healthcare Quarterly* 12 (1): 38–47.

Hollander, M., and M. Prince. 2008. "Organizing healthcare delivery systems for persons with on-going care needs and their families: A best practices framework." *Healthcare Quarterly* 11 (1): 42–52.

Hudson, R. 1997. *The Future of Age-Based Public Policy*. Baltimore, MD: Johns Hopkins University Press.

International Observatory on End of Life Care. 2007. *Mapping Levels of Palliative Care Development: A Global View*. Lancaster, UK: Lancaster University.

Johnson, T., Ed. 1999. *Handbook on Ethical Issues in Aging*. Westport, CT: Greenwood.

Joseph, A., and B. Hallman. 1996. "Caught in the triangle: The influence of home, work and elder location on work-family balance." *Canadian Journal on Aging* 15 (3): 393–412.

Keating, N., et al. 1999. *Eldercare in Canada: Context, Content and Consequences*. Ottawa: Statistics Canada.

Keating, N., Ed. 2008. *Rural Ageing: A Good Place to Grow Old?* London, UK: Policy Press.

Keefe, J. 2002. "Home and community care." In M. Stephenson and E. Sawyer, Eds, *Continuing the Care: The Issues and Challenges for Long-Term Care*, 109–40. Ottawa: cha Press.

Keefe, J., et al. 2000. "The impact of ethnicity on helping older relatives: Findings from a sample of employed Canadians." *Canadian Journal on Aging* 19 (3): 317–42.

———. 2007. "Developing new strategies to support future caregivers with disabilities: Projections of need and their policy implications." *Canadian Public Policy* XXXIII (supplement): 65–80.

Keefe, J., and P. Fancey. 1997. "Financial compensation or home help service: Examining differences among program recipients." *Canadian Journal on Aging* 16 (2): 254–78.

———. 2002. "Work and eldercare: Reciprocity between older mothers and their employed daughters." *Canadian Journal on Aging* 21 (2): 229–41.

Keefe, J., and B. Rajinovich. 2007. "To pay or not to pay: Examining underlying principles in the debate on financial support for family caregivers," *Canadian Journal on Aging* 26 (supplement 1): 77–90.

Kramer, B., and J. Lambert. 1999. "Caregiving as a life course transition among older husbands: A prospective study." *The Gerontologist* 39 (6): 658–67.

Kuhl, D. 2002. *What Dying People Want.* Toronto: Doubleday Canada.

Lai, D. 2007. "Cultural predictors of caregiving burden of Chinese-Canadian family caregivers," *Canadian Journal on Aging*, 26 (supplement 1): 133–49.

Laumann, E., et al. 2008. "Elder mistreatment in the United States: Prevalence estimates from a nationally representative study." *Journals of Gerontology. Series B, Psychological Sciences and Social Science* 3B (4) 6: S248–54.

Lawton, P., Ed. 2000. "Focus on the end of life: Scientific and social issues." *Annual Review of Gerontology and Geriatrics* 20: 1–320.

———. 2001. "Quality of life and the end of life." In J. Birren and W. Schaie, Eds, *Handbook of the Psychology of Aging*, 593–616. New York: Academic Press.

Leichtentritt, R., and K. Rettig. 2001. "The social construction of the good death: A dramaturgy approach." *Journal of Aging Studies* 15 (1): 85–103.

Leming, M., and G. Dickinson 2011. *Understanding Dying, Death, and Bereavement,* 7th edn. Cengage: Belmont, CA.

MacAdam, M. 2008. *Frameworks of Integrated Care for the Elderly: A Systematic Review.* Ottawa, ON: Canadian Policy Research Network.

Maclean, M., Ed. 1995. *Abuse and Neglect of Older Canadians: Strategies for Change.* Toronto: Thompson Educational.

Martin-Matthews, A. 2000. "Intergenerational caregiving: How apocalyptic and dominant demographies frame the questions and shape the answers." In E. Gee and G. Gutman, Eds, *The Overselling of Population Aging*, 64–79. Don Mills, ON: Oxford University Press.

Martin-Matthews, A., and J. Phillips. Eds. 2008. *Aging and caring at the intersection of work and home life: Blurring the boundaries.* New York: Lawrence Erlbaum Associates.

Martin-Matthews, A., and J. Sims-Gould 2010. "Strategies used by home support workers in the delivery of care to elderly clients." *Canadian Journal on Aging* 29 (1): 97–107.

Matthews, S. 2002. *Sisters and Brothers/Daughters and Sons: Meeting the Needs of Old Parents.* Bloomington, IN: Unlimited.

McDonald, L. 1997. "The link between social research and social policy options: Reverse retirement as a case in point." *Canadian Journal on Aging/ Canadian Public Policy* supplement (spring): 90–113.

McDonald, L. 2011. "Elder abuse and neglect in Canada: The glass is still half full." *Canadian Journal on Aging* 30 (3): 437–65.

McDonald, L., et al. 1991. *Elder Abuse and Neglect in Canada.* Toronto: Butterworths.

———. 1995. "Issues in practice with respect to mistreatment of older people." In M. Maclean, Ed., *Abuse and Neglect of Older Canadians: Strategies for Change*, 5–16. Toronto: Thompson Educational.

McDonald, L., and A. Collins. 2000. *Abuse and Neglect of Older Adults: A Discussion Paper.* Ottawa: Health Canada, Family Violence Prevention Unit.

McDonald, L., and B. Wigdor, Eds. 1995. "Elder abuse research in Canada." *Canadian Journal on Aging* 14 (supplement 2): 1–140.

McGuire, F., et al. 1999. *Leisure and Aging: Ulyssean Living in Later Life.* Champaign, IL: Sagamore.

McKee, M., et al. 2007. "So no one dies alone: A study of hospice volunteering with rural seniors." *Journal of Palliative Care* 23 (3): 163–72.

Mellor, J., and P. Brownell, Eds. 2006. *Elder Abuse and Mistreatment: Policy, Practice and Research.* Binghampton, NY: Haworth.

Mindszenthy, B., and M. Gordon. 2002. *Parenting Your Parents: Support Strategies for Meeting the Challenge of Aging in the Family.* Toronto: Dundurn Press.

Mitchell, B. 2003. "Would I share a home with an elderly parent? Explaining ethnocultural diversity and intergenerational support relations during adulthood." *Canadian Journal on Aging* 22 (1): 69–82.

Molloy, D., et al. 1996. *Let Me Decide.* Toronto: Penguin.

Montigny, E.-A. 1997. *Foisted upon the Government? State Responsibilities, Family Obligations and the Care of the Elderly in Late-Nineteenth Century Ontario.* Montreal: McGill-Queen's University Press.

Motiwala, S., et al. 2006. "Predictors of place of death for seniors in Ontario: A population-based cohort analysis." *Canadian Journal on Aging* 25 (4): 363–71.

NACA (National Advisory Council on Aging). 2006. *Seniors in Canada: 2006 Report Card.* Ottawa: NACA.

NACA (National Advisory Council on Aging). 1991. *Intergovernmental Relations and the Aging of the Population.* Ottawa: NACA.

National Citizens' Coalition for Nursing Home Reform. 2007. *The Faces of Neglect: Behind the Closed Doors of Nursing Homes.* Washington: National

Citizens' Coalition for Nursing Home Reform. http://nursinghomeaction.org.

National Seniors Council (NSC). 2007. *Report of the National Seniors Council on Elder Abuse, December 11, 2007*. Ottawa: National Seniors Council. www.seniorscouncil.gc.ca.

Navon, L., and N. Weinblatt. 1996. "The show must go on: Behind the scenes of elderly spousal caregiving." *Journal of Aging Studies* 10 (4): 329–42.

Neimeyer, R., and J. Werth. 2005. "The psychology of death." In M. Johnson, Ed., *The Cambridge Handbook of Age and Ageing*, 387–93. New York: Cambridge University Press.

Northcott, H., and D. Wilson. 2001. *Dying and Death in Canada*. Aurora, ON: Garamond.

Parliamentary Committee on Palliative and Compassionate Care. 2011. *Not to be Forgotten: Care for Vulnerable Canadians*. Ottawa: Parliamentary Committee on Palliative and Compassionate Care.

Patsios, D., and A. Davey. 2005. "Formal and informal community care for older adults." In M. Johnson, Ed., *The Cambridge Handbook of Age and Ageing*, 597–604. New York: Cambridge University Press.

Pearlin, L., et al. 1996. "Caregiving and its social support." In R. Binstock and L. George, Eds, *Handbook of Aging and the Social Sciences*, 283–302. San Diego: Academic Press.

——. 2001. "Caregiving by adult children: Involvement, role disruption, and health." In R. Binstock and L. George, Eds, *Handbook of Aging and the Social Sciences*, 238–54. San Diego: Academic Press.

Ploeg, J., et al. 2009. "A systematic review of interventions for elder abuse." *Journal of Elder Abuse and Neglect* 21: 187–210.

Penning, M., et al. 2006. "Home care and health reform: Changes in home care utilization in one Canadian province, 1990–2000." *The Gerontologist* 46 (6): 744–58.

Podnieks, E., et al. 1990. *National Survey of Abuse of the Elderly in Canada*. Toronto: Ryerson Polytechnical University.

Rabiner, D., et al. 2006. "Financial exploitation of older people: Challenges and opportunities to identify, prevent, and address it in the United States." *Journal of Aging & Social Policy* 18 (2): 47–68.

Raina, P., et al. 2004. "Understanding the influence of the complex relationships among informal and formal supports on the well-being of caregivers of persons with dementia." *Canadian Journal on Aging* 23 (supplement): S49–59.

Roberts, P. 2004. "Here today and cyberspace tomorrow: Memorials and bereavement support on the web." *Generations* 28 (2): 41–6.

Romanow Commission. 2002. *Building on Values: The Future of Health Care in Canada*. Ottawa: Royal Commission on the Future of Health Care in Canada.

Rosenthal, C., and E. Ansello, Eds. 2007. "Special issue: Hidden costs/invisible contributions of caregiving." *Canadian Journal on Aging* 26 (Supplement 1): 1–161.

Ross, M., et al. 2002. "End of life care for seniors: Public and professional awareness." *Educational Gerontologist* 28 (5): 353–66.

Schroepfer, T. 2006. "Mind frames towards dying and factors motivating their adoption by terminally ill elders." *Journal of Gerontology: Social Sciences* 61B (3): S129–39.

Seale, C. 2005. "The transformation of dying in old societies." In M. Johnson, Ed., *The Cambridge Handbook of Age and Ageing*, 378–86. New York: Cambridge University Press.

Settersten, R. 2003. "Rethinking social policy: Lessons of a life-course perspective." In R. Settersten, Ed., *Invitation to the Life Course: Toward New Understandings of Later Life*, 191–222. Amityville, NY: Baywood.

Shapiro, E. 2002. "Home care." *Health Transition Fund Synthesis Series*. Ottawa: Health Canada.

Silverstein, M., et al. 2002. "Reciprocity in parent-child relations over the adult life course." *Journal of Gerontology: Social Services* 57B (1): S3–13.

Sims-Gould, J., and A. Martin-Matthews 2007. "Family caregiving or caregiving alone: Who helps the helper?" *Canadian Journal on Aging* 26 (supplement 1): 27–46.

Skinner, M., and M. Rosenberg. 2002. "Health care in rural communities: Exploring the development of informal and voluntary care." SEDAP Research Paper no. 79. Hamilton, ON: McMaster University. http://socserv2.mcmaster.ca/sedap.

Snell, J. 1990. "Filial responsibility laws in Canada: A historical study." *Canadian Journal on Aging* 9 (3): 268–77.

——. 1996. *The Citizen's Wage: The State and the Elderly in Canada, 1900–1951*. Toronto: University of Toronto Press.

Snyder, L., and A. Caplan, Eds. 2001. *Assisted Suicide: Finding Common Ground*. Indianapolis: Indiana University Press.

Statistics Canada. 2011. *Family Violence in Canada: A Statistical Profile*. Catalogue no. 85-224-X. Ottawa: Minister of Industry.

Stewart, M., et al. 2006. "Accessible support for family caregivers of seniors with chronic conditions: From isolation to inclusion." *Canadian Journal on Aging* 25 (2): 179–92.

Stobert, S., and K. Cranswick. 2004. "Looking after seniors: Who does what for whom?" *Canadian Social Trends* 74 (autumn): 2–6.

Stones, M., and M. Bédard. 2003. "Higher thresholds for elder abuse with age and rural residence." *Canadian Journal on Aging* 21 (4): 577–86.

Strain, L., and A. Blandford. 2003. "Caregiving networks in later life: Does cognitive status make a difference?" *Canadian Journal on Aging* 22 (3): 261–73.

Tam, S., and S. Neysmith. 2006. "Disrespect and isolation: Elder abuse in Chinese communities." *Canadian Journal on Aging* 25 (2): 141–51.

Teaster, P., and K. Roberto. 2004. "Sexual abuse of older adults: APS cases and outcomes." *The Gerontologist* 44 (6): 788–96.

Thomas, R., et al. 2006. "A literature review of randomized controlled trials of the organization of care at the end of life." *Canadian Journal on Aging* 25 (3): 271–93.

Torres-Gil, F. 2005. "Ageing and public policy in ethnically diverse societies." In M. Johnson, Ed., *The Cambridge Handbook of Age and Ageing*, 670–81. New York: Cambridge University Press.

Tulloch, G. 2006. *Euthanasia: Choice at Death*. New York: Columbia University Press.

Turcotte, M., and G. Schellenmberg. 2006. *A Portrait of Seniors in Canada*. Ottawa: Statistics Canada.

Ward-Griffin, C. 2002. "Boundaries and connections between formal and informal caregivers." *Canadian Journal on Aging*, 21 (2): 205–16.

Ward-Griffin, C. 2004. "Nurses as caregivers of elderly relatives: Negotiating personal and professional boundaries." *Canadian Journal of Nursing Research* 36 (1): 92–114.

Ward-Griffin, C., et al. 2011. "Compassion fatigue within double duty caregiving: Nurse-daughters caring for elderly parents." *Online Journal of Issues in Nursing* 16 (1): 1-21.

Weeks, L., et al. 2004. "A gendered analysis of the abuse of older adults: Evidence from professionals." *Journal of Elder Abuse and Neglect* 16 (2): 1–15.

Weeks, L., and K. Roberto. 2002. "Comparison of adult day services in Atlantic Canada, Maine and Vermont." *Canadian Journal on Aging* 21 (2): 273–82.

Weir, R. Ed. 1997. *Physician-Assisted Suicide*. Indianapolis: Indiana University Press.

Wilber, K., and D. McNeilly. 2001. "Elder abuse and victimization." In J. Birren and W. Schaie, Eds, *Handbook of the Psychology of Aging*, 569–92. New York: Academic Press.

Williams, B., et al. 2006. "The feminization of bereavement among community-dwelling older adults." *Journal of Women and Aging* 18 (3): 3–18.

Wilson, D. 2002. "End of life issues." In M. Stephenson and E. Sawyer, Eds, *Continuing the Care: The Issues and Challenges for Long-Term Care*, 387–420. Ottawa: CHA Press.

Wilson, D., et al. 2008. "Researching a best-practice end-of-life care model for Canada." *Canadian Journal on Aging* 27 (4): 319–30.

Wilson, K., et al. 2007. "Desire for euthanasia or physician-assisted suicide in palliative cancer care." *Health Psychology* 26 (3): 314–23.

Wilson, K., et al. 2010. "Aging and health: An examination of differences between older Aboriginal and non-Aboriginal people." *Canadian Journal on Aging* 29 (3): 369–82.

Wilson, K., et al. 2011. "Aboriginal peoples. Health and healing approaches: The effects of age and place on health." *Social Science and Medicine* 72: 355–64.

Wister, A.V., and C. Moore. 1997. "First Nations elders in Canada: Issues, problems and successes in health care policy." In A.V. Wister and G. Gutman, Eds, *Health Systems and Aging in Selected Pacific Rim Countries: Ethnic Diversity and Change*, 83–104. Vancouver: Gerontology Research Centre, Simon Fraser University.

World Health Organization. 2002. *Missing Voices: Views of Older Persons on Elder Abuse*. Geneva: World Health Organization.

Wu, Z., and R. Hart. 2002. "Social and health factors associated with support among elderly immigrants in Canada." *Research on Aging* 24 (4): 391–412.

Yahnke, R., Ed. 2003a. "End-of-life decisions, Part 1." *The Gerontologist* 43 (1): 140–3.

———. 2003b. "End-of-life decisions, Part 2." *The Gerontologist* 43 (2): 285–8.

Yon, Y., et al. (2013). "A national comparison of spousal abuse in mid- and old-age." *Journal of Elder Abuse and Neglect*. DOI: *10.1080/08946566.2013.784085*.

Zukewich, N. 2003. "Unpaid informal caregiving." *Canadian Social Trends* (autumn): 14–18.

Index